# MOBILIZING FOR MODERN WAR

MODERN WAR STUDIES

# MOBILIZING FOR MODERN WAR: THE POLITICAL ECONOMY OF AMERICAN WARFARE, 1865–1919

PAUL A. C. KOISTINEN

UNIVERSITY PRESS OF KANSAS

Published by the University Press of Kansas (Lawrence, Kansas 66049), which was organized by the Kansas Board of Regents and is operated and funded by Emporia State University, Fort Hays State University, Kansas State University, Pittsburg State University, the University of Kansas, and Wichita State University

Library of Congress Cataloging-in-Publication Data

Koistinen, Paul A. C.
Mobilizing for modern war: the political economy of American warfare, 1865–1919 / Paul A. C. Koistinen.
p. cm. — (Modern war studies)
Includes bibliographical references and index.
ISBN 0-7006-0860-5 (alk. paper)
1. War—Economic aspects—United States—History. 2. United States—Defenses—History. 3. Industrial mobilization—United States—History. I. Title. II. Series.
HC110.D4K643 1997
338.4'76233'0973—dc21 97-19148

British Library Cataloguing in Publication Data is available.

Printed in the United States of America

10 9 8 7 6 5 4 3 2 1

The paper used in this publication meets the minimum requirements of the American National Standard for Permanence of Paper for Printed Library Materials Z39.48-1984.

In memory of
Bernard O'Rourke
and
Ralph Cox

# CONTENTS


Preface ix

1 The Political Economy of Warfare in America 1

Part One—The Industrial Stage, 1865–1916 9

2 The Rise of a Modern Political Economy 11

3 Modernizing the Navy 19

4 Modernizing the Army 58

5 The Role of American Elites 100

Part Two—Economic Mobilization for World War I 105

6 Preparedness and Participation 107

7 Economic Mobilization, 1914–1916 139

8 The National Defense Advisory Commission, February–July 1917 166

9 The War Industries Board, August 1917–March 1918 198

10 The War Industries Board, March–November 1918 230

11 Other Agencies and the Economic Consequences of World War I 254

12 Reconversion 268

13 The Challenge and Effect of Mobilizing for Modern War 288

Notes 299

Bibliographical Essay 373

Index 377

# PREFACE

This volume constitutes the second of a five-volume study of the political economy of warfare in America—the means the nation has employed to mobilize its economic resources for defense and hostilities. The volume begins in 1865 and concludes in 1919. Volume 1—*Beating Plowshares into Swords: The Political Economy of American Warfare, 1606–1865*—covers the colonial period through the Civil War; volume 3 will deal with the interwar years; volume 4, World War II; and volume 5, the years after 1945, essentially the period of the Cold War. In chapter 1, I set forth the paradigm for the whole work and summarize the contents of the five volumes. Essentially the same chapter appearing in volume 1, it is for the benefit of those who have not read the earlier book and to remind readers of the major themes of my larger study.

In previous publications I have traced the origins and development of the so-called military-industrial complex from World War I to the Cold War years. In this volume I have the opportunity to analyze economic mobilization for World War I in greater depth and to examine at length the political economy of warfare during the Gilded Age. Scholarly work on the politics and economics of the late nineteenth century is extensive and sophisticated; it is less so for the rich and rewarding history of the armed services.

There is a general evolutionary pattern to the political economy of warfare. The preindustrial stage, which includes the Revolutionary War, bore a striking resemblance to developments in the twentieth century, even though the technology of war was unsophisticated. War mobilization had a profound and lasting effect on the nation in both eras, and civil-military relations were exceptionally tumultuous. The preindustrial and industrial stages, therefore, were periods in which economic mobilization created multiple problems for and threats to the society. That was not the case in the transitional stage between the two, exemplified best by the Union during the Civil War. Economic mobilization in that stage was comparatively easy, civil-military relations remained stable, and the postwar legacy of harnessing the economy for hostilities was not great. In short, mobilizing the economy in this stage presented few hazards to the social system. After the Civil War, America entered the industrial era in which big business, big government, a professional military, and sophisticated weaponry combined to require economic planning during major wars or periods of extended conflict. World Wars I and II and the Cold War cumulatively demonstrate the enormous impact that economic mobilization has had on an advanced industrial society, including the fundamental transformation of civil-military relations.

Analyzing the political economy of warfare also means studying power in America. My previous work on World Wars I and II demonstrates that focusing on economic mobilization offers a nearly unequaled opportunity to examine the development of society and the relative strength of various social groups and institutions. The demands of war tend to reveal social realities that can remain obscure in times of peace. It is not too much to say that one can make a fairly accurate assessment of the nation's growth, development, and power operations by examining economic mobilization for America's many wars.

Economic mobilization for war is shaped at the national level by the interaction of political, economic, and military institutions and by the sophistication of weaponry. Yet no general history of economic mobilization exists for wars of the eighteenth and nineteenth centuries that is systematic in nature and based on an analytic paradigm. More and better scholarship on the political economy of warfare in the twentieth century is available, but a great deal remains to be done. For instance, no synthesis of the economics of warfare from the Spanish-American War to the present has been written, and although World War I has been analyzed with sophistication in recent years, the interwar years generally have been neglected. Moreover, economic mobilization for World War II has received little attention since official histories and memoirs of participants were published shortly after the conclusion of hostilities, despite the availability of probably the finest and best-organized document collections for any period in American history. Works of varying quality on the political economy of the Cold War are numerous to the point of being overwhelming, yet an authoritative synthesis of the post–World War II period that draws upon the past to help explain the complexities of the present is missing.

My goal in this multivolume series is to provide scholars and other readers with a source that is now unavailable: a comprehensive, schematic, and interdisciplinary study of the economics of America's wars from the colonial period to today. In doing so, I demonstrate the impact of the political economy of warfare on domestic life and highlight the realities that economic mobilization for defense and war reveals about the nature and operations of society. I also seek to expand on the study of military history by examining in depth and breadth an aspect of warfare that is often ignored or treated in a perfunctory manner. This particular perspective leads to different insights and conclusions about civilians, soldiers and sailors, and warfare. If I raise as many questions as I answer, I will have more than accomplished my purpose.

It is also important to point out what I am not doing. I am not studying logistics, tactics, or strategy in any organized way. I touch upon those subjects, particularly logistics, throughout the series but only as they pertain directly to the political economy of warfare or serve to illuminate that subject. I examine, for example, the development and construction of the "new navy" in the late nineteenth and early twentieth centuries, but I do not study naval warfare. My focus is on how the nation mobilized its economic might in order to conduct war, not on the conduct of war itself.

Nonetheless, economic might has played a major role in how the United States has fought its wars. In the preindustrial stage, an underdeveloped economy forced Americans to fight defensive wars of attrition during the Revolution and the War of 1812. Growing economic maturity in the transitional stage allowed the United States to operate offensively during the Mexican War. A decade or so later, the Union relied on its enormous economic might to overwhelm the Confederacy through a strategy of annihilation. The South bungled its strategy of attrition—in which it sought to win by not losing—largely because it failed to mobilize effectively the region's less-developed economy. The North's strategy during the Civil War anticipated the total wars of the industrial stage in which the nation relied on its superior economic power virtually to crush the enemy—what Russell F. Weigley calls "the American way of war."

For the years 1865 through the Progressive Era—approximately one-third of the book—I have organized the material to elucidate systematically major economic, political, and military developments and the state of military technology. By 1917 major institutions in those areas had reached maturity and no longer need to be surveyed. Consequently, the focus of the remainder of the book shifts to preparation and economic mobilization for war. Nonetheless, I briefly recast the analysis according to the pattern of the earlier chapters at the conclusion of the section on World War I for consistency and continuity.

In a work as ambitious as this one, scholarly collaboration is not a choice; it is a necessity. My enormous debt to numerous historians, economists, and political scientists is clearly set forth in the notes. Of particular importance are the "new military historians." In the past few decades, they have broadened the study of the armed forces, defense, and warfare to include most of society and have thus enriched military history and the study of the past in general.

A few words about the notes are in order. To cut down on the number and length of citations, I have employed "cluster noting" for the sections on the Gilded Age and Progressivism, simply listing in one note the numerous primary and secondary sources I have relied upon in analyzing these periods. When the analysis depends heavily on primary documents, as is the case throughout the remainder of the book in dealing with World War I, I return to the more usual procedure.

I have benefited greatly from the assistance of others in putting this second volume into its final form. My son and daughter, David J. Koistinen and Janice H. Koistinen combined their excellent critical and copyediting talents to help turn a rough and long manuscript into one that was briefer and more readable. Later, Terry J. Woulf proved equally valuable as an assistant. At California State University, Northridge, John J. Broesamle and Ronald Schaffer read the entire manuscript and provided me with invaluable insights and advice. Finally, Russell F. Weigley and Edward M. Coffman used their unequaled expertise and keen analytical skills to point out errors on my part and to suggest textual revisions that improved the volume. I could not ask for more from a publisher than the services provided by the University Press of Kansas. Michael Briggs, editor-in-chief, oversees the project with a sure but gentle hand, and his capable and dedicated staff—including Susan Schott, marketing manager, and Rebecca Knight Giusti, production editor—go about the wonders of converting manuscripts into published volumes with a high level of professionalism.

My debt to all of these people is matched only by my appreciation for their labors and contribution. Needless to say, I, not they, am responsible for all that is and is not said in this book.

Much precedes the review and publication of a manuscript. John Taylor and Wilbert Mahoney, Textual Reference Division, National Archives, provided me with invaluable assistance in coping with the voluminous records involving World War I. Nancy Bressler of the Princeton University Library helped guide my work in the Papers of Bernard M. Baruch and Frank A. Scott. The staff of the Manuscript Division of the Library of Congress facilitated my review of the Papers of Woodrow Wilson, Newton D. Baker, and George W. Goethals. A number of people at the U.S. Chamber of Commerce Archives in Washington, DC, went out of their way to assist my research. Without the Oviatt Library at California State University, Northridge (CSUN), especially its interlibrary loan services, I would have been hard-pressed to complete this work. Charlotte Oyer, Donald L. Read, Michael Barrett, and Felicia Cousin worked endlessly on my behalf. For word processing of the various drafts, I appreciate the skill and good humor of Marcia M. Dunicliffe, formerly of the History Department, and Pamela Fowell, formerly with the College of Social and Behavioral Sciences. Finally, the continued support, encouragement, and love of my wife, Carolyn Epstein Koistinen, is crucial to what I do.

For financial support, I have had many benefactors over the years, including research fellowships from Harvard's Charles Warren Center for Studies in American History, the American Council of Learned Societies, and the National Endowment for the Humanities. Furthermore, CSUN's History Department, College of Social and Behavioral Sciences, and the university as a whole have assisted me in numerous ways for many years.

The volume is dedicated to the memory of two close friends dating back to my undergraduate years, Bernard O'Rourke and Ralph Cox. They frequently led the way as we explored together the fascinations and frustrations of trying to reconstruct the past. Although now long gone, they will not be soon forgotten.

# 1
# THE POLITICAL ECONOMY OF WARFARE IN AMERICA

Scholars have begun analyzing warfare and the military with increasing breadth and sophistication, but they have not paid much attention to how America has mobilized its economic resources for war and defense—the political economy of warfare—a subject that is important for a number of reasons. Logistics are basic to warfare and depend upon the nation's ability to marshal effectively its economic might. Over the centuries, economic mobilization has followed a discernible evolutionary pattern that illuminates the study of warfare and the military. Furthermore, how the United States has mobilized its economy reveals a great deal about institutional and power structures. Indeed, the stress and demands of warfare make manifest social patterns that are less evident or obscured during years of peace.

The political economy of warfare involves the interrelationships of the political, economic, and military institutions in devising the means to mobilize resources for defense and to conduct war. In each war, the magnitude and duration of the fighting have dictated *what* the nation had to do to harness its economic power, but prewar trends have largely determined *how* this mobilization took place. Four factors are essential in determining the method of mobilization. The first is economic—the level of maturity of the economy; the second is political—the size, strength, and scope of the federal government; the third, military—the character and structure of the military services and the relationship between them and civilian society and authority; and the fourth is the state of military technology.

Patterns of economic mobilization for war have passed through three major stages over the course of American history. The Revolutionary War, the Civil War, and twentieth-century warfare best characterize these stages, which I have labeled preindustrial, transitional, and industrial. Altering the four factors—economic, political, military, and technological—modifies each stage of mobilization. The factors have seldom changed at the same time or pace, but over time each has had to keep pace with the others so that viable patterns of economic mobilization could be maintained.

## STAGES OF ECONOMIC MOBILIZATION

The preindustrial stage of economic mobilization for war extended from the colonial period to approximately 1815 and included the Revolutionary War and the War of 1812. During the American Revolution, economic, governmental, and military institutions were in an embryonic state and were not clearly distinguished from one another. Military technology was rather primitive and varied little from production in the peacetime economy. Hence, economic mobilization involved increasing civilian output and diverting products from civilian to military use in order to supply the armed forces without converting the economy. Nonetheless, to maximize output, comprehensive regulation of the emerging nation's economic life became essential. Yet the undeveloped nature of economic, political, and military institutions not only prevented such regulation from ever working well but also resulted in private and public, civil and military activities becoming inextricably intertwined. Merchants simultaneously served as public officials and military officers while they continued to conduct their private affairs.

The effects of harnessing the economy for war carried over into the years of peace. By highlighting the weaknesses of the Articles of Confederation, economic mobilization helped to create the momentum for the ideas underlying the Constitution. And, during the early national period, conflict intensified between the factions that became the Federalist and Republican parties over the strength and policies of the national government under the new charter. This strife weakened the federal government and stunted the growth of the armed services, a major source of dispute. Consequently, although the economy was much stronger in 1812 than in 1776 and military technology had changed little during that period, economic mobilization for the War of 1812 did not improve measurably over what it had been for the Revolutionary War.

The second, or transitional, stage of economic mobilization extended from 1816 to 1865. During this period the economy developed enormous productive capacity; it became diversified and quite industrialized, and specialized functions emerged in manufacturing, marketing, and banking, although the size of firms was comparatively small. The federal government was limited in size, scope, and activity, but it was capable of expanding in order to handle economic mobilization effectively and efficiently. Both the army and navy, for their part, had professionalized to the point where they had definable structures and missions. But military technology still had not undergone any dramatic change. Since weaponry remained basic, economic mobilization required only expanding and diverting civilian production, not economic conversion.

Harnessing the economy for war was more readily accomplished in the transitional stage than in those stages that preceded and followed it. The pattern was evident in the Mexican War but was best demonstrated by the Union during the Civil War. Operating under the direction of the president, the War, Navy, and Treasury Departments acted as the principal mobilization agencies. They relied on market forces in a strong competitive economy, not on the elaborate regulation characteristic of the preindustrial and industrial stages, to maintain economic stability while meeting the enormous demands of war. Moreover, institutional barriers were not breached. In the economic realm, little mixing of activities and personnel occurred among private and public, civilian and military affairs. The only major exception involved the railroads, which had begun to organize modern corporations before hostilities; the telegraph system followed a similar trend.

Union success contrasted sharply with the Confederacy's failure. The South was closer to the preindustrial than to the transitional stage. Like the colonies/states during the revolutionary years, the Confederacy experimented with comprehensive economic regulation without much success. Weak economic and political systems consistently undermined the Confederacy's economic mobilization effort and played an important role in the South's defeat.

Modern warfare in the twentieth century represents the third, or industrial, stage of economic mobilization. By 1900 the United States had become a mature industrialized nation with a modified capitalist system. Although market forces remained significant in the production and distribution of goods, the administered decisions of several hundred modern corporations exercised strong, at times dominant, influence over the economy's direction. In order to make concentrated and consolidated economic power more responsible to the public and to stabilize an enormously complex economy, the federal government began to act as economic regulator. The growth of huge bureaucracies in the corporate and governmental spheres began to blur the institutional lines between both. Businessmen often staffed the government's regulatory agencies, and, as during the preindustrial stage, the affairs of government and business touched or merged at many points. A government-business regulatory alliance began to emerge during the Progressive Era.

For a time during the late nineteenth century, the military services entered a period of relative isolation in America as the nation became absorbed in industrialization, the threat of war receded, and the army and navy became intensely involved in professionalizing their functions. A technological revolution in weaponry in the later years of the nineteenth century, however, drew the civilian and military worlds back together. The consequences of this revolution were first manifest in the navy. In order to build a new fleet of steel, armor, steam, and modern ordnance, a production team consisting of political leaders, naval officers, and businessmen was formed. Although the composition, responsibilities, and operation of such a team have varied over the years, it has continued to exist. The army was slower to feel the impact of technology, but it eventually experienced the same needs and a relationship with industry and civil authorities similar to the navy's.

By the eve of World War I, therefore, the federal government, the industrial community, and the military services had developed complex, modern, and professionalized structures, each dependent upon the others in terms of national defense. Economic mobilization for World War I (unlike the brief and limited Spanish-American War) forcefully demonstrated this institutional interdependence. The quantity and sophistication of military demand meant that increasing and diverting civilian production was no longer adequate; market forces could not be relied upon. Production had to be maximized and industries had to be converted in order to manufacture the often specialized military hardware. Priority, allocation, price, and other controls had to be introduced, and existing governmental departments and agencies were unequal to the task. New mobilization bodies had to be created, the most important being the War Industries Board (WIB). Through the board, centralized control over a planned economy was established and carried out by representatives of the government, the business community, and the military. The process obscured institutional lines. Civilian and military, private and public activities once again combined. For very different reasons and with quite different results, the first and the third mobilization stages are strikingly similar.

World War I mobilization left an indelible imprint on national life. During the interwar years, direct and indirect economic planning patterned after the WIB was tried. Congress and other governmental bodies repeatedly investigated the methods and consequences of harnessing the World War I economy in order to understand better what had taken place, to prevent future mobilization abuses, and to head off the perceived threats of modern warfare. Moreover, close ties between the civil and the military sectors of the government, the industrial community, and other new and old interest groups were maintained in order to design, produce, and procure specialized munitions and to plan for industrial mobilization. During World War II, a modified form of the World War I model was used to mobilize the economy for meeting the astronomical and often highly specialized demands of the armed forces and

America's allies. With the Cold War following World War II, the nation for the first time in its peacetime history supported a massive military establishment, one that became inordinately expensive because of its size and because of a continuing transformation of weaponry through scientific and technological advancement. As a result, a defense and war "complex" included and affected most private and public institutions in American life.

## ELITES AND ECONOMIC MOBILIZATION

Economic mobilization has been carried out largely by political, economic, and, ultimately, military elites. Economic and political elites are closely related and comprise the nation's upper classes. In the late eighteenth and early nineteenth centuries they included merchants, planters and large landowners, and professional elements. As the economy matured, the people involved with banks, railroads, and manufacturing gained in importance, and the twentieth-century economic elite is primarily based on the vast corporate and financial communities.

Military elites did not work in close association with economic and political elites until the industrial stage. In the preindustrial period, no clear line separated the military from the civilian world. During the transitional stage, both the army and navy distanced themselves from civilians as they began to professionalize and to acquire separate identities. But in the industrial stage, military leaders out of necessity had to join their political and economic counterparts in order successfully to mobilize the economy for war.

Elites shaped economic mobilization in a number of ways. The federal executive—or what approximated it during the Revolution—devised and implemented the methods for harnessing the economy for war. Throughout American history, the highest appointed officials in the executive branch have been drawn predominantly from among the nation's wealthy or the individuals associated with them. Moreover, the federal government has turned to the nation's business leaders to assist in economic mobilization. They have acted as temporary or permanent advisers to government mobilizers, served in established or newly created federal agencies with or without pay, or engaged in some combination of these activities.

Harnessing the economy for war has generated a great deal of political controversy in America because economic mobilization highlights the nation's most basic contradiction: an elitist reality in the context of a democratic ideology. During years of peace that dynamic contradiction tends to be obscured; during years of war it is magnified by elitist economic mobilization patterns.

Excluded interest groups and classes inevitably challenge the legitimacy of mobilization systems run by the few as unrepresentative and as failing to protect larger public interests. This resentment is exaggerated by the widespread aversion to and fear of government at the national level. Moreover, economic mobilization for war elevates the armed services to positions of central importance, which intensifies the strong antimilitary strains in American thought. Opposition to war among nonelites also often leads to adverse critiques of economic mobilization policies. There is a close correlation between antiwar and antielite attitudes.

Controversy over the political economy of warfare has been greatest in the preindustrial and industrial stages. By requiring a form of planning, underdeveloped and highly developed economies have made elites quite visible. Market economies do not have that effect because mobilization agencies combining political and economic elites are unnecessary. Consequently, economic mobilization caused comparatively little political turmoil in the transitional stage.

Mobilizing the economy for the Revolutionary War was tumultuous. For over a quarter of a century after hostilities, the new nation was engulfed in basic political strife involving the nature of government at the federal level under first the Articles of Confederation and then the Constitution. Disputes between Federalists and Republicans became so intense that the former attempted to use the military in settling its differences with the latter. Early in the nineteenth century, the torn and distracted nation drifted unprepared toward a second war with Britain. The consequences of political divisions dating back to the Revolution prevented Americans from effectively mobilizing their economy for the War of 1812.

Conflict over the political economy of warfare in the industrial stage began with the building of a modern navy in the late nineteenth century and has never fully subsided. Mobilizing the World War I economy intensified the discord manyfold, and battles over economic mobilization continued throughout the interwar years. Those struggles enormously complicated the means used for harnessing the World War II economy. During the Cold War years, the dispute over the economics of defense and war grew in prominence and level of sophistication. The number of critics multiplied rapidly and focused on the comprehensive consequences of the military-industrial complex, in effect a weapons-driven industrial policy.

Compared with other periods, the political economy of warfare in the transitional stage was politically placid. The Union's economic mobilization is largely remembered for its corruption, a matter that has been greatly distorted and, more important, that generally ceased after the first year of war. Because the market acted as regulator and existing executive departments carried out the functions of economic mobilization, the centralized planning that took place in the preindustrial and industrial stages was avoided. Hence, harnessing the Union economy did not emphasize the elitist contours of power at the federal level. Among the states, however, elite mobilization patterns were blatantly evident. The Northern states played an important role in economic mobilization, especially during the first year of war. In every state of the Union, political and economic elites—who also often acted as military elites—combined for purposes of economic mobilization to the point that the public and private spheres became virtually indistinguishable. This development caused few political problems because it only exaggerated during an emergency practices that were standard during peacetime among the states and localities. State and local elites are usually more visible to and less troublesome for the general population than elites at the national level, partly because they are more familiar to the public and wield less power.

The Confederacy differed in fundamental ways from the Union. It was economically underdeveloped, and the planter-slave system made the South the most obviously elite-dominated section of the nation. To maximize its limited economic strength for fighting a much stronger foe, the Confederacy had to plan its wartime economy. It did so by relying heavily on the South's commercial and professional elements, transplanted Northerners and individuals from abroad, and officers trained at West Point and Annapolis. Ultimately, economic mobilization in the Confederacy failed. The planter elite consistently thwarted effective planning efforts both by what it did and did not do. Their behavior alienated the Southern white masses and significantly weakened the Confederacy's ability to hold off the advancing Union.

Throughout the course of American history, the role of political, economic, and military elites in economic mobilization for defense and war can be understood fully only within the four-factor, three-stage paradigm. If the preindustrial stage is dated from 1765 to 1815 (instead of including the entire colonial era), it lasted only about fifty years, approximately the same duration as the transitional stage. Accelerated physical and economic growth quickly modified institutions and power operations, altering in the process the stages of economic mobilization. Rapid industrialization after the Civil War ushered in the last stage of mobilization, one that has had a permanence of sorts to it. Since the late nineteenth century, political, economic, and military elites have been absorbed in creating and refining planning structures to cope with the ongoing weapons revolution, a revolution that has comprehensively affected the way that America prepares for and conducts warfare.

# PART ONE
# THE INDUSTRIAL STAGE, 1865–1916

Economic mobilization for the Spanish-American War (April–December 1898) differed significantly from the methods of the Union during the Civil War, although it resembled in many ways the approach taken during the Mexican War (1846–1848). Still, as in most wars, the economics of the Spanish-American War had its unique qualities, an observation made clear by analyzing the political, economic, military, and technological factors that shape the political economy of warfare.

By 1898 the federal government was just beginning to restructure itself in order to cope with the far-reaching changes of rapid industrialization. Nonetheless, the executive branch was sufficiently developed to allow William McKinley to act as a strong commander-in-chief by directing almost all facets of the war. For its part, Congress was supportive without being passive.

The economy by the turn of the century was approaching industrial maturity, with advanced technology widespread, the modern corporation established, and consolidated economic power emerging as a means for maintaining stability. In terms of production potential and financial resources, the mighty American economic machine could meet demands many times that of the Spanish-American War without the least stress.

Given adequate federal and massive economic structures, the success of mobilizing the economy depended heavily on the effectiveness of the military services. The Navy Department performed well. With relative ease it expanded its fleet and manpower to fight a two-front war. By comparison, the War Department stumbled badly. Although it ably produced and procured weapons and supplies, it repeatedly fell down in transportation, distribution, and camp organization and operation. Both the army and navy had gone through a far-reaching modernizing and professionalizing process before the war. Even so, the army was unprepared to fight efficiently. As a result, with the conclusion of hostilities, Elihu Root as secretary of war began the final stage of army reform by restructuring fundamentally the land forces' command system and by making other related changes.

Technological advancement accounted in part for the difference between the two services. Between 1881 and 1898 a new navy of steel, steam, armor, and modern ordnance had come into being. Building such a fleet transpired under outstanding civilian leaders at the highest levels of government, working in tandem with naval officers and industrialists. The nation's elite power system was adapted to the realities of industrialization in the late nineteenth and early twentieth centuries through the interaction of big government and big business. Civilian leaders ensured that the navy was prepared for war in terms of command, weaponry, and supply systems. Without a comparable transformation, the army was denied effective civilian leaders. Root stepped in to correct that situation, but even his reforms were not fully implemented until World War I, when civilians intervened again to save the army from disaster.

# 2
# THE RISE OF A MODERN POLITICAL ECONOMY

Rapid industrialization in the late nineteenth and early twentieth centuries created the modern political economy based on big government and big business. Big business came into existence first. The emergence of the modern corporation led to extreme concentration of economic power, necessitating a large federal government to act as economic regulator and social welfare agent. During the Progressive Era, big government and big business began combining their strength to constitute the new American elite. Representatives from the corporate, financial, and legal communities held key positions in the federal executive. This elitist system of power was evident during years of peace in staffing and policymaking at the national level and became much more explicit when economic mobilization for war led to direct planning.

Twentieth-century elites are both continuous with and different from the elites of pre–Civil War America. Continuity stems from the fact that political leadership, particularly at the national level, comes principally from the nation's wealthiest groups or those associated with them. Wealth distribution, after the Civil War as before, is heavily skewed toward the upper classes. As a consistent pattern, the richest 10 percent come close to owning 60 percent of all wealth, the poorest 30 percent have almost nothing, and the rest goes to the middle classes. Some variation usually occurs. Economic inequality lessened from roughly 1929 to 1944, and in the last fifteen years the wealthy have gained more than ever before in American history.

Most of the wealthy are tied to business, and they often have generational depth reaching back as far as the colonial period. Business leaders in the 1870s through the 1890s came in large numbers from the railroads and in the twentieth century increasingly from industry and finance. Even during the Gilded Age, when professional politicians supposedly reigned supreme and the national government was relatively small and unimportant, the principal positions in the federal executive were filled by individuals from or associated with the economic elite. Elite rule became even more predominant and significant in the Progressive Era as the federal government streamlined its operations and grew in size and power.

Industrialization did not alter the major American paradox of an elitist reality operating within the context of a democratic ideology. Except for women and blacks, voting as a percentage of those eligible was more extensive during the Gilded Age than in any period before or since. With suffrage becoming universal in the twentieth century, the potential voting base expanded even further. Yet elite control has persisted at the local, state, and national levels.

Modern elites, however, differ in significant ways from their predecessors. Primarily, they have greater permanence. Although the industrial-financial community and the federal government have changed over time, they still maintain the foundations created in the late nineteenth and early twentieth centuries. Second, elite domination has been more prevalent in foreign and defense policy than in domestic concerns as the nation became a global power. Third, the military has been integrated into the elitist structures.

## POLITICS AND GOVERNMENT DURING THE GILDED AGE AND THE PROGRESSIVE ERA

After the final phases of Reconstruction, the nation entered a period between 1876 and 1896 in which the political and economic systems were more separated from one another than has ever before or since been the case.[1] This extreme fragmentation came about as the sectional ideology that had fueled politics before and after the Civil War became irrelevant. The principal new issues arose from the nation's wrenching transition from an agrarian to an industrial society. Yet the two major political parties could not quickly reorient themselves to this dramatic change. They could neither come to terms with the industrialization taking place nor devise policies for handling the problems it caused. A drift set in, and elected offices became more important than issues, leading to elaborate and sophisticated political machines and campaigns for turning out the vote and to a high level of political corruption.

In the midst of drift some positive developments occurred. Between approximately 1885 and 1900 party and congressional leaders used party caucuses, committee structures, and new or modified regulations to streamline procedures and transform the two houses of Congress into a reasonably effective national legislature. Meanwhile, beginning with Rutherford B. Hayes and continuing under his successors, the various one-term presidents restored some authority to an executive branch that had been badly weakened by the impeachment of Andrew Johnson and the political incompetence of Ulysses S. Grant. By restoring authority, they helped pave the way for an effective presidency—the sine qua non of reformed government—and specifically for the presidency of William McKinley.

The political adjustment to industrialization took place first on the periphery rather than at the center of the social system. This reaction was evident in the operations of the urban political machines—which in a rather feudal manner ministered to the needs of the immigrant masses—and in the growing agrarian protest movements. Simultaneously, reform was taking hold within traditional political and governmental circles at the local, state, and national levels. Generally, these movements were led by mugwump and new professional elements from the middle to upper classes who were seeking to make the social system more efficient or humane and sometimes both. Their efforts included improved social services, updated public utilities, and more effective forms of governance.

Local and state reforms in time forced Washington to take a more active role in coping with the widespread effects of industrialization. Most important, the national government had to address the consolidation of economic power under the modern corporation as the most significant result of the industrial revolution. It did so with the Interstate Commerce Act of 1887, and, at least symbolically, with the Sherman Antitrust Act of 1890. By setting up an independent regulatory commission with the former statute, Congress created the most basic institution of the twentieth century for dealing with the complexities of a modern industrial economy.

Lasting reform at the national level depended on breaking the stalemate that paralyzed the two parties between 1872 and 1892 and that kept them focused on elections rather than on issues. Beginning in 1884, the party system entered a period of exceptional turbulence that led to the fundamental realignment of 1894–1896, in which the Republicans emerged as the nation's majority party based on winning the cities. Industrialization had destroyed the third party system and ushered in the fourth.

Despite its shortcomings, the third party system was in many ways quite remarkable. In a passive, negative fashion it saw the nation through the most trying period of industrialization. By focusing on local and state issues, the third party system, along with the various third parties, helped to keep the people loyal to the existing social system during a twenty-year period of enormous stress. The two parties acted to ameliorate, rather than to intensify, class antagonisms; intense appeals to class interests were made only during the 1896 campaign. Even then, the Republican party was able to win the support of the urban masses at least in part because major party leaders such as McKinley and

Marcus A. Hanna had positive labor records. During the repeated industrial eruptions of the late nineteenth century, party leaders sought to calm the animosities between capital and labor and to persuade the former to adopt a more flexible attitude toward unions. Moreover, since a large part of the population, particularly urban inhabitants, were immigrants, both parties had to be sensitive to ethnic, cultural, and religious interests. By paying attention to such concerns, the political parties tempered class antagonisms, a strategy that was reasonably effective except during the repeated periods of economic depression. Ethnocultural issues became less consequential in the early twentieth century as the economy experienced greater stability, government at all levels became more involved in economic and welfare measures, rates of immigration fell, and labor unions grew in strength.

The fourth party system (1896–1932), like the third, started with a strong executive. McKinley led with a firm hand and Theodore Roosevelt even more so. Unlike in the third party system, the dominance achieved by the executive branch in the fourth would be permanent—a necessity in a modern, complex society. During the Progressive years, strengthening the executive depended on furthering domestic reform.[2] That effort began with Roosevelt, both advanced and faltered under William Howard Taft, and was brought to fruition by Woodrow Wilson. By combining his own New Freedom with Roosevelt's New Nationalism, Wilson achieved a new Progressive synthesis: a government-business regulatory alliance as the principal mode of twentieth-century American political economy. A larger government would begin to act as social welfare agent and to regulate business—but under conditions in which either the regulated would actually be the regulator, or the regulator would share at least the interests and ideology of the regulated. The people-in-the-street would be included in the bargain through a modest welfare state that ameliorated the worst features of capitalism and kept the general public committed to the system.

Wilson's accomplishments were substantial; he completed what Roosevelt had started but could not finish because the New Nationalism was too blatantly elitist and too clearly statist. By finesse and indirection, Wilson succeeded in legitimizing corporate capitalism with a larger federal government while obscuring the latter with rhetoric about the virtues of competition, democracy, and individualism.

The workings of the new Progressive synthesis remained elusive during the years of peace because the activities of government, business, and the people appeared to proceed largely on different planes that overtly touched only on occasion. But a planned wartime economy made the new system clear and palpable. The functioning of the War Industries Board during World War I fully revealed the dynamics of the government-business regulatory alliance; the operations of the larger wartime economy manifested the main features of a modest welfare state.

Although Progressivism was exceptionally complex and contradictory, its political economy at the local, state, and national levels had a consistency of sorts. Elite patterns were evident at all levels and centered on limiting democratic trends. This effort took place directly through measures restricting the franchise and indirectly through the creation of independent regulatory agencies staffed by officials who were appointed rather than elected, operated largely outside the public eye, came from the middle- to upper-class elements, and were designated as professional experts. The trend was of course most important at the national level since the federal government, the fulcrum of the new regulatory alliance, was growing at the expense of both local and state government. The importance of appointed officials in Washington was evident in the growing size and power of the executive branch and in agencies such as the Interstate Commerce Commission, Federal Trade Commission, and Federal Reserve Board.[3]

## THE TRANSITION TO A MODERN ECONOMY

The shaping force of the Gilded Age was the transition from an agrarian to a mature industrial economy in a short period of thirty-five years.[4] The United States was already a manufacturing nation of importance in 1860, but by 1900 it had become the world's industrial giant, and by 1910 it was unsurpassed in the output of most industrial products. The Gross National Product in stable prices grew from $6.2 billion in 1870 to $30.1 billion in 1910—an annual growth rate of over 4 percent, or 2 percent per capita. Although agriculture accounted for part of this outstanding record, the manufacturing sector was key.

In analyzing the growth, most scholars recognize the importance of expanding demand from a population that jumped from 36 million in 1865 to 100 million in 1914. The supply side of growth matched or exceeded the contribution of demand. Technological innovation, adaptation, and diffusion became exceptionally important in the late nineteenth and early twentieth centuries and multiplied manyfold the productive capacity of American industry. Mass production techniques were especially important in that regard.

Between 1869 and 1899 agriculture reversed positions with industry, dropping from 53 to 33 percent of value added in commodity output even though gross farm output nearly tripled between 1860 and 1910 with the enormous push into the Great Plains, greater mechanization, and improved farming techniques. These trends acted to establish more firmly the regional agricultural specialization that had begun before the Civil War and that still continues today.

A national market was basic to the economic growth of both industry and agriculture in the late nineteenth century. Regardless of the numerous academic disputes involving the railroads, most scholars agree that they were essential in transforming the United States from a collection of regional markets to a national market in which raw materials and semifinished goods could be moved quickly, reliably, cheaply, and flexibly to centers of production and finished products could be distributed throughout the nation and abroad with similar ease.

Scholars also generally agree that the railroads pioneered in the organization of the modern corporation, which was later adapted and refined by industrial firms. Multimillion- and ultimately multibillion-dollar enterprise with a national and even international reach required new and effective management methods. Although corporate structures took many forms, three characteristics stand out. The first involved separating policymaking from operations, with the top executives determining strategy, coordinating the various divisions, and planning for the future. Second, control of operations was specialized and turned over to middle management, which regularly reported to corporate heads. Third, elaborate financial controls, including modern accounting systems, were implemented to facilitate sound operations. Here was born business bureaucracy, with separate divisions for production, marketing, and finance.

The evolution of the corporate structure placed in the hands of managers the means for determining rational prices internally rather than relying on the pressures of the marketplace. But they could do so only by controlling the external as well as the internal business environment. The external environment turned out to be a harsh one, involving brutal and destructive competition, which led corporations to seek security through the consolidation of economic power. The methods used varied according to the nature and needs of the industry involved; the holding company eventually becoming the favored approach. In the drive for stability and predictability to facilitate planning, the invisible hand of the marketplace, to use Alfred D. Chandler, Jr.'s felicitous phrase, gave way whenever possible to the visible one of the corporate manager.[5]

By the turn of the century, the modern American economy had emerged with a dualistic nature. At the center stood so-called big business—oligopolistic industries consisting of a few large, mass-production firms that did not compete in terms of price, tended to recognize market shares and specialties, and generally conducted their affairs more through corporate decisionmaking than by market forces. These industries were capital intensive, benefited from economies of scale, and discouraged entry; examples include steel, oil, and chemicals. Several hundred corporations constituted this core. In 1901, even before the massive merger wave begun in 1897 had crested, one-third of manufacturing value added took place in industries where four firms accounted for at least 50 percent of the industry's output.

On the periphery were the industries subject to competition. What they lacked in size and clout, they made up in numbers, consisting of thousands of firms. These industries included principally small- to medium-sized firms that were often labor intensive, were unable to benefit substantially from economies of scale, and regularly faced new competitors because of easy entry. The textile, lumber, and clothing industries fell into this category.

Rapid industrialization left no part of the economy untouched. Mass production, for example, brought mass distribution at the expense of the middleman. Though the middleman declined in distribution, in finance his function, numbers, and importance grew after the Civil War. The exponentially expanding economy created new wealth and required vast amounts of investment since the large corporations at this stage depended heavily on external financing. The role of the financial intermediaries was to coordinate saving with investment. Almost all intermediaries, including commercial and savings banks, trusts, building and loan associations, and insurance companies, grew vigorously in size and assets from 1865 to 1910 and served the purposes of encouraging saving, providing investment funds, and increasing the mobility of capital. The outstanding institutions for the rise of big business were the investment banking houses, the most important of which was J. P. Morgan and Company.

The economic reach of these firms became so substantial that some scholars and other observers have concluded that in the late nineteenth and early twentieth centuries the American economy entered a phase of "finance capitalism"—becoming in effect an economy dominated by bankers. If such conditions did exist, they were only temporary and had ended before the close of World War I. The twentieth-century American economy was basically one of corporate, not finance, capitalism.

The corporations in the core industries were professionally managed. However, the notion that the separation of ownership and control, another distinctive feature of the modern economy, created a form of private socialism is far from the mark. More often than not, managers were also owners and shared the latter's ethic; and, as the J. P. Morgan and Company directors on the boards of hundreds of companies dramatically demonstrated, owners, no matter how widely dispersed, could affect corporate operations. The larger truth is that stock ownership since the late nineteenth century has always been exceptionally concentrated and able to influence, even shape, corporate policymaking.

In 1900 as in 1860, therefore, the United States had a vigorous capitalist economy, although one that big business had significantly modified by the turn of the century. Although the nature of the economy per se did not change substantially between 1901 and 1917, the nation's political economy did change fundamentally due to the rise of big government.

# 3
# MODERNIZING THE NAVY

The Gilded Age and the Progressive Era were critical periods for the military services. Yet on one level, this was not apparent. Drastically reduced in size and importance after the Civil War, both the army and navy returned to their antebellum, peacetime pursuits. For the army that meant frontier duty; for the navy, showing the flag and protecting commerce. At the same time, however, both services began a process of professionalization that fundamentally altered their outlook, structure, and role and prepared them to handle the technological revolution that was transforming weaponry. Although the professionalization process reached maturity only with World War I, it was already well advanced by the early years of the twentieth century. The navy's progress was faster, its task perhaps simpler, and the pressures of technological change greater.

## DECLINE AND REVIVAL

With massive Civil War expansion, the navy in 1865 had one of the world's most formidable fleets.[1] By the early 1880s, though, the navy was no longer an international contender, rating no higher than twelfth in the world. This precipitous decline stemmed partly from severe postwar reductions in ships and personnel. Within eight years the navy was reduced from 700 to 165 ships and from nearly 7,000 officers and over 51,000 enlisted men to about 1,600 and 10,000. Many of the ships weeded out after hostilities were unfit because of poor design and hurried construction. Even if all the vessels had been of good quality and the nation had maintained its wartime numbers, the United States would still have had an inferior fleet in the 1870s. A naval revolution that had begun in the 1840s had produced ships of iron and steel, steam, propeller, and advanced ordnance and armor. The modern battleship, around which offensive fleets sailed, was evolving. The nation participated in the move to steam and propeller, iron and armor before the Civil War and made numerous advances in those categories during hostilities. But after the war, decline set in. The American navy was soon left without any armored vessels, and its blue-water fleets returned to sail power even when ships were equipped with steam locomotion.

According to most naval historians, the years from 1866 to 1881 were the dark ages. The nation allowed its navy, top-heavy with officers who faced a bleak future in terms of assignments, promotion, and experience, to rot and rust. Stagnation and neglect, corruption and demoralization were the lot of the navy, both afloat and on shore.

There is of course some truth to the charges. After Gideon Welles left office, a string of inexperienced or incompetent secretaries of the navy served from 1869 to 1881 with curious, often unfortunate, results. President Ulysses S. Grant's first secretary of the navy, Adolph E. Borie (March–June 1869), was a stand-in for Adm. David D. Porter, who used his position as de facto secretary of the navy to prepare for an unlikely war with Great Britain that he desired and to subordinate the staff in general and the Bureau of Steam Engineering in particular to the domination of the line.

Borie's successor was George M. Robeson (June 1869–March 1877), a New Jersey attorney with no particular qualifications for the job. He received the appointment through the influence of New Jersey's senator Alexander G. Cattell. For the next eight years, Cattell, his family and associates, and Robeson enriched themselves by bending or violating Navy Department regulations to buy naval supplies from favored contractors without competitive bidding and by ignoring conflicts of interest to use Jay Cooke and Company as the navy's fiscal agent.

Much more money was lost and greater harm done to the navy by the practice of constructing new ships under the guise of repairing old ones. This subterfuge came about because Congress, although it provided for ten new ships during Robeson's years in office, generally frowned on new construction. As a result, the secretary of the navy rebuilt existing ships, including deteriorated monitors large and small, at public and private yards. When funds for rebuilding ran low, the secretary ignored governmental policies by turning monitors and other vessels earmarked for sale over to private contractors for scrap in return for continued construction. The rebuilding process shackled the navy with obsolete ships, costing nearly twice the amount that England and France were paying for up-to-date ironclads.

Inefficiency also prevailed at the navy yards, which were rent by line-staff conflict, fragmented by the operations of the bureaus, and subject to party politics. Private yards had a better record, but efficiency was often sacrificed to politics as influence-peddling, party contributions, and kickbacks became a standard part of the contracting process. John Roach, the nation's leading shipbuilder, was not the incompetent, unscrupulous, and corrupt contractor that contemporaries and numerous historians have portrayed. Nonetheless, in building, rebuilding, and repairing ships for the navy, he engaged in the expected practice of sharing some of his contracting dollars with Robeson and other Republicans.

Repeated congressional investigations exposed nearly all of Robeson's shady operations and questionable practices. However, partisanship obfuscated the issues, and the revelations did not prevent Robeson from serving two terms in the House of Representatives between 1878 and 1882. Richard W. Thompson (March 1877–December 1880) followed Robeson as secretary. He did little more than try to improve the Navy Department's reputation by following the letter of the law until he was fired for agreeing to act as a front man for Ferdinand de Lesseps's Panama Canal Company while still secretary of the navy.

Malfeasance, misfeasance, and inactivity are only peripheral complaints among twentieth-century scholars disenchanted with the navy in the early decades of the Gilded Age. As disciples of Alfred Thayer Mahan, their real complaint is that the United States lost its Civil War dominance and did not keep abreast of the naval revolution so as to maintain a world-class force. A number of dissenting historians, particularly Kenneth J. Hagan and Lance C. Buhl, trenchantly point out that this approach is ahistorical.[2] During the Gilded Age, America faced no major threats to its security and was absorbed in continentalism and commercialism. Continentalism meant turning away from Europe to fill out borders and to develop the enormously rich internal market; commercialism meant maximizing trade with Europe and with countries that today are called the Third World. Those goals required only a modest navy. To protect the continent, the United States followed its traditional policy of harbor defense and commerce raiding; to maximize trade, it relied on stability in Europe and concentrated on policing the Third World with small naval squadrons that were more than a match for any local adversary. As the dominant branch of government during the Gilded Age and the primary author of naval policy, Congress repeatedly rejected the importunities of individuals seeking a better navy and checked their attempts to foment war with Europe and to acquire colonies in the Pacific and Caribbean, which would have made an expanded navy imperative. Focused on internal development and international commercial opportunity, the nation was satisfied and secure with an admittedly inferior navy and had no desire to match its policies or situation with Europe's. Had it been otherwise, the navy would have been an end in itself, "no small matter," according to Buhl, "in a society whose Constitution clearly treats the military as instrumental to civilian concerns."

Congress was hardly parsimonious toward the postwar navy. It allowed Welles to keep an exceptionally large peacetime fleet between 1865 and 1867 until all foreign threats faded. Budgets declined thereafter, but they were generous compared with the antebellum period. In unadjusted dollars, average annual appropriations for the navy ran around $13 million between 1851 and 1861, rose to $79 million between 1862 and 1865, and dropped to $22 million between 1866 and 1881. Hence, in the dark ages the nation spent almost twice the amount on the navy that it had in the decade before the Civil War.

Indeed, inexperienced and incompetent secretaries of the navy, corruption, and politicized navy yards did not first appear in the Gilded Age; these problems were commonplace by 1860. Furthermore, the United States and its leaders showed a certain wisdom in allowing Europe to engage in the expensive, troublesome experiments of the naval revolution. Much of the technology was unperfected, and change progressed at a swift pace. Ships, guns, armor, and steam machinery could be obsolete before vessels even put to sea. Frequently damned for not hurriedly embracing the new technology, cautious and skeptical navy officers and their civilian supporters were often simply being responsible. When the United States began to build a new fleet in the 1880s, it greatly benefited from European experience.

When the time did come for a new fleet, leadership and expertise had to originate in the naval officer corps, qualities that were lacking in the 1860s and 1870s. Traumatized and demoralized by postwar demobilization, the bloated officers corps displayed its worst tendencies in the decades after hostilities. The line and staff fought intensely over control of the navy. Officers schemed to advance their careers and engaged in endless petty quarrels and stratagems. Without strong, knowledgeable secretaries to impose order, the fractured service was in no position to approach Congress with proposals for reform or material improvement.

In the midst of the navy's disarray, a professionalizing process, which had begun before the Civil War, was reactivated and grew in strength and accomplishment. Key to this progress was the creation of several institutions and the introduction of new practices. The former included the U.S. Naval Institute, founded in 1873, the Office of Naval Intelligence, created in 1882, and the Naval War College, established in 1884. Beginning in 1881 and continuing into the twentieth century, the secretaries of the navy, acting alone or at the direction of Congress, created various boards of naval officers to advise and assist them with the composition of the fleet, ship construction, navy yard operations, differences between the line and staff, and, in conjunction with the army, coastal fortification. Additionally, as international tensions mounted, existing and ad hoc agencies began to plan for war. These efforts gradually led to modifications in the navy's command structure. Secretary of the Navy John D. Long created a Naval War Board to assist him with command functions during the Spanish-American War. After hostilities, the secretary made this arrangement more permanent by establishing the General Board of the Navy in 1900 to act as a rudimentary general staff. Although a formal general staff never emerged, the chief of naval operations, created by statute in 1915, became the navy's counterpart to the army's chief of staff. Restructuring the shore establishment and command functions usually also involved reform of the bureau system.

The Naval Institute was organized at Annapolis about the same time that mobilization of the navy for a crisis with Spain over Cuba late in 1873 revealed how unprepared the fleet was. Although line officers led in founding the institute, staff officers supported and participated in the effort at naval modernization. Disregarding rank, officers from the lowest to the highest grade joined in a scholarly debate on vital issues, such as tactics and strategy, technology and ship construction, officer training, and manpower. The institute's *Proceedings* became an effective and respected means for disseminating knowledge, attracting new members, and influencing policy. By formalizing and broadening debate, the institute helped to energize the navy and bridge its divisions.

The Office of Naval Intelligence (ONI) was the nation's first agency charged with systematically gathering information on the military affairs of foreign powers. Through its small Washington office and a network of naval attachés abroad, the agency was intended to provide the navy with practical information on modern naval weaponry and to stimulate public interest and support for revamping the American fleet. Intelligence operations abroad presented few challenges because major powers made no attempt to restrict access to their fleets until the early years of the twentieth century. Having gathered vital information on the strength of foreign navies, the ONI in time began to plan for war. Various officers looked on this process as logical since they considered the office as the first step toward creating a general staff for the navy.

Establishing the Naval War College (NWC) constituted the most significant move in professionalizing the naval officer corps during the Gilded Age. The intense and ongoing resistance to the college is one measure of its importance. Viewing it as a threat to their status and authority, conservative officers of the line nearly succeeded in sinking the new school during its tumultuous first ten years.

The Naval War College was the brainchild of Rear Adm. Stephen B. Luce, the true father of the modern American navy if any one person can claim that distinction. Luce was a rare combination of the cerebral and practical naval officer. Exceptionally although eclectically well read, he was also a first-rate seaman. At the age of thirty-six, while serving as head of the Department of Seamanship at the Naval Academy in 1863, he compiled *Seamanship,* which quickly became the standard work on handling sailing vessels. When the navy turned its back on his proposal for improving the training and quality of seamen, Luce successfully lobbied business leaders and members of Congress to achieve legislation setting up a nautical school for boys in 1874. The rear admiral was also one of the leaders in creating the Naval Institute and was among its most prolific authors.

These activities were a prologue to his principal goal of thoroughly professionalizing the officer corps in its specialty, the science and art of conducting war. Only when that was accomplished, Luce was convinced, would naval officers gain a proper role in shaping the nature and function of their service. Influenced by Social Darwinism and military thought, the rear admiral believed war to be inevitable because nations and peoples were aggressive, especially where economics was involved. Basing his views on his own studies, the work of colleagues such as Commodore Foxhall A. Parker, the German example, and the influence of Generals William T. Sherman and Emory Upton, Luce believed that immutable laws governing military strategy could be discovered and conveyed to the officer corps. Since no literature of note existed on naval strategy, that of the army had to be applied to warfare at sea. Fighting a type of army battle was feasible since steam and propeller made it possible to maneuver navies predictably and precisely. Over time, however, evolutionary and revolutionary changes in military weaponry affected only the tactics, not the strategy, of warfare. If officers bogged down in "technicism" or focused excessively on their roles as seaman, engineer, hydrographer, and the like, they not only fragmented their service but also compromised their primary function of providing for the nation's security.

The Naval War College was created as a postgraduate school to put Luce's ideas into action. Starting with a few students in rundown facilities at Newport, Rhode Island, in September 1885, the NWC began with a program of lectures and independent study, advanced to war problems, games, and planning and tactical fleet exercises, and became a research center for the General Board. Together, the board, the ONI, and the NWC acted as the general staff the navy lacked. Luce served as the college's first president, followed by Capt. Alfred Thayer Mahan, who had two tours, 1886–1889 and 1892–1893. In a sense, the presidency of Capt. Henry C. Taylor, between 1893 and 1897, was among the most important in the institution's history. As politically astute and strategically talented as Luce, and as the moving force on behalf of a general staff for the navy, Taylor saved the NWC from its numerous enemies within the navy by reaching out to businessmen, politicians, and community leaders for protection.

Mahan was the college's most famous president and faculty member. Selected by Luce in 1885 to fill the chair in Naval History and Strategy, Mahan's lectures on the subject were published in 1890, *The Influence of Sea Power upon History, 1660–1783.* The book included the now-familiar proposals for controlling the seas with a modern navy, overseas bases, an American-controlled Isthmian Canal, and an enlarged merchant marine. Luce, Taylor, Mahan, and their colleagues in and about the NWC filled out this general outline by insisting that the American fleet must be offensive in nature, concentrated around the battleship, and prepared in years of peace to protect overseas naval bases and the commercial fleet and in years of hostilities to seek out and destroy the enemy fleets as far from American shores as possible. It was to be, in short, a navy for empire and world domination.

Little that Mahan wrote was original, since he dealt much better with past rather than with present or future naval strategy. Moreover, he was tactically inept. Luce, Taylor, and other civilian and naval figures were much more talented thinkers. Nonetheless, Mahan's importance should not be underestimated. He systematically set forth for the first time how navies should be used in peace and war. More important, he was a talented synthesizer and propagandist who made the "science of naval warfare" graspable, and in some instances creditable, to American leaders and laypersons. Most important, he attracted and influenced national leaders who played a vital role in converting the American navy from insignificance to first-class status.

Yet it was Luce who made the most of the initial contacts. Unlike the vain, aloof, and priggish Mahan, Luce was a politically shrewd, outgoing, gifted, and persistent lobbyist. Accurately anticipating the resistance that the NWC would encounter, he used the *Army-Navy Journal* as the mouthpiece for the college and then turned to the civilian world for help. His first recruit was Nelson W. Aldrich, the powerful senator from Rhode Island, where Luce intended to locate the NWC. William E. Chandler, while and after he served as secretary of the navy, proved to be critically important. Distantly related by marriage to Congressman and later Senator Henry Cabot Lodge of Massachusetts, Luce exploited that advantage and invited Theodore Roosevelt to lecture at the college at the first available opportunity. Furthermore, the founder of the NWC never missed a chance to reach out to members of the Naval Affairs Committees of both houses of Congress. Luce's contacts usually became Mahan's as well, and once the *Influence of Sea Power* was out and other publications followed, prominent men appeared anxious to share the spotlight with Mahan and to use his work to assist their drive for an expanded navy. The Roosevelt-Lodge-Luce-Mahan ties were particularly important in that regard.

The year 1881 marks the beginning of the new navy. It was then that Pres. James A. Garfield appointed William H. Hunt as his secretary of the navy. Although serving for only a year, from March 1881 to April 1882, Hunt's tenure represented a clear departure from the secretaries of the past. He was the first of six successive secretaries of the navy of good to excellent abilities who guided the modernization of the American fleet in the last decades of the nineteenth century. Never before had the navy had such capable leadership over a twenty-year period. This was even more remarkable because control of the White House and Congress alternated between Democrats and Republicans from 1885 to 1897 in a highly charged partisan atmosphere. Bipartisanship was evident, if not fully in force, in relation to the navy, however. Modernization proceeded in two distinct phases. The first, extending from 1881 to 1889, involved technologically updating the fleet more effectively to carry out its defensive mission. The second, beginning in 1889 and extending into the twentieth century, entailed gradually and at times deceptively changing the fleet's mission to an offensive one along the lines Mahan had set forth.

Modernizing the fleet made sense in the 1880s. American warships had passed obsolescence en route to becoming relics while Europe's progress on modern naval weaponry had reached the point where the United States could genuinely benefit from its experience. Professionalization also unified support for reform within the navy. Moreover, by the 1880s, the pace of industrialization was slowing and the pain of the Civil War was becoming sufficiently distant that the nation appeared willing to spend time and money on the navy if that appeared necessary. Money was not a problem as Washington struggled with budget surpluses. And the war scare with Spain in late 1873 over the *Virginius* affair demonstrated that the navy lacked the ability to perform adequately even in its home waters.

In the 1890s the building of an offensive fleet began as America fundamentally altered its foreign policy. The international scene grew increasingly volatile in the late nineteenth and early twentieth centuries as Germany, Italy, and Japan challenged the stabilizing balance of power and the great powers engaged in another round of imperialism and menacing arms races. As long as the United States remained aloof from the scramble, two oceans still shielded it from hostilities and no enemies were in sight.

Nonetheless, emerging as the world's most economically powerful nation, the United States itself began expanding late in the nineteenth century. Its diplomatic and military intervention in Latin America grew throughout the 1880s and 1890s, leading to the Spanish-American War, in which the United States emphatically designated Latin America as its sphere, closing the door to foreign intervention. In taking the Philippines, the nation did not innocently stumble into the Asian tinderbox but rushed forward to begin achieving dominance in the Pacific and to play a leading role on the Asian mainland. As William Appleman Williams and his students have explained, America's imperialism was formulated and executed by a civilian elite and fueled by a complex mixture of economics, power politics, and idealism. The United States could have expanded into Latin America and still remained aloof from international tensions while maintaining a defensive military strategy. Once expanded into the Pacific and Asia, however, the United States joined seriously in the ongoing restructuring of international power balances, which increased the possibility of war. To match strategy with diplomacy, an offensive American navy became a necessity.

Washington moved to square strategy and diplomacy in a subtle, even deceptive way. After converting from outmoded to modern ships in the 1880s, the United States began to shift the fleet's mission in the 1890s from harbor defense and commerce raiding to a defensive mission achieved offensively. Only after the Spanish-American War and the acquisition of colonies on both sides of the continent did the nation overtly give the fleet an offensive role and set its sights first on a navy second to one and then, with the outbreak of World War I, on a navy second to none.

Civilians determined the major outlines of America's expansionist foreign policy, and civilians in the executive and legislative branches also made the critical decisions involving the navy, the officer corps providing the necessary support, expertise, and advice. As the fleet grew in size and sophistication, its circle of supporters expanded to include, besides imperialists and navalists, multiplying interest groups that benefited directly or indirectly from the new navy.

America's new diplomacy and strategy were debated, often with intensity in and outside the halls of government throughout the late nineteenth and early twentieth centuries. The argument was usually of a truncated nature, however, taking place after, not before, the defining event. Such was the case with the acquisition of the Philippines. With growing support in Congress, the federal executive deftly moved the United States from continentalism to imperialism without full public scrutiny. The general public found the new diplomacy and strategy to its liking, remained unaware or unconcerned about these distant developments, was subject to patriotic manipulation, or assumed some combination of the three responses.

William Hunt took over as secretary of the navy in 1881 already disposed to reform the department, since one of his sons was a naval officer. The navy's neglected condition had become a matter of national and international ridicule. By then the American fleet consisted of 140 ships, 17 of iron construction, only 52 considered worthy of duty, and none mounting modern ordnance.

Guided by Admiral Porter, Hunt convened a Naval Advisory Board of nine line and six staff officers to review the existing fleet and to make comprehensive recommendations for a new building program. After deliberating for four months, a divided board recommended that the navy immediately acquire eighteen unarmored steel cruisers and twenty wooden cruisers equipped with both steam and sail locomotion, five rams, and ten torpedo boats. In the next eight years, the board favored building an additional ninety-one cruisers, twenty-one of which would be armored, and twenty-five more torpedo boats. The relatively small and lightly armed nature of the recommended ships clearly showed that the board envisioned an updated but still defensive navy.

Congress, which had regularly investigated the navy since the days of Secretary of the Navy Robeson and was quite knowledgeable on the subject, held hearings to gather further information. Hunt and Pres. Chester A. Arthur lobbied extensively and effectively for a building program. At the same time, the secretary of the navy began educating the aloof naval officer corps, which tended to be hostile toward civilians, on the need to respect and work with Congress to advance the service's cause. For political reasons, Hunt was forced out as secretary of the navy in favor of William E. Chandler before Congress completed naval legislation. Nevertheless, before leaving office, Hunt made a good start on the so-called naval renaissance and capped his contribution by issuing a general order creating the Office of Naval Intelligence.

Chandler was controversial before, during, and after serving as secretary of the navy. A major Republican political operative, he had served for a short time in the navy's bureaucracy and acted as an influential Washington lobbyist for, among others, John Roach, the largest shipbuilder and a major naval contractor. Picking up where Hunt left off, Chandler organized another Naval Advisory Board, which helped formulate a more modest, politically realistic building program of three unarmored cruisers and a dispatch boat. Congress accepted the proposal, and in the authorizing legislation required that these vessels be made of domestic steel, armed with breech-loading rifled cannon, and capable of operating by sail or steam. By limiting repairs to 20 percent, in some cases 10 percent, of the cost of building a comparable ship, the enabling statute also forced the retirement of numerous worn-out vessels. Here were the origins of the new navy. For the first time since the Civil War, Congress voted to build a number of technologically advanced ships of war. Henceforth, the fleet would steadily increase in size and quality as the United States rather rapidly ascended from twelfth to as high as second place among navies of the world in the early twentieth century.

Because the navy yards were unprepared for such construction, Chandler sought competitive bids from private shipyards. Possessing the only yard integrated backward to include steel production and the manufacture of marine steam engines, Roach won contracts for the four vessels (called ABCDs after the initials of their names) for his Chester, Pennsylvania, establishment over the accusations of other firms that he and Chandler were engaged in collusive contracting. Although unsubstantiated and untrue, the charges cast a cloud of suspicion over the venture and led to further complications when Roach failed to complete any of the vessels by 1885, leaving him to deal with the succeeding, hostile Democratic administration.

Chandler's contribution to the new navy did not end with contracts for ships. He ignored senior admirals to establish the Naval War College by general order in 1884. Chandler also sought to rationalize the navy yards. He succeeded in closing those at Pensacola and New London but did not dare move against the ones at Boston and Portsmouth because they were part of the political fiefdoms of Congressmen Lodge and Thomas R. Reed. Politics also prevented Chandler from weeding out incompetents to reduce the enormous surplus of officers plaguing the navy. But the secretary nonetheless ignored protests from the officer corps and its political supporters to uphold dismissals of officers for cause, deny officers assignments of convenience, and end senior officers' use of navy ships for personal and private purposes. These steps advanced professionalism and raised morale. Indeed, Chandler was a successful secretary who accomplished a great deal during three years in office.

Grover Cleveland's election to the presidency in 1884 gave the Democratic party its first opportunity to appoint a secretary of the navy since before the Civil War. The president turned to William C. Whitney, a wealthy businessman and political protégé of Samuel J. Tilden, the Democratic presidential candidate in the disputed election of 1876. Whitney had played an active role in breaking up New York's Tweed ring. He was a highly partisan, self-righteous reformer who made war on his predecessor, Chandler, by rejecting the one vessel completed by Roach, driving him into bankruptcy, and having the navy complete the other three ships in Roach's former yards. Congress' annual naval appropriations under Whitney averaged $21 million, a 25 percent increase over those for Hunt and Chandler, which speeded up shipbuilding considerably. Like his predecessors and successors, Whitney appointed a board of naval officers to advise him on construction. Approximately thirty ships joined the fleet during the secretary's four years in office, ranging from heavily armored and gunned cruisers, later redesignated as second-class battleships, to small service vessels.

Several points stand out in relation to this building program. The cruiser *Charleston* was the first warship to dispense with sails, setting a standard that all other naval vessels soon followed. Further, the self-propelled "automobile torpedo" made the ram obsolete, led to the realignment of gun placement on ships, and constituted another formidable weapon of war. Finally, although building what could be considered offensive men-of-war, the strategic doctrine, such as it was, remained defensive, creating considerable confusion within and outside the navy.

The confusion was compounded because Whitney, again turning against Chandler's work and listening to disgruntled line and staff officers, almost succeeded in doing away with the Naval War College. While undermining the service's most promising agency for strategy and planning, Whitney insisted that he lacked proper advice on the technical and military aspects of the navy and unsuccessfully attempted to have Congress reorganize the bureaus into a more effective operational and advisory system.

Perhaps more important than Whitney's building program were steps he took to free the United States from dependence on Europe for building its new fleet. The ABCDs were designed by European-trained naval architects, and the navy depended on the ONI and naval attachés to keep abreast of current technology. Whitney purchased abroad plans for some of the most advanced ships built during his term. The big guns, armor, armor-piercing shells, brown powder, and even shafts and some steam machinery and equipment came from Europe. Seeking to strengthen domestic construction capabilities, Whitney in 1887 consolidated several years' worth of armor and armament requirements. He then offered Bethlehem Iron Company a large enough order at a high enough price ($4.5 million) for building a steel forging plant to handle the contract. Thus the navy subsidized the large-scale steel forging industry in the United States. Whitney also participated in creating a gun factory at the Washington Navy Yard and, along with the army, worked to develop production facilities for brown powder and projectiles. By the next decade, the United States had satisfactorily developed the ability to domestically design, construct, equip, and arm the most sophisticated ships of war. Despite a mixed record, Whitney made a substantial contribution in modernizing the navy.

Benjamin F. Tracy, Pres. Benjamin Harrison's secretary of the navy between 1889 and 1893, is generally considered the most important and talented of the men holding the office in the post–Civil War nineteenth century. Tracy deftly led the transition from a defensive to an offensive navy. He instituted revisions in doctrine, launched an impressive shipbuilding program, and furthered reform of the shore establishment. In a sense, Tracy was an unlikely candidate for this critical role. A Civil War veteran, he was an attorney, a jurist, and an identified member of Thomas C. Platt's New York Republican machine. Harrison appointed Tracy—an "honest spoilsman"—to placate Platt.

Tracy showed few signs before 1889 of being the aggressive navalist and expansionist he became after taking over as secretary of the navy. Among his early acts was rescuing the Naval War College from line hostility. More broadly, he began a six-month process of educating himself about the service and its needs. He consulted widely with line and staff officers, principal strategists such as Luce, Mahan, and James R. Soley (a professor at Newport and Annapolis who became assistant secretary of the navy in 1890), influential members of Congress, such as Speaker Reed, Charles A. Boutelle (R-ME), Lodge (R-MA), Hilary A. Herbert (D-AL), and William McAdoo (D-NJ)—all important members of the House Naval Affairs Committee—Sen. Eugene Hale (R-ME) of the Senate Naval Affairs Committee, and other navalists such as Theodore Roosevelt and Charles A. Dana. The new secretary also proved to be shrewd at public relations. In November 1889 he organized the first "squadron of evolution"—the nucleus of a permanent fleet consisting of three cruisers and a gunboat—to test at sea the NWC's tactical and strategic doctrines and to visit Europe so that foreigners could see the new navy. Tens of thousands of Americans visited the ships before they departed, with the publicity continuing as the fleet visited various European ports.

Historians have labeled Tracy's first annual report to the president in November 1889 as "revolutionary" and "radical"—the first state paper to endorse an offensive naval policy based on the capital-ship theory. In the report, Tracy maintained that only heavily armored battleships and auxiliary vessels in the Atlantic and Pacific would give the nation the capacity to defend its interests through offensive operations. As a start in that direction, the secretary of the navy recommended building twenty armored battleships. His bold, blunt report reflected the views of navalists and imperialists in general and bore the clear imprint of Admiral Luce and Mahan. With the president recommending eight battleships and the first fully Republican-controlled Congress since 1875 ready seriously to consider a building program of eight battleships, two armored monitors, three cruisers, and five torpedo boats, Tracy appeared to be in a strong position.

Before the congressional debate was fully under way, however, the secret report of a Policy Board, headed by Commodore William P. McCann, that Tracy had appointed months earlier to advise him on a building program was leaked to the press. In it, the board proposed a long-range building schedule, including 35 battleships, 24 armored cruisers, 15 torpedo-cruisers, and over 100 light torpedo boats, which could give the United States a navy second only to Great Britain's. The leaked report aroused and galvanized the opposition of the small-navy advocates (individuals favoring a substantially enlarged and modernized navy but with a defensive strategy), who included former Secretary of the Navy Chandler and editors at Luce's once-loyal *Army-Navy Journal;* the report even drew the ire of some expansionists, who labeled it as "naval fanaticism." Antiexpansionist, isolationist, and pacifist elements throughout the nation, particularly from the Midwest, also joined the fray. The combined attack threatened to scuttle any expansion of the fleet. Congressman Boutelle saved the navy for Tracy and his supporters by cutting the expansion program to three battleships, relabeled as "sea-going coast-line battleships" with limited cruising ranges, which were supplemented by a protected cruiser, a torpedo cruiser, and a light torpedo boat. Labels aside, the three battleships were rated by the British upon completion as at least a match for any ships afloat, and no future American battleships had restricted cruising ranges.

Before Tracy left office, nineteen steel warships had been added to the fleet and another nineteen were under construction. Annual appropriations averaged $29 million, nearly 25 percent higher than those of his predecessor. In four years, Secretary Tracy basically changed American naval strategy and laid a firm foundation for an offensive fleet.

Aggressive and impetuous, Tracy sought to acquire colonies and coaling stations to buttress the nation's enhanced sea power. He played a major role in the blatant, failed attempts to acquire base sites in Haiti and Santo Domingo and to annex Hawaii. The only success here was the acquisition of a coaling station at Pago Pago in Samoa. If Tracy had had his way, the navy would have been tested in a war against Chile that threatened on several occasions in 1891–1892 when the United States became involved in the revolution rocking that nation. From the outset of the conflict, the secretary of the navy created a board to write war plans and ordered a full-scale naval mobilization. As in his first annual report, Tracy kept no one guessing as to his policies and ambitions.

Tracy had the virtue of almost total consistency. He was the first Gilded Age secretary to direct the department in an organic way. Having decided on a strategy, he approached the composition of the fleet, building programs, training, and shore establishment with the aim of effecting his strategy. Hence his rescue of and heavy reliance on the NWC made sense, given his aspirations for an offensive fleet, as did his insistence that quality be the major criterion in the selection of Annapolis candidates. A navy could be no better than the quality and training of the men who ran it.

Tracy applied the same approach to the shore establishment. To improve and speed up the construction of ships and to free himself from endlessly playing mediator, Tracy set up a Board of Construction (also known as the Board on the Design of Ships) shortly after taking office. It consisted of the chiefs of the five bureaus involved in shipbuilding: Construction and Repair, Equipment, Yards and Docks, Ordnance, and Steam Engineering. The board was to agree on the plans for all ships and then take full responsibility for the completed product. The system allowed the bureaus to maintain their identity while significantly reducing the fragmentation that had led to poor design and construction delays by making one body accountable for the ship as a whole.

Tracy's attempts at reform extended to the private sector. With Bethlehem holding up ship construction by failing to deliver armor on schedule, the secretary in 1890 persuaded Carnegie, Phipps and Company to join in as a contractor. An expanded production base allowed Tracy to insist that contractors take up the manufacture of nickel-steel and then Harveyized-steel armor when tests showed them to be superior to simple forged steel.

Further, Tracy gave attention to naval procurement and the navy yards consistent with his conviction that efficiency and economy were essential for a fighting navy. Picking up where Whitney and previous secretaries had left off, Tracy centralized purchasing, auditing, and accounting in the Bureau of Provisions and Clothing, aptly renamed the Bureau of Supplies and Accounts in 1892. This effort carried over to the navy's subunits. Each navy yard appointed a general storekeeper and each ship a paymaster who acted as central buying and storing agent answerable to the Bureau of Supplies and Accounts. The navy thus achieved a centralized system for procurement, accounting, auditing, and inventory. Moreover, over the loud and long protests of his own party, the secretary of the navy ended the spoils system in the navy yards, setting up a system of hiring and evaluation by merit and introducing civil service rules and procedures.

Tracy could not remake the navy in the space of a few years; many of his changes and reforms had not advanced far beyond the stage of planning or initial implementation. Nonetheless, he left the navy quite different from how he found it, and he certainly ranks among the most important civilians involved in modernizing the American fleet.

Hilary A. Herbert followed Tracy as secretary of the navy. A former Confederate officer and a Democrat, his years in office indicated that support for an enlarged, offensive navy had become bipartisan and had gained backing in the South. Few men came to the office better prepared than the Alabamian. During sixteen years in the House of Representatives, he had served for three sessions on the Naval Affairs Committee, including once as chair. As a small-navy man, Herbert had opposed Tracy's building program and came to office unfriendly to the Naval War College.

Once in office, though, exposure to national and international naval realities and to Mahan's *Sea Power* quickly converted him to the large-navy position. Herbert eventually not only supported the NWC but also used it for war planning during various crises facing the Cleveland administration. His recommendation for extensive building in 1893 went unsupported by the president—a declared opponent of imperial expansion and a fiscal conservative—or by Congress, which was unwilling to spend during a depression. Face-offs with Great Britain over Nicaragua and Venezuela in 1895, the beginning of trouble with Spain over Cuba the same year, earlier military intervention in the Brazilian revolution, and the rising naval prominence of Japan after its victory over China in 1894–1895 made Congress more receptive to Herbert's continued insistence upon expanding the fleet, however. His argument that naval contracts would accelerate, not retard, economic recovery proved particularly telling. For 1895 and 1896, Congress authorized the construction of five battleships and sixteen torpedo boats.

Herbert asserted that growing turbulence in Latin America and the Pacific required increased naval might to protect American interests. His assistant secretary, William McAdoo, also once a small-navy man and who anticipated the style and substance of his successor, Theodore Roosevelt, was much more aggressive than Herbert and an outspoken jingoist. He was among the first to call for abandoning small squadrons and concentrating ships in two major fleets in the Atlantic and the Pacific to meet challenges in Latin American and Asia. The nation soon adopted this policy. As war threatened with Spain, the assistant secretary called for a board patterned after the British Board of Admiralty to advise the secretary on strategy, tactics, and technology. This group anticipated the Naval War Board set up during the Spanish-American War and the General Board, which came after hostilities. Herbert and McAdoo clearly demonstrated that in terms of naval and foreign policy, very little separated Democrats from Republicans, Cleveland's putative anti-imperialism notwithstanding.

Like Tracy, Herbert had troubles with the steel firms over armor. In 1894, Carnegie, Phipps was charged with delivering defective armor plate to the navy, leading to a substantial fine that the president reduced in severity. When Herbert a year later sought to reduce the price of armor purchased from Carnegie and Bethlehem, the companies proved recalcitrant, would not cooperate in an investigation of costs ordered by Congress, and were discovered to be selling to Russia for $250 per ton the same armor they were providing the navy at $625 per ton. Herbert concluded that $400 per ton was more than a fair price but left office before he could resolve the issue. The episode hardly died with Herbert. Growing more acrimonious after the Spanish-American War, the incident led the navy, already managing a substantial industrial plant for the manufacture of guns, torpedoes, powder, and projectiles, to build an armor plant. The imbroglio additionally provided documentation for anti-imperialist and antinavalist elements, who argued that naval growth encouraged profiteering and corruption and compromised relations between the government and industry.

Herbert encountered corruption of the old style as well as the new. The government did not have yards and docks that could keep up with the increased output and size of the navy ships. Attempting to remedy this situation, the secretary of the navy faced intense opposition on the East Coast to new or expanded naval facilities on the West Coast. Building on the work of Tracy, Herbert did manage to improve the operation of the bureaus. In 1894 he concentrated responsibility for ship construction even further by making the Bureau of Construction and Repair the primary agency for designing and building ships. This reform worked out well. Herbert also refined the policies and practices that Tracy had introduced to centralize navy buying, storage, auditing, and financing. In 1896 the secretary could report that during his term in office the U.S. Navy had risen from ninth to sixth place in the world as measured by battleship strength.

## THE SPANISH-AMERICAN WAR

Developments after 1881 left the navy better prepared for the Spanish-American War than for any previous conflict. Hilary A. Herbert had begun to face the tensions that led to hostilities before he left office, but the major naval responsibility in the conflict with Spain fell to William McKinley's secretary of the navy, John D. Long. An attorney and a politician from Maine, Long's appointment was political, and he was not particularly qualified for the office. The secretary in many ways resembled the president. Affable, low-key, competent, and not easily pushed around, he wanted to avoid war and imperialism but went along with trends he felt to be larger than his own wishes.

Assistant Secretary of the Navy Theodore Roosevelt was just the opposite. Aggressive, bellicose, and impetuous, he treasured an offensive navy, fully accepted Mahan's theories, and welcomed war and expansion abroad. Almost from the day he took office, Roosevelt worked to prepare the navy for war with Spain. Long and Congress blocked his way; the secretary of the navy was not anxious to further enlarge the navy, and Congress was of a like mind.

Actually, the navy was already in good shape to fight a weak adversary such as Spain. In 1897 the American navy had four first-class battleships, two second-class battleships, eighteen cruisers, and seventy lesser vessels, with five first-class battle wagons, sixteen torpedo boats, and a submarine under construction. By this time the United States could design, build, equip, and arm its own vessels. The service's authorized strength was 1,232 officers and 11,750 men. With improvements in the education at Annapolis and training fostered by the Naval War College and other institutions, the officer corps had probably never been of higher caliber. The enlisted men had also improved in quality, with over 70 percent being citizens. Two weaknesses stood out. First, none of the eleven navy yards could handle large ships. New York's Dry Dock no. 2, completed in 1901, was the first government facility that could service the large vessels in the fleet. Second, the struggle with the steel companies over armor continued, slowing down the completion of ships. By 1897 Congress had become so agitated over the matter that it seriously looked into building a public plant. The legislature backed away, and Long paid a higher price for armor than was believed justified.

Besides building up an impressive fleet, the navy had made significant headway in planning for its use in the event of hostilities. The Naval War College and the Office of Naval Intelligence started planning for war with Spain as early as 1894, and Herbert convened a special naval board to settle differences between the two agencies. Without resolving the matter, Long in June 1897 created a Naval War Board to continue the planning and later replaced it with a body of the same name to prepare for and direct the war. The first board was dominated by Roosevelt and his hawkish group. From the various plans emerged the strategy of destroying the Spanish fleets in the Philippines and in the Caribbean, an action that would leave those areas open to American imperial domination and provide apparent validation for the capital-ship theory of warfare. Before Roosevelt left the department, he virtually ordered Alfred Thayer Mahan to come out of retirement and return from Europe to serve on the Naval War Board. Meanwhile keeping his own counsel and authority, Long relied heavily on the advice of the board throughout hostilities. Roosevelt also played an important role in selecting Commodore George Dewey to head the Asiatic squadron in October 1897. Before war had broken out, Long and Roosevelt had selected the principal commanders for the Atlantic, instructed them on basic strategy, and prepared their orders.

Throughout the months of fighting, the various Atlantic squadrons, unlike Dewey's, found their every move dictated directly from Washington. Once Dewey had destroyed the Spanish fleet in Manila Bay, however, he too was subject to close control from Washington, given the delicacy and the importance of conditions there.

Throughout the war, President McKinley was a strong commander-in-chief. He set up a war room in the White House with the appropriate maps, telephone connections with his cabinet members and Congress, and telegraphic hookups with overseas bases. The president read, approved, or revised all important orders, consulted the secretary of the navy and the secretary of war and their chief advisers, his cabinet, or both groups on major decisions, and coordinated navy and army operations. The president and the Navy Department found their decisionmaking eased by the elaborate intelligence system the ONI set up in Europe, and to a lesser degree in Asia, which provided information on Spanish war preparations and ship movements.

The Navy Department began expanding its fleet in March 1898 by purchasing ships abroad and at home, taking over vessels from other government departments, and accepting gifts. One hundred twenty-eight ships were added to the navy in 1898, ranging from protected cruisers to luxury yachts. Dewey purchased several vessels in Asia to augment his squadron. During the war, naval manpower more than doubled to 2,088 officers and 24,123 enlisted men, including 2,600 from the naval militia and 1,800 other militiamen serving in an auxiliary capacity. Appropriations for 1898 totaled $57 million, and Congress in May of that year provided for three additional battleships, twelve torpedo boat destroyers, twelve torpedo boats, one gunboat, and thirty-eight other vessels—the largest spurt of naval building since the Civil War.

Mobilizing the navy for the war proved relatively simple and ultimately efficient. Streamlined and reformed bureaus and navy yards, and especially centralized procurement under the Bureau of Supplies and Accounts, facilitated mobilization and kept the profiteering and corruption that inevitably accompanies war to a low level. Although supplies of ammunition were more adequate than ample, no military operations suffered from shortages. Most other supplies were readily provided by the navy yards, where the work force almost doubled during hostilities, or were procured by the bureaus without major difficulties through contracts with private firms or open-market buying in the robust industrial economy. Facing war, Long set up Key West as the principal naval base for Caribbean and Atlantic operations, and it operated with few difficulties. Coordinating a number of squadrons in the Atlantic and Pacific was a major challenge for the Bureau of Navigation, but it proved equal to the task.

The war revealed several areas where improvements were imperative. Naval gunnery was exceptionally poor, with only a 3 percent hit record. The navy also needed an improved command system and better coordination with the army, including the transportation of troops and the conduct of amphibious warfare.

Both services were accorded the opportunity to improve joint operations during the three years of brutal, mostly guerrilla warfare that followed Spain's ceding the Philippines to the United States. In the first brown-water war of the twentieth century, the navy played a vital role in transporting troops, softening up landing spots, invading areas with sailors and marines, interdicting insurgent supply efforts, and disrupting guerrilla communications. With the army in better shape and with pressure lower than during a declared war fought in two oceans, the two services worked more successfully together than they had in the Caribbean, even though the navy found it difficult to provide the ships and men needed in the Philippines and on the Asian mainland.

Generally, the navy performed well during hostilities, particularly when compared with the army. Long's leadership had proven sound, though not outstanding. He drew upon the navy's professional and material strengths, built up since the early 1880s, to good effect.

The war also served to ensure continued growth for the navy and an expanded role for it in American diplomacy. With colonies or bases in the Philippines, Hawaii, Guam, and Wake, in addition to Samoa, and with active military and diplomatic involvement in the crumbling Chinese Empire, the United States had quite suddenly become a major imperial power throughout the Pacific and Asia. Moreover, the nation's hold on the Caribbean and its role in Latin America in general was much greater than it had ever been before. Imperial diplomacy meant imperial strategy, which for the moment principally involved the navy.

## A NAVY SECOND TO NONE

The Spanish-American War removed many of the prior restraints on naval building and allowed the Progressive administrations to aim for a second- and later a first-place navy. Various scholars have pointed out that the heavy American building schedules were strategically unnecessary since Great Britain was friendly, virtually withdrawing its fleet from the Caribbean; since a naval race between Britain and Germany focused the attention and might of both powers in Europe; and since Japan faced insuperable obstacles in mounting an attack on the West Coast of the United States.[3] These commentators assume that Washington's primary interest was defensive and continental, but the United States clearly had begun to move toward global domination and required a navy to match its ambitions.

The rapid building began under John D. Long during the Spanish-American War. Among the navies of the world, America moved from sixth to fourth between 1900 and 1902. Theodore Roosevelt—who appointed a total of six naval secretaries but actually acted as his own—made the navy one of his top priorities, achieved a thoroughly remarkable building program, and moved the navy to third place, possibly second, among the nations of the world before leaving office in 1909. Between 1901 and 1909 total naval appropriations approached $1 billion, averaging over $106 million annually. Shipbuilding absorbed a large share of the appropriations. Between 1900 and 1909 America constructed 101 naval vessels: eighteen battleships, including dreadnoughts, seven armored cruisers, three protected cruisers, three scout cruisers, thirty-one submarine torpedo boats, twenty-three torpedo-boat destroyers, and sixteen miscellaneous vessels, for a combined size of approximately 600,000 tons. By the end of Roosevelt's term, the United States had built or was building twenty-seven battleships, compared to forty-eight for Great Britain and thirty for Germany. To man this vastly expanded fleet, the officer corps increased from 1,588 in 1899 to 2,630 in 1909 and the number of enlisted men from 14,766 to 44,903 over the same period.

Roosevelt's building program followed guidelines laid down by the General Board in 1903. The board at that time reported to the secretary of the navy that the United States should have by 1920 a navy of forty-eight first-line battleships with auxiliaries in proper proportion. The recommendation was not published until 1913, but it carried great weight among presidents, secretaries of the navy, and Congress because it bore the imprimatur of Adm. George Dewey and other important naval officers. The aim was to achieve and maintain for the United States a navy second to one. This goal was accepted by every Progressive administration and Congress, Republican and Democratic alike. Differences arose among the majority only over the pace of building and whether armored cruisers and early first-line battleships should be included in the forty-eight. If they were, the nation had already reached its goal by 1915. A minority element throughout the Progressive years wanted a navy second to none; their position prevailed by 1915–1916.

After Roosevelt left office, naval expansion continued under the William Howard Taft administration even though the president and Secretary of the Navy George von Lengerke Meyer were much less persistent and aggressive than Roosevelt. From 1909 to 1913 a total of sixty-six ships was authorized, including six battleships, with appropriations averaging $123.6 million per year. Officers and men increased during those years to 3,273 and 48,929. Under Taft, the navy slipped from any claim of second place to third, behind Germany.

Ironically, it was the Woodrow Wilson administration that pushed American naval policy to its logical conclusion: a navy second to none. The president at first left naval policy largely to his secretary of the navy, Josephus Daniels, who held a curious mixture of civilian and military values. During his first years in office, he supported only a modest building program, although the General Board wanted more. Daniels became converted to the course of a much larger navy when Wilson began to favor preparedness, beginning in mid-1915. The pressure from hawkish advisers such as Secretary of State Robert Lansing and Edward M. House combined with Mexican conflict and various consequences from the outbreak of World War I to change Wilson's mind on the armed services. In time the president and the secretary of the navy endorsed a General Board program for making the United States the world's preeminent naval power within five years. Congress cut the timetable to three years and in 1916 voted to start the largest naval expansion in U.S. history with four battleships and four battle cruisers. America's entry into the war interrupted the building program but not the nation's determination to have a fleet in the future ready to face any potential enemy or combination of enemies, including Great Britain, Germany, and Japan. Between 1913 and 1916 naval appropriations averaged $142.2 million annually and manpower in those years increased to 4,022 officers and 56,354 enlisted men.

## CREATING A NEW SYSTEM OF COMMAND

The navy's basic system of command and administration was modified during the years between the Spanish-American War and America's entry into World War I. These critically important matters had plagued the navy since its origins and took on greater urgency as the service was professionalized and a new fleet built. The Spanish-American War highlighted the contention of reformers that a secretary of the navy, advised by a collection of disparate bureau chiefs, could not effectively command a small, peacetime navy, much less a modern one on constant alert for military action and war. What was needed was a body comparable to a general staff. In the absence of such an agency, the Naval War College and the Office of Naval Intelligence performed such staff functions, supplemented by various ad hoc boards on fleet size, building programs, and war planning.

Long's creation of the Naval War Board during the Spanish-American War turned out to be a significant step in the direction of a general staff. After the war, the secretary of the navy, recognizing the need for a better command system but sharing the views of many congressmen that a naval staff created by statute could threaten civilian control of the navy, compromised by creating the General Board in March 1900 by general order. Without authority or responsibility, the board was directed to advise the secretary of the navy on war plans, policies, and facilities and to coordinate the activities of the NWC and the ONI. The board was made up principally of line officers, the chief of the Bureau of Navigation, and representatives from the NWC and the ONI, aided by the cream of the junior officer corps, who served as staff assistants. Long gave the board wide latitude to deliberate and to make recommendations on most issues facing the navy and strengthened the body enormously by selecting Dewey, the most prestigious military officer, to act as its president, a position he held from 1900 to 1917. Neither a reformer nor a reactionary, Dewey set a middle course for the General Board and the navy it helped to direct. The admiral had a keen eye for talent, could persuade diverse and differing individuals and groups to cooperate for a common cause, and managed to maintain harmony through policies of compromise. Besides planning for war, the board concentrated on administering the fleet and America's new empire, setting goals for shipbuilding and manpower, and reforming the shore establishment.

In July 1903 the secretaries of war and navy set up the Joint Army-Navy Board to coordinate the efforts of the two services where that was necessary. Dewey headed this barebones agency, which proved to be helpful in strategic planning. But that did not solve a fundamental flaw in military planning: It took place in a vacuum. The navy's principal war plans, Black and Orange, aimed at Germany and Japan and with an obsessional emphasis on the former, had what one scholar labels an unrealistic, "rigid and deterministic" quality. Indeed, the Black plan was predicated on Germany's fleet invading the Caribbean to challenge the American navy for hemispheric dominance.

Naval planning was obviously not carried out in systematic consultation with the State Department and the presidency, the sources determining foreign policy. Without such a dialogue, diplomacy and strategy could not be synchronized. Disturbed by that reality, members of the Naval War College in 1912 proposed the creation of a Council of National Defense, made up of the secretaries of war, state, and navy, appropriate members of Congress, the military heads, and chief strategists of the army and navy, to coordinate foreign and defense policies. Congressman Richmond P. Hobson (D-AL) introduced a bill incorporating these recommendations, but it did not get far in a Congress that, unlike the military, was not focused on war.

Shortly after Long left office, Roosevelt and Secretary of the Navy William H. Moody proposed that Congress create a general staff–chief of staff system for the navy similar to that of the army. Reformers such as Admirals Stephen B. Luce and Henry C. Taylor had long advocated this move. Opposition from the bureaus, their congressional allies, and those concerned about diluting civilian control of the navy defeated such proposals. Although efforts at reforming the command structure continued throughout Roosevelt's years in office, the president refused to give them priority because he feared jeopardizing his primary goal of increasing the size of the fleet as much as possible.

Basing his approach on a number of studies and recommendations on command and administrative functions, Taft's secretary of the navy George von Lengerke Meyer tried to create a chief of staff by making an end run around Congress. Consulting the nation's legislators but acting on his own authority, he set up a system of four aides, covering fleet operations, material, inspections, and personnel, to whom the various bureaus would report. Just before leaving office and under pressure from his aide for operations, Rear Adm. Bradley A. Fiske, Meyer elevated Fiske to the position of liaison man between the secretary and all the bureaus and offices in the department. If Meyer's successor had accepted the idea, Fiske could have emerged as the de facto commanding officer of the navy.

From the outset, Josephus Daniels, Woodrow Wilson's secretary of the navy, squelched all attempts to circumvent his authority. He never approved of Meyer's aide system and allowed it to wither. A firm believer in civilian control of the military, Daniels also favored military professionalism. He accorded the General Board respect without becoming its captive; he breathed life into the Naval War College by making attendance at it important for all officers and mandatory for senior officers; he insisted upon regular periods of sea duty for all officers; and he generally sought to improve the lot of the enlisted men and, in his own way, that of the officers as well.

The earthy, unpretentious Daniels repeatedly clashed with Fiske, who fit almost perfectly Peter Karsten's idea of the "naval aristocrat."[4] A technical genius in terms of ordnance and fire control, Fiske was contemptuous of civilian control of the navy. In his view, the secretary of the navy should be no more than a figurehead for the professional naval officers who alone were qualified to run the service. After war broke out in Europe, Daniels continued to make policy at variance with the advice of Fiske, the General Board, and other naval officers. In January 1915 Fiske joined forces with Capt. William S. Sims and other second-generation navy reformers (the protégés of Luce, Taylor, and Mahan) to free the navy of the secretary's control. Working secretly with Congressmen Hobson and Augustus P. Gardner (R-MA), Senator Lodge's son-in-law, Fiske and his associates authored a bill that would place the fleet and its preparation for war under a chief of naval operations.

Once alerted to this stratagem, Daniels used his own extensive and friendly ties with Congress to have the proposed bill modified so that the new chief would serve under the direction of the secretary of the navy. When the bill became law, Daniels forced Fiske into retirement and appointed Capt. William Shepherd Benson as the navy's first chief of naval operations. Benson was an able but not an outstanding officer who would not challenge Daniels's authority.

Daniels then created an Advisory Council, consisting of the assistant secretary, Benson, the bureau chiefs, the judge advocate general, and the commandant of the Marine Corps, to assist him in running the service. Daniels was thus in an ideal position for controlling the navy. With the chief of naval operations directing the fleet, the bureaus collectively handling the department's business, and both sides of the department reporting only to him, the secretary of the navy alone could coordinate their activities. The new arrangement was inelegant and depended heavily on personal compatibility for success, but it was still the best naval command system since the creation of the service.

## REFORMING NAVAL ADMINISTRATION

Attempts to reform naval administration, or the business side of the service, took as much or more time as matters of command between 1900 and 1917. Four problem areas stood out: the status of steam engineers vis-à-vis the line, ship design, the navy yards, and the general operation of the bureaus. The first involved the conflict between steam engineers and line officers that had waxed and waned since the Engineer Corps had been created in 1842. Officers with technical specialties insisted on equal rank and similar perquisites to those of the line. Sensing a threat to their status, the line treated the engineers as inferior until the Civil War increased the latter's importance and Secretary of the Navy Gideon Welles gave them equivalent rank. Admiral David Dixon Porter reversed this decision when he served as de facto secretary of the navy for a few months in 1869. But the importance of steam engineering could not be denied, even though Annapolis had two tracks for its cadets between 1871 and 1899: cadet-midshipman and cadet-engineer. As the new navy emerged after 1881 and sail disappeared, the division became increasingly untenable. The issue was finally settled in 1899, when engineers were amalgamated with the line, the two-track system at Annapolis was abolished, and steam engineering was incorporated into the Annapolis curriculum. Although officers in general did not become proficient steam engineers, a failing that frequently had unfortunate consequences, most officers at least gained some knowledge of steam engineering, the Naval Academy gradually improved its level of steam engineering education, and the longstanding and destructive line-staff dispute was settled in the only feasible way.

Related personnel matters included setting criteria other than seniority for the promotion of officers and establishing a reserve of officers and enlisted men for emergencies. After years of controversy, Congress passed legislation in 1899 allowing the navy to remove ("pluck") from the service blatantly incompetent, unfit, or unnecessary officers so as to allow faster promotion for supposedly able officers. More drastic reform occurred in 1916 when the nation's legislators authorized the navy to base promotion decisions on perceived merit, a system known as promotion by selection. Action on reserves took place at about the same time. During the Spanish-American War many flaws surfaced in the state naval militia organized between 1888 and 1898. Consequently, in 1900 and 1916 Congress passed statutes creating a national naval reserve system to help staff the growing fleet and to provide officers and men during war or hostilities. The reforms involving promotion and the reserves had mixed results.

The second problem area dealt with disputes over ship design and construction. In the 1880s the navy had to send officers to Europe for training, and it had to buy plans abroad. By the 1890s this deficiency had been remedied through reforms in higher education. Compared with the army, the navy relied more consistently on civilian institutions for graduate work, but not totally so. As an intermediate step, Adm. Stephen B. Luce arranged in 1893 to have the Massachusetts Institute of Technology create a School of Naval Architecture at which naval constructors could be trained. The Naval War College was of course the most prominent and important of the navy's schools. Additionally, by 1880 a Torpedo School opened at Newport, Rhode Island. After ending the cadet engineering program at Annapolis in 1899, the navy created an advanced school of marine engineering, electrical engineering, and ordnance in Washington, DC. In 1909 the school moved to Annapolis and eventually became the Postgraduate Department of the Naval Academy.

Administrative reforms were also instituted to deal with technical problems. Secretary of the Navy Benjamin F. Tracy had created the Board of Construction to coordinate the five bureaus involved in shipbuilding, and his successors had improved upon this reform with generally positive results. Nonetheless, line officers complained that the staff produced ships that were poorly designed and built, specifically in such critical areas as the placement of armor, the location, mounting, and distribution of guns, and the handling of ammunition. Moreover, compared with Europe, the United States was slow in constructing ships, and its vessels were deficient in speed.

When their complaints went ignored, a group of second-generation insurgents, led by William S. Sims, Bradley A. Fiske, and Comdr. Albert L. Key, made their quarrel public in 1908 through an article appearing in *McClure's Magazine*. President Theodore Roosevelt personally intervened to protect the insurgents against retaliation by their superiors and had their grievances investigated. A solution was worked out that gave seagoing officers the opportunity to pass on the design of warships when the Board of Construction was abolished and its functions transferred to the General Board in 1909. This reform was related to reforms involving modern fire-control methods that Fiske the inventor and Sims the hard-hitting line reformer had been pushing for years over the intense resistance of traditionalists in the line and staff.

The third area of concern related to the first two and involved the various navy yards and stations. Near the turn of the century, the navy had twelve yards and stations on the Atlantic Coast, two on the Gulf Coast, and two on the Pacific Coast in addition to bases in the Pacific and the Caribbean. Navy facilities had retained the odor of the pork barrel since the eighteenth century, and civilian and military advocates of the navy continued to play upon the possibilities of largesse to win support and appropriations for the service. The building of the new navy and the comparatively huge annual naval budgets proportionately increased the political and economic significance of navy yards and stations.

Various secretaries in the nineteenth century attempted to handle the problem without much success other than to concentrate production of items such as rope, sail, chain, anchors, and so forth in the Boston yard and ordnance at the Washington yard, henceforth called the Naval Gun Factory. Proposals to close various yards or stations were usually blocked in Congress or quickly reversed when another secretary of the navy came into office.

The politically shrewd Josephus Daniels followed the most sensible and effective route. He kept open or reopened all existing facilities, assigning them logical specialties—i.e., large or small ship construction, submarine building and maintenance, repair, aviation, or the manufacture of certain products—and gave all vessels a regular home port. By improving yard and station efficiency and increasing capacity through modifications, additions, expansions, and reform and incentive programs, and by placing growing amounts of new construction and repair in public instead of private facilities, Daniels kept the yards busy year round, saved the government money through reduced costs, and substantially decreased the political pressure on behalf of the individual yards and stations.

Daniels was able to make the yards, docks, and stations function efficiently because of the basic reforms that preceded him. Once Tracy, Herbert, and other secretaries replaced the spoils system with one based on merit, two fundamental and related problems remained at the navy facilities. First, they were headed by commandants from the line on two-year assignments who were unqualified to fulfill their duties; second, the five bureaus involved in building and repairing ships tenaciously guarded their independence and maintained separate power plants, repair shops, and supply centers that were often duplicative in nature. This interbureau feuding turned the yards into decentralized entities and prevented the goal of integrated, centralized production facilities.

This situation was radically changed in a matter of months by Truman H. Newberry, Roosevelt's last secretary of the navy, who served from December 1908 to March 1909 after three years as assistant secretary. Newberry terminated bureau jurisdiction within the navy yards and stations, centralized industrial activities under a naval constructor who acted as technical assistant to the commandant, and restricted the latter and line officers in general to inspecting completed work. For the first time, navy yards could function as centralized industrial facilities under competent direction. Regrettably, Newberry left office before he could fully implement his reforms. His successor, George von Lengerke Meyer, left the changed system intact while making some modifications that diluted the impact of Newberry's scheme, which had been inspired basically by Naval Constructor Holden A. Evans.

Daniels, drawing on some of the initiatives of his predecessor Meyer, consolidated Newberry's reforms by decisively separating the military and industrial functions of the yards and stations. The commandant then reported to the aide for operations and later to the chief of naval operations; the naval constructors reported directly to the secretary of the navy. Like Daniels's new system of command, the reforms in the navy yards and stations were not ideal, but they were the best arrangement the Navy Department had yet worked out.

The fourth problem area involved the bureaus and was central in various ways to the line/staff controversies, ship construction and design, and yard and station operations. Although the bureaus had basically the same form in 1917 as in 1865, some important changes had been made. Tracy and his successors had successfully centralized most procurement, audit, and financing functions in the Bureau of Supplies and Accounts. In 1910 Meyer, with congressional authorization, abolished the Bureau of Equipment as duplicative and dispersed its duties to the remaining seven bureaus. He also ruled that bureau chiefs could serve for no more than eight years. This move acted to bring in new blood and to reduce the political power of the bureaus and their strong congressional alliances. Daniels allowed Meyer's aide system, in which the various bureaus served under four assistants reporting to the secretary, to die. However, Daniels did create an Advisory Council to assist him in directing the bureaus and coordinating their efforts with the line. The system worked well under the strong, energetic leadership of the secretary of the navy, but it depended excessively on personalities and did not have enough structure to ensure success.

Between 1881 and 1917, then, the United States had become one of the major naval powers of the world, fast advancing to the position of having a navy second to none. By 1917 that navy was commanded by the newly created chief of naval operations, who acted under the secretary of the navy. The business side of the navy was handled by seven bureaus and a number of yards and docks at home and abroad that reported to the chief of naval operations for military purposes and to the secretary of the navy for industrial purposes. The General Board continued as an advisory body to the secretary of the navy and the chief of naval operations on naval policy, building programs, ship construction, and such matters. However, war planning was the province of the chief of naval operations, and the General Board would gradually diminish in significance until it was completely phased out in 1951. Though this multifaceted structure was not ideal, it functioned with considerable efficiency. One of its principal virtues was the fact that the service stayed in a state of readiness for hostilities and would not face great problems in mobilizing in the event of war. Clearly, the navy was fundamentally transformed in size, organization, and strategy in the years between 1881 and 1917.

## CONGRESS AND THE NEW NAVY

The role of Congress in the navy's transformation is instructive. Generally, the nation's legislators responded to executive initiatives instead of coming up with their own. Although it rejected, modified, and altered the pace of proposals coming from Republican and Democratic administrations, Congress never set its own naval policy. Between 1881 and 1916, the drive to make an insignificant navy into a peerless force took on nearly inexorable qualities that Congress seemed unable to control. Persistence by the executive branch and international developments acted to break down congressional opposition first to a modern navy, then to an offensive one, and finally to a navy second to none.

In the 1880s and 1890s only a few congressmen and senators fully understood the technology and strategy involved in building the new navy they were authorizing through statutes and appropriations. Nonetheless, through frequent hearings and investigations conducted by or for one or both houses, legislators at least became increasingly conversant with the major issues involved in building a new fleet. The two Grover Cleveland administrations helped to make naval policy bipartisan or nonpartisan, an outcome facilitated by ending the spoils system in the navy yards. Of course, politics continued to affect Congress' response to the navy in small and large ways. Members of Congress were swayed by the location and work performed at the navy yards, by ties with bureau officers, and by the direct and indirect effects of a modern navy on their districts, states, and regions.

The Republican party more consistently favored naval growth; the Democrats tended to be skeptical about the strategic necessity and expense of the new navy, and more of its congressional members were ardently antinavy. Yet congressional majorities in both parties opposed the shift from a defensive to an offensive navy, which began under Secretary of the Navy Tracy (1889–1893). Manipulation and deception were required to start the building of battleships, and thereafter war scares, imagined enemies, and statistical sleights of hand, along with appeals to nationalism, patriotism, and duty, were standard techniques in shaping legislation in the navy's favor.

After the Spanish-American War, a navy ranking second in the world became national policy, although in both parties significant minorities strongly and often vociferously opposed navalism. Their primary strength was in the agrarian regions of the Midwest and South. Although this minority made its voice heard, a more important faction was the one associated with Theodore Roosevelt, Sen. Henry Cabot Lodge, Cong. Richmond B. Hobson, and the naval aristocracy, which wanted a navy second to none. This group's position became official policy when in mid-1915 Wilson dropped his indifferent-to-hostile attitude toward the military services and embraced preparedness for World War I. Repeatedly, at every major step in the construction of a modern navy, Congress engaged in a bruising debate over first-place status for the fleet, only to follow the executive branch's lead.

## INDUSTRY AND THE NEW NAVY

Two related and vital issues must still be addressed: the relationship the service developed with private industry in building a new fleet, and the significance of that relationship for modern defense and warfare. Shipbuilding firms did not cause great problems for the navy since an industry existed that required some, but not exceptional, adjustment to modern naval output. In contrast, the manufacture of armor and ordnance had to begin from scratch and involved elaborate and complicated relations between public and private, civilian and military individuals and institutions both at home and abroad. These relations suggested the complications and consequences that would arise from the large-scale production for the military in a modern economy.

When the Navy Department sought bids for building the ABCDs early in the 1880s, an American shipbuilding industry already existed. Although the United States lost its status as a major international ocean carrier before and during the Civil War, it still had a modest merchant marine in the post–Civil War period in addition to various packet and passenger lines. Many of these ships were constructed at home, and American firms also built for sales abroad. Moreover, considerable building of vessels for coastal and inland waters also took place. Although most shipyards in the late nineteenth century still built wooden vessels, iron shipbuilding had begun by 1868, with the transition from iron to steel occurring between 1875 and 1885. In 1874 the nation had sixteen firms building iron steamships. Ten were on the Atlantic Coast, with the heaviest concentration on the Delaware River; three were located on the

Great Lakes, and three were on the Ohio and Mississippi Rivers. With the construction of the Union Iron Works in San Francisco in 1884 and the Newport News Shipbuilding and Drydock Company in 1891, the Pacific Coast and the South Atlantic became important centers of modern shipbuilding. Before navy contracts, American shipbuilders were already constructing sizable vessels of steel; they also built ore ships for the Great Lakes and oil tankers for inland and ocean usage.

The Spanish-American War created a short-run stimulus for new building as the navy's need for vessels of all kinds suddenly escalated. Demand remained high as the war in the Philippines stretched out and the United States oversaw a new empire in the Pacific and Caribbean. Inadequate private-sector capacity for building navy vessels existed only where submarines were concerned. Two companies organized by inventors involved in submarine development, the Electric Boat Company and the Lake Torpedo Boat Company, built submersibles of varying quality early in the twentieth century. Lake Torpedo went out of business in 1924, leaving Electric Boat with a practical monopoly, which the navy offset in part during the interwar years by making Portsmouth Naval Shipyard into a center for designing and manufacturing submarines.

The Navy Department relied on private shipyards to construct most of the new fleet. Ships from private firms cost less, although those from public yards were better built. Until Daniels became secretary of the navy, the department preferred to deal with private yards out of ideological preference, the desire to stimulate private capacity so that emergency needs could be met, or for both reasons. Daniels began to channel more new building into the navy yards, but private builders still did most of the construction. Of the seventy-three vessels authorized between 1882 and 1897, only two second-class battleships and two protected cruisers were built in navy yards. In 1905 twelve firms were building thirty-one ships, and they had subcontracted with sixty-five companies to supply steel and with 318 for engineering materials. The biggest shipbuilding contractors were Cramp and Sons of Philadelphia and the Union Iron Works.

The high level of naval demand had a definite effect on the shipbuilding industry. From 1882, the service became the single most important customer for the industry, and it attracted new firms, such as the Newport News Shipbuilding Company. Naval shipbuilding also had some effect on the steel industry. For the ABCDs—the first steel ships of the new fleet—navy specifications provided for rolled, open-hearth steel plates of a quality in terms of tensile strength and ductility never before achieved in the industry. Naval inspectors rejected nearly all the initial plates. Within a matter of months, however, navy specifications were exceeded and rejection rates were relatively low, although all steel firms appeared to have lost money on the venture. The new ships also required steel castings for stern and stem posts that reached fifty tons and more, exceeding anything the industry had previously produced. Not only did naval demand push the steel industry to new levels of accomplishment, but naval experts also worked with the steel companies to help attain the desired quality of output and published technical papers on how the results were achieved.

Although the navy's demands may have hastened the steel industry's progress, the overall impact was not great. The industry was already well advanced in the technology of rolling and casting steel, and it was beginning to diversify from rails into bridge and structural shapes, wire, pipes and tubes, and nails. Commercial demand would have produced the same results as the military, although the pace of advance might have been somewhat slower.

The contribution of the navy to steel technology was greater, involving the manufacture of armor and heavy ordnance.[5] Armor and ordnance required heavy forging, not rolling or casting, and the steel industry was unprepared for such production. Hence, throughout the 1880s and into the 1890s, armor and ordnance purchased from abroad equipped the ships of the new navy. This situation was considered to be unacceptable since foreign supply could be unreliable and unavailable in an emergency. National defense demanded that the United States produce its own armor and ordnance; as the sole consumer, the government had to take the lead in adapting the steel industry to meet its demands. To accomplish this end, civilian and military officials in the United States worked closely with U.S. steel executives and with their counterparts abroad.

The organization of the Gun Foundry Board in 1883 marked the beginning of this effort. Made up principally of naval officers, with some army representatives, the board was charged with recommending the best means for domestically manufacturing heavy ordnance. Its investigation took ten months and covered both domestic and foreign industries. By publishing its report early in 1884, the board provided the nation with the first systematic information on the technology of modern heavy forging and established that American firms could only manufacture ordnance up to six-inch caliber, not cannons with calibers as large as sixteen inches as the military required. Moreover, domestic firms would be interested in upgrading their capacity only if the government ensured orders large enough to cover all costs.

In addressing the question of whether production should be private, public, or mixed, the board opted for mixed. This crucial issue had been debated in different circumstances since the founding of the nation. Basing its decision on the country's past experience and the European example, the board concluded that private production could leave America subject to the will and manipulation of unscrupulous individuals and firms, public production could be excessively expensive and could lead to stagnation, but a combination of the two could maintain the progress and vitality necessary for optimal output. The Gun Foundry Board specifically recommended that steel firms prepare the heavy gun forgings and that military facilities finish them.

The Gun Foundry Board was asked to make its recommendations more specific, and three additional investigations took place. In 1885 the army appointed a Board on Fortifications and Other Defenses (known as the Endicott Board, after Secretary of War William C. Endicott who chaired it) to consider rebuilding coastal fortifications. The board came up with an extravagant proposal for protecting the coasts but essentially agreed with the Gun Foundry Board on the issue of ordnance production. Some months earlier, the Senate had created a Select Committee on Ordnance and War Ships and the House appointed a Commission on Ordnance and Gunnery, which reviewed the same matter addressed by the two military boards. The Senate committee's work was more thorough and included extensive testimony by steel industry representatives. Basically, the committee agreed with the Gun Foundry Board about mixed production of heavy ordnance, but it favored having private firms handle armor alone. In an elliptical manner, the House Commission on Ordnance and Gunnery favored making both armor and ordnance the exclusive reserve of private enterprise.

Although some differences existed, by 1885–1886 a consensus had begun to emerge from the various investigations in favor of mixed enterprise for the manufacture of heavy ordnance, with armor left to private firms. This approach was generally favored by the steel industry, which did not want to undertake on its own new lines of production with limited markets. One problem remained unresolved: How could the government guarantee adequate orders to induce industry to participate in the production of armor and ordnance? The investigatory agencies had considered this delicate question but did not arrive at any solution.

Secretary of the Navy William C. Whitney during his tenure from March 1885 to March 1889 used his executive authority to implement the vague decisions reached by the Gun Foundry Board and other investigating bodies. By mid-1886 Whitney had accumulated in excess of $4 million in past and current congressional appropriations for armor and ordnance, enough to interest the Bethlehem Iron Company in undertaking the desired production. At the time, Bethlehem was experiencing one of the periodic downturns in the steel market and sought to diversify from its heavy dependence on rail production. However, since a new production line involving new technology was involved, Whitney could not rely on normal contractual relations. Neither a traditional negotiated contract, if such were possible, nor a contract awarded through competitive bidding would guarantee that the navy receive the products it wanted, i.e., all-steel armor of the quality produced at the plant of Henri Schneider at Le Creusot, France, and steel forgings equal to those of Joseph Whitworth at Sheffield, England. The French and the English companies both had reputations for manufacturing the best products in the world, and Whitney insisted that the navy would settle for nothing less. Bethlehem therefore would have to go abroad to obtain the expertise needed to win the Navy Department contracts.

To achieve his goal, Whitney, between July 1886 and March 1887, engaged in secret, intricate, and illegal negotiations involving Bethlehem, Schneider, Whitworth, and naval officers on active duty who had signed on as exclusive American agents for the two foreign firms. The secretary of the navy opened negotiations with Bethlehem in mid-1886 to ensure that the company would be prepared to win the competitive bidding to be held the following year. Bethlehem then turned to Schneider to gain patent rights and technical assistance for producing armor. The negotiations turned out to be long and difficult and probably would not have been successful without the intervention of Lt. Comdr. F. M. Barber, an active-duty naval officer who had served on the Gun Foundry Board and become Schneider's exclusive agent in the United States. Barber helped to arrange an agreement in which Bethlehem received patent rights and assistance in producing Schneider armor in exchange for a share of the American firm's profits.

Relations with Whitworth were much easier, principally because of the role played by Lt. William H. Jaques, also an active-duty naval officer who had served on the Gun Foundry Board, who had been tapped for the position of secretary of the Senate Select Committee on Ordnance and War Ships because of his reputation as a steel expert and who became Whitworth's exclusive commercial agent in the United States. After Bethlehem received the armor and ordnance contract in 1887, Jaques, unlike Barber, who remained in the service, resigned from the navy to serve as Bethlehem's ordnance engineer. Jaques, like Barber, had first attempted to import the product of the foreign firm he represented, but Whitney adamantly held out for domestic production. Consequently, Whitworth authorized Jaques to approach Bethlehem with an offer for the latter to duplicate in the United States the former's plant. The offer was quickly accepted for a hefty price. Ultimately, Bethlehem invested around $3.5 million in its factory for manufacturing armor and ordnance.

Whitney's action in 1886–1887 ensured that Bethlehem would receive the naval contracts when bidding took place. Nonetheless, before the bidding occurred, the secretary of the navy began correspondence with Carnegie, Phipps and Company and Midvale Iron and Steel Company to encourage them to make bids as well. Eventually Bethlehem, Midvale, Cambria Iron Company, and the Cleveland Rolling Mills submitted bids that were opened in March 1887. Whitney had structured the bidding process so that Bethlehem could not lose, and when Cambria underbid Bethlehem on gun forgings, the secretary of the navy persuaded the favored company to match the lower bid so that it could get the entire $4.5 million contract. Prices on the contract were set at levels intended to allow Bethlehem to recoup its investment for government production, in effect a subsidy. Moreover, Bethlehem claimed that the secretary of the navy had promised it additional contracts and perhaps all future armor work.

In August 1886 Whitney drew upon a million-dollar appropriation from Congress to set up a Navy Gun Factory at the Washington Navy Yard to finish forgings provided by steel firms. By 1889, ahead of schedule, Bethlehem was supplying the Navy Gun Factory with semifinished products, possible because a Whitworth plant had been built and tested in England before being shipped and set up in the United States. Key to the operation of the plant was the hydraulic forging press, which would quickly become the standard tool for heavy forging in the United States. By slow stages, American firms achieved the ability and capacity to produce the largest and most technologically sophisticated breech-loading, rifled ordnance possible. Efforts to produce armor did not encounter the same success. Schneider relied on heavy steam hammers to forge his armor, tools that Bethlehem had exceptional difficulty in building. Consequently, by 1890 the steel firm had delivered no armor and was far behind its contractual deadlines, leaving the navy with ships waiting to receive their protective cover.

Whitney left the armor problem for Tracy, the new secretary of the navy, to handle. As it turned out, Bethlehem's complication worked to the navy's benefit. By 1889 Schneider was producing nickel-steel armor, a great advance over his all-steel armor and the compound armor (iron plates with steel welded on the front) favored by the English. In tests at the Annapolis Proving Ground, the compound armor shattered and the all-steel armor cracked, but the nickel-steel armor remained unscathed.

Facing the realities of improved armor, an accelerated building schedule of enlarged ships, and Bethlehem's nonperformance, Tracy turned to Carnegie, Phipps. Tough negotiating by Carnegie produced a contract in 1890 favorable to the firm. The company would manufacture nickel-steel armor at the same inflated price paid to Bethlehem; it was promised future orders; the navy would pay royalties to Le Ferro Nickel, the Schneider-controlled firm holding the patent on the new process; and the service would provide Carnegie with the necessary nickel, which was short in supply and high in price. To deliver the nickel, Tracy had earlier contracted with S. J. Ritchie, who represented Canadian nickel-mining interests, to deliver the metal to the United States at a set price. A $1 million authorization to purchase nickel was rushed through Congress in September 1890 under conditions of secrecy based on national security. Moreover, as part of his negotiations with Ritchie, Tracy probably played a part in having nickel put on the free list in the highly protective McKinley Tariff of 1890.

Despite the overly generous terms Tracy granted, Carnegie, Phipps did not produce armor in the few months promised. Indeed, over two years passed before the company began delivering armor with some regularity and only after Tracy had persuaded Lt. C. A. Stone, a navy ordnance expert, to take a two-year furlough to assist the company. Stone later resigned to join the firm. Before Carnegie's production hit its stride, another naval officer perfected a process of face hardening armor further through a method developed by Augustus Harvey. Even this system was improved on by Carnegie and Bethlehem with the so-called Corey process of reforging Harveyized plate. By 1895 Carnegie finally completed its contract with the navy. Although many years late, the company was producing armor reputed to be the best in the world.

Bethlehem, the nation's pioneer in modern armor, had greater difficulties than Carnegie, Phipps. After years of effort it had to give up the Schneider steam hammer for the Whitworth hydraulic press. Tracy assisted the firm as he had Carnegie by furloughing another ordnance expert, Lt. J. F. Meigs, to work with Bethlehem. In time, Meigs also traded his commission for a position with the steel firm. By 1893 Bethlehem was beginning to deliver armor with regularity, was making Harveyized and Coreyized nickel-steel armor equal to Carnegie's, and in 1895 finally completed its 1887 contract.

Most of the unorthodox procedures the Navy Department employed to acquire modern armor and ordnance were uncovered through investigations by Congress and other groups. The resulting political furor was magnified manyfold by several other incidents. The first involved revelations that in late 1893, Carnegie, Phipps fraudulently passed off on the navy below-standard armor plates. Then in 1895 President Cleveland substantially reduced the fines leveled against the company as a penalty. Second, through the influence of former Lieutenant Meigs, Bethlehem contracted with Russia in 1894 to manufacture armor for about $250 per ton while it continued to charge the navy an average of $625 per ton. The higher price had been set to cover the costs of initial investment. By 1896 both Bethlehem and Carnegie had more than recouped all costs.

The result of these scandals was over twenty years of acrimony, investigations, and accusations of profiteering, collusion, price setting, and warmongering during the Populist and Progressive Eras. As improved armor came into being, the conflict grew when the steel companies insisted on increased prices, and some people in the government asserted that this behavior amounted to little more than robbery. The running controversy kept prices lower than they otherwise would have been. But when the government attempted to set prices at levels the steel firms thought to be too low, the companies refused to accept contracts, which in time forced the government to back down. Out of frustration and after years of agitation, investigation, and threats, Washington in 1916 finally authorized the building of a government armor facility. The navy began building a plant in South Charleston, West Virginia, in 1917, but it was never completed and was abandoned in the 1920s.

The construction of a modern navy eventually spawned a large collection of industries dependent to varying degrees on continued naval growth. In 1903 Midvale Steel Company joined the armor industry controlled by Bethlehem and Carnegie. By 1902 six firms made ordnance for the navy, nine companies manufactured projectiles, and seventeen constructed various kinds of vessels. Subcontractors numbered in the hundreds. Between 1902 and 1917 the number of firms involved in production for the navy grew substantially and then expanded enormously during World War I.

Numerous contemporaries, commentators, and scholars have argued that these industrial interests combined forces in 1903 under the banner of the Navy League to work for a larger navy from which they would economically benefit. Although the Navy League was not a vulgar collection of merchants of death, many of its members were probably motivated as much by pecuniary gain as by patriotism, nationalism, and ideology. Whatever the motive, the Navy League from the outset served as the civilian voice of advocates in the navy pressing for an ever-larger fleet, performed valuable services for its namesake, and did not have an identity separate from that of the service.[6]

## THE NEW NAVY AND THE ORIGINS OF THE MIC

Various authors have rightly pinpointed the construction of the new navy as originating the military-industrial complex (MIC).[7] For the first time the nation experienced military-industrial relations of a new order on a continuing basis. In defining the nature of this new order, it is necessary to distinguish between the peripheral and the central. Of minor importance were the conflicts of interest, illegal contracting, profiteering, and like behavior. Such practices were common, expected, and dated back to the founding of the nation. Even the excesses of the Gilded Age do not invalidate the point.

Also peripheral was the impact of the new navy on the development of the steel industry. Contrary to the claims of various authors, the navy was neither responsible for the emergence of the steel industry nor did it play a significant role in improving the production of various forms of steel. At best, the demands of the new navy acted to speed up to some degree technological advancement in the industry, particularly in high quality rolled steel and heavy forgings. Without the building of a modern fleet, the steel industry would have made the same advances, albeit at a slower pace.

Several characteristics of the new order of civil-military relations are of central importance and distinguish the experience of the navy in the late nineteenth and early twentieth centuries from the past. First, the building of a new fleet required a production team composed of government officials, naval officers, and industrialists that eroded the barriers between private and public, civilian and military institutions. On a limited basis, personnel began to circulate among the various institutions because of their interrelationship and the need to fulfill special functions. The institutions in question were huge, modern, complex bureaucracies. Relating them—the federal government, the navy, and the corporate structure—to one another in order to construct a new navy generated enormous tensions that would take decades to resolve. Once resolved, however, disengaging the various institutions could be at least as difficult as engaging them.

Second, this production team was a permanent, not a temporary, phenomenon. It had come into being because of the sophisticated nature of military technology; it would remain in being in different forms because technology continued to advance, making ships larger and more complex and their predecessors obsolete or inferior. Furthermore, building the new ships of war required long lead times; a modern navy of substance could not be assembled quickly. For the first time in U.S. history, these realities led to the nation's permanently maintaining a large and growing fleet. This outcome broadened and deepened the government-navy-industry production team necessary to develop, build, and maintain the naval forces. As that growth occurred, increasing numbers of economic, political, and military groups became committed to an expanding navy.

Third, these developments had started and would have continued with the construction of a defensive navy; they were exaggerated manyfold by the creation of an offensive fleet. Once the fleet became offensive, two forces acted to continue its expansion. The first was foreign policy. As the principal military arm for expansion abroad, the navy grew along with America's outward thrust. Second, as an ambitious world power, the nation gauged its fleet against the fleets of perceived or potential enemies at a time when the major powers were engaged in an arms race. The Spanish-American War removed many of the objections to a growing offensive fleet, since the United States by then had a modest empire to police in the Caribbean and the Pacific. As America's perspective became increasingly global after the outbreak of World War I, the Wilson administration elected to build a navy second to none.

To locate the origins of the MIC in the building of a modern navy in the late nineteenth and early twentieth centuries is not to say that a complex per se existed at that time. It did not. The government-navy-industry production team was still rather crude and embryonic. Although naval officers and various political and economic allies had already begun to work steadily for an expanded service and had identified real or imagined enemies to justify their fears or aspirations, they could still be checkmated by countervailing coalitions or groups opposed to navalism. Spending for the navy had not yet become so great or lengthy as to create interest groups with the power to determine naval policy. Presidents and secretaries of the navy still controlled the naval bureaucracy, as is evident in the differing policies and priorities implemented from Arthur through Wilson. On the whole, the navy adapted to the nation's foreign policy instead of shaping it in any significant way. Nonetheless, in retrospect, the building of a modern navy at least suggested that heavy military spending over a prolonged period of time in an industrialized economy could lead to circumstances in which the armed services could significantly and dangerously distort the nation's defense and foreign policies and its economic structure. Therefore, analyzing the historical roots of the military-industrial complex that emerged in the Cold War years must begin in 1881 when the construction of a new navy commenced.

# 4
# MODERNIZING THE ARMY

## DECLINE

The army's transition to peace at the end of the Civil War was more severe than the navy's because the relative size and role of the former was so much greater than the latter's.[1] An army of over 1 million men in May 1865 was cut to a little under 200,000 by December of that year. In 1866 federal troops numbered somewhat in excess of 57,000, fell to 37,240 in 1870, and dropped to approximately 28,000 in 1872, remaining near that level until the Spanish-American War.

The trauma of these drastic reductions was compounded many times over by the bitter controversies over the army's role in postwar domestic affairs. The army remained in the South after defeating the Confederacy, first as an occupying force and then as a principal agent for carrying out congressional (radical) Reconstruction. Until Pres. Andrew Johnson left office early in 1869, the army was caught up in the power struggle between the executive and legislative branches. In a constitutionally dubious manner, it answered to Congress on Reconstruction policies and to the executive on defense policies. For a few years, the nation suffered the peculiarity of having, in effect, two armies: one for Reconstruction under the authority of the legislative branch, and the other for frontier duty and national defense under the president as commander-in-chief.

Throughout the Reconstruction period an inadequate number of troops had the thankless task of trying to enforce the law in the face of increasing Southern hostility and resistance and despite the waning interest and commitment of the North. Convinced that federal troops had helped save the presidency for the Republican party in the intensely disputed election of 1876, Democrats from the North and South, returning to Congress in full strength, looked to settle scores with the army.

No sooner was the army pulled out of the South than it began to be used to police industrial conflicts, beginning with the railroad strike of 1877.

Although sent in by the executive, troops unsupervised or poorly directed from Washington usually sided with management over labor, which alienated the latter and its friends and allies.

Even when pursuing the more traditionally military role of fighting Indians, soldiers became enmeshed in bitter controversies. After the Civil War, the transcontinental railroads gave the westward push the proportions of a stampede. Indian resistance naturally grew, especially when the government adopted the policy of confining various tribes to reservations. This action resulted in a state of nearly constant "warfare" from 1866 until the Indians were collectively ground down by 1891. Here was another trying and thankless task. Humanitarians and other friends of the Indians damned the army for its often ruthless and brutal conduct while frontiersmen complained that the troops were insufficiently homicidal.

Controversies over Reconstruction, industrial strife, and Indian removal generated strong emotions and negatively affected Congress' response to and legislation concerning the land forces. By comparison, the navy was spared the consequences of such close involvement in domestic political events.

Like the navy, however, the postwar army was significantly larger in size and received much more generous funding than before the Civil War. During the 1850s the army's annual strength averaged about 15,317 and its budgets $15.8 million. Between 1866 and 1871, comparable annual figures were 44,773 and $112.5 million. Between 1872 and 1897 annual averages were 27,020 men and $42.9 million. Thus, after the extended adjustment to peace, Gilded Age armies were nearly twice the size of those in the decade before the Civil War, and army appropriations in unadjusted dollars almost tripled.

Despite nearly twelve years of involvement in the South's Reconstruction and at least twenty years of policing strikes, the majority of troops served on the frontier, where Indians absorbed most of their attention. By 1870 half of all regulars were on duty in the West, and that figure jumped to at least 70 percent in the subsequent twenty years. These troops in 1875 occupied some 129 camps, posts, and forts, which usually housed no more than two or three companies and frequently fewer. Troop barracks at the various garrisons were generally crude, dirty, crowded, and unhealthy. They were barely illuminated shanties and hovels, devoid of bathing and sanitary toilet facilities, common areas, reliably pure water, and other amenities. Officially designated as temporary facilities, the army sites were selected and buildings constructed and repaired by untrained and inexperienced officers and troops who used local materials, including sod and green logs. Assistant Surgeon General John S. Billings lamented that the United States had "the best-fed and worst-housed Army in the world."[2] Although the rations remained plentiful when delivered, they were monotonous, improperly balanced, often badly stored, and usually poorly prepared. Companies depended on their own gardens and livestock, and hunting and fishing by the troops, to make their diets tolerable. Medical care remained backward. The army disestablished its fine Civil War hospital system and relied on post hospitals, two special hospitals, and only one general hospital, all with limited patient capacity. Medical doctors were in short supply. The pleas of various surgeon generals for organizing a hospital corps to evacuate and treat the sick and wounded went unanswered until 1887, and a regular nurses' corps was established only during the Spanish-American War.

Consistent with past practices, the supply of troops east and west of the Mississippi fell principally to the Quartermaster, Subsistence, and Ordnance Departments. For nonperishable clothing, equipment, and supplies, the army simply drew upon its vast surplus of war stock until early in the 1870s. Thereafter, the Quartermaster Department resumed procurement by advertised bids, manufactured numerous items such as clothing at department facilities, and relied on the Ordnance Department to make or provide most leather items in addition to knapsacks, haversacks, and canteens. The Ordnance Department, of course, continued to manufacture, distribute, maintain, and when necessary alter most weapons and accoutrements. As a new trend, the Quartermaster Department had shoes, boots, harnesses, kettles, pans, chairs, and other articles produced in the military prison at Fort Leavenworth. Quartermaster General Montgomery C. Meigs, however, stubbornly resisted most proposals for additional manufacture of army supplies, such as wagons, by the service as uneconomical and as politically unwise, since it would needlessly antagonize civilians selling to the army.

The supply bureaus operated out of several large depots, centers, and arsenals in cities such as New York, Philadelphia, St. Louis, New Orleans, Springfield, and San Francisco. Although the general trend in the late nineteenth century was to centralize procurement in Washington, DC, the Quartermaster Department encouraged open-market purchasing in local areas for forage, lumber, fuel, and other such products as long as prices were reasonable when transportation costs were factored in. As the army moved further west, the Subsistence Department followed the same practice for food items like fresh meat, flour, and produce. Generally, procurement and production for a comparatively small army in a burgeoning economy was a relatively simple matter.

Transportation was the major problem facing the bureaus in general and the Quartermaster Department in particular, since it moved most goods. Supplying posts and forts scattered over thousands of miles of sparsely settled plains, deserts, and mountains harboring hostile Indians was a major, daunting task that was not always carried out. "The sufferings endured at remote, inaccessible posts," observes the Quartermaster Department's official historian, "were as intense as any experienced at Valley Forge."[3] Besides the difficulties and dangers involved, transportation constituted the major army expense in the West, and the Quartermaster Department waged a relentless battle to reduce the cost of moving men and supplies.

As before the Civil War, most late-nineteenth-century transportation was handled by private carriers, the most economical method. After hostilities, the Quartermaster Department quickly divested itself of the railroads under its charge, sold all boats and ships except a few retained for harbor and seacoast duty, and significantly cut back the elaborate wartime system of wagons and teams. Nevertheless, the army required an irreducible minimum of government-owned wagons in the West to meet emergencies such as unanticipated troop movements, contractor failure, and fire, floods, and other disasters. Additionally, each army unit had a specified number of wagons for executing military missions. In Arizona, New Mexico, and the Rocky Mountains, pack mules had to be used even though the troops were not well trained in their management.

Immediately after the Civil War, a large part of army supplies was moved by privately owned freight companies, which received annual contracts through competitive bidding. Stagecoach lines, such as Wells Fargo, also moved some passengers and goods. Whenever possible, hired steamboats transported freight and passengers to forts and distribution centers and at times played a vital part in military campaigns against the Indians. Railroads, of course, served the military extensively east of the Mississippi, and the Quartermaster Department used their services in the West as quickly as they became available. The Union Pacific Railroad started carrying army goods in 1867 even before the transcontinental line was completed. When that occurred in 1868 and other railroad lines began service throughout the West, the department increasingly relied on rail transportation.

At times, transportation systems worked in tandem as loaded wagons were lashed to flat cars and mules carried in closed ones. Competition from the railroads forced the price of wagon transportation down, but the army never freed itself from this more expensive and slower mode of moving supplies. After 1867 railroads and wagon trains started to divide the carriage of military supplies in the West. As late as 1897 railroads moved 48,745 tons of freight for the army in the West, but wagons hauled 32,647 tons, and even stagecoach lines continued to handle some army goods. The army was still ahead of the railroads in some areas, and even when that was not the case, supplies had to be moved from railroad and military stations to the widely scattered posts, camps, and forts.

Once the Indian wars ended in 1891, military supply in the West became much easier and cheaper. The War Department reduced the number of Western posts to seventy-nine in 1890, a 40 percent reduction from 1875. The number was still much too large and the garrisons usually too small to serve military purposes. Nonetheless, local pressures for military protection and economic stimulation prevented a more rational pattern.

In the twentieth century, the army began maintaining a few relatively large, well-placed, and properly built military bases with amenities to improve the lives of both the officers and enlisted men. Actually, Adj. Gen. R. C. Drum began instituting reforms on behalf of the troops early in the 1880s. Change had become essential to attract and keep enlisted men. Up to 50 percent of the troops were immigrants during the Gilded Age. Desertions averaged 15 percent annually and could go as high as 33 percent, and drunkenness and disciplinary problems abounded. Horrible living conditions, low pay, limited opportunities to advance, severe, rigid, and capricious disciplinary systems, and the absence of social and recreational facilities drove men to despair. Reforms included more regular pay periods, shorter terms of enlistment, less arbitrary military customs, a more equitable system of military justice, better social, educational, and recreational activities, consolidated mess halls with trained cooks, and post exchanges in place of the often greedy and exploitative traders and sutlers licensed by the secretary of war. Greater changes came in the future when a professionalized and enlarged army stressed more and better training and target practice, welcomed initiative, adopted new weapons of war, and offered more advancement.

Despite its flaws and failures, the army met most of the challenges of the frontier reasonably well between 1866 and 1891. It did so through steadiness of discipline and routine, not innovation and daring. The army ran as if it were on autopilot, for in a meaningful sense it had no driver. Unlike the navy, the army lacked a genuinely talented, qualified, and interested civilian secretary between Edwin M. Stanton, who departed in May 1868, and Elihu Root, who assumed office in August 1899 (the peculiar appointment of Gen. John M. Schofield, June 1868–March 1869, and the competent service of Redfield Proctor, March 1889–November 1891, excepted). Of the twelve men serving as secretary of war during those years, most were selected for political purposes. One, William W. Belknap (October 1869–March 1876), served for more than four years but resigned suddenly to avoid impeachment for corrupt practices; three served a full four-year term; and the remainder were in office for terms ranging from two months to less than three years. Few secretaries during this period stirred themselves except to beat back efforts by Generals William T. Sherman and Philip H. Sheridan to give the office of the commanding general more power.

With inattentive secretaries of war and largely ceremonial commanding generals, power within the War Department–army system gravitated to the supply and service bureaus. Most bureau heads were able Civil War veterans who ran their departments expeditiously and resisted changing a system that had produced a great Union victory. To economize, standardize, reduce irregularities and fraud, and enhance their own power vis-à-vis the line, beginning in 1867 and accelerating in the 1880s and 1890s the bureaus centralized control over supply in Washington at the expense of the commanding generals of the various geographical departments. Thus most procurement required extensive, tedious, and time-consuming paperwork that started in the field, was ultimately routed to the nation's capital, and then returned along the same path. Over the protests of the bureaus, Congress complicated procurement even more in the late 1860s and 1870s by legislating line-item appropriations with prohibitions against transferring funds even between subdivisions of a bureau, with regulations that limited expenditures to the fiscal year for which funds were appropriated, with separate accounting for each appropriation, and with impractical procedures for the sale of public goods.

The army's supply system worked well during peacetime, including the limited and ongoing skirmishes with Indians on the frontier. A certain level of contractor failures and malfeasance in transporting supplies and providing provisions occurred, but compared to the earlier years of the nineteenth century it had been reduced to a minimum. Procurement through competitive bidding probably cost the army more than open-market purchasing, but it reduced the opportunities for abuse. In 1865–1866 the Quartermaster Department discovered gross irregularities, mismanagement, fraud, and corruption in its operations throughout the West, which had been under volunteer officers during the war and had not received much scrutiny from Washington. After hostilities, Quartermaster General Montgomery C. Meigs moved quickly to replace almost the entire staff in the area and to set right misdoings that had been allowed to grow while he was distracted.

The Ordnance Department continued to be slow and overly cautious in responding to technological advances in weaponry, but its affairs were otherwise conducted responsibly and efficiently. Although the Medical Department endured severe cutbacks after hostilities, it began to make a comeback with the creation of the Hospital Corps in 1887. The Corps of Engineers continued to work on forts and other projects for the military along with civilian works involving rivers and harbors. The Signal Corps, the newest bureau, not only set up and operated military telephone and telegraph lines but also branched out to help create the U.S. Weather Bureau. The supply bureaus during the Gilded Age were on the whole mature institutions, staffed by knowledgeable, capable officers tested in the fires of an extended war and operating in a dynamic, booming economy. They had every reason to function reliably and effectively, and they did so.

Despite that reality, more was wrong than right in the bureaus' affairs. Their maturity and leadership enhanced their ability to dominate the army, but they did so as individual units, not as a collective whole. Each bureau was an independent, highly specialized unit proud of its expertise and jealous of its turf. Since the bureau heads acted as the principal advisers to the inexperienced secretaries of war, the department operated without central direction. Moreover, by the last decades of the nineteenth century the bureaus had become hidebound, narrow, and addicted to red tape. The centralized system of supply intended to reduce abuse during times of peace could present insuperable obstacles to massive and rapid expansion during war. Meaningful planning for emergencies could have reduced such threats, but it did not occur. Hence, the army was unprepared for war. The intricate, improvised, but effective system of command and administration that Abraham Lincoln, Edwin M. Stanton, Henry W. Halleck, and Ulysses S. Grant had devised during the Civil War had quickly and predictably given way to prewar patterns. The Spanish-American War graphically revealed that the army's organizational structure was fundamentally flawed.

## REFORM

Those structural flaws led to Elihu Root's reforms early in the twentieth century. Actually, a group of officers had been advocating an overhaul of the army since shortly after the Civil War. General William T. Sherman led the way for change, serving as a bridge between postwar reformers and their antebellum counterparts such as Dennis Hart Mahan. Unlike navy reformers, the army's were not influenced significantly by technological advance. Although the land forces felt the impact of changed weaponry in the late nineteenth and early twentieth centuries, the major breakthroughs came during World War I. The Civil War was the primary force motivating Sherman and his allies. That total, relentless war of attrition had seared into them the lesson that armies existed to fight and that victory depended on marshaling a nation's strength to the fullest and methodically using that might to destroy the enemy. During years of peace, the military's primary goal was to prepare for war. Preparedness required effective command and administrative systems, reliable methods for expeditiously mobilizing and training mass armies, and the selection, evaluation, and training of high-quality officers to lead the troops. The lesson the

American Civil War taught was reinforced by Prussia's earlier victories in the 1860s, the Franco-Prussian War of 1870–1871, and the English translation of Clausewitz in 1873. The army reformers proposed to professionalize and modernize the army thoroughly.

Throughout the late nineteenth century, the reformers insisted that effective preparation for and the conduct of war required that the army be directed by a commanding general and his staff, not by the supply and administrative bureaus or an untutored secretary of war or both. They demanded that the nation resolve the critical and controversial issue of how officers of the line could command the army without violating civilian control of the military. With no enemy in sight and the army facing an indifferent-to-hostile political climate, the reformers were ignored until the army's botched performance in the Spanish-American War gave the advocates of fundamental change the opening they needed.

The drive for an effective system of command began soon after the Civil War ended and continued for the rest of the century. Once Ulysses S. Grant became president and Sherman took over as commanding general of the army in March 1869, the line appeared to have an open road. Grant's wartime leadership had virtually written the script for how a commanding general should function, and Sherman had been his chief lieutenant and good friend. The president moved quickly to place the bureaus under Sherman's control and to require that all communication to and from the president and secretary of war pass through the commanding general's office.

This arrangement lasted about three weeks. Secretary of War John A. Rawlins, Grant's wartime chief of staff, convinced the president that the general order involving the commanding general was illegal and had to be rescinded with the authority of the secretary restored. Rawlins in fact allowed Sherman to act as commanding general, but the secretary died in office and was replaced by William W. Belknap in October 1869. Belknap, who had served as a volunteer officer under Grant and Sherman in the West and risen to the rank of brigadier general, worked with sympathetic members of Congress to maximize the powers of the secretary and to reduce the commanding general to a virtual cipher. After five years of terrible frustration and anger, Sherman in October 1874 followed the example of Winfield Scott by moving his office from Washington. Relocated in St. Louis, Sherman officially commanded little more than a few aides.

When Belknap hurriedly resigned in March 1876, his successor, Alphonso Taft, lured Sherman back to Washington with orders placing the army under his control and having the adjutant general and inspector general, whose administrative bureaus were both critical to running the line, report directly to him. Taft was satisfied attending to the War Department's fiscal and legal affairs. The pattern continued under the next four secretaries of war, three of whom were appointed by Rutherford B. Hayes and James A. Garfield. These conditions made Sherman's final years as commanding general both contented and fruitful. Yet no permanent progress was made because Sherman's authority, having no legal basis, depended on general orders of the army and his own prestige.

That reality became clear when Sherman retired as commanding general in November 1883 in favor of Gen. Philip H. Sheridan. The latter moved quickly and aggressively to establish his authority over the entire army at the expense of the bureaus and the secretary of war. Holding the office of secretary between 1881 and 1885, Robert Todd Lincoln, who had deferred to Sherman out of respect and lack of interest in his position, rose to defeat the new commanding general's challenge and to keep him subordinated until retirement in August 1888.

Lieutenant General John M. Schofield succeeded Sheridan and remained in command until September 1895. He brought to the office exceptional talents and experience. A West Point graduate who had seen army duty as both a regular and a volunteer, Schofield also served as a compromise secretary of war from June 1868 to March 1869 when Andrew Johnson and Congress locked horns over Reconstruction policies. Drawing on his varied background, Schofield concluded that a professional officer could command all parts of the army only if he subordinated himself to and allied himself with the secretary of war, rather than challenging his power. Consequently, Schofield acted as principal military adviser—in effect chief of staff—to four secretaries and used their authority to command the line and the bureaus in all but routine administrative matters.

Schofield's insights and innovations held promise for resolving the tangled and undefined relationships among the secretary of war, the bureaus, and the commanding general. This promise went unfulfilled because Schofield's experiment remained incomplete and never produced any changes in statute. Schofield's replacement, Lt. Gen. Nelson A. Miles, according to Russell F. Weigley, was probably the "least qualified man to serve as commanding general since the inception of the post."[4] Actually, Miles, who ascended from the ranks of Civil War volunteers, was an outstanding combat officer. But he got along with almost no one, and he was intent on using the office of commanding general to advance his fanciful ambitions for the White House. Along with Secretary of War Russell A. Alger and the supply bureaus, he played a major role in bringing disrepute upon the army and the War Department during the Spanish-American War, thereby setting the stage for the reforms of Secretary of War Elihu Root.

The vexatious relationships between the commanding generals and secretaries of war became an important source of concern for Congress in the late nineteenth century. Throughout the 1860s and 1870s, it strove mightily to give the army a more sensible command system but had no more success than the executive branch.

The nation's legislators focused on the army because many members had seen wartime service, understood its operations, and acted as both strong advocates and intense critics of the land force. From 1865 to 1870 the army in general and the line in particular faced a friendly Congress. James A. Garfield, who had risen to the rank of major general of the volunteers during the Civil War, chaired the influential House Committee on Military Affairs and acted as a knowledgeable supporter of the army.

In July 1866 the legislators called upon the secretary of war to present Congress with regulations for governing the army. Grant was serving as interim secretary at the time, and he appointed a board made up of Generals Sherman and Sheridan and Col. Christopher C. Augur. The board wrote rules that not only placed the commanding general in charge of both the line and the bureaus but that also restricted the secretary of war to administrative responsibilities. A bill incorporating these provisions sailed through the Senate but was blocked in the House because Garfield would not support legislation over which the army and War Department were acrimoniously divided. Garfield continued to seek a more rational command system in 1868–1869 but without legislative results. As long as soldiers differed over how the army should function, congressional divisions and uncertainties over the land force were simply too great to impose a solution. That reality gave the bureaus and the secretary of war the opportunity to defend themselves against the initiatives of the line.

During the 1870s Congress grew much more critical of the army and less favorable to the line. With Southern Democrats returning to Congress, the Democratic party often controlled at least the House of Representatives during the quarter-century of party stalemate. War and Reconstruction had strengthened the party's antipathy to the military. Antimilitary trends also grew as the army was used against strikers, and pressure mounted to cut armed services' costs during the depression of the 1870s. Democrats did not always lead moves against the army. Few regular army critics were as severe, vindictive, and influential as John A. Logan (R-IL)—volunteer major general during the Civil War, founder of the Grand Army of the Republic (GAR), Jacksonian advocate of the democratic citizen-soldier as opposed to exclusive regulars, and bitter enemy of Sherman, who, he was convinced, had denied him command of the Army of the Tennessee. Replacing Garfield as chairman of the House Military Affairs Committee in 1869, Logan succeeded in having the pay of Sherman and other generals cut and the Command of the Army Act repealed. Elected to the Senate in 1870, he continued his running battle with the regulars, occasionally while acting as chair of the Military Affairs Committee, and cooperated with Belknap in driving Sherman from Washington.

Over half a dozen hearings were held during the 1870s to reorganize the army and to reduce its budget. None was stacked against the service, and most investigating bodies included military personnel, with representatives coming from the line and the staff. For example, in 1876 the two houses of Congress created a bipartisan commission headed by Secretary of War James D. Cameron that included Commanding General Sherman and Quartermaster General Meigs. It rather thoroughly reviewed most aspects of army structure and spending but was not able to file a report because of the obstructionist tactics of Cong. Henry Banning (D-OH), chair of the Military Affairs Committee and a former Union general. Banning was a curious mixture of army reformer and persecutor, and it was not always possible to tell what he sought to accomplish. After the disputed presidential election of 1876 went to Hayes, Banning led congressional Democrats on a legislative rampage aimed at the army. Although Congress turned back proposals to cut the army's size drastically, it adjourned in March 1877 without making appropriations for the War Department. After June of that year, all soldiers, from the lowest private to the highest ranking general, went without pay and the service without funds. This emergency was remedied only in November 1877 when a special session of Congress passed an Army Appropriations bill after a month of heated debate.

In 1878 Garfield moved to end the army's position as a pawn in Republican-Democratic battles by organizing a joint committee of Republicans and Democrats, including former Confederates, once more to recommend legislation for reorganizing the army. Senator Ambrose E. Burnside (R-RI), a former Union general, chaired the body, which held periodic hearings from June to December 1878. In 1879 the committee presented a seventy-seven-page bill to Congress that would trim the army's size, enact many long-overdue reforms involving officers and enlisted men, and institute various organizational changes for strengthening the line. Several attempts to advance the bill failed, and it never stood much of a chance of passing because, among other reasons, the bureaus lobbied against it with great effect.

The proposed legislation appeared to have a cathartic effect, however, and the army ceased to be a scapegoat for regional tensions. Appropriations bills henceforth passed without major traumas, and Congress satisfied itself with minor, commonsense reforms. Major divisive issues thus were avoided. The ineffective command system remained, but the army was no longer pilloried for political reasons.

Despite the executive and legislative stalemate over the army's system of command, the cause of reform continued within the service. Most of the progress was initiated by Sherman or had his support. Among many other accomplishments, Sherman nurtured and supported the talents of Emory Upton, whose ideas and proposals helped shape army thinking on reform for decades. Opposition to the radicalism of Upton's thought explains in part the resistance to change in and outside the service.

A West Point graduate who had a meteoric career during and after the Civil War and who pioneered in infantry tactics, Upton traveled to Asia and Europe in 1875 to study foreign armies. He had become a close associate of Sherman, who sent him abroad to make informed proposals for reforming the American army. Dazzled by the German military, Upton, first in *The Armies of Asia and Europe* (1878) and then in *The Military Policy of the United States* (uncompleted at his death in 1881 and published posthumously), proposed not simple reform but a fundamental reordering of the American army.

Upton asserted that the nation's future depended on a professional, not an amateur, army. This force had to be large enough in peacetime to serve as cadre for a vastly expanded national reserve during war: a reserve—presumably raised through conscription—that would be trained, equipped, officered, and controlled by the federal government and hence able quickly to take on professional qualities. The militia, in contrast, would have peripheral responsibilities to the degree that it was used at all. The army would be directed by a general staff rigorously trained by a professional army educational system. The staff would prepare war plans, collect intelligence, direct training and military education, and write legislation to maintain exacting standards of army performance. Civilians would have little influence over the army. The president would have to yield to professional judgment; the secretary of war would handle only business matters; and Congress, lacking qualifications, could reject but not author legislation for the army.

Only with such policies, Upton insisted, could the nation avoid the disasters of the fundamentally defective practices of the past, when excessive civilian control had crippled the army and invited and needlessly prolonged war. Since the United States lacked a usable military past, he argued, it had to look to Europe, and particularly to Germany, for proper models. However, Upton remained deeply pessimistic about America's seeing the light and adopting military policies capable of redeeming its future.

Upton's analysis and conclusions were embraced by a generation of officers, hardly surprising since Upton was not an especially original thinker. He only systematized prevalent thought about military professionalism and legitimized it through historical analysis and supposedly irrefutable truths revealed by the past. Those realities, combined with the fact that his work was the first, albeit unfinished, military history of the nation, almost instantly made Upton a prophet after his death. In his brooding pessimism—Upton eventually committed suicide—he had begun to view himself as one. That his prescriptions had no relevance to America's heritage appeared unimportant to the author and his advocates. Perhaps their detachment from American traditions was necessary to sustain an increasingly professionalized officer corps through its dark ages of hostility, neglect, and obscured mission. Sherman's position accurately exemplified the cul-de-sac that army professional thought had entered. Although the commanding general played a key role in almost all army reforms, he, unlike Adm. Stephen B. Luce, remained inexplicably obtuse about the civilian context in which military change had to take place.

The price for the army's unrealistic thinking was high. Supporters of drastic Uptonian change were ignored. For example, during the Burnside Committee hearings in 1878, almost all the line officers, including Sherman and Upton, supported the latter's ideas on reform. The committee incorporated many of Upton's proposals in its bill, which, not surprisingly, ensured its defeat. Variations of that scenario had already been played out numerous times before Congress in the 1860s and 1870s. Many of Upton's specific reforms were adopted in the twentieth century, but only after they had been separated from German-style militarism and incorporated into a system consistent with American military traditions.

Indeed, before the turn of the century, advanced schools for military education were already well under way. Sherman, looking to further professionalism whenever he could, played a vital role here, especially between 1876 and 1883 when his powers as commanding general were at their height.

The first step occurred in 1868, when Sherman revived John C. Calhoun's Artillery School at Fortress Monroe, which had been closed in 1860. Sherman made his most important contribution in 1881, when he created the School of Application for Cavalry and Infantry at Fort Leavenworth, Kansas. Beginning without a clear mission and as a basic training school for officers, the school evolved in the late nineteenth and early twentieth centuries into two institutions, the Army School of the Line and the Army Staff College, to prepare outstanding officers for high command and general staff work. Colonel Arthur L. Wagner and Capt. Eben Swift played key roles in adapting German educational methods to the United States and in emphasizing "military art," which included tactics, strategy, logistics, and military history. Under the two educational giants, Leavenworth became noted for its applicatory method of tactical training, which used map problems, war games, terrain exercises, and the issuing of practice orders. After Root's reforms, Brig. Gen.

J. Franklin Bell, commandant of Leavenworth beginning in 1903, and Maj. John F. Morrison, instructor and head of the Military Art Department between 1906 and 1912, shaped the schools for their twentieth-century function. Although Leavenworth had little impact on the Spanish-American War, during World War I its graduates played a critical role in the success of the American Expeditionary Forces (AEF).

Various branch schools, with a narrower focus than the School of the Line and the Staff College, were also established in the late nineteenth and early twentieth centuries. These included the Engineer School of Application in 1866, the Cavalry and Light Artillery School in 1891, the Army Medical School in 1893, the Signal School in 1904, the School of Musketry for the infantry in 1907, the Field Engineering School in 1910, the School of Fire for the field artillery in 1911, and numerous others.

Although army higher education in general thrived, West Point stagnated. It was separated from the Corps of Engineers in 1866, and its curriculum was broadened to include more aspects of military education, though the emphasis on mathematics continued. In the postwar years, the academy lost its distinction as a leading engineering school, stressed form over content, shunned innovation, and prepared the cadets at best for junior officer assignments.

As part of the modernizing process, army officers led in establishing professional organizations and publications. With Sherman's encouragement, Maj. Gen. Winfield Scott Hancock in 1878 helped set up the Military Service Institution of the United States—the counterpart of the United States Naval Institute—to encourage study and publication on military science and military history. It published the *Journal of the United States Military Service Institution,* and in 1879 a similar publication, the *United Service,* was launched. As offshoots of military schools, most branches also established professional associations that published journals. Hence, in 1885 the Cavalry Association was founded and three years later began publishing the *Cavalry Journal.* A group of officers at Fort Leavenworth in 1893 organized the Infantry Society, which, after going through a number of name changes, began publishing the *Infantry Journal.* Over time, associations and their publications merged, were absorbed, or adopted more appropriate names. In addition to journals, various monographs were published. Besides Upton's, some of the important volumes included Wagner's *The Service of Security and Information* (1889) and *Organization and Tactics* (1895) and John Bigelow, Jr.'s *The Principles of Strategy* (1894) and *The Campaign of Chancellorsville: A Strategic and Tactical Study* (1910). These specialized publications, together with the schools and professional associations, interacted to further military knowledge, open debate on key issues, and advance the interests of the army and its specialized branches.

The army also established a unit that assumed intelligence and planning duties and appropriately became part of the General Staff in the twentieth century. With the army increasingly interested in military developments abroad and concerned about hemispheric security, the adjutant general's office in 1885 created an agency later called the Military Information Division (MID). The division's work abroad was strengthened when Congress created the attaché system in September 1888. By 1892 the rather small and amorphous agency began to grow in size, taking on greater responsibilities. They included gathering intelligence on the geography, economic resources, and armed forces of the United States and foreign nations, directing the attaché program, preparing military maps, maintaining a reference library, collecting information on the militia and assisting in its training, and planning for the mobilization of the regulars, volunteers, and militia in the event of an emergency.

Always squeezed for funds, office space, and manpower, the MID never managed to do much planning, but its intelligence work was good. The MID was well prepared for the Spanish-American War in the Caribbean, although months of work were required to create an adequate intelligence network in the Philippines. After the war, the MID began to cooperate with Naval Intelligence, played a role in the nation's expansion in the Caribbean and Pacific, and assisted in the background work for organizing what became the General Staff. Once the staff began operating, the intelligence unit became caught up in bureaucratic struggles and encountered hostility from several well-placed and influential officers. The MID was ultimately placed under the direction of the Army War College, was absorbed by that institution, and virtually lost its identity and function between 1910 and 1916. With the nation close to war in 1917, the MID made a comeback, was incorporated into the General Staff, and played a vital role in military operations during World War I.

Late in the nineteenth century, Congress adopted a few proposals from reformers for improving the quality of the officer corps. Retirement at age sixty-four became compulsory in 1884. Changes eight years later based promotions on seniority within each arm, corps, or staff department instead of by regiment, and all ranks below major required examinations. By the mid-1890s the War Department required annual efficiency reports on all officers. Moreover, with the consolidation of army posts, officers engaged in field training with whole regiments, and in the late 1880s a number of regiments came together for exercises as a single infantry unit for the first time since 1869.

Army reform was not driven by technology, a reality reflected by the state of late nineteenth-century weaponry. From 1865 to 1872 the infantry made do with the wartime Springfield rifle muskets modified to load at the breech and fire a metallic cartridge, and the cavalry used a mix of commercial carbines, particularly those of Spencer and Sharps. In 1873 shoulder arms were standardized with the adoption of the 1873 Springfield rifle and carbine, a single-shot, .45-caliber weapon. Twenty years later, the army finally adopted an excellent repeating shoulder arm, the Danish .30-caliber Krag-Jorgensen rifle and carbine, a bolt-action weapon with a five-round magazine that fired smokeless cartridges. All or most of these weapons were manufactured at army arsenals.

Some progress also was made in terms of artillery. By the 1880s muzzle-loading, cast-iron cannon were replaced by rifled steel guns ranging in caliber from 3.2 to 7 inches and manufactured at the newly established Army Gun Factory at the Watervliet Arsenal. As with the navy, private firms provided the factory with gun forgings and carriages and in some instances manufactured finished weapons. Generally, however, the nation trailed Europe in advanced artillery, as Ordnance was only beginning to experiment with recoil-absorbing devices, elevating, traversing, and sighting instruments, steel carriages, explosive shells, and so on, which were already in use on the Continent. Moreover, smokeless power production in both public and private facilities was still much too limited to handle a major emergency. Initial advances in ordnance probably owed more to the navy than to the army. In 1883 the navy-led Gun Foundry Board presented the first survey of modern ordnance development and proposals for public-private production to assist the armed services in procuring up-to-date weapons.

In 1885 Congress created the army-led Board on Fortifications and Other Defenses, headed by Secretary of War William C. Endicott, to consider rebuilding coastal fortifications. The board found America's harbor defenses to be obsolete and useless against modern weaponry and proposed rebuilding twenty-seven coastal and Great Lakes sites at an estimated cost of $127 million in ten years. Congress was taken back by the high figure and troubled by the lack of an identifiable enemy, but it still made an initial appropriation in 1890 to begin the work. Two years earlier it had provided for a Board of Ordnance and Fortification within the army to oversee plans devised by the Corps of Engineers. Progress in the 1890s was slow; old forts at major harbors were gradually abandoned in favor of earthworks or armor-protected concrete pits. Ten- to twelve-inch rifled guns were installed on disappearing carriages. On the eve of the Spanish-American War, though, only 30 of the 500 heavy guns and 70 of the over 1,000 mortars recommended by the Endicott Board had been mounted. Appropriations picked up in 1896 and continued at a reasonable level until 1905, when a scaled-down program costing a little over $30 million came to a conclusion. As the United States expanded abroad, built a world-class navy, and reassessed the international situation, it no longer needed the elaborate coastal defenses proposed in 1885. The twenty-year effort nonetheless updated these defenses to some extent and focused the army's attention on the effects of the naval revolution on coastal defense as well as on modern developments in ordnance, armor, and weaponry in general.

The army made limited progress during the Gilded Age on the vital but touchy issue of reserves. Commitment to a national reserve modeled on Upton's ideas created nothing but controversy, leaving the nation with the state militia. By 1896 most states had followed the lead of New York by redesignating their volunteer militia companies as National Guard, even though they remained essentially state-directed units. After languishing during the 1860s and 1870s, state militias started to rebuild in the 1880s with larger budgets, modified laws, new armories, and improved training. The War Department tallied 114,000 officers and men in state units in 1897. The quality of state formations varied greatly, but the National Guard as a whole was not a ready reserve, boasting and propaganda to the contrary. Weapons were discards from the national government; clothing, equipment, and accoutrements were seldom sufficient, with no reserves of these supplies in existence; and training was at best inadequate.

The army assisted the states to some degree by lending weapons, detailing officers for training and inspection, and even arranging joint maneuvers. The results were questionable. Units with elected officers and lax discipline functioned like social clubs more than as military units. Moreover, the militia's legal obligation to the national government was ambiguous in terms of presidential authority over it, terms of service, and the possibility of use outside the United States. One weapon the militia did possess was political clout. The National Guard Association was organized in 1877 and proved an effective lobbying agency for state troops. Although its weaknesses far outweighed its strengths, the National Guard simply could not be bypassed.

Professionalization of the army in the late nineteenth century was broad-based. It included the struggle for an effective command system at the executive and legislative levels, Uptonian absolutism and the more prosaic but steady progress for change through military higher education, professional organizations and publications, intelligence work, promotion reforms, some officer training with large bodies of troops, new weapons technology, and proposals for manpower mobilization.

The nature of this professionalizing process has set off a significant, and potentially fecund, debate. John M. Gates concludes that Samuel P. Huntington is wrong in his assertion that the soldier was physically, socially, and intellectually isolated from the civilian in the late nineteenth century and that such isolation was an essential condition for professionalizing the officer corps.[5] The differing interpretations are significant because they say a great deal about civil-military relations; the debate is potentially fecund because both authors basically rely on fragmentary, impressionistic evidence to support their cases. One needs much more knowledge about the officer corps of both services and their interaction with civilian society before reasonably concluding that either Huntington or Gates has the better argument, but the analysis by both authors is sophisticated, intricate, and subtle.

Civil-military relations were continuous during the Gilded Age; there was no sharp break from the past, although the evolution necessary to prepare for the future did occur. In a larger sense, the military services' isolation from or closeness to civilian society is not the key issue; whether their reforms prepared them for a global role as part of a mature industrial society is. And on that point, neither the navy nor the army was able to succeed without close and continuing civilian guidance.

## THE SPANISH-AMERICAN WAR

The Spanish-American War highlighted the major strengths and weaknesses of the army's professionalization process in the late nineteenth century. Without a proper command system, progress in the army's individual parts did not lead to an effective whole. Devising a command system that was consistent with the nation's traditions, giving order and system to the army's parts, and making the National Guard a meaningful reserve required civilian leadership that was creative and flexible enough to provide the army with the balance it lacked.

Recent scholarship has demonstrated that army mobilization for the Spanish-American War was not the unmitigated disaster that is often portrayed, that much of the chaos resulted from vast expansion within a few months, and that the president and his advisers enormously complicated the War Department's task by abruptly changing military strategy. Although such assertions are true, they do not detract from the reality that an undemanding war clearly revealed a fragmented War Department–army structure badly in need of reform.[6]

War Department problems began at the top. Secretary of War Russell A. Alger, a wealthy Michigan businessman and former national commander of the GAR, had only limited political experience, was not a good administrator, tended to be impulsive and unpredictable, and often clashed with other people over matters of pride. Commanding General Nelson A. Miles was worse. Extremely ambitious and vain, Miles feared conspiracies against him and was constantly at odds with his colleagues. He lacked the temperament, insight, and perspective that his position demanded. Predictably, Alger and Miles were soon at odds and proved unequal to the enormous tasks facing them. As a result, Miles was simply pushed aside and Alger took direction from Pres. William McKinley. The president relied increasingly on Adj. Gen. Henry C. Corbin, a skillful administrator who acted, in effect, as a chief of staff.

Once war was declared McKinley became a strong commander-in-chief who determined and coordinated diplomacy and military strategy from a war room in the White House. Since the navy was ably run, the president directed it only generally, but the multiple problems of the army forced him into much more detailed management of that service. Moreover, the Army and Navy Coast Defense Board created by Alger and Long never functioned well, and McKinley had to act as coordinator and mediator between the two services.

The biggest problem facing the army was a tenfold increase in its size in a matter of months. On March 17, 1898, on behalf of the War Department Cong. John A. T. Hull (R-IA) introduced a bill in Congress for a type of Uptonian expansible army of 104,000 men, with the state militia relegated to an auxiliary role. Supporters of the National Guard, backed by Southern Democrats and Populists—who continued to harbor animosity toward regulars—forced a quick retreat. The administration negotiated a settlement in which an April 22 law provided for a volunteer army of National Guard units. Another law of April 26 increased the regular army to 65,700 men. To the surprise of many observers, McKinley on April 23 called up all available guard units under his order for 125,000 militiamen; most reported within six weeks. Late in May the president called up an additional 75,000 state volunteers; 17,000 more joined the army as federal volunteers. These troops, in combination with the expanded regulars, gave the army nearly 275,000 officers and men at the time of the armistice on August 12, 1898.

Initial plans to keep the volunteers in state camps for extended periods proved impractical. They were quickly moved to large facilities, with the regulars at Tampa, Florida, and Chickamauga, Tennessee, as well as at other sites and in Pennsylvania, Virginia, Kentucky, Alabama, Florida, Louisiana, and California. Contrary to the promises of state officials, most guardsmen arrived at camps with little training, few weapons, limited equipment, and poor or no military clothing.

Rapidly changing strategy put additional pressure on the army. In late April the McKinley administration decided to limit army operations against the Spanish in Cuba to sporadic forays. Four days later, it was decided to attack Havana no later than mid-June with a relatively large force of 50,000 men. On May 26 even that strategy was scrapped in favor of immediately launching a 25,000-man campaign against Santiago.

Major General William R. Shafter's Fifth Corps did not sail from Tampa until June 14, however, and then with only 17,000 soldiers. The port turned out to be a disastrous choice for a major point of embarkation. It might have been able to handle the small army units for which it was originally intended but not the large concentration of soldiers who traveled there. Shafter's expedition against Santiago was followed up by another last-minute decision to allow Commanding General Miles to invade and occupy Puerto Rico in late July and early August with a total of 17,000 troops. Finally, while struggling with the Caribbean kaleidoscope, the McKinley administration early in May faced the need to send an expedition to the Philippines after Adm. George Dewey's destruction of the Spanish fleet in Manila Bay. Plans for a 5,000-man expedition expanded to 20,000 men under Maj. Gen. Wesley Merritt's Eighth Corps, who were transported to the Philippines in a number of contingents between May 25 and August.

Supply, not mobilizing and transporting soldiers to the various camps, was the army's main problem. Initially overwhelmed, the major supply bureaus were at least competently led by Civil War veterans, even though Quartermaster Gen. Marshall I. Ludington took over only in February 1898 and Commissary Gen. Charles P. Eagan did not assume office until May 1898. Chief of Ordnance Daniel W. Flagler had held his position since 1891. The bureaus made preliminary preparations for war in March and April 1898 by expanding production at Quartermaster depots and Ordnance arsenals and by surveying actual and potential private suppliers. They could do little else, since regulations rigidly restricted spending, and they could make no contracts ahead of appropriations. Moreover, reserves of supplies, equipment, and weapons were relatively limited. The Quartermaster Department, for example, was prepared to clothe and equip only the existing army of about 28,000 officers, plus 8,000 to 10,000 others, for three months.

Once war broke out and ample funds became available, the bureaus quickly stepped up their supply operations. The Quartermaster Department expanded output of clothing, tents, and other items at depots in Philadelphia, Jeffersonville, and San Francisco and introduced electric cutting and stitching machines at the depot in Philadelphia. Still, department facilities could not meet the exponential increase in demand. Consequently, depots throughout the nation let contracts to private firms for over one hundred different items of clothing and equipment, almost exclusively through competitive bidding. For most of the war, bids had to go to Washington for approval; to expedite contracting, the quartermaster general finally delegated authority to the depots toward the end of the hostilities. Departmental flexibility was essential since few firms were capable at first of producing fabrics or tent canvas that met army specifications. The department made do with lesser quality until plants could gear up for more demanding production. Moreover, the Quartermaster Department never devised a suitable uniform for the tropics.

The most troubling problem for the Quartermaster Department undoubtedly involved wagons. The department had sold most of its fine, sturdy wagons in 1895 during an economy drive. With the outbreak of war it needed 5,000 new ones. But the previous manufacturers, particularly the Studebaker Company, had sold off their material and machinery for army production and only could deliver the required amounts in nine months. Consequently, the department basically had to settle for farm wagons of much lower quality. Ambulances were even harder to obtain. In contrast, purchasing 16,618 horses and 20,182 mules presented no problems.

When the Quartermaster Department did hit its stride in production and procurement it was efficient. In less than two weeks, the New York depot produced 100,000 complete uniforms ready for delivery to the field. Within three and a half months, the department had equipped an army of 275,000 men and held adequate reserves. Two-thirds of the clothing and tentage had come from the private sector, as had all vehicles and animals. The quality of purchased items was good and prices fair. Moreover, there were virtually no supply scandals, shoddy materials, fraud, or other failings common in the past.

The Ordnance Department also performed well. It too depended on a mix of production from its own and private facilities. The Krag-Jorgensen shoulder arm could be produced only at the Springfield Arsenal, and output could not be expanded fast enough to provide all troops with the weapon. As a result, only the regulars and the Rough Riders regiment received the Krags at the outset. The volunteers were armed from the Ordnance Department's stockpile of 260,000 .45-caliber Springfield rifles—a quality arm, although the black-powder ammunition gave off smoke when fired, revealing the shooter's position. As production of the Krags increased, volunteers received that weapon as a replacement for the Springfield. However, the smokeless powder used by the Krags was in short supply because the army lacked a stockpile, and private and naval production was never sufficient. As a result, the two services created a priority system for distributing smokeless powder. Since the war was short and most troops never saw combat, the limited supply did not adversely affect many of the fighting forces.

The Ordnance Department had ample amounts of cannon and artillery on hand for the war, and Ordnance and private concerns could produce additional carriages, ammunition wagons, and so forth as needed. To supplement its own production at Philadelphia's Frankfort Arsenal, Ordnance contracted with numerous firms to produce small-arms ammunition, artillery shells, and fuses. The department was also responsible for cartridge belts, knapsacks, haversacks, and eating utensils, along with saddles and animal harnesses. Production was increased at the Rock Island Arsenal, but private firms also had to be brought in, and the department contracted with some 130. Inexperienced firms often produced inferior products or failed to meet delivery dates. Like the Quartermaster Department, however, the Ordnance Department met its commitments to the expanded army before hostilities ended, with the single exception of mess kits. Although the department's operations were also free of malfeasance, the chief of ordnance was never as satisfied with private production as the quartermaster general, in part because contracting with private companies to produce the highly complex Ordnance materials placed a greater strain on the department.

The Commissary Department was the supply bureau best prepared for war. The commissary general alerted all subordinate units early in April 1898 to have ample rations on hand and to maintain lists of firms that could immediately supply the army with necessary food items. The department easily met the army's demands for food. The regulars traveling to Chickamauga Park or Tampa carried thirty days' worth of rations with them, and the Commissary Department had contractors regularly deliver food items to each camp as it opened and expanded. For the first time, the army used refrigerated beef instead of fresh beef on the hoof. The department also relied on a product called fresh roast beef, actually cooked canned beef, instead of on corned beef as the principal meat in the field ration. Although the diet was unimaginative and heavy, it could be palatable if properly prepared, especially if fresh vegetables and baked bread were available.

Commissary General Eagan was an aggressive executive who purchased huge quantities of food with spirit and confidence. No one ever complained that there was not enough to eat. Indeed, a frequent complaint was that excess rations on hand created storage problems. The Commissary Department, like the two other principal supply bureaus, operated without charges of corruption. The other bureaus involved in supply—the Medical Department, the Signal Corps, and the Corps of Engineers—did not purchase in great volume and usually ran into the normal complications and delays in contracting, buying on the open market, or having specialized equipment manufactured, but they did not face inordinate problems.

In general, the principal supply bureaus operated with reasonable efficiency after a slow start. Within a month of the declaration of war, supplies were moving to camps with regularity, by mid-June shipments were enormous, and by mid-August all or most troops were clothed, equipped, armed, housed, and fed.

Several points stand out in regard to this record of production and procurement. The supply bureaus had matured in such a way that they could rapidly and efficiently conduct enormous business ventures virtually free of graft, fraud, and corruption—a laudable feat for any public or private institution. Moreover, the American business and industrial system had grown in size and sophistication to the point that it could produce most military items quickly, even without previous experience. These realities accounted for the remarkable speed with which the bureaus initiated a massive supply program. Indeed, producing and procuring most items on a scale at least ten times greater than in peacetime had become almost routine for the bureaus.

Although the Quartermaster Department excelled at procurement and production, grave difficulties arose in the distribution of goods to thousands of soldiers in camps scattered across the country. The department often encountered bottlenecks, such as that at Tampa, and the supply system as a whole ran into serious trouble and for a time nearly broke down. The well-known record of supply failures during the Spanish-American War was neither fiction nor exaggeration.

Two critical failings stand out in the army's chaotic distribution system: coordinating the railroads and organizing base depots. Water transportation also became a problem, but never on the scale of the other two.

In the three areas, the Quartermaster Department by 1898 had lost its knowledge and experience from the Civil War. In the earlier conflict, the department and related units had made innovative use of railroads, telegraphs, water transportation, and often the three in combination, to accomplish wartime logistical feats that for the time were breathtaking. The accomplishments of Herman Haupt, Daniel C. McCallum, and Lewis B. Parsons were especially impressive. On a more day-to-day level, Ulysses S. Grant's base depot at City Point for operations against Richmond exceeded in size, level of activity, and organizational efficiency any business, industrial, or transportation center of the day.

In 1898 the bureau chiefs, including the quartermaster general, were Civil War veterans, yet none seemed aware of what had been accomplished less than thirty-five years before. In any case, the army should not have had to rely on the memory of aging veterans. The logistical lessons of the Civil War should have been taught, practiced, and planned. Though the army set up numerous specialized schools in the late nineteenth and early twentieth centuries, including classes for bakers and cooks, no institutions existed for teaching logistics, transportation, or the operation of base depots. The various Quartermaster depots gave effective schooling in the management of production and procurement, but that experience obviously did not provide training in quickly setting up base depots that could handle the needs of thousands of troops, working with the railroads under emergency conditions, and acquiring and using water transportation efficiently. In the first months or more of war, the Quartermaster Department violated almost every cardinal rule Haupt had devised for the effective use of railroads in an emergency. Moreover, the errors occurred after decades of advance in railroad and telegraph systems had made the department's job in the 1890s much easier than it had been in the Civil War.

If the quartermaster general showed himself incapable of managing modern logistics, then the commanding general or the secretary of war should have stepped in to correct the problem. Miles's performance and judgment in the area were seriously lacking and therefore of no benefit. More could be expected from Alger, a businessman associated with some of the largest industrialists and financiers in the nation. The secretary of war did what he could in the supply area. He met daily with the bureaus to solve problems and was generally helpful in freeing their procedures from stultifying peacetime routines, granting subordinate units the right to purchase in the open market when necessary and loosening up the prewar requisition system, which permitted supplies to be issued only when ordered by unit commanders and demanded an enormous amount of paperwork. In June, as more camps became necessary, the secretary of war also improved procedures for selecting the sites. Meanwhile, Adjutant General Corbin, acting on his own and for the president, dealt with numerous matters to expedite the army's vast expansion. Yet no one official in Washington brought centralized direction to the mobilization effort, and the shortcoming was evident throughout the army.

Without centralized control, the army's misuse of the railroads caused serious problems. Alger considered bringing in a railroad executive to coordinate rail transportation for the army but decided against it because the movement of troops was going so well. From April to August 1898 the railroads efficiently, economically, and without mishap moved over 450,000 enlisted men and officers in day coaches and sleeping cars.

Moving troops presented few problems, but handling them once they arrived at the camp sites did. The new camps lacked loading docks, sidings, and warehouses. Into these camps poured tons of supplies from all the bureaus in unmarked cars, with bills of lading specifying their contents arriving days and even weeks later. Quartermaster supplies were at times shipped in the same car as medical provisions and ordnance stores. The only way to determine the contents of a railroad car was to unload it, yet the facilities, manpower, and wagons for doing so were lacking or in short supply. Incredible traffic jams resulted, which were made even worse because most camps were in the South, whose railroad system was less developed than the North's.

No camp suffered from worse congestion than Tampa, the major camp and port for operations against Cuba. Only two railroads connected Tampa with the North, and only one line ran from the city to the port. To make matters worse, the two lines were not particularly well run, and they competed in a way that undermined the operating efficiency of both. At one point, boxcars were backed up halfway to the nation's capital. When McKinley ordered ships to sail for Santiago on June 7, pandemonium set in. Units disregarded preparations for embarkation to race for the port as rumors circulated that there were not enough vessels to take all the troops.

Coordinated use of the railroads could have prevented much of the confusion that occurred at Tampa and most other camps. Since properly trained Quartermaster officers were lacking, railroad executives should have been brought in to institute policies ensuring that supplies were shipped only as needed and with proper marking and paperwork, a move that would have solved many (though not all) problems. The various camps were unprepared to receive troops or supplies because of a shortage of competent staff officers. When war broke out, the Quartermaster Department had an authorized strength of fifty-seven officers and eighty quartermaster sergeants, the Subsistence Department twenty-two officers and ninety-six commissary sergeants. (During the war the Quartermaster Department grew to 155 officers and 105 quartermaster sergeants, and the Subsistence Department to 129 officers.) Few of these officers and noncommissioned officers could be spared for the field. Their National Guard counterparts usually lacked the training and experience to take over supply operations at the newly created camps. Moreover, the commanding officers at the camps seldom had any experience in handling large bodies of troops and did not know how to use a staff in establishing control. That was certainly the case with General Shafter at Tampa, and even after Commanding General Miles joined Shafter, nothing improved. Consequently, confusion, congestion, and disorder at the camps were inevitable.

Chaos gradually gave way to order. Railroad officials joined army officers in restoring method to rail transport. Usually at their own expense, the railroads built additional platforms and sidings, and railroad agents cooperated with the army to smooth the flow of men and goods. Between June and July the quartermaster general required that a list of contents precede all rail shipments to their final destination, that boxcars be labeled as to contents, and that rush shipments be telegraphically followed to ensure arrival. The bureaus also altered their practices to facilitate mass supply operations. For example, the Quartermaster Department's Clothing and Equipage Division in mid-May began shipping bulk supplies to concentration points without waiting for requisitions. Commanding officers, their staff officers, or both in time gained enough experience or guidance to bring some order to the camps.

Water transportation also plagued the War Department. Quartermaster General Ludington in March 1898 began surveying the availability of ships on the Atlantic and Gulf Coasts for moving troops. Not many suitable vessels were at hand. The American merchant marine was small, East Coast shipowners blocked foreigners from transferring their vessels to American registry, and international law prohibited the use of foreign ships. The navy also beat the army to the existing market. To complicate matters further, the shallow waters off Cuba and Puerto Rico denied the army some of the best ships because of their deep draft. The Quartermaster Department, consequently, had to depend on small, slow, and worn ships used in the coastal trade on the Atlantic and in the Gulf. Moreover, the department chartered vessels only when the need for them was absolute. With the McKinley administration repeatedly shifting strategy, this practice left the Quartermaster Department constantly scrambling to catch up. As a result, the ships that carried Shafter's men to Santiago were not intended to be troopships. They were hurriedly and inadequately converted for carrying soldiers, were without proper cooking facilities, and turned out to be crowded, poorly ventilated, and unsanitary. The crowding stemmed partly from the Quartermaster Department's miscalculation that the thirty-one ships chartered could carry Shafter's 25,000 men. In fact, 17,000 fit aboard and only then when packed in too tightly.

Loading the ships at Port Tampa in late May and early June produced another trauma. There were no docks at the port, only a pier that could not accommodate more than two ships at once. The one rail line from the city and camp to the port stopped fifty feet short of the wharf so that freight had to be hauled over sand to the pier. The logistics of loading supplies and men under such conditions were nightmarish. Shafter's chief quartermaster, Col. Charles F. Humphrey, had no experience in loading ships, which made circumstances much worse. The assistance of a civilian shipmaster claiming twenty years of service in runs between Florida and Cuba did not seem to help. Although the charges are disputed, ships apparently were loaded in a haphazard way, medicine and other Medical Department goods packed beneath other freight, and a great many supplies had to be left at the port because of a lack of cargo space. By most accounts, the embarkation of troops was a mad scramble since they had not been properly assigned as units to ships in advance.

Debarkation was if anything worse than embarkation. The ships sailed from Tampa on June 8, were called back because of a false alarm about the presence of Spanish warships, finally got under way on June 14, and reached the vicinity of Santiago some six days later. Landing took place at Daiquiri and Siboney, seventeen and nine miles east of Santiago. Neither of these so-called ports was sheltered or had adequate landing facilities. Landing the troops was not difficult, but supplies were another matter. Most of the boats and barges intended to serve as lighters broke down, sank, or deserted en route from Tampa, leaving just one steam lighter to unload the ships. The navy could provide little assistance. Additional ships sent from the mainland were lost in a storm, and a New York company hired to take over much of the debarkation and transportation functions did not arrive in Cuba until Santiago surrendered, when its services were no longer needed.

With only one boat to handle thirty-one ships, ammunition, food, and some medical supplies had priority for unloading. Ships remained offshore as warehouses instead of returning to the United States for reinforcements as had been intended, exacerbating further the already desperate shortage of ships.

On land, incredibly harsh terrain in the height of the rainy season reduced the movement of supplies inland to a minimum. Wagons could barely operate on steep and rugged jungle trails. Mules carried a considerable part of the limited provisions unloaded from the ships to the troops, who suffered from great privations of every sort. Much of the cargo was not unloaded until Santiago fell; some of it returned with the ships to the United States.

Many of the problems at sea and on land stemmed from the diversion of an expedition originally intended for Havana to Santiago, where conditions were quite different, but the complete absence of planning compounded the difficulties. The Military Information Division had done extensive intelligence work on Cuba, yet its efforts apparently were ignored.

The troops and supplies sent to the Caribbean after the troubled departure of the Fifth Corps benefited from some basic reforms. In mid-June Secretary of War Alger decided to supplement chartered ships with purchased vessels that would form a permanent army transportation fleet. To assemble the government flotilla, he brought Frank J. Hecker, a Detroit banker and railroad executive, into the War Department. For a time Hecker operated as a civilian agent, but in mid-July Alger and Quartermaster General Ludington created a new two-branch Transportation Division in the Quartermaster Department. Hecker headed the branch dealing with water transportation; Col. Charles Bird, a Quartermaster officer, handled the branch for railroad transport.

Hecker ultimately spent $16.5 million on a fleet of modern passenger liners, freight ships, a refrigerator ship, and smaller vessels that could comfortably handle 14,000 troops and 7,000 animals. Additional ships were chartered and others returned from Santiago. These vessels were refitted according to new specifications designed to avoid the worst features that the Fifth Corps had endured. Moreover, at the urging of the quartermaster and other officers, Alger decided in early June to abandon Tampa as the port of embarkation because of the severe and irremediable conditions there. Troops in and around Tampa would still depart from that port, but those in Northern camps remained in the healthier climate with more comfortable facilities instead of being transferred to the humid coastal lowlands. When reinforcements were needed for Santiago or troops were mobilized for Commanding General Miles's expedition to Puerto Rico, they shipped out of New York, Newport News, and Charleston. Ample rail connections and proper wharf facilities at these ports simplified embarkation of men and equipment.

Actions that Alger, Ludington, and their colleagues finally took on the East Coast resembled events unfolding in the West. The McKinley administration began assembling troops on May 3 for the Manila expedition. The task force ultimately encompassed 20,000 troops—5,000 regulars and the rest volunteers from the West Coast. On May 12 Maj. Gen. Wesley Merritt, the second ranking general in the army, took command of what became the Eigth Corps. Merritt was a West Point graduate and Civil War veteran who had commanded competently at the divisional level and hence knew how to handle large bodies of troops.

The experience showed. He aggressively selected capable fellow generals who helped him organize a staff made up mostly of regulars. He placed his second-in-command, Maj. Gen. Elwell S. Otis, in charge of chartering and fitting out transports. Using the threat of seizure, Otis secured fourteen passenger ships, which were carefully converted to troopships with accommodations and facilities necessary for transporting military units some 7,000 miles. The soldiers were well housed, equipped, and trained before departure, and they left the large and well-equipped port of San Francisco in approximately five orderly contingents on ships that had been properly loaded. The troops arrived in Manila in good shape. Although the transports did not carry many landing craft, upon arrival in Manila Merritt's quartermaster improvised a landing fleet composed of boats from the troopships, navy launches, and native lighters in order to unload men and equipment efficiently. Ground transportation also had to be improvised.

These challenges were handled in an effective manner that resembled the last days of the Civil War; in constrast, Tampa evoked memories of the early days of that long conflict. The difference stemmed from the quality and experience of the commander, proper planning, and the correct use of staff.

The failures of the brief mobilization for the Spanish-American War could have been forgotten easily in the joy and relief of victory, in the acrimony over imperialism following the war, and especially because of the ongoing conflict in the Philippines. But the epidemics of typhoid, dysentery, malaria, and perhaps yellow fever that swept the camps in Cuba and at home created such a furor that the conduct of the war became a matter of intense controversy just before and after the armistice in mid-August. Out of 5,462 deaths in the armed services in 1898, 379 resulted from combat; most of the others were caused by disease.

Because of location, primitive conditions, inadequate supplies, and climate, 75 percent of the Fifth Corps in Santiago suffered from malaria, complicated by dysentery, typhoid, and possibly yellow fever in July and August. Conditions became so desperate that the entire corps had to be rushed in August to a special camp at Montauk on the northern tip of Long Island. But the botched evacuation of the troops resembled the corps' embarkation at Tampa and debarkation at Santiago.

Public shock at sickness and death among the troops abroad grew when typhoid swept through the camps at home. Of the 200,000 volunteers called up in 1898, only 35,000 ever left the country. The rest remained in camps in Tennessee, Virginia, Florida, and elsewhere. Sanitary conditions were often abysmal and medical facilities inadequate. When the epidemic hit in July and August, army medical facilities in the camps simply gave way, requiring an all-out War Department effort to control the situation and to implement medical attention and sanitary conditions.

The Medical Department simply failed to carry out its mission during the war. It was as if the medical experience of the Civil War and the efforts of the U.S. Sanitary Commission in that conflict had not occurred. Surgeon General Dr. George M. Sternberg was an outstanding research scientist but an incompetent administrator. The department attempted without much success to re-create the hospital system of the Civil War, failed to keep tabs on the sanitary conditions in the camps, and inadequately ordered, distributed, and monitored availability of medical supplies, stores, and equipment. Sternberg and his assistants were caught off guard by the conditions in the camps and by the diseases that their neglect helped to spread.

Although the Medical Department suffered from a lack of prestige and power within the army, astute leadership would have made its voice heard. Moreover, if the Medical Department were not doing its job, the War Department should not have remained ignorant of that reality, as it did. The Inspector General's Department, intended to alert higher authorities to real and potential trouble, did not sound an alarm about the Surgeon General's failure. Having lost a power struggle with the Adjutant General's Office, it had become virtually dysfunctional. Nonetheless, the president, the secretary of war, the commanding general, or someone else should have moved to correct the situation.

The medical calamity exposed the weaknesses in the War Department and army, created serious political problems for the McKinley administration, and set off a search for a scapegoat. Secretary of War Alger became the victim.

Although not an outstanding secretary, Alger was at least competent, but under attack his worst defensive traits became manifest. His position was made even more difficult when Commanding General Miles, seething with frustration and anger over McKinley and Alger's having ignored him during the war and over his inability to become a wartime hero, publicly charged that the army's use of refrigerated beef treated with harmful chemicals (embalmed beef) and unauthorized fresh roast beef contributed significantly to the unusual amount of sickness among the troops. To quell the public clamor, McKinley in September 1898 appointed a commission headed by Grenville M. Dodge, a Civil War general and railroad executive, to investigate army administration. After lengthy hearings covering in great detail most of the problems, the commission concluded that the War Department leadership had not been fully in control of the mobilization effort, which had reduced both efficiency and performance. The commission recommended various reforms to correct that situation; otherwise, it found that the department and the army had struggled earnestly and mightily to solve problems not of their own making. There had been no neglect, corruption, or incompetence. Dodge and his fellow commissioners closely examined the charges Miles and other critics had made and found them to be without merit.

The media and the public generally looked upon the Dodge Commission's work as a whitewash. But the commission did serve the McKinley administration's purposes by taking the spotlight off the White House. Soon after the commission's report was in, Alger resigned as secretary of war, or, more accurately, was pushed out by the administration. He had not only become a scapegoat of the public but also of the president. If Alger was not to blame for the numerous failures of the war, that left only the president, whose decisions Alger loyally supported and executed throughout the grueling months of war.

McKinley had used the army in a rather cynical and ruthless manner to defeat Spain quickly and to pick up large parts of its crumbling empire while keeping his opponents at home off balance. Mobilizing the entire National Guard won support for the president and bought time while he worked out the details of war and empire. It also left 165,000 unnecessary troops in camps that became sinkholes of filth and disease due to the incompetence of the National Guard and the inattention of the U.S. Army.

The Spanish-American War was the swan song of the old army. Although the army's problems were not entirely of its own making, the short conflict unmistakably revealed the need for a new command system, an effective logistical structure, reliable reserves, and training for handling mass armies. McKinley's politically oriented strategy had pulled the War Department and the army too quickly in too many directions at once. But that did not excuse the chaos at Tampa and Santiago, the failure to use rail and water transportation systems effectively, the breakdown of the Medical and Inspector General Departments, which led to disaster in the camps at home, and the spectacle of the commanding general petulantly attacking his own service. Miles's pathetic behavior signaled that the army was out of tune with the society in which it functioned.

The world's strongest economy could produce almost any materials the military wanted with little lead time. It could also muster remarkable financial reserves. The war from April through August cost approximately $250 million, which was easily financed through bond issues and the assessment of miscellaneous minor taxes. Moreover, the nation could mobilize hundreds of thousands of men without any problem. But the army was critical in converting this economic and political might into military power. A nation that was now a global power with an empire in the Pacific and the Caribbean could no longer tolerate the old army; it needed a new one.

Interestingly enough, the conditions for a modern army already existed in 1898. On the West Coast, Wesley Merritt had demonstrated the kind of action that talented and qualified military leadership could accomplish. The professional preparation of the army was already well under way with a higher education system, new thinking about command systems as exemplified by Schofield, and the necessity of dealing realistically with the National Guard and mass mobilization of armies. The War Department and the army simply needed fresh, capable, outside leadership that would help break old molds so that the energy and creative forces within those institutions could reshape the land force in a new and modern way.

## ELIHU ROOT'S REFORMS

William McKinley, among the most enigmatic of American presidents, gave to the War Department the leadership necessary for remolding in Elihu Root. The president was apparently motivated by the desire to have a capable executive at the head of the army to run the new colonial empire. There may have been more to McKinley's choice of Root, however. Not much escaped the president's attention; the army unquestionably needed reform, and it was also quite clear that the best talent for achieving change lay with the individuals in and about Theodore Roosevelt's neo-Hamiltonian circle.

Root was an exceptionally able and respected New York corporate attorney with no background in military affairs. Nonetheless, during his term in office between 1899 and 1904, he laid the foundations for a modern army. His efforts included instituting the chief of staff–general staff system and other less important reforms intended to keep the army under line control, rationalizing the army's postgraduate education system, and persuading Congress to pass the Militia Act of 1903, which began restructuring the National Guard as a more effective reserve force.

The chief of staff–general staff system was by far Root's most important accomplishment. It was designed to give the army an effective system of command while maintaining civilian control over the military. The chief of staff replaced the commanding general and served as the principal military adviser to the secretary of war. Hence the secretary of war stood between the president, as commander-in-chief, and the head of the army, the chief of staff. The latter, in the name of the secretary, commanded both the line and the administrative and supply bureaus. The chief of staff depended on the General Staff to carry out those duties and to plan for future operations, help define army policies, write army legislation, conduct intelligence, oversee the higher education system, and perform any other tasks assigned by its chief. If the chief of staff ever found himself at odds with the president or the secretary of war, it was his professional duty to resign. Members of the General Staff were appointed for four years. Thereafter, they had to serve for a minimum of two years in the regiment in which they were commissioned before returning to staff duty. The same rules applied to the administrative and supply bureaus after existing staff officers retired. Circulation between the staff and the line was intended to keep the command and administrative structure in touch with the fighting forces, thus preventing the staff from building up a political power base in Washington that could be used for its own purposes but to the detriment of the army.

Root's ideas were not original. Assistant Adj. Gen. William H. Carter, who became the secretary of war's closet adviser on reform, familiarized the secretary with prevalent ideas for change within the army and introduced him to the writings of Emory Upton. Root read other books on a general staff system and on the German example in particular. Root's principal tasks were adapting the general staff concept to American traditions and institutions and then persuading Congress to accept it. He proceeded astutely and cautiously. On the recommendation of a board of officers, he appointed a War College Board in 1900 to advance army education and to study military policy. This body acted as an embryonic general staff, carrying out military planning and examining further the idea of a permanent general staff. In 1902 Root had introduced in Congress legislation that Carter had written creating a general staff, but Commanding Gen. Nelson A. Miles, the bureau heads, and other opponents were able to stop its progress. Root then modified some of the more controversial parts of the bill, mobilized military and civilian support for the War Department legislation, and outmaneuvered his opposition. On February 14, 1903, Congress voted to establish the chief of staff–general staff system. Once the General Staff was in existence, the secretary of war replaced the War College

Board with the Army War College. The latter acted as the capstone of the army's postgraduate education system, supervised the army's education structure, trained General Staff planners, and engaged in military planning.

Although not without accomplishments before World War I, the General Staff began to fulfill its potential as a planning and an executive body only during the last year of the war. Several reasons account for the slow progress. First, officers selected for General Staff duties often did not know what they were supposed to do or had conflicting ideas about staff work. Time, experience, and experimentation were necessary to adapt the new command system to the needs and the traditions of the nation; copying the activities of general staffs in Germany and elsewhere was simply not feasible.

A second and more important reason was that the change Root spearheaded required strong, able, and aggressive secretaries of war and chiefs of staff who worked well with one another. Those conditions were missing from February 1904 to May 1911. After Root a series of weak or inattentive secretaries held office: William Howard Taft (1904–1908), Luke E. Wright (1908–1909), and Jacob M. Dickinson (1909–1911). And the first three chiefs of staff—Lt. Gen. Samuel B. M. Young (1903–1904), Lt. Gen. Adna R. Chaffee (1904–1906), and Maj. Gen. John C. Bates (January to April 1906)—were old Indian fighters without administrative abilities or the stomach for bureaucratic infighting.

Major Gen. J. Franklin Bell (1906–1910), who had previously had an important role in the development of the Fort Leavenworth schools, was the first chief of staff who had ability and was interested in making the General Staff work. He understood that it had to develop in two areas. The first involved coordinating and administering the bureaus, and the second dealt with planning and intelligence. In Bell's view, the key to success in the first area was for the staff to learn the bureaus' functions and guide their conduct in a general way without bogging down in minutia, as had occurred beginning in 1903. Bell made some headway but at the cost of losing direct control over the planning and intelligence functions, which he left to the president of the Army War College. Though an improvement over his predecessors, Bell was still not an outstanding chief of staff.

In 1910–1911 drift in the War Department and army came to an end when Maj. Gen. Leonard Wood took over as chief of staff (1910–1914) and Henry L. Stimson became secretary of war (1911–1913). Wood was a bright, even brilliant, but an overaggressive, ambitious, and unorthodox evangelist of preparedness who had his eye on the White House. Stimson was a law partner and protégé of Root who had an unusual interest in and talent for military matters. Both Wood and Stimson were in the Theodore Roosevelt coterie; both men were also fully dedicated to the proposition that armies existed to fight and that to fulfill that mission they had to be run by the line, not by the bureaus.

During their years in office, the secretary of war and the chief of staff for the first time combined the power of their two offices directly to confront the collective power of the administrative and supply bureaus. The resistance of these bureaus to the authority of the chief of staff and the General Staff was third, and probably the principal, reason that the new command system did not work well until the World War I years. Under weak secretaries of war and chiefs of staff between 1904 and 1911, power in the War Department–army structure remained with the bureaus, where it had been before 1899 and essentially stayed from 1899 to 1904.

Leading the bureaus' opposition to the chief of staff was the adjutant general, Maj. Gen. Fred C. Ainsworth. He was a talented administrator and bureaucratic intriguer who had developed substantial political clout with Congress over the years through his control of the army pension records. He also sided with congressmen who favored keeping open the numerous, small frontier posts that provided benefits to local communities instead of consolidating the troops in a number of large camps to facilitate training and administration. Many officers in the line favored the advantages of large camps, and Wood was an outstanding example. Ainsworth had manipulated Root to bolster his position and further enhanced his powers under the previous insubstantial secretaries of war and chiefs of staff. The adjutant general fully understood that a peacetime army operated through mundane routine and, as a peculiarly bureaucratic type, had probably convinced himself that administrative detail and records were possibly the primary function of an army. Wood realized that to bend the bureaus to the chief of staff's will, he would first have to rein in Ainsworth. Backed by Stimson, who was in turn supported by Pres. William Howard Taft on key points, Wood attacked Ainsworth on his own turf: control over everyday matters such as the routing of orders, instructions, and information, the operation of recruiting centers, and the supervision of recordkeeping. Wood's firm and steady insistence that these areas were legally his, not Ainsworth's, prerogatives, drove the latter to rank insubordination and then led him to retire to avoid a court-martial.

Wood had unquestionably established the supremacy of the chief of staff over all parts of the army, but he paid a high price for this control. Ainsworth fought back through his numerous friends and allies in Congress, particularly the chairman of the House Military Affairs Committee, John Hay (D-VA). In 1912 the former adjutant general collaborated with Hay and other members of Congress, particularly neo-Jeffersonian elements from the Midwest and South who felt that the General Staff threatened militarism in the United

States, to pass a law that reduced the staff from forty-five to thirty-six and to pass the so-called Manchu Law, which forbade officers below the rank of major from being on detached service unless they had spent two of the previous six years with their assigned regiment. The latter law created difficulties in assigning officers to the General Staff and advanced schools. In the National Defense Act of 1916, Congress increased the size of the General Staff to fifty-four but placed severe restrictions on how many staff officers could serve in the capital. When the United States went to war in April 1917, only nineteen General Staff officers were on duty in Washington. Additionally, the 1916 act, among other measures, restricted the General Staff to planning and stripped it of all power over the bureaus. Newton D. Baker, who had just taken over as secretary of war, in a bold stroke wrote a legal decision that in effect invalidated those congressional restrictions.

Nonetheless, the General Staff was rather severely weakened between 1912 and 1916. Its operating divisions that dealt with administering the army, the bureaus, and training all but withered. The process of atrophy was facilitated after Wood left office in 1914 by two more weak chiefs of staff, Major Generals William W. Wotherspoon (April–November 1914) and Hugh L. Scott (November 1914–September 1917). Secretary of War Lindley M. Garrison (March 1913–February 1916), a spirited but ineffective leader, did not help much. Yet the General Staff continued to grow during this time through its War College Division, which Wood had created in 1910 to handle planning and intelligence. From then until America's entry into World War I, the division's planning and intelligence functions prepared the army for the conflicts with Mexico and preliminarily for operations in Europe.

The difficulties the chief of staff–general staff system encountered from 1903 to 1917 were predictable and probably inevitable in a country so distrustful of the military. Root's reforms represented fundamental change that affected not only the army but also civil-military relations. Though time, experience, and exposure reduced resistance to the General Staff, it received final approval only during the crisis of World War I. In retrospect, Wood and Stimson's victory over Ainsworth was the major turning point. With the outcome of that confrontation, in the words of Russell F. Weigley, "The center of gravity of the War Department shifted from the bureaus to the General Staff."[7]

The second part of Root's reforms, which involved postgraduate education, was the most immediately successful because it was easy to implement and uncontroversial. In 1900 the army's educational structure was effective but piecemeal, and most officers did not receive formal military education. To advance army professionalization, Root and his military advisers envisioned a system in which all officers would continuously benefit from a fully rationalized system of postgraduate education. Colonel William H. Carter drew up a proposal that was implemented by a general order in 1901. It created a tiered system of education that dealt with basic tactics at the garrison level and proceeded to a higher level of tactics at the branch schools for artillery, engineering, the Signal Corps, and other categories that had been in existence since the nineteenth century and that were now formalized and expanded. The tactics of combined arms up to the division level were taught at the Leavenworth School of the Line, the Leavenworth Staff College gave instruction in handling a corps and in General Staff duties and logistics, and the system culminated with General Staff planning and an attempt to place it in the context of national strategy at the Army War College. Only the best students proceeded from one level to the next. The school system became an integral part of the promotion process, and it served as an effective means of selecting officers for command duties reaching to the very top of the army structure. It was this system that prepared the officer corps for two world wars in the twentieth century.

Root's third area of reform dealt with reserves for the regular army and in one sense was probably the least successful of his efforts. Military advisers such as Carter attempted to push the secretary of war in the direction of a federal reserve system envisaged by Upton. Root, realizing the political impracticality of such an approach, joined with Cong. Charles W. Dick (R-OH), the principal congressional spokesman for the National Guard, in writing what became the Militia, or Dick, Act of 1903, the first basic revision of the militia law since 1792.

The act continued the idea of a universal military obligation for all eligible males in a Reserve Militia but stopped there to focus on the National Guard as the Organized Militia. The National Guard would have an obligation for federal service of nine, not three, months and would be supported by the federal government with money and equipment to the degree that it conformed to national standards in terms of organization, training, and the selection and retention of personnel, including periodic drills and summer camps. To facilitate the achievement of higher, uniform standards, regular army officers would instruct and inspect the National Guard units, and the guard would join the regular army for joint exercises whenever possible.

These reforms, and several others in 1908 and 1914, met with only limited success as National Guard mobilization during the height of the crisis with Mexico in 1916 demonstrated. Nonetheless, the reforms served an important purpose by gradually weaning regular army officers away from their commitment to an Uptonian reserve as the only acceptable way of expanding the army in an emergency. In one way or another, citizen soldiers would have to serve that function in the future as they had in the past. Wood not only accepted that reality but looked for the best method quickly but thoroughly to train civilians for military service. Unwilling fully to surrender Uptonian standards, Wood never found a satisfactory solution. He advocated a politically unacceptable massive federal reserve system as part of Secretary of War Garrison's Continental Army Plan and gave increasing support to the Plattsburg Movement to gain political support for preparedness.

While Wood thrashed about for solutions, Capt. John McAuley Palmer, a thoughtful and talented General Staff officer, was also searching for ways that the nation could mobilize mass armies to meet the needs of modern war. Palmer ultimately concluded that Upton's ideas on reserves had to be totally scrapped. Once that step was taken, Palmer arrived at the logical solution, suggested for nearly a century by Winfield Scott and other observers, that citizen soldiers, when properly led by qualified and trained officers, could be prepared for warfare in a matter of months. Palmer had the ear of Stimson and other colleagues and was laying the theoretical foundations for the American mass conscript armies that fought World Wars I and II.

The Root reforms tied into and strengthened one another. The General Staff and educational reforms gave the army the structure and training essential for full professionalization. Reforms of the National Guard advanced the officer corps' thinking about the use of citizen soldiers in mass armies. Although Root's reforms appeared incomplete and in some instances failed during the early years of the twentieth century, World War I demonstrated their viability and enormous importance.

Root by no means devoted all or even most of his time to army reform. Indeed, during his first two years in office he exerted a great deal of effort in devising and implementing a colonial administration that included a major role for the army in both the Pacific and the Caribbean.

The secretary of war also had to ensure that the army remained large enough to carry out its regular and colonial duties, including intervention in China during the Boxer Rebellion. With the Philippine insurrection under way, Congress early in 1899 kept the regular army at 65,000 and authorized 35,000 volunteers to serve until July 1, 1901, at which time the regulars would revert to their prewar strength of 28,000. After taking over as secretary of war, Root began working for a permanently enlarged army. He succeeded when Congress in February 1901 set the maximum strength of the regular army at 100,000, with the actual size determined by annual appropriations. Between 1902 and 1916 the total strength of the regular army hit a low of 64,170 in 1907 and reached a high of 108,399 in 1916, an average of somewhat over 83,000 for the fifteen-year period. Appropriations over that period ranged from a low of $112.3 million in 1902 to a high of $183.2 million in 1916 with an annual average of $169.6 million. Hence, after the Spanish-American War, the annual average peacetime strength of the army was over three times greater than in the period 1872 to 1897, and average annual budgets in unadjusted dollars were almost four times as large. As in the past, the army remained substantially larger after a war than it had been during the previous peacetime period, and average annual costs increased faster than the army's size.

The concentration of troops in a few posts, desired by many reformers to facilitate training and administration, did not take place during the early years of the twentieth century. Because communities opposed closing camps for economic reasons and the army was habituated to them, fully sixty-five posts existed at the turn of the century, and the number did not change much as the army enlarged existing camps instead of building new ones to accommodate the growth in its increased size.

Root had hoped that a General Staff would help keep the army current with technological development. Although the army made some advances in weaponry, the General Staff apparently had little to do with them. The army adopted the Model 1903 Springfield rifle, a bolt-action magazine rifle; by 1908 the army and most of the National Guard were equipped with the weapon, which remained the standard shoulder arm until the eve of World War II. Ordnance moved more slowly on automatic rifles and machine guns, but that was not the case with field guns. The bureau started production on the Model 1902 three-inch gun with optical sights and a recoilless carriage, a weapon equal in quality to any in Europe. In 1905 the Ordnance Department for the first time began production of smokeless powder at the Picatinny Arsenal in New Jersey.

The Quartermaster Department approached the automobile and truck with caution. Nonetheless, by 1906 it had purchased its first cars. Though experimentation with internal combustion vehicles continued, the real breakthrough did not occur until the punitive expedition against Mexico in 1916. For that operation the army quickly purchased and used 588 commercial trucks, 57 tanker trucks, 10 motor machine-shop trucks, 6 motor wrecking trucks, 75 automobiles, 61 motorcycles, and 8 tractors. Since thirteen types of trucks from eight manufacturers were in use, maintenance presented major problems. In general, the automobile companies were unwilling to begin specialized military production until the army was ready to buy in volume, a practice that started thereafter.

The army was even more cautious about the airplane. The Signal Corps established an aeronautical division in 1907 and by 1913 had organized its first

Aero Squadron. The outbreak of war in Europe and the use of the airplane in combat stimulated greater American interest. With eight planes, the Aero Squadron served with Gen. John J. Pershing's troops in Mexico and proved valuable for reconnaissance, although all craft were wrecked within six weeks. The military would not make full use of the airplane until after World War I.

Various authors lament that the army proceeded so cautiously on technologically advanced weapons.[8] These complaints are often devoid of historical context, however. Although military budgets were growing, Congress still kept the army on a short financial leash—and rightfully so since the United States faced no military threats that could justify huge budgets for technological experimentation. Most of the army planning that took place involved operations in the Western Hemisphere and the Pacific. Moreover, technological advance was so rapid that obsolescence was a major factor in any weapons program. It was not a catastrophe that the United States had to rely on British and French rifles, field guns, and airplanes when it entered World War I because it could not mass-produce enough of its own weapons. Such dependence did not interfere with the conduct of the war. The future danger for America was not technological conservatism by the military but the growth of a weapons culture devoted to the most modern military hardware possible, regardless of the consequences, including cost and practicality. By comparison, these were sane years for military weaponry.

Root, most army reformers, and the bureaus recognized that improvements were essential in the area of supply. After studying the Spanish-American War, the Dodge Commission made specific recommendations for improving the operations of the Quartermaster Department; most were considered and many tried in the years between 1899 and 1917, with uneven results. One reform intensely resisted by all the bureaus was the short detail system, which required bureau personnel to return to the line after four years. This change, instituted by law, ignored the need for specialization at a time when the military services were becoming more complex. Emphasizing that reality, the bureaus made inroads against the law, achieved some congressional modifications, and nearly succeeded in having it repealed before 1917.

A sensible reform was consolidating the Quartermaster, Subsistence, and Pay Departments into one bureau. Some reformers even wanted to create an army Department of Supply that would function like the navy's Bureau of Supplies and Accounts. Besides procuring its own products, such an agency would purchase common items for the service, i.e., goods required by more than one bureau. Root attempted to achieve this reform in 1901 but backed away in the face of stiff opposition. In 1912 Congress finally passed a bill combining the three departments under the designation of the Quartermaster

Corps but did not give the agency the power to procure common goods. The same statute created a uniformed service corps, advocated for decades by the bureau, consisting of 6,000 craftsmen, laborers, teamsters, and so forth to perform jobs previously done by civilians or men detailed from the line.

In 1908, before the consolidation took place, the Quartermaster Department moved to decentralize procurement so as to speed up its response to emergencies and to avoid the terrible tangle of paperwork that occurred during the Spanish-American War. Much of the responsibility for procurement was delegated to the commanders of the army's geographical departments and their quartermasters. Considerable flexibility was permitted in acquiring needed supplies, with many of the details and the paperwork of procurement also performed at the geographical department level.

The Quartermaster Corps also attempted to follow the Dodge Commission's recommendations that a four-month reserve of articles and equipment for 100,000 men be maintained. Because Congress never appropriated enough money for the corps and various emergencies arose, such as the mobilization of virtually all National Guard units in 1916, reserve stocks were usually low and in 1917 almost nonexistent. Nevertheless, the Quartermaster Corps was able to handle all rapid mobilization action between 1900 and 1917 in the United States, in the colonies, and in Latin America and Asia.

The Quartermaster Corps' record in transportation, so troubled during the Spanish-American War, improved greatly in the early decades of the twentieth century. The Quartermaster Department created an Army Transportation Service, an outgrowth of the wartime Transportation Division, to move men and goods by water to the nation's newly acquired colonial empire. The service took over the troop and supply ships purchased during hostilities, added to that fleet, and acquired a collection of smaller vessels for harbor duty and water transport among the Philippine islands. The Transportation Service enabled the Quartermaster Department to meet the numerous calls for transporting men and supplies in the Pacific, Asia, and Latin America without the chaos that had characterized the Spanish-American War. As American operations in Cuba, the Philippines, and elsewhere dwindled, the maritime industry, usually backed by various secretaries of war, sought to have transportation services taken over by private firms as an economy measure. The Quartermaster Department resisted this drive with some, although hardly total, success, and was still operating sixteen transport ships in 1917.

Resolving the problem of railroad transport was much more demanding than addressing difficulties in water transportation. After all, the army could not easily purchase and operate railroads. But it could and did plan how best to use the roads in an emergency by gathering full information on routing, the types of rolling stock and equipment owned by various rail companies, systems for marking box cars, and so on. In doing so, the Quartermaster Department secured the cooperation of the American Railway Association and planned for that organization to set up an office in Washington in the event of an extended emergency. Convinced that the cooperation of the railroads was ensured, the Quartermaster Corps thought no further steps were necessary.

The corps was opposed on this issue by the General Staff and various civilian sources, who believed that it was essential to pass laws that compelled the railroads to follow government direction in a major war, provided for penalties in the event of resistance, and created government agencies to regulate and coordinate railroad operations. Such action seemed even more imperative after war broke out in Europe in 1914. The corps refused to be persuaded, appearing more interested in protecting its turf against General Staff incursions. The dispute seemed to distract both the staff and the bureau from recognizing the simple realities that the Spanish-American War had made clear. For example, the railroads could not operate properly unless the various bureaus adequately coordinated their use, and rapid turnaround of railroad cars required proper storage facilities. The last point was highlighted by the problem that in 1916, freight cars loaded with exports for Europe were backed up for hundreds of miles from the Atlantic seaboard because of the insufficiency of ships. Since army planners appeared blind to basic truths involving the railroads, another disaster involving the roads was almost guaranteed once the United States entered World War I.

Another major sign of trouble was indicated when after war broke out in Europe in 1914 the Quartermaster Corps saw no need for emergency preparations, convinced that the United States would not become involved. The complacency was extended in September 1916 when Maj. Gen. Henry G. Sharpe, who had spent most of his career as a Subsistence officer, took over as quartermaster general. "The Corps," writes the bureau's official historian, "was as unprepared in 1917 as it had been in 1898."[9]

In some respects that judgment may be too harsh. Having transported and supplied expeditionary forces in Cuba, Puerto Rico, the Philippines, China, Mexico, and elsewhere, the Quartermaster Corps was prepared to move massive numbers of troops and supplies abroad over an extended period of time. But it was not prepared for the national economic mobilization effort that modern warfare required, as its attitude toward handling the railroads in a national emergency indicated. The General Staff had a somewhat broader purview, but its outlook was still far from sufficient. Indeed, at no level of the War Department–army structure was planning for mobilization of the national economy, or even adequate planning for procuring necessary supplies, taking place. The military still thought of mobilization principally in terms of manpower, not economic power.

But the army was not alone in its myopia regarding the imperatives of economic planning for modern warfare. Civilians, including principal political and economic leaders, also remained in the dark on the subject.

# 5
# THE ROLE OF AMERICAN ELITES

## THE POWER ELITE

The transformation of the economic and political systems during the Gilded Age and the Progressive Era created the modern American "power elite."[1] The elite consists of those people controlling a core of about 200 corporations, largely in heavy and high-technology industries, and high officials in the federal executive, particularly the president, his chief advisers, and the most important cabinet members.

These two components of the elite have separate, though hardly unrelated, power bases with definite upper-middle- to upper-class orientations. Although both groups share a common capitalist ideology, significant differences over means exist within and between the corporate and governmental spheres. The federal executive is not an executive committee for the people who own and run the economy. The operations of power are much too complex and tangled for such a simple formula.

Some students of power propose that the government and the corporate community are entirely separate, but their analysis is faulty. To make it consistent, they must accept the interpretation set forth by Adolf A. Berle, Jr., and Gardiner C. Means in 1932 and later developed more explicitly by Berle. This thesis proposes that a separation has occurred between ownership and management in the corporate world. Such an analysis is questionable in whole or in part. Most top corporate managers reflect the values of the owners and have substantial investments in the companies they direct. Where such circumstances are not the case, because ownership (broadly defined to include financial institutions as well as individual and family stockholders) is highly concentrated, the owners and their associates can usually set the major strategies for their corporations and hire and fire managers at will. Control of all the intricacies of the so-called technostructure of a corporation is not essential for determining its larger policies even though elaborate bureaucracies tend to possess a rather intractable quality.

Consistently throughout the twentieth century, this corporate structure, along with its financial and legal allies, has provided the staffing for most of the important offices of the federal executive. As the government has grown in size and scope during the twentieth century, the ties between it and the corporate community have naturally become both greater and more complex. Those ties are more homogenous in areas involving foreign and defense policies—e.g., the State, War, and Navy Departments (later, Defense Department)—than the ties concerned with domestic policy, where more variety in appointments prevails and the presence of the corporate structure is less consistent.

As far as the military is concerned, several points are in order. As the officer corps professionalized in both the army and the navy, and especially in the latter, it took on an upper-class bias.[2] This trend was particularly true of academy graduates and of officers in the higher ranks. Furthermore, the importance of the military in the American system of power grew as the twentieth century wore on and the United States continued to expand on the world scene, facing the necessity of balancing strategy with diplomacy. Yet the military certainly is no more monolithic than business or government, although, as in the latter two, differences within and between the armed services tend to be more over means than ends. Most important, it is a gross exaggeration to view the military as either beyond civilian control, on the one hand, or as having no power of its own, on the other. Reality lies somewhere between the two extremes. But the essential point is that the military traditionally has been and through the twentieth century has remained a derivative or secondary, not a primary, power grouping. An essential service group for the elite, the military is not of the elite itself. Hence, though, the armed forces are a center of power to contend with, without aberrational developments they can be managed by civilians.

The outlines of the power elite need not be elaborated upon at this point; the analysis of the political economy of twentieth-century warfare will provide comprehensive detail. Whenever the nation explicitly planned its economy—during World War I, with the National Recovery Administration during the Great Depression, and during World War II—the power of corporate America within government was made blatantly clear as were the close relationships between the corporate structure and the military services.

## THE POLITICAL ECONOMY OF WARFARE

Using the four factors—economic, political, military, and weaponry—to assess the political economy of warfare during the Gilded Age and Progressive Era yields a number of significant insights. First, the maturity of the economy shaped the entire period and particularly the Gilded Age. Industrialization and the rise of the corporate structure meant that mobilization of the economy for another major war would be significantly different from that process in the Civil War. The economy could produce an almost endless stream of goods ranging from the simplest to the most complex during hostilities, but it had to be carefully and closely controlled. That reality was not made clear during the Spanish-American War because the conflict was so brief and undemanding. Furthermore, the massive corporate structure that came into being during the Gilded Age and the early years of the twentieth century created the basis for a new American elite. This elite acquired final form only when the federal government was able to regulate the new corporate structure and to provide the larger population with various necessary services that the private sector was unprepared to deliver.

Second, the size, strength, and scope of the federal government went through dramatic change from 1865 to 1917. The political system was at first simply overwhelmed by the speed and consequences of economic growth. It fell into a holding pattern during the Gilded Age in which some political cohesion existed at the local, state, and regional levels but very little at the national level. Gradually, as the pace of economic change slowed and the shape of the new society became more evident near the end of the century, Washington began to respond at least symbolically and ceremoniously to the multiple demands facing it. During the Progressive Era, with elements of both parties dedicated to reform, the federal government was rather rapidly revitalized. By taking on the role of economic regulator and social welfare agent, it acted to legitimatize the new order and to give balance to the elite structure. Such a development was essential for America to reach its economic potential during both peace and war.

Third, the character and structure of the military services and their relationship with the larger civilian society and authority also changed significantly during these years. Both services were modernized and professionalized. Technological change acted as a major spur for the navy, but the army was motivated more by the need for effective systems of command and control. The short and relatively undemanding Spanish-American War revealed that reforms had made the navy reasonably efficient but that the army required a fundamental restructuring. Civilians played a vital, indispensable role in modernizing both the army and navy, although the impetus for change came from within the services. Civilian involvement in military change began with Congress. Even during the Gilded Age, Congress, led by members specializing in army and navy affairs, remained basically informed about the armed forces while legislating and appropriating funds for their operations. This development was even more pronounced during the Progressive Era, when the quality of the nation's legislature generally improved.

Yet both the Gilded Age and the Progressive Era clearly demonstrated that the executive branch, not the legislative, had to provide the leadership to restructure the services where necessary and to make them function properly. From 1881 to 1902 a remarkable collection of good-to-excellent secretaries of the navy, backed when necessary by the president, led a group of naval officers intent on modernizing the service. Since Theodore Roosevelt acted as his own secretary of the navy, the quality of civilian chiefs of the navy dropped somewhat under him, picked up to a degree under William Howard Taft, and returned to excellence under Woodrow Wilson. By 1917 the navy was more than sound in terms of command and administration, education, and professional standards.

Despite a strong push for reform in the army, change was slow in coming until the shock of the War Department's and the army's performances during the Spanish-American War. That recognition led to the appointment of Elihu Root as secretary of war and reforms in command and administration, education, and manpower mobilization, which he deftly achieved through his own political skills and the expert advice of army reformers.

Unlike the navy, the army did not benefit from consistently able civilian leadership. Indeed, between 1868 and 1916 the War Department had only two outstanding secretaries, Root and Henry L. Stimson. The army also faced much greater resistance to change than did the navy from Congress, the National Guard, and civilians in general. Consequently, modernizing and professionalizing the army was slower, harder, and more controversial than it had been for the navy. Basic changes in the army took place in spurts under Root and Stimson, with strong, at times critical, backing from Presidents Roosevelt and Taft. Periods of reaction followed. Moreover, unlike the navy, and despite the reforms, the army was not actually prepared for World War I, and it was only during that extended emergency that the Root reforms came to full fruition.

The fourth and last criterion, the state of military technology, is in some respects the most intriguing for the 1865–1917 period. To build a new navy of steel, steam, armor, and modern ordnance required a production team of civilian government officials, naval officers, and industrialists, especially for the manufacture of armor and ordnance. In one way or another, that production team has remained in existence through today. And in that coalition are located the origins of the military-industrial complex.

No complex as such existed during these years. Nevertheless, patterns of abuse that could afflict the military services and the nation when military spending was great and sustained were already evident and stood as a warning of the dangers that lay ahead. The professionalization of the military services largely eliminated the gross corruption and other irregularities to which the armed services had been subjected and in which they participated before the Mexican War. Industrialization and the new pattern of civil-military relations it dictated presented much greater threats to the armed forces and to the society than the comparatively simply malfeasance involved before the 1840s.

Moreover, patterns that reached back to the very foundations of the nation indicate that even limited military spending could cause problems similar to those arising in an MIC. Throughout the various eras, but particularly for the late nineteenth and early twentieth centuries, Washington faced great difficulty in cutting back, closing down, or moving army and naval bases that had been in existence for any length of time. Communities and their representatives in Congress often appeared more interested in the economic stimulation and political benefit of the army's and navy's presence than in the well-being of those services. Indeed, in the Gilded Age and Progressive Era the navy lacked proper dry docks to service its ships, and the army was denied large posts with substantial numbers of troops to facilitate training so that nonmilitary purposes could be accommodated. And, over time, the army and navy came to accept such policies and practices as normal and necessary. If this situation held true when the military services were small, in the army's case not yet technologically advanced, and without a world role, the probability of a fundamentally abusive MIC when all or most of those conditions changed was high.

Looking at both the third and the fourth criteria, which involve basically civil-military relations, significant change occurred in the civilian and military spheres. Both of these areas were driving the United States toward a much more active role in world affairs, a position that would require a larger, more active military as strategy had to be balanced with diplomacy. In terms of the strategic planning carried out by both the army and the navy, the armed services had not yet realistically adjusted their sights to the new direction, but they would do so under civilian direction.

The last point is perhaps the most important. Despite enormous change, the direction of American society, including the military services, was under firm civilian control.

# PART TWO
# ECONOMIC MOBILIZATION FOR WORLD WAR I

Mobilizing the economy for World War I was an experiment that was still evolving at the time of the armistice. The foundations for a planned economy were based on the government-business regulatory alliance that had begun to emerge during the Progressive Era. The effort of various groups and individuals launched the mobilization experiment in mid-1915 with the creation of the Naval Consulting Board. Limited in what it could do, the board was, in effect, replaced by the Council of National Defense–National Defense Advisory Commission late in 1916. Once the nation entered the war, that weak structure and subordinate agencies carried out economic mobilization functions until the War Industries Board was created in July 1917 and strengthened significantly early in 1918.

The WIB and its predecessor agencies gradually devised the methods and regulatory controls essential for harnessing a wartime economy. Since these agencies operated without adequate statutory authority, they depended on the federal government's general powers and the voluntary cooperation of the business community for organizing supply. Although legally tenuous, the makeshift system worked well enough to meet the relatively limited mobilization needs in 1917 and 1918.

Before it could be perfected, however, this mobilization scheme was almost destroyed by the military, which constituted organized demand and by law had the mobilization authority. The problems did not stem from the Navy Department. As during the Spanish-American War, the navy used its reformed structure to expand for hostilities with relative ease. The War Department was the major source of difficulty. Elihu Root's reforms involving command and administration had not yet taken effect. As a result, the decentralized supply and administrative bureaus carried out mobilization functions in such an uncoordinated, chaotic way that they badly distorted the economy. By winter 1917–1918 the entire economic mobilization program began grinding to a halt. To cope with the crisis, the Woodrow Wilson administration forced the War Department to institute centralized control over the supply bureaus and to coordinate their operations with those of the WIB. Throughout 1918, the WIB and the armed services gradually devised mobilization policies that mutually met civilian and military needs. The system had not been fully worked out before the war ended.

The principal difficulty in mobilizing the World War I economy, therefore, stemmed not from the political or economic realms, since the federal government and the business community worked in reasonable harmony from the outset. Neither were the tools of war a significant problem. The navy, for example, was building or could build the most sophisticated ships of war with few difficulties. Under the right conditions, most of the armed services' demands in 1917–1918 could be met.

It was the military, particularly the army, that was the major obstacle to harnessing the economy for war successfully. Once that reality became fully manifest, the army had to pattern itself after the WIB as the price for maintaining control of its supply operations. In doing so, the service began an intricate process of institutional adaptation that affected the political economy of American warfare in ways that still endure.

# 6
# PREPAREDNESS AND PARTICIPATION

## PROGRESSIVE REFORM, FOREIGN POLICY, AND PREPAREDNESS

Mobilizing the American economy for World War I reflected the divisions that characterized the enormously protean Progressive Age.[1] Scholars have long recognized that domestic and foreign policies in the late nineteenth and early twentieth centuries were closely related and interacting. The dawning of the era of domestic reform paralleled the Spanish-American War, continued within a context of increasing expansion and involvement in world affairs, and culminated in America's participation in World War I and peacemaking at Versailles. Expansion abroad could be as divisive as reform at home, and some rough correlations existed in responses to policies in the two areas.

Neo-Hamiltonians dedicated to a strong, active state at home and whose strength was centered in the Northeast, favored a "large" policy abroad.[2] Although Theodore Roosevelt stood out among this group, few reformers and only a minority of New Nationalists followed him down the path of strident and martial imperialism. Conservatives such as Henry Cabot Lodge were inclined toward Roosevelt's view of foreign affairs, yet even they tended to be more cautious and evenhanded than the intense Rough Rider.

Some neo-Jeffersonians were as dedicated to anti-imperialism, if not isolationism, as the Roosevelt set was to expansion. This stance was especially true of agrarians who evolved out of Populism, came predominantly from the South, Midwest, and West, looked to William Jennings Bryan as their spokesman, and defined their Jeffersonian creed in a way opposed to foreign adventurism and the militarism they associated with it. Empire required a big state, which they opposed as much for domestic as for foreign policy reasons.

With some variation, these positions carried over in response to America's entry into World War I. Anti-interventionist sentiment was increasingly voiced by progressive Republicans from the Midwest and West, such as Sen. Robert

M. LaFollette (R-WI), and some Bryanite Democrats from those regions and the South. Vociferous, if not rabid, interventionists like Roosevelt and Lodge were reduced to marginal numbers. Wilson was able to isolate the Roosevelts and to reduce the LaFollettes to manageability by pushing for intervention based not on rampant nationalism, militarism, imperialism, and realpolitik, but instead on idealistic promises of law and international peacemaking.

Wilson found middle ground on foreign policy as he had done with domestic reform. By combining the New Freedom with the New Nationalism, the president had formulated a Progressive synthesis built around a government-business regulatory alliance.[3] Similarly, Wilson steered between anti-imperialists and imperialists to include a world role for Progressivism. He was able to do so because the views of most reformers involving foreign policy were not fixed, and he convinced them that under existing conditions international and domestic reforms were compatible and mutually supportive.

The controversy over preparedness between 1914 and 1917 further illuminated Progressive attitudes and aspirations. With the outbreak of war in Europe in 1914, the War Department launched a campaign to expand considerably ground forces numbering approximately 100,000 regulars and 120,000 National Guardsmen. This effort did not pay off until 1916. Wilson's first secretary of war, Lindley M. Garrison (March 1913–February 1916), resigned when the president refused to back his plan for a continental army in the face of congressional opposition. Such an Uptonian army would have consisted of 400,000 fully trained reservists raised over a period of three years. These men would have been ready immediately to join the regulars, expanded from 100,000 to 142,000, and the National Guard would have been relegated to an insignificant role. The president, his new secretary of war, Newton D. Baker (March 1916–March 1921), and Congress ultimately reached a compromise with the National Defense Act of 1916. The army would slowly increase to 175,000, expand to 286,000 in an emergency, and be supplemented by a force of National Guardsmen eventually numbering 400,000 and more fully under the control of the federal government.[4] More important, the Wilson administration in 1916 threw its full weight behind legislation for a massive program of naval expansion with the ultimate goal of making the American navy "second to none."[5]

The administration moved slowly and reluctantly in supporting military preparedness despite intense pressure from elite circles. When Gen. Leonard Wood was reassigned in 1914 from chief of staff to commander of the Eastern Department, he intensified his efforts to expand the army.[6] A shrewd politician, Wood concluded that a rather unfocused army and an uncertain national government in conjunction with widespread antimilitary sentiments meant that preparedness could be advanced only through the efforts of civilians. Wood set about gaining the support of the "best" elements. In 1913, while chief of staff, he began moving in that direction by organizing summer military training camps for high school and university students, who paid their own way. He also sought to introduce a type of ROTC program at various universities and by 1915 had had a measure of success at Harvard, Princeton, and Yale. A Society of the National Reserve Corps of the United States, established in 1913, attempted to coordinate some of these efforts.

Wood got an enormous boost in 1915 when a Committee of One Hundred, centered at the Harvard Club and including the sons of prominent national leaders, such as Grenville Clark, Elihu Root, Jr., and Theodore Roosevelt, Jr., persuaded the former chief of staff to train business and professional men militarily. This step led to the so-called Plattsburg Movement, which included summer training camps at the New York site and three others in the West and Midwest. The participants, overwhelmingly from the upper classes and socially prominent, became enthusiastic supporters of and proselytizers for military preparedness. Early in 1916, under the prodding of Clark, a Military Training Camps Association (MTCA) was formed. Intended to unify the voluntary training efforts that had begun since 1913, it acted as a well-connected lobbying organization pushing for an enlarged military. The War Department ultimately proposed that the MTCA take a role in training reserve officers.[7]

In 1913 Wood also combined efforts with Frederick L. Huidekoper, an elite Washington lawyer, amateur military historian, and preparedness enthusiast, in establishing an Army League to serve as the War Department's counterpart to the Navy League. This organization turned out to be smaller and neither as well financed nor as influential as the naval group. Still, it spoke out and lobbied on the army's behalf when regulations, traditions, or discretion forced silence on those in uniform.

More important, other civilian groups formed without prodding from the military. In October 1914, Cong. Augustus P. Gardner (R-MA), Lodge's son-in-law, moved to launch an investigation of the nation's defense. Most of the urban press quickly took up the cause. The agitation led to the formation of the National Security League (NSL) in late 1914. S. Stanwood Menken, a New York lawyer, headed the group; its members came from the most prestigious social clubs and from the ledgers of the Social Register. The league became a leading advocate for preparedness and was soon joined by the National Civic Federation, the U.S. Chamber of Commerce, and other business and professional groups.

By 1916 proponents of the scattered preparedness efforts sharpened their focus. Robert Bacon, the new president of the NSL and a former Roosevelt secretary of state and J. P. Morgan partner, moved to coordinate the activities of the NSL, Navy League, Army League, Aero Club, and other bodies. Thus a range of societies stretching from the Plattsburgites to the U.S. Chamber of Commerce became aware of the others' activities, if not fully and meaningfully coordinated. Although nationwide in scope, the preparedness drive was centered in the East, particularly New York, and was mostly urban and middle and upper class. Though not a partisan issue in 1914–1915, it was identified more with Republicans than with Democrats.

The preparedness advocates ultimately committed themselves to universal military training (UMT), which members of the military had favored for years. Many of Wood's endeavors had been intended to create a mindset conducive to such a scheme. By 1916 an Association for National Service and a well-heeled Universal Military Training League, supported by Bacon, John T. Pratt, George H. Perkins, and J. P. Morgan, Jr., was organized specifically to further the cause of universal service. The NSL, Chamber of Commerce, other important organizations, and some government officials became backers. Most of this support coalesced around proposed legislation written by Capt. George Van Horn Moseley and introduced in Congress by Sen. George E. Chamberlain (D-OR).

Congress seriously examined the proposal in the early months of 1917, but the War Department's unwillingness to support a bill not its own and Germany's declaration of unlimited submarine warfare killed any chance of passage. Facing war, the nation needed troops quickly, not in the future, as UMT proposed. Indeed, business and public support for UMT began to wane as the National Guard was quickly mobilized to deal with the convulsive Mexican revolution in summer 1916. Indiscriminate military service could be disruptive; for a mature industrial system, selective instead of universal service was a more rational solution.

The preparedness movement was paradoxical and odd. The army's plans for expansion were obsolete. Because army planners held on to a defensive strategy, they had to hypothesize a transoceanic attack by Germany, Japan, or some other enemy to justify a large military. In August 1915 Wilson ordered an end to any military planning for involvement in the European war, but his admonition appeared unnecessary since few officers were inclined to think in those terms. Even the plans and legislation for naval expansion were unrealistic, given the way the European powers fought the war at sea. Military planning, therefore, was not tightly related to foreign policy, and the War, Navy, and State Departments and the White House moved as separate units rather than as coordinated centers for making vital decisions.

Most civilian preparedness advocates failed to see the unrealistic nature of their proposals. Their dedication to the cause grew as the war in Europe continued, even though few appeared to be hard-core interventionists despite their Anglophilia. The army seemed to be using the European war to push for a long-desired expansion in size; but the middle- to upper-class preparedness enthusiasts appeared determined to use hostilities for achieving greater order, stability, and control in American life, in addition to finding adventure and validating their masculinity and character. Some Progressives such as Roosevelt matched the desire for a more regimented society with the goal of intervention in the war and expansion abroad. Still another set, including the *New Republic* group of Herbert Croly and Walter Lippmann, John Dewey, and moderate socialists such as Morris Hillquit, saw preparedness and war as a supreme opportunity for achieving a planned and just society at home. Among civilians, preparedness often had more to do with social control and reform than with defense per se.

A rural-dominated Congress consistently frustrated the urban-based preparedness movement. In the House, Majority Leader Claude Kitchen (D-NC) headed a group of about thirty "peace" Democrats from the rural South and West. They were supported by a few Northern urban reformers, usually with labor constituencies, and some Midwestern Republicans. Although for the most part not pacifists, this group opposed enlarging the military, which they held in suspicion, favored governmental economy, and objected to the United States taking on a world role. Kitchen stacked the House Military Affairs and Naval Affairs Committees with like-minded colleagues. Antipreparedness strength in the Senate was significant but less than that in the House. LaFollette, Albert B. Cummins (R-IA), and James K. Vardaman (D-MS) stood firmly against most preparedness measures. The lineup in Congress against preparedness, therefore, was principally, although not exclusively, rural, neo-Jeffersonian, and reformist.

Opposition to preparedness among the general public resembled that in Congress but was somewhat broader. The biggest bloc consisted of farmers, who overwhelmingly opposed or were indifferent to a strengthened military. Organized labor, despite Samuel Gompers's efforts to the contrary, stood quite solidly with the rural community. So too did German-Americans and most Socialists. Antipreparedness feeling thus came mostly from rural areas and from elements of the lower and lower-middle classes. Among the urban middle and upper classes, antipreparedness attitudes were usually associated with social-welfare Progressives, radicals, and religious pacifists.

Peace societies vocalized the sentiments and focused the efforts of the various antipreparedness groups. The anemic peace movement of the post–Civil War years grew in size and strength in the late nineteenth and early twentieth centuries as the United States began to expand abroad. But it was as riddled with contradictions as Progressivism itself. By 1914 some sixty-three peace organizations existed in the United States. They ran the gamut from the elite, genteel, and well-financed Carnegie Endowment for International Peace, which viewed war as irrational and avoidable through arbitration and internationalism, to radical organizations that saw capitalism as the principal cause of war, militarism, and exploitation at home. In the early years of the twentieth century, the respectable establishment groups clearly held sway.

The outbreak of World War I initially shattered the peace movement as conservative, elite adherents wavered in their dedication to plowshares over swords, often becoming enthusiastic supporters of war as the way to peace, through such organizations as the League to Enforce the Peace. The more dedicated, radical, and religiously oriented pacifists regrouped to fight for their beliefs more effectively. A new, modern peace movement was emerging, made up of two distinct groups: pacifists and internationalists. Despite their fundamental and ideological differences, the two wings were or would become much more sophisticated about the causes, consequences, and possibilities for avoiding war than had been the case before World War I.[8]

Nevertheless, both the pacifist and internationalist forces in and outside government arrayed cogent arguments against military preparedness. They insisted that although unrealistic in terms of the immediate crisis, the proposed military buildup could lessen security by leading to war, would cost huge sums and divert resources from reform, would favor the rich over the poor, and would not distribute the burdens of war equally. If a bigger defense effort were necessary, they maintained, it should involve improving coastal defenses, building submarines, and strengthening the militia—efforts that would be relatively inexpensive and that would avoid militarism.

The antipreparedness elements largely had their way into 1915 because Congress and Wilson dragged their heels, but the *Lusitania* crisis in May 1915 weakened their influence. The reality of war and an aroused public motivated the president to throw his weight behind the preparedness drive. With his changed outlook, Wilson faced the unenviable task of trying to reconcile the varied positions in his divided administration and party on the complex and vexatious preparedness issue.

The political heat was increased enormously by the threat that hard-line Republicans led by Roosevelt would snatch the preparedness issue from Wilson and his party and use it for partisan reasons. Compromise was ultimately possible because the president sensed that national attitudes were not firm and that important congressional leaders were antimilitary but not pacifistic. Given those political realities, Wilson adroitly moved to unite his party to the degree possible behind the National Defense Act of 1916 and a massively expanded navy, which had never aroused American fears of militarism as had the army.

With foreign policy and preparedness as in domestic policy, Wilson maintained control of events, reined in the disparate Democratic factions, and isolated the most rabid Republican partisans. His accomplishments were hardly unalloyed, however. America was drifting toward war, yet measures for enlarging the military in the future, based on questionable strategy, did not address the impending crisis. John Patrick Finnegan, a careful scholar of the period, observes that "one of the most disturbing aspects of the prewar defense movement was its lack of connection between power and policy."[9] Since the Wilson administration's policies were so fluid, the nation so divided, the military services so mired in traditional thinking, the preparedness advocates influenced by so many peripheral or irrelevant issues, and the antipreparedness forces so numerous, the results were predictable and probably inevitable. Nonetheless, Finnegan maintains, without the preparedness movement, the United States could not have intervened in World War I when and to the extent that it did.

> A mass army was now acceptable. The incessant propaganda for universal military training had conditioned the public to accept conscription. The General Staff had already drawn up plans to train men under universal service in batches of 500,000 dispersed among sixteen localized training divisions. These plans were readily adapted to fit the needs of a national army raised by the draft. The Plattsburg Movement provided the necessary framework to recruit and train the vast number of reserve officers which the huge wartime force needed. . . . Over a two-year period, preparedness had steeled America to meet the demands of total war.[10]

With national conscription under the Selective Service Act of May 1917, America adapted its dual military traditions of citizen soldiers and regulars to raise mass armies for fighting abroad. No huge standing armies or elaborate national reserves were needed. Instead, as Winfield Scott had demonstrated a century earlier, regulars could quickly and effectively train and lead citizen soldiers. By basing a draft on the universal obligation of actual or potential citizens, administering it through local boards staffed by volunteer citizens, and relying on selective service with deferments to meet economic and social needs, the Wilson administration defused strong and widespread opposition to a major new direction.

National conscription, like building a new navy and reforming the army, required civilians stepping in to lead the way. The insights and advocacy of Leonard Wood and John McAuley Palmer could never alone extricate the army from Emory Upton's professional myopia; that required the boldness of Theodore Roosevelt, the more subtle qualities of Woodrow Wilson, Henry L. Stimson, Newton D. Baker, and the organization and advocacy of a substantial portion of the economic elite.[11] At least through World War II, there was no question about military subordination to civilian control in America.

## J. P. MORGAN AND COMPANY AS ALLIED PURCHASING AGENT AND FINANCIER

The movement for industrial preparedness was even more uncertain than that for military preparedness—and with good reason. The nation had extensive experience in dealing with its military services; they had been modernized to a substantial degree and had even recently fought in a limited war. But aside from the confused and halting experience of the European nations, no precedents and no guidelines existed for mobilizing a modern industrialized economy. Most advocates of preparedness included industrial mobilization in their proposals, but such plans were always quite vague. The opponents of preparedness had raised the issues of government munitions production, drafting capital as well as men, and so on, without going into particulars.[12] Industrial mobilization required experimentation with a process in which the difficulties dwarfed the problems involved in raising an army and a navy.

The nation's awkward experiment in industrial mobilization began, at least indirectly, in early 1915 when J. P. Morgan and Company became the purchasing agent for Great Britain and later for France. Buying for the Allies and helping finance their purchases ultimately became for Morgan virtually the same operation. The sums involved were massive. From late 1914 to the end of 1921, the House of Morgan, first as purchasing agent and later only as disbursing intermediary, made payments in the United States for Great Britain and France in excess of $24 billion, with Britain accounting for about two-thirds of the total. In the period when the company acted as purchasing agent—January 1915 to April 1917—payments totaled $10 billion, of which Morgan itself placed contracts for over $3 billion. While acting as purchasing agent, J. P. Morgan and Company also arranged financing for the Allies that, when combined with the buying and paying, involved accounts of approximately $48 billion in the aggregate.[13]

These figures were without precedent in the early years of the twentieth century. Equally extraordinary is the fact that by these operations, a private banking firm was sustaining two of the world's most powerful nations in a global war that would shape the nature of the future international community. As a member of J. P. Morgan and Company observed in 1923, the firm's purchasing, paying, and financing services "assumed in many of their aspects a governmental rather than a commercial character."[14] Few private or public leaders on either side of the Atlantic in 1914 or early 1915 fully grasped the incredible flow of goods and wealth that hostilities would require or the elaborate and innovative economic organization that would be necessary to deliver them. Now more than then, it is clear that the functions performed by the House of Morgan for the Allies from 1915 into 1917 began making America aware of the enormous demands and impact of modern warfare—forces that shaped the very destiny of nations.

The Allies began extensive purchasing programs on their own in the United States shortly after the outbreak of war in Europe in August 1914. Most of the buying was done by Great Britain and France, but Russia, Italy, and lesser powers also participated. Because the buying was carried on without centralized direction or coordination, it threatened the Allied war effort and created turbulence in the American economy. England and France, and even different departments of the same nations, competed among themselves in what became a mad scramble for goods. The confusion was aggravated by the circumstance that much of the procurement involved munitions for which there were virtually no manufacturing plants in existence in the United States. Allied representatives, many of them unfamiliar with the operations of the American market and, except for the British, dealing in a foreign language, often carried out transactions with manufacturers and a plethora of merchants, commission agents, and war brokers who were commonly incompetent and irresponsible. By the end of 1914, Allied buying was essentially a chaotic tangle of duplicate orders, overtaxed or incapable manufacturing firms or both, and spiraling prices.[15]

Great Britain was the principal buyer in the United States. Unlike the Continental powers, it had not maintained large mass armies and lacked the ability to supply them quickly. The navy and the industries sustaining it constituted Britain's first line of defense.

These realities led Britain to assume the lead in regularizing Allied procurement in America. The first significant opening occurred when Britain sent members of its Treasury to the United States in October 1914 to explore matters of foreign exchange and payment for purchases under conditions in which international financial norms had virtually been paralyzed by the war. The talks soon broadened to include the need for selecting a bank in the United States to handle British accounts, for centralizing purchases in America, and for financing continued procurement in America, which Great Britain could not sustain on its own for much longer. In August 1914 J. P. Morgan and Company had offered its financial services to Great Britain to facilitate procurement in America. The British representatives in the United States explored the proposal with Morgan in October–November, and the talks moved to London in November. Henry P. Davison, the senior Morgan partner, traveled to England that month to join members of the London affiliate, Morgan, Grenfell and Company, in negotiating a contract that required attention at the highest levels of British government, including Prime Minister Herbert Asquith, Chancellor of the Exchequer David Lloyd George, Financial Secretary Edwin S. Montagu, and governor of the Bank of England, Lord Cunliffe.

On January 15, 1915, J. P. Morgan and Company officially became the Commercial Agents in the United States for His Majesty's Government. This contractual agreement was limited to procurement, but much more was involved. In the tough negotiations that extended over a period of several months, critically important "understandings" were reached, which, at least tacitly, formed an inextricable part of the Commercial Agency Agreement. According to the understandings, since the buying power of Great Britain and its allies was limited, J. P. Morgan and Company would work out a system of credits to facilitate procurement and, when the time was right and if the funds were spent exclusively in the United States, would float loans as well. Moreover, during the process of working out the Commercial Agency Agreement, Davison became Britain's adviser on developments within the United States, and particularly on the political scene insofar as it involved the Allies and the conduct of the war. The House of Morgan continued to perform this role until the United States became a belligerent.[16]

In the negotiations that led to the Commercial Agency Agreement and related understandings, a bargain of sorts was struck between Great Britain and J. P. Morgan and Company. Britain was interested primarily in establishing a centralized procurement system in the United States, preferably under the control of Morgan. For Morgan, the first priority was acting as paying agent for Britain. Although not opposed to acting as buyer, the bank was unenthusiastic about undertaking responsibilities in an area that was not its specialty. Early on, however, British representatives made it clear that the procurement and financing functions had to be a package arrangement. As long as Britain was agreeable to the terms of the Commercial Agency Agreement, which was the case, the House of Morgan was willing to accept the British requirements.

J. P. Morgan and Company and the British agreed early in their negotiations that the success of any centralized buying arrangement in the United States depended in part on coordination among the Allies. Britain became even more committed to this idea when it realized that it would have to help finance the French and Russian war efforts. London, therefore, backed Morgan in its attempts to work out an agreement with France that paralleled the one signed with England. This effort was not accomplished until May 1915. Decisionmaking within French circles was tangled; competing U.S. financial institutions, particularly the National City Bank and William P. Bonbright and Company, sought the French contract and received varying degrees of support within that country; and the French strove to obtain better terms than the English, especially firmer commitments on financing in exchange for the procurement contract. Early in February 1915, both France and Russia were ready to join Britain in identical contracts with Morgan for the sake of common interests. The top levels of the British government then unexpectedly became obstreperous and ultimately torpedoed this approach, fearing that they might lose their preferred position in the United States. Thereafter, France and J. P. Morgan and Company slowly worked toward the same agreement as had been devised with Great Britain, but with the understanding that British interests would remain unharmed.

While J. P. Morgan and Company did act as commercial and financial agent for France, the relationship between the two was never as close, as smooth, or as trusting as that between the company and Great Britain. Since the House of Morgan did less buying and financing for France than for Britain, the former was less dependent on the company and hence gave the financial house less latitude than did their ally.[17]

Britain's decision to contract with J. P. Morgan and Company, which logically led France to follow suit, did not stem from a lack of options. London was fully aware that half a dozen New York firms would make considerable sacrifices to land the Commercial Agency Agreement. Indeed, the National City Bank actually offered Whitehall better terms than those proposed by Morgan. The National City Bank was a well-placed competitor. In October 1914 it had issued $10 million in short-term bonds for France, an act constituting the first loan to a belligerent and one sanctioned by the State Department.[18]

Whitehall's choice, however, was logical and predictable. As the most powerful and prestigious financial banking house in America, J. P. Morgan and Company could be relied upon to execute all buying and financing functions successfully. Moreover, the company's political advice and clout could be as valuable as its economic services, as proved to be the case in the months leading up to the Commercial Agency Agreement. Additionally, the House of Morgan, with branches in London and Paris (Morgan, Harjes and Company), had more experience about and knowledge of the complexities of international exchange than any other American firm. Finally, close personal ties existed between members of the Morgan firm and the economic and political elite in Britain and, to a lesser extent, in France. The Morgan affiliates in

London and Paris facilitated these relationships. J. P. Morgan and Company never hesitated to make clear its dedication to the Allied cause once hostilities broke out, despite the Wilson administration's call for genuine neutrality. In retrospect, once it became clear that the Allies required massive assistance from the United States to continue the war while the nation still remained officially neutral, the selection of J. P. Morgan and Company as the economic intermediary was a foregone conclusion.[19]

Morgan's desire for the Commercial Agency Contract was as explicable as Britain's desire to award it in both the short and long run. Morgan and Company had risen to power through its link to British and European banks, and its future as well as its past closely bound the firm to the Allied cause. Moreover, with the British controlling the seas in a world war, the export trade and the production for and financing of it would remain largely in Allied hands, with London playing a pivotal role. As a virtual partner of the British, J. P. Morgan and Company was assured even a more powerful place at the center of international economic activity.

The arrangement proved profitable. J. P. Morgan and Company made over $34 million on the Commercial Agency Contract alone. Renegotiations and adjustments resulting from tough bargaining on Whitehall's part reduced this sum to about $30 million once Morgan agreed to pick up the expenses of the bank's buying department in the United States. Morgan also made profits on numerous related transactions.

Exactly how much Morgan gained from investments related to manufacturing for the Allies in the United States is hard to measure. J. P. Morgan and Company was contractually obligated to inform its foreign clients of all contractors with which it was financially involved. Of the nearly 1,000 prime contractors, the House of Morgan reported that it had direct investments in only about fifteen. The bank also provided some financing to contracting firms between 1915 and 1917, but it avoided revealing details. It stated merely that outstanding loans to contractors never exceeded $5.6 million, releasing no information on which companies those loans had been made to. It is known, for example, that Morgan and the First National Bank of New York were the biggest buyers of three-year, 5 percent gold notes issued by Remington Arms–Union Metallic Cartridge Company in 1916, taking almost $1 million apiece. When difficulties developed with rifle makers and other companies, the Allies encouraged J. P. Morgan and Company to buy the firms out, but Morgan refused to go along.

The Morgan partners were anxious to avoid any relationships with contractors that smacked of improprieties or war profiteering, but the bank disclosed its involvements in a way that cast it in a favorable light. In the 1930s, the Senate Special Committee Investigating the Munitions Industry, chaired by Gerald P. Nye (R-ND), atypically did not examine this evidence. Thus, while Morgan had direct investments in only fifteen prime contractors, these companies were among America's giant corporations, and some were the largest producers for the Allies, including United States Steel Corporation, International Harvester Company, Midvale Steel and Ordnance Company, Baldwin Locomotive Works, and General Electric Company. Furthermore, Morgan's figures on investment and financing included only prime, not subcontractors, and there were many more of the latter than the former. Moreover, economic gain did not derive solely from direct investments. According to the Pujo Committee—a 1912 subcommittee of the House Banking and Currency Committee, headed by Arsene Pujo (D-LA)—and scholars of varying ideology, J. P. Morgan and Company, at the time America's leading banking house, made great use of trusts, interlocking directorships, cliques, networks, and inner groups, including the formation of syndicates for marketing securities. These devices were designed to produce profits as well as to maximize power and rationalize the corporate capitalist system. Morgan's specialty, of course, should not be overlooked. The bank floated loans and arranged credits for the Allies worth billions of dollars, and these transactions presented ample opportunity for profitmaking.

How much pecuniary gain Morgan realized from the different aspects of wartime business is unknown. Reliable records are available only on the Commercial Agency Agreement. Financial matters involving the House of Morgan and Allies between 1915 and 1917 and after became so tangled and complex that only an expert in international finance with full documentation could discern precisely what transpired. Even after months of study, the Nye Committee was unable to figure out many aspects of J. P. Morgan and Company's operations during the war years.[20]

Establishing with finality the wartime profits of J. P. Morgan and Company is probably not the key consideration, because the firm was interested in more than short-run gains by providing services to the Allies. Long-run international economic dominance for the United States, which inevitably would enormously enhance the wealth and power of the House of Morgan, always played a major role in the thinking of the Morgan partners.[21] Various scholars have examined the crucial point that the United States was beginning to reach out from a national to an international base before World War I, a move that represented the first phase in America's replacement of Great Britain as the world's dominant economic power. World War I accelerated this process. By the end of the war, the United States had become the world's largest creditor, with developed, semideveloped, and undeveloped nations dependent on its wealth. As buyer and financier for the Allies, J. P. Morgan and Company was participating in one of the major alterations of power in modern times. Thus positioned, Morgan was able to expand its power, influence, and prestige at home and abroad in a truly extraordinary manner; again, the bank's conduct was more like that of a nation than of a commercial agency. In a larger political sense, since America's international ambitions were always closely associated with those of Great Britain, the House of Morgan, by supporting that nation in a war fought for world domination, was also acting to secure its own future and that of the United States.[22]

Economics and politics blended at home as well as abroad. J. P. Morgan and Company was interested in rationalizing the American economy. The Commercial Agency Agreement presented the company with an unprecedented opportunity to work closely with leading manufacturers in almost every major category. The agreement also increased the company's influence over the economic system in general. In the short run, the role of Morgan allowed it to protect the economy against the chaos that uncoordinated Allied buying had created at the outbreak of war. Of course, the long-run effects were of much greater importance. Mobilizing the economy for World War I proved to be a watershed for the American political economy. Morgan initiated the process. Although the bank could not have known exactly in 1914 and 1915 where matters would end, neither could it have been completely ignorant about the possibilities and consequences of a world war that was reshaping all that it touched.[23]

Testifying before the Nye Committee in 1936, the senior Morgan partners insisted that they had jumped to the assistance of England to preserve the free world against a brutal German onslaught.[24] That explanation is even more simplistic than one proposing that the partners were motivated only by the pursuit of short-term profit. J. P. Morgan and Company, like the United States itself, was moved by power, prestige, profits, and economic well-being, combined in a complicated pattern of short- and long-run strategies. National security considerations and ideology under the rubric of "freedom" were no doubt involved, but only to the degree that they coincided with the larger goals of power rather than as absolutes standing alone.

The Commercial Agency Agreement with Great Britain and France made J. P. Morgan and Company almost overnight the world's largest buyer of goods. Its purchases for the Allies—basically Britain and France, but with Britain also buying for Russia, Italy, and a few lesser powers—totaled nearly $3.16 billion. Most of the buying took place between January 1915 and April 1917.[25] Approximately two-thirds of the purchases went to Great Britain and the remainder to France. Some 4,000 prime contracts were negotiated with 948 firms, almost all of which were in the United States. Including subcontractors, perhaps over 20,000 firms were involved. Though prime contracts ranged as low as $13.80, over 87 percent of contracts exceeded $1 million in value and went to 167 firms; ten contractors received over $1.3 billion, 42 percent of all dollar-value contracts. E. I. Du Pont de Nemours Powder Company headed the list, with contracts worth about $425 million. Most regions received some prime or subcontracts, but not surprisingly, the bulk went to the Northeast. Fifty-eight percent of all Morgan contracts involved munitions and "essential war materials"; the other 42 percent included hardware, machine tools, acids, foodstuffs, draft animals, and other goods.[26]

This huge purchasing operation made Morgan the world's largest single exporter. The volume of orders played a vital role in the growing American prosperity from 1915 to 1917. American exports between June 1915 and June 1917, as compared with June 1911 to June 1913, jumped from $6.7 billion to $15.2 billion in current dollars. Of the latter figure, about $9.8 billion went to the United Kingdom, France, Italy, Russia, and Canada. The House of Morgan accounted for over 32 percent of that trade—21 percent of U.S. exports and 84 percent of all American sales abroad of munitions and war materials.[27]

J. P. Morgan and Company carried out its vast procurement duties through a newly created Export Department. The Morgan partners had initially considered doing the buying through brokers or the purchasing organization of a large industrial firm such as the Western Electric Company. They ultimately decided to keep operations and control within the firm, however. Edward R. Stettinius, president of the Diamond Match Company and an officer and director of the Babcock and Wilcox Company, both of which had executive offices in New York, was selected to head the new enterprise. Though lacking national prominence, Stettinius was well respected within business circles for his breadth of experience and successful performance in large corporations. Stettinius was also well known by senior Morgan partners for his role in rescuing a corporation in which their bank had been involved.[28]

Organizing the new enterprise in January 1915, Stettinius assembled a reasonably well-functioning staff in a matter of weeks and by mid-1915 had nearly perfected the operations of the department. His staff eventually numbered about 175 people. The department was structured along functional lines with carefully selected experts heading sections on big-gun ammunition, propellants, explosives, and heavy chemicals; heavy equipment; hardware; food and livestock, and so on. In choosing a staff, Stettinius relied more on engineers and manufacturers than on people with strictly commercial experience since he was convinced that a technical background, involvement in production, and experience in handling a large labor force constituted the best training for dealing with new problems. Many of his chief lieutenants came from J. P. Morgan and Company, were associated with the bank, or were in one way or another well known to it, principally because reliability, discretion, and loyalty were defined as essential in an enterprise handling information that was classified in both a military and an economic sense. Although Stettinius delegated responsibility and authority, he closely supervised all parts of his department and also served as liaison between the Allies and the House of Morgan.[29]

Success in the Export Department depended on bringing some order to the chaos of Allied procurement. Stettinius first moved quickly to stabilize the demand side of the war business. (Throughout the war years, Export Department purchasing for the British was principally for the army, under the War Office, because army needs were the greatest. The navy, under the Admiralty, required less and insisted on doing most of its own buying.) Working with the British War Office, the Export Department set up procedures for establishing reliable requirement statistics, delivery dates, and other essential data on goods to be furnished by the United States. This enormously demanding assignment was executed at the outset by the War Office and later by the newly created Ministry of Munitions. The War Office in the first half of 1915 received the almost indispensable assistance of Morgan's London branch, Morgan, Grenfell, and Company. Similar arrangements were later worked out with France through the aid of the Paris affiliate, Morgan, Harjes, and Company, and by mid-1915 the two Allies had devised the means for coordinating their purchasing through the American firm. It must be emphasized that bringing order to the demand side did not mean that the Export Department had stable, long-range production goals upon which to base its operations. The Allies' ability to project requirements was never precise, and their needs constantly changed according to military vicissitudes.

While perfecting the demand side of the war trade, the Export Department simultaneously moved to rationalize supply. Stettinius and his department first decided that they would deal only with principals. By eliminating all middlemen, they strengthened their own control over procurement and cut costs for their clients and themselves. That decision alone had an enormous impact in clearing the avenues of exchange. Filling Allied orders for raw materials, foodstuffs, or existing products seldom presented problems once the Export Department was functioning well. The American economy had ample sources of supply and J. P. Morgan and Company had a nearly unrivaled fund of information about the reliability of firms. The crunch point was munitions, which constituted a substantial portion of Allied orders in the early years of the war. Outside the War and Navy Department arsenals, the United States had little or no experience or plan for meeting the massive demands of modern warfare. Reflecting on the critical situation that existed in 1915, Stettinius explained several years later that in creating a private munitions industry, he and his department were guided by the quality and character of a firm's leadership, and especially its technical staff, instead of by the company product. Product, plant, and machinery were less important than a proven manufacturing record.[30]

Combining the wealth of knowledge the Morgan associates possessed about industrial America with the collective expertise of the Export Department's staff, Stettinius had at his fingertips a detailed who's who of the American manufacturing community. More often than not, the Export Department had a wide range of contractors from which to choose. At times, however, the desired firms were reluctant to take the risk of engaging in new or expanded production for a temporary or an unpredictable market. The Export Department usually persuaded the hesitant companies to cooperate since the Allies offered almost irresistible terms, including generous advances, big orders and high prices to cover capital outlays and to ensure substantial profits, and lenient attitudes about production deadlines. Moreover, the potential contractors realized that they had the power and prestige of America's foremost financial house behind them should they encounter unanticipated difficulties.

Stettinius's dictum that the Export Department choose contractors according to men, not plants, was only partially followed. An analysis of contract distribution reveals that firm and managerial experience in the munitions field played a critical role in the awarding of contracts. For example, wartime production of rifles, carbines, pistols, and a small amount of artillery was carried out with rare exception by the Remington Arms Company, the Winchester Repeating Arms Company, and other firms that already manufactured weapons on a limited scale. The same held true for rifle cartridges and powder. Though a greater variety of companies produced explosives or the ingredients of explosives like trinitrotoluol, guncotton, picric acid, and nitrocellulose during the war, powder corporations and chemical firms still dominated. Contracting for artillery shells most closely approximated Stettinius's description of the firm-selection process. Since the nation had almost no shell-manufacturing capacity in 1915, new firms had to be selected, and the Export Department spread the contracts among more companies than it did for any other single product. But even in this instance, the range of manufacturers was small; most were iron and steel or metal-working firms.[31]

Whatever process the Export Department used to select its contractors, the statistics I have cited indicate that most Allied purchasing was concentrated in the hands of relatively few corporations. Those companies were often among America's largest economic enterprises. The top ten J. P. Morgan and

Company contractors received almost 42 percent of all dollar-value contracts. The leading four, Du Pont, Bethlehem, American Smelting and Refining Company, and U.S. Steel, were among the nation's biggest one hundred corporations. They alone received over $1 billion in contracts and accounted for almost one-third of all dollar-value contracts awarded by the Export Department. Stettinius explained after the war that his department had a defined policy of contracting with the fewest number of firms possible so as to concentrate responsibility. Not unexpectedly, therefore, the pattern of Allied purchasing through the House of Morgan matched the concentrated nature of economic power in American manufacturing and may have prompted even further consolidation (see Table 6.1).[32]

Formally, the Export Department was only the agent for the Allies, with the obligation to collect competitive bids and to disburse funds. Actually the department did much more. Although all contracts were ultimately signed between the various American firms and the Allies, the Export Department played a critical role in screening potential contractors, selecting and often persuading companies to undertake new lines of production, getting manufacturing under way, and helping to set prices and other terms of contracts. Stettinius and his associates also helped firms in securing financial assistance and in locating qualified and reliable subcontractors. Moreover, the Export Department acted as a general adviser to both the American firms and the Allied governments and also provided technical advice to facilitate cooperative relationships. Finally, the Export Department helped arrange transportation of goods from the United States to Europe. Stettinius and his associates learned to avoid rigid functional divisions in their organization so as to allow the closest possible coordination of procurement, production, and inspection activities. Apart from inspection, which was performed by Allied representatives, Stettinius and his staff were fully engaged in all aspects of the vast Allied purchasing program in the United States.

Export Department purchasing made a critically important, if not indispensable, contribution to Allied victory. In mid-1916 (at the time of the Battle of the Somme) for example, Great Britain was receiving nearly three-quarters of its light field artillery shells from the United States. Throughout the war, the Allies in general acquired most of their smokeless powder and high explosives from this nation. France bought large amounts of raw materials and semifinished products but relatively few finished goods from America. Great Britain, by contrast, procured heavily in all categories. Two-thirds of all Export Department buying until April 1917, or about $2 billion worth, involved supplies and parts for big gun ammunition. Nitrocellulose powder alone accounted for almost $430 million. Also of great importance to Britain, although not to France, were

Table 6.1. Top Ten Contractors for Allies Through the Operations of J. P. Morgan and Company, 1915–1917

| | Product | Adjusted Value of Contracts in Millions of $ | Morgan Interest | Bunting List of 100 Corporations, 1896–1905 | Chandler List 1917 by Rank |
|---|---|---|---|---|---|
| E. I. Du Pont de Nemours Powder Company | Explosives and ingredients | 424.9 | No | Yes | 8 |
| Bethlehem Steel Company | Shells, billets, forgings, misc. | 241.6 | No | Yes | 3 |
| American Smelting and Refining Company | Copper, brass discs, cadmium | 234.6 | No | Yes | 13 |
| U.S. Steel Products Company | Bars, forgings, wire, rope, rr material, misc. | 121.9 | Yes | Yes | 1 |
| Hercules Powder Company | Explosives and ingredients | 66.7 | No | Yes | 176 |
| Aetna Explosives Company | Explosives and ingredients | 52.5 | No | No | 197 |
| Baldwin Locomotive Works | Shells and components, locomotives and rr parts | 52.3 | Yes | No | 75 |
| New England Westinghouse Company | Rifles | 40.6 | No | No | — |
| Butterworth Judson Company | Explosives and ingredients | 40.5 | No | No | — |
| Midvale Steel and Ordnance Company | Shells, shell forgings, howitzers, tube forgings | 40.2 | Yes | Yes—as Cambria | 6 |
| | TOTAL: | $1315.8 of total Morgan contracts of $3160.0 million or 41.6% of all contracts. | | | |

*Source:* Nye Committee, *Hearings,* part 25, pp. 7691–7714; David Bunting, *Statistical View of the Trusts* (Westport, CT: Greenwood Press, 1974); and Alfred D. Chandler, Jr., *The Visible Hand: The Managerial Revolution in American Business* (Cambridge, MA: Belknap Press, 1977), pp. 503–12.

shipments of small arms—rifles, machine guns, pistols, and the like—which had a value of nearly $181 million. Only some $12.5 million worth of lathes, machine tools, and machine tool equipment was bought for the Allies. Nonetheless, this category of goods, which was basic to all munitions output and production in general in an industrial economy, involved a greater number of individual contracts than any other type of product, thus causing extraordinary problems and demanding exceptional efforts in all Allied countries and the United States.

The purchasing effort extended far beyond these items, touching nearly every industry in the United States. "Out of the Export Department's dragnet," relates the J. P. Morgan chronicler, "came anything from hobnails to locomotives, from micrometers to giant lifting-jacks, from clinical thermometers to rectifying stills, from catgut to heavy cordage, from antitoxins to liquid chlorine, from pocket-knives to lances."[33]

Allied purchasing through the Export Department played a significant role in preparing the United States for World War I. By April 1917 an industrial structure for the massive production of munitions had been created. Plants manufactured 15,000 to 20,000 British Enfield and Russian rifles daily and had an annual capacity of 70,000 machine guns. From 1914 to 1917 the annual capacity of private firms for producing rifle cartridges increased from small amounts to 2.25 million rounds. In the same period, the private production of powder increased from 15 million pounds per year to 360 million. The output of artillery shells was even greater and included the production of components such as fuses, cases, and primers. Private firms could annually produce more than 36.5 million shells in sizes between three and twelve inches. Further, elaborate plants were built for manufacturing various explosives and their ingredients. In addition to plants and equipment, production for the Allies trained a large work force in the often exacting demands of munitions output. As it turned out, the nation did not use this capacity as wisely or as expeditiously as it should have when it entered the war, but that does not detract from the accomplishments that J. P. Morgan and Company had helped to achieve.[34]

It is impossible to separate the Export Department's buying program for the Allies from J. P. Morgan and Company's extensive efforts for financing purchases in the United States. From the outset, the two critical functions were different sides of the same coin. Great Britain had awarded its contract for banking and buying in the United States contingent upon commitments for financing, France had been even more emphatic in this regard, and J. P. Morgan and Company had accepted the terms. In late 1914 and early 1915, the Allies had no idea of the magnitude of buying in the United States that the war would force upon them. Yet even when the Allies anticipated only modest procurement, financing was considered imperative. As hostilities continued and the demand for American munitions and other goods became virtually insatiable, U.S. financing of these purchases took on greater urgency. The financing crisis grew until the United States entered the war in April 1917. Since paying for goods was a critical issue between 1915 and 1917, the Export Department's purchases in these years cannot sensibly be set apart from J. P. Morgan and Company's extensive and imaginative programs for providing the Allies with the capital to balance their accounts. The Morgan partners unequivocally, repeatedly, and emphatically insisted before the Nye Committee that there was no relationship whatsoever between the buying and the financing, but appropriately, few observers took their denials seriously.[35]

Until America entered the war, private financing for the Allies created grave problems for the Wilson administration and J. P. Morgan and Company. The trouble started almost with the outbreak of hostilities in Europe. In August 1914, Morgan approached Washington about the propriety of floating a loan to France. The inquiry elicited Secretary of State William Jennings Bryan's private observation that money was the worst contraband "because it commanded everything else" and his public declaration that loans to belligerents would be "inconsistent with the true spirit of neutrality."[36]

Without the administration's sanction, no bank would engage in financing belligerents. There matters remained until October 1914. At that point, Robert Lansing, counselor to the State Department and, in effect, assistant secretary, won Wilson's approval for the establishment of "bank credits of belligerent governments in contradistinction to a public loan floated in this country." The distinction grew out of a French request to the National City Bank for financial assistance that ultimately involved $10 million. Lansing acted at the request of, and perhaps under pressure from, the National City Bank and J. P. Morgan and Company. All parties recognized that this was a test case that could fundamentally alter American financial relations with the Allies. The matter was so sensitive that no official announcement of this change in policy was made until March 1915. Indeed, in January 1915 the administration denied to the Senate that the August 1914 pronouncement had been modified. Under the revised policy, American bankers, with J. P. Morgan generally in the lead or as a major participant, arranged loans or credits for France, Russia, and Italy totaling over $160 million between November 1914 and October 1915.[37]

J. P. Morgan's most extensive loan activity with a belligerent in 1915 and after involved Great Britain. The Morgan partners serviced Britain's purchase account as well as one for buying sterling to maintain the desired exchange rate. Britain consistently overdrew both accounts. The overdrafts were labeled the British Demand Loan and were backed by uncommitted British collateral that was never specifically deposited or even earmarked for that purpose. J. P. Morgan and Company always carried the bulk of this loan, although it was assisted by New York and other banks along with the participation of giant corporations such as International Harvester, U.S. Steel, and American Telephone and Telegraph Company. The amount of the loan varied with the level of Morgan's purchasing activity and the rate at which Britain made payments by shipping gold and American securities from Britain and the Commonwealth countries. The balance on the loan would have gone into billions of dollars had not most of it been paid off by private, short- and long-term American financing. The Demand Loan reached a peak of $437 million on April 25, 1917, an amount that exceeded any other loan floated in the United States for Britain. Ultimately, through direct or indirect means, Washington paid some or all of the Demand Loan outstanding in April 1917. That amount must be added to the sum of private financing of the Allied cause before America entered the war.[38]

Both Britain and the Morgan partners knew in late 1914 and early 1915 that the Allies, and especially Britain, would at some point have to float public loans in the United States to continue buying in America. In April 1915 senior Morgan partners began pressing Whitehall to consider loans and to confront the difficulties such an enterprise would encounter in the United States. America lacked the institutions and practices for rapidly absorbing large quantities of publicly marketed securities and certainly not the paper of a foreign belligerent. Divisions and anxieties over the war, and Washington's opposition to loans to belligerents, created further barriers to American public loans. London initially resisted Morgan's importunities because Whitehall was distracted by governmental reorganizations, the course of the war, conflicting advice from another American banking house, and an unwillingness to accept the harsh economic realities reported from Wall Street. By mid-1915, though, Britain begrudgingly agreed that publicly floated loans had become essential. But it insisted, contrary to the strong recommendation of the Morgan partners, that they be unsecured.

Once Britain accepted the need for public issues, the biggest immediate obstacle to such an undertaking was the opposition of the Wilson administration. London had considered forcing Washington's hand on loans by acting to destabilize the dollar. That strategy was not implemented, but a similar one was. On August 14, 1915, J. P. Morgan and Company inexplicably halted the purchases of sterling that were maintaining a stable exchange rate, and London ceased mobilizing its economic resources to allow the New York banker to do so. This move reversed a practice that had been standard for over six months.

Within days, the pound fell from $4.71 to $4.51, which threatened to disrupt the flow of goods from the United States to England by making American products more expensive to the British.

At the same time, the Morgan partners, together with Secretary of the Treasury William G. McAdoo; Benjamin Strong, governor of the Federal Reserve Bank of New York; Edward M. House, one of Wilson's closest advisers; Robert Lansing, by then secretary of state; and others in positions of power mounted a campaign to persuade the president to revise the official policy against loans to belligerents. McAdoo presented to Wilson the bluntest argument in favor of such loans: "To maintain our prosperity, we must finance it. Otherwise, it may stop and that would be disastrous."[39] By late August 1915 the president cautiously and inconspicuously allowed the ban on loans to be lifted. Despite pressure from members of his administration, he would not endorse any loans to the Allies. Nonetheless, his action cleared the way for marketing an Anglo-French loan in October 1915 worth a total of $500 million. The loan was unsecured and the amount much less than the Allies, particularly Great Britain, wanted. As J. P. Morgan had repeatedly warned London, the securities were difficult to sell and attracted limited support outside the East and even less from noninstitutional investors. After this first loan, public loans of another $1 billion were made to the Allies. In April 1917 the Allies' debt to private investors totaled approximately $2.7 billion, in addition to $800 million in outstanding contractual obligations.[40]

Throughout the years 1915 to 1917, Allied orders, American loans to the Allies, and America's wartime diplomacy formed an intricate tangle that placed J. P. Morgan and Company in a highly sensitive and often awkward position. These conditions are best illustrated by difficulties that developed in 1916 over the American production of rifles.[41] By late 1915 Winchester Repeating Arms Company, Remington Arms–Union Metallic Cartridge Company, and Remington Arms Company (owned by Midvale Steel and Ordnance Company) had contracted with Britain to produce nearly $200 million worth of rifles and bayonets. Advance payments reached about $50 million. The American companies encountered serious obstacles by mid-1916 and fell far behind the delivery schedule in the contracts. Extremely frustrated, Britain indicated a desire to cancel the breached contracts on 1.8 million rifles worth about $55 million.

The simple suggestion of cancellation caused extraordinary concern in American financial and industrial circles. In elaborate and anxious negotiations that stretched out through October 1916 and eventually involved face-to-face meetings of J. P. Morgan, Jr., Henry P. Davison, the chief Morgan partner for relations with Britain, the chancellor of the exchequer, the minister of munitions, and the prime minister, the New York bankers repeatedly warned the British that cancellation would have dire consequences. To protect themselves, they argued, other American manufacturers would contract with the Allies only if offered excessive prices and exceptional terms. Much more important, cancellation would jeopardize future loans from the United States that the British desperately needed. Another factor was that some of the nation's largest financial concerns, including the Chase National Bank, the First National Bank of New York, the Guaranty Trust Company, Lee, Higginson and Company, and Kidder, Peabody and Company, had an important stake in the economic welfare of the three rifle manufacturers as either stockholders, bondholders, or general creditors. J. P. Morgan itself was involved.

The officers of the rifle companies were well known and in communication with most other munitions manufacturers. They argued that British problems in designing and inspecting the rifles, not their manufacturing methods, had caused the delays. To complicate matters further, the attitude of the business community and the public toward Great Britain had begun to sour because of that country's escalated violation of neutral rights while Germany had greatly curtailed submarine warfare after the *Sussex* crisis. Under these circumstances, no more bond issues for Britain could be floated successfully in the United States. The first United Kingdom Loan for $250 million had been issued on September 1, 1916, and the second for $300 million would be floated on November 1, 1916. The timing of the rifle controversy could not have been worse. Davison considered this crisis the most serious one the Export Department had faced in its years of operation.

Once fully apprised of the high stakes involved, Britain accepted a settlement worked out in London and the United States in October 1916—a settlement virtually dictated by the rifle companies and their creditors and one that the Morgan partners felt to be unfair but necessary. Britain was forced to buy most of the physical assets of the rifle companies that had been added for wartime production. The formal transfer of title did not take place until the United States entered the war, and the House of Morgan employed various deceptive devices to maintain at least a semblance of American neutrality. After all, direct ownership by a belligerent of firms producing munitions in a neutral country would have rendered any reasonable definition of neutrality totally meaningless.

A similar situation developed with the Eddystone Ammunition Corporation, a firm created by the Baldwin Locomotive Company in 1915 to produce ammunition and shrapnel for the Russians. Britain had advanced the firm $10 million. The Chase National Bank and the Mechanics and Metals National Bank were the firm's principal financiers, and Morgan eventually became involved. During the summer 1916 Eddystone experienced production difficulties and also became embroiled in a controversy with the Russians and the

British, which threatened to halt output. To ensure continued production, which the Allies wanted and needed, the British again had to buy out the firm, but, as with the three rifle firms, avoided taking title. Subterfuge was employed once more, with J. P. Morgan and Company taking a principal role in the transaction. Such manipulation disturbed Stettinius because of its shady nature and also because it created problems in protecting British investments.[42]

In addition to compromising dilemmas involving Allied interests and American neutrality, J. P. Morgan and Company faced conflicts between Allied requirements and American preparation for possible military encounters with Mexico beginning in early 1916. Britain was worried that U.S. orders could interfere with American production for the British, and the Export Department acted to protect British interests. Remington Arms–UMC Company, Bethlehem Steel Company, Eddystone, and Midvale assured the United Kingdom through the Export Department that American contracts were not slowing deliveries to the Allies and that in cases of conflict, Britain would be granted first priority. Midvale was forced to live up to its pledge. Due to pressure from Great Britain and the Export Department, the steel firm in mid-1916 delayed fulfilling contracts it had previously signed with the American government for twelve-inch artillery shells, in order to meet later contractual obligations with Great Britain.[43]

Conflicts over financing needs, not competing demands on munitions capacity, turned out to be the major problem between the United States and the Allies before April 1917.[44] By November 1916 Allied buying in the United States was at a peak, and so, too, was the demand for financial assistance. Yet private loans were becoming increasingly difficult to negotiate. At no time had the various Allied bond issues sold easily. Most were absorbed either by large Eastern banks, manufacturers, shippers, and the like that had direct or indirect economic ties to the Allied cause or by the munitions makers, which the Morgan partners had pressed hard to buy securities to the limit. The holders of these securities could only resell them at a loss; as a result, the nation's principal creditors were loaded down with Allied issues and hardly anxious to acquire more. Even if it had been possible to sell more bonds, Britain could no longer raise the necessary collateral or at least did not want to face the consequences of doing so. And unsecured public loans were out of the question, as J. P. Morgan and Company had repeatedly warned its skeptical client. The British plight was worsened by the fact that Britain was financially supporting France, Russia, and other belligerents in addition to meeting its own astronomical demands. Between 1914 and 1917, Britain lent its allies approximately $4 billion.

To mobilize additional American credit for the British under unpromising, if not forbidding, financial circumstances, Morgan and the Allies devised a scheme for issuing, refunding, and reissuing a series of ninety-day unsecured British Treasury Bills. Under ideal conditions, this scheme would have provided the Allies with the benefits of a $300 million long-term bond issue without the commitment of any collateral. Since the bills would be sold mainly to banks, the Morgan partners felt compelled to consult the Federal Reserve Board. Just a few weeks earlier the board had rejected a proposal to grant France $100 million in industrial credits. Nonetheless, the Morgan partners expected assistance from the Federal Reserve Board because they had played a key role in persuading the board in 1915 to accept short-term Allied paper as a means of substantially expanding credit for their clients in the United States. This time, the board proved not only uncooperative but delivered what the Morgan partners and Britain considered a crushing blow to Allied finances.

On November 27, 1916, the Federal Reserve Board issued a public announcement urging American bankers to be cautious in foreign lending. It warned them in particular against investing in unsecured foreign treasury bills, and in an unprecedented step, extended the alert to private investors as well. The board's action arose from a disagreement at the highest levels of the American government about how the power of American finance should be used to influence international events and from fears among some observers that a high level of foreign lending could endanger the American economy. Benjamin Strong, governor of the Federal Reserve Bank of New York and a commanding figure in the Federal Reserve System, wanted American bankers to assume leadership, even dominance, in international finances. He was also pro-Ally, an Anglophile, and a close friend and confidant of J. P. Morgan, Jr., and several of the senior partners of the Morgan house. From 1914, Strong sought to advance financing for the Allies in the United States in every way possible, including granting them credits, accepting their paper, negotiating a correspondence agreement in 1916 between the Federal Reserve Bank of New York and the Bank of England, and, finally, allowing the British and French publicly to float loans in America. These acts were simultaneously pro-Ally, pro-Morgan, and, most important, pro-American. Strong could fully agree with Davison's arguments on behalf of more financial aid to the Allies in late 1916:

> We are now in a fair way of becoming the masters of the world. The more we stimulate [Allied] trade, and the more loans we make to these foreign countries, the more we increase our predominance.[45]

By late 1916, Strong was ill and not participating in the Federal Reserve Board's operations. Other members shared his ambitions for making the

United States the world's principal financial power, but some were not pro-Ally and others were certainly not in the Morgan orbit. Indeed, W. P. G. Harding, governor of the Federal Reserve Board, insisted that American financial might could dictate the outcome of the war and had to be used with discretion. "The carnival of death and destruction has gone far enough," he stated, and the United States should not act mindlessly to perpetuate it.[46] Harding and his colleagues also worried about the domestic consequences of the seemingly unending flow of capital to the Allies. In the worst case, these loans could mean disaster for the American economy, and in the best case they would contribute to increasing prices and tighter credit at home. Harding and his supporters perceived continued financing of the Allied cause as being fraught with extreme peril in the short and the long run. By acting to rein in this lending, they were determined to meet their responsibilities to the newly created board and, thereby, to increase its strength and protect its future.

When Morgan approached the Federal Reserve Board in November 1916 with the proposal for using British Treasury Bills to extend Allied credit, Strong was not there to support the company, and Harding and like-minded members pushed their views. The issue was of such importance that the president was ultimately consulted. Wilson agreed with Harding's position and indeed encouraged the board to strengthen a proposed public declaration opposing further loans.

Wilson apparently had his eye on the foreign as well as on the domestic scene. He was about to offer his last peacemaking effort and seemed to welcome the Federal Reserve Board's action as a way to warn Britain, by then blatantly violating neutral rights, to beware. This action was one of the first displays by the president that he, along with Strong and his supporters, intended to use America's newly gained economic predominance to control Britain and to shape a world community along the lines that he desired. Wilson and Strong simply disagreed in November 1916 about the best means of pursuing those aims.

For the British, the Federal Reserve Board's declaration constituted a crisis more extreme than the submarine menace. J. P. Morgan and Company labeled it the worst financial development since the outbreak of war and believed it would have fearful consequences. Harking back to the exchange crisis precipitated in 1915, which had forced the Wilson administration to lift its ban on loans to belligerents, Morgan proposed that the Allies cut back purchasing so as to put an economic squeeze on the United States and to create a public backlash against the Federal Reserve Board's statement. Britain had good reasons to ignore this advice. In October 1916 Whitehall had conducted a high-level, interdepartmental study of its economic dependence on the

United States. The findings were chilling in every way. Without American supplies, Britain could not continue the war; without American financing of almost $10 million a day to pay for those goods, Britain would exhaust its reserves of gold and securities by March 1917. Its dependence was total. Cutting back procurement would cause distress in America but would produce disaster in England.[47]

The Federal Reserve Board's late-November 1916 warning against foreign investment temporarily ended hopes of a publicly floated loan for the Allies. Yet purchasing continued at very high levels until the United States entered the war in April 1917. J. P. Morgan and Company reluctantly financed this procurement through further extensions of the Demand Loan, with the assistance of the National City Bank, the First National Bank, and other financial institutions. Public loans again became possible once diplomatic relations between the United States and Germany were broken. A third United Kingdom Loan worth $250 million was floated in February 1917 and sold well because Wilson for the first time since the outbreak of war allowed his administration and the Federal Reserve Board publicly to endorse the sale of belligerent bonds and to encourage their purchase. Nonetheless, British credit continued to deteriorate. J. P. Morgan and Company pleaded with its client to act in a way that would guarantee liquidity. Nothing was done, and Britain and Morgan proceeded as if no day of reckoning would arrive. On April 4, 1917, Great Britain and France had outstanding unsecured loans of $855 million, the former owing the greater amount. Morgan's British Demand Loan alone stood at $345 million; Allied debt held privately by Americans totaled $2.7 billion.[48]

Despite these harsh realities, Great Britain's anguish over its desperate economic situation appeared to dissipate in late 1916 and early 1917. Years later, the Nye Committee was extremely puzzled by this state of affairs. After searching through the documentation and examining witnesses, the committee became convinced that Whitehall was operating on the assumption that the United States would shortly come into the war and act to relieve its plight. Nye and his colleagues also believed that American government officials at the highest level had informed Great Britain of this probability and had taken steps to modify the severity of the Federal Reserve Board's action of November 1916. J. P. Morgan and Company was obviously privy to this information and had conveyed some of it to the Allies. Once the United States entered the war, Morgan publicly expressed the belief that Washington would bail out the Allies financially and their American financiers.[49]

Whether or not the Nye Committee's analysis is correct is less important than the fact that America's entry into the war relieved the financial plight of the Allies.[50] After April 4, 1917, Washington became the Allies' financier. The

United States lent them almost $7.1 billion before hostilities ceased and nearly $3.3 billion thereafter. Less than $1 billion of the money lent by the American government was ever repaid, but all of the approximately $3 billion owed to private U.S. investors was. Had the United States not intervened in the war and taken over the failed loans, it is safe to say that some or most of the privately held debt would have gone unpaid, as occurred with the publicly held loans.[51] American public loans to Great Britain were used to pay approximately $650 million of the privately held debt, mostly British, and not including the Demand Loan contracted by the Allies before April 4, 1917. This action violated the spirit, if not the letter, of the laws authorizing Washington to assist the Allies financially.

Furthermore, Secretary of the Treasury McAdoo slowly and reluctantly reversed policies and commitments made to Congress that American loans to the Allies would be used only to purchase goods in the United States. In practice, those loans also financed purchases in other countries and supported the price of the pound and franc. The Nye Committee estimated that $1.7 billion was used for the latter purpose but ultimately concluded that it was almost impossible to establish accurately how the loans were spent.

Indeed, American dollars were used to settle Allied, and particularly British, accounts throughout the world. This practice occurred because once the United States entered the war, the government believed, despite grave reservations, that it could not or should not tell the Allies how to spend the money mobilized on their behalf. Given this view, McAdoo and some associates wanted to use American loans at least to ensure that the United States was not underwriting aggressive Allied war aims. They also pondered using American economic power as a lever on the Allies in behalf of a peace settlement designed to avoid future conflicts. Secretary of State Lansing vetoed even this approach.

McAdoo, in spite of dogged resistance and vehement protests, also failed to prevent the U.S. government from helping to pay off the British Demand Loan, which had grown to $400 million and was held principally by J. P. Morgan and Company. Washington only settled this account after a year of delicate negotiations, the intercession of House and Strong, great finesse by England, and the development of procedures for hiding the transaction from the American public and its elected representatives. Had Congress or the public learned that Liberty Loans were being used to pay off Morgan, there would have been a major political eruption. As late as the mid-1930s, the Morgan partners and two former Treasury officials, one of whom became a Morgan partner, continued to deny to the Nye Committee that Washington had covered Morgan's private loans to Great Britain. McAdoo finally agreed to Britain's using Treasury advances for making payments on the Demand Loan because not only would that prop up British finances, he realized, but the government also needed the assistance, expertise, and influence of J. P. Morgan and Company successfully to market American bonds essential for financing the American and Allied war efforts.[52]

American entry into World War I logically ended the quasi-governmental role that J. P. Morgan and Company had assumed in working with the Allies between 1914 and 1917. However, the Morgan partners' role in financing the now-expanded war did not end at that point, nor did the Export Department's purchasing and disbursing functions quickly stop. On February 2, 1917, and again on April 4, J. P. Morgan, Jr., had personally offered the services of his organization to Wilson. The president politely declined.[53]

Both the Allies and Morgan realized that a basic reorganization in buying had to occur because the United States was the major claimant and was financing virtually all procurement taking place in the country. Nonetheless, the Allies to varying degrees wanted the Export Department to continue in some form, and Morgan unquestionably desired such an outcome. No quick resolution was possible because the United States was slow to fashion machinery for effectively mobilizing the economy. Finally, in August 1917, after the creation of the War Industries Board, the Allied Purchasing Commission was set up, in effect, to take over the functions that the Allied governments and J. P. Morgan and Company had handled among themselves. Gradually, outstanding orders and inquiries that the Export Department had handled since 1915 and in the interim between April and August 1917 were transferred to purchasing departments set up by the Allies in the United States to deal directly with the American mobilization agencies. The process was nearly completed by January 1918.

Although Morgan's purchasing operations all but stopped in 1917, disbursements continued. The Export Department paid Allied bills after April 1917 as it had done before. The department actually made its greatest outlays in 1918 a sum of over $2.1 billion for Great Britain and France. This amount reflected deliveries of past orders and the fact that financing from the American government allowed the Allies to buy at a level never before possible. In 1917 and 1918 the pattern of Allied buying changed as purchases of raw materials and food outweighed finished goods. At the end of 1921 the Export Department transferred to Allied agencies any accounts still open and figuratively closed its doors.[54]

The Export Department was a gigantic enterprise that made almost $10 million a day in purchases alone at the height of its activity. It was the largest endeavor in private procurement undertaken to that time. The $500 million Anglo-French loan in 1915, which helped finance the buying, was also a landmark, exceeding by fourfold the value of any previous public loan. Lending abroad was quite new for America and ultimately reached levels earlier unknown in the United States. The purchasing and financing operations carried out by the Morgan partners involved day-to-day contacts and negotiations with high-level officials in the world's most powerful nations, including Britain's prime minister and America's president. This cast Morgan's activities in a quasi-governmental role. Acting in such a capacity, J. P. Morgan and Company played a leading part in making a mockery of American neutrality and in putting the nation on the road to war.

Through the Morgan operation, America's business community experienced for the first time the immense consequences of modern warfare. The Export Department accomplished for the Allies a process that the nation worked out for itself after April 1917 on a scale encompassing the entire economy. The American mobilization effort after April 1917 did not use the unmatched knowledge and experience of Stettinius and his staff in any direct and systematic way, however. Representatives from J. P. Morgan and Company sat in on various conferences as Washington strove to devise the necessary mobilization machinery. At the request of Edward M. House, Stettinius in May 1917 provided the Wilson administration with a memorandum on how economic mobilization should be carried out. These recommendations appeared to have no effect.[55] In 1917 two direct offers of the Export Department's services to the Wilson administration were turned aside. Stettinius was finally called to duty in the War Department in early 1918. He remained into 1919 but was shuffled around from one largely nominal post to another. Members of his staff fared much better, with several eventually holding high and powerful positions in the various mobilization agencies. Leland L. Summers and Waddill Catchings stand out in that regard.[56]

Stettinius's fate stemmed from his identification with J. P. Morgan and Company. He had, in fact, become a partner of the firm on January 1, 1916. To many Americans, the House of Morgan embodied abusive capitalism. Pre-1914 hostility toward the company had increased during the neutrality years; opponents of the war, antibusiness elements, competitors, disappointed contractors, and excluded middlemen contributed to growing criticism and suspicion of America's foremost financial house, which the war had at least temporarily strengthened. If Wilson had given the Morgan partners a central role in economic mobilization, he would have left himself open to sharp political attacks as his administration set out on an already difficult and sensitive mobilization process.

Though the Wilson administration could choose largely to ignore the Export Department, especially its chief, that option was not open in regard to J. P. Morgan and Company as a whole. The Export Department dealt with industry, which was not the specialty of the Morgan partners and for which alternate and perhaps even better experts could be found. This situation was not so for finances. As McAdoo discovered when he attempted to prevent Washington from making payments on the British Demand Loan held largely by Morgan, an end run could not be made around the nation's predominant financial house. The realities and symbols of power are best illustrated by comparing the treatment of Stettinius with that of Thomas W. Lamont, one of the most aggressive of the Morgan senior partners.[57] After the United States entered the war, Lamont served as a financial adviser to House and later to the American delegation to the Paris Peace Conference. In 1917 he also managed to be appointed chief of the American banking group participating in consortiums for China. In that key slot, Lamont acted, as J. P. Morgan and Company had acted in the neutrality years, to protect the interests of the bank, Great Britain, and, according to the firm's definitions, the United States.[58]

The role of J. P. Morgan and Company in economic mobilization between 1915 and 1917 demonstrates a basic point: Private economic power, if exercised shrewdly and at times ruthlessly, can be strengthened enormously through public operations. If the National City Bank had won the Commercial Agency Agreement instead of the Morgan partners, the contours of power in the American financial community would have been changed significantly. Based on its existing strength, the House of Morgan got the contract. Using this position, together with imagination and enormous assets, J. P. Morgan and Company protected and advanced its power and prestige in the political and economic whirlwind of World War I. In the process, the House of Morgan showed the complexities that economic mobilization for war involved and demonstrated the type of economic leadership required of corporate America in using hostilities to benefit itself and the nation.

# 7
# ECONOMIC MOBILIZATION, 1914–1916

In contrast to their involvement in the preparedness movement, economic and social elites did not lead in creating governmental agencies to mobilize the economy for World War I. Many corporate leaders failed to see the need for centrally directing a wartime economy. Some of the largest corporations—already absorbed in munitions and other production for the Allies—acted as if J. P. Morgan and Company's Export Department, or a similar agency, would be enough for handling an emergency. Even if big business had anticipated the war's requirements, corporate America would have been loath overtly to assume leadership for economic mobilization since, unlike with military preparedness, its interests and power were directly involved. If United States Steel Corporation, First National Bank of New York, or firms associated with them had taken the lead, harnessing the economy would have been harmed more than helped. Instead, the initiative came from business associations, the navy and army, management specialists and other professionals, and individuals seeking to advance their political ambitions.

This development was consistent with the Progressive movement. Many or most Progressive reforms originated among the middle- to upper-middle classes, with new professional groups of especial importance. No reform could go far, however, unless it took into account the economic elite. The corporate structure and its financial, legal, and other allies, after all, constituted the hub around which the entire economy turned.[1] America's corporate giants figuratively sat back to let others work out the means for controlling a wartime economy, confident that any approach had to be based on their power, institutions, and personnel.

Economic mobilization for World War I grew out of the Progressive political economy, but the demands of war were always much greater than those of peace. Devising the right mobilization approach was slow and controversial. As late as December 1917, Frank A. Vanderlip, president of the National

City Bank of New York, observed, "We are just beginning to understand what it means to go to war in the modern sense and what it means to prepare America for war."[2]

## THE U.S. CHAMBER OF COMMERCE

The U.S. Chamber of Commerce, Progressives dedicated to efficiency and scientific management, and a few magnates such as Bernard M. Baruch who were detached from the Eastern elite led the drive to prepare the nation economically for war. They were joined and assisted to some degree by the military services and various individuals within the Woodrow Wilson administration. On the whole, however, the administration responded cautiously to numerous importunities for action on economic mobilization as America's entry into the war seemed imminent. Congress moved even more slowly, stirring itself to action only when prodded by the Wilson administration and individuals and groups outside government.

The Chamber of Commerce played an important part in economic mobilization, and some of its prewar practices were adapted for wartime uses.[3] Maturation within the business community led to the creation of the chamber. From 1890, modern trade associations grew in number and size, expanded their scope from the local and regional to the national level, and increasingly stressed practices designed to rationalize the marketplace and to mitigate destructive competition. Along with the National Association of Manufacturers (NAM), the American Bankers' Association, the National Board of Trade, and similar organizations, trade associations lobbied government, especially at the federal level. Local and state chambers of commerce and other such groups had also grown in size, function, and sophistication. A national federation such as the U.S. Chamber of Commerce was a logical outgrowth of these developments and was necessary for furthering business unity.

A few talented and far-sighted business leaders initiated the action that culminated in the organization of the Chamber of Commerce in 1912. Moderate publisher John H. Fahey, Progressive merchant Edward A. Filene from the Boston Chamber of Commerce, and Harry A. Wheeler of the Chicago Association of Commerce, who was also vice-president and later president of the Union Trust Company of that city, headed the drive. They were assisted by William Howard Taft administration officials, particularly Secretary of Commerce and Labor Charles Nagel.

Wheeler became the first president and was virtually indispensable during the chamber's formative stages. Shrewd, energetic, and tactful, he had keen insight into what the new organization must and must not do in order to succeed. He and Fahey, who served as the second president from 1915 to 1917, drew upon their extensive associational experience in charting the chamber's course. They established three cardinal principles, which proved of great importance: political impartiality, balance to ensure fair representation for all members, and moderation toward organized labor.

These tactics facilitated growth. Between 1915 and 1920, the number of affiliates increased from around 624 to 1,321, i.e., 17 percent of the nation's commercial and industrial associations were members and 16 to 50 percent of the commercial and industrial population of most states was represented. Membership was greatest in the Northeast, Midwest, and Far West but weaker in the South and Northwest. In general, however, representation was distributed throughout the country.

Most of the chamber's membership came from small- to medium-sized businesses. The largest enterprises did not join for a number of reasons. Their absence probably strengthened the organization by not scaring off many potential members. Furthermore, the chamber's influence with the public and the government was enhanced by its widespread representation, freed from suspicions of control by the trusts.

Ultimate success for the Chamber of Commerce depended on uniting businessmen around key issues of political economy to bring about desired government action. Its priorities coincided almost perfectly with those of the Wilson administration. Through compromise, the administration was determined to break the national stalemate in Progressivism and enact needed legislation on tariff, banking, and consolidation of economic power.

Because of division within its own ranks, the chamber maintained a relatively low profile on the heated struggle over the Underwood Tariff of 1913. After the passage of the act, the chamber led a drive for creating a permanent, nonpartisan tariff commission to balance the needs of adequate protection against the necessity of encouraging foreign trade. The proposal was both popular and familiar, having originated in the late nineteenth century. The chamber joined the industrial and financial elite represented in the National Tariff Commission League, and their combined strength produced a measure of success with the Rainey Act in 1916. Chamber leaders also worked hand-in-hand with the Commerce Department beginning in 1913 to strengthen its general services to business. Once World War I broke out, the chamber, along with most of the business community, moved from bitter opposition to grudging support for legislation that became the Wilson administration's 1916 Shipping Act.

The chamber took a much more direct and active role in banking reform. Wheeler mobilized the chamber's membership in organizing a middle-of-the-road business coalition that proved essential in securing passage of a modified and amended Glass-Owen Act. Wilson recognized the crucial role the chamber had played in the passage of the legislation by nominating Wheeler as a member of the Federal Reserve Board (FRB), an honor he turned down. The chamber was also gratified to have Congress incorporate into the Glass-Owen bill a provision for a Federal Advisory Council to the FRB, consisting of one member elected by the board of directors of each of the twelve Federal Reserve Banks. Whether the advisory council originated with the chamber, as its leaders claimed, is uncertain, but the chamber was the council's most persistent advocate and probably deserves credit for the creation of the adjunct body.

Though banking was obviously important to the chamber, the government's policy on economic consolidation had even higher priority.[4] Businessmen were anxious and uncertain as antitrust strategies shifted between the Theodore Roosevelt and Taft administrations, and the Supreme Court's "rule of reason" in 1911 promised flexibility. Given the strong emotions on the antitrust issue in the business community and from the public, Chamber of Commerce leaders faced a major challenge in working out a position that would satisfy most of the membership and still convey a sense of responsibility and sensitivity to the public, Congress, and the Wilson administration. The organization's future would stand or fall on this issue. The challenge was adroitly met.

In dealing with the vexatious problems of competition, cooperation, and the consolidation of economic power, the chamber's leadership maneuvered, indeed manipulated, with extreme skill. It used vague, innocuous, and diluted referenda in which only about one-third of its constituents voted to create the impression that a consensus existed over what became the Clayton Antitrust and Federal Trade Commission Acts.[5] Among the small- to medium-sized businesses that constituted most of the chamber's membership, consensus simply was not the case. At best, most businessmen were ambivalent about national regulatory agencies. Nonetheless, chamber spokesmen articulated positions that were more their own than a reflection of the rank and file's inchoate views.

According to chamber leaders, the Sherman Antitrust and Clayton Acts, if enforced at all, should be administered by or subject to the recommendations of the Interstate Commerce Commission (ICC), the FRB, and the Federal Trade Commission (FTC). Better yet, the entire question of trade restraints should be left to the FTC, which would be guided by concepts of reasonableness and elasticity instead of by the arbitrary and rigid antitrust statutes.

To indicate their cooperative attitude and to attempt to influence the operations of the commission, chamber leaders appointed a voluntary nine-man advisory committee to the FTC early in 1915. Wheeler, the chamber's chief strategist on antitrust policy, appropriately headed the committee, which, unlike the advisory council to the FRB, lacked the sanction of law; the FTC was under no obligation to meet or even to listen to the chamber's representatives. Nevertheless, the commission and the advisory committee, known as the Federal Trade Committee, between 1915 and 1917 developed a good working relationship through frequent meetings and exchanges of ideas on major issues. Although the chamber called for the FTC to demonstrate strength and independence in combating unfair competition and in protecting the public, it was pleased when the commission proved to be a pliable friend of business rather than a stern regulator.

By 1914–1915 the chamber had passed through an organizational phase and clearly established itself as the largest and most influential business association. Bridging the gap between their neo-Hamiltonian orientation and the neo-Jeffersonian or ambiguous views that characterized much of their membership, chamber officials guided the organization in a firm but conciliatory manner in the direction of a larger regulatory state. This process involved a measure of the leadership's manipulating the membership. These tactics and goals apparently were acceptable to most members since the chamber attracted more affiliates than it lost. With a larger regulatory role for the federal government a certainty, most businessmen seemed to accept the inevitable and agreed with the chamber leadership that businesses' interests were best protected by working with the government instead of by adopting a passive or an antagonistic attitude toward it. The organization's democratic form disguised the essentially elitist nature of its operations. During this period, the Chamber of Commerce was clearly much closer to the outlook of the National Civic Federation than to the National Association of Manufacturers.

Although not yet fully conceptualized or articulated by 1915, the chamber had already come close to proposing a government-business partnership for dealing with the complexities of a mature industrial system. Any such partnership would almost inevitably operate more to the benefit of the industrial and financial giants than to the small- to middle-range of businesses. The "moderately prosperous"[6] bankers, manufacturers, and merchants who led the Chamber of Commerce fell somewhere between the bulk of their constituents and the economic elite in America's business hierarchy. Whether they were fully aware of subordinating their constituents' interests to those of big business is problematic.[7]

Nevertheless, before World War I the Chamber of Commerce played a significant role in assisting business and government to adjust to new economic and political realities. Chamber-devised methods, such as voluntary advisory committees to the Federal Reserve Board and the Federal Trade Commission, created both precedents and patterns for the dollar-a-year-man system and commodity section–war service committee structure that were basic to mobilizing the American economy for World War I.

With the outbreak of World War I in August 1914, Chamber of Commerce leadership shifted from familiar issues to face the challenge of preparedness. Here the association displayed uncommon insight, innovation, and even daring. In September 1915 chamber leaders appointed a Committee on National Defense. Bascom Little, a Cleveland contractor, chaired the committee, which consisted of representatives from the army, navy, National Guard, and business. At its first meeting in January 1916, the committee divided itself into two subcommittees, one for dealing with the armed services and the other for economic matters. The committee and its subcommittees prepared referenda that were distributed to the membership in spring 1916 and that followed the standard practice of being vague and allowing the leadership wide latitude for interpretation. For the first time, half the membership voted. As usual, the constituency approved the leaders' work by wide margins.

Based on the referenda, the Chamber of Commerce supported strengthening the army and navy and emphasized a commitment to universal military training. Such training would prepare the nation for war and a "virile, substantial peace" as well as inculcating the virtues of discipline, morality, learning, health, and patriotism, which would improve the quality of youth and create a better work force, as had supposedly occurred in Germany. The chamber's dedication to UMT did not stop with military service. During time of war, it desired controls on the laboring population through a system of national service. Although chamber spokesmen used the concept of equality of sacrifice in justifying UMT and national service, and even alluded to instituting controls on management, the thrust of their proposals was aimed at the blue-collar, working population.[8]

Economic preparedness obviously interested the chamber more than military matters. Preparing the economy for war, the association argued, required new statutory institutions. A council of national defense, headed by a civilian director equal to the army chief of staff and the chief of naval operations—which would include prominent businessmen—would coordinate the armed services as well as advise the president and Congress on policies of national defense. A staff of industrial mobilization would direct industry. It would immediately survey industrial plants, determine production from firms during hostilities, negotiate educational orders to prepare selected plants for large-scale munitions production and to build up stockpiles, and arrange options for Washington to lease industrial facilities in the event of war at a price yielding a "living wage" to the owners but preventing wartime profiteering. Privately owned, not public, facilities would be the only reliable and economically feasible source of munitions production in the event of war, the chamber warned. Moreover, firms producing armaments for the Allies should not be allowed to wither without contracts during hostilities. They could serve as a skeletal structure capable of quickly expanding to meet the exigencies of war. As with the chamber's proposal for UMT, this recommendation drew heavily upon a perception of the German experience and attracted many neo-Hamiltonians and various efficiency devotees such as Howard E. Coffin.[9]

Some of the chamber's national defense proposals have to be read more as indices of the social attitudes of businessmen more than as serious propositions for mobilization. Nonetheless, they indicate that the association, with remarkable foresight, perceived that a mobilized economy would accelerate enormously the achievement of the chamber's peacetime goal of a government-business regulatory partnership. "Commerce and industry have become the handmaids of war," declared a March 1916 Chamber of Commerce editorial in its publication, the *Nation's Business.* Going one step further, the magazine announced in June that chamber mobilization plans "will make individual manufacturers and business men and the Government share equally in responsibility for the safety of the nation."[10]

Writing to the Du Ponts in December 1916, the chamber's Committee on National Defense chairman Little candidly set forth one of the motives behind the chamber's defense plans:

> The Chamber of Commerce of the United States has been keenly interested in the attempt to create an entirely new relationship between the Government of the United States and the industries of the United States. It is hoped that the atmosphere of confidence and cooperation which is beginning in this country, as shown by the Federal Trade Commission, the Federal Reserve Board and other points of contact which are now in existence, may be further developed, and this munitions question would seem to be the greatest opportunity to foster the new spirit.[11]

With American entry into the war a certainty, the chamber became more bold in its public pronouncements. In February 1917, the *Nation's Business* declared:

> Before the advent of the National Chamber, business thought and acted in small units. The change from that old order is almost startling. It is so complete that when the recent crisis in our international relations arose, there was one voice to speak for the business of the country, to

> tell where it stood. *The formulation of national policies is its new ideal.* To this end it has familiarized the individual with the meaning of such words as solidarity, cooperation, service, sacrifice.[12]

By combining policy formation with patriotism, the chamber acknowledged that winning an enhanced role for businessmen in government required refurbishing the tarnished image of industry and commerce.[13] The war, association leaders reiterated, provided an unequaled opportunity for regaining the momentum business had lost during the reform decades.[14] But the chamber clearly intended no regimentation of industry during mobilization. Instead, the business community would join hands with government in a largely cooperative and voluntary national effort.

In January 1917, after months of encouraging its members to work diligently for national defense measures, the chamber offered its services to Secretary of War Newton D. Baker. The chamber president explained that his organization could serve as a source of communication, information, and recruitment for mobilization agencies. Washington was not yet ready to accommodate the chamber's ambitions, however, and the federation had to begin its efforts for national defense at a less exalted level. At the request of the Wilson administration in February 1917, the Chamber of Commerce appointed voluntary and uncompensated committees from its membership to assist local army Quartermaster depots spread throughout the nation. Those committees performed varied and useful services connected with procurement, including advice on the price, quality, and design of products; aid in expanding the range and number of contractors; and, in some instances, assistance in financing when funds ran out and additional appropriations had not been made. As the number of local Quartermaster depots increased, so too did the chamber's committees. They continued to serve until early in 1918, when the War Department's supply services were reorganized.[15]

Except for assistance to local quartermasters, the chamber's direct influence on and participation in industrial preparedness activity was rather restricted until the United States entered the war. One reason for this circumscription was that the chamber's proposals for economic preparedness and mobilization were at best intelligent speculation about the requirements of modern warfare and hence had limited value. Since America lacked any knowledge or precedents involving economic planning for modern war, it had to begin not with an abstract, comprehensive blueprint but with circumscribed, tentative steps that could be expanded upon as experience and need grew. Mobilization structures had to evolve rather than suddenly be established.

## THE NAVAL CONSULTING BOARD

The creation of the Naval Consulting Board (NCB) in July 1915 proved to be the Wilson administration's first step toward harnessing the economy for World War I. With the administration proposing a vastly expanded navy as the first line of defense, and because less controversy surrounded the navy than the army, the Navy Department was well positioned to seek civilian assistance in dealing with the demands of industrialized warfare. Thomas A. Edison had earlier proposed that the United States could best defend itself by using a relatively small number of scientists and engineers to perfect new weapons of war and to survey the nation's industrial plants in anticipation of mass munitions production. Secretary of the Navy Josephus Daniels organized the board to achieve those rather vaguely conceived aims.

Actually, both Daniels and Edison viewed the latter's proposals as a means for preparedness that would limit expenditures and avoid war—a truly defensive, not an offensive, military posture. The two men devised the NCB, headed by Edison, whose folk-hero image and antiwar orientation could win wide support for the board and limit opposition to it. The board would consist of two representatives from the eleven leading engineering and scientific societies. It was intended to serve primarily as an agency for evaluating and developing inventions so that the navy could better cope with mechanized conflict. This aspect of the board's activities became the most enduring, though not the most important, contribution of the NCB during the World War I years.[16]

The most significant outcome of the Naval Consulting Board was a subdivision eventually labeled the Industrial Preparedness Committee (IPC). Daniels apparently did not anticipate the ambitious role that the IPC would assume in the economic preparedness movement but proved supportive when possible and never took any action to impede its efforts.

Discovering that neither the army nor the navy had adequate information about the nation's industrial potential, the committee from January through September 1916 relied on the five largest engineering societies to inventory some 30,000 plants to determine their capacity for war production. The societies organized at the state and in some instances the local level to carry out the task. The detailed work was done by voluntary effort and private financing (estimated at a cost of $250,000) under the direction of the then virtually unknown Walter S. Gifford, chief statistician for the American Telephone and Telegraph Company (ATT). John J. Carty, the company's chief engineer, president of the American Society of Electrical Engineers, and an army reserve officer, had arranged for ATT to donate Gifford's services. He was eager to serve. A preparedness enthusiast, Gifford had participated in Gen. Leonard Wood's Plattsburg training camp for businessmen and professionals.[17] But the prime mover behind the IPC was Howard E. Coffin, vice-president of the Hudson Motor Car Company in Detroit.

Coffin's preparedness efforts were merely an extension of his peacetime endeavors. In 1910, as president of the Society of Automobile Engineers (SAE), he, with the help of colleagues, had transformed the society and the auto industry by bringing about the standardization of specifications and materials. Coffin's accomplishments were part of the Progressive Era's larger, multifaceted Taylorite Movement, which looked to engineers as the new "industrial intelligentsia" that would resolve America's social conflict through detached, neutral leadership. Engineering, along with the other modern professions that emerged in the late nineteenth and early twentieth centuries, had become acceptable occupations for the children of the well-to-do and the socially aspiring. Coffin, Carty, and Gifford fit this pattern, as did other participants in the IPC. Most were well-connected, well-educated businessmen-engineers, or in the minds of many people, engineer-businessmen. The Industrial Preparedness Committee, therefore, reflected the enlightened elitism so prevalent in Progressive reform. There were close ties and a great deal of personal interchange between the Plattsburg Movement and the IPC. Both groups emphasized values of elitism, social control, efficiency, discipline, and nationalism.[18]

Rationalizing the productive process and promoting industrial organizations were continuing interests of the restless, imaginative, and even visionary Coffin. When war broke out in Europe, he almost immediately became absorbed with problems of economic preparedness. He foresaw the threats and possibilities of industrial mobilization as few of his contemporaries did.

"Twentieth century warfare," Coffin insisted, "demands that the blood of the soldier must be mingled with from three to five parts of the sweat of the man in the factories, mills, mines, and fields of the nation in arms."[19] World War I was "the greatest business proposition since time began." Although he and other industrialists were moved by "patriotism" along the lines of Progressive rhetoric, just as important was the coldly realistic desire to protect their own interests. Only industrialists and engineers were qualified to run a mobilized economy, Coffin averred. Under such leadership, war could be fought without untoward damage to the economy.[20]

Coffin seized the opportunity presented by the creation of the Naval Consulting Board to push it far beyond the rather limited role Daniels apparently had in mind. He persuaded the board members to divide themselves into numerous committees covering a wide range of activities relating to munitions. Guided only by general rules, each committee operated almost autonomously.

With such latitude, Coffin launched the industrial survey project, personally financing the central office in New York at a cost of over $30,000. Then he and his colleagues worked out the broader goals for the IPC. The industrial inventory would be completed and refined and plans drawn up to expand the nation's manufacturing base. Next, a program for educational orders would be initiated.[21] Finally, a system of labor control would be developed to prevent essential skilled labor from being drafted, enlisting, or leaving employment. (Whether such labor-control mechanisms would be antilabor in nature under Coffin's plans is uncertain. Coffin, like many individuals in the National Civic Federation, manifested an understanding of labor issues and a sympathy for the working population. But other members of the IPC, such as Grosvenor B. Clarkson, were at best condescending toward unions and workers.) These three goals together constituted the basis for a preparedness and mobilization scheme that would require an agency or agencies with authority to implement them.

Drawing on his experience with both the SAE and Hudson, Coffin perceived that the success of the industrial inventory and the general preparedness measures required a high-powered publicity campaign to educate business, public officials, and the nation's population. Clarkson was called upon to handle the drive. He had previously managed publicity for the automobile industry, had a background that included newspaper and political work, and at the time operated his own New York public relations firm. Using his extensive media contacts, Clarkson won the cooperation of the United and Associated Press Services, various prestigious magazines and newspapers, and other sources to launch an extensive news blitz on behalf of preparedness. The media campaign also included movies, billboard displays, speakers, and so forth. In general, the Industrial Preparedness Committee's educational and propaganda effort was the most elaborate, sustained, sophisticated, and effective of its kind to that time. It facilitated the work of the IPC and advanced the general cause of preparedness.[22]

Central to the IPC's proposals was the theme that the economic status quo could be preserved in the face of modern warfare only by careful preparation and planning. Time and information were essential for preparing industry for massive munitions output. To ensure balance and stability, all or most manufacturers had to be included in the mobilization effort. Coffin and Gifford were especially concerned that lesser industries and firms not be excluded and their interests protected. To allow war preparation and production to fall into the hands of the economic giants would threaten to rend the economy's intricate fabric and also immeasurably intensify the Progressive argument over political economy. Moreover, the munitions question was highly controversial; allegations about promised riches as a cause for war always threatened to prevent or inhibit preparedness and popularized the notion of government munitions production. Only a united business community backed by substantial public support could plan and implement a feasible scheme for mobilizing the economy. Without such support, no planning and certainly no implementation would be possible, and the nation could face economic and political chaos in the event of hostilities.

Public backing was essential for the larger goals of the IPC, but the business community was the committee's primary target. Business would be the principal mover in economic mobilization, and its cooperation was essential for the industrial survey, the first step in the IPC's program for economic preparedness. Even though the Chamber of Commerce referenda suggested wide support for economic preparedness, the Industrial Preparedness Committee inventory revealed that commitment was thin. Outside the Northeast, attitudes toward preparedness were at best lukewarm, and the people conducting and participating in the surveys often responded lethargically. The larger industries already producing for the Allies also lacked enthusiasm. They were already doing what Coffin and others were preparing to do and resented the War Department's refusal to assist them in initiating munitions production out of its desire to maintain a neutral stance.

The IPC inventoried thousands of factories, but this information proved of limited value because it did not indicate plant conversion potential and had been gathered in a vacuum. Until at least the general outlines of a war production program existed, no informed and intelligent survey could take place. The industrial inventory, therefore, proved to be simply a method for building support for preparedness and groping for the means to mobilize the economy instead of a concrete step in the direction of industrial preparedness.[23]

Despite its limitations, Coffin's Industrial Preparedness Committee still accomplished a considerable amount. It initiated and to some degree popularized the idea of economic preparedness and possible mobilization, devised plans for implementing the idea, and supervised activity for instituting the plans. Moreover, and of crucial significance, the committee and its parent body, the Naval Consulting Board, brought to the cause of economic mobilization America's new generation of professionals: engineers, statisticians, mathematicians, and scientists. No modern war could be fought without them. Additionally, since the IPC worked within the government structure, it spoke with more authority and attracted more attention than groups such as the Chamber of Commerce, which operated from a private base. With its elevated status, the IPC gave more concrete meaning to ideas the Chamber of Commerce had also advocated: voluntary service and private financing, which would be basic to the commodity section–war service committee and dollar-a-year-man systems, and the crucially important principle that a successful economic mobilization scheme had to have the support and involvement of all or most of the business community, not just the elite, and had to be free from charges of warmongering, war profiteering, and other unsavory practices of the munitions makers. More specifically, the Naval Consulting Board laid the foundations for the Council of National Defense–National Defense Advisory Commission and set the pattern of wide latitude that leaders within that structure would use to devise a workable scheme for mobilizing the economy for war.

## THE ARMY GENERAL STAFF

Activities of the army's General Staff complemented the work of the Industrial Preparedness Committee, gave greater force to the IPC's efforts, and produced the first legislation on industrial mobilization. This action was appropriate since the army, much more than the navy, would vastly expand in the event of hostilities.

Beginning in 1915 and continuing in 1916, the General Staff, working through the supply bureaus, attempted to study the requirements of preparedness and the probable impact of war on the army and the economy. But a lack of funds, personnel, and insight made the endeavor rather piecemeal and desultory. Nevertheless, the War College Division of the General Staff analyzed the available information and recommendations. In November 1915 it advised that the War Department support legislation granting the president, acting through his department heads, emergency authority to place mandatory orders and educational orders with qualified firms. The War College Division also called for granting the commander-in-chief the power to create a Board on Mobilization of Industries Essential for Military Preparedness, staffed by government officials and "skilled representatives of industries . . . selected by the industries concerned."

At the War Department's request, these provisions were included in slightly modified form as Section 120 (educational orders were provided for in Section 123) of the National Defense Act of June 3, 1916. The government's power was further strengthened by defining violation of these statutory provisions as criminal and giving the president the right to commandeer plants. The act also authorized the secretary of war to survey all plants capable of producing munitions with or without conversion. This provision resulted from Coffin's work with Secretary of War Baker, Secretary of the Navy Daniels, and Sen. George E. Chamberlain (D-OR), chairman of the Senate Military Affairs

Committee. The navy was granted similar powers, less the mobilization board, in the Naval Appropriations Act of 1916.[24]

Section 120 gave the IPC and the General Staff the authority, except for labor controls, that those agencies had claimed was essential for economic preparedness and mobilization. In fact, however, the statutory provisions did not have great importance. Limitations on funds, personnel, and will continued to curtail action by the services on procurement, with the result that nothing was done on plant inventories or educational orders.[25] The power to place compulsory orders, commandeer plants, and establish price controls would be useful during the war, but America's entry was still almost a year away. Potentially the most significant part of Section 120 granted the president the authority to create an undefined Board of Mobilization of Industries (details about its composition had been deleted). Wilson never made use of the vast power to create a legislatively sanctioned mobilization agency for the same reason that rendered the Chamber of Commerce's recommendations infeasible: Without information and experience, an effective mobilization or preparatory agency could not be created. Even if decisive action had been possible, an administration that moved with such caution in military and diplomatic matters was unlikely to proceed boldly in the area of economic preparedness. Thus, the efforts of the General Staff and the IPC on behalf of a legislative base for economic mobilization ended in a cul-de-sac. A more modest, indirect, and flexible approach was necessary.

The National Defense Act of 1916 had one immediate consequence for economic mobilization: The Kernan Board was created to try to resolve the conflict over private versus public munitions production. The industrial preparedness advocates predicated their plans on the assumption that private industry would supply most munitions in the event of war. Opponents of preparedness targeted the munitions makers in an effort to discredit the drive for an enlarged military, claiming that a government monopoly on munitions production would curtail warmongering motivated by the pursuit of profit. Almost to a man, military personnel opposed the proposition as impractical. It would be prohibitively expensive and would not provide the armed forces with the quantity of munitions needed for war, they maintained. Industry, of course, took a similar stand, especially since the armaments industry was threatened by the cutback in Allied orders as new factories in Europe came on line.

Section 121 of the National Defense Act of 1916 authorized a board of three military officers and two civilians to study the troublesome matter and make recommendations. They met in November and December 1916 under the direction of Col. Francis J. Kernan. Benedict Crowell—chairman of the Crowell and Little Construction Company of Cleveland, a partner of Bascom

Little, chairman of the Chamber of Commerce's Committee on National Defense, and later assistant secretary of war—and Pres. R. Goodwyn Rhett of the Chamber of Commerce served as the civilian members. The Kernan Board's study relied heavily on the work of the IPC. Coffin, Edward R. Stettinius, other individuals involved in industrial preparedness, and actual and potential munitions makers lent their advice.

After inspecting government arsenals and the private plants of some leading American manufacturers, the board, given the nature of its membership, predictably reported that it was "not desirable for the Government to undertake, unaided by private plants, to provide for its needs in arms, munitions, and equipment." In the event of war, the government should depend "largely upon private plants for war material." The board did not stop there. Reading like an editorial from the *Nation's Business,* the report praised businessmen for their patriotism in preparing for an emergency and assured the nation that industry would continue to cooperate in the future. On more immediate issues, the board recommended that plants producing munitions for the Allies not remain idle when orders were terminated and called for a comprehensive plan for industrial mobilization.[26]

Sections 120, 121, and 123 of the National Defense Act of 1916 had another advantage; they forced Congress for the first time to focus meaningfully on economic mobilization and to seek the advice of the armed services. The results were enlightening but not encouraging. Few members of Congress, either on the military affairs committees or in the body as a whole, demonstrated any grasp of or particular interest in this vital subject. Some, such as Senator Chamberlain and Congressmen Frank L. Greene (R-VT), John Q. Tilson (R-CT), and Julius Kahn (R-CA), demonstrated concern and insight on the issues but in a sporadic and disjointed way.

Generally, military witnesses were lamentably bad. Secretary of War Lindley M. Garrison and Assistant Secretary Henry Breckinridge all but pleaded ignorance about the matter. Chief of Ordnance William Crozier appeared to have some narrow awareness of modern military problems; Quartermaster General James B. Aleshire lacked even that. Only Gen. Leonard Wood manifested an appreciation of the wholly new conditions that modern warfare had created. Wood's ability to anticipate future needs and developments grew in part from a dedication to preparedness. Although supporting preparedness did not ensure insight into economic mobilization, such advocacy was characteristic of the people in and out of public life who displayed some grasp of the realities involved.

In contrast, the critics of preparedness, such as Jane Addams and Lillian Wald, did not mount effective arguments against armaments and war and tended to voice objections that sounded too much like clichés. This response was quite different from the later interwar years, when the opponents of war began to understand its institutional consequences and mounted a theoretically devastating critique of war. Before the advocates and opponents of warfare in the twentieth century could fully grasp its impact, they had to experience it firsthand.[27]

## THE COUNCIL OF NATIONAL DEFENSE–NATIONAL DEFENSE ADVISORY COMMISSION

Before the Kernan Board had reported, Congress in August 1916 created the Council of National Defense (CND). The council, unlike Article 120, proved to be the correct approach for beginning the mobilization process. Howard E. Coffin and the Industrial Preparedness Committee continued to have the greatest influence in the formation of the CND, but various other individuals and groups also played a significant role.

Bernard M. Baruch's influence was considerable because of his access to the highest officials in the Wilson administration, including the president. Baruch had been restively seeking a more exalted outlet for his talents after accumulating a fortune as a Wall Street speculator. With the Democratic victory in 1912, he began using his prestige and money to win favor within the Democratic party and the Wilson administration. His activity in the preparedness movement paved the way for a long and intermittently successful political career.

From late 1914, Baruch belonged to or supported most of the prominent preparedness organizations and activities. By mid-1915 he concentrated his energy and attention on economic mobilization. Like the Chamber of Commerce, Coffin, the IPC, and, with qualifications, the army General Staff, Baruch was convinced that only businessmen were qualified to direct industrial mobilization. In June he outlined his ideas to General Wood and in September personally presented a plan to Wilson. His scheme was general but centered on the notion that a commission of industrialists and financiers, in coordination with the military supply bureaus, could devise the means for harnessing the economy for war. He believed that the Naval Consulting Board could be expanded for that purpose. Throughout 1915 and 1916, Baruch pressed the president and Edward M. House to act on his proposal and to take other steps he believed were even more necessary to improve the administration's image and reputation among businessmen, thus giving his plan a sound basis. Characteristic of his future political role, Baruch had become the self-appointed adviser to the administration on economic preparedness and government-business relations; and self-promotion was never far from any advice he offered.[28]

Organized medicine and science also lent their voices and strength to the push for economic preparedness, which resulted in the creation of the Council of National Defense. In medicine, Franklin H. Martin and Franklin F. Simpson led the way. Both were prominent, respected medical doctors devoted to the growth, professionalization, and organization of their fields. Martin concluded years of organization in medicine in 1913 with the formation of the American College of Surgeons; Simpson played an even more active role in founding the American Gynecological Club. Witnessing firsthand the impact of war in Europe, the two doctors quickly grasped the role that medicine would play in modern warfare and the need for further organization to maximize its contribution. In April 1916 Martin and Simpson assembled representatives from the significant medical associations to form the Committee of American Physicians for Medical Preparedness, which began surveying the nation's medical personnel. It outlined to the president, Baker, Daniels, and other influential public officials, along with heads of private organizations like the Red Cross, the enormous range of activities and responsibilities the medical field could perform in preparation for and during war. Throughout 1916 and into 1917, Martin and Simpson, with the endorsement of Wilson, indefatigably lobbied for preparedness and medicine's place in it. Martin also joined forces with Surgeon General William C. Gorgas to help strengthen the Army Medical Corps.[29]

What Martin and Simpson were doing for medicine, the prominent astronomer George Ellery Hale was accomplishing in science. Hale displayed the same dedication to professionalism and organization as the two medical doctors. Before the war, he had devoted long hours and much energy to furthering the National Academy of Sciences. With the advent of World War I, Hale extended his reach. He headed the academy's preparedness committee and in mid-1916 led in organizing the National Research Council, a coordinating agency for applying the efforts of scientists to war preparation.[30]

The activities of businessmen, engineers, the military, medical doctors and scientists, and other professionals on behalf of economic preparedness had a growing impact. By 1916 the president, major officials within his administration, and some members of Congress were committed to the idea. Converting theory into practice then became the central concern. The Naval Consulting Board's activities suggested a possible approach, but the NCB was too narrowly based and had lacked congressional sanction for over a year; Section 120 of the National Defense Act was too general and ambitious. Something in between was necessary. The Council of National Defense emerged as a compromise. Hollis Godfrey precipitated the action that immediately led to the creation of the CND, and its foundation served to pull all or most preparedness advocates together into one organization.

From a patrician background with an education to match, Godfrey was an engineer who became a disciple of Frederick W. Taylor and his principles of scientific management. A career of applying Taylorite ideas to industry and local government led him in 1913 to the presidency of the Drexel Institute, a Philadelphia institution for industrial training and management education. Like many in the Taylor circle, Godfrey was nearly obsessed with the idea of management education as the high road to industrial efficiency. A trip to Europe in 1906 convinced him that war was imminent and that the ideals of efficiency through management would serve the nation in war as well as in peace. While in Britain, Godfrey was taken with the plan for a Council of Imperial Defence, which government officials were then considering. Such an agency resembled the Council of National Defense that had been proposed, considered, but rejected by Congress in 1910 and later. The idea of an American council varied according to the intent of various advocates, which included the Democratic party in its 1912 platform. Almost all adherents shared the belief that such an agency, consisting of representatives from the executive branch, Congress, and the armed forces, was essential for defining and implementing a national defense policy. Enthusiastic about such a council, Godfrey began defining for it a different responsibility: economic preparedness and mobilization.

The outbreak of war in Europe pushed Godfrey to move from vague speculation about economic preparedness to formulating more concrete proposals. He began enumerating the raw materials necessary for a wartime economy, locating their geographical sources, and drafting plans for an economic mobilization agency. He was assisted by Henry E. Crampton, a Columbia University zoologist and curator of the American Museum of Natural History. Godfrey also called upon the help of numerous businessmen and some faculty members from the Drexel Institute.

With his preliminary surveys under way and his ideas for a mobilization agency still in embryonic form, in May 1915 Godfrey began working with General Wood, the military official most knowledgeable about the subject. In doing so, Godfrey sought to give greater shape to his proposal for a government body to gather, classify, and act on information and statistics essential for a mobilized economy. After getting the approval of Secretary of Commerce William C. Redfield, Godfrey during summer 1915 presented his scheme to Secretary of War Garrison. The secretary was impressed, taking steps to expedite the material surveys, including providing the military data essential for conducting them.

Drafting legislation to put Godfrey's plan into effect was the next step. Crampton and Elihu Root, with the advice of such luminaries as Benjamin Strong, governor of the Federal Reserve Bank of New York, and Nicholas Murray Butler, president of Columbia University, sketched out a preliminary statutory outline. Godfrey maintained that it was at this stage that the idea emerged of a two-tiered Council of National Defense. The council would consist of cabinet members who would be aided by an advisory commission of experts from various sectors of the economy. The first draft of the bill was reworked and refined through consultation with members of Congress, including Senators John W. Weeks (R-MA) and Chamberlain and Congressmen James Hay (D-VA) and Rollin B. Sanford (R-NY). Edward M. House then reviewed the draft bill, suggesting some changes. Early in 1916 Godfrey finally had the opportunity to present his efforts and ideas to Wilson, who, Godfrey reports, enthusiastically endorsed his work. Numerous consultations with Baker, the new secretary of war, followed; he also responded favorably.

After almost a year of activity and pressure, the Wilson administration in March 1916 was ready to move forthrightly for preparedness. As a result, the final stage in writing legislation to create a Council of National Defense began. Starting with the proposals and drafted bills of Godfrey, Baruch, and their associates, Baker had Judge Advocate General Enoch H. Crowder begin writing a final statute. Writing and rewriting took place as ideas were exchanged within the administration. The secretaries of war and navy and the president played the leading roles in this process, and Godfrey, Coffin, Baruch, and other advocates were also involved.

Once the administration's bill was completed, another series of negotiations occurred between the executive and legislative branches. Various members of Congress had significant disagreements with the administration's plans. Ultimately, however, the administration had its way on every key point. Senator Chamberlain and Congressman Hay, chairmen of the Military Affairs Committees in the two houses, arranged for the final version of the bill to be incorporated as Section 2 of the Army Appropriations Act of August 1916. As with Sections 120 and 123 of the National Defense Act passed in June, there was little congressional scrutiny of the proposal through hearings or debate. The subject was a new one on which relatively few members of Congress had strong views or adequate information. For those who did, direct consultation and negotiation with the administration replaced the more traditional means of elucidating and resolving conflicts. Except for minor details, Section 2 was wholly a product of the administration, not of Congress.[31]

Section 2 created a Council of National Defense "for the coordination of industries and resources for the national security and welfare." On this council sat the secretaries of war, navy, interior, agriculture, commerce, and labor. The CND was to nominate and the president appoint a National Defense Advisory Commission (NDAC) consisting of seven civilian experts. The NDAC would assist the CND in investigating and advising the administration on issues of defense and emergency conditions, including rail, inland water, and seagoing transportation; army and navy mobilization; the economic potential for munitions production and the possibilities of expanding this potential; and

> the giving of information to producers and manufacturers as to the class of supplies needed by the military and other services of the Government, the requirements relating thereto, and the creation of relations which will render possible in time of need the immediate concentration and utilization of the resources of the Nation.

The commission members were to serve without compensation, except for incurred expenses. Subject to presidential approval, the CND would adopt rules governing its operations and the NDAC's. Section 2 specifically authorized the council to create subordinate bodies to help it fulfill its responsibilities. The NDAC and other subdivisions were to report periodically to the CND and the council to the president or the appropriate executive departments. The president would then make an annual report to Congress. Congress appropriated $200,000 to launch the Council of National Defense–National Defense Advisory Commission.[32]

The process of selecting the members of the NDAC began in June 1916 before Section 2 had become law. Secretary of War Baker, who would head the CND, directed the effort although Wilson was also involved. Coffin, Godfrey, Baruch, and others involved in preparedness attempted to influence the selections. Godfrey, in addition to surveying material and natural resources, had compiled rosters of personnel for economic mobilization purposes. The CND made its final recommendation in mid-September. With one key change, Wilson approved the work of his subordinates and the names were made public on October 11. To cover the areas of responsibility set out in Section 2, the appointments included Coffin, Godfrey, Baruch, and Martin; Daniel Willard, president of the Baltimore and Ohio Railroad; Julius Rosenwald, president of Sears, Roebuck, and Company; and Samuel Gompers, president of the American Federation of Labor (AFL). The medical community had lobbied hard and long to have a representative on the NDAC but so too had the scientists. For a time, a compromise solution was contemplated by having one representative cover both fields. Medicine ultimately won, principally because of the recognition that the National Academy of Sciences' National Research Council could act as a separate coordinating body on science for the federal government.

The Council of National Defense and the National Defense Advisory Commission did not meet jointly until December 1916. Shortly thereafter, Gifford and Clarkson from the Industrial Preparedness Committee were officially selected as the CND's director (comparable to an executive secretary) and secretary. Their duties also included overseeing the NDAC.[33]

The CND–NDAC structure was ingenious. It was both restricted and supple: restricted in that the council and commission could only investigate, advise, and recommend; supple in that their purview was defined so broadly that they encompassed all possible aspects of industrial mobilization. Congress had not prohibited the CND–NDAC from doing anything; this latitude virtually allowed it to do everything. Only the imagination of the participants restricted the range of their purview. In essence, with Section 2 the Wilson administration broadened the official base of the Naval Consulting Board to include five cabinet members in addition to the secretary of the navy and expanded the unofficial IPC base of Coffin and his engineers-scientists-businessmen with six more advisers, all now covered by statute and hence having greater prestige and influence, though not authority. The law also authorized initiatives of the sort that had given the IPC, through the Naval Consulting Board, its grand opening; the CND could create subordinate bodies that it believed essential. The place of Coffin, Gifford, and Clarkson on the NDAC indicated the importance of the IPC in the creation of the commission. But Godfrey, Martin, and Baruch had also been recognized for their ideas, talent, and contribution to the cause of industrial preparedness.

The CND–NDAC was also ingenious in that it embraced both continuity and change. It was continuous with the American past in that the War Department and its secretary, and to a lesser degree the Navy Department, remained the principal source of public authority over economic mobilization. Yet it recognized the changed nature of warfare by broadening the public mobilization base to include other departments and, more important, by integrating industrialists, financiers, and other businessmen into the exploratory industrial mobilization structure. Even the last innovation had roots in the past in that an approximation of it had been used to run the Union railroads and telegraphs during the Civil War.

Although the image of the IPC appeared clearly in the CND–NDAC, Coffin's committee had not emerged from or worked in a vacuum. The proposals of the industrial preparedness advocates were so similar that a cross-fertilization of ideas had taken place. Coffin, Godfrey, and their colleagues were in regular contact with one another. For example, William L. Saunders, chairman of the board of Ingersoll-Rand Company and president of the American Institute of Mining Engineers, who was vice-chairman and later chairman of the Naval Consulting Board and a member of the IPC, had also served on the Chamber of Commerce's Special Committee on Antitrust Legislation. Numerous other contacts existed among the chamber, the IPC, and various preparedness advocates. The military services also worked closely with Coffin and Godfrey and had some contact with most other individuals involved in economic preparedness.

Indeed, all or most individuals or groups working for industrial preparedness at least touched base with General Wood and had frequently supported military preparedness before turning to the economic field. A high percentage of the people involved in industrial preparedness had financially supported or participated in the Plattsburg Movement. Colonel House, because of his strategic position in the Wilson administration, was at least as popular and important as Wood to Godfrey, Baruch, and their counterparts. Baruch made it his business to know anyone of importance in his field of endeavor and therefore met and exchanged ideas with virtually all industrial preparedness enthusiasts. With such an elaborate interaction of persons and groups occurring, designating which ideas originated with whom is nearly impossible and not particularly important. Rather, what is important is that early in 1916 Secretary of War Baker, at Wilson's signal, began drawing most groups and individuals together to produce enabling legislation for the CND–NDAC.[34]

Despite some variations in their proposals, the leading economic preparedness advocates shared two critically important convictions: Private businessmen and professionals had to direct the mobilization of the economy, and the basic structure of the nation's economic system had to be preserved during this process. In their view, the government lacked the personnel, information, and experience necessary for economic mobilization, and success in the task was critical for maintaining the liberal capitalist system intact. Without the involvement of the people who owned and managed the economy, the nation's mature industrial system could be severely damaged, even paralyzed. With the exception of the army General Staff, the Wilson administration and Congress responded to the schemes of Coffin, Godfrey, Baruch et al. rather than initiating their own programs. The national government thus appeared to accept the two crucial propositions that underlay the businessmen's plans.[35]

The IPC had demonstrated in a crude way the means by which the government could tap the private economic talent for purposes of mobilization, which had been refined with Section 2. To use Coffin's imagery, the NDAC, through the CND, became the device for "clutching" (or connecting) a privately owned and operated economy with the national government for mobilization purposes. The CND–NDAC refinement of the IPC also saw the blooming of the "dollar-a-year-man" phenomenon. This development occurred despite statutes of 1905 and 1906 placing definite limitations on voluntary service in government. Once the casual duty of Coffin and his committee became more formalized with the CND–NDAC, caution and discretion dictated that at least nominal attention be paid to existing law.[36]

The formation of the CND and the NDAC involved vital issues of power between the public and private sectors and the executive and legislative branches of government. Wilson lacked detailed knowledge of the structure and operation of the nation's economic system, but he had an exquisite eye for the operations and nuances of power. Though willing to use representatives from business to prepare for possible war mobilization, he was not about to surrender public power to them. The NDAC—staffed by businessmen and professionals familiar with, but not from, the corporate elite—could go no further than the CND would allow, and the council was fully accountable to the president since it was made up of cabinet members. Until the mobilization system was reasonably well perfected in the early months of 1918, Wilson, although relying on his advisers, made the key decisions himself. Even after that time, he remained abreast of events and saw to it that the agencies for harnessing the economy remained generally answerable to him.

Wilson also guarded his authority in relation to Congress. In the negotiations over Section 2, some members of Congress wanted NDAC nominees to be subject to the advice and consent of the Senate. The Wilson administration insisted on complete freedom in choosing commission members in order to avoid the delays and inevitable wrangling that would occur and also to prevent excessively political appointments to a body that was essentially managerial. The president and his administration astutely perceived that they needed congressional sanction to initiate economic preparedness, but because the mobilization process involved so many unknowns and possible pitfalls, they wanted maximum latitude to maneuver in order to meet exigencies as they arose. Congress was willing to cooperate with the administration because preparedness of some sort was necessary, legislating it without background knowledge was virtually impossible, and Section 2 authorized little more than commissions of cabinet members and advisers who could, on paper, only recommend policies. For the conditions of the time, the tentativeness and fluidity of the CND–NDAC met the interests of most people concerning economic preparedness, including the Wilson administration, Congress, and the private sector of the economy.

Appointments to the NDAC had to be made with extreme care because the creation of the commission brought together two explosive issues: the political role of business, especially big business, in economic planning, and war preparedness. Passions surrounding both questions were calmed rather than inflamed by the choice of NDAC members. Though all except Gompers were identified with or supported preparedness, they were not rabid on the subject, and none could be charged with warmongering.

Godfrey, Martin, and Gompers, representing education, medicine, and labor, raised few hackles. Coffin, though a businessman, was sensitive to the interests of small business and was more visible as a member of the engineering profession than as an industrialist. Willard and Rosenwald already had reputations as business statesmen: Willard for inviting government to play a constructive role in railroad regulation and labor relations, and Rosenwald as an innovative and imaginative merchandiser and philanthropist. Moreover, neither was associated with heavy industry since they came from railroads and retailing.[37] Baruch was the one potential problem. His career of Wall Street speculation conjured up the worst images of abusive capitalism. But as a lone operator, Baruch had the advantage of being apart from the elite. Furthermore, soon after becoming seriously interested in industrial preparedness in late 1915, Baruch had divested himself of stock in corporations producing munitions to protect his name against charges of conflict of interest. Such charges were leveled against him several months after he joined the NDAC. A congressional investigation exonerated him, and he benefited from the widespread publicity.[38] With a membership that did not offend the public and could indeed be identified with its interests, the NDAC could test the limits of its influence without crippling debate over the motives of the men who staffed it.

The NDAC members had differing motivations. They were legitimately concerned about preparedness, a possible war, and the implications of those conditions for the economy. The group did not view war as either an unmitigated or a necessary evil. The industrial preparedness enthusiasts and planners were, almost without exception, neo-Hamiltonians. Organization, rationalization, standardization, efficiency management, planning, and, for some, regimentation were cherished ideals that became virtually inseparable from the idea of progress. The demands of modern warfare could further those goals and hence were not necessarily an experience to be avoided. Even though Germany was emerging as the enemy, the incredible precision and the machinelike operation of its economic mobilization system, whether real or imagined, were repeatedly cited with awe and envy as the model the nation must match in the event of war.[39] Within the larger New Nationalist ideal operated more limited group interests and personal ambitions. Coffin, Godfrey, and Martin saw preparedness and possible war as advancing the interests of their professions and furthering professionalization within them. As enlightened businessmen, the cooperative ideal and the quest for a government-business partnership appealed to Willard, Rosenwald, and Coffin. Baruch, more than anyone else on the NDAC, had his eye on his own advancement. His fine feel for power made him realize that key to any mobilization system was the nation's industrial elite.[40]

Baruch's grasp of the realities of power was instrumental in the way he came to overshadow the other members of the NDAC and of subsequent agencies. Economic mobilization for World War I laid bare the system of power that had evolved from the rapid industrialization of the late nineteenth century. The peacetime economy revolved around the giant, consolidated corporations in heavy industry.[41] Consequently, those corporations had to be the nucleus of a planned wartime economy. That reality was vaguely recognized from the outset but became increasingly formalized in the mobilization structure as the demands of warfare relentlessly grew. The engineers, efficiency experts, and other professionals did not, as in the ideal of Thorstein Veblen, Frederick W. Taylor, and other thinkers, direct the economic system; they were instead a subordinate group servicing corporate capitalism. War mobilization also exposed as a grandiose dream the Chamber of Commerce's aim of a unified business community forming a regulatory partnership with government. The acquiescence of the small- to middle-range of businesses was essential for economic mobilization, but they generally operated within a framework designed by the industrial and financial elite.

The NDAC's initial strength as an agency that could win, or at least not alienate, public support was also its major source of weakness; the economic elite was not represented. Indeed, for political reasons, the Wilson administration kept the business community at a distance from the initial planning for economic mobilization. (Aside from the offer of J. P. Morgan and Company's Export Department, however, big business did not rush forward to present its services to Washington.) Even the Chamber of Commerce's offer of assistance was rejected, leaving that federation to exercise its energy for industrial preparedness at the local level in conjunction with army quartermasters and in an advisory function such as on the Kernan Board. Wilson's political positioning aside, the NDAC had to devise means for integrating the business community, particularly the corporate elite, into its operations to achieve any measure of success. That effort would be a major challenge, testing the commission, the Wilson administration, Congress, business, and the nation.

Despite its haphazard structure and grave weaknesses, the Council of National Defense–National Defense Advisory Commission system was of the greatest significance. It signaled the beginning of a government-industry partnership in national security. The initiative had come from private sources, but from necessity the federal government, and especially the military services, appeared willing to go along. When announcing the appointment of the NDAC members, the president observed, "The organization of the Council [of National Defense] . . . opens up a new and direct channel of communication and cooperation between business and scientific men and all departments of the Government."[42] Coffin and his colleagues believed that the CND–NDAC would be a permanent agency whether or not the nation entered the war and had great ambitions for it. Writing to the Du Ponts in December 1916, Coffin observed:

> Private industry in all the varied lines of Governmental supply must be encouraged and not discouraged. It must be educated, organized, and trained for the national emergency service. A closer and more mutually satisfactory business relation must be established between the industrial lines and every Department of the Government, and the work of the newly created Council of National Defense must be directed to this end.
>
> The first meeting of the Council of National Defense and its Advisory Commission will be held in the office of the Secretary of War, December 6th, and within six months thereafter, it is our hope that we may lay the foundation for that closely knit structure, industrial, civil and military, which every thinking American has come to realize is vital to the future life of this country, in peace and in commerce, no less than in possible war.[43]

The CND–NDAC became agencies for war, not peace; and they served as the primary economic mobilization bodies until March 1918. Lack of experience explains in part the failure to create a better, more powerful system. No one was fully able to anticipate what was required, so the nation had to go through the pragmatic process of working out solutions as problems arose. More important, the desire to avoid permanent political and economic change during the war was widespread. It was hoped that makeshift organizations like the council and the commission, without clearly defined authority and headed by existing departmental secretaries, would be sufficient to meet war needs. When hostilities ceased, they could easily be disbanded.[44]

Moreover, vital issues of political economy shaped the scheme for industrial mobilization. Divisions among Progressives were still great over the proper role of government in the economy, and any attempt to set up new, powerful mobilization machinery could end in paralyzing debate in Congress and the nation.

Thus, the president and Congress consistently avoided facing issues of economic mobilization whenever possible. Not until the mobilization program was on the verge of collapse during winter 1917–1918 did Wilson strengthen the industrial mobilization apparatus. Even then, only the minimal changes essential to the continued operation of the economy were made.

# 8
# THE NATIONAL DEFENSE ADVISORY COMMISSION, FEBRUARY–JULY 1917

The National Defense Advisory Commission began operating in earnest in February 1917. During the next four months the commissioners struggled with methods for mobilizing the economy. They first devised ways to include business representatives in the NDAC structure and then experimented with directing the economy through controls involving requirements, clearance, priority, and pricing.

The commission's progress was constantly obstructed by the military services and especially by the army. With wartime demands swamping the service's supply system, the War Department worried that the NDAC would try to take over military economic functions. Army supply bureaus welcomed and benefited from NDAC assistance with procurement while insisting that the commission's activity altered nothing legally. The department used its statutory authority over supply and Secretary Baker's position as chairman of the Council of National Defense both to protect army prerogatives and to thwart the NDAC from gaining more than advisory powers.

These circumstances produced chaotic conditions that highlighted decision-making in the Wilson administration. President Wilson and Baker—his chief adviser on economic mobilization—resisted more effective mobilization methods because they were uncertain about what had to be done and they wanted to minimize the institutional impact of warfare. More important, basic matters of political economy were involved. Better civilian mobilization agencies meant strengthening both the federal government and the corporate structure, trends that Wilson and Baker opposed, particularly where private economic power was involved. Economic mobilization, therefore, proceeded by drift.

The turmoil involved in mobilizing the economy also accentuated leadership potential within the NDAC. Bernard M. Baruch emerged as the outstanding member of the commission. Advised by industrial experts and backed by the corporate elite whom he had mobilized for war production, Baruch determined quite early the structures and policies necessary for successfully harnessing the economy. As drift in the economic mobilization program produced inevitable problems, President Wilson increasingly turned to Baruch for guidance in handling the crises.

## THE NDAC IN OPERATION

Secretary of War Baker convened the first joint meeting of the Council of National Defense and the National Defense Advisory Commission on December 6, 1916, after the presidential election. The meeting was inconclusive, and for two months thereafter the agencies met separately and together only infrequently, with few accomplishments and little focus. Though some members of the council and commission viewed their responsibilities in terms of long-range planning, most acted on the assumption that they were intended to prepare for possible war. The ambiguities of the mission and structure of the CND–NDAC inhibited definite direction and action. The break in relations with Germany on February 3, 1917, spurred the council and commission into full action, however. Continuous meetings to treat with the emergency conditions began, and in early March Daniel Willard was elected permanent chairman of the NDAC.[1]

Once they began full operations, the CND and NDAC were quickly transformed from basically advisory bodies to administrative agencies for mobilizing the economy. Two critically important characteristics emerged during that process and remained constant throughout the CND–NDAC's most active and influential period. First, the commission, like the Industrial Preparedness Committee before it, took the lead in working out the means for mobilizing the economy; the council played the rather passive role of approving and supporting or disapproving and resisting the NDAC's proposals and recommendations.[2] Second, the commissioners chose to create the most efficient organization possible with the least disturbance to the economic status quo. Thus the federal government would accept, use, and adjust itself to the patterns and configurations of power in the private sector of the economy.

To mobilize the economy with minimum disruption, the NDAC first divided itself into semiautonomous committees (though called committees, they actually consisted of a commissioner and his staff) corresponding to the natural subdivisions of the economy. Willard took charge of transportation and communication; Howard E. Coffin, munitions and manufacturing;

Bernard M. Baruch, raw materials, minerals, and metals; Julius Rosenwald, general military supplies like clothing, shoes, and hardware; Hollis Godfrey, engineering and education; Samuel Gompers, labor; and Franklin H. Martin, medicine. The commissioners then faced the crucial issue of how to incorporate business spokesmen into their structure. Almost immediately, a low-key but extremely critical struggle ensued between CND–NDAC director Walter S. Gifford and Baruch over the method for selecting the businessmen.

Gifford favored business participation through broadly based democratic procedures.[3] National trade associations would choose an authentically representative advisory committee to serve under the commissioner with responsibility for its industry. For unorganized industries and business sectors, the CND–NDAC would facilitate organization. To accomplish his purpose, Gifford began working with the Department of Commerce and the U.S. Chamber of Commerce to gather data on existing business associations and methods for expanding their numbers. Gifford's goals were close to the chamber's emphasis on the total business community, sensitivity toward small- to medium-sized business, rationalizing industrial and commercial life, and improving business ethics. His aims also reflected some of the ideals of the IPC. Coffin, Godfrey, and Rosenwald supported Gifford's approach, perhaps in part because none of them came from oligopolistic heavy industry.

Baruch's elitism contrasted sharply to Gifford's business democracy. Baruch wanted the commissioners themselves to select the most prominent man or men in the various lines of business to advise and assist them. Such leaders, or their representatives, had or could get the information necessary for mobilization and could facilitate and expedite action when essential. Baruch's approach was based more on experience and reality than on an aspiration or ideal. His Wall Street experience with companies producing steel, copper, tungsten, and rubber had brought him into contact with the economy's high and mighty and had given him keen insight into how the economic system functioned. Since 1915 he had consistently held to the notion that any mobilization program had to be based on the giant corporations in heavy industry. With raw materials, minerals, and metals as his bailiwick, he was in an ideal position to put his convictions into practice. Dealing with oligopolistic industries with few firms that maintained close contacts facilitated Baruch's ability to tap the top men to speak for the sector. Organizing war production in such industries was also relatively easy, particularly since most firms sold one or a small line of semifinished products or raw materials. By comparison, coordinating companies that manufactured finished goods presented much greater obstacles, making the organizational tasks of Rosenwald, Coffin, and Martin more difficult than Baruch's.

The CND–NDAC ultimately approved the approaches of both Gifford and Baruch and hence never really selected between the two. In December 1916 the agencies granted Baruch permission to begin implementing his ideas, then gave more formal sanction to Gifford's proposal on February 12, 1917, without rescinding their earlier action. As a result, the various commissioners were left to decide for themselves which method to employ. Of course, the structure of power and the degree of market concentration in the industry to be organized played an important role in determining which scheme was used. Reality placed severe restrictions on Gifford's method. Trade associations were relatively few in number and frequently too young, small, and unsophisticated to provide a basis for authentic national representation. Organizing new associations in a matter of months outside the oligopolistic industries was virtually impossible, since rivalry and suspicion were rife. Creating business associations during peacetime had always been tedious and frustrating work. With the hectic pressures surrounding America's entry into World War I, neither the government, business, nor business groups like the Chamber of Commerce were in a position to persuade new organizations or unified industries to select the democratic spokesmen that Gifford and his colleagues desired. By necessity, the various commissioners had to adopt the most expedient methods possible.

Two important consequences grew from the industrial representation system. First, it helped to cause and then to reinforce the decentralization that characterized the NDAC almost from the outset. Each of the commissioners went his own way, relying only on casual relations with the others and lacking meaningful direction or even complete information from the CND, the director and his staff, or the NDAC as a whole. The advisory agencies had become executive mobilization bodies without proper authorization; they operated in a loose-jointed fashion with few if any checks against abuse and could not even explain their activities effectively to other executive departments, Congress, or the public. Those conditions inevitably led to severe criticism. Furthermore, such questionable operations badly weakened the mobilization process. Second, industrial representation based on prestige, power, prominence, or the judgment or favoritism of a commissioner left many firms in most industries without a voice in the mobilization scheme. Resentment among the excluded business elements was bound to grow. A divided, suspicious, and quarreling business community inevitably weakened, even crippled, efforts at harnessing the economy for war. If the mobilization program were to work effectively, the giant corporations would have to serve as the foundation for mobilization but only within a setup giving most of business at least a sense of representation.

In effect, the CND–NDAC needed a method of industrial representation that incorporated the approaches of both Baruch and Gifford. Baruch was much more astute than Gifford about locating and exploiting sources of private power for industrial mobilization. But Gifford was much more attuned to the ultimate organizational pattern that a mobilized economy would necessitate. He also knew the forms of industrial representation within mobilization agencies that would be essential for uniting, instead of dividing, business and for winning at least the acceptance if not the total confidence of the Wilson administration, Congress, and the general public. Before the end of 1917, the Baruch and Gifford systems merged, but only after the methods of the former provoked intense debate and agitation.

By February 1917 the NDAC members had begun organizing what came to be called cooperative committees, usually consisting of three or more representatives from the industries, trades, or organizations in a commissioner's area of specialization. At first, the cooperative committees served as sources of information on production capacity, expansion and conversion potential, plant location, raw materials, and transportation requirements, the work force and the probable effects of war upon it, and other data essential for mobilizing the economy for war. After the nation entered hostilities in April, the cooperative committees, as affiliates of the CND–NDAC, acted as vital parts of the nation's de facto economic mobilization structure.[4]

The February 12, 1917, decision to allow the various commissioners to operate separately and to organize cooperative committees generated a great deal of hectic, often inchoate activity. Since the cabinet members on the CND were overloaded with departmental activities, the council continued to play a passive role. As heads of the vastly expanding military departments, Secretary of War Baker and Secretary of the Navy Daniels held dominant positions and wielded enormous power. Of the two, Baker was the more important since the army grew much more rapidly and became much larger than the navy. The secretary of war, as chair of the CND, became and remained Wilson's chief adviser on industrial mobilization until March 1918. Both Baker and Daniels, however, used the CND to protect their departments' prerogatives against encroachments from the NDAC and other wartime mobilization bodies rather than to build the council into a mobilization agency.

The tentative and uncertain nature of the CND–NDAC meant that its work would be only the first phase in mobilizing the economy for war. Those institutions would ultimately be replaced by ones with more authority and a better structure. In the meantime, given the CND's passive role, the NDAC largely determined how the mobilization scheme ran and what its future shape would be.

In retrospect, the principal reality molding the operations of the NDAC and successor agencies was the ability of the various commissioners to combine private and public power for the purpose of harnessing the economy. Although talent, ambition, and foresight played a significant role in the success of the various commissioners, the most important factor was the base of power they had in the private sector of the economy. The NDAC, in effect, became a testing ground for leadership under new and intensely demanding circumstances.[5] Only Baruch survived the brutal shakedown.

The other NDAC executives lost their footing for a number of reasons. Most members either lacked support outside the commission or spoke for secondary power groups, others were unable to navigate the transition from planning to implementing economic mobilization, and a few lacked the drive or the know-how for getting to the top. Baruch had boundless ambition and ability to match it. He used those qualities to build a base of support among the corporate elite and within the Wilson administration that led to the chairmanship of the War Industries Board.

Walter S. Gifford never became a powerhouse in the CND–NDAC. Since the various commissioners always acted independently, Gifford's efforts to establish a semblance of coordination in the dual agency proved futile. The centrifugal force of each commissioner operating on his own prevented cohesion. Moreover, and more important, Gifford had no base of power within the economy. Although he helped devise the means for economic rationalization for war, he never controlled the rationalizing process itself. When the CND–NDAC was finally pushed to the sidelines in March 1918, Gifford lost even the appearance of exercising power.[6]

Among the NDAC commissioners, Hollis Godfrey's fall was the fastest and most complete. He had been elected temporary chairman of the commission in December 1916, only to be replaced by Willard in March after it became apparent that Godfrey could not rise above his penchant for theory, information, and long-range planning to focus on immediate problems. Even if Godfrey had manifested sterling leadership qualities, however, he would never have gone far. As the commissioner in charge of engineering and education, he headed sectors of the economy that were vital but not powerful. Godfrey organized six cooperative committees, made up mostly of engineers, officers of engineering societies, representatives of small- to medium-sized businesses, university presidents, professors, and other educators. Those committees did some significant work, such as recruiting engineers for the military, but their efforts became increasingly peripheral.[7]

Howard E. Coffin, one of the most important prewar preparedness figures, faltered once actual mobilization began. He appeared stuck in the mindset of the Industrial Preparedness Committee and constantly pressed the NDAC to continue the work the IPC had started rather than squarely facing the exigencies of war. As commissioner for munitions and manufacturing, he did organize cooperative committees on gas and electricity and automobile transportation as well as a committee from the membership of the National Industrial Conference Board, which included some of the nation's largest corporations. But this was the smallest number of committees organized by a commissioner, and Coffin allowed them to languish. His most significant contribution was the creation of new agencies for standardizing munitions and facilitating their procurement. Once they began operation, however, Coffin neglected his duties on those bodies. After April 1917 he concentrated almost exclusively on aircraft production—a botched effort leading to intense dispute and recrimination. Essentially, Coffin faced almost insuperable odds. Organizing the entire manufacturing sector was beyond the grasp of one man. Munitions manufacturing, involving some of the largest corporations, was more manageable but also difficult and frustrating. Military requirements were unknown, existing capacity was limited, and new facilities would cease production when the fighting stopped, conditions that acted as a disincentive to investment. Though Coffin's power base in the economy—automobiles—was better than Godfrey's, that sector was still amorphous and embryonic. Coffin thus floundered about, unable to prevail as a leader of industrial mobilization.[8]

Franklin H. Martin and Samuel Gompers remained active and useful in their fields, but they dealt with activities and organizations that remained subordinate within the mobilized economy. Martin was exceptionally enterprising, organizing sixty-three cooperative committees and subcommittees (more than any other commissioner) in medicine, sanitation, public health, research, education, and supplies and equipment. He and his committees were useful to civilians and especially to the military. Nonetheless, though medicine was indispensable to warfare, it was not central to industrial mobilization. Consequently, Martin remained active throughout the war without having any great influence on the general problems of economic mobilization.[9]

Gompers had quite an active role in industrial mobilization throughout the war years. He organized some thirty-two bodies on mediation, wages and hours, the employment of women, health conditions, and so forth. On these committees sat numerous labor officials, prominent industrialists, public officials, academics, and public-spirited citizens. Labor, however, was essentially limited to narrow issues of manpower and industrial relations. Even there, when new agencies were created, the public and management had a role, which drew power away from the labor representatives. Gompers, other labor leaders, and some of the committees managed to have labor questions considered in most decisions (including wages, hours, and working conditions) and were able to protect and even advance trade-union interests (particularly the right to organize and bargain collectively). The price of these gains was surrendering a free hand to management and government to work out in the CND–NDAC and successor agencies the means for mobilizing the economy largely free of labor influence.[10]

Julius Rosenwald was also elbowed aside in the scramble for war mobilization. His Committee on Supplies was probably the most active in the NDAC. From February to August 1917 it gave massive and critically important assistance to the army's Quartermaster Corps in purchasing clothing, shoes, leather goods, food, and so forth. Rosenwald's section worked through seven prestigious and effective cooperative committees that included officers of the National Associations of Cotton and Wool Manufacturers, the president of Libby, McNeil and Libby, the secretary of the H. J. Heinz Company, and a representative from the Simmons Hardware Company. After months of hectic and useful service, however, the power of Rosenwald's committee began to erode. It ultimately lost control of food to Herbert Hoover's Food Administration, created in August 1917 under the Lever Act. When the War Department began reorganizing its supply system in December 1917, Rosenwald's staff and cooperative committees were partially absorbed by the Quartermaster Corps.

By March 1918 Rosenwald sat on the NDAC but had little to do. Actually, he had virtually retired months before, turning his duties over to his chief assistant, Charles Eisenman, a retired Cleveland textile manufacturer. Eisenman and the Committee on Supplies came under constant attack for alleged favoritism and corruption, which resulted in several congressional investigations. Although the controversy sullied the committee and its activities, Rosenwald and his assistants were never in a position of dominance within the mobilization scheme because they dealt with industries producing consumer goods. Within that sector, there were not many large corporations; it was mostly made up of smaller and highly competitive firms that were not at the center of the economic system.[11]

Daniel Willard rose to the top of the economic mobilization structure but did not remain there. He appears to have been the least self-serving individual on the NDAC; he also joined the commission as its most prominent member, having gained a reputation as a business statesman. Those qualities and his general business acumen led to his selection as permanent chairman of the NDAC in March 1917, a position he held until the conclusion of hostilities.

Willard had responsibility for transportation and communication and began organizing the railroads for emergency conditions early in 1917 around a cooperative committee based on the American Railway Association. Subsidiary committees were created to match the nation's six military districts. Eighteen cooperative committees in all existed. In addition to the rail boards, they covered the telephone and telegraph industries as well as railroad service and production. With little difficulty, Willard gained the cooperation of the railroad industry in order to operate the various lines virtually as a continental system. Nonetheless, a disjointed industrial mobilization program, the financial distress of the railroads, and the severe winter of 1917–1918 dislocated the railway system so badly that the federal government had to take it over in December 1917.

Secretary of the Treasury William G. McAdoo, who was appointed director-general of the U.S. Railroad Administration, basically used the system Willard had developed to administer the railroads. Indeed, without the unified structure established by Willard, temporary nationalization would have been difficult if not impossible. Nevertheless, Willard lost his base of power. From the outset, the railroads were not the best foundation from which to operate. Though critically important to all aspects of industrial mobilization, they were the arteries rather than the heart of the economic system. Further, Willard allowed himself to be drafted as chairman of the crippled War Industries Board in late 1917, which detracted from his image as a leader. Like Gifford, he could not use his position of leadership in the decentralized NDAC to establish broad-scale control of industrial mobilization. Ambition might have led Willard to overcome the liabilities he faced as a war mobilizer, but that he did not have. He was committed to the Baltimore and Ohio Railroad, which he headed, and he was philosophically skeptical about public life, into which he had been drafted. Consequently, like almost all the NDAC commissioners, he did not survive the testing period of industrial mobilization.[12]

Baruch emerged supreme in the mobilization scheme, becoming chairman of the reorganized WIB in March 1918. His base of strength rested with the heavy industries, from which he organized some thirty-five cooperative committees and subcommittees as commissioner for raw materials, minerals, and metals. These industries were central to the operation of the economy and were organized around the modern corporation. Generally, these modern corporations were capital-, energy-, and manager-intensive; they were also integrated, multiunit, and multifunctional in that they carried out both mass production and mass distribution and owned or controlled their sources of supply. In all or most of these firms, to use Alfred D. Chandler, Jr.'s phrasing, the invisible hand of the marketplace had given way to the visible hand of managers in pricing, production, and marketing.

Almost all such companies operated in oligopolistic industries with traditional competition eliminated. Of the 278 largest industrial corporations in

1917, which accounted for more than one-quarter of the nation's net manufacturing, Baruch's NDAC area of specialty—mining, chemicals, petroleum, coal, rubber products, and primary metals—included 120, or 43 percent. In primary metals alone, which involved more huge enterprises than any other industry, nineteen of thirty-nine firms were directly represented on various cooperative committees Baruch helped to create. Baruch's NDAC position placed him squarely at the center of America's dynamic economy. Not only was he dealing with nearly half of the nation's largest corporations, but most of those companies, to quote Chandler, were in industries "central to the growth and well-being of the economy."[13]

Baruch organized by far the most impressive and powerful cooperative committees in the NDAC.[14] The staffing of those committees reads like a who's who of corporate America and included almost 170 prominent industrialists. Elbert H. Gary, chairman of the board of the U.S. Steel Corporation and president of the American Iron and Steel Institute, headed the Cooperative Committee on Steel and Steel Products and eleven subcommittees. For aluminum there was a committee chaired by Arthur V. Davis, president of the Aluminum Company of America; for brass, Charles F. Brooker, president of the American Brass Company; for copper, John D. Ryan, president of the Anaconda Copper Company; for nickel, Ambrose Monell, president of the International Nickel Company; for oil, Alfred C. Bedford, president of Standard Oil Company of New Jersey; for rubber, H. Stuart Hotchkiss, president of the General Rubber Company; and for zinc, Edgar Palmer, president of the New Jersey Zinc Company. In the competitive industries like lumber, Baruch often relied on trade association officials such as Robert H. Downman, president of the National Lumber Manufacturers' Association. Where trade associations were nonexistent or weak, Baruch turned to the outstanding businessmen in the trade. Gradually and carefully, he expanded his committee structure until it incorporated industries in raw materials, metals, chemicals, and so forth.

Baruch's strength depended not only on dealing with many of America's most powerful corporations but also on mastering a method to use them for mobilization purposes. No one person could conceivably have the information and expertise essential for directing such an array of industries. To make up for his deficiencies, Baruch, more than any other NDAC commissioner, gathered about him a collection of knowledgeable assistants. The first was Leland L. Summers, a chemical engineer-consultant who had become an expert on artillery and explosives through European travel and study before World War I. In 1915 he joined the J. P. Morgan and Company Export Department as head of the heavy gun and shell purchasing section.

Summers had an unusual grasp of the economic consequences of modern warfare and was able to anticipate the kind of economic mobilization the nation would require should it enter the war. Baruch had begun tapping Summers's knowledge and insight in November 1916, shortly after his appointment to the NDAC. Several months later he lured Summers away from Edward R. Stettinius's Export Department and brought him on to his own staff. Baruch thus gained the services of an extraordinarily gifted individual and benefited from the private mobilization experience of J. P. Morgan without the opprobrium the latter name elicited.[15]

Summers ultimately was only one of the many specialists with whom Baruch surrounded himself to make up for his lack of information and experience in industry, chemicals, and engineering as they related to war. Other experts included Eugene Meyer, Jr., from the Guggenheim empire; Alexander Legge, vice-president and general manager of the International Harvester Company; and George N. Peek, vice-president of John Deere and Company. These individuals were part of the managerial revolution basic to the rise of modern corporate America.

Drawing upon his chief lieutenants and his cooperative committees, Baruch began determining how economic controls should be exercised in a mobilized economy and started experimenting with them or at least advocating their adoption. By the time the nation had been at war for almost three months, Baruch and his aides had generally determined what a mobilization agency must do, how it should be organized, and what powers it must have. The ultimate form of the War Industries Board thus took shape in Baruch's mind early on; he then worked steadily for the implementation of his ideas.

In doing so, he never lost control of the cooperative committees that were his source of power as Rosenwald and Willard had done; he grew as an executive instead of stagnating or drifting as Godfrey and Coffin had done; and, unlike Martin and Gompers, he headed a vital, indeed the most powerful, sector of the economy. And unlike most other commissioners, Baruch had no company, industry, or organization of his own to distract him from his goals. Moreover, in contrast to Willard, he was intensely ambitious and would not allow himself to be used in ways that would weaken his grasp or tarnish his image.

A quiet ruthlessness and steady concentration guided Baruch's every effort. Once he had fully established himself with the leaders of the heavy industries, he was virtually impossible to waylay, for no one could predict that another leader would emerge who could match his success in organizing and controlling the sinews of the economy. Although Baruch had many rivals and enemies within the economy and the Wilson administration, he also had strong supporters (including William G. McAdoo) who proved to be invaluable allies on Baruch's behalf, notably with the president. Moreover, Baruch had begun to establish a relatively open door to the White House himself and had gained Wilson's confidence and respect as an industrial mobilization leader. The fact that he had become a loyal Democrat and made generous donations to the party strengthened his position considerably. Not of the industrial and financial elite but closely in touch with it, possessing a shrewd political eye, demonstrating the capacity to master the complexities of economic mobilization, and displaying an uncanny ability for timing, Baruch had emerged by mid-1917 as one of the dominant mobilization figures. His star would continue to rise as those of his counterparts fell or faded.

Individuals, institutions, and power from the private and public sectors mixed in a complicated and intricate way in the NDAC's cooperative committees, a feature that was characteristic of the entire industrial mobilization process during World War I. To the degree that a commissioner gained the cooperation of the industries in his area of responsibility and avoided having his duties absorbed in whole or part by existing governmental bodies, he succeeded in creating a new mobilization agency that was neither public nor private but a combination of the two. The government lacked the experience, the information, and the personnel to build a mobilization system on its own. Private industry had those elements, but it often lacked the unity necessary to apply them effectively, a firm legal base for achieving unity, and the authority to apply the various controls needed to harness the economy. The NDAC, in combination with the cooperative committees, was a curious public-private amalgam. With only advisory powers, the NDAC had to rely on industry's voluntary cooperation; if industry did cooperate, the combined efforts of the commissioner and industry still had only advisory status. The committees had no legal base of authority for the mobilization functions they began to perform. Even the trappings of power and prestige were absent. The commissioners and their cooperative committees served for a dollar a year or without compensation (nonsalaried personnel authorized by the 1916 legislation creating the CND–NDAC) and, because of inadequate funding for the CND, often paid their own expenses, including those for clerical help and even office space.

Organizing cooperative committees was neither simple nor neat and orderly. Martin and Gompers apparently had the easiest time of it because they operated with effective private organizations and in sectors where the power considerations were, realistically, not so great.[16] Because Godfrey and Coffin did little in organizing or directing cooperative committees, they faced few of the tensions that such committees generated.

Rosenwald and his chief assistant Eisenman, as directors of the Committee on Supplies, encountered severe strains in dealing with the highly competitive textile, shoe, and leather industries. Numerous producers were suspicious of one another and of government authority and harbored resentments stemming from past tribulations and often alleged corruption in military contracting. Organizing these industries required endless patience. Usually Rosenwald and his associates would pick a talented industrial executive who was known for his ability to work with others. That individual would then seek the assistance of trade associations, prominent members of the trade who carried weight with their fellow businessmen, or both. A long process of skillful negotiations and careful persuasion, stretching out as long as six months and sometimes a year, then ensued in the endeavor to achieve some semblance of unity within the industry in order to regulate it and to make it capable of dealing with the government on a centralized basis.[17]

Willard had an easier task, since he dealt with the oligopolistic or monopolistic railroad and communication industries, which already had some effective trade associations and rather naturally lent themselves to coordination and unity.[18] For Baruch, organizing highly concentrated industries like steel, copper, and aluminum proved relatively easy once the leading corporations took an interest. These industries were already imbued with the cooperative ethic and most had been involved with the House of Morgan's Export Department in supplying the Allies. Hence, they had some notion about the imperatives of the economics of warfare and were inclined toward cooperative committee structures. In the less concentrated industries like zinc, lead, and especially lumber, Baruch encountered many of the same difficulties as Rosenwald.[19] Cooperative committee patterns, in short, were as varied as the economy itself.[20]

Simply organizing a cooperative committee did not ensure successful mobilization of an industry. The NDAC commissioners and cooperative committee leaders often had their tasks complicated manyfold by the lack of motivation from industry and the attitudes and actions of other government agencies. Many if not most firms seemed uninterested in government contracts and therefore were not easily persuaded of the need for organization. The firms that did want contracts often preferred to rely on market conditions and their own bargaining power rather than on industrial organization to achieve their goal. In the months just before and after the United States entered World War I, flush economic conditions and the absence of highly visible shortages and other manifestations of a wartime situation took away the sense of urgency necessary for business in general to see the need for and fully participate in the drive for such organizations as the cooperative committees.

Where the spirit of cooperation did exist, the law and law enforcement agencies tended to dampen it. Unless exempted, the cooperative committees were in violation of the antitrust laws even though they had been formed at the urging of government agencies. Soon after Willard began organizing the railroad industry in early 1917, the attorney general repeatedly warned that his committees could not violate the letter or spirit of the antitrust laws.[21] These laws and other statutes and regulations governing purchases by government departments hung like a sword of Damocles over the cooperative committees and even the commissioners of the NDAC. If the government was not inclined to use these powers, disaffected businessmen could always bring suits to force the court's attention to the antitrust problem. Threats of such action were not rare.[22] The Wilson administration never seriously tried to deal with the ominous antitrust problem. The entire mobilization structure, with its unwieldy mixture of public and private interests, defied close definition and invited paralyzing debate.

Once an industry had been at least partially organized through a cooperative committee, it usually began formulating and implementing mobilization policies under the general direction of an NDAC commissioner and his staff. Those efforts were undertaken most seriously after the United States entered war, but for many industries the process began before hostilities. Working with the commissioners, cooperative committees collected information on their industries vital to informed decisionmaking, began considering the means for expanding or converting production capacity according to war needs, and started developing rudimentary price, priority, and other controls. In conjunction with the military services and other public and private agencies, the cooperative committees also made recommendations for the distribution of contracts within industry. In some instances, they actually (although not formally) awarded the contracts.[23]

The enormous difficulties in operating the cooperative committees created conditions in which power tended to accrue in the hands of participating businessmen rather than with the NDAC commissioners. Having no authority to compel industry, the commissioners had to rely on the voluntary cooperation of business. Consequently, in organizing and operating the cooperative committees, the initiative frequently passed to industry's representatives, trade association officials or prominent industrialists. More often than not, these leaders and not the commissioners selected the committee members and then insisted on considerable latitude in defining and carrying out their responsibilities. Industrialists recruited for cooperative committees under vaguely defined public authority could draw on private sources of power that the commissioners did not have. Representatives from giant corporations in oligopolistic industries who headed a cooperative committee could use their prestige or the market power of their firms to persuade or force other companies to acquiesce in the committee's will. Such was the case with Elbert H. Gary and the Cooperative Committee on Steel and Steel Products, which was actually an extension of the American Iron and Steel Institute. Gary not only chose and largely set policy for his committee, but he also took the initiative in organizing eleven subcommittees. In the more competitive industries, like lumber, with Robert H. Downman as head of the cooperative committee, an elaborate and slow process of balancing and bargaining was essential to achieve organization and action. The cooperative committees, therefore, reflected quite accurately the nature and operation of the various industries in peacetime. Given the manner in which a cooperative committee functioned, it could have greater power than the commissioner himself.[24]

The growth of the cooperative committees between February and July 1917 involved a strong measure of industrial self-regulation on an enormous scale. Nearly every industry of any importance was organized to some degree. The NDAC commissioners and the CND at best had only partial control over the actions of the numerous committees. Industry was using public authority with few safeguards against abuse. The honesty and integrity of businessmen acted as the principal regulatory mechanism; only their talents ensured competent management. Within the competitive industries, countervailing power resulted in a form of pluralism that tended to reduce abuse or threatened to expose it; in the oligopolistic industries even that check did not exist. In the hectic months just before and after the nation entered the war, the development of the cooperative committees was so confused and amorphous that few people other than the participants could discern what was happening. Once information began to reach Congress and the public, the operations, and even the existence, of the cooperative committees became an extremely volatile political issue, threatening the Wilson administration and the entire economic mobilization program.

The NDAC commissioners were not without actual power, and they had considerable potential power. It stemmed from the goals that most commissioners and many businessmen shared: the desire for economic stability and for preserving as much of the status quo as possible under the strains of war in a planned system. The pursuit of these goals had led the commissioners to initiate the move toward cooperative committees, encourage their growth, and generally establish their aims and guidelines. Moreover, in dealing with many industries, the commissioners inevitably had a broader outlook than the businessmen on the committees. The commissioners also gained information from various sources about the dimensions of the total war demand and its implications for the industries with which they worked. This overview and information placed them in a better position than the cooperative committees to discern the shape of the ultimate mobilization structure.

As long as industry lacked a sense of urgency about wartime organization and controls, it could afford to look upon the commissioners and the NDAC casually. Once wartime pressures and demands began creating shortages, disorganizing peacetime production and exchange, dislocating transportation facilities, and threatening to shut down industries nonessential for the war, businessmen began to take governmental agencies more seriously. They advocated a better, more centralized mobilization administration than the Council of National Defense–National Defense Advisory Commission, one that would have some real authority. When that point was reached, public authority grew because business then needed the government as much as the government needed business. Furthermore, to keep a mobilization program going without a radical reordering of power within the economy, the cooperative committees, or some similar bodies, had to remain at the foundation of any program for harnessing the economy. Those committees not only required the mantle of public authority to give them legitimacy, but they also had to be restructured so as to separate private and public functions more effectively and to ensure at least the appearance of public regulation of private power.

The economic mobilization program for World War I ultimately became a massive government-business regulatory partnership based on mutual need: The government needed business because it owned the means of production and distribution; business needed the government to give shape, direction, and control to the planning system. Neither private nor public interests could be protected in conditions of modern warfare without the participation and cooperation of both parties.

The NDAC, with its cooperative committees, constituted the means for organizing and controlling the private sector of the economy to supply wartime needs. The methods were crude and piecemeal, but they could be perfected. The outline of this system took shape quite early in the war. Relatively rapid progress was possible because a measure of government-industry cooperation on behalf of economic regulation during the Progressive Era had prepared both the public and private sector to a degree for wartime conditions. Nevertheless, the economic mobilization program floundered for almost a year. Organizing supply—the civilian economy—was not enough; demand—the multiple needs of claimant agencies like the army and navy—also had to be controlled. Throughout the war, demand exceeded supply. Consequently, unless war contracts were distributed with care and in order of priority, economic equilibrium could not be maintained. The NDAC, however, had no authority over the claimant agencies, which were free to do as they liked.

A crisis was avoidable as long as the claimant agencies procured in an orderly manner and cooperated with the NDAC. Some procurement administrations functioned efficiently, but others did not, and none coordinated consistently with the NDAC. As a result, the commission's attempts to organize supply were disrupted, and the general mobilization program, lacking centralized direction, drifted and lurched. Those circumstances became increasingly intolerable as wartime demand mounted and the business mobilizers gained experience and a greater awareness of the agencies and controls that were essential for harnessing the economy effectively. The growing tensions between the procurement and mobilization structures were relieved only after a major and enormously threatening crisis erupted in winter 1917–1918.

## THE MILITARY THWARTS ECONOMIC MOBILIZATION

Most procurement agencies had established or had fashioned reasonably efficient systems for wartime purchasing, as was the case with most new administrative bodies. For example, the Food and Fuel Administrations set up in August 1917 and the Emergency Fleet Corporation, a subdivision of the U.S. Shipping Board that had been established in September 1916, were quite flexible because they did not have rigid bureaucracies that had built up over the years.[25]

The Navy Department, among the nation's oldest executive departments and, after the War Department, the largest procurement agency, also adjusted to hostilities without major difficulty. The department had been in a state of semipreparedness since the late nineteenth century and had maintained the capacity to expand rapidly based on the existing system. Between April and December 1917 the number of navy personnel grew from 64,000 to 300,000 with relative ease. Compared with the army, which had over 3.5 million men before the end of hostilities, the navy's growth was quite modest. Reorganizations begun in the late nineteenth century had given the Navy Department an excellent, modernized supply system. Although six bureaus had a role in supply, centralized control was maintained. The Bureau of Ordnance procured guns, shells, and armor plate, and the Bureau of Supplies and Accounts bought almost all other supplies. In the latter bureau, the very able John M. Hancock headed the Purchasing Division, and buying was carefully structured along commodity lines. Local purchasing, compulsory orders, and commandeering of plants were strictly checked to avoid rivalry and conflict within the navy. During the war years, the navy continued competitive bidding whenever it could and used tough safeguards against abuse when turning to negotiated contracts.[26] Inadequacies in the purchasing systems of the Navy Department and other claimant agencies, therefore, did not threaten NDAC activities. Weaknesses that existed were corrected without major upheaval or restructuring.

That was not the case with the War Department, the largest and most powerful procurement agency. The flagrant inadequacies of its supply apparatus undermined the efforts of the NDAC at almost all levels. When war broke out, five, and later eight, bureaus—the Quartermaster Corps, the Ordnance Department, and others—procured for the army.[27] Unlike the navy's centralized supply system, the army's was decentralized and uncoordinated. Each bureau had its own purchasing staff, handled its own funds, transported and stored its own goods, and distributed its own supplies. Each bureau also tended to operate in a different manner from the others in these areas. The War Department subdivisions often used their differing systems to procure identical or similar items. Determined to meet their own needs, the bureaus competed with one another and other claimant agencies. Contracts were let indiscriminately, equipment hoarded, facilities commandeered without plan, and supplies transported without regard to need. This disorganized setup made it virtually impossible for the War Department to provide reliable statistics on requirements. Only in October 1917 did the army finally adopt a thirty-division American Expeditionary Forces (AEF) program to be filled by December 1918. Before that point, and sometimes even afterward, each bureau, without proper executive guidance and with partial or inaccurate information, calculated or guessed at the size of the army it was preparing to supply and used different formulas to arrive at these estimates.

War Department difficulties, of course, did not start with the war. The politics of supply had been a source of aggravation within the department since the Revolutionary War. The chief of staff–general staff system created by Secretary of War Elihu Root between 1899 and 1904 had been intended in part to bring the bureaus under centralized direction. But the tenaciously independent bureaus successfully resisted control.[28]

Consequently, the staff-bureau conflict continued as the United States entered World War I, fundamentally weakening the army's ability to meet the exigencies of war. Secretary of War Baker would not move forcefully to resolve the conflicts rending the department. A Progressive dedicated to applying local solutions to modern problems, Baker opposed temporary changes in the federal government during the war, fearing that they might become permanent. Moreover, the former mayor of Cleveland consistently tried to avoid controversy. Attempting to reach a compromise in the nearly irreconcilable differences between the General Staff and the bureaus, Baker allowed the War Department to drift toward disaster. With two weak chiefs of staff in Generals Hugh L. Scott and Tasker H. Bliss between April 1917 and May 1918, and an uncertain secretary of war, the bureaus continued to dominate the department. The War Department/army structure, therefore, moved and spoke with many voices, not one.

Congress compounded the War Department's dire problems in several critical ways. The bureaus' success in maintaining independence stemmed partly from close ties with key members of Congress. The latter body tended to look upon War Department affairs in parochial terms and viewed army centralization under the chief of staff–general staff system, which was patterned along German lines, as a militaristic threat. Those attitudes and bureau lobbying resulted in legislation after 1904 that kept the General Staff small and otherwise restricted in relation to the multiple responsibilities it faced. Matters grew even worse with the National Defense Act of June 1916. The staff's size was reduced, in effect, to approximately twenty, and it was supposedly restricted to planning, not administration. Baker used his authority to maintain the General Staff as a supervisory body, and its size was substantially increased after the declaration of war. But in the vital months before hostilities, the staff simply lacked the personnel needed for adequate planning and preparation for war. In April 1917 the General Staff had nine officers in Washington; the Army War College had eleven. The National Defense Act of 1916 also provided for expanding the peacetime army to 175,000 over a period of five years and 286,000 in the event of war. Thus the army, unlike the navy, which began massively increasing in size in 1916, could not begin expanding to wartime size until the actual outbreak of hostilities. With the declaration of war, the five-year expansion program was compressed, and the Selective Service Act of May 1917 established the statutory basis for what became nearly a 4-million-man army. Nonetheless, exponential growth from almost nothing had to take place under the pressure of war.

The process of expansion was particularly difficult for the supply bureaus. The Quartermaster Corps, which had a peacetime budget for 1917 of $186.3 million, spent over $8 billion during the war. Its officer staff grew from 347 to 6,431 between April and December 1917 and expanded even further in 1918. Wartime expenditures by the Ordnance Department exceeded $4 billion and its officer staff jumped from 96 to 5,000. Since regular army officers were needed for handling the thousands, ultimately millions, of new recruits, the supply bureaus had to rely heavily on reserve officers, volunteers, and draftees to fill their ranks, which meant training thousands of officers while trying to manage the exploding requirements of war.

Appropriations further plagued the War Department. Unlike the Navy Department, which received some funds for expansion in 1915 and a huge budget for 1916, the first large War Department appropriation did not occur until June 1917, with additional billions of dollars coming in October. For six months, therefore, funding lagged far behind contractual needs. The secretary of war maneuvered around this difficulty by placing orders before Congress acted, but no contracts could be signed until specific appropriations were made. Although industry was usually cooperative, in the numerous instances where money or a signed contract was essential for financing the acquisition of special equipment or for building or expanding plant capacity, budget restrictions caused severe delays, difficulties, or both. Additionally, Congress appropriated money for the War Department on a bureau-by-bureau, item-by-item basis, with strict provisions against the transfer of funds. Since the War Department as a whole was doing little more than guessing about its needs throughout most of 1917, this procedure was a serious obstacle. In April 1917 the War Department tried unsuccessfully to get Congress to adopt lump-sum appropriations as it had done for the Navy Department.

Other regulations and statutes further delayed or complicated both army and navy supply. Specific appropriations were required for employing additional personnel or acquiring more office space. With a slow budgetary process, the military services in 1917 worked in ridiculously restricted quarters with insufficient office staff. The acquisition of land and the erection of buildings were also subject to bureaucratic red tape. Many of the congressional restrictions were circumvented in one way or another, but delay and frustration almost inevitably resulted.

The Navy Department consistently fared better than the War Department before Congress, partly because the navy faced legislators from a reasonably unified position. In contrast, the parts of the War Department carried their differences to Congress; the latter body responded to the parts rather than to the whole, and the entire department suffered badly as a result.

The General Staff–bureau controversy also partially accounted for the army's failure to anticipate the nature of twentieth-century warfare. The General Staff to some extent perceived that industrial production was of equal or greater importance than tactics or strategy for military success and that relating the procurement apparatus to a mobilized economy was part of the military mission in modern times. But the staff lacked the time and personnel to explore or fully develop its ideas. Moreover, at the time the General Staff and its subdivisions had a limited impact on the army and the War Department as a whole. By contrast, the Navy Department was much more attuned to the imperatives of modern warfare because of the continuous contact it had had with the economy beginning in the late nineteenth century, as it built and maintained a new navy.[29]

Had the General Staff–bureau conflict ended with the onset of war and had an efficient supply system been fashioned, the army could have adjusted to emergency conditions with relative ease and, in the process, begun adapting its thought to the changed imperatives of warfare. Since that did not happen, the army nearly lost control of supply by threatening the entire civilian economy. Out of total war costs approximating $32 billion, the army spent $14.5 billion between April 1916 and June 1919.[30] Pouring such vast amounts of money into the economy through the department's antiquated supply system unavoidably produced havoc.

To mitigate the effect, the NDAC, while organizing supply and attempting to devise some wartime economic controls, was forced to assume responsibility for coordinating supply and demand. No other agency existed for that purpose. The task was almost impossible. The procurement agencies had the statutory authority; the NDAC had no more than advisory powers. The Navy Department had an efficient supply apparatus and would not voluntarily lend itself alone to continuous NDAC direction, and neither would the numerous civilian claimant agencies. The War Department, the largest and least competent procurement agency, created the greatest problems for the NDAC. Had the department handled supply more effectively and been more willing to cooperate with the NDAC, the other procurement agencies, because of the War Department's power and influence, might have been persuaded or forced to accept a coordinating role by the NDAC.

The NDAC's difficulties with the War Department stemmed from two sources. First, according to military dictum, the authorities who controlled strategy must also control supply. The army thus looked upon civilian mobilization agencies not just as a threat to its power over supply but as a threat to its overall military prerogatives. The weakness of the army supply system served only to strengthen the suspicion. Although the navy was just as determined to maintain control of its supply operations, the strength of its system made it less anxious about the incursion of civilian agencies. Indeed, the Navy Department seemed most concerned that the inadequacies of War Department procurement operations would necessitate the takeover of all military procurement by civilian administrations.[31]

Second, the War Department's supply network did not correspond to that of the civilian economy. The bureaus were organized along functional lines—Quartermaster, Ordnance, and so forth—but the economy was informally structured according to commodities, such as raw materials and industrial products.[32] This mismatch made effective coordination of supply and demand impossible. Logically, the army should have reformed its supply system and restructured it along commodity lines as the navy had done before World War I. The army stubbornly resisted the changes until early in 1918, which discouraged or prevented other procurement administrations from cooperating with the NDAC. The War Department was disrupting the entire industrial mobilization effort.

Baker's appointment as chairman of the CND Defense and his position as President Wilson's chief adviser on industrial mobilization helped the War Department to resist change. Baker was unable to bring order out of confusion in the department and failed to rise above departmental interests as chairman of the CND. Rather, he used his position to preserve the army's prerogatives. With the support of Josephus Daniels and other cabinet members on the CND who were also out to protect their turf, Baker operated on the assumption that the NDAC should assist the military services in fulfilling their goals on the terms laid down by the army and navy. As in past wars, and despite the changed nature of warfare, the War and Navy Departments were to act as the principal economic mobilization agencies. Since Wilson maintained Baker as his secretary of war and chief aide on economic mobilization, he obviously shared some or most of Baker's views. For almost a year after the outbreak of war, therefore, the War Department insisted that the civilian economy adjust to its decentralized, inefficient, and functional supply system rather than vice versa. The tail was wagging the dog.[33]

## THE MUNITIONS STANDARDS BOARD AND THE GENERAL MUNITIONS BOARD

At first, the NDAC accepted the War Department's terms. It attempted to make the department system work by serving more or less as a bridge between the industrial and military worlds. In mid-February 1917, even before the United States entered the war, the NDAC insisted that the services provide it with full requirements and specifications for raising, equipping, and fielding a 1-million-man army. Neither the army nor the navy was able or willing to supply such details. Consequently, the commission obtained the services of a retired army colonel, J. F. Reynolds Landis, to assist it in compiling such estimates in order to facilitate planning. Working with their staff and the War Department, the commissioners in March determined the goal of a 1-million-man army as a basis for procurement planning.[34]

Once war broke out, the NDAC had to focus on more pressing demands as the army bureaus were unable effectively to manage the huge demands suddenly imposed on them. At first, the NDAC attempted to get the CND to initiate legislation that would permit the army to transfer funds among bureaus and items to be purchased and to eliminate the obstacles to expanding the military supply agencies' personnel and office space. The CND refused to act. Then the recently organized cooperative committees began performing procurement activities. Individuals and committees aided the army in distributing contracts within the industries they represented. Julius Rosenwald's Committee on Supplies built a procurement system around parts of the Quartermaster Corps and assumed many of its functions. Aid from the NDAC unquestionably kept the army bureaus from being totally swamped. But the system that emerged from the emergency had drawbacks. The commission's operations were often illegal. Industrialists awarded contracts to themselves and their colleagues, in fact if not on paper. Small groups of businessmen engaged in collusive activity sanctioned by the government. Army regulations and the antitrust laws were being violated.[35]

The expediency rather than the illegality of the NDAC's operations bothered its members. Need forced the NDAC to assume the responsibilities of a general mobilization agency without the authority to do so. As a result, the procurement agencies used or ignored the commission as they chose. The NDAC needed the power to require the various claimant agencies to work with it for the purposes of coordination. This authority would enable the NDAC to end the competition within and among those agencies and to work out rules and controls for facilitating a relatively smooth and orderly economic mobilization process. Until the War Department reformed its supply system, however, army cooperation was futile and impossible. What the War Department did or did not do remained key to realizing the NDAC's goals.

Out of frustration, the commission began pressing the CND to sanction a more effective organization even before war was declared. The council reluctantly yielded to the NDAC's entreaties after agonizing deliberation, and it always granted less than was essential.[36] The first breakthrough came with the organization and staffing of the Munitions Standards Board (MSB) on March 3, 1917, based on recommendations made by the NDAC and accepted by the CND.

The idea for the MSB originated with Howard E. Coffin. Although the board's charges were exceptionally vague, Coffin and his colleagues intended for a group of knowledgeable industrialists to join military personnel in reviewing the army and navy specifications and drawings for munitions, to standardize where possible the requirements of the two services, and to begin preparing industry for quantity production. Through this initiative, Coffin sought to give some specific direction to his NDAC responsibilities for munitions and manufacturing and to take action essential for fulfilling the commission's calculations for equipping a 1-million-man army. The committee members, selected principally by Coffin, included Samuel M. Vauclain, vice-president of Baldwin Locomotive Works; W. H. Van Dervoort, president of Root and Van Dervoort Engineering Company; Francis C. Pratt from General Electric Company; John E. Otterson, vice-president of Winchester Repeating Arms Company; Edward A. Deeds from Dayton Engineering Laboratories Company (Delco); and Frank A. Scott, vice-president of Warner and Swasey Company. With one exception, the companies represented had been or still were, through the J. P. Morgan and Company Export Department, supplying the Allies with munitions or the means for producing munitions. The executives on the MSB were defined as experts in that field. At that point, the MSB represented the most extensive and direct tie to develop between Edward R. Stettinius's operations and those of the government mobilization system that had been evolving since late 1915.[37]

Scott was elected chairman, probably because he was from Cleveland and had Baker's confidence. The secretary of war had prevailed upon Scott to serve on the board, and he remained a central figure in mobilization through October 1917. Scott was talented, exceptionally dedicated, and shared Baker's view that the civilian mobilization agencies were subordinate to the military and existed to assist the armed services in fulfilling their mission. He had made warfare and military systems a hobby from the age of ten, traveling extensively in the United States and Europe to study those subjects. His firm produced machine tools for the Allies, but Scott had also become involved in preparedness by representing the American Society of Mechanical Engineers for Ohio on the IPC.[38]

The Munitions Standards Board met once on March 21 with the secretary of war and the Ordnance heads of the army and navy. The industrial and military representatives expressed an interest in combining their efforts to facilitate munitions output, but they were puzzled about procedures since the secretary of war, Coffin, and Scott appeared unable to give meaningful direction. The board ultimately divided itself into subcommittees covering artillery, projectiles, gauges, dies, small arms and munitions, and so on and recruited other industrialists to assist them. The MSB never met again as a whole. Some subcommittees pursued their specialties and made considerable progress. Without centralized direction from the board, however, their efforts were scattered and piecemeal. Before the end of March, the MSB had for all intents and purposes dissolved, though no official action marked its demise.[39]

The MSB experience revealed several important realities. Baker either did not understand what mobilization required or hesitated to encourage agencies outside the military services to take action. Without guidance from the secretary of war, Scott could not provide leadership. Furthermore, the executives on the MSB, whose firms had been producing Allied munitions for almost two years, had no grasp whatsoever of what warfare meant for a mature industrial economy. They appreciated only the industrial process and the details needed to produce munitions. Although Coffin, almost alone, understood the larger implications of industrial mobilization, he lacked the ability or the tenacity to convert his insight into an organization capable of carrying out the necessary action. He had led the move to found the MSB and was able to set forth in general terms what the board should do, but at that point he virtually abandoned the effort. Even if Coffin had devoted his full energies to the MSB, it would never have succeeded because its focus was much too limited. Concentrating on standardization and the details of munitions production without first coordinating all wartime procurement and devising controls for managing the economy was an exercise in futility. The MSB ended almost before it had begun because its intent was wrongheaded and misguided.

The General Munitions Board (GMB) replaced the MSB on March 31, 1917, and continued operating until July of that year. In the latter part of March, Baker appointed Scott and the NDAC selected Coffin, Baruch, and Rosenwald to make recommendations concerning the evident need for coordinating the military services' procurement. Scott and the NDAC representatives joined forces with CND–NDAC director Gifford to draft plans for the GMB, which the NDAC approved on March 30 and the CND consented to a day later. The board was to coordinate military procurement, expedite the acquisition of raw materials and manufacturing facilities for war production, establish a priority system, and act to resolve conflicts in purchasing between the War and Navy Departments. The GMB was specifically prohibited from engaging in direct purchasing, a prerogative that was to remain with the existing departments. The enabling resolution empowered the chairman of the CND to choose the chairman of the new body. Baker, predictably, selected Scott, who reflected his thinking on industrial mobilization.

At the outset, the board consisted of seven army and eight navy members—principally representing the various supply bureaus—and members appointed by Baruch, Coffin, Martin, and Rosenwald, who were intended to represent the NDAC committees most vitally affecting military supply. Eventually, representatives from the Emergency Fleet Corporation, the National Research Council, the American Railway Association, and other agencies joined the board. The GMB also absorbed the various subcommittees of the MSB, had at its disposal the cooperative committees of the four NDAC commissioners, and over the months created about a dozen subdivisions of its own. Originally consisting of twenty-two members, the GMB at first tried to conduct its operations through the board as a whole. That procedure quickly proved to be too unwieldy. Hence an executive committee, composed of the chairman and members from the army, navy, and the relevant civilian agencies, met daily to make most decisions and to handle the day-to-day work. Important decisions had to be approved at weekly meetings of the entire board.[40]

The General Munitions Board was a poor compromise at best. Baruch, Coffin, Willard, Rosenwald, and other NDAC commissioners had already concluded that a civilian agency with centralized authority, superior to the armed services, and able to extend its power over the entire economy was necessary for successful industrial mobilization. But Baker, with the support of Wilson, Daniels, and most other CND members, would not relinquish the procurement prerogatives that he and the War Department held, although he recognized that some agency with responsibilities more clearly defined than the NDAC's was essential. The GMB, therefore, was given responsibility but no actual authority. Indeed, as a creation of the CND, which itself had only advisory powers, the GMB technically could not have authority. The operations of the board further confused the already tangled mobilization system. It complemented rather than replaced the NDAC. Some commission committees operated through the GMB, a few did so only partially, and others not at all. It was impossible to discern where the NDAC started and the GMB stopped. No one was satisfied with the GMB.[41] No attempt to go beyond the NDAC would have been irresponsible, but going further than the GMB before war was declared was virtually impossible. Had the GMB succeeded in coordinating demand, especially from the military, it would have taken a giant step forward. Since that did not occur, the board did not go far.

Despite its limitations, the General Munitions Board began to explore and refine the various economic controls that mobilization required. That step was possible because the GMB, unlike the NDAC, brought together the military supply bureaus, other procurement agents, and representatives of the most important NDAC committees for the purpose of joint decisionmaking. Under the GMB, some set procedures were introduced for clearance, priority, and price control—all vital steps if economic stability within a mobilized economy were to be achieved.

Clearance was the GMB's first attempt to coordinate military purchasing. By clearing orders or proposed contracts, the board tried to ensure that adequate facilities, materials, labor, transportation, and so forth existed in a given geographic area. If the means of production were inadequate or the area was operating at capacity or had excessive commitments, the board moved to increase the supply of raw materials, transportation, and so on, divert contracts to less congested regions where it had located qualified manufacturers, or take other actions designed to avoid unbalancing the economy in the various regions of the nation. At first the board itself strove to clear all military contracts. When that procedure proved too cumbersome, the GMB created a Clearance Committee to act on the military, Allied, and other contracts involving its list of materials already in short supply. This list grew constantly and rapidly and was later replaced with the "congested districts" approach.

Had the clearance function worked, the GMB would have begun centralizing control of purchasing and accumulating the data vital to a regulated program of economic mobilization. That never happened. The CND and the War Department granted the GMB the right to clear orders but with the escape clause that the military supply bureaus had discretion in using the board's services. The Navy Department never officially granted the GMB any authority over its operations, although it cooperated at times with the board. As a result, most contracts were let without board action, and even when the board located alternate manufacturers, the military preferred the established and reliable firms in the Northeast. That region quickly became flooded far beyond its capacity with contracts. With the military services using or ignoring the GMB to suit their own purposes, and with the board establishing no provisions for follow-up when the military services did cooperate, the clearance operations of the GMB never went forward meaningfully.[42]

Clearance was always tied in closely with priority, the process of determining which contracts were most essential so that they could receive raw materials and other inputs ahead of others. Clearance dealt with existing orders and contracts; priority involved future or prospective, as opposed to immediate, production. Shortages existed even before the nation entered the war, and conditions grew progressively worse as hostilities continued. With demand exceeding supply, economic balance depended on an effective priority system.

Shortly after its creation, the General Munitions Board began pressing the CND, through the NDAC, for an overall outline of war needs so that the board had some way of knowing the level of urgency of different requirements. The council did no more than state in late April that for one year, naval demand would have precedence over army needs and that the building of wooden ships would have the top priority unless other goods became more urgent. Although such guidelines were of some use, the board itself could not apply them effectively, and they fell far short of the kind of specificity that the business representatives on the GMB and the NDAC believed essential.

Mounting pressure from those agencies ultimately led the CND to sanction a GMB Priority Committee in mid-May 1917. The committee was headed by Maj. Gen. James B. Aleshire (naming a military man as the head of a committee with such a broad economic purview indicated Baker's continuing protective stance) and eventually included representatives from the army, navy, Departments of Agriculture, Interior, and Commerce, and the Federal Trade Commission. The committee was to determine priority where conflicts existed between the army and the navy, between the military and civilian sectors, and, in conjunction with an NDAC–related committee, between different parts of the civilian economy. But the committee could not act where conflicts existed between Allied and American civilian demand, and it was restricted in areas where Allied purchasing conflicted with that of American procurement agencies. Although the Priority Committee's reach was reasonably broad, its power was not. Directives from the CND were vague and uncertain; the supply bureaus, as with clearance, ignored the committee when they chose to do so; and authority over civilian firms was legally dubious. The last obstacle led the Priority Committee to make requests rather than issue directives to the nation's corporations. This approach proved remarkably effective, principally because many businessmen wanted meaningful priority controls and kept pressing the GMB for action in the area. Despite all that it was not, the Priority Committee experienced more success than the Clearance Committee because its task was more limited. It continued operating in a different form in subsequent mobilization administrations.[43]

Just as priority was related to clearance, price control was inextricably involved with both those functions.[44] Without a reasonably stable price structure, economic controls could not have much effect because prices would outrun appropriations and thereby undermine planning. Foreign demand and war-induced prosperity had driven prices up by more than 50 percent between August 1914 and March 1917; prices of war-related commodities, such as most metals, had jumped almost 150 percent during the same period. Once the United States entered the war, inflationary pressures grew much more intense. Business mobilizers such as Baruch recognized that some form of price control was imperative. As the NDAC commissioner of raw materials, Baruch negotiated in March 1917 with the copper industry the sale of a large order to the government at substantially below the prevailing market price. He later arranged similar one-time agreements with the steel, zinc, aluminum, and lumber industries. Such ad hoc accomplishments were no substitute for a systematized pricing policy. At the time of its creation, the GMB faced skyrocketing prices and the urgent need to act to contain them. Nonetheless, the board accomplished even less with pricing than it did with clearance and priority.

In mid-April Baker authorized the GMB to determine equitable prices on military goods, but only upon the request of the armed services. The NDAC committees had already been doing so before the formation of the GMB and continued to do so, along with the GMB committees, afterward. Moreover, GMB subdivisions assisted the military departments and other procurement agencies with a "cost plus" type of contract. The one attempt at general price controls stemmed from Baruch's persistence. He and his supporters constantly prodded the CND, NDAC, and GMB to move in the pricing field. Finally, late in April, the CND directed Scott to head a Special Price Committee of representatives from the Departments of Commerce, Agriculture, and Interior, the Federal Trade Commission, and possibly other agencies to study the price question. The committee was specifically instructed to consult Baruch. Early in May the committee reported that pricing for important items was needed immediately. Prices should be set high enough to attract high-cost producers so as to maximize output and should apply to the Allies as well as to the United States. The committee asserted that those ends could best be realized through negotiations between a centralized governmental agency and the nation's largest corporations. Committee members were hopeful that their report would stir the CND to act. Despite repeated efforts throughout May and June to achieve that goal, no action took place. The impasse occurred principally because the president and his administration were divided over and uncertain about how to handle this politically sensitive issue, and Congress was beginning to focus on pricing as part of the larger matter of economic mobilization.

In mid-July, after months of deadlocked negotiations between mobilization committees and the copper, steel, coal, and shipbuilding industries, Wilson lashed out at businessmen for putting profits ahead of patriotism. The president declared that the Federal Trade Commission was conducting studies to guide his administration in determining prices and that prices for the government would also apply to the civilian population and the Allies.

Wilson's assertions hardly clarified the confused price control issue. Based on executive power and various bills passed before and after America entered hostilities, the administration had ample authority to set prices on goods required for the emergency. But converting that authority into concrete action proved endlessly complex and controversial. Moreover, extending that authority to the Allies was questionable, and trying to apply it to the public in general was legally untenable. Congress never authorized blanket price controls during World War I. By necessity, therefore, prices were set through negotiations and agreements between the government and various industries. By July 1917, months after its creation, the GMB had made no progress in defining or implementing a price control policy.

The one highly significant function that the General Munitions Board never embraced was requirements. From the outset, the board members recognized that meaningful clearance, priority, and pricing decisions depended on reliable requirement figures, and they pleaded with the CND to lend some guidance on this issue. Since the military services could not produce figures and the dimensions of American involvement remained obscure, the council could do little more than provide the GMB with some vague generalizations. In this episode, the CND displayed the passivity that had characterized it since its creation. The council acted only in response to GMB pressure, provided a minimal answer, and made little effort to seek out information or to provide a sensible framework within which the GMB could function. As a result, the GMB constantly worked in a vacuum. Devising effective clearance, priority, and pricing policies, given sensible requirement figures, would have been difficult enough under the conditions the GMB faced; without those figures, the task was virtually impossible.[45]

By mid-1917 the GMB had proved unequal to the task of economic mobilization. It had made little progress in centralizing control over war purchasing through clearance; it had made some, but not enough, progress in priority; and it had made no progress in pricing and requirements. As spring 1917 gave way to summer, confusion was rife and efforts to harness the economy were bogging down.

The GMB's central problem was that the military representatives dominated its operations. Moreover, the military members of the board were not unified. Each army and navy supply bureau was represented on the board. The competition between the War and Navy Departments thus continued, and, even worse, the War Department's decentralized and chaotic procurement structure carried on without reform. The army's bureaus, each with its own rather unique system, continued to operate in their own ways and often competed with one another. The Navy Department feared that its efficient, centralized system would be disrupted by War Department methods and the attempts of the GMB to bring some order to general military purchasing. As a result, the navy insulated itself as much as possible from War Department confusion and GMB coordinating efforts; its cooperation with the GMB was always minimal and reluctant. Since the overwhelming number of representatives on the GMB came from the armed services, the military set the general parameters within which the board operated. The military's influence on the GMB Executive Committee, which made the day-to-day decisions, was significantly diluted, with the result that its recommendations were much less parochial. Nonetheless, major policy matters had to receive the board's approval, which almost always reintroduced the narrow military orientation of the armed services.

In instances where the GMB manifested initiative and reached out for authority, it encountered resistance from the Baker-dominated CND. The council allowed the board to try implementing various economic controls but always in a way that left the War and Navy Departments' prerogatives undiminished. Thus the GMB, for all intents and purposes, was without authority and hobbled to the point of near-paralysis. Board chairman Scott did not move decisively to change those circumstances. He, like Baker and the armed services, was convinced that civilian mobilization agencies should only aid the military. Consequently, he was always slow to push for more power for the agency he headed, willingly accepted the obstruction or hesitancy of the CND and the military services, and almost never displayed the vigor or leadership the board required. Scott appeared committed to trying to make an untenable mobilization agency work instead of forcefully seeking to extend its power or change its structure.

The driving force for change came from the business mobilizers on the GMB and the NDAC. Separating the actions of the board from the commission is virtually impossible. Almost all requests, recommendations, and observations from the GMB to the CND passed first through the NDAC. Furthermore, Baruch, Rosenwald, and Martin had chosen representatives on the board (Coffin never designated anyone to speak for his committee and attended board meetings only irregularly). With Baruch leading the way and Willard and other commissioners and their designees on the GMB playing an active role, the civilian mobilizers pressured the CND either to strengthen the GMB or to consider creating a new agency that would be headed primarily by business representatives, would be able to achieve centralized control over the mobilization process, would have the authority to enforce its decisions, and would be superior to the military services.

Baruch and his counterparts acted according to their own beliefs about the requirements of a successful mobilization system. Their actions were also influenced by the pressure and advice they were receiving from the business community, articulated by the cooperative committees. Once the nation began to experience the economic distortion and destabilization that modern warfare produces, the corporate community, and especially its members on the cooperative committees, began insisting that centralized purchasing, clearance, priority, and price controls were imperative for restoring economic balance and achieving some sense of predictability for the future. No later than June 1917, Baruch and other members of the NDAC and GMB were agitating for more effective mobilization agencies and policies, with the substantial support and even the urging of the business community.[46]

Between February and July 1917, the National Defense Advisory Commission and related bodies determined how to mobilize the American economy for war. The guiding principle was using and preserving the existing economic system. Hence, temporary governmental agencies, patterned roughly after the economy's contours and overseen generally by public spokesmen, relied heavily on business and industrial leaders to convert and run the economy for war purposes. This approach was representative in that most sectors of the economy were included; it was elitist in that big business was dominant.

A mobilization system based on the status quo depended on organized demand—principally the armed services—adapting to organized supply. In resisting that imperative, the army challenged the guiding principle of economic mobilization. Successfully harnessing the economy for hostilities after July 1917 therefore hinged on the War Department's accepting the pattern of the civilian mobilization agencies. Otherwise, America could not fight.

# 9
# THE WAR INDUSTRIES BOARD, AUGUST 1917–MARCH 1918

In July 1917 the Woodrow Wilson administration replaced the National Defense Advisory Commission and related agencies with the War Industries Board. Although a major step forward in terms of organization and the use of business advisers, the new agency was hobbled by a lack of authority. Operating free of WIB control, the War Department and other procurement agencies continued to thwart the board's attempts centrally to direct the economy. The results were dire. By winter 1917–1918, economic mobilization was in shambles. To reestablish order, the Wilson administration in March 1918 increased the WIB's power so that it was able to act as the general coordinating agency for harnessing the economy—a function the board performed with growing proficiency throughout 1918 under the chairmanship of Bernard M. Baruch. Key to the WIB's success in the last months of hostilities was the cooperation of the procuring departments, a development made possible by a radical reorganization of the War Department's supply structure.

During summer 1917 and winter 1917–1918, Congress spurred the hesitant Wilson administration in reforming the economic mobilization system. The president and his chief advisers balked at creating new agencies such as the WIB that were dominated by the corporate community and had real authority over the procuring administrations. Growing crises, however, forced the Wilson administration to work out a compromise, one in which the WIB was strengthened enough to do its job, but never so much that the board threatened the independence of the War Department and other government agencies.

In its final form, the WIB became a government-business regulatory partnership that enhanced both public and private power. Wilson and Secretary of War Newton D. Baker had tried to avoid the growth of power in either sector during the war years, a position that explains in part why the administration approached the political economy of modern warfare with such uncertainty.

## CREATING THE WIB

By late May/early June 1917 a change in the nation's mobilization structure had become imperative. The General Munitions Board was clearly unable to meet the demands of war, as indicated by growing confusion within the economy and the rising demand for better methods by business mobilizers and businessmen. Escalating war demands guaranteed that the situation would grow worse unless significant modifications were made. The first step toward new methods came on May 31 and June 1. The Council of National Defense instructed the National Defense Advisory Commission and the GMB that henceforth no new committees, subcommittees, or new members for existing committees were to be appointed without the approval of the council and that all subdivisions of the CND should seek the approval of the director before initiating new inquiries or actions. Furthermore, from mid-June, the CND refused the GMB's requests for further power or expanded activity on the grounds that a reorganization of the mobilization system was being considered. From that point until the end of July, the GMB remained in a state of limbo despite mounting demands on its services and the increasing tempo of economic activity.[1]

Beginning in late May, President Wilson took an active role in resolving the conflict over economic mobilization that was racking his administration. After the creation of the CND–NDAC in 1916, the president had largely left mobilization matters to those agencies, which were under Secretary of War Baker's control. Growing divisions between Baker and the business mobilizers forced the president to address the conflict. Action by Wilson was further necessitated by the question of Allied purchasing. In early May, J. P. Morgan and Company was phasing out its role as financier and procurement agent for the Allies, with the federal government taking on both functions. Secretary of the Treasury William G. McAdoo would handle financing for the Allies and would logically have a voice in determining how Allied purchasing in the United States would be managed. Since the Wilson administration elected to continue purchasing through a centralized body like Edward R. Stettinius's Export Department, McAdoo committed to the idea of a centralized purchasing agent or mobilization board to handle American and Allied procurement. Business mobilizers such as Bernard M. Baruch thus had an influential supporter within the administration. From early May, McAdoo not only vociferously advocated a centralized mobilization system but also became wedded to the notion that Baruch was the most qualified person to direct such an endeavor. Until May, the only CND member who supported the business mobilizers' position was Secretary of the Interior Franklin K. Lane. McAdoo's added support gave them an effective counterweight against Baker's influence.[2]

In late May and early June, Wilson called a series of conferences at the White House that included Baker, Daniels, McAdoo, Hoover, and Baruch. Purchasing, priority, pricing, and Allied procurement were reviewed, but no resolution emerged on any of these major issues. The fundamental division over centralization versus decentralization remained, with Baruch, supported by McAdoo, insisting on the former and Baker adamantly advocating the latter. The secretary of war maintained that controlling the economic mobilization machinery was beyond the capacity of any one person and that a powerful mobilization agency, which businessmen would necessarily dominate, would be totally unacceptable to the public. The existing departments, assisted by experts from the economy, must continue to supervise industrial mobilization. Baker did acknowledge that a better agency than the GMB was necessary, and he had already begun sketching out a model.[3]

Mounting criticism and attacks in Congress immeasurably strengthened the impetus within the Wilson administration to change the mobilization structure. The Council of National Defense–National Defense Advisory Commission and General Munitions Board had assumed new responsibilities and spawned hundreds of subdivisions without consulting or even informing the nation's legislators. Indeed, the CND and its subordinate units themselves lacked consolidated data on the activities of the mobilization agencies. Government officials and war mobilizers had given the distinct impression in various hearings that the mobilization machinery was out of control. Members of Congress and their business constituents who were excluded from contracting or the cooperative committees complained bitterly that the wartime bureaucratic maze had become impenetrable. Charges of conflicts of interest, corruption, favoritism, profiteering, and other abuses proliferated.

By May 1917 Congress had sufficient information about the functioning of the mobilization machinery to be thoroughly alarmed. The dollar-a-year-man and cooperative committee systems were especially vulnerable to attack. A situation in which private businessmen served as government officials and often had a role in awarding contracts to themselves and their colleagues took on the proportions of a national scandal when publicized. In addition to distress over the growing dissent from the press, public, and disaffected businessmen, Congress was concerned about the basic soundness of the economic mobilization scheme and chagrined by the legislature's exclusion from the process.[4]

The operations of the CND and its subordinate bodies were involved in an acrimonious congressional debate stretching from late April to early August over what became the Lever Food and Fuel Control Act. High war demand, shortages, and hoarding had created runaway prices for food and fuel, resulting in a public outcry and demands for action. In April 1917 the Agriculture Department presented a bill to Congress designed to give the president authority to stabilize conditions by creating new agencies, increasing production, instituting price controls, and taking other measures. For more than three months, the bill went through revisions extending from the establishment of comprehensive price controls to allowing market forces to operate uninhibited. Ultimately, through intense lobbying, pressure, and appeals to the public, the administration secured passage of a measure that allowed the president considerable discretion for dealing with the critical food and fuel situation. Before the compromise was reached, however, the administration had to muster its strength and influence to beat back an amendment creating a type of Civil War joint committee on the conduct of the war.

This provision had been introduced earlier by Sen. John W. Weeks (R-MA), was reintroduced with Democratic backing in July by the same senator, and was adopted by the Senate 52 to 31 when fourteen disaffected and mostly Southern or agrarian Democrats joined forces with thirty-eight Republicans. Support for the amendment was obviously somewhat partisan. Nonetheless, the general confusion and ineffectiveness of the administration's economic mobilization system, the alleged corruption and extravagance in war contracting, the rampant conflicts of interest upon which the entire mobilization system was based, and the desire to reestablish some congressional control over mobilization generated substantial backing for the idea of placing a congressional watchdog over the executive. Wilson viewed the Weeks amendment as a divisive, an obstructive, and even a sinister challenge to his authority and managed, by one vote, to have it killed in conference. Weeks unsuccessfully sought to have the proposal adopted several months later.[5]

The Wilson administration also fought intensely, and with only partial success, against another amendment to the Lever bill introduced by the Senate Committee on Agriculture, which directly affected economic mobilization. This amendment made it illegal for any government employee, agent, or adviser to contract or influence the contracting for any supplies in which that person had any kind of pecuniary interest. It was obviously aimed at the dollar-a-year men and the cooperative committees. The measure would have wiped out or severely impaired the entire mobilization system built up since the creation of the CND–NDAC, a reality readily acknowledged by the business mobilizers and the Wilson administration. Julius Rosenwald, an NDAC commissioner, early in July told the president:

> It is vital that the cooperation which has already been established should be maintained and, furthermore, it is of the greatest importance that

> confidence exist between government and industry and that suspicion, which has existed on the part of both, be eliminated.

A few days later he publicly labeled the restrictive amendment as "stupid, shortsighted, nonsensical, and foolish."[6] Although tactless and blunt, Rosenwald expressed the sentiments of other commissioners and most businessmen involved in economic mobilization. The commissioner's utterances harmed more than helped the cause for which he spoke by creating a furor in Congress. To prevent the adoption of the amendment, the president had to step personally into the fray. On July 9 he pleaded the necessity of business advisers with Sen. Kenneth D. McKellar (D-TN), a strong supporter of the amendment and a leading critic of the existing economic mobilization structure:

> If anything in the law should make it necessary to dispense with the services, the Government would be seriously and perhaps fatally embarrassed, inasmuch as we must in the circumstances have the cooperation, and the active cooperation, of the men who are in actual control of the great business enterprises of the country. I should find myself hampered in a degree which I think you cannot realize if I were deprived of the opportunity to use these gentlemen as they are willing to be used.[7]

The most vocal spokesmen and ardent supporters of the restrictive amendment were Southern Democrats and Midwestern Progressive Republicans, politicians of a decidedly neo-Jeffersonian bent in matters of political economy. The amendment had considerable support outside those ranks precisely because the mobilization structure was so open to criticism and subject to abuse. Since an attempt to defeat the amendment outright might well have failed, the administration instead sought compromise. Senator Atlee Pomerene (D-OH) offered a substitute for the committee's amendment. Pomerene's proposal prohibited a government agent from seeking contracts in which he had an interest but allowed such an individual to recommend a contract as long as he declared his involvement in writing. Speaking for the ardent neo-Jeffersonians, McKellar ridiculed the Pomerene substitute as farcical; a simple written statement, involving information already known, would allow the dollar-a-year men and the cooperative committees to continue as before. Most members of Congress appeared to recognize the validity of McKellar's arguments, but they also seemed to grant the legitimacy of Wilson's appeal that without the cooperation of the industrial giants as well as most other businessmen, economic mobilization would be virtually impossible. Without a radical reordering of the economic system, the CND–NDAC approach or some variation of it was necessary for modern warfare. In July eighteen senators, principally neo-Jeffersonian in outlook, followed McKellar in voting against the Pomerene substitute, but fifty-three supported it, many of them believing they had no alternative if economic mobilization for war were to continue. The House backed the unsatisfactory compromise, which was in reality mostly a symbolic gesture recognizing the discomfort and doubts about the CND and its subordinate bodies.[8]

Even the Pomerene substitute probably would have been inadequate to defeat the McKellar amendment had Wilson not informed Congress early in July that he was about to reorganize the mobilization structure in a way that would eliminate the widespread conflicts of interest. The administration had begun considering a reorganization early in May. Baker was the principal architect, although a preliminary draft he submitted to Wilson on May 28, 1917, was revised considerably in consultation with the CND. On June 13 the secretary of war presented a reworked plan to the president nearly identical to the one adopted almost six weeks later. From June 13 through the end of July, creating a new coordinating agency for industrial mobilization was one of the administration's main concerns. It was during those weeks that the GMB's repeated requests for more and better economic controls and the organization of new committees or the expansion of old ones were postponed pending the reorganization. The inadequacy of the GMB and the debate in Congress had virtually brought the process of industrial mobilization to a standstill.[9]

The reorganization was delayed for about six weeks for two principal reasons. First, a muted but intense struggle was taking place within the administration over the nature of the new mobilization agency. To varying degrees, everyone involved in the debate agreed that it was necessary to have businessmen run the mobilization apparatus and act as advisers to it. Secretary of the Navy Daniels, who reflected most closely the attitudes of the neo-Jeffersonian Progressives like Senator McKellar, had the greatest reservation about that approach. Everyone also agreed, some with greater reluctance than others, that it was necessary to devise tactics that would allow businessmen to continue advising economic mobilizers without holding official or quasi-official positions as they had on the cooperative committees. At that point, agreement broke down. Baker, who remained Wilson's main adviser on economic mobilization, argued that a reshuffled GMB without much additional power would meet prevailing needs. Most important, the military services would surrender none of their prerogatives to civilians and hence would remain the key centers of authority within the administration's decentralized mobilization apparatus. At the opposite pole stood most business mobilizers in the NDAC and the GMB, with Baruch and McAdoo their most outspoken and active advocates. They wanted a centralized administration with real power in which the military services would be subordinate to civilian executives who were businessmen.

Some members of the CND, like Secretary of the Interior Lane, sought a compromise between Baker's and Baruch's positions by giving the new coordinating agency a moderate degree of power. Wilson's thought appeared close to that of Baker, but the president, along with the other CND members, believed that a new agency had to be more than merely a reshuffled GMB.

Second, the reorganization was postponed because of congressional battles over the Food and Fuel Control Act, which ran from April until early August 1917. There was a real possibility that Congress would enact a full program of price controls, pass the Senate Agricultural Committee's amendment and thereby dismantle the entire economic mobilization structure, and shackle the administration with a committee on the conduct of the war. Therefore, Wilson could not move on the reorganization proposal until the main disputes in Congress were either settled or seemed manageable. The president used the promise of reorganization to beat back or modify legislative provisions his administration opposed.

Once it seemed that Congress would pass a bill acceptable to the administration, Wilson was ready to move on industrial mobilization. He could not go too far, however. During the months of April to July, his administration had been repeatedly attacked by neo-Jeffersonians, Republicans, and even some loyal Democrats for abusing executive power through the creation and operation of the multiple mobilization bodies. Even if the president had shared the visions of Baruch and McAdoo, given the mood of Congress he would have been politically irresponsible to create a centralized mobilization administration that put real power in the hands of one man to whom the statutory powers of the War and Navy Departments were subordinate. Forming such an agency without precipitating a congressional revolt would have required some legislative sanction more forthright than that on which the CND was based. Gaining approval from Congress for such a measure when that body fought tirelessly, during wartime, over the Weeks and Agricultural Committee proposals and army appropriations would have been almost impossible. Baker's position in favor of a new mobilization agency principally under the CND and the War and Navy Departments was politically the only realistic approach during summer 1917, though it was not the best administrative solution. Baruch and McAdoo were astute in terms of need, but not of possibility. Wilson, who took a rather enigmatic stance throughout the war years over economic mobilization, mixing neo-Jeffersonian ideals with neo-Hamiltonian realism, basically supported Baker in the crucial months of June and July because the president seemed to favor this approach and because he had few practical alternatives.[10]

Baker's dominant position during the summer months is demonstrated by the fact that the NDAC—still in a sense the main mobilization agency—was not even shown the reorganization plan he had been working on since May until July 9. Smarting under congressional criticism, growing anxious over the stalled mobilization process, and operating without official knowledge of a new mobilization agency that had become a matter of repeated press speculation, the commission began pressing the CND for information and action in early July. The GMB in mid-June had initiated a study on how to achieve greater efficiency and purpose in economic mobilization. To mollify an irate NDAC, though not to seek input from it, Baker finally revealed his plan.

The commissioners were furious at the secretary's decentralized scheme, which was the opposite of the centralization they sought. Through Edward M. House, Baruch and Hollis Godfrey communicated their dissent to Wilson. The NDAC as a body then presented a compromise plan written by Franklin H. Martin to the CND. The commissioners' response, combined with the months of advocacy for centralization by McAdoo and Baruch, had some impact on Wilson. He personally revised Baker's final draft to make it more palatable to the NDAC businessmen and McAdoo, giving the business mobilizers a more prominent place in the new mobilization agency than Baker had desired. The secretary of war had become so alarmed by the demands of Baruch and his supporters for a centralized administration under business control that he had proposed putting the business mobilizers in an even more subordinate position in the new administration than they had occupied on the GMB. Baker appeared especially hostile toward Baruch, whom McAdoo persistently backed as the most qualified person to direct a centralized mobilization agency under civilian control.[11]

On July 28, 1917, the Wilson administration, through the CND, finally unveiled its plans for the new agency—the War Industries Board—which would replace the GMB on August 1. The WIB would

> act as a clearing house for the war industry needs of the Government, determine the most effective ways of meeting them and the best means and methods of increasing production, including the creation or extension of industries demanded by the emergency, the sequence and relative urgency of the needs of the different Government services, and consider price factors, and, in the first instance, the industrial and labor aspects of the problems involved, and the general questions affecting the purchase of commodities.

In terms of requirements, clearance, priority, price controls, and other aspects of industrial mobilization, this charge was the clearest and most forthright yet set out for a World War I agency. Moreover, unlike the Munitions

Standards Board and the General Munitions Board, the War Industries Board, as its name implied, was broadened from an agency tied to the needs of the armed forces to one that embraced all the nation's industry. Although the NDAC was to remain in existence, the subdivisions of the commission and the CND, which corresponded to the WIB's responsibilities, were to be transferred to the board's jurisdiction. The NDAC had clearly been eclipsed, and the nation for the first time had one centralized organization, or at least the basis for such an organization, for controlling industry.[12]

The WIB consisted of seven members. Frank A. Scott carried over from the GMB as chairman; Lt. Col. Palmer E. Pierce represented the army and Rear Adm. Frank F. Fletcher the navy; and Baruch, Hugh A. Frayne, Robert S. Brookings, and Robert S. Lovett had responsibility for raw materials, labor, finished goods, and priorities. Frayne, Brookings, and Lovett were new faces. Wilson had made it clear that he wanted a representative from labor on the board. Secretary of Labor William B. Wilson recommended Frayne, an AFL organizer, probably at the suggestion of Samuel Gompers. Brookings, a close friend of and mentor to Secretary of Agriculture David F. Houston, had had access to the White House for years. A retired St. Louis merchant, Brookings was a philanthropist who concentrated on public and educational issues and institutions. In effect, he took responsibility for the areas Howard E. Coffin and Julius Rosenwald had covered on the NDAC, since the two men had declined in influence during the hectic months of 1917. Lovett, who was known to Baker, was apparently the secretary's choice. He had simultaneously been president of the Union Pacific and Southern Pacific Railroads and at the time of his appointment was on the executive committee of the former and working with the Red Cross. Baruch, Brookings, and Lovett, along with Hoover on issues involving food, were also designated as the Allied Purchasing Commission, an arrangement that closely tied Allied buying to the general coordinating functions of the WIB.[13]

On paper, the WIB represented a considerable step toward the centralization of mobilization functions. Allied purchasing was effectively made a part of the board's responsibilities, and the military services had one representative each instead of every supply bureau having a member, as had been the case with the GMB. Further, the services were outnumbered five to two by civilians. Nonetheless, since the WIB was officially appointed by and answerable to the military-dominated CND and chaired by Baker's associate Scott, the board's success would depend to a considerable degree on cooperation from the War and Navy Departments. If they did not go along, the WIB would be little more than a refined and streamlined version of the General Munitions Board.

Among the first priorities of the WIB was devising the means by which the cooperative committees could continue to operate while escaping the censure of Congress, the public, and dissatisfied businessmen. As his principal tactic for defeating the McKellar amendment, Wilson had assured Congress that the conflicts of interest would be ended. In announcing the appointment of the WIB, the administration declared that among the board's purposes was to establish

> clearly and definitely the important tasks indicated upon direct representatives of the Government not interested in commercial and industrial activities with which they will be called upon to deal, and to make clear that there is *total disassociation of the industrial committees from the actual arrangements of purchases on behalf of the Government.* It will lodge responsibility for effective action as definitely as is possible under existing law. It does not minimize or dispense with the splendid service which representatives of industry and labor have so unselfishly placed at the disposal of the government.[14]

The appointment of Baruch, Brookings, and Lovett to the board was a major step toward resolving the issue of business representation. The three men, especially the first, favored industrial mobilization through a government-business partnership, yet none could be accused of conflicts of interest. Baruch had covered himself on that issue long before; Brookings was retired and had a public-service image; and Lovett, though on leave from the Union Pacific, was free from suspicion since the railroads remained under Willard's direction in the NDAC and Lovett's service with the Red Cross gave him the appearance of detachment. Scott had always been above criticism, and few people would criticize the labor representative, Frayne, since he was a former businessman and had a reputation as a conciliator in industrial relations. Brookings and Lovett, identified with a border state and the South, and Frayne of labor also gave greater regional and class representation to the WIB. Wilson personally made Baruch, Brookings, Lovett, and Frayne full-fledged members of the WIB after Baker had placed them in a subordinate status. The president was anxious to give the business mobilizers, and through them the entire business community, adequate recognition and representation on the board, a necessary move if industrial mobilization was to be based on private economic power.

The Pomerene amendment, which had become Section 3 of the Lever Act, required modification of the cooperative committees, a necessary step in order for the Wilson administration to live up to its commitment of separating public and private power in the operations of the WIB. Baker and Scott, who both favored and indeed recognized the essentiality of the organization of business through cooperative committees as long as military prerogatives were left intact, first attempted to have the committees continue as they were with their members declaring in writing conflicts of interest that occurred. The secretary of war and his lieutenant thus sought to exempt the members of the cooperative committees from the criminal penalties of Section 3 with only minimal changes in procedure. Attorney General Thomas W. Gregory scotched this approach by ruling that no such blanket exemption was possible; the ambiguities of Section 3 were such that in certain situations where contracts were awarded, the cooperative committees could run afoul of the law despite the declaration of conflicts of interest. Even before the attorney general's opinion was handed down, businessmen concerned about their status under Section 3 were leaving or threatening to leave the cooperative committees. Gregory's action accelerated the trend. A new approach was essential if the WIB were to maintain its business advisers and yet meet the demands of Section 3. A different scheme was also necessary to reassure Congress, the public, and discontented business elements.[15]

Walter S. Gifford, still director of the CND, led the move to reorder the business advisory system. In doing so, Gifford merely returned to the approach that he had advocated, as opposed to that favored by Baruch, shortly after the NDAC was organized: broad-based, representative, democratically selected advisory committees. He turned to the U.S. Chamber of Commerce to achieve this goal. Actually, the CND director had never given up on his hopes for representative national industrial organizations and consequently had maintained good relations with the chamber, the largest and most representative of the various commercial associations. Close ties with the chamber were ensured when Gifford appointed Waddill Catchings as one of his assistants in June 1917. Catchings was president of ironwork firms in New York and Ohio and had served in various responsible positions in the J. P. Morgan and Company Export Department from June 1915 to January 1917. In summer 1917 he was appointed chairman of the chamber's Committee on Cooperation with the CND. The chamber had suggested Catchings's appointment to Gifford as a means by which the chamber could be informed of the mobilization program, pass the information on to the general business community, and offer its advice and service to the economic mobilization agencies. Outside the mobilization administrations themselves, the chamber was perhaps the best informed and most enlightened body on economic mobilization. It desired almost the same goals as the business mobilizers. Moreover, it had participated in industrial mobilization in limited ways since early 1917 and was always on the lookout for a larger and more important role.[16]

As Gifford and chamber officials agreed in September 1917, the chamber would supervise the formation of new industrial advisory committees and certify them. Industries with trade associations or similar societies would "democratically" elect members to represent them before the WIB. Precautions were to be exercised to ensure that nonmembers had a voice. For unorganized industries, the chamber would facilitate organization and, in cases where forming a trade association was impractical, would select a representative body for an industry. The elected or selected bodies were called war service committees. Unlike the NDAC, MSB, and GMB committees, their members were private, not public representatives; industry financed their operations, and they were to remain in an advisory rather than an administrative or executive role. The chamber had been advocating such a system since before the war. It was based in part on the British mobilization experience and reflected the organization's long-term goals for the American political economy.[17]

The war service committees secured business far more immunity from the antitrust laws than even the most sanguine advocates of industrial cooperation had espoused during the Progressive years. A private commercial body, not the federal government, certified that the committees represented the collective interests of business. The Gifford-chamber strategy also led to the coming of age of the modern trade association movement. Associations grew rapidly in number and importance during the war years.

The change from the informal, legally tenuous NDAC cooperative committees—which were reminiscent of the ambiguous relations between government and industry during the Progressive years—to fully private, nongovernmental councils had important effects. The creation of the war service committees recaptured the full support of most industrial elements for economic mobilization. Without that support, the task of harnessing the economy for war would have been difficult if not impossible. Furthermore, by allowing the committees to be formed, the federal government dropped its reservations about trade associations. This step was born of necessity, for industry could treat with the government only on an organized basis.

The creation of the committees also served the long-term goals of the Chamber of Commerce. Writing in the *Nation's Business* in August 1918, Chamber of Commerce president Harry A. Wheeler, who had been called back to the presidency to use his enormous prestige and ability to lead the organization during the war crisis, declared:

> Creation of the War Service Committees promises to furnish the basis for a truly national organization of industry whose proportions and opportunities are unlimited. . . . The integration of business, the expressed aim of the National Chamber, is in sight. War is the stern teacher that is driving home the lesson of cooperative effort.[18]

The war was also having an impact on the chamber's organization and focus. Prior to World War I, the strength and numbers of the organization had rested with the local, state, and regional bodies. With national trade associations growing in number and the demands for forming war service committees, the chamber assumed a much more national orientation.[19]

Industry in general responded positively to the war service committee approach, but key members of the WIB did not, the most important being Baruch and Lovett. The latter distrusted trade associations in general, and the former, reflecting the views and values of the moguls to whom he was closely tied, remained convinced that his flexible and elitist approach was superior to and more realistic than the so-called democratic methods. This division had curious consequences. In late 1917 and early 1918, when Gifford, backed by the Chamber of Commerce, sought to have the War Industries Board officially endorse the standing and the work of the war service committees, the board refused to do so. Baruch and Lovett's aversion to war service committees was one aspect, but the WIB proved uncooperative because it wanted to avoid sanctioning chamber-certified committees that might come under the same censure as the cooperative committees they replaced. In any case—and characteristic of the entire World War I mobilization structure—the less an agency's duties were defined and the more ambiguous its status remained, the more latitude it had to function and carry out its declared or understood responsibilities.

Moreover, the WIB, always fighting for a measure of power, would not consider giving an organization like the chamber any official status that might detract from the limited authority the board possessed. The WIB did sanction various war service committee agreements, and board officials appointed numerous war service committees on their own, which the chamber then certified. Nonetheless, relations between the WIB and the chamber, though often close, remained on an unofficial basis throughout the war years. To give more formal recognition to the efforts of the Chamber of Commerce, Gifford later sought to have the Commerce Department certify the war service committees. Secretary William C. Redfield wisely declined. Why should his department take responsibility for unofficial bodies with which it had no connection and which might make it vulnerable to criticism from the public or Congress?[20]

From September 1917, the war service committee system was slowly phased in while the cooperative committees were being disbanded. In October–November 1917 Gifford exercised the authority he had to order an end to the cooperative committees. Nonetheless, in some instances the old committees were not fully phased out and the new war service committees established until as late as June 1918. Baruch's cooperative committees on raw materials were some of the last to be reorganized along war service committee lines. Since the range of the WIB was constantly growing as the effects of war reached more and more industries, especially in 1918, many of the war service committees were new, e.g., refractories and locomotive cranes. Others, like those dealing with steel, were essentially the old groups with new names and minor changes involving expansion in the size and number of their subcommittees. Some were hybrids between the old and new systems, as was the case with petroleum and textiles.[21]

The organization of war service committees, or the reorganization of the cooperative committees as war service committees, necessitated a restructuring of the WIB. This process began in fall and winter 1917 but did not get fully under way until spring and summer 1918. Almost from the outset of the NDAC, the cooperative committees had moved from being advisory bodies to performing executive functions. Once those committees began to be phased out, the WIB was left without experts to determine policy for and to administer the nation's industries. To fill this vacuum, the WIB executives began organizing what came to be called commodity sections. The sections consisted of a chief and assistants, who usually came from the industry to be regulated, and representatives from the army, navy, and other claimant agencies. Quite often, the board simply made the existing cooperative committee into a WIB commodity section and then had a war service committee appointed to advise it; such was the case with lumber and cotton goods. In other cases, executives like Baruch, Rosenwald, and Brookings had begun to recruit specialists outside the cooperative committees to advise them before reorganization began in fall and winter 1917. Hence, they already had the nucleus of a commodity section and simply had to expand and formalize existing procedures. Baruch had made more progress than the others in recruiting expert assistants. This enabled him to organize commodity sections with relative ease for chemicals and steel, based on the assistance of Leland L. Summers, who had been advising Baruch since late 1916 and had served in J. P. Morgan and Company's Export Department, and of J. Leonard Replogle, president of the American Vanadium Company, who was tapped by Baruch in August 1917. In many other industries, such as optical glass and cranes, commodity sections had to be built from scratch.

The WIB ultimately organized fifty-seven commodity sections, and the Chamber of Commerce certified about 300 war service committees. Some of the former operated individually within the board; most of the more important ones, however, were grouped into divisions that followed the natural patterns of the economy: iron and steel, chemicals, textiles, hides, leather, and leather goods, and so forth. The war service committees operated with the commodity section to which they corresponded.[22]

In order to meet the demands of Section 3 of the Lever Act and to prevent a repeat of the public and congressional dissent over the operations of the cooperative committees, the war service committees, not officially part of the WIB and certified only by the Chamber of Commerce and not by any government body, were only supposed to "advise" the commodity sections. The quasi-official historian of the WIB, Grosvenor Clarkson, has described the commodity section–war service committee system's operation:

> Through the commodity sections on the side of Government and the war service committees on the side of business, all industry was merged in the War Industries Board. Subject to the veto of the Chairman of the Board, as the supreme interpreter of the national good, industry imposed its own emergency laws and regulations and assumed nine tenths of the burden and responsibility of enforcing them.

Clarkson further maintained that the commodity section–war service committee system was the very nerve center and major source of policy of the WIB. The board was a form of industrial self-regulation writ large.[23]

The reality that Clarkson implied or omitted was that the control of the WIB over the commodity section–war service committees was always tenuous, that no real or imagined line separated the official commodity sections from the unofficial war service committees, and that conflicts of interest and other abuses were rife throughout the WIB. These patterns became most evident when the board began functioning with greatest effectiveness from spring 1918 under a reorganized structure and with a new chairman, but they actually existed from the beginning of the NDAC and continued through the MSB, the GMB, and the first organization of the WIB.

Almost without exception, the commodity sections and the war service committees constituted an organic unity in which any division between public and private interests was obliterated.[24] Most commodity section chiefs and their staffs not only came from the industry that they directed but also were often from an industry's trade association, its war service committee, or both. Harry T. Dunn, president of the Fisk Rubber Company, was selected as head of the Rubber and Rubber Goods Section. Edward E. Parsonage, who became chief of the Agricultural Implements and Wood Products Section, was secretary and manager of the John Deere Wagon Company and had been president of the National Implement and Vehicle Association. Charles C. Hanch, chief of the Automotive Products Section, was treasurer of the Studebaker Corporation; Murray Sargent, secretary of Sargent and Company, was chief of the Hardware and Hand Tool Section; and Ramsey Penquet, secretary of the Silk Section, was secretary of the Silk Association of America. Although the nature of relations between the new bodies varied from industry to industry, in all instances a commodity section had to pay close attention to the wishes of its war service committee or committees. In some cases, the committee set the parameters within which the section operated. It was not atypical for the commodity section staff as well as the war service committee to be selected in a manner designed to balance the various interests and power groups within an industry. Since so many diverse interests and needs within an industry had to be recognized and satisfied in order to guarantee the smooth operation of the commodity section and its war service committee(s), the chief of a commodity section was frequently chosen more for his ability to get along with diverse groups and individuals than for his technical expertise.

Because industry provided the personnel for staffing the key sectors of the WIB, it also controlled the information that the board required for mobilizing the economy. Dominance through personnel and information meant that industry shaped essential wartime controls such as clearance, priority, and pricing.

The stronger the commodity sections–war service committees were, the more independent of the WIB executives they could afford to be. The sections could and did deny them full information as to their actions. Even if the WIB chairman had full knowledge of what transpired, effective control was simply beyond the reach of one man and his relatively small staff. The commodity sections, in effect, ran like small war industries boards with only general, not detailed, direction from the top. The presence of representatives from the military and other claimant agencies in the commodity sections put some checks on the power of business, as did the fact than in certain industries, rival factions vied for power within the commodity section–war service committee structure. But these restraints were not consistent or reliable.

The operations of power within the WIB dictated two crucially important and interrelated realities. The board was a rather crude and inefficient planning mechanism. Fifty-seven centers of power instead of one gave the board a decentralized quality. And the WIB was dominated by a business ideology dedicated to the notion that industries, individually and collectively, deserved as much favorable treatment and protection as they could possibly get while they mobilized the economy for war. What was best for fifty-seven particular industries did not and could not determine what was best for the war effort, the economy as a whole, or the public. Such was the case for industries like steel, aluminum, oil, nonferrous metals, munitions, and the like, let alone those that were less essential. Once the impact of war was felt throughout the economy, industries such as locomotive crane firms and businesses such as fire insurance companies rushed to the board to be included as commodity sections even though the basic rationale for a section—i.e., demand exceeding supply—did not exist. The board officials were reluctant to turn away any industry that sought membership within the WIB.

With war shortages growing and board controls expanding in number and coverage, most industries, many of which had resisted cooperating with the economic mobilization earlier in the war or in the prewar months, realized that membership in the WIB was the best way to protect their interests. Within the board, industries had access to information they would otherwise be denied or have difficulty getting; they could help shape the controls to which they would be subject and ward off arbitrary action; and through the commodity section, the war service committee, and their trade associations, they could devise collective strategies that would protect and benefit all or most firms within an industry.

The WIB, in short, provided industry with the attributes of planning but few of the drawbacks. An agency dominated by industry controlled the process of harnessing the economy while remaining free of the encumbrances and threats of the antitrust laws. The more enlightened business elements had sought such a situation before the war, and once the war began, increasing numbers of businessmen were seeing the virtues of planning. Essential for war purposes, planning also served many private ends at the same time.

Especially important to the operations of the WIB was the limited efforts by the chairman and principal officials to reduce conflicts of interest and real or possible abuse.[25] They did discourage the appointment of trade association or war service committee officials to commodity section positions. At times they also sought to have someone from outside the trade appointed as head of a commodity section. In almost every instance, however, their wishes and suggestions were ignored, and industry dictated the selection of personnel while paying little attention to the sensitivities and putative authority of the WIB executives. Board officials passed a resolution in June 1918 requiring all commodity section personnel to declare their affiliations and interests; they further sought to get section members to notify the board when they dealt with matters involving their firms and to absent themselves from negotiations in which their firms had an interest. The WIB also suggested that commodity section officials not continue to be reimbursed by their companies.

It is surprising not that these requests were made but that they were few in number, gently stated, and late in coming. Moreover, these suggestions and regulations were not enforced. Individuals who avoided conflicts of interest and declared where their involvement with firms overlapped the board's or their own activity did so more because of personal choice or from firm or industry policy than because of the WIB's effort. Furthermore, most evidence indicates that the suggestions for not taking compensation from a company were almost totally ignored. The preponderance of individuals, except for a relative few at lower levels within the board who received government compensation, served for a dollar a year and received their salaries elsewhere. Overall, little effort was made to establish, and certainly not to enforce, regulations to minimize conflicts of interest and abuse or possible abuse. In view of the wide field of operation of the WIB, this state of affairs was truly extraordinary. Never in the nation's history was so much public power placed in private hands with so few checks.

In permitting this situation to arise, the business war mobilizers like Baruch became trapped by their own ideology.[26] They had argued that public power could be safely turned over to industry for mobilization purposes without the risk of abuse or any real conflict of interest because business would act responsibly out of its own self-interest and a concept of the public good. Yet Baruch and other business mobilizers did not move to enforce the selection of disinterested personnel or to limit conflicts of interest and other abuses for two reasons. First, forcing these moves on industry would have threatened its cooperation—the basis of the entire mobilization structure. A showdown with the representatives of industry in the WIB could have led to intransigence, thereby paralyzing the mobilization effort. Second, for Baruch and his colleagues to have attempted coercion would have contradicted their ideal of voluntary cooperation. They were out to prove the virtues of industry and its "patriotism." Calling insistently for an end to conflicts of interest and moving to enforce their will would have been tantamount to admitting that they had been wrong and their assumptions false. The point is illustrated by the request of Baruch and other mobilizers that commodity section officials forgo private compensation, but Baruch did not push for this change. Indeed, he did not really desire it. Instead, he wanted to hold dollar-a-year men up to the public as proof of business' sense of sacrifice and dedication to public service. Business mobilizers actually argued along these lines. The point was largely moot in any case since few businessmen would operate without outside salaries, and government compensation was out of the question. The ideological claims of Baruch and his counterparts aside, the dollar-a-year-man phenomenon truly demonstrated the business community's recognition that lending its executives to the WIB was a sound investment since these executives ensured business control of the board.

Besides the lack of checks on abuse and conflicts of interest within the WIB, the other remarkable characteristic of the agency is that businessmen and board executives remained convinced that the only reason for efforts in the direction of probity was to satisfy an unsophisticated Congress and public. As a group, they viewed themselves as beyond the need of policing. They thought that vast power could be turned over to them safely and without anxiety because their morality warranted it. It seems that many businessmen and war mobilizers were true believers in the rhetoric of altruistic capitalism regularly appearing in the *Nation's Business.* In a real sense, the WIB, like its predecessor agencies, operated outside public scrutiny and control throughout the war. In the view of Baruch and his colleagues, to do so was not a problem. Indeed, there could be no problem, almost by definition, because business was in control and could be trusted. Baruch, who had such sensitivity for business prerogatives, lacked a comparable sense for public prerogatives. He was incensed by Section 3 of the Lever Act—intended to reduce conflicts of interest in government contracting—because it reflected ill upon his ideology and that of the business community. He argued that the commodity section–war service committee substitute for the cooperative committees was a charade imposed upon the people. He seemed to expect the public and Congress to accept the cooperative committee system because, in effect, no abuse or real conflict of interest existed. Hence, when the commodity sections and war service committees were introduced, he did little or nothing to change the system and went along, ever so reluctantly, with the charade.

Despite its shortcomings, the WIB was a giant step forward. It made effective industrial control possible. The board organized or put into motion the process of organizing private industry, it allowed coordinated mobilization, and it brought together a body of trained personnel. Within a six-month period, the nation had devised the system for mobilizing the economy. Whether it worked depended on the Wilson administration's willingness to empower the War Industries Board.

## HOBBLING THE WIB

As it turned out, the president and his advisers still dragged their heels. The reorganization of July 28, 1917 did not deal with the fundamental flaw in the mobilization system: The War Industries Board, like its predecessors, lacked authority. Officially created by and answerable to the Council of National Defense, the WIB had only advisory powers. The board's formation had been a victory for Secretary of War Baker and the War Department. They had resisted the concerted drive for an agency independent of and superior to the military services, and in giving the WIB only limited powers, Wilson had backed them.[27] The army still had the authority to force its methods on the economy, and the WIB had to stand by helplessly. An impasse had been reached: Either the army had to give way or the mobilization program would halt. The latter occurred before the former.

Most of the problems that had plagued the National Defense Advisory Commission, the Munitions Standards Board, and the General Munitions Board in the early months of the war continued with the War Industries Board from August 1917 to March 1918. The board was a collection of partially related parts, not an organic whole. Baruch continued to expand his responsibilities in raw materials in terms of industries covered and assistants added, such as Replogle, who took charge of steel, and Pope Yeatman, a consulting engineer who headed nonferrous metals. As in the past, Baruch was building the most authoritative and efficient center of economic power within the mobilization agency, an accomplishment that would propel him to the top of WIB operations. Brookings, in charge of finished products, also proved forceful and energetic. He gained control of Rosenwald's supplies committees and began organizing commodity sections on machine tools, electrical equipment, army vehicles, and so forth.[28] Baruch, Brookings, and Lovett together served as the Allied Purchasing Commission. But Lovett's suspicion of Baruch as a former Wall Street speculator prevented the selection of a chairman, which left the commission without effective leadership. Baruch brought in Alexander Legge, vice-president and general manager of International Harvester Company, who gradually began to direct Allied purchasing. Legge was limited in his work, however, until the purchasing commission had a chair who was able to delegate authority.[29]

Progress by individual commissioners did not equate to progress for the WIB as a whole. The consequences of the WIB's lack of authority showed up almost immediately as Baruch, Brookings, and their commodity section chiefs attempted to bring some order to wartime purchasing. Without the power to enforce decisions on the business community and the claimant agencies, not much could be done. The procurement agencies remained the central problem. In carrying out buying, the army and navy personnel continued to use or to ignore the WIB as it suited their purposes. The War Department was more cooperative than the Navy Department in some respects, but the War Department's decentralized and inefficient supply mechanism prevented it from becoming an effective partner. The department was simply incapable of meaningfully coordinating its activities with those of the board. The Navy Department, desirous of protecting its efficient supply apparatus from confusion in the War Department and the limpness of the WIB, refused the board any authority over its purchasing. Consequently, both the War and Navy Departments operated much more outside the WIB system than inside it.

Civilian contractors therefore often found it advantageous to ignore the WIB also and to work directly with the military services.

This result inevitably produced competition among contractors for access to the armed services and vice versa and heightened the general economic dislocation. Even full military cooperation would not have ensured smooth mobilization under the WIB, however. The U.S. Shipping Board, the Aircraft Production Board, and other civilian claimant agencies were not represented on the WIB and hence not subject to its coordinating efforts. By late 1917 and early 1918 those agencies were purchasing goods at significant levels; the increased number of claimant agencies led to greater economic confusion. Still, the military services constituted the chief problem since they did the overwhelming amount of buying. Until they were brought under control, the civilian claimant agencies were an additional problem but not the principal source of difficulty.[30]

The WIB did an even poorer job in clearance, priority, and pricing than in coordinating purchasing. The Clearance Committee that had been organized under the GMB continued under the WIB. The committee was unable to persuade the military services to clear all contracts with it for the purpose of balance and stability, not really surprising since it represented a continuation of patterns under the GMB. What was surprising was that Baruch and other WIB civilian executives proved uncooperative. They viewed the committee as an appendage of the War Department because Chester C. Bolton, a reserve colonel from Cleveland and a friend of Baker, chaired it. With opposition or noncooperation coming from within and outside the board, the Clearance Committee had little opportunity to succeed.[31]

The Priority Committee of the WIB did much better, but it suffered from the same flaws that enervated the WIB as a whole. Lovett, as commissioner of priorities, inherited a committee from the GMB. A driving, energetic, and capable manager, he quickly set about strengthening the rather ineffective agency. First, he expanded his staff with recruits from the railroads, other businessmen and attorneys, and most significantly, Edwin B. Parker, from a prominent Houston law firm. Lovett then asked a Price, Waterhouse and Company consultant to survey the operations of the Priority Committee and recommend a reorganization, which was accomplished in November 1917 and was so successful that the new setup continued as the basic priority structure for the remainder of the war. Even before the reorganization, Lovett had issued the first priority order, Circular no. 1, on September 21, 1917, which provided the basis for classifying all orders for steel. Although this order set a major precedent, it was not followed up in a timely manner by priority orders for additional products. Lovett greatly strengthened the structure and functioning of the Priority Committee, but like his fellow commissioners on the WIB, his efforts were limited by lack of authority. As elsewhere, the War Department cooperated in part, the Navy Department and other claimant agencies hardly at all, and civilian producers only sporadically. Although it tried, the Priority Committee failed to prevent the military services from using their statutory authority to commandeer supplies and plants. Unlike the Clearance Committee, the Priority Committee had the personnel and the structure necessary to do a competent job. Nevertheless, it lacked sufficient authority, and without it there was not much that it could do.[32]

The WIB spent as much time on the price control issue as on any other matter, but no final policy emerged until after March 1918.[33] For once, Baker and the WIB business executives were in agreement on a broad issue of policy: maximize output while avoiding excessive profits. To achieve those two goals, Baker, Baruch, and other individuals generally favored executive agencies setting prices at a level that would allow high-cost producers to continue or begin operations and an excess-profits tax to recoup the unwarranted earnings of the low- or medium-cost producers. The WIB executives faced opposition to this strategy from many sides. There was a rising cry from the public against price inflation, and members of Congress were beginning to grow restless over this critically important matter. Congress almost enacted total price controls as part of the legislation that became the Lever Act before backing off from that drastic proposal. Board executives ultimately opposed price controls dictated by legislation, fearing that they could be rigid or require the mobilization leaders to take action they would consider unwise. Further, producers of steel, copper, and other primary metals opposed a WIB price-fixing program. Nearly continuous negotiations had taken place since March 1917 without much success. Late in September WIB officials and the steel and copper industries finally agreed on compromise prices, which could have served as a precedent for a general price-fixing policy, but it did not. Future price regulation was sporadic and incremental.

The stubborn and shortsighted position of executives in the steel, copper, and other industries on voluntary price controls created conditions in which Congress might institute mandatory price regulations. It also cast considerable doubt on the business mobilizers' claim that once a mobilization program was under way, industry's cooperation could be depended upon. Industry's intransigence also highlighted the WIB's weaknesses, as the WIB executives could do little in the face of business resistance. An industry like steel, with a limited number of producers, could theoretically be commandeered, but everyone involved wanted to avoid such drastic measures. In an industry such as lumber, where there were thousands of producers, government seizure was simply beyond the realm of the possible.

Moreover, the president's stance presented problems for the WIB's push for price regulation. By resisting the movement toward a clearly defined policy, Wilson was as responsible as recalcitrant business people for inflationary pressures and price gouging. He had rushed in to protect the cooperative committees when they were threatened by the amendments to the measures that became the Lever Act, but he was much more reluctant to assuage business on the price issue. In a public declaration in mid-July, he indirectly criticized steel, copper, and other industries for putting profits ahead of patriotism, insisted that any policy would have to ensure "just" prices, and averred that prices set for the government would have to apply to the Allies and the civilian economy. In reality, statutory authority existed for price controls for military purchasing, controls for Allied purchasing were legally dubious, and controls for the general economy lacked any legal base. The president confused the issues involved without advancing the movement for price control.

Clearly, most of business, like the WIB executives, wanted a systematized, rational, broad-based pricing policy. The issue was at least as important as any facing government, yet Wilson was slower to move on it than on any other. Unlike most other mobilization questions, he would not delegate authority to Baker, perhaps because of the sensitivity of the subject. Decisive presidential action on prices alone, however, would not have solved the problem. As WIB personnel repeatedly emphasized, pricing policies could not be resolved in a vacuum. They could be worked out satisfactorily only within the context of coordinated buying, priority, clearance, and so on. The WIB, like its predecessors, helped procurement agencies set prices on individual contracts, but a meaningful overall price-control policy awaited a strengthened civilian mobilization agency.

There were no effective policies for purchasing, clearance, priority, and pricing. Yet the need for these controls grew as the mobilization program expanded. Thus, matters appeared to get worse, not better, as the war effort gained momentum. Indeed, the chances of instituting the necessary economic controls appeared to recede as the confused war economy expanded in size and complexity and became more difficult to manage.

As in the past, the WIB business mobilizers, prodded by their commodity section chiefs who were being pressured by the business community, pressed the CND and Wilson to give the board some real authority. Their efforts encountered the executive passivity that had characterized the council from the beginning. Furthermore, WIB chairman Scott opposed reforms. He continued to hold to the conviction that the civilian mobilization agencies existed only to help the military fulfill its duties and reflected the attitude of Baker and the War and Navy Departments that the WIB, like its predecessor agencies, should not interfere with military prerogatives. [34]

With Scott as chairman, the War Industries Board at least functioned. Early in September 1917, however, after agonizing months spent in government service, Scott's health broke, and on October 26 he officially resigned. Despite his limitations, Scott had inspired the confidence of Baker and the military because he shared their views. As chairman of the GMB and the WIB, Scott served as a bridge between the civilian mobilization agencies and the military. Once he resigned, the armed services and the CND, dominated by Baker, had more reason to suspect and resist the WIB.[35] The WIB, which had faltered under Scott, stumbled after his departure. Lovett reluctantly took over as acting chairman in October and was replaced late in November by Daniel Willard, whom Baker and Wilson virtually drafted. On January 11, 1918, Willard quit in disgust at the board's impotence. After mid-January rapid deterioration occurred; a crippled WIB simply could not fulfill its functions. Various sections remained active, but there was no overall direction. Like a convulsed person, WIB's limbs twitched without central motor control. For a time, a so-called War Council, made up of representatives from leading war agencies and other groups, tried to provide leadership, but without much success. A crisis was at hand. A new WIB chairman was not appointed until March, since no one who was considered qualified would take the job unless sweeping changes were inititated.[36]

The paralysis gripping the board was matched by that in the economy. Uncontrolled procurement overloaded Northeastern manufacturers with contracts far beyond their capacity to meet them. In the unusually severe winter of 1917–1918, fuel was critically short, and the railroad and shipping industries virtually halted in some sections of the nation. The mobilization effort, indeed the entire economy, appeared to be grinding to a halt. To remedy the transportation crisis, in December 1917 the administration was forced to bring the railroads under national control. But overall coordination of procurement and production was also essential to resolve the economic crisis. On that crucial issue the Wilson administration was at a stalemate.[37]

## STRENGTHENING THE WIB

In the absence of executive leadership, the Senate Military Affairs Committee, under the Democratic maverick Sen. George E. Chamberlain of Oregon, moved on its own. The committee conducted an investigation of the War Department from December 12, 1917, until the end of March 1918—one of five major investigations of the war effort launched by Congress when it came into session in the first days of December. The inquiry established beyond question the chaos in army supply and highlighted its effects on the economy.

The Chamberlain Committee was greatly influenced by Waddill Catchings, chairman of the War Committee of the U.S. Chamber of Commerce. Catchings had served as an assistant to CND director Gifford until resigning in November 1917 when the chamber's bitter criticism of the chaotic state of the administration's program of industrial mobilization made his presence on the CND untenable. Catchings argued before the Chamberlain Committee that chamber members had devoted months of full-time effort to perfecting the nation's mobilization machinery, only to have conditions deteriorate rather than improve. Businessmen found their economic fortunes threatened not by government regulation but by government chaos. With a united chamber behind him, Catchings recommended that the United States follow the British example: separate procurement from the military and place it under a civilian-controlled ministry of munitions and create a war cabinet to direct the overall national war effort.[38]

In January 1918 the Chamberlain Committee presented two bills to Congress incorporating the chamber's recommendations. The proposed legislation led to the most extended and knowledgeable debate on economic mobilization heard in the halls of Congress during World War I. Unlike the June–August 1917 debate involving the Weeks, Pomerene, and other amendments to the Lever Act, this debate concentrated less on the abuses of mobilization and more on the inadequacies of the mobilization agencies and the obstruction by the War Department. Legislation for a ministry of munitions was seriously considered although the war cabinet idea was not. To circumvent the pending legislation, the army began to reform its supply system.

More important, the Wilson administration came forth with the Overman Act, written by Judge Advocate General Enoch H. Crowder and introduced by Sen. Lee S. Overman (D-NC). The bill gave the president nearly unlimited authority to reorganize all parts of the executive branch of government to meet the demands of warfare. With the full weight of the administration behind the compromise proposal, the Chamberlain Committee's legislation never stood a chance. In May 1918 the Overman bill passed with only slight opposition.[39]

The compromise succeeded only because in March Wilson put an end to the War Department's domination of the economic mobilization program. Using his powers as president and commander-in-chief, Wilson separated the WIB from the CND and placed it directly under his leadership. After the passage of the Overman Act, Wilson confirmed this action with an executive order. To chair the strengthened board, the president selected Bernard M.

Baruch. According to Wilson's instructions, the WIB's specific and general powers were great indeed, and authority over the board was centered in the office of the chairman. Baruch was to have general authority over mobilization, including the coordination of purchasing, clearance, and priority, and he was to obtain advance information on all requirements so as to facilitate planning. "In brief," Wilson's letter of instructions read, the WIB chairman "should act as the general eye of all supply departments in the field of industry." Since the reformed WIB still did not have statutory authority, however, its power was limited because much of the board's action would remain legally tenuous. Moreover, the president's directive was vaguely qualified on many points, and Baruch was specifically instructed to leave alone those areas that were operating smoothly and to "interfere as little as possible with the present normal processes of purchase and delivery in the several Departments." Nevertheless, with Wilson's full backing, the nearly complete support of business, and the critical conditions in the economy, the WIB was in a position to achieve a significant degree of centralized control over the mobilization process. The winter crisis, therefore, was resolved with the military services maintaining control of supply but not of the economy.[40]

Probably without anyone fully realizing its consequences, the Overman Act set a most important precedent for twentieth-century warfare in the United States. Unlike the military in most belligerent nations, the U.S. military services continued to procure their own munitions and therefore remained in a position to affect the economy, most directly and vitally during war but also in peacetime. In contrast to the American experience, Great Britain and France during World War I separated procurement to varying degrees from the services and placed it under civilian-controlled munitions ministries. Even in prerevolutionary Russia, the armed services did not maintain unqualified control of their own purchasing. In Germany quite a different pattern emerged. The economy was largely mobilized under military authorities in league with large industrial elements.[41]

Maintaining procurement in the hands of the armed services was dictated more by realities of the American political economy than by military necessity. Businessmen had directed economic mobilization since April 1917 because they were the only people qualified to do so. Yet Wilson, members of his administration, Congress, and the public at large doubted the ability of business to place the interests of the nation above its own and resisted giving businessmen additional power.[42] Such attitudes, combined with the desire to avoid political and economic changes during the war, led to industry's receiving a great deal of latitude for improving the mobilization machinery while ultimate authority continued to reside with the traditional procurement agencies. Only when that expedient failed did the business-dominated WIB gain some authority through the Overman Act.

To many government officials, going further than the Overman legislation by separating procurement authority from the armed services was both undesirable and politically hazardous. It would have meant turning over to industry direct responsibility for billions of dollars worth of contracts. The ministry of munitions legislation supported by the Chamberlain Committee was no more than a general grant of authority for a director of munitions to perform procurement functions. The director would have had to depend heavily on the WIB or some agency controlled by businessmen to carry out his responsibilities. Of course, even in the WIB system, some contracts were virtually in industry's hands, and the board had considerable influence over others. Nonetheless, as long as the armed services maintained the legal right to procure for themselves, real or ceremonial distinctions between government and business were preserved. Since the commodity section–war service committee system nominally separated private and public interests, Congress appeared resigned to WIB operations.

Yet the dollar-a-year-man and commodity section–war service committee practices—the very lifeblood of the WIB—proved vulnerable. They came under repeated attack during 1917 from neo-Jeffersonian elements, and in January 1918 legislation was introduced to prohibit the use of industrial advisory committees and government officials serving on a nominal salary. Instead, the impetus was for the wartime economy to be run by paid employees free of compromising affiliations.[43] The legislation failed, and critics of abuses in the NDAC and the WIB were largely ignored. Had Congress moved to place procurement in the hands of the WIB or attempted to write detailed legislation to guide civilians in performing procurement functions, the WIB's modus operandi for mobilization would have been jeopardized, as the debate over the Pomerene amendment to the Lever Act had fully demonstrated.

The Overman Act allowed the administration and Congress to dodge the vexatious problems of industrial mobilization—a solution satisfactory to few people but better than any other readily available alternative. The WIB was strengthened without in any way disturbing its operations or clearly defining its authority. Moreover, the War Department—the major obstacle to successful mobilization—was forced into line. Issues almost too complex for direct resolution in the unique context of the American political economy were thereby avoided.

Business representatives had every reason to support the Overman compromise and did so. Appearing before the Chamberlain Committee, the business members of the CND and WIB insisted on the need for real authority centered in the WIB, but none of them favored a ministry of munitions.[44] As members of the Wilson administration, they could not have done otherwise. As long as the president was willing to strengthen the WIB, they had no reason to press for the new ministry. Furthermore, businessmen within the government were conscious of the threat a ministry of munitions would present to the existing mobilization machinery. While still chairman of the crippled and helpless WIB during the winter crisis of 1917–1918, Daniel Willard argued to the Chamber of Commerce leaders in early December that their proposal for a munitions ministry was too extreme. Businessmen, he maintained, had been called to Washington to supplement, not to replace, government. Should the ministry of munitions be implemented, he doubted "if [businessmen] would find as sympathetic a point of contact with the governmental agencies as they were able to find at the present time." Several months later, in the pages of the *Nation's Business,* Willard pleaded with businessmen not to support a supply ministry. It was a risky experiment requiring legislation, he maintained, implying that such legislation was undesirable.[45] Grosvenor B. Clarkson and Gen. Hugh S. Johnson, both intimately involved with the wartime economy, concluded that the flexibility granted the NDAC and the WIB by the lack of specific statutes was a decided advantage.[46] The attitude of businessmen within the administration apparently influenced the business community. In February 1918 the Chamber of Commerce, which had been largely responsible for the Senate Military Affairs Committee bill, switched its support to the Overman Act and defended the legislation against its critics. "Those in charge of the administrative machinery of Government" were opposed to more extended legislation, announced a chamber member. Through the Overman Act, the desired ends could be achieved without going through an unduly cumbersome legislative process.[47]

During the crisis that led to reorganizing the WIB in March 1918, widespread discontent with the mobilization structure had spread throughout the industrial community, producing demands for a major overhaul. Industry was responding more from fear than from any considered commitment to planning per se. Since late 1915 the Chamber of Commerce had been working diligently not only to perfect plans for a rationalized wartime economy and to have its proposals accepted by the Wilson administration but also to convince businessmen of the need for effective mobilization agencies to meet emergency conditions without disturbing the status quo. The chamber further sought to advance its peacetime goal of promoting the cooperative over the competitive ethic. That effort was a principal reason that Catchings joined the CND as Gifford's assistant, but it was also to gain greater authority for the War Bulletins, which the chamber regularly published to keep business abreast of mobilization developments. Until winter 1917–1918, the chamber's efforts did not have much impact.

Yet the WIB's virtual paralysis and growing economic chaos created desperation within the business community—a condition that won broad support for the chamber and the reforms it favored. When Catchings testified before the Chamberlain Cómmittee in December 1918 and called for a munitions ministry and a war cabinet, he came as close as any one person could in speaking for the general business community. In whole or in part, the Chamber of Commerce had the backing of most of the business press. Specific as well as general anxieties moved industry in the direction of demanding a mobilization structure that could cope with the exigencies of war. By late 1917 exponentially increasing war demand was causing shortages, cutbacks, and interrupted production felt by most industries—a situation that had not been experienced before.

Two developments during fall and winter 1917 brought these realities home to businessmen with enormous impact. First, in October 1917, Priority Commissioner Lovett issued WIB Priority Order no. 2, listing a group of "nonessential industries" that would be denied unlimited access to rail transportation. His action had been preceded by a request to steel manufacturers to sell alloy steel only to industries engaged in war production. Atypically for the WIB, those decisions had been made without consulting the industries involved. A storm of protest engulfed the board, and the largest and most directly affected industry, automobiles, led the way in vociferous complaint. The adverse reaction was so great and the WIB at this point so weak that it had to retreat quickly from the restrictive action.

Nonetheless, the WIB's move revealed a truth that industry had been unwilling to face: The demands of war would inevitably force the curtailment or shutdown of industries not producing for hostilities. The less effective the planning, the more capricious and haphazard this effect would be. Howard E. Coffin had constantly reiterated this point from the time he joined the Naval Consulting Board: the better the planning and the better the preparation for war, the greater the opportunity for preserving the basic structure of the existing economy. This preparation had always been a major argument of the Chamber of Commerce and other war mobilizers as well. The so-called nonessential industries and the business community in general, finally seeing and feeling the validity of Coffin's position, belatedly demanded an effective wartime planning machinery to protect their interests.

The second shock was even broader in scope than the first. In late January the fuel administrator, Harry A. Garfield, moved dramatically to deal with the fuel and transportation crisis by ordering industrial plants east of the Mississippi to close down completely for nine consecutive Mondays. Even more than the nonessential industries directives, this move convinced business of the drastic impact that war could have on the economy and of the dire consequences that would occur unless governmental agencies had the ability and the authority to deal with emergency conditions. The government's takeover of the railroads no doubt put industry on notice again of the extreme action that war could necessitate. As Washington daily exerted greater power over the economy, businessmen felt compelled to shape the government's operations in order to protect their own interests and those of the nation as they defined them.

Unlike the mobilization crisis of spring and summer 1917, the fall and winter 1917–1918 crisis was much more severe and generated enormous pressure from business, Congress, and the public for a resolution. The support of industry was especially important. For the first time, a broad spectrum of business leaders backed the business mobilizers within the Wilson administration in demanding real authority to plan the economy so that the requirements of the conflict would be met and the basic nature of the economic system preserved.[48]

Baruch's selection as chairman was as important to the WIB as its new grant of authority.[49] Indeed, Baruch played an instrumental part in writing the letter of charges that Wilson sent to him on March 4, 1918. In late January 1918 Baker and Baruch began a series of negotiations for fashioning, in effect, a new WIB. Baker had testified at length before the Chamberlain Committee, proving to be an elusive, even disingenuous, witness. He refused to grant that any fundamental flaws existed in the mobilization structure or the War Department and insisted that the administration was handling the crisis. His stance was actually untenable in the context of existing conditions, a fact he admitted in private. At Wilson's direction, Baker sought to work out with Baruch a resolution to the mobilization crisis that would bring order out of chaos and maintain control in the hands of the administration, instead of allowing Congress to take the lead. Baruch was the logical candidate to negotiate with Baker. Among the business mobilizers, Baruch was the only carryover from the NDAC on the WIB; Brookings and Lovett were relative newcomers. Baruch's staying power and steady but not overbearing insistence upon real power for the WIB had put him in a strategic position during the winter crisis. In typical fashion, he maximized his opportunities.

Baruch and Baker agreed in advance on the essential powers to be granted to the WIB in Wilson's March 4 letter. Baruch insisted that the chairman, not the board, be the source of authority, a position that Baker and Wilson ultimately accepted. The Baker-Baruch agreement was strengthened by indirect support from the CND late in February. Although Wilson made the final decision about the March 4 instructions to Baruch, the president relied heavily on the joint efforts of his subordinates. Moreover, on February 7 Baruch met personally with Wilson in order to ensure that his position was understood.

Undoubtedly Baruch also sought to advance his candidacy for the chairmanship of the strengthened WIB, an important decision yet to be made.

Baruch, the person best suited to negotiate with Baker over the powers of the reformed WIB, was also the logical candidate for WIB chairman. Nonetheless, his selection was not without controversy. Baker, Redfield, Houston, and Lane in the cabinet and Lovett and Gifford in the mobilization administration opposed or had reservations about Baruch because of his speculative career, his style, or both, or because they questioned his administrative ability. The Chamber of Commerce strongly opposed Baruch's appointment as did other business elements, partly because they believed an industrialist, not a banker or financier, was needed in the job. As alternates to Baruch, Edward R. Stettinius, John D. Ryan, president of the Anaconda Copper Company, and other businessmen were considered but rejected; the first because of his Morgan connections and the others because support for them within the cabinet was marginal. Ultimately, the respect for and trust in Baruch that Wilson had gained came into play. That fact, combined with McAdoo's support and the backing of Daniels and presidential adviser Joseph P. Tumulty—all of whom believed Baruch deserved the position for his loyalty to Wilson and the Democratic party as well as for his talents—swung the decision in favor of Baruch.

In the last analysis, Wilson had few options other than Baruch. The latter knew the workings and potential of the WIB better than anyone else, and the president was determined to make the board work. Though Baruch had opponents, he had gained more than sufficient respect within the WIB and from the business community, Congress, and the public to direct a board that carelessly and grossly mixed private and public interests and functions. A new appointee would require months to gain Baruch's experience without any guarantee that he could make the board work, and the nation did not have the luxury of time. Personal factors also favored Baruch. The new WIB head would replace Baker as the president's chief mobilization adviser, or at least complement the secretary of war while bringing a new approach to the task of economic mobilization. Wilson had already established good relations with Baruch; a new face would lack that important advantage. The realities were propitious for Baruch. His talent, experience, and highly successful maneuvering delivered to him the position he so desperately coveted.

The months between July 1917 and March 1918 saw both progress and deterioration in mobilization efforts. The War Industries Board was a major step forward in centralizing control over a wartime economy. By mitigating the crudest features of the NDAC's cooperative committees, the board's commodity section–war service committee system allowed Washington to continue the indispensable practice of using private businessmen to harness the economy. Indeed, broadened and systematized industrial representation within the WIB facilitated that risky, contentious venture by obscuring the elitist nature of the mobilization structure. As war demand grew, so too did heavy industry's hold on the mechanism for planning the economy. That reality was basic to Bernard M. Baruch's rise to the top.

Yet an improved form for civilian mobilization agencies without added authority led to decline as the disruptive forces of warfare spread. By winter 1917–1918 the Wilson administration rescued the floundering mobilization system by intricately dividing power between private and public sectors. The fundamental change involved adapting the War Department's supply system to that of the WIB. Although multiple details had to be worked out, economic mobilization could proceed because the armed services accepted the fundamental principle of a wartime system built upon the foundations of a peacetime economy. Although temporarily emphasizing the demands of war, the economic system during hostilities remained essentially civilian and elitist.

# 10
# THE WAR INDUSTRIES BOARD, MARCH–NOVEMBER 1918

## REFINING THE WIB

By March 1918, when Bernard M. Baruch assumed the chairmanship, the War Industries Board was nearing its final stage of organization. However, some tightening of structure and change in major personnel did occur. Ultimately, in addition to the commodity and miscellaneous divisions and sections, eleven major divisions or offices formulated policy for the board, the most important being Priorities, Price Fixing, Requirements, Facilities, and Conservation. The WIB itself consisted of ten members. Besides Baruch and the military representatives, there were Alexander Legge, who served as vice-chairman and head of the Requirements Division; Robert S. Brookings, head of the Price Fixing Committee; Edwin B. Parker, who replaced Robert S. Lovett as chief of Priorities; George N. Peek, who took over Finished Products from Brookings; J. Leonard Replogle, who continued to direct policy for steel; Leland L. Summers, who from the beginning of his service with Baruch acted as general technical adviser; and Hugh A. Frayne, who chaired the Labor Division.[1]

Baruch's executive style became more visible in the chairmanship, but those qualities were already characteristic by March 1918. The chairman carefully selected his subordinates to ensure that they had his confidence, then delegated responsibility and authority and backed them during any crisis or challenge. Baruch tended to operate with a relatively small coterie that got along well as a group, often included idea people, deferred to the "boss," and collectively passed upon the credentials of newcomers. Baruch preferred active industrialists who were in midcareer and moving up to positions as owners and controllers of firms or as financiers—individuals who had knowledge and experience and were probably the movers and shakers of the firms they served but who had not yet reached national prominence.

The chairman also had a penchant for business executives from the Midwest, especially from the Chicago area. Peek believed this was so because businessmen not from the Northeast presumably had broader vision and were more flexible. Perhaps, as Replogle and Clarkson maintained, since the chairman of the WIB often had to operate beyond traditional methods and without precedent, he found Midwesterners to be more attuned to such necessities. Additionally, as an outsider and as a Democrat from the predominantly Republican world of Wall Street, Baruch no doubt felt more comfortable with, and maybe less threatened by, people removed from the center of the nation's corporate and financial elite. Surely the chairman of the WIB knew that given the board's extraordinary mixing of private and public interests, lesser-known industrialists would cause less opposition than the big business moguls and their key men. Whatever the case, Legge, Peek, and Arch W. Shaw—head of the Commercial Economy Board, a Chicago businessman, publisher, and an ardent advocate of rationalizing industry—fit the mold that appeared to be Baruch's ideal executive type, and they were from the Middle West. As the second most important member of the WIB, Legge had a hand in formulating most policies of importance.

If the executives of the WIB were not archetypes of the corporate establishment, the latter were fully represented, directly or indirectly and with a full range of ages, talents, reputations, and authority, on the advisory bodies to the mobilization agencies. This situation had been true of the NDAC's cooperative committees and had continued with the WIB's war service committees. Elbert H. Gary—chairman of the board of the U.S. Steel Corporation and president of the American Iron and Steel Institute—for example, headed the iron and steel advisory committees in both the NDAC and the WIB. In one way or another, all or most of industrial and financial America's major groups were represented in the WIB, which was necessary for the board's success.[2]

The WIB executives and subdivisions acted primarily through the various commodity sections or divisions and the war service committees. These groups already existed for most industries or were in the process of being reorganized from the cooperative committees of the NDAC. For those industries not yet represented in the WIB and for which war demand was becoming urgent, commodity section–war service committee structures were created. Generally speaking, under Baruch's chairmanship the commodity sections–war service committees were strengthened and became the major source of power, information, and policymaking and implementation within the WIB.[3]

The most significant changes in the WIB's operations after March 1918 involved clearance, requirements, priority, and pricing, the last two being the most important. In all four cases, however, new methods or approaches redounded to the advantage of the commodity section–war service committee system, reflecting the realities of power within the board.

The Clearance Committee, which had originated with the General Munitions Board and continued in the WIB between July 1917 and March 1918, reached its final form with the reorganized board. The committee became more effective and less significant at the same time. It continued to pass on contracts to ensure that raw materials, parts, labor, transportation, and so on were available, that they were not placed in congested areas, and that new plants were not unnecessarily built. Previously, the Clearance Committee had foundered because its task was impossible, and claimant agencies had bypassed it at will. Once the commodity sections–war service committees were functioning reasonably well, the Clearance Committee—now the Clearance Office—turned to them to perform its functions. It gathered, classified, and recorded orders along commodity lines and passed them on for action to the commodity sections, on which both industrial and claimant agencies were represented. After deliberating on the various orders the commodity sections returned them, through the Clearance Office, to the procurement agencies with recommendations. Once the Clearance Office had referred contracts to the appropriate commodity section, it simply checked to ensure that recommendations were made and acted upon, proper records maintained, and all parties kept informed of action taken or pending.[4]

The Clearance Office actually became a subordinate unit to the much more important Requirements Division, created in June 1918. This division had the formidable task of assembling the prospective needs of the various procurement agencies and expediting the action necessary to meet them. The Clearance Office restricted itself to immediate needs; the Requirements Division dealt with future demand. Accurate information on both supply and demand had been the most crucial limiting factor for the whole mobilization program from the outset. Gradually, through the cooperative committees and then the commodity sections, the mobilization agencies acquired reasonable statistics on the supply side. Demand, however, always remained a problem because of the inability of most claimant agencies to provide reliable statistics. By mid-1918 the procurement bodies, and especially the army, were able to provide at least a semblance of projected requirements to guide the WIB's operations. The Requirements Division, which included representatives from all procurement agencies and various divisions of the board, therefore became in theory, if not in practice, among the more important sections of the WIB. Once the division began to accumulate the necessary information, however, like the Clearance Office, it depended on the commodity sections to review prospective demand in depth and to consider the steps that would be essential to meet it. As with the Clearance Office, the Requirements Division became an agency that received, categorized, recorded, and followed up on information rather than one that deliberated and made decisions based on it. For both immediate and long-run demand, the commodity sections became the subdivisions that weighed detailed information and took action based on this data.[5]

Key to ensuring the production of the projected wartime demand was a system for rating the flow of material and semifinished and finished products according to the urgency of need—a priority system.[6] Lovett had reorganized the rather haphazard and withered Priority Committee that he had inherited from the GMB after the WIB was founded in July 1917. Though the new structure was quite efficient, it lacked the authority essential for any real impact. In March 1918 Wilson, when selecting Baruch as chairman of the WIB, specifically instructed him to establish a priority system to deal with shortages involving wartime production. On March 27 the old Priorities Committee was expanded into a new Priorities Division headed by Parker.[7] On it sat representatives from the army and navy, the Food, Fuel, and Railroad Administrations, the U.S. Shipping Board, the Emergency Fleet Corporation, and the War Trade Board. Unlike the WIB, these administrations had statutory authority, which could serve to grant greater legitimacy and power to the Priority Division's actions.

The ideal of the WIB executives was that the Priority Division would act as a source of centralized authority for the board, channeling the flow of goods according to the demands of war. That did not occur in practice, however. Establishing priorities played a vital part in the economic mobilization program, but control over priorities became dispersed rather than remaining concentrated within the Priority Division. Since it did not have statutory authority, the WIB often had to rely on the Railroad, Fuel, and other administrations to give some force to its priority decisions. This circumstance made the board partly reliant on the cooperation of outside agencies for accomplishing its responsibilities. Those agencies, and in particular the Railroad Administration, were not always compliant. Furthermore, the military services maintained the crucial right to commandeer goods and facilities. The board only obtained informal powers to coordinate commandeering in June 1918 and official sanction to do so in September. Along with the Emergency Fleet Corporation, the armed services were also granted the right, subject to the review of the Priority Division, to set priorities on their most important contracts.

Primarily, the dilution of the Priority Division's authority stemmed from the reality that administering a priority system to embrace the entire economy was simply beyond the division's capacity. It set up a system of classifying orders into five major categories, with subdivisions in each category, according to the urgency of first war and then civilian needs. This approach was supplemented by a Preference List used to classify industries, which became increasingly important when the entire industrial structure was placed under priority regulation. As first set up, the Priority Division passed on each request; with applications running into the thousands per day, the division became swamped rather quickly. To relieve the pressure, in July 1918 the division adopted a system of automatic priorities in which manufacturers rated the orders they placed and the contracts they received, except in the categories with highest priority.

This system could have quickly spun out of control had it not been for the commodity sections. From the time that the Priority Division was strengthened in March 1918, the sections insisted on having a major voice in priority decisions. Their demand had force for a number of reasons. Since they were effectively performing the clearance and requirements functions and were the primary source of information concerning the nation's industries, the commodity sections were the logical place for making determinations on priority. Moreover, without statutory authority, much of the Priority Division's action was legally dubious, could be challenged at numerous points, and ultimately depended on the voluntary cooperation of industry. The commodity sections, along with the war service committees, constituted the core of voluntary industrial cooperation. For the Priority Division to ignore the commodity sections was to invite impotence or chaos. In the end, the commodity sections–war service committees generally made and implemented priority decisions. If a war service committee dominated a commodity section, that meant the industry as a whole imposed its own priorities; if the commodity section had some independence from the industry, this decisionmaking was shared; and if the commodity section and war service committees were weak, individual manufacturers could largely proceed on their own. Thus industry nearly always directly or indirectly imposed its own priorities.

Depending on other mobilization agencies to help enforce its will, never establishing full control over the military and other claimant bodies, and having to delegate much of its responsibility to the commodity sections and manufacturers acting individually or as a group, the Priority Division was hardly a source of centralized control within the WIB. Nonetheless, the priority system that evolved after March 1918 was a vast improvement over the previous system and was a chief source of wartime stability.

Price control was as important to economic mobilization as a system of priority.[8] Yet less progress had been made in this area by March 1918 than on any other mobilization function. Both the war mobilizers and much of industry had pushed for set policies on pricing from the outbreak of war. Unlike on most mobilization matters, Secretary of War Newton D. Baker agreed with Baruch and the other mobilizers about the need for controls and the desirable approach for establishing them. But Wilson refused to move in this crucial matter as the various reorganizations of the mobilization system took place. Finally, with the March 1918 reorganization, the president consented to the creation of a Price Fixing Committee (PFC); it was an anomaly. The PFC was within the board yet independent of it, and its chairman—Brookings, whom Wilson himself selected—reported directly to the president. Wilson proceeded so cautiously on the price-fixing question because it was the aspect of mobilization most visible to the public. Placing control over prices directly with the WIB, given that agency's rampant conflicts of interest, would have invited the wrath of a public and a Congress that had already sharply criticized the operations of the WIB and its predecessor agencies.

Besides Brookings and ex officio-member Baruch, the PFC was composed of representatives from the army and navy, the Fuel Administration, the U.S. Tariff Commission, the Federal Trade Commission, labor, and agriculture. Among the agencies operating under or in association with the WIB, the PFC was the one least dominated by industry and most staffed by public representatives. The committee had four assignments: to advise on prices for basic materials, coordinate general pricing policy, review procurement agency contracts upon request, and establish prices for commandeered goods. Plans called for the PFC to rely on the FTC as its primary source of information in fulfilling its responsibilities.

The Price Fixing Committee neither acted as the detached, objective judge over pricing that the Wilson administration proposed, nor did it establish and enforce the centralized, coherent policy that the war mobilizers desired. This outcome resulted from the same factors that limited the operations of the Priorities Division. Without statutory authority, the PFC had to rely on voluntary cooperation from business. Furthermore, the procurement agencies, and especially the military, maintained the right to determine their own pricing. The first rather than the second factor was the more important in influencing the committee's behavior.

At no time during World War I did the PFC establish general policies to guide its decisions; however, several major assumptions existed behind most PFC actions. Price policy should maintain and strengthen the existing economic system, maximize output for war, and prepare for intensified international competition after the war. Furthermore, price setting that did take place would be for an entire industry, not individual firms, and prices would be fixed at a level that permitted marginal firms to keep producing to ensure maximum output and to guarantee the industry's status quo. The high profits accruing to low-cost firms from such policies would be recouped by the government through excess-profits taxes.

Acting on these assumptions, the PFC did not set prices but negotiated with representatives from industries on a reasonable price for their output over a future period, usually three months. In the negotiating process, the committee relied mostly on industry-provided information since the Federal Trade Commission proved an ineffective source of data and analysis. In arriving at the desired "reasonable" price, the PFC turned to the war service committees or similar groups, which usually meant a role for the commodity sections. Indeed, the commodity sections, backed by the war service committees, fought from the outset of PFC operations for the right to participate in setting, if not setting outright, prices in the industries for which they had responsibility. The commodity section's activity on pricing ranged from investigating and recommending prices to the PFC to requiring the PFC to turn over to the section the task of working out an agreement with an industry. Once an agreement was reached, the PFC, through the commodity section–war service committee structure, depended on industry to administer and enforce the decision. In highly competitive industries violations were common, in the oligopolistic industries, rare.

The nature of the process of fixing and administering prices was largely determined by the competitive forces in an industry. In monopolistic or oligopolistic industries like aluminum, copper, steel, oil, and so forth, it was rather easy to arrange meetings with industrial representatives, arrive at mutually acceptable prices, and rely on the industry to administer and enforce the decisions made. This process had been taking place for a long while through the earlier cooperative committees (although it created great controversy at times) and was really no more than an extension of peacetime practices. At the other end of the spectrum, in highly competitive industries made up of numerous firms, subject to easy entry, and without strong trade associations or a history of cooperative efforts, the pricing process was often long, tedious, and frequently acrimonious, as was the case in textiles, lumber, hides, and leather and leather goods. The PFC and the commodity sections–war service committees had to go through a difficult period of assembling the appropriate industry representatives, followed by a period of patient persuasion and pressure to convince the business spokesmen to accept the need for setting prices and then to agree on a price. Once agreement was reached, administering and enforcing the decision was another frustrating and not always successful task.

Generally, and despite the agonizing deliberation required in some, most industries ultimately looked at price fixing in a positive light. After all, the process provided a source of stability to some industries for the first time and did so in a period when runaway prices threatened to undermine the balance provided by the WIB and the PFC. Moreover, price setting fit in with the growing cooperative spirit many industrialists desired and allowed a temporary respite from the antitrust laws. This spirit of cooperation and sense of mutuality characterized most of the negotiations the PFC conducted. Members of the committee and representatives from industry realized that no real compulsion existed, yet almost all participants shared a desire for stability. Consequently, the negotiations, despite some acrimony, were conducted with considerable grace in order not to undermine a delicate arrangement, which, if thrown off by a lack of balance, could result in a standoff that would discredit industry in general and the WIB and PFC in particular.

Besides the prices set for "basic materials," the PFC also took price-fixing action in cases where procurement agencies sought assistance on their contracts. At these times, prices were usually established in the commodity sections with the understanding that the military services or other procurement agencies approve the decisions that were made. The military services also became involved in general pricing through their insistence that when the commodity sections were included in pricing decisions, their representatives had to be available.

Like priority setting, pricing was decentralized, with most power in the process going to industry through the commodity section–war service committee system. Since the sections and committees also dominated clearance, requirements, and priorities, it is understandable that they became, to use Clarkson's imagery, the heart, nerves, and muscle of the WIB's mobilization process.

Several other divisions of the WIB played significant roles in the mobilization process, though not on the level of priority and pricing. They included the Conservation Division, the Facilities Division, the Resources and Conversion Section, and the Division of Planning and Statistics. The Conservation Division had begun as the Commercial Economy Board, created by the CND in late March 1917 at the instigation of Arch W. Shaw, a Chicago publisher. The board had devoted itself to conserving materials, labor, fuel, and other inputs of production and distribution by working with manufacturers and retailers to increase standardization, to reduce the range of styles, varieties, colors, finishes, and so forth, to curtail excessive deliveries, and to increase the efficiency of business in other ways. Most of the Conservation Division's efforts were directed at nonwar activity and were intended both to release more productive potential for the war effort and to protect the existing economic fabric by minimizing the cutback of nonwar economic activity.[9]

The work of the Facilities, Planning and Statistics, and Resources and Conversion Divisions blended. Like the Conservation Division, these divisions were devoted to maximizing war production while preserving as much of the peacetime economic structure as possible. Based on projections of wartime demand, the Facilities Division passed on proposals for new construction and, if approval was granted, ensured that the new facility's location and need for materials, transportation, labor, and so forth were consistent with the overall mobilization program. The WIB was interested in limiting construction of new plants as much as possible in order to conserve resources and to use existing facilities to the maximum. Key to the Facilities Division's success was accurate information. It drew in part on the Planning and Statistics Division, which ultimately had the broadest view of the war effort through the statistics it compiled from government agencies. Of particular importance to the Facilities Division was the Questionnaire Section, which continued the work of industrial inventories that Howard E. Coffin had started with the Naval Consulting Board. In addition to information supplied by the commodity sections, data from the Questionnaire Section guided the Facilities Division's functions. The division, however, worked even more closely with the Resources and Conversion Section.[10]

The Resources and Conversion Section was the brainchild of Charles A. Otis, a Cleveland financier and member and former officer of the local and national Chamber of Commerce.[11] Beginning as early as 1915, Otis had participated in a movement of Cleveland businessmen to organize northern Ohio for Allied war orders and later for American ones. A rather extensive system of committees and subcommittees structured along commodity lines was created to attract and expedite war orders in the Cleveland area. Drawing on this experience, Otis, a personable individual of great enthusiasm and some vision, concluded that businessmen in other metropolitan areas should emulate Cleveland's actions. By surveying the capacity in their area, industrialists could make known to the WIB the facilities that were available for war production or convertible to war output. Thus, the unnecessary expansion of industrial facilities would be avoided and nonessential or nonwar firms could take up war work as production was cut back due to priority restrictions. Otis's ideas took on increasing importance for smaller businesses as the war effort cut ever deeper into the economy.

Loud protests came from owners facing the shutdown of their plants. The issue was sufficiently important that the WIB in November 1917 called George N. Peek to Washington to deal with the entire issue of plant expansion and the fate of nonessential industries. Peek immediately set to work with the Commercial Economy Board and the U.S. Chamber of Commerce to persuade nonwar industries to undertake conservation and efficiency measures to avoid curtailment or shutdown. This effort staved off dissent for a time, but by May 1918 a more concerted approach was necessary. At that point, the Resources and Conversion Section was created and Otis selected to head it. Peek and Otis worked closely with the Chamber of Commerce to create a regional structure that would complement the national structure of the commodity sections. Eventually, the nation was divided into twenty-one regions headed by a regional adviser, with subdivisions similar to those in Cleveland.

This regional organization was intended to channel information to Washington about existing facilities, inform local, state, and regional firms of contractual opportunities, and aid industry in converting to war production. The approach was partially comparable to the advances the Ordnance Department had already accomplished under the leadership of Col. Guy E. Tripp, former chairman of Westinghouse Electric and Manufacturing Company. The department had created ten Ordnance Districts in order to decentralize its purchasing and to reach more potential contractors. Although tension developed between the Ordnance Department and the Resources and Conversion Section over regional operations, on the whole the two bodies worked together to include smaller business units in the war production efforts.

Otis had grandiose dreams for totally organizing the nation's industrial strength along local, state, and regional lines through the Resources and Conversion Section. His ideas, like so many of Coffin's, met a definite need but never reached full fruition. The section doubtlessly made more potential contractors available to the government, and it was only through such a decentralized system that smaller producers could be located. Furthermore, small nonwar firms that faced shutdown got contracts they otherwise might not have received. Still, the system did not flourish for several reasons. Otis believed in working more through personal, usually elite, contacts than through concerted organization. As a result, the various regions became little more than lobbying organizations for different parts of the nation's decentralized economy. The Resources and Conversion Section was also created so late in the war that it had limited time to experiment adequately and perfect its organization. Most important, even with excellent organization and ample time, the nation's metropolitan, state, and regional firms could never be anything but peripheral. The center of wartime production rested with the industrial giants in the commodity sections, not with the small firms in and associated with the Resources and Conversion Section.

Nonetheless, to achieve a sense of unity and to quell dissent, it was essential for the WIB to pay attention to the needs of small business during the war. Strangely, Baruch was slow to recognize this, just as he was reluctant to replace the cooperative committees with the commodity sections–war service committees and never showed much interest in working with the Chamber of Commerce. The pressure for creating the Resources and Conversion Section came from outside the WIB from such people as Otis and Secretary of the Navy Josephus Daniels and was supported by Peek and others within the board. Baruch acquiesced but without much enthusiasm, interest, or conviction. He seemed to prefer outright elitism.

Despite the varied efforts to maximize the use of existing facilities and to minimize building, the WIB ultimately faced the need to restrict production in nonessential industries. Growing war demand and limited supplies of fuel, raw materials, and so forth forced the WIB to take action. The issue was so sensitive that the board and the Wilson administration approached the problem with the utmost care and deliberation. The voluntary cooperation of business, upon which the entire WIB structure rested, could be threatened if the curtailment of nonessential industries were handled in a reckless manner. The board experienced a severe reaction when in October–November 1917, without consulting industry or making prior preparations, it announced that nonessential industries would face significant cutbacks. A virtual explosion occurred that forced the board quickly to retreat from this position.

Thereafter, it proceeded with exceptional caution. When curtailment again became an issue in May 1918, the Priorities Division had responsibility for the matter. The division first sought the assistance of the U.S. Chamber of Commerce in educating business about the situation, WIB procedures, and measures industry could take to protect its interests. Wilson created a committee to study and advise him on the delicate issue and followed that up in June 1918 by forming an Industrial Adjustments Committee in the Priorities Division, consisting of representatives of the principal mobilization agencies, to aid industry in adjusting to curtailment. The Priorities Division then held trade conferences with the industries involved, including household appliances manufacturers, bed manufacturers, and others. The usual procedure was to negotiate an agreement that involved curtailment along with conservation and standardization. Since the last two approaches served the long-run interests of manufacturers, most industries were eager to cooperate. In exchange, the Priorities Division, using the weakest rather than the strongest firms in an industry as a gauge, worked out procedures whereby companies received enough materials to survive, although at a substantially reduced level of production. In no instance were directives imposed on an industry. As with prices, a long, patient bargaining process occurred. Industries facing curtailment, however, were small ones without substantial market power. The WIB's action protected them, and most were appreciative.[12]

One major exception to the relatively smooth progress of curtailment was the automobile industry. Here was neither a small nor an insignificant industry but one that included some of the largest corporations and that had relatively strong trade associations able to make a united stand. The industry's strength was matched by its consumption of a range of materials, steel being the most important, and by the extensive use of skilled labor, machine tools, and so on, all vital to the war effort. By any definition, the automobile industry was both nonessential and a luxury.

The WIB made its first move to curtail car production in late 1917, only to pull back in humiliation before an onslaught of protest from the industry. Once the board was further strengthened in March, it again took up curtailment in negotiations with the industry. The bargaining process became extremely acrimonious and reached the breaking point on several occasions, with auto representatives accusing the WIB of failing in the areas of transportation and fuel and hence unnecessarily threatening their supply of steel. Throughout the bargaining process, the industry comported itself in the worst possible manner, hoarding raw materials, being disingenuous, and engaging in various protective stratagems. Finally in August an agreement was reached in which automobile production would be curtailed for the last six months of 1918 to 25 percent of the 1917 output levels, or 50 percent of usual production. Total conversion to war production could occur beginning in January 1919.

This was no victory for the board since many of the larger car companies—including Ford Motor and General Motors Companies—were already using at least 75 percent of their capacity for war production. Where that was not the case, the evidence indicates that shortages of materials on the market, not WIB power, brought about the cutbacks that did occur. The armistice came before the production quotas were reached. With limited powers, the WIB could not compel firms to do its will, and the auto companies were sufficiently important to steel that the latter industry would probably deliver its product to the car manufacturers despite WIB pressure. Even if the WIB had had the power to coerce the industry, it probably would have held back. The board was committed to volunteerism. To become engaged in a drawn-out confrontation with autos, steel, and other major industries would have discredited the WIB's approach and indicated that voluntary cooperation was no basis for mobilization. That revelation would have reflected ill upon the WIB and the entire business community, especially the industrial elite.[13]

The WIB faced a dilemma similar to the problems over priorities and curtailment in regard to the application of price controls to goods produced strictly for civilian use.[14] The board's price fixing for munitions and related products had some statutory basis, though it stemmed largely from the powers of established departments that were represented on the WIB. Its right to fix prices on these goods would have been clearer had Wilson delegated his price-fixing powers to the board, but this surrender never occurred. Existing legislation also provided some justification for setting prices on goods sold to the Allies. However, the legality of fixing prices on strictly civilian products seemed dubious to most people who seriously considered instituting such a program. Nonetheless, certain individuals saw the need for price fixing.

The most forthright advocate was the Price Fixing Committee's head, Robert S. Brookings. Bringing to the WIB his prewar National Civic Federation ideals of harmonious relations between capital and labor, Brookings saw wartime conditions lending themselves to sharpening class antagonism. Rising and unchecked prices for shoes and clothing, Brookings argued, would inevitably lead to cries for wage increases. Not only would that heighten the likelihood of strikes, but it could also price the United States out of markets in postwar competition, which would create stagnation and rising class conflict at home. For immediate and long-run reasons, therefore, Brookings favored general retail price controls for consumer goods similar to the system introduced in Great Britain to maintain the buying power of the working population.

George N. Peek tended to agree with Brookings, but for different reasons. He was moved not by some ideal goal of social harmony but by the fear of a mass upheaval if economic stability were not achieved. That consequence would force stronger and more widespread state control, an outcome that was undesirable and avoidable if industry was farsighted enough to act to avoid it. Baruch was also concerned, though less enthusiastic about undertaking a broad price-fixing scheme and the elaborate controls such an endeavor would entail. Wilson, typically, manifested the same doubts but was willing to allow the WIB to search for answers or to experiment with controls.

Rather than introducing any wholesale scheme at once, the WIB, while going on record early in August 1918 for consumer price controls, decided to experiment with the shoe industry. This approach stemmed from a larger scheme advocated by Brookings in which the government would oversee the production of mass-produced, standardized Liberty products, like clothing and shoes, for the working population. Prices on these items would be fixed by the government. Starting with the boot and shoe industry made some sense, since by early August the Conservation and Priority Divisions had negotiated agreements with it to standardize products and to increase productive efficiency in return for getting on the preference list for fuel and transportation.

The WIB's attempt to go beyond general agreements with industry and to implement closely supervised programs to manufacture Liberty items at fixed prices led businessmen to rebel. They strongly objected to the WIB closely monitoring the specifics of production and protested even more strenuously the board's becoming involved in wholesale and retail pricing on consumer goods. Feelings ran so strong that the WIB executives were publicly berated for their "socialistic" schemes and "radical," unconstitutional business practices. Facing such opposition, the board elbowed aside Brookings, its most socially conscious member, and began a long series of negotiations that produced a compromise solution. The shoe industry agreed to reduce its output to four basic lines with a price range for each. Most of the WIB's earlier ideas, including the Liberty line, government inspection, and specific controls on wholesale and retail pricing, were scrapped.

The whole attempt at consumer pricing came to naught. The agreement for shoes was not officially to take effect until late spring 1919, and realistically, little would be done until months after that. Some talk of a similar program for workers' garments took place but led nowhere. Had the WIB actually tried to implement the boot and shoe scheme it had worked out, most of the board's experience indicates that difficulty, if not failure, would have resulted. Trying to police the prices of raw materials was difficult enough. Enforcing prices at the retail level would have produced almost insurmountable problems. The WIB lacked even the beginnings of the necessary administrative machinery to handle such difficulties and had no statutory basis for doing so. Moreover, industry was most resistant, and the resentment probably would have grown had the implementation stage been reached. The divisions within the board and the Wilson administration over consumer pricing would have made any progress difficult. The board was fortunate to avoid this vital issue in terms of retaining its image of successful business cooperation. A failure could have helped increase the social disturbance it had hoped to avoid with the consumer price-fixing scheme.

The problems the WIB encountered with priorities, price fixing, and curtailment, especially in relation to nonessential industries like autos and necessities such as shoes, fundamentally tested its authority and inevitably raised the matter of seeking a statutory mandate for its manyfold activities. This issue, of course, had been a matter of central concern for war mobilizers even before the nation entered the fighting. Once the nation was at war, legislation giving the WIB and its predecessor agencies the power to enforce decisions was a primary goal for many people. The drive was directly proportional to the ineffectiveness of the mobilization machinery and, hence, constantly grew in strength from April 1917. It reached its peak during the mobilization crisis of 1917–1918. After the reorganization of the WIB between March and May 1918, establishing a legislative base for the board's action was less urgent, yet it remained a significant issue until the war's end.

Brookings from the outset favored legislation for the PFC, correctly foreseeing enormous difficulty in carrying out his functions without that authority. Robert S. Lovett and Edwin B. Parker agreed with Brookings and sought legislation for their priority duties. However, Baruch's legal adviser, Albert C. Ritchie, consistently argued against legislation for priorities and pricing, even after Baruch had arranged to have introduced in Congress a bill written by Lovett and supported by Brookings and Parker. Ritchie put forth two main arguments. First, the act of seeking legislation would call attention to the fact that the board's actions were illegal or questionable. Second, the situation would become intolerable if the desired legislation was denied, a very likely outcome. Baruch sensed these dangers and did not want Congress probing the WIB's operations. The bigger issue, which Baruch seemed to appreciate, Willard knew, and which Grosvenor Clarkson and Hugh Johnson became aware of, was that any attempt at legislation could threaten the WIB's entire operation, as the introduction of the Chamberlain bill during the winter crisis had demonstrated. The WIB had to live with its limited authority or face wholesale change since the commodity section–war service committee and dollar-a-year-man systems would most likely not receive sanction from Congress. Moreover, legally prescribed powers for the WIB would have undermined the business cooperative ideal, the very foundation of Baruch's thought and that of his chief lieutenants.[15]

By mid-1918 then, the WIB had put the finishing touches on its operations. With new, revised, or strengthened systems in clearance, requirements, priorities, and pricing and the basis for meaningful programs in facilities, conservation, and curtailment, the board could manage industrial mobilization on the supply side. And it could do so despite the limitations it faced in working through a commodity section–war service committee system based on cooperation, not compulsion. Nonetheless, the system of controlling supply could not achieve effective economic mobilization unless demand, and particularly that emanating from the War Department, was coordinated with it. The prospects for successful management of demand were better after March 1918 than ever before.

## ADAPTING THE MILITARY TO THE WIB

Newton D. Baker had begun to reform the army's supply structure during late summer 1917.[16] The effort consisted mostly of shuffling personnel and responsibilities to improve the old bureau system. A more decisive step occurred in November 1917 when the secretary of war appointed Benedict Crowell as assistant secretary to replace the ineffectual, if not incompetent,

William M. Ingraham. Crowell, chairman of the Crowell and Little Construction Company of Cleveland, had been interested in military affairs for years prior to World War I (like the first WIB head, Frank A. Scott). In 1916 Baker had appointed Crowell to the Kernan Board. With American entry into war, he accepted a commission in the Ordnance Department, where he was serving when tapped for the assistant secretaryship. An ambitious individual, Crowell was committed to the principle that army supply should be under the general direction of the secretary of war and particularly the assistant secretary. Baker had selected Crowell from the desire to increase his control over the bureaus and to rationalize the army's chaotic supply system in the process.

The escalating winter crisis of 1917–1918, with the mobilization program approaching paralysis and the Senate Military Affairs Committee threatening the army's prerogatives, forced Baker to pursue reform assiduously in order to prevent a complete rout of the department. To appease his congressional critics and assuage rising business criticism, Baker in January 1918 appointed Edward R. Stettinius to a post that ultimately became second assistant secretary of war, serving under Crowell, to supervise purchases and supplies. With the appointments of Crowell and Stettinius, Baker was still attempting patchwork change in the War Department's supply structure in order to contain the spreading crisis.

The growing demands in Congress for a munitions ministry, however, ultimately convinced Baker that fundamental, not piecemeal, change was essential to prevent procurement from completely escaping the War Department's control. That conclusion ultimately led to the establishment of centralized control over the supply bureaus and the coordination of their operations with the WIB by the chief of staff and General Staff, not by Baker and his two assistants.[17]

The growing mobilization crisis from summer 1917 was perceived by the chief of staff and the General Staff as an opportunity for the staff to assert the kind of control over the supply bureaus that had been intended by the Elihu Root reforms of the turn of the century. Chief of Staff Maj. Gen. Hugh L. Scott, who was succeeded in September 1917 by Maj. Gen. Tasker H. Bliss, had created and supported various committees in the General Staff to study army supply and to suggest modifications. From September 1917, plans for reorganizing the supply system under General Staff control began flowing from the War College branch of the staff. Consequently, when the winter crisis erupted, the General Staff had fully developed proposals for dealing with the emergency. The staff had become as alarmed as Baker at the prospect of the army losing control over supply. Baker soon perceived that the General Staff could carry out the reforms essential for preserving army control over supply more expeditiously than his office. Consequently, he stopped relying on Crowell, and later on Stettinius, to bring about the needed changes and embraced the plans of the General Staff. This shift was an agonizing and reluctant move on Baker's part since he had resisted for months any such drastic revisions; his decision was a recognition of the real threats he and the army faced.

The General Staff was reorganized beginning in January 1918 in order to establish effective staff supervision of the bureaus and to better coordinate army operations with the civilian economy. To carry out the coming radical changes, Baker summoned Gen. Peyton C. March from Europe that same month to take over as chief of staff. He was appointed acting chief in March and chief of staff in May. With ruthless efficiency, the dynamic, aggressive March revitalized the War Department; the days of drift were over. Baker had selected the right man and given him the widest possible latitude. In record time, the competent but heavy-handed March fashioned a powerful agency out of the withered General Staff he had inherited from Scott and Bliss, each of whom lacked the command capabilities the office demanded.

General George W. Goethals—the famous "builder" of the Panama Canal—became March's chief lieutenant for supply and procurement. Baker called Goethals back to active duty in December 1917 after he had already served the war effort by acting as general manager of the Emergency Fleet Corporation and then by assisting the New York Port Authority in reorganizing for war operations. Goethals's appointment as head of the Quartermaster Corps began the radical reorganization of army supply. The departing quartermaster general, Maj. Gen. Henry G. Sharpe, and his Ordnance Department counterpart, Maj. Gen. William Crozier, were made members of a newly created War Department War Council as a face-saving measure. The council had a short life and little significance. Goethals received the same staunch support from March that the latter received from Baker. Drawing on his Panama experience, Goethals believed he had to establish direct control over supply by consolidating the bureaus rather than just supervising them. Based on powers granted by the Overman Act and through successive steps initiated in January 1918, Goethals directed a near-revolution that broke down the old bureau structure and replaced it with a centralized system of supply. It was a herculean task and provoked intense resistance in the bureaus. At the time of the armistice, the job was incomplete.

Goethals ultimately became an assistant chief of staff and ran supply operations through a subdivision of the General Staff called the Division of Purchase, Storage, and Traffic. The new division took over the responsibilities of the Quartermaster Corps and the supply functions of the other bureaus, including purchase, storage, transportation, and finance. Only the procurement, production, and inspection of aircraft, ordnance, chemicals, and other highly technical items were excluded. In the process of consolidation, army purchasing operations were organized along commodity instead of functional lines, which brought the War Department's supply system into conformity with that of the WIB. At last the army was adjusting to the civilian economy. Reforms also included methods for obtaining reliable information on requirements, centralized procurement of common items, and standardization of the forms and procedures for letting contracts.

Goethals's radical restructuring methods were extraordinary in that they violated basic General Staff principles. The staff was intended by its principal architects to be a planning and coordinating body, not an executive and administrative agency. But Goethals, facing the need to bring order out of chaos in stabilizing the economic mobilization program and to meet the ever-growing requirements of the AEF, saw no other alternative to concentrating supply activities to the point of delivery in Europe in one administrative unit under his control.

This stance brought him into conflict not only with the bureaus but also with Assistant Secretary of War Crowell, and to a lesser degree with Second Assistant Secretary Stettinius, who was intent on establishing control over supply operations in his own office. In July–August 1918, when Goethals was at a critical stage in absorbing the bureaus into his Division of Purchase, Storage, and Traffic, even the intrepid Chief of Staff March hesitated to back such a radical departure from traditional General Staff operations. For over a month, March refused to authorize the necessary orders. When he did so, they were couched in language that could be interpreted as confining Goethals to planning and supervisory duties rather than giving him direct control, which would leave him subject to Crowell's authority. Goethals immediately challenged March on this vital matter. He insisted that he could fulfill his responsibilities only with operational control; that his division must hold a powerful position in the department, accountable only to the chief of staff and the secretary of war; and that Crowell must be kept out of the operations of the Division of Purchase, Storage, and Traffic. Recognizing the practical if not the theoretical strength of Goethals's arguments and desiring to retain his services, March acceded to his demands. Henceforth, Crowell, under the title of director of munitions, largely confined his activity to ordnance. Any threat from Stettinius to Goethals's position had been removed in July when Stettinius was sent to Europe, where he ultimately became the American representative on the Inter-Allied Munitions Council.[18]

In a sense, Goethals conceived of his Purchase, Storage, and Traffic Division as a weak substitute for a munitions ministry. Hence, he would not allow theory about the General Staff to impede his concept of organizational necessity.

When he first assumed the duties of acting quartermaster general in December 1917, Goethals viewed the disarray in the bureaus as so serious that it would best be resolved by a civilian-directed ministry of munitions. His military experience as an engineer and his civilian work as a consulting engineer had given him both a civilian and a military outlook and spared him the parochialism of many military officers. However, since the Wilson administration and especially the secretary of war were adamantly opposed to a munitions ministry, Goethals had to work within the War Department structure.

Goethals viewed most bureau activity as essentially an enormous purchasing program rather than as a particularly military operation. Therefore, the more he could use the authority of the General Staff to consolidate bureau activity while keeping his operations outside the traditional military chain of command the greater his chance of successfully controlling supply. These ideas affected not only Goethals's views of structure and command but also his approach to staffing. He turned to some high-quality officers known to him from past experience or by reputation to fill some of the key positions in his service, and he also had transferred back to supply operations various knowledgeable clerks and other prewar civilian personnel who had acquired commissions and were serving elsewhere. Increasingly, however, Goethals turned to civilians. The bureaus had relied heavily on commissioned civilians or activated reserve officers to meet the burgeoning demands of war. Goethals followed this practice but modified it in several important regards. He purposefully kept many civilian recruits out of uniform so that they would have greater latitude and not fall victim to the army's hierarchy of rank. (This procedure was contrary to the practice, for example, of the Ordnance Department.) Goethals was also fully willing to use civilian businessmen as key advisers in aiding the army to restructure its supply system. As a result, the Purchase, Storage, and Traffic Division was honeycombed with civilians, in mufti or uniform, in executive or advisory slots.

Shortly after returning to active duty, Goethals persuaded Robert J. Thorne, president of Montgomery Ward and Company, to serve as his chief assistant. In mid-June, Gerard Swope, vice-president of the Western Electric Company, joined Goethals's staff. Swope played an instrumental role in devising the plans for fully consolidating the bureaus under the Purchase, Storage, and Traffic Division. Earlier, Oliver D. Street, general manager of distribution for Western Electric Company, and members of his staff had devised and implemented a system with which the army could handle the flood of supplies to be stored and distributed in wartime. Among the other important individuals aiding the Purchase, Storage, and Traffic Division on a permanent or temporary basis were Harry M. Adams, a vice-president of the Missouri Pacific

Railroad; C. B. Seger, president of the Union Pacific Railroad; Otto H. Kahn, of Kuhn, Loeb, and Company; Christopher D. Norton, president of the First National Bank of New York; Herbert H. Lehman of Lehman Brothers; F. Carrington Weems, of J. P. Morgan and Company; Charles G. Dawes, president of the Central Trust Company of Chicago; Rodney Hitt of White, Weld, and Company; and R. H. Hayes of Stone, Webster, and Company. Furthermore, in the numerous reorganizations of the General Staff and War Department between December 1917 and November 1918, the Statistics Division, headed by Leonard P. Ayers of the Russell Sage Foundation, was transferred by stages in early 1918 from the Council of National Defense to the General Staff, to provide the latter with vital information it lacked. Finally, John D. Ryan, president of the Anaconda Copper Company, who had become director of Aircraft Production in April 1918, replaced Stettinius as an assistant secretary, with the new responsibility of supervising the army's entire aircraft program.[19]

The evolution of supply within the War Department that began in December 1917 was a curious mixture of tradition and nonconformism. It was traditional in that Baker, in dealing with the winter crisis, reverted to the Elihu Root–Henry L. Stimson policy whereby the secretary of war allied himself with the chief of staff in order to bring the bureaus under control. It was nonconformist in that the Purchase, Storage, and Traffic Division not only had direct control over operations, as opposed to just supervisory powers, but was also virtually a civilian institution in terms of operations, staffing, and attitudes.

The unorthodox nature of the army's reorganized supply system created conditions in which the War Department and the WIB could find common ground. The departmental reforms had been intended to preserve the War Department's independence and to obviate the need for a strengthened civilian agency; facilitating the operations of the WIB had not been an original aim. Nevertheless, on returning to active duty, Goethals quickly concluded that the department's cooperation with a strengthened civilian mobilization agency was essential for meeting army requirements. His business advisers and assistants confirmed these convictions.

In March and April 1918, WIB and military officials conferred on ways to implement Wilson's instructions to Baruch on coordinating the entire mobilization effort. As early as December 1917, Navy Department supply leaders had suggested that the war program might best be run through the commodity section structure of the WIB. In late March Edwin B. Parker, the WIB's priorities commissioner, drafted a proposal to put this concept into effect. Drawing on ideas from the WIB and the military, Parker proposed that a body (which became the Requirements Division) collect information on the prospective needs of the various claimant agencies, collate and classify it, and send it to the relevant WIB commodity sections for action. With such information, the sections could make intelligent decisions on plant expansion, curtailment, priorities, pricing, and other functions essential for a successful mobilization program. The military services, along with other procuring departments, would be represented on the commodity sections. Since the sections were the key arms of the board, the procurement agencies would be fully integrated into the chief mobilization body. Further, the army and navy would continue to have representatives on the WIB itself, as well as on the major divisions, including Requirements, Priority, Price Fixing, Conservation, and Facilities.[20]

Integrating the navy into the commodity sections was relatively simple because its supply system was organized along those lines. The Emergency Fleet Corporation, the Red Cross, and other claimants were already structured by commodities or easily reorganized their systems in that way and thus presented no problems. For the army, however, commodity organization was a new and wrenching experience.[21] Brigadier General Hugh S. Johnson, who had previously served as deputy provost marshal general and played a major role in planning and implementing the Selective Service System, was the one person in the army most responsible for reorganizing army supply operations along commodity lines. In April 1918 Johnson, Thomas N. Perkins (a Boston corporation lawyer representing the WIB), and Charles R. Day (a prominent Philadelphia engineer and efficiency expert representing the War Department) had been selected to serve as a committee to make recommendations for modernizing the War Department's supply system. Several weeks after its appointment, the so-called Committee of Three outlined and presented in general terms a rationale for the agency that ultimately became the Purchase, Storage, and Traffic Division. That month, Johnson was appointed director of Purchases and Supply, with Gerard Swope of Western Electric serving as the assistant director. From that time, Johnson remained one of Goethals's most important aides. Drawing on his study with the Committee of Three and the knowledge he had gained in working with the WIB, Johnson immediately began reorganizing army procurement according to commodities. He and Goethals also served as the chief army representatives on the WIB.

Integrating the military services into the commodity sections provided no magic resolution to industrial-military relations during World War I. Accommodation, familiarity, and confidence slowly had to develop before the representatives from two quite different worlds could work smoothly together. Army and navy personnel initially viewed the WIB with suspicion—the suspicion of civilian institutions that had grown since 1916. Soon, however, they began to see that the WIB could help secure rather than threaten military prerogatives by aiding the services in fulfilling their responsibilities. Businessmen also had to forget or ignore their resentment toward the military services for having undermined the mobilization program for well over a year. The increasing number of civilian businessmen working in the supply bureaus and representing the army in the WIB also served to ease tensions.

The crunch point arose over the question of authority within the commodity sections. The WIB and the military had never clarified whether the entire section, including representatives from the procurement agencies, or the section chairman was the ultimate source of authority. In such an ambiguous situation, the chairman continued to operate as a power unto himself, the commodity sections often failed to invite the military representatives to their meetings or keep them fully informed of developments, and, at times, the sections dealt with military supply subdivisions outside the army's and navy's commodity committees. As long as such practices took place, the military not only resented and distrusted the WIB but also refused to send representatives who could speak and act with authority to the various subdivisions of the board.

Through the repeated demands of Johnson and other military representatives and the sympathetic attitude and efforts of WIB officials such as George N. Peek, chief of the Finished Products Division, the commodity section as a whole (not just the chief and a few of his assistants) ultimately became the source of authority, and the various sections negotiated agreements with and established procedures acceptable to the military. As that system developed, the armed services' confidence in the WIB grew, and they began to send to the commodity sections and other levels of the WIB structure officials who could make decisions.

By the war's end, then, through similarly structured organizations and a growing spirit of cooperation, the WIB and the military—and most important the War Department—had finally reached a modus operandi. It was based on a compromise along the lines Wilson had spelled out in his directions to Baruch of March 4, 1918: The WIB was to have general coordinating authority over the entire mobilization effort, but the chairman was to leave alone that which was running smoothly, particularly the operations of the claimant agencies. To achieve those ends, a cooperative spirit from the military, the other claimant agencies, and the WIB was essential. Over time, these bodies exercised sufficient flexibility to resolve the crisis in the economic mobilization program that had peaked during winter 1917–1918.

Yet it would be wrong to say that the mobilization machinery ran smoothly and lacked major flaws or that the munitions picture was bright at the war's end. Other than the rather ineffectual War Cabinet—periodic, brief meetings convened by the president beginning in March 1918, at which the heads of the various war agencies shared information and reviewed the mobilization program—no agency directed the total national effort. On many issues, the Emergency Fleet Corporation, War Trade Board, War and Navy Departments, and other claimant agencies acted independently. They set their own requirements; the WIB determined only how they were met. Reliable statistics on the overall wartime economic effort remained incomplete. As late as September 1918, Alexander Legge, chairman of the Requirements Division, complained that the claimant agencies were still not submitting their requirements to the division on a regular basis, and the WIB had no way to compel them to do so. Hence, the Requirements Division, which should have been the core around which all WIB activities revolved, never acquired that status. Without full information on demand and without authority over requirements, the WIB could not plan a production program that was feasible for the economy. Nonetheless, as long as demand did not seriously outrun supply, economic equilibrium could be maintained. But when hostilities ceased, demand was rapidly expanding. Had the fighting continued, the WIB would have faced the need to limit demand in order to avoid another mobilization crisis.[22]

The actions of the claimant agencies affected the functioning of the WIB but none as greatly as the War Department, since it was the largest and least efficient procurement body. Although Goethals's reforms dramatically improved army supply, the army was still unable to predict its needs with the necessary degree of certainty. The Emergency Fleet Corporation did little better in this regard than the War Department. In contrast, the Navy Department did an excellent job of calculating requirements, as it had before the war.

But more was involved than figures; attitudes also played an important role. Although Goethals, Johnson, and representatives from other procurement agencies developed reasonably amicable relationships with the WIB, that was not the case with army chief of staff March. His subordinates in the supply bureaus tended to see the WIB as a coordinate body with superior status, but March viewed it as an obtrusive agency that was perhaps the War Department's inferior. As major shifts in military requirements occurred, March was slow to share information about them with the Purchase, Storage, and Traffic Division and refused to inform the WIB. Only a major showdown between Baruch (who admired the hard-driving chief of staff) and March resolved the matter in favor of the board. Realizing that the armed services tenaciously guarded the right to determine their needs, the WIB never attempted to institute review procedures. Had the war continued, with demand multiplying faster than supply, the military requirements riddle would have become an explosively divisive issue.

Plans called for expanding the thirty divisions of the 1918 AEF program to eighty in 1919 in preparation for a great Allied offensive in the middle of the year; Gen. John J. Pershing was holding out for even more. Throughout 1918 the AEF commander insisted that his forces were critically short of needed supplies, including ordnance, signal equipment, motor vehicles, and medical provisions. By fall, conditions were reported to be desperate. Goethals pessimistically predicted that a shortage of ships would undermine, if not destroy, the army's 1919 effort to supply its troops in Europe. In the minds of some army officers, only the armistice spared the nation the trauma of testing Goethals's prediction.[23]

Nonetheless, when hostilities ceased, a mobilization scheme that worked existed. In many respects it was a makeshift system, based on compromise and made to function through improvisation under the pressures of wartime demand. Still, the armed services had preserved their control over supply, and reasonable economic stability had been restored despite the exigencies of war. The basic pattern was sound although the mechanics involving the principal civilian mobilization agency and the major claimants, particularly the armed services, required perfecting. Lines of authority throughout the entire mobilization structure, furthermore, needed to be rethought, clarified, and ideally defined by law.

In shaping the functions of the War Industries Board, decisionmaking and power gravitated to the commodity sections–war service committees, a natural development since the board in microcosm duplicated the economy. At the board's hub were the one hundred or so huge corporations around which the American economic system turned, with the periphery made up of thousands of medium-to-small industries and businesses.

Size and demand, however, made the military central to the operations of a mobilized economy, a reality magnified by the fact that the armed services had the statutory authority that the War Industries Board lacked. Even when the War Department was forced to adapt its supply system to that of the WIB, the latter could not carry out its responsibilities until the army and navy were granted a meaningful voice in commodity section–war services committee decisions. The economics of modern warfare highlighted and reinforced the elitism of the American system and introduced the military as a new factor in that system's enormously complex equation of power.

# 11
# OTHER AGENCIES AND THE ECONOMIC CONSEQUENCES OF WORLD WAR I

An analysis of the political economy of World War I is incomplete without an examination of mobilization administrations other than the War Industries Board and its predecessors. Most of these agencies, such as the U.S. Food Administration, followed the patterns and methods of the WIB although the labor offices differed in that regard. A broader view of the entire mobilization system also facilitates assessing the economic consequences of World War I.

## OTHER MOBILIZATION AGENCIES

The War Industries Board was the chief economic mobilization agency during World War I, but numerous temporary bodies helped mobilize the wartime economy. Though the importance of the agencies varied, as a group they played a significant role in maximizing the nation's economic might for hostilities. The more significant new agencies included the U.S. Food Administration, the U.S. Fuel Administration, the U.S. Railroad Administration, the U.S. Shipping Board, and the War Finance Corporation.

Several important points can be made about these bodies. Unlike the WIB and its predecessors, these agencies had statutory authority to act. This fact had both helpful and harmful consequences. It helped in that the various agencies had much more authority for fulfilling their responsibilities than did the WIB; it was harmful in that each guarded its prerogatives intensely and thereby avoided effective coordination with other mobilization administrations. Nonetheless, these agencies largely depended on the same voluntarism and cooperation to carry out their duties that underlay the operations of the WIB. Although in theory most of the activities of the agencies might have been carried out by the WIB, that was impossible in practice. The agencies operated in relatively self-contained sectors of the economy that lent themselves to independent treatment and demanded concerted attention before the reorganized WIB began functioning with some decisiveness after March 1918. The agencies had come into being through congressional mandate before March 1918 because of their circumscribed responsibilities as compared with the WIB's. Placing the other mobilization bodies in or under the WIB in March 1918 or after, had this been possible, would probably have swamped the shaky agency, worked out under Woodrow Wilson's vulnerable compromise. Even at the end of the war, the WIB was sufficiently amorphous that additional responsibilities could well have done it severe harm.

Though establishing the independent mobilization agencies was essential, the failure to coordinate their activities with each other and especially with the WIB put enormous strain on the economic mobilization program. Only Wilson's ineffective War Council existed to focus the entire economic mobilization effort, which meant that no true focus existed. The WIB was the logical coordinating body. To serve in that role, however, it would have required much stronger powers and a firm legislative sanction. Wilson would have invited trouble by placing statutorily authorized mobilization agencies under the control, or even the coordination, of a WIB that lacked legal legitimacy. Although the WIB was the linchpin of the mobilization program, its weakness tended to draw strength away from the agencies around it.

The genesis of the Food, Fuel, and Railroad Administrations is to be found in the committees of the National Defense Advisory Commission, which handled supplies, raw materials, and transportation.[1] In time, NDAC action was inadequate to meet the growing crisis in food, fuel, and railroad transportation. After acrimonious and extended debate, Congress authorized Wilson to create the Food and Fuel Administrations with the passage of the Food and Fuel Control Act (the Lever Act) in early August 1917. Herbert Hoover was selected to head the former agency and Harry A. Garfield the latter.

The nation's legislators were pressed to move on the food issue because of skyrocketing prices, rapidly escalating demand, and declining supply. Acting through a centralized administration that coordinated and directed several government corporations and an elaborate series of state, county, and local voluntary organizations, Hoover succeeded in stimulating production, curtailing usage and waste, and stabilizing prices. He rejected rationing in favor of moral suasion and powerful persuasion and moved adroitly in effect to set prices on all commodities but cotton, which Southerners in Congress had exempted from his reach. With all Allied and American military purchasing channeled through his organization, Hoover exercised extraordinary market control. Despite the enormous power that he and his assistants wielded, the food administrator constantly emphasized the largely voluntary nature of his organization—nearly 800,000 people, almost all of whom served without compensation—and the cooperative instead of coercive controls exercised.[2]

During the congressional deliberations over measures that became the Lever Act, more attention was paid to food than fuel, but the latter received due notice. Of particular importance was coal. The tumultuous bituminous coal industry, and to a lesser degree anthracite, had been the subject of a long dispute over pricing. The controversy led to a congressionally ordered investigation by the Federal Trade Commission that started in 1916 and concluded in mid-1917. To deal with the shortages, high prices, and generally unstable conditions that threatened almost every aspect of the economic mobilization program, the FTC recommended full control of the industry by the federal government. Garfield's powers over production, distribution, and (through the FTC) pricing, were as broad as Hoover's. Like the food administrator, he worked mainly through local, county, and state voluntary organizations, although, again like Hoover, he was not afraid to move forcefully in emergency conditions. The Fuel Administration managed to increase production, institute conservation, stabilize prices, and facilitate distribution and also harmonized labor relations and manpower supply problems in the strife-torn coal industry. Less attention was paid to petroleum than to coal and coke. Nonetheless, the Fuel Administration, working principally through industry-staffed war service committees, managed to stabilize oil prices and maintain adequate supplies for the expanding requirements of both the nation and its Allies.[3] In carrying out their responsibilities, both the Food and Fuel Administrations relied more heavily on the state Councils of National Defense and their personnel than did the WIB or most other mobilization agencies. But the Fuel Administration proved much more willing to use these councils than Hoover's agency.[4]

Wilson placed the railroads under federal control during the winter crisis of 1917–1918, based on authority granted to him in the Army Appropriations Act of 1916 and further defined by legislation in March 1918. This action had become essential to bring greater order to the nation's most important transportation system. The administration had moved previously to facilitate movement on highways and inland and coastal waterways, which had become clogged by huge increases in usage stemming from the war. Such action, however, was always minor compared to the railroads, which carried the bulk of goods and people. As head of the U.S. Railroad Administration, William G. McAdoo largely worked through the organization that Daniel Willard had created almost a year before under the NDAC. By strengthening the financial situation of the distressed railroads, McAdoo and his assistants rationalized the rail system to the point that it efficiently carried the nearly impossible load imposed upon it.[5]

The work of the U.S. Shipping Board (USSB) actually tied in closely with the War Trade Board, created in October 1917 and headed by Vance C. McCormick. The War Trade Board, like the three agencies just described and the WIB, functioned primarily through representatives from the industries it was supposed to regulate. It directed almost all American import and export activities and, in conjunction with the Allies, extended as much control over global trade as was possible.[6] The U.S. Shipping Board had a quite different charge. Created in September 1916, the board was empowered to regulate the shipping industry and to acquire and build vessels according to emergency needs. After a period of conflict involving major shifts in top executive positions, the Shipping Board in July 1917 came under the direction of Edward N. Hurley, a self-made millionaire recently retired from the Federal Trade Commission. Hurley's leadership hit its stride in April 1918 when he selected Charles M. Schwab, chairman of the board of the Bethlehem Steel Corporation, to head the Emergency Fleet Corporation (EFC), the board's principal arm for building ships. The USSB and EFC by gradual steps took complete charge of the construction, acquisition, and use of ships throughout the United States. Like most other wartime agencies, these administrations worked with and through industry representatives. The accomplishments of the USSB remain a subject of controversy, but at war's end it commanded a huge fleet that had been virtually nonexistent in 1916.[7]

The War Finance Corporation, created by Congress in March 1918, played a role in the larger program of financing the war. This same legislation also established the Capital Issues Committee. Both the corporation and the committee were dominated by a close partnership between the Treasury Department and the Federal Reserve Board. The committee was to oversee the issuance of new securities; the corporation, through the national banking structure, would help finance industries and economic endeavors vital to national security.[8]

The actions of the Food, Fuel, and Railroad Administrations, the War Trade Board, the U.S. Shipping Board, the Emergency Fleet Corporation, the War Finance Corporation, and the Capital Issues Committee affected each other and the WIB. Some cooperation had to take place among them, and most bodies had representatives on the WIB. But coordination was always piecemeal, intermittent, and disjointed and, as a result, the entire economic mobilization effort displayed the same qualities. One characteristic that these agencies and administrations did share was a similar mode of operation. To varying degrees, they worked through the industries they were supposed to regulate, and they stressed voluntary and cooperative approaches instead of acting as detached civil servants with coercive powers. Most of these bodies had powers for imposing their policies, but shows of force were rare. Reflecting the realities of power in the economy, the various mobilization bodies functioned in a manner similar to the WIB. Thus to a substantial degree they provided for the welfare, protection, and profits of their constituents, often at the expense of consumers and the larger public interest.

## ORGANIZED LABOR

Organized labor exercised less control and influence over the wartime agencies formed to deal with it than any other economic group. Moreover, where it did have representation, labor was actually, if not nominally, confined to the area of management-labor relations and manpower-supply programs instead of exercising influence over the entire economic mobilization effort as business did. This situation was not surprising since the organized labor movement was still comparatively weak, its strength confined to a relatively limited number of occupations like transportation, the building trades, printing, clothing, and mining. Unions were largely excluded from the heavy mass industries so crucial to the war effort. Furthermore, the labor movement was deeply divided between conservative trade unionists and radicals. Although unions and the working population made gains through increased union membership and improvements in wages, hours, and working conditions, labor paid a high price for these advances. The American Federation of Labor joined the Wilson administration and business in crushing radical unions like the Industrial Workers of the World (IWW), curbing dissent against the war, and, in effect, lending its support to a war effort and a corporate capitalist order that were far from universally supported within even moderate labor circles.[9]

Labor's limited role in economic mobilization and its co-option within a liberal corporate order cannot be overemphasized. Labor's influence on the overall mobilization movement was slight—even though Samuel Gompers was a member of the National Defense Advisory Commission, Hugh A. Frayne sat on the War Industries Board and its Price Fixing Committee, labor had representatives in other mobilization agencies, and the Gompers-inspired General Trade-Union Conference of March 1917 called for a voice for labor in all mobilization agencies. Gompers's primary role on the NDAC involved educating the other commissioners about what they should and should not do to win working-class support for the war. He also used his position to advocate, with some success, the creation of new agencies for dealing with labor issues. These bodies were established outside the NDAC structure, however. Gompers organized a full complement of committees within the Labor Section of the NDAC to handle labor affairs, but generally they proved to be weak. On the WIB, Frayne appeared reasonably successful in presenting labor's views, especially in providing for higher wages when high prices were set and in adjusting blatant wage inequities in price negotiations. Yet outside those areas labor rarely spoke, was seldom heard, and appeared uninterested in venturing beyond its narrowly defined sphere.

Nevertheless, the significance of labor's representation on the NDAC and the WIB, limited though it was, should not be minimized. Progressive attitudes toward unions were ambivalent to hostile, and except for the National Civic Federation (NCF), most businessmen were still antagonistic, and often extremely so, toward labor. Hence, Gompers, Frayne, and other labor leaders sitting in high government circles signaled an important breakthrough. Several factors explain this dramatic change. First, any reasonable analyst who grasped the realities of modern warfare realized that enlightened labor relations and manpower programs were indispensable for a successful mobilization of the economy. Howard E. Coffin was among the most astute in this regard, and even the U.S. Chamber of Commerce recognized the importance of the issues, having advocated a system of national service for the working class before the United States entered the fighting. For people whose insight was less keen, the chaotic labor situation—with more than three times as many strikes in 1917 as 1915, severe labor shortages, and extremely high turnover rates after the United States entered the fighting—forcefully brought home the necessity of working out effective policies for dealing with the working population.

That need explains the second principal reason for labor's newly elevated and legitimized position: Only with the cooperation of moderate-to-conservative labor elements could manpower be used intelligently and labor stability achieved. Traditionally, the AFL had been pacifistic and antimilitary and had manifested a healthy suspicion of government. Beginning in 1914, however, the AFL leadership had swung to a pro-Allied, propreparedness, and prowar position. But much of the federation's rank and file, associated with or sympathetic to the antiwar Socialists and the IWW, continued to harbor the earlier views or remained uncertain. Requiring mass support to fight an unpopular war and to mobilize the economy, the Wilson administration needed Gompers and his lieutenants to carry along the AFL and the working class and to isolate labor's radical elements who continued to oppose the war effort.

The first step in this direction was to include labor representatives in the mobilization administrations, as well as working out policies and setting up agencies to win labor support. The new bodies would be staffed by labor spokesmen and individuals such as Frank P. Walsh, who had chaired the U.S. Commission on Industrial Relations during Wilson's first term. Including labor within the mobilization apparatus and ostensibly allowing it to share fairly in war prosperity made a great stride toward winning labor's support for the war and mobilization. Where that tactic did not suffice, the Wilson administration, with the support of the AFL and prowar Socialists and other radicals, moved forcefully against dissenting workers and radicals through suppression, incarceration, and provoked violence. The insidious propaganda of the Committee on Public Information and front organizations like the American Alliance for Labor and Democracy played an important role in this attack.

Through this dual approach, the Wilson administration in effect adopted the tactic used earlier by the National Civic Federation: working with the labor center against the radical left and hardline-management right. In doing so, the administration bolstered the economic status quo and strengthened a war effort related to defending the system and firming up its capitalist base. To enhance its own position, power, and status, the AFL was fully willing to go along with this process of co-option.

Actually, the working population and organized labor were most immediately affected by government action outside the NDAC and the WIB. Hostilities quite suddenly made the War Department, the Navy Department, the Fuel Administration, and other agencies into major contractors with vital interests in and influence over labor matters. Most immediately, the 1912 law requiring an eight-hour day for all federal contractors took on new significance; more generally, government agencies as contractors now had authority to deal with all questions of wages, hours, and working conditions.

The War Department set the pattern in handling these immense issues. Early on, Secretary of War Baker appointed a special assistant for labor, a post filled successively by Felix Frankfurter, Walter Lippmann, and Stanley King. With the department facing severe problems in building cantonments, Baker and Gompers agreed in June 1917 to the creation of a Cantonment Adjustment Commission, consisting of representatives from government, labor, and the public. The commission rendered quite liberal decisions on wages, hours, and working conditions. Similar bodies proliferated within the War Department, the Navy Department, the Railroad Administration, the Fuel Administration, and other agencies.

Late in April 1918 Wilson created the National War Labor Board (NWLB), consisting of five labor and five management members and a dual chairmanship under Frank P. Walsh and William Howard Taft. The body served in effect as a court of last resort for disputes that other agencies could not settle or that were not covered by a separate body. The board agreed that strikes and lockouts would be prohibited; that union organization and collective bargaining were legitimate, with union and nonunion shops remaining as they were but without prejudice against union membership; that women would receive equal pay for equal work; that the eight-hour day would be accepted in principle; and that local standards would serve as the guideline for wages, but only if a "living wage" prevailed. The NWLB had its greatest impact in areas where special government labor boards had not been created and was quite successful in settling conflicts.

Shortly after the creation of the NWLB, Wilson established the War Labor Policies Board (WLPB) within the Department of Labor. Headed by Frankfurter and including representatives from the departments and agencies dealing with labor issues, the new board was charged with attempting to coordinate, unify, and standardize the labor policies of government agencies. Although the second board had not made great progress by November 1918, more coordination was attempted in the labor field than was true for the mobilization program in general. The bodies dealing with labor issues were created without any specific congressional mandate. As in the case of the WIB, they thus had wide latitude and avoided the paralyzing debate that could have occurred had congressional approval been sought. Furthermore, the Department of Labor, through the determined and skillful efforts of Secretary of Labor William B. Wilson and Assistant Secretary Louis F. Post, maintained significant control over its areas of responsibility that related to economic mobilization. By contrast, the Department of Commerce had to surrender most of its jurisdiction temporarily to mobilization agencies such as the WIB.

The issue of labor supply received considerable attention during the war years. The Department of Labor assumed an even more dominant role in this instance than it did on labor relations. On the eve of World War I, labor distribution was without national direction, handled mostly by private employment agencies, employers themselves, various federal bodies, and some state efforts. With shortages, inefficient usage, and maldistribution mounting in 1917, the Labor Department succeeded in having its emerging U.S. Employment Service (USES)—actually established under that name in spring 1918—designated as the principal labor supply agency.

When it received proper funding in late 1917, the service began performing the centralized role that Secretary of Labor Wilson had sought for it as early as 1914. Its efforts were strengthened considerably in June 1918, when a presidential proclamation called upon all employers engaged in war work to recruit exclusively through the service and encouraged the working population to heed its call for labor. Moreover, a month earlier the Selective Service Act was amended to provide for a "work-or-fight" order, in which men eligible for the draft were required to transfer from nonessential to essential employment or face induction.

Under such conditions, the USES was able to do a reasonable job of channeling labor according to requirements, especially in unskilled categories.

The work-or-fight order suggested a darker side to wartime labor supply. Compared to the brutal acts perpetrated against the International Workers of the World, controlling the work force involved attitudes and aspirations more than implemented policy, but the attempt is nonetheless worthy of note. From the outset of the preparedness movement to the mobilization process itself, some individuals sought to draft labor through a system of national service in which the federal government would direct the working population for the duration of the war. Advocates ranged from such men as Howard E. Coffin, who in the vein of the National Civic Federation sought to regulate labor as part of a thoroughly rationalized mobilization program—one in which labor would be represented and its interests protected—to neo-Hamiltonian elites who wanted regimentation, order, and patriotism under their own control, to reap the benefits they believed existed in Germany. In between were organizations such as the Chamber of Commerce, which favored labor supply programs from the perspective of aiding employers and which also believed that any national service system could strengthen management, weaken unions, or both. Other than the work-or-fight order, these proposals never got beyond the advocacy stage, probably because doubts about an enlarged government were still so strong that few people would embrace the notion of Washington running the daily lives of a majority of the population.[10]

In general, labor fared reasonably well during World War I, though it hardly prospered. Unions increased their membership from slightly more than 3 million in 1916 to over 4 million in 1919. Despite considerable inflation, real wages in 1918 were about 4 percent above the levels of 1914 (a recession year). This was not a great gain but was better than the experience of white-collar and salaried employees who saw a drastic loss in real pay during the war years. Furthermore, the Wilson administration moved to check the erosion of protective labor legislation and even made advances in reducing the official workday and restricting the abusive use of women and child labor. Nonetheless, through willing co-option, labor had made itself quite vulnerable and allowed its militancy to erode without any guarantee that its long-term interests would be served. The 1920s revealed the dangers of this course.

## ECONOMIC CONSEQUENCES

Labor fared the worst as an economic interest group during World War I. Farmers as a group did much better. Their real income in 1918 was about 29 percent over that of 1915, a relatively prosperous year itself, even though output remained fairly constant. However, Southern cotton growers saw their economic position deteriorate badly because of seriously eroded foreign markets.[11]

The economic group that gained the most, not unexpectedly, was the well-placed corporations directly or indirectly involved in war production. According to the Federal Trade Commission, the U.S. Steel Corporation in 1917 had profits based on invested capital that were six times higher than the average level of 1912–1914. (These were conservative calculations, which did not take into account cost padding, high management salaries and bonuses, and various questionable or deceptive cost accounting methods.) Ten less integrated steel firms benefited from profits in 1917 ranging from 30 percent to 320 percent. Twenty-one copper companies saw their average after-tax profits shoot up from 12 percent in 1913 to 24 percent in 1917. Among those businesses leading in wartime profits were the four largest meat-packing firms; their aggregate average profits jumped from $19 million in 1912–1914 to $140 million in 1915–1917, more than a sixfold increase. Total corporate profits rose much less dramatically, increasing from approximately $4.2 billion in 1915 to nearly $8 billion in 1918, when government wartime regulations and controls were more firmly established.

In a hard-hitting report on wartime profiteering, the FTC explained that in some industries, like zinc, no unusual profits occurred; in others, such as nickel, elevated profits resulted primarily from increased output rather than higher prices. But most big earners, (besides those just discussed) including firms in petroleum and its products, flour millers, and leather and leather goods companies, relied on high prices that they maintained themselves or that were set by the government. The FTC concluded that although fixing prices to stimulate output in an ascending market helped increase production, it also punished the consumer, strengthened the low-cost producer, and put high-cost firms in a vulnerable position when demand dropped after the war. On the matter of wartime profits, the FTC declared:

> The commission has reason to know that profiteering exists. Much of it is due to advantages taken of the necessities of the times as evidenced in the war pressure for heavy production. Some of it is attributable to inordinate greed and barefaced fraud.[12]

In general, given the rudimentary nature and slow evolution of the mobilization structure, the nation's economic performance during World War I was reasonably good. The Gross National Product (GNP) in 1918, measured in 1914 dollars, was 15 percent above that of 1914, but 5 percent below

1917. In 1916 total manufacturing for the war years reached a high of 39 percent above 1914, then fell from that level by a percentage point in 1917 and by another in 1918. This drop meant that planning succeeded in converting the economy to war production but did not increase the amount of economic output by much and did not, after 1916, increase manufacturing output at all, despite the stimulative effect of the billions expended for the war. Nonetheless, in industries such as steel, aluminum, ships, and locomotives that were essential to the war effort, considerable and even spectacular gains were made. These advances came at the expense of production for the civilian economy, however.[13]

American war financing was superior to that of the other belligerents but was only fair compared to the financing of America's other wars. Of war expenditures totaling nearly $38 billion, $13.7 billion, or about 36 percent, was paid by taxation and the remainder raised through borrowing. Taxation paid for a lesser percentage of war costs during the Civil War but for a greater percentage for World War II. The vast expansion in credit and only moderate dependence on tax revenue helped feed the inflationary flames that pushed the general index of wholesale prices 95.7 percent above the base year of 1913, with 42.1 percent of the increase occurring in 1917 and 24.5 percent in 1918. Manufactured goods followed approximately the same pattern. Raw materials experienced the greatest price controls, which were most effective in 1918. Raw material prices rose faster than wholesale and manufacturing prices in 1917 but increased at rates 6 to 9.5 percent below those figures for 1918. Hence, the policies that sought to stabilize raw material prices can be judged a moderate success.[14]

In general, then, economic policy during World War I, including remuneration, financing, and pricing, tended to reflect the economic and political power in the nation. Not surprisingly, the various wartime agencies carried out economic policies and mobilization practices that were fully consistent, if not identical, with each other.

World War I had profound and enduring effects on the nation's political economy. In one area, this consequence was immediately evident. Through the economic stimulus of the war, both before and after the United States entered hostilities, economic power was further concentrated and the conditions were created for another wave of mergers. After the first modern merger movement from 1895 to 1904 (with most activity concentrated in the years 1898–1902), there had been limited economic consolidation from 1904 to 1914. In 1915 merger activity sped up and continued intermittently through 1920. This new wave of mergers can be interpreted as the upswing that culminated in the second major wave of mergers from 1925 to 1929.

Based on Ralph L. Nelson's data and analysis, several observations are in order concerning World War I and the reinvigoration of the merger movement.[15] Periods of high merger activity roughly correlate with eras of strong industrial growth rates, a generally favorable business climate, and buoyant securities markets. In 1914 the American economy was in a recession, and the economic system from 1905 to 1914 was unpropitious for mergers. World War I stimulus, both before and after the nation entered the war, created the essential conditions for reviving the rather inactive merger process. On average, there were 139 mergers per year from 1915 to 1920 (considerably below the annual average of 301 for the 1895–1904 period but above the 100 annual average for the years 1905–1914). The 1915–1920 period witnessed the first occurrence of exceptionally large mergers since 1898–1904.

The mergers of the earlier period differed strikingly from those of the later one. Turn-of-the-century mergers were primarily by consolidation (i.e., the "simultaneous multiple-union" of firms into one corporation), but mergers in the World War I era were generally by acquisition (i.e., that one firm took over another, either as a single action or as one step in a more elaborate strategy).[16] Although mergers in and of themselves need not create greater market control, the movement of 1895–1904 enhanced industry domination dramatically, and the one beginning in 1915 and peaking in the late 1920s further restricted market forces. That effect stemmed from the circumstance that most mergers in both periods were horizontal rather than vertical, or diversified, and strengthened in various ways oligopolistic structures and practices. Furthermore, although primary metals and food products remained at or near the top of lists of mergers per industry in terms of number and capitalization in the late nineteenth and early twentieth centuries, beginning in 1915 and continuing into the 1920s the "new" dynamic, high-growth industries were moving to the top of merger activity. These included petroleum products, chemicals, and transportation equipment—with a shift from railroads to automobiles, trucks, and parts.

The war had a direct impact on the economy, not just indirect effects, as in the case of mergers. Total spending for the war in 1914 dollars constituted about 7 percent of the aggregate GNP for the years 1914–1918; if the time period is extended to 1919, the figure is 8 percent. In 1914 and 1915 war spending constituted less than 1 percent of the GNP, but by 1918 it had risen to 23.3 percent and in the last quarter reached 28.6 percent. The spending ran the gamut from purchases of food and textiles to munitions and included construction of all sorts. Munitions for World War I were more highly specialized than in the Civil War but less so than for World War II, and were a far cry from today's weaponry. The nation had begun to develop the expertise and to create the products and plants for building the modern navy beginning in the late nineteenth century. Allied demand from 1914 to 1917 virtually created whole new industries in this country to produce rifles and small arms and massively expanded the output of explosives and powder.[17]

Once it had entered the war, the U.S. built on these foundations to equip and arm itself while still assisting the Allies. Only about 20 percent of war demand consisted of specialized equipment requiring specialized plants; the rest involved standard goods produced in ordinary civilian factories. Even so, in some areas the United States never met its needs for specialized equipment, and in others it failed rather miserably in attempting to do so, as was the case with artillery and aircraft. In general, the nation did much better in producing supplies for the navy, where it had greater experience, than for the army.

The genuine problems of World War I, however, concerned planning and managing an economy under stress from a high level of demand rather than converting a civilian economy to the massive production of specialized munitions. Nevertheless, wartime demand pulled the nation out of the economic doldrums and produced the rather lavish prosperity of World War I, even though the overall growth of the economy was not spectacular, and war demand often occurred at the expense of production for civilians.[18]

World War I also acted to alter the power position of banks vis-à-vis industry, or at least to create conditions for change in their relationship. The dominant position of financial, or investment, banks, the most prominent of which was J. P. Morgan and Company, was probably weakened from 1919 as manufacturers found alternate sources for credit, first from the federal government and then internally from their high wartime profits and the prosperity of the 1920s. New financial centers also grew in the West, and commercial banks entered the securities and investment fields. These changes and new competition enhanced the strength of industry in relation to the financial houses by making manufacturers less dependent on them. Moreover, the war made the United States the world's creditor, a fact that changed in both blatant and subtle ways the role of industry, finance, and the federal government in the operations of the international economic system. Such profound developments inevitably affected power operations in the United States.[19]

The most far-reaching impact of World War I involved planning the wartime economy and the consequences of that experience for the future. In this instance, as in others, the war accelerated existing trends rather than introducing new ones. Big business, first on its own in the late nineteenth century and then in combination with the government during the Progressive Era, attempted to stabilize the economy, using various forms of planning. The results were always incomplete and unsatisfactory.

Focusing on the corporation and its leadership, Alfred D. Chandler, Jr., has established that the major oligopolistic industries had gone far in the early years of the twentieth century in replacing the marketplace with administered decisionmaking in pricing, production, and so forth. Although Chandler observes that the large corporation managed in a modern fashion was already established by 1917, some important structural weaknesses still existed. Because management was not yet fully professionalized, with a proper division of labor between middle and top-level managers, corporations could not effectively adapt their operations to short-term market fluctuations. More important, corporate leaders continued to concentrate on the daily operations of the firm instead of confining themselves to setting major policies and planning for the future. Chandler maintains that further refinement of the corporate system and fuller professionalization of management in the 1920s acted substantially to correct both these flaws.[20]

A major drawback to Chandler's otherwise rich and perceptive book is that he pays little attention to World War I and considers government to be largely inconsequential for the corporate and economic development in the late nineteenth and early twentieth centuries. But the war and the government were of the greatest significance for that development. Mobilization for World War I impressed corporate leaders, serving both as government officials and in the private sector, with the importance of short- and long-term planning and exposed the defects in their own operations. Never before had the corporate structure been required to concentrate so fully on its production potential, production scheduling, pricing, conservation, and the coordination of activities among firms and with the government through trade associations and similar organizations. That experience held true for companies that participated directly in war production and for those that did not. In a short but extremely intense period, World War I convinced corporate management of the importance of planning through its own structure and through trade associations and acted as a stimulus for rationalizing further corporate and economic structures in the 1920s.

Moreover, the war forcefully established for corporate executives the reality that their welfare depended on a government actively involved in the operations of the economic system, either formally or informally. In short, World War I acted to accelerate, shape, and bring to a level of completeness the twentieth-century American political economy.

# 12
# RECONVERSION

Reconversion, or returning the economy to its peacetime pursuits, involved much effort and generated a great deal of controversy. Analyzing the problems is worthwhile not only because the transition to peace was important but also because the struggle over that process highlights many of the salient qualities and legacies of war mobilization.

The effect of World War I on advancing economic planning is evident in the demobilization as well as in the mobilization process. Like most of the World War I mobilization experience, prevailing attitudes were confusing and uncertain about what role, if any, the government should take in guiding the reconversion of the war economy to peacetime conditions. Within that ambiguous context, two major trends are discernible: First, at varying times there was widespread support for the government to play an active role in reconstruction or readjustment (the noun selected to describe the process had important implications for the plans advocated); second, for a complex set of reasons, the government's part in reconversion turned out to be minimal. Even after the decision to minimize the government's role was finally and supposedly firmly made in late November and early December 1918, that path was not followed. An Industrial Board was created early in 1919 and remained in existence for several months to ease the transition to peace and to further the cause of industrial cooperation in the postwar years.

## THE TRANSITION TO PEACE

The Council of National Defense–National Defense Advisory Commission made the first definite move involving reconversion as early as March 1918. With the War Industries Board separated from the CND, the latter organization faced extinction. To prevent such an occurrence, help ensure an active role for the council during the war and the years of peace that lay ahead, and meet their convictions about the need for peace preparation, Grosvenor B. Clarkson and to a lesser degree Walter S. Gifford, still secretary and director, began a campaign to have the CND designated as the agency to direct reconversion planning. With the support of the members of the CND and the NDAC, including Secretary of War Baker, President Wilson on June 19, 1918, agreed to allow the CND to "coordinate" existing studies on reconversion and "suggest procedures" for accomplishing the goal.

Thereafter, working mostly through a small staff and various advisers directed by Clarkson, the CND–NDAC carried out in-depth studies and worked up rather elaborate plans for reconversion. As the CND–NDAC moved from vague investigations to more concrete proposals and the war's end approached, divisions over the proper course of reconversion and the role of the CND–NDAC in it became evident. The CND–NDAC's work received enthusiastic support from Samuel Gompers, Franklin H. Martin, and Hollis Godfrey on the NDAC, with Bernard M. Baruch providing encouragement but not participating in the effort, and from Secretary of Commerce William C. Redfield and, to a lesser degree, Secretary of the Interior Franklin K. Lane on the CND. Commission members Daniel Willard, Julius Rosenwald, and Howard E. Coffin, along with Gifford, were somewhat hesitant, believing that the CND–NDAC would require more authority to fulfill its new goal. Typically, Baker, like Wilson, appeared uncertain and hence was at best courteous and tolerant about the CND's reconversion efforts.

Shortly after Wilson's positive nod to the council on June 19, Gompers, Martin, and other supporters pushed through the NDAC a resolution for creating a "special commission on reconstruction"—which could have been the CND–NDAC itself—with real authority for dealing with the matter. The CND, however, pigeonholed the resolution. Thereafter, the work under Clarkson went forth apace but without fruition. At a critical point in November, a meeting of the WIB and the State Councils of National Defense was about to take up reconversion policies, which might have presented a meaningful opening for the CND, but Wilson, on the advice of Baker and Secretary of Agriculture David F. Houston, squelched the move. The CND–NDAC continued to exist and plan for reconversion into 1921, but its efforts never produced tangible results.[1]

The CND, of course, was only one source of advocacy and planning for demobilization. The Department of Commerce, the War Labor Policies Board, other temporary and permanent government bodies, and numerous business, labor, agricultural, and publicly oriented groups came forth with specific recommendations or at least insisted that the matter receive serious attention. Organized labor, including the AFL as a body and Samuel Gompers and

Hugh A. Frayne, and others in various government agencies, especially the WIB, vociferously supported an active role for government in guiding the nation through the transition to peace.

Numerous proposals involving demobilization were drawn up or introduced in Congress. The most notable included a bill creating a joint congressional committee on reconstruction, authored by Sen. John W. Weeks (R-MA), and a measure for setting up an executive-appointed commission favored by Sen. Lee S. Overman (D-NC). Wilson was as adamantly opposed to the Weeks proposition as he had been to the senator's proposal for a joint committee on the conduct of the war; he also discouraged the Overman initiative. Except in a few minor areas, the advocates of a defined reconversion program had no greater success than had the CND. The nation returned to peace as unprepared as it had gone to war.[2]

The most significant struggle over reconversion took place within the WIB and continued among some of its principal leaders after the board was disestablished. Since the WIB was the principal mobilization agency and incorporated the representatives of most of industrial America, the controversy is not surprising. What is surprising is the fact that the WIB did not take up the issue seriously until October and November 1918, when it became clear that the war was ending. The delay can be explained partly through immediate causes. The WIB was struggling to refine its operations until the end of the fighting and simply lacked the time and energy for more long-term issues. Further, most members expected the war to extend into 1919; indeed, military and economic planning was directed toward a major Allied offensive in mid-1919. Such a schedule allowed ample time to prepare for demobilization to the extent that it was necessary. But long-term factors were at work. Great Britain, France, and Germany had created institutions for reconversion quite early in the war. Although this action stemmed partly from their greater need for such bodies, a more fundamental factor was involved. Industrial mobilization in those nations, unlike in the United States, was firmly based in law. Since the method of harnessing the European economies had a statutory basis, those nations could also statutorily prepare for the unharnessing that would inevitably occur. Because the United States lacked a legally grounded basis for economic mobilization, it was inclined to enter the economic transition to peace in the same indirect and piecemeal fashion.

Wilson largely set the parameters for demobilization, just as he had set the guidelines for World War I mobilization. Throughout the war years, the president had manifested a distinct discomfort with the burgeoning emergency government. To the degree possible, he relied on the existing statutory departments to carry the burden of economic mobilization, aided by the CND–NDAC and their successor agencies, until that expedient broke down during winter 1917–1918. Only then, and under intense pressure, did Wilson grant the War Industries Board a measure of independence and authority. One who was so resistant to institutional innovation in the face of national catastrophe was unlikely to sanction new ventures and new institutions as the war was ending unless another crisis of extreme dimensions threatened. Late in 1918 fears about a depression were widespread, but the indications of a downturn were not evident. In short, Wilson opposed a major state role in demobilization because of his continuing ambivalence toward big government and the fear that if the war administration was not cut back quickly, it could become permanent.

Once the need for a demobilization policy emerged in October–November 1918, Wilson laid out his position quite clearly: There would be no commission or agency for reconversion; the WIB and most though not all emergency war administrations would be disestablished and controls removed within a reasonable time and manner; and war agency functions that would be useful for postwar readjustment and in peacetime would be transferred to existing statutory departments. Until fall 1918, Wilson remained open to reconversion planning as long as it committed him to nothing, as was the case with the activity of the CND. Even during the autumn, he seldom said no firmly to the numerous proposals and advice he received, with the exception of Senator Weeks's bill for a joint congressional committee. Instead, the president evaded the issue or remained ambiguous. Wilson clearly was opposed to new agencies and to a large role for the state in demobilization but still entertained ideas of short-term emergency action and long-term policies that did not significantly conflict with the expeditious restoration of peacetime government. Given Wilsonian principles, his stance was pragmatic and politically astute. With so many pressure groups and agencies pressing him for positive action, he would have been politically insensitive to brush them aside brusquely; with so many uncertainties about reconversion, he would have been foolhardy to reject irrevocably a state role in the demobilization process.

The outcome of the November 1918 elections served only to strengthen Wilson's reconversion convictions. The incoming Republican Congress would weaken his position at Paris and at home. With Republican conservatives ascendant and demands for retrenchment in federal spending growing, the president had every reason to avoid a big role for the government in demobilization in order to protect his political flank. On December 2, in his address to Congress prior to departing for Europe, Wilson announced more boldly than ever that the nation was already in the demobilization process, that the procedures were going smoothly, and that little else from his administration was required. Still, the president did not exclude the possibility of reconversion and some long-range programs if they were needed; and he made no move to disestablish government controls over the railroads, the shipping industry, the merchant marine, and the coal and wheat subsidy programs. A considerably enlarged state still existed and the door was left open for some maneuvering, but Wilson had clearly set forth his determination to return to a government of peacetime size and function with all deliberate speed.[3]

The president's position on reconversion created problems for Baruch and the top WIB leaders. Tactically, if not strategically, most of the board's executives agreed with Wilson's decisions on reconversion, but only after a period of agonizing deliberation. Many board members favored a carefully planned demobilization program, and some refused to modify their thinking after Wilson's speech of December 2. Even if they did not agree with the president, they were under intense pressure to continue planning from the commodity sections, trade associations, and other business groups like the U.S. Chamber of Commerce. Supporting the president's decision, therefore, was not easy.[4]

In assessing the response of business to the state's role in reconversion, chronology must be considered. Just before and after the armistice, a condition of near-panic was widespread throughout the business community and the WIB commodity sections. A quick end to the war, with the sudden cancellation of contracts and a threatened drop in demand, could trigger a severe economic downturn. Since virtually no planning had been done by the WIB itself for the war's end, anxiety was high, and for a short period of time, businessmen overwhelmingly demanded that the WIB immediately undertake a program to ensure stability as the nation made the transition to peace. The demand was strongest in the heavy industries that depended greatly on wartime production.

Toward late November, however, the immediate fears generated by the armistice began to subside as the mental adjustment to peace was made and economic prospects brightened. In the changed circumstances, the insistence of the commodity sections and of business for quick and forthright action by the WIB began to diminish, though it remained high. The U.S. Chamber of Commerce reflected the change most dramatically. In late October and early November, the association and its president, Harry A. Wheeler, insisted that business anxieties could be calmed only by a substantial government reconversion program. Yet by the time the chamber's Reconstruction Congress of American Industries met December 3–6, 1918, the leadership and delegates agreed that the economy was in transition to peace with unexpected ease and that all wartime controls should be removed as quickly as possible.

The outlook of business on reconversion varied according to the type of program under consideration. Although some commodity-section and business spokesmen and organizations ultimately backed away from favoring a major government role in reconversion, few gave up the notion that a variation on the wartime planning experience should be continued after the war. They envisioned short-term moves to smooth the adjustment to peace, followed by permanent government involvement in the operations of the economy through basic revisions in the antitrust laws. Planning for reconversion actually blended in with the desire for a fundamental change in the legal framework of the economic system. For purposes of clarity, I shall discuss reconversion programs first.

Beginning early in November 1918 and subsiding toward the end of the month, the commodity sections put forth numerous and varied reconversion proposals. They ranged from a minimum program of continuing the efforts in standardization and conservation to the maximum stance of continuing the full panoply of WIB controls, including pricing, priorities, and allocations for as long as a year, with regulations phased out as the economy gradually converted to full peacetime operations. The more an industry's output was tied to the war effort, the greater the tendency to favor extensive controls. Heavy industry in particular supported continued regulation. On November 13, in a lengthy meeting with WIB members, steel spokesman Elbert H. Gary requested that the board guarantee maximum prices for an extended period so that buyers would not delay purchases in the hope of a rapid price drop. He also asked the board to coordinate all cancellations of foreign and domestic contracts, initiate a program of extensive government buying, and take all other possible action to guide the economy through the transition to peace. Out of perceived necessity and principle, in early November many top WIB executives such as George N. Peek were quite disposed toward the board's assuming a major role in reconversion. As a long-time advocate of economic rationalization, Baruch shared these views, at least in theory.

Despite the convictions of Baruch and his chief lieutenants, the WIB never played a major role in demobilization for varied and complex reasons. First was Wilson's opposition. Baruch's rise to the chairmanship of the WIB had been achieved in part through his ability to discern the president's wishes and adjust his position accordingly. Regardless of his beliefs and those of his principal advisers, the WIB chairman was unlikely to pursue a line contrary to that of the president.

During a few critical weeks in November, however, Wilson still appeared to be somewhat in doubt about the reconversion program and possibly open to a strongly and cogently argued case for the WIB's pursuing an active role in it. Moreover, during the winter crisis of 1917–1918, Baruch had joined numerous other war mobilizers in pressuring the president to resolve the mobilization crisis, and ultimately he had won. Baruch made no such effort concerning demobilization.[5] His decision not to push for an active part for the board in reconversion involved reasons other than the president's attitude.

Actually, Baruch and a few of his key advisers had manifested considerable uncertainty about reconversion once it became a pressing issue in November. The WIB and its predecessor agencies had guided the industrial community through the throes of industrial mobilization and constantly assured the commodity sections and war service committees that its principal goal was maintaining economic stability and keeping the prewar economic structure intact during the trauma of war demand. For practical reasons and from a sense of obligation, Baruch and the other WIB executives believed that the board should aid demobilization for the same purposes of stability and continuity. Nonetheless, those leaders had to face other realities. Although there was nearly unanimous support for a WIB conversion program in early November and still great support for it in late November, no consensus existed about what such a program should entail. The prospects for working out a compromise were not auspicious. Even if a compromise could be reached, there was no assurance that it could be enforced. The WIB had largely worked through voluntary cooperation based on industrial self-interest and national need. With the war over or coming to a quick end, the emergency conditions essential to the whole mobilization scheme were slipping away. There was no guarantee that the WIB was needed for reconstruction. Indeed, with only a minor effort, industry might be able to carry itself through the process of readjustment.

Furthermore, even if the WIB pursued a reconversion policy, it could not depend on the numerous other war agencies, and especially the military services, to cooperate. Cooperation had at best been strained during the war; in the transition to peace, conditions for a coordinating role for the WIB were even less favorable. Without the cooperation of other governmental bodies, any WIB program could rather quickly be thwarted. Hence, the whole tenuous nature of the WIB as a mobilization agency—both its internal relations with industry and its external relations with other agencies—cast major doubts on the wisdom of its pursuing a major reconversion program. What the program would be and whether it would be acceptable to industry and other governmental bodies was extremely problematic. Wilson and Congress by indirection had avoided facing the hard questions about industrial mobilization. Issues not faced during the intense crisis of war were unlikely to be confronted as peace approached.

Baruch and his major advisers faced a situation in which they would have to pursue a legislative mandate for the WIB if they wanted to give the board a substantial role in reconversion. Only through congressional action could the board's internal and external authority be ensured, since the WIB's position was simply too precarious without statutory powers. The situation had reached an all-or-nothing status.

Baruch and prominent WIB executives such as Arch W. Shaw and Charles F. C. Stout, and especially legal counsel Albert C. Ritchie, rejected the legislative route quite quickly. Neither Wilson nor Congress was likely to welcome a WIB–sponsored reconversion bill. Even if they did, there was no promise that Congress could resolve vital issues of political economy that had been evaded during the war. Furthermore, Baruch, Ritchie, and other board members were inclined to avoid legislation on reconversion for the same reason that they had done so with pricing and priorities: to raise the issue of WIB authority could cast doubt on the legality of board operations during the war. Steadily, over time, Baruch and his lieutenants had made a virtue of necessity. The lack of statutory sanction had provided enormous latitude and allowed business largely to regulate itself. Creating a statutory agency at the end of the war could reduce the flexibility the WIB had enjoyed and introduce the threat of regulatory agencies not controlled by business. The political turmoil that inevitably lay ahead after the outcome of the November election gave the WIB leadership even further pause when pondering legislative solutions for possible reconversion problems. So touchy had the WIB leadership become about keeping its agency out of political conflicts that Baruch asked Wilson to consider having Congress pass legislation, as it had after the Civil War, retroactively legalizing all government actions during the war. Baruch never pushed the matter, and no such bill was ever passed.[6]

Always prominent in the minds of Baruch and his principal advisers as they approached reconversion was the reputation of the War Industries Board. They rightly perceived that it had established an estimable reputation with business and the public, one that Baruch and his coterie had carefully cultivated. The image of unstinted business cooperation and sacrifice based on patriotism had been the constant refrain of the WIB and its business partners. Had the WIB entered the reconversion fray, either by asserting its own authority or through legislation, it could have become embroiled in enormous controversies involving open conflict with elements of the business community that opposed its programs and with other agencies that resented its policies. Baruch, always sensitive about his own image and the WIB's, ultimately decided that the reputation of the board's war effort had to be protected by forgoing its role in reconversion. That view, next to Wilson's stand, is the most important reason for the WIB leadership's turning against a significant role for the board in the demobilization process.

But even the positions of Baruch and Wilson were based on a larger truth: The United States was so divided over questions of political economy that it was impossible directly to confront and resolve fundamental issues about how to mobilize the economy for war and how to avoid a potential crisis in demobilization. Basic, controversial issues over the operations of power within the economy were involved. Moreover, the hostilities and resentments that had built up during the war would have a deleterious effect on any situation of postwar crisis. There were too many differences and pent-up doubts and frustrations from the war years, and reconversion was an insufficient reason to submerge discord for reasonable harmony. Indirection had worked, though poorly, during the emergency, but the threat of disorganized demobilization was not great enough to make indirection work after the war. The end of the war created circumstances in which the unofficial reality of business control over much of the economy would have to become overt if it were to continue. Bringing this reality into the open would be unwelcome to Wilson, Baruch, and much of the governmental structure and public. For that central reason, America drifted into demobilization, just as it had drifted into mobilization.

Certainly Baruch and the WIB leadership did not simply fold up their tents after the armistice and walk away. They felt a practical and moral obligation to industry and to the nation to ease any difficulties of reconversion. Even if he had not been so disposed, Baruch would have been uncharacteristically impolitic to ignore the great concern expressed about the consequences of the war's end and the innumerable importunities awaiting WIB action. While the board was struggling to formulate an official position on reconversion, the statements of the chairman were imprecise and often contradictory. When panic gripped the board's subdivisions and the business community at the time of the armistice, Baruch indicated that the WIB would continue with an active policy until the economy had made the transition to peace. As the fear began to wane and his own ideas jelled, Baruch, much like the president, still avoided categorical statements. He maintained a stance of being open to advice and repeatedly suggested to the commodity sections, to the president, and to other concerned parties actions that the board and other governmental bodies could or would take to ease the transition to peace. These moves included scheduling the cancellation of contracts, clearing raw materials as peacetime production increased, avoiding a sudden dumping of finished products on the market, discharging troops in a way that would least disrupt the labor market, and transferring the board's standardization and conservation offices to the Commerce Department.

In some respects, the chairman was grossly exaggerating objectives that the board and other agencies would or could achieve. Nonetheless, Baruch sincerely worked for various goals from the desire to smooth the way to a peacetime economy. Even after the decision to disestablish the board quickly was made, Baruch remained guarded in his public statements. If it was necessary to end the WIB's role in the wartime economy expeditiously in order to protect the board's image, it was likewise necessary to give business and the public the impression that the WIB was doing everything possible to fulfill its responsibilities during the period in which it continued after the armistice. Like Wilson, Baruch ultimately justified a limited or nonexistent role for the WIB in demobilization by suggesting that in the transition to peace and in the long-term effort for prosperity, the nation must depend on expanding markets abroad and at home through lowered prices and business cooperation.

In the whole reconversion imbroglio, Baruch was not free to operate as a potentate, given the restrictions on the chairman's power that remained even after March 1918. Various WIB executives fought ruthless bureaucratic battles; hence, the confusion caused by Baruch's uncertainties and contradictions was compounded as other board members spoke for the WIB. Reports appeared in the press that were obviously floated by board officials pushing for an active WIB role in reconversion. Moreover, WIB executives at times argued for a closely controlled demobilization on grounds that were more appealing than accurate. Continued WIB controls were as necessary to check inflation and limit profits, the arguments often ran, as they were to head off deflation and maintain profits. Yet ensuring profits was the main concern of the strongest advocates of a WIB–coordinated demobilization program. The public relations battle grew to such proportions that Robert F. Himmelberg has concluded that WIB executives were engaging in well-calculated and disingenuous propaganda campaigns in order to pressure Wilson into supporting an active role for the board in reconversion.[7]

Despite the infighting and uncertainty, Baruch could not postpone decisions on reconversion indefinitely. Without setting forth a comprehensive blueprint for the dissolution of the WIB, Baruch and his chief lieutenants started disestablishing controls in the last weeks of November. Step by step, price agreements were allowed to expire, priorities orders lifted, and conservation procedures ended. In the process, the commodity sections were virtually given carte blanche to work with their industries and any part of the board or other government agencies in developing demobilization programs. On several occasions, however, the board insisted that the commodity sections recognize that any actions they took were merely advisory. Finally, under intense pressure from some sections to sanction production pooling and price fixing that would extend beyond the life of the board, Baruch and his aides gave a tentative and then a definite no.

On November 27 Baruch informed Wilson that the WIB was virtually dissolved and submitted for the president's approval a letter of resignation. It became official on November 29, and he set January 1, 1919, as the termination date for the board. In the letter, Baruch, like Wilson himself, hedged his bets by allowing for renewed action in the event of a sudden downturn in the economy.[8] A few days later, Baruch proposed modifications reflecting his views contained in a November 30 letter from Secretary of War Baker to the president, prompted by a meeting of war agencies convened by the CND in which the council, in effect, called for the quick removal of all controls and a rapid retreat by the federal government.[9] Baker's attitudes toward federal versus local and state government had changed during the war, but on the reconversion issue, he and Wilson once again held the same views. Baker's outlook contrasted with that of Baruch, who favored a continuing and substantial role for the government in the economy but decided not to push for those goals because of expediency.

After Baruch sent his November 27 letter, the WIB division and section heads were left to determine when they should shut down. Baruch had already been tapped to go with the president to Paris. When the former chairman departed, George N. Peek took over as acting chairman and Albert C. Ritchie served as the liquidating official. As January 1 approached, the commodity sections and other subdivisions of the WIB ground to a halt in a disorderly and unscheduled manner. The board ended much as the NDAC had started—in a piecemeal, disjointed fashion.

The WIB's demobilization role, in which the parts continued or ended without centralized direction, was characteristic of the Wilson administration's approach to reconversion. There was neither a set reconversion program nor an agency to carry it out. Board offices dealing with conservation and standardization, planning and statistics, and minerals were transferred or were intended to be transferred to the Commerce Department, other regular departments, or other wartime agencies so that the work could go on at least temporarily. The military services and the USES made some effort to rationalize the massive discharges of troops, and the cancellation of contracts received some attention. The agencies and programs for the railroads, fuel, food, farmers, and other divisions were maintained for a time.[10] Generally, however, little was done to regulate demobilization. The lack of planning may not have been the only cause of the rapid inflation, severe depression, and labor strife and violence that the nation suffered between 1919 and 1921, but its absence certainly contributed significantly to those economic and political convulsions.

## INDUSTRIAL BOARD AND ANTITRUST REVISION

The termination of the WIB did not end industry's drive for government-controlled demobilization or the business community's desire fundamentally to alter the antitrust laws so as to permit corporations to engage legally in intraindustry planning. These two goals were never really separate, and under a peculiar set of circumstances, persistent efforts to gain them coalesced to produce the Industrial Board in February 1919. The board had a short but nonetheless significant life, ending abruptly in May of the same year. From examining the board's experience, one can make important observations about war mobilization, the reconversion imbroglio, and the astuteness of Baruch and his lieutenants in quickly ending the WIB's tenure once hostilities had ceased.

Industry's interest in modifying the antitrust laws so as to allow for intraindustry collusion, cooperation, or, as it was often euphemistically called, the New Competition began during the Progressive years and reached a culmination of sorts with the passage of the Federal Trade Commission Act in 1914. Antitrust policies were only partially and ambiguously altered before the war, partly because they were highly controversial. Although large corporations in the oligopolistic industries staunchly favored revision, the National Association of Manufacturers and other associations representing smaller businesses feared that any relaxation of the legal requirements for competition would redound to the benefit of big business and threaten their existence. The Chamber of Commerce found middle ground, with its leaders astutely pushing their small- to medium-sized constituents toward cooperation.

World War I significantly changed this lineup. The huge corporations continued to support revision, but they were now enthusiastically backed by the Chamber of Commerce, the NAM, most trade associations, and a good part of the business community. This shift stemmed from these less powerful groups experiencing the benefits of planning through the War Industries Board, from a recognition that cooperation was essential for economic stability, and from the realization that during the war large business and the government had behaved so that smaller business units were not injured and certainly not destroyed. The role of the chamber in the formation of the war service committees and the manner in which they functioned helped greatly to create a broad-based sense of confidence in industry. Furthermore, the war mobilization effort encouraged trade association growth, so that organizations existed in many more industries in 1919 than had been the case in 1916. By nature, trade associations were committed to cooperation.

Because of these changed attitudes, support for antitrust revision was strong in business circles. As early as May 1918 the NAM went on record damning the Sherman Act as a fundamental infringement on basic rights. Numerous trade associations supported antitrust revision as a way to aid reconversion and also as a means of realizing long-term goals of industrial cooperation. At its Reconstruction Congress of American Industries early in December 1918—which was actually a meeting of the war service committees—the Chamber of Commerce devoted more attention to antitrust revision than to any other topic, assuming national leadership in the agitation for it. Although opinions on the type of revision varied among business groups and businessmen, a consensus emerged that trade associations should be allowed to go beyond the generally legal activities of standardization, uniform accounting, lobbying, and so forth to pursue cartel-like policies of setting prices and production levels.[11]

Several attempts were made to implement these changes. The first effort, which began in mid-November 1918, involved preparations to transfer the WIB's Conservation Division to the Commerce Department. George N. Peek, division officers including Arch W. Shaw, and Secretary of Commerce William C. Redfield assented to the Conservation Division's suggestion that an ambiguously worded bill accomplishing the transfer, with the cooperation of the FTC, could be used to circumvent the antitrust laws. Redfield believed that the proposed legislation could get through Congress with the support of the WIB, FTC, and Commerce Department. These maneuvers were aborted when the transfer was accomplished by executive order, a sure indication that Baruch was not sympathetic to or informed of the attempted ploy.

Thereafter, the priorities commissioner, Edwin B. Parker, and the assistant administrator of the Fuel Administration, Mark L. Requa, drew up bills that more forthrightly addressed antitrust revision by allowing industries to establish production quotas. One or both of the bills were considered at length by Baruch, Peek, other WIB members, government officials, and businessmen. They were impressed by the proposed legislation and thought it served the interests of business and the public. Peek was the most enthusiastic, convinced that the legislative approach was politically feasible; how far Baruch was willing to go in pushing it is uncertain. What is certain is that Albert C. Ritchie played a key role in withholding the WIB's endorsement. He argued that such bills would not get through Congress, that proposing them was not the WIB's responsibility, and that Baruch and the board would sully their reputation by identifying themselves with schemes so far removed from prevailing attitudes on political economy. Businesses looking to modify market forces legally turned to the WIB to carry the fight for antitrust revision because the board's imprimatur would give the legislation a more official and impartial introduction. If business wanted such legislation, Ritchie concluded, it should proceed on its own. Baruch seemed to agree. For many of the same reasons that the WIB did not proceed with reconversion plans, it pulled back from lobbying for antitrust revision.[12]

Business continued to support antitrust revision and won a more willing partner in Secretary Redfield's Commerce Department than with the WIB. For years, Redfield had been an enthusiastic supporter of industrial cooperation encouraged and coordinated by the government. He had viewed the planning effort with a sense of satisfaction throughout the war and was among the most prominent government spokesmen for active government reconversion programs and antitrust revision. The evidence strongly suggests that Redfield and WIB officials did not stop seeking antitrust revision despite the failed attempt to achieve it through legislation transferring the Conservation Division to Commerce.

With the Conservation Division renamed as the Industrial Cooperation Service, Redfield in late November began working through it to facilitate the growth and operation of trade associations. In December he went one step further by creating an "advisory board" that would assist the department with trade association activity and also act in any way that would be "helpful" to industry. The board was made up entirely of highly placed businessmen from moderate to large firms who were in the process of leaving the WIB. Its members included Peek, his assistant William M. Ritter, Samuel P. Bush of the Facilities Division, and George R. James, chief of the Cotton and Cotton Linters Section. The group launched the most concerted and daring of all efforts to achieve demobilization stability through price and possibly production controls. Its members believed that success in that area would eventually lead to a basic revision of the antitrust laws.[13]

In late December 1918 the growing threat of deflation regenerated anxiety within the business community and triggered action by the new advisory board. Acting on his own, Ritter, in the latter part of January 1919, authored a proposal for creating what came to be called the Industrial Board, which would act to readjust inflated prices to counteract depressionary trends. Between late January and early February, Ritter's plan was the subject of numerous high-level administration meetings. The proposal was sponsored by Redfield and the Commerce Department and received the endorsement of the department's advisory council, Secretary of the Interior Franklin K. Lane, Secretary of Labor William B. Wilson, Walker D. Hines, head of the U.S. Railroad Administration, and most important, Secretary of the Treasury Carter Glass.

By early March the Industrial Board was staffed and in operation. It consisted of the members of the Commerce Department's advisory board plus

Thomas Glenn, another former WIB member; a representative for labor and the consumer selected by Secretary Wilson; and Thomas C. Powell of the U.S. Railroad Administration, sitting in for that agency and other government purchasers. The former WIB members on the Commerce Department's advisory board and Industrial Board came from the Midwest or South, which was obviously more than coincidental. The arrangement was probably intended to assuage any remaining fears among small- to medium-sized businesses and the public about Eastern and giant corporations dominating the board. Moreover, some of the most progressive businessmen came from the Midwest, a region that had been overrepresented in the top echelon of the WIB.[14]

Selected by Secretary of Commerce Redfield as chair, George N. Peek rather quickly emerged as the leader of the Industrial Board. The former WIB executive had been one of the leading advocates on the board for reconversion. He had also authored an elaborate plan for categorizing all soldiers according to occupation and discharging or furloughing them based on the needs of industry and especially of the farm community (policies beneficial to his own firm). In this class-biased proposal, which never got off the ground and was actually a form of national service, business executives, professionals, and small businessmen would have been singled out for special attention and early discharge. Throughout the war years, Peek had also worked more closely with the Chamber of Commerce than any other WIB official, contacts that continued after he left the board. Early in December 1918 optimistic economic projections led the chamber to retreat from its previous, vociferous demands for strong government reconversion policies. With the transition to peace again appearing troubled in late December, however, the chamber resumed its strong advocacy of government-business cooperation in order to facilitate economic stability and communicated its change in position to Peek. Peek, therefore, was acting not only on his own convictions but also because of agitation from the largest and most prestigious business association.[15]

Almost from the outset, divisions over the role of the Industrial Board were evident. Redfield was most interested in facilitating long-range economic rationalization through trade associations and government-mandated industrial cooperation. Peek, Ritter, and other members shared this goal, but they believed that the first priority was immediate economic stability. Once having achieved this and established its credentials, they thought, the Industrial Board could then proceed to the larger goal of antitrust revision, which would make possible the permanent intraindustry planning that most former WIB representatives and Redfield favored. Here, then, was the closest merging of the short- and long-term economic planning that had been so prevalent both within and without the WIB for months.

The Industrial Board, however, could not proceed without Woodrow Wilson's approval. After agreeing on its charges, Redfield and Glass wired the president in Paris on February 6 that, with his approval, the board would work for voluntary price reductions so as to stimulate buying by the Railroad Administration and other governmental agencies in the anticipation that such activity would encourage general buying and thereby counteract an economic downturn. Although absorbed in peace negotiations, the president had reasons to be concerned about the home front, especially since Joseph P. Tumulty—his secretary and closest, most trusted adviser in Washington—had telegraphed Wilson on January 30 that economic conditions were ominous, a depression was expected early in the spring, and the administration would be held responsible. Baruch, in Paris with the president, advised him that the proposal for the Industrial Board was "good." However, the former WIB chairman read between the lines and warned Wilson that it was a proposal for setting minimum prices, which might violate the Sherman Act. Wilson noted this caveat without emphasis in the approval that he wired to Redfield on February 11.

Indeed, Redfield, Baruch, and Wilson had broached this subject much earlier. On November 25 Redfield had spelled out to the president a vague but ambitious role for the Commerce Department in reconversion and had implied that Baruch agreed. Wilson had partially and tentatively given his approval the next day. Furthermore, in his November 27 letter to the president calling for an end to the WIB, Baruch much more explicitly, but with some remaining ambiguity, set forth the possibility of establishing an agency to aid in reconversion. The advisory board to the Commerce Department matched Baruch's proposal and some of the duties of the Industrial Board as well. This similarity suggests that plans or possible plans for the Industrial Board were set before Baruch left office, with Wilson wittingly or unwittingly complying. Such an awareness would account for Baruch's ability to explain to Wilson with such clarity the real intent of the Industrial Board's proposal. Yet, the board simply may have grown out of obvious and overt developments within the WIB and the business community. Current evidence permits only speculation.[16]

It is beyond doubt, however, that the former WIB members, with at least the acquiescence of Redfield, intended from the outset to use the Industrial Board not for the innocuous purposes wired to the president but for the price fixing Baruch had warned Wilson about. The subterfuge had begun even before Wilson was consulted. Ritter advocated that the Industrial Board attempt price reductions by fixing prices, which would then be sanctioned by the attorney general. Walker D. Hines and Carter Glass squelched this scheme, the former suspecting an attempted end run around the Sherman Act. However, after the president's approval of the board, and with backing for it from the Chamber of Commerce, the NAM, many trade associations, and a governors' conference on readjustment, the former WIB members immediately returned to the price-fixing approach. They clearly believed they had the political muscle to overcome any obstacle.

George N. Peek and his counterparts maintained that only solidly based minimum price agreements could ensure economic stability; otherwise, the chance of price wars or buyers waiting for anticipated drops could precipitate an economic decline or inhibit growth. Prices were not excessive, the argument ran, and guarantees at current or objectively determined levels, with extensive government buying to back them, would encourage public confidence, increase economic activity, and secure the interests of the public and the business community. The only trouble with this argument was that the board never attempted objectively to set prices. Its handling of the steel industry illustrates the point.[17]

The Industrial Board opened negotiations with the steel industry in the latter part of March. The conference was crucial. Success in this endeavor would significantly advance the board's efforts to set minimum prices and would also pave the way for revision of the antitrust laws. Peek and Elbert H. Gary articulated exactly these sentiments at the meeting. An acceptable agreement would secure desirable policies for the transition to peace and at the same time create a basis for fundamentally altering the relationship between business and government. The agreement would achieve the latter goal by winning public confidence in the intent, goals, and good faith of industry and in the virtues of government-business cooperation, as evidenced by the anticipated prosperity such joint action would bring about. But the steel executives chose to act in a short-sighted way. Despite the efforts of the Industrial Board significantly to lower price schedules, the steel representatives insisted on a schedule of prices only 10 to 20 percent below existing levels and effective throughout 1919, a level that many observers considered to be much too inflated. The board nonetheless acquiesced, writing an agreement with the steel executives to achieve those ends.

Soon thereafter, the Industrial Board ran into enormous and ultimately fatal obstacles. First, the Railroad Administration refused to be bound by the prices contained in the steel agreement of March 21. Then on March 22, the Federal Trade Commission implied that the board's procedures violated the antitrust laws, an opinion officially confirmed, although not publicly announced, by the attorney general's office on April 1. Peek, attempting to make the board's work more overt and seeking the necessary legal sanction, had sought the approval of both agencies prior to the conference. Before receiving the opinions, he had assured the steel magnates that the board's work was immune from the antitrust laws and would be honored by the Railroad Administration and other government buyers. Even after the FTC's opinion and the Railroad Administration's refusal, Peek and his colleagues, apparently confident they ultimately would win, organized additional conferences with coal and other industries, assuring executives that their action was legal and would be acceptable to the entire Wilson administration. In part, Peek's obduracy may have stemmed from widespread backing and from his conviction that the Industrial Board's approach was eminently sound. There was also the belief, right or wrong, that he had Wilson's ear through Baruch. On March 24 Peek wired Baruch, asking him to convince Wilson to order the Railroad Administration into line. Baruch failed to answer.

For a short time late in March, the Industrial Board's aggressive, unauthorized, and illegal approach appeared to be on the brink of success. Railroad director Hines began to waver under pressure, and on March 27 Redfield and Harry A. Garfield, who as fuel administrator attended the coal meetings, wired Paris in support of the Industrial Board. Matters swung against the board at the end of March, however, when Glass joined Hines in opposition to the Industrial Board's approach and wired his dissent to Wilson. Thereafter, other cabinet secretaries lined up against Peek, Redfield, and the board. After waffling, Wilson was forced to intervene. The Industrial Board's negotiations with industry were stalled, the battle within the administration was growing more bitter and leaking to the press, and no resolution was in sight. On Tumulty's advice, Wilson directed Hines on May 3 to end all contact with the Industrial Board. On May 8 Redfield signaled defeat by announcing the resignation of all Industrial Board members.

Several significant conclusions can be drawn from the Industrial Board's experience. First, businesspeople were so intent on a reconstruction program and antitrust revision that they virtually stopped at nothing to achieve those aims. Such aggressiveness grew from the success and popularity of the industrial cooperation practiced during the war. Even though industry did not want government to become excessively active in its affairs, it still desired that government act as partner; even though the goals of business were never fully achieved, it always found a number of public officials sharing its viewpoint and willing to push its agenda. Nonetheless, businesspeople in and outside government misread the times in that they believed the war had created conditions that would allow them to do as they chose. Peek, Redfield, and their colleagues repeatedly ignored obvious signals of opposition and plunged ahead with a recklessness that could stem only from gross misjudgment.

Second, the seemingly final decision of the president and the War Industries Board in November against a defined reconversion program and antitrust revision turned out to be far from immutable. The decisions were based on the assumption of a smooth transition to peace and were hedged in the event that serious trouble might arise. The negative responses from Wilson and Baruch to a reconversion program, and, in the case of the former and perhaps even the latter, to antitrust revision, appear to have been firm only concerning the WIB's involvement. Wilson was anxious to dismantle the large, unwieldy, and legally dubious mobilization apparatus as quickly as possible because he was uncomfortable with its structure and operation. Baruch wanted to follow the president's lead and to protect the board's image. Both men seemed willing to experiment with the Industrial Board—perhaps because it was under a statutorily established department and no longer tied to the defunct WIB—though they apparently understood its implications for reconversion and perhaps even for antitrust revision.

Third, the leadership of Wilson and Baruch emerged both tarnished and enhanced by the Industrial Board episode: tarnished in that the two men supported an experiment they should have known was fundamentally flawed and that would cause endless controversy; enhanced in that the board's fate made their earlier decisions to disestablish the war mobilization machinery quickly, without plans to guide reconversion or alter the nation's future political economy, appear exceptionally astute. Decisionmaking from Europe was doubtlessly difficult, but in Baruch's case the imbroglio suggests that without the advice of aides such as Ritchie he could veer badly off the track. Viewed another way, the Industrial Board highlighted the weak leadership potential of men like Peek when they lacked Baruch's guidance. Even Redfield emerged from the experience diminished, although he had been more cautious than Peek.

Ultimately, the Industrial Board experience demonstrated that government-sanctioned, industry-directed economic mobilization and planning could take place in the United States only in an emergency of the magnitude of World War I. Divisions within the government, among the public, and to some degree, within business, were simply too great for an industry-sponsored partnership to work in peacetime. Such an experiment required the sense of urgency and sacrifice engendered by war. Measures that the Industrial Board attempted differed little from practices that had repeatedly taken place during wartime. The times, not the practices, had changed. Moreover, the Industrial Board exposed more than objectionable collusion among industrial elements; it also revealed the intense insecurity and greed of the business community. The steel magnates' insistence on high postwar prices was not inspiring. Again, such behavior had not been unusual, and was perhaps even typical, during World War I, but it had not been as successfully challenged and thwarted during wartime as in 1919.

In terms of political economy and business behavior, the Industrial Board anticipated in many ways the fate of the National Recovery Administration of the depression years. Even a dire peacetime emergency was not enough to create the right atmosphere for an overt, full-blown government-business planning partnership. Conditions of war—when a sense of patriotic sacrifice was high and prosperity widespread—created the nearly unique conditions necessary for such an endeavor to succeed in America. That they understood that fact was one measure of the political and economic astuteness and caution of Woodrow Wilson, Bernard M. Baruch, and their advisers. Because of such insight, the War Industries Board emerged from the war with a positive image; the Industrial Board looked ill-advised, shabby, and rather sinister.

# 13
# THE CHALLENGE AND EFFECT OF MOBILIZING FOR MODERN WAR

Mobilization for World War I set in motion two principal and related developments: the creation of a government-business partnership for the purpose of mobilizing the economy, and the integration of the military services into the mobilization system. Discerning the motivations of the president, his advisers, Congress, and the business mobilizers in that extraordinarily complex process is particularly important.

The government-business planning partnership of World War I was an extension of the government-business regulatory partnership that began emerging during the Progressive years and that constituted the dominant trend in twentieth-century political economy. It was initially brought about by the need for a larger state to counterbalance the concentration of economic power that had occurred in the late nineteenth and early twentieth centuries through the growth and maturation of the modern corporation. In assessing the intricate patterns that evolved during the war, it is essential to emphasize that a partnership in the true meaning of that term was involved. The War Industries Board and its predecessor agencies gave industry enormous latitude within which to operate, but the parameters were always set by the federal government—directly by the executive and more indirectly, but significantly, by Congress. Hence "partnership" is a more apt description of World War I mobilization than "industrial self-government."[1] Industry largely regulated itself in terms of plant expansion and conversion, conservation, the distribution of orders, allocation, pricing, and so forth, but it never controlled or meaningfully influenced the huge demand emanating from the government claimant agencies, either civilian or military. More significantly, the various controls that businessmen-volunteers worked out were largely academic until Woodrow Wilson in March 1918 separated the War Industries Board from the Council of National Defense and gave the board a measure of authority. Even after that date, the WIB largely relied on the cooperation of business and government agencies to carry out its program.

The limitations that an ambiguous presidential mandate and competition from other administrations—such as the War Department and the U.S. Railroad Administration—placed on the WIB was matched by the board's internal restraints. Even if the board had had solidly based statutory power for its actions and attempted actions, the performance of the WIB leadership indicates that it would not and could not have imposed its will on industry, except in rare and isolated instances, because of practical and ideological considerations. In practical terms, the WIB was too makeshift, too young to work out effective controls, and too lacking in the vast information and independent personnel necessary to control America's enormously complex economy effectively. Ideologically, war mobilizers such as Baruch and the businessmen in the commodity sections and the war service committees (WSC) were committed to the notion of having a huge government oversee war mobilization without such a government really existing because, the rhetoric ran, business was actually mobilizing itself. Hence, the writings of Grosvenor B. Clarkson, the final report of Baruch, and related works portray the paradox of a huge governmental apparatus with total control over industry operating side by side with a virtually invisible government free of compulsion and patriotic and selfless businessmen voluntarily carrying out the essential mobilization functions.[2]

The curious aspect of this paradox is that there is some truth to both images. Led at the outset by what Robert D. Cuff has described as "business politicians" or "synthesizers" such as Baruch, the industrial community through its own representatives largely devised and implemented the mobilization scheme.[3] But within the WIB as it was finally established, there were few business politicians aside from Baruch and Robert S. Brookings. Almost all its members were active businessmen on temporary leave. Given WIB staffing and the WSC systems, the lines of demarcation between government and business were broken down so completely that it was almost impossible to identify whether most men on the board (or in other agencies) were public officials or private businessmen. Indeed they were both simultaneously. Not an invisible but a virtually undefinable (or partial) state arose to meet the emergency of war.

The participating businessmen were motivated by need; if they did not volunteer, their own and the nation's vital interests would be fundamentally threatened. Some were motivated by the possibility of reform since the war presented opportunities for economic rationalization that they had long supported. Others were motivated by greed since the possibilities for plunder were endless. And many, perhaps most, were moved by a mixture of motives.

Certainly there was more to the reality of the system than the publicized selfless image. There were numerous instances of self-sacrifice and great generosity. However, working within a governmental structure gave businessmen more opportunities to improve and exercise power than had ever existed before. In every way, the industrial community benefited from the war more than any other interest group in society.

If the selflessness of business was a mirage, so too was the notion of an invisible state. Probably more than most industrialists cared to admit, they had become significantly beholden to the state. That state shared a good part of their own ideology but nonetheless constituted a power outside themselves. Before America entered the war, the mobilizers could not begin to experiment with their ideas and plans until the state legitimized them by setting up the Naval Consulting Board and the Council of National Defense–National Defense Advisory Commission. With the means for mobilization worked out, further legitimization was required with the reorganization and redefinition of the WIB. Although government needed business for successful mobilization, business needed government to legitimize the functions that it had learned were essential. Because business and government needed each other, compromise usually prevailed. But many businessmen and business leaders refused to see this process of compromise, which led to the illusion of the invisible state. Their myopia, even hubris, could be indulged during the war years without detriment. When it continued after the war with the Industrial Board, by which former WIB executives such as George N. Peek thought they could manipulate the state for what they defined as the good of government and industry, they were brought up short. The struggle over reconversion tells us as much about state versus private power during mobilization for World War I as does the demobilization process itself and clearly supports the idea of partnership more than the interpretation of business self-regulation.

Greater cooperation within the industrial community was essential for the government-business wartime partnership to work effectively. Although they had not pioneered the patterns of mobilization, the giant corporations dominated the process and received most contracts. Yet no mobilization program could proceed smoothly without a reasonable measure of representation for all business groups. Not realizing that fact was one of Baruch's greatest flaws as a leader. He was so imbued with an elitist outlook that he virtually flaunted big business' domination of the NDAC system until the entire mobilization structure came under withering attack from a Congress responding to public and business dissent. Even in the face of this challenge, Baruch appeared uncharacteristically reluctant to give way. Walter S. Gifford, closely cooperating with the U.S. Chamber of Commerce, had to devise the WSC approach.

Thereafter, Peek and other WIB executives saw the need to work with the broad-based business representation of the chamber. Without the "democratic" representation that the commodity section–war service committee system provided, it is highly doubtful that Wilson could have mustered the political support necessary to strengthen the War Industries Board as he did in March 1918. Indeed, the process of refining business representation on the board was still going on when it was reorganized and strengthened.

Although plagued by major flaws—which colleagues and advisers such as Gifford, Peek, and Albert C. Ritchie acted to save him from—Baruch had great talents as a war mobilizer. He used his base of power among economic elites to master the enormously complex and ambiguous World War I mobilization system. In the process, he sought out and listened to the right assistants and allowed them to lead in ways he might not favor without losing control of the limited authority his office commanded.

Another aspect of Baruch's leadership qualities was his shrewd sense of what Woodrow Wilson wanted and would tolerate. That attribute was absolutely crucial for any successful wartime leader since the president maintained remarkable control over the industrial mobilization process—more so, for example, than Franklin D. Roosevelt did during World War II.

Wilson was a rather shadowy, enigmatic figure during World War I. The president seemed to harbor greater suspicion about large government than about large business. There was evidence of this tendency before the war, and it became more obvious during hostilities. His outlook may have stemmed in part from the fact that huge, consolidated corporations in the major industries were an accomplished reality and enlarged government was only an emerging phenomenon. Like many Progressives, Wilson seemed willing to accept, although with reservations and suspicions, the existing power of the corporations but generally held back or moved cautiously in expanding the government.

Newton D. Baker remained Wilson's chief adviser on industrial mobilization throughout 1917, principally because he occupied the most powerful position below the president in the established framework of government and shared, perhaps even exceeded, Wilson's reluctance to take steps that might permanently expand the size and role of the state. Therefore, the president and the secretary of war were willing to allow industry, especially huge industry, wide latitude for mobilization within jerry-built agencies as long as this activity was not given full authenticity through solidly founded governmental institutions. When this expedient broke down under the weight of the burgeoning mobilization effort during winter 1917–1918, Wilson, under intense pressure from all sides, made the minimum changes essential to keep the mobilization program going; Baker, partly from the desire to guard his own bailiwick and partly because of inflexibility, was hesitant to do so. Wilson's suspicion of big government persisted after the authority of the WIB was expanded; his determination to maintain more control over the mobilization apparatus than over business no doubt stemmed from his continued suspicion.

Two important points about Wilson need to be emphasized. First, he kept the mobilization system, particularly the WIB and its predecessor agencies, answerable to himself. He took an active part in writing the legislative mandate for the CND–NDAC and in the choice of personnel; he played a decisive part in resolving the mobilization crises during summer 1917 and winter 1917–1918; although his day-to-day involvement after March 1918 was less intense, he still appeared to be on top of matters; and he set the general conditions for demobilization. No official was so powerful that he could proceed on his own or excessively manipulate conditions against the president's will, as Secretary William C. Redfield and the members of the Industrial Board discovered when Wilson was overseas and fully absorbed in more pressing events.

The second point involves the degree to which Wilson was aware of what was taking place within the War Industries Board and its predecessor agencies and his response to those developments. More than one WIB participant testified that the president displayed a keen interest in the intricacies of the mobilization process. In the administration's struggle with Congress, led by Sen. Kenneth D. McKellar (D-TN) in summer 1917 and Sen. George E. Chamberlain (D-OR) during winter 1917–1918, Wilson seemed to perceive events clearly and knew what had to be done to keep the embattled mobilization scheme going. Wilson's instructions to Baruch in March 1918, although written by Baruch and Baker, were apparently worked out under the president's directions. In short, the evidence indicates that Wilson was aware of how the mobilization mechanism worked, accepted its essential nature as the best that could be achieved given war demand and the American political economy, was sufficiently wary of the WIB's power and sensitive enough to congressional and public criticism that he kept the board in check with a limited mandate and the power of established departments, and ended the board's existence as quickly as possible once the emergency passed.

Although Wilson had doubts about corporate power, he also realized that changing that pattern during peacetime, or certainly during war, would involve radical departures for which neither he nor the Progressive reform movement had any predilection. Industrial mobilization for World War I accurately reflected the patterns of power in the economic system. For the mobilization program to have been different, the system itself would have to have been different. Wilson, without enthusiasm but with quite clear vision, accepted that reality.

Some members of Congress were not prepared to be so pragmatic. Congress in general was jealous of its prerogatives in the face of growing executive power. As a result, in 1917 it nearly adopted the proposal of Sen. John W. Weeks (R-MA) for a committee on the conduct of the war. But congressional disturbance over mobilization policies stemmed from more than jealousy. A substantial majority was sufficiently upset about the rampant conflicts of interest in the NDAC that it was ready to put an end to the dollar-a-year-man/advisory committee system. These legislators backed off with an innocuous compromise only after intense lobbying by the president himself. Thereafter, most members of Congress, like the president, appeared to view the operations of the WIB as an unavoidable necessity, acceptable as long as the Wilson administration took steps to achieve some balance in the mobilization apparatus among different business interests and at least gave the appearance of guarding the public welfare. Indeed, during the winter crisis of 1917–1918, the Senate, by threatening more far-reaching solutions, helped force the administration to give some power and better direction to the WIB. When the economic system and the war effort were threatened, the nation's legislators were willing to increase the power of mobilization agencies run by business while the president and his advisers seemed paralyzed.

That episode notwithstanding, there was always a minority of Southern and Midwestern neo-Jeffersonian Progressives in Congress who would not accept the realities of American power and who were thus the most agonized elements during the war years. They saw clearly the questionable nature and consequences of the mobilization process but were unable to provide feasible alternatives. They insisted for a time that rigid lines be maintained between the public and private sectors, with competition used to meet war needs. In time, the impracticability of that approach became so evident that they started to advocate a vastly expanded state, though they feared big government as much as big business. But creating government departments staffed by civil servants to run a mobilized economy would have been extraordinarily expensive and wholly impractical because the public sector lacked the necessary expertise.

Following the pattern of the neo-Jeffersonians throughout the Progressive years, these dissenters offered a good, at times trenchant, critique of the nation's political economy and articulated doubts and fears that other observers repressed. But their solutions always fell short because, unwilling to advocate radical change, they looked for dated means to deal with modern problems of power. They flirted with authentic state capitalism, in which government would be clearly separated from interest groups, or with some form of socialism; but they always retreated, seeing these cures as worse than the disease. Throughout the war years and even after, various neo-Jeffersonians remained perceptive critics of the political economy of warfare without offering viable alternatives to previous and ongoing activities.[4]

The scrutiny of the neo-Jeffersonians and their colleagues in Congress served to keep the nation's legislative branch meaningfully engaged during the war years. Congress had not yet surrendered much of its power to a rising executive, and that resistance forced the president along routes that he might not otherwise have taken.

For the president, Congress, the war mobilizers, various interest groups, and the public, the experience of economic mobilization for war confirmed what had already become a truism: nations prepare for and fight wars according to the patterns of their peacetime traditions and institutions. The nature of the modern American political economy had in reality been quite well established by 1917, but that system was not yet fully accepted in theory or in practice. The antitrust, competitive instincts were still strong, and a legitimately radical movement, advocating a form of socialism, lacked adequate strength and appeal to be consequential.[5] As a result, a compromise solution, even before the war, began to emerge in the form of a government-business regulatory partnership. The progress made, however, was incremental and uncertain. By necessity, the war sped up enormously the formation of this new partnership, so much so that most people in and out of public life could not or would not accept fully the reality of its existence. Consequently, agencies embodying this partnership carried out economic mobilization without a clear legislative or even an explicit executive mandate. Matters were always approached ambiguously and indirectly. Practices that could not be overtly accepted had to be left undefined or only partially defined. As a result, the economic mobilization agencies, especially the War Industries Board and its predecessors, always had an illusory quality to them. Indeed, in discussing the mobilization experience, Clarkson, Baruch, and their counterparts offer a dual portrait of a realized Hamiltonian dream and a gigantic voluntary, self-help, American effort.

Despite the dual image, industry was usually portrayed as exceptionally virtuous by the early historians of the movement such as Clarkson, most of whom were little more than publicists. Business and its leaders appeared anxious to sell the image of great and selfless accomplishments, as much to themselves as to the public. That process continued, even grew, in the Dollar Decade of the 1920s.[6] By contrast, economic mobilization has never been held up as the finest hour of the presidency or of Congress. Indeed, in the years immediately following hostilities, the most pervasive responses to wartime government were doubt, anger, and the desire to forget the painful episode. The image-making involving business, however, was very much in the Progressive tradition and reflected its proponents' uncertainties.[7] This observation is evident when one realizes that mobilization for World War II had no publicity blitz; if anything, more coverage went to the critics of mobilization than to its supporters. But the New Deal as a reform movement was quite different from that of the Progressive movement. By 1941 Americans accepted the realities of the nation's political economy more readily than did the early twentieth-century reformers.

Although twentieth-century American political economy was well advanced by 1917, civil-military relations were not, especially those involving the role of the armed services in the economic system, which modern warfare had made so important for the military. Two points should be made in this regard. First, the military had not yet gone beyond civilian control, or civilians had not yet taken on the military ethic, depending on how the phenomenon is defined.[8] Wilson oversaw the entire mobilization process, including the role of the armed services. Secretary of War Baker and Secretary of the Navy Daniels were very much in charge of their departments and at least set the outlines for the way the services participated in mobilization. An important indication of continued civilian direction of the military was the circumstance that the armed services were almost constantly at odds with civilian mobilization administrations, although to a diminishing degree toward the end of the war. Though military prerogatives in the mobilization scheme served as a check on the WIB and its predecessor agencies, the crucial part played by industrialists in mobilizing the economy also served as a check on the services, a restraint that broke down later.

The second point of significance is that the encounter between the mobilization administrations and the armed services was not, as is often portrayed by scholars and other writers, essentially a struggle between civilian and military elements over domination of economic mobilization.[9] The conflict arose as civilian and military institutions adjusted to the realities of modern warfare, where it was no longer economically possible to maintain rigid lines of demarcation between the two spheres. Civilian administration adapted with greater ease to the new conditions. The War Department resisted the minimum changes essential for the successful mobilization of the economy. The Navy Department made the adjustment more easily, due to its reorganized supply system, extensive interaction with the business community in building the modern fleet, and constant state of preparedness. But the chaos created by the War Department made the Navy Department more protective of self-defined interests than would otherwise have been the case. Moreover, as much the smaller of the services, the Navy Department's adjustment to civilian administrations would not have served much purpose until the War Department cooperated. Nonetheless, the Navy Department still harbored suspicions of civilian institutions and, like the War Department, only slowly made the changes in attitude and behavior essential for successful economic mobilization. In doing so, it generally followed the War Department's lead.

Throughout a good part of World War I, a divided War Department was barely able to manage its own affairs and certainly could not control the economy. Its resistance to civilian mobilization agencies resulted from isolation from, suspicion of, and ignorance about the civilian economy more than from a desire to dominate it. A central cause of the friction was Baker's hesitance to make the institutional changes necessary to bring under control the army supply bureaus (which were more civilian than military, given their close ties to Congress and detachment from the line). And Chief of Staff Peyton C. March's arrogant attitude toward civilian institutions reflected a failure to grasp that it was no longer possible to compartmentalize civilian and military functions.

Civilians were not anxious to take over military roles. The first concern of the business community and its representatives, who were largely responsible for industrial mobilization, was finding the means for mobilizing the economy without endangering the overall economic status quo. Nonetheless, from the beginning, circumstances made the military services central to any mobilization scheme. Therefore, while perfecting their own institutions, members of the National Defense Advisory Commission, War Industries Board, and private businessmen and business organizations worked hand in hand with army personnel to modernize military supply procedures. Events reached the point that the Purchase, Storage, and Traffic Division became a heavily civilian-staffed body. Ultimately, the War Industries Board proved to be the right means for harnessing the economy.

Civilians, and particularly businessmen, with the critical support of Congress, would not permit the War Department to ruin the system they had carefully worked out to protect their own and the nation's interests. The army either had to adjust to the WIB or lose its procurement prerogatives. Since separating procurement from the armed services was politically undesirable, the former rather than the latter solution was adopted with the Overman Act. The critical role of private power in public institutions was possible because of the emergency, but only when that role was left undefined. Severing supply from the army and navy could have threatened the entire enterprise. Out of those conditions, then, economic and military institutions were partially integrated during the war effort, and the institutional adjustment for an industrial-military complex—which had begun with the building of a modern navy—were further advanced.

The World War I mobilization experience left an indelible imprint on twentieth-century life. By accelerating the emerging Progressive political economy, it strengthened the cooperative planning ethic within business and government. It also sped the transformation in civil-military relations that modern warfare made necessary and introduced the idea and practice of industrial preparedness. These adjustments, although at a slower and less visible pace, continued after the war, reached a point of fruition with World War II, and have remained established patterns, albeit dynamic and shifting, to the present day.

Robert D. Cuff, in his impressive work on the War Industries Board, maintains that the continuity thesis is a misconception: that the World War I mobilization experience was unique because the WIB's structure and operation were quite crude and amorphous, and that it is wrong to try to connect wartime industrial mobilization with Progressive political economy or to see World War I as a harbinger for the future in terms of political economy, civil-military relations, or even industrial mobilization.[10]

I do not agree with this line of reasoning. My response amounts to more than the usual differences between historians, for it involves matters of vital importance in the life of the nation since World War I—matters that continue to be crucial today. There is no question that the World War I mobilization process was only partially worked out and that it was uncertain and crude in many ways. Given the magnitude of the problem, the lack of experience with modern warfare, the short period of time the nation was actually engaged in hostilities, and the momentous issues involved, it would have been extraordinary had that not been the case.

Nonetheless, World War I appears unique, as all things do, only if it is viewed in isolation. The interwar years served as an intense period for analyzing the positive and negative aspects of war mobilization and for planning for future conflicts. Moreover, mobilizing the World War I economy would have been quite different had the American political economy in the early twentieth century been different. As Alfred D. Chandler, Jr., observes, the corporate and business communities in 1917 were much closer to 1970 than to 1870. Accordingly, economic mobilization for World War I closely resembled that of World War II and differed basically from that of the Civil War principally because the nation's political economy was approximately the same throughout the twentieth century but different from what had existed in the nineteenth century. Although more complex, civil-military relations during World War II were significantly shaped by World War I and the interwar developments. Finally, the military-industrial complex of the Cold War years was built on foundations rooted in the late nineteenth century; the MIC was not an institutional structure suddenly emerging without antecedents. When economic mobilization for World War I is considered within the context of the entire twentieth century, continuity, not uniqueness, stands out in every area of importance.[11]

Related to the idea of continuity, as opposed to singularity, is a point that emerged from World War I: Modern warfare had an enormous impact on reform. It accelerated secondary aspects of reform such as union growth and welfare measures but twisted, warped, and contorted the efforts of many reformers, especially in the broader reaches of the political economy. The reversal of many Progressive reforms in the 1920s harshly emphasizes that observation. Indeed, World War I made emphatically clear that in twentieth-century America, war much more than reform would shape the nation's values, institutions, and ideology. During World War I, the nation had taken a major and seemingly irrevocable step in the direction of becoming a warfare or national security state.[12]

The World War I economy highlights the four historical factors shaping economic mobilization. Concerning the first and second of these factors—the maturity of the economy and the size, strength, and scope of the federal government—the war advanced and refined the emerging government-business regulatory alliance as the principal mode of twentieth-century political economy. For the third factor—the military services and their relationship to civilian society and authority—the war vastly accelerated a major transition in civil-military relations that had just begun in the late nineteenth century. In order to meet the military demand of modern war, the armed services had to join the government and the industrial community in mobilizing the economy. At the time, no one could fully predict the consequences of transformed relations between the military and the civilian worlds. But it was clear that the growing sophistication of military technology—the fourth factor—was also acting to draw industrial, military, and governmental elements together. Unlike the Spanish-American War, therefore, World War I made manifest the dynamics and presaged the consequences of the political economy of warfare in the industrial stage.

# NOTES

## CHAPTER TWO. THE RISE OF A MODERN POLITICAL ECONOMY

1. The discussion of politics during the Gilded Age and beyond is based on John D. Hicks, *The Populist Revolt: A History of the Farmers' Alliance and the People's Party* (Minneapolis: University of Minnesota Press, 1931); F. W. Taussig, *The Tariff History of the United States* (New York: G. P. Putnam's Sons, 1931); Matthew Josephson, *The Politicos, 1865–1896* (New York: Harcourt, Brace, 1938); Robert G. McCloskey, *American Conservatism in the Age of Enterprise, 1865–1910: A Study of William Graham Sumner, Stephen J. Field and Andrew Carnegie* (Cambridge: Harvard University Press, 1951); C. Vann Woodward, *The Origins of the New South, 1877–1913* (Baton Rouge: Louisiana State University Press, 1951); Samuel P. Hays, *The Response to Industrialism, 1885–1914* (Chicago: University of Chicago Press, 1957); Paul P. Van Riper, *History of the United States Civil Service* (Evanston, IL: Row, Peterson, 1958); Margaret Leech, *In the Days of McKinley* (New York: Harper and Brothers, 1959); Leonard D. White, *The Republican Era: A Study in Administrative History, 1869–1901* (New York: Macmillan, 1958); Harold U. Faulkner, *Politics, Reform and Expansion, 1890–1900* (New York: Harper and Row, 1959); Paul W. Glad, *The Trumpet Soundeth: William Jennings Bryan and His Democracy, 1896–1912* (Lincoln: University of Nebraska Press, 1960); Ari Hoogenboom, *Outlawing the Spoils: A History of the Civil Service Reform Movement, 1865–1883* (Urbana: University of Illinois Press, 1961), Hoogenboom, *The Presidency of Rutherford B. Hayes* (Lawrence: University Press of Kansas, 1988), and Hoogenboom, *Rutherford B. Hayes: Warrior and President* (Lawrence: University Press of Kansas, 1995); J. Roger Hollingsworth, *The Whirligig of Politics: The Democracy of Cleveland and Bryan* (Chicago: University of Chicago Press, 1963); H. Wayne Morgan, *William McKinley and His America* (Syracuse, NY: Syracuse University Press, 1963), Morgan, *From Hayes to McKinley: National Party Politics, 1877–1896* (Syracuse, NY: Syracuse University Press, 1969), and Morgan, ed., *The Gilded Age*, 2d ed., rev. (Syracuse, NY: Syracuse University Press, 1970); Norman Pollack, *The Populist Response to Industrial America: Midwestern Populist Thought* (Cambridge: Harvard University Press, 1962); Walter T. K. Nugent, *The Tolerant Populists: Kansas, Populism and Nativism* (Chicago: University of Chicago Press, 1963); Nugent, *From Centennial to World War: American Society, 1876–1917* (Indianapolis, IN: Bobbs-Merrill, 1977); Ray Ginger, *Age of Excess: The United States from 1877 to 1914* (New York: Macmillan, 1965); David J. Rothman, *Politics and Power: The United States Senate,*

*1869–1901* (Cambridge: Harvard University Press, 1966); Robert Wiebe, *The Search for Order, 1877–1920* (New York: Hill and Wang, 1967); John A. Garraty, *The New Commonwealth, 1877–1900* (New York: Harper and Row, 1968); John G. Sproat, *"The Best Men": Liberal Reformers in the Gilded Age* (New York: Oxford University Press, 1968); Walter B. Burnham, *Critical Elections and the Mainsprings of American Politics* (New York: W. W. Norton, 1970); Paul Kleppner, *The Cross of Culture: A Social Analysis of Midwestern Politics, 1850–1900* (New York: Free Press, 1970), Kleppner, *The Third Electoral System, 1853–1892: Parties, Voters, and Political Cultures* (Chapel Hill: University of North Carolina Press, 1979), and Kleppner, *Continuity and Change in Electoral Politics, 1893–1928* (Westport, CT: Greenwood Press, 1987); Richard Jensen, *The Winning of the Midwest: Social and Political Conflict, 1888–1896* (Chicago: University of Chicago Press, 1971); Robert D. Marcus, *Grand Old Party: Political Structure in the Gilded Age, 1880–1896* (New York: Oxford University Press, 1971); John M. Dobson, *Politics in the Gilded Age: A New Perspective on Reform* (New York: Praeger, 1972); James Gilbert, *Designing the Industrial State: The Intellectual Pursuit of Collectivism in America, 1880–1940* (Chicago: Quadrangle Books, 1972); Samuel T. McSeveney, *The Politics of Depression: Political Behavior in the Northeast, 1893–1896* (New York: Oxford University Press, 1972); Melvyn Dubofsky, *Industrialism and the American Worker, 1865–1920* (New York: Crowell, 1975); Lawrence Goodwyn, *Democratic Promise: The Populist Movement in America* (New York: Oxford University Press, 1976); Herbert Gutman, *Work, Culture and Society in Industrializing America: Essays in American Working-Class and Social History* (New York: Alfred A. Knopf, 1976); Carl N. Degler, *The Age of the Economic Revolution, 1876–1900,* 2d ed., rev. (Glenview, IL: Scott, Foresman, 1977); Thomas L. Haskell, *The Emergence of Professional Social Science: The American Social Science Association and the Nineteenth Century Crisis of Authority* (Urbana: University of Illinois Press, 1977); Morton Keller, *Affairs of State: Public Life in Late Nineteenth Century America* (Cambridge: Belknap Press, 1977)—in his sequel to this volume, *Regulating a New Economy: Public Policy and Economic Change in America, 1900–1933* (Cambridge: Harvard University Press, 1990), Keller perceptively analyzes developments in the early twentieth century; R. Hal Williams, *Years of Decision: American Politics in the 1890s* (New York: John Wiley and Sons, 1978); David Montgomery, *Workers' Control in America: Studies in the History of Work, Technology, and Labor Struggles* (New York: Cambridge University Press, 1979), and Montgomery, *The Fall of the House of Labor: The Workplace, the State, and American Labor Activism, 1865–1925* (New York: Cambridge University Press, 1987); Justus D. Doenecke, *The Presidencies of James A. Garfield and Chester A. Arthur* (Lawrence: University Press of Kansas, 1981)—the author cites the major critiques of the so-called new political history in the bibliographic essay, p. 198; Richard P. McCormick, *The Presidential Game: The Origins of American Presidential Politics* (New York: Oxford University Press, 1982); William E. Nelson, *The Roots of American Bureaucracy, 1830–1900* (Cambridge: Harvard University Press, 1982); Stephen Skowronek, *Building a New American State: The Expansion of National Administrative Capacities, 1877–1920* (Cambridge: Cambridge University Press, 1982); Alan Trachtenberg, *The Incorporation of America: Culture and Society in the Gilded Age* (New York: Hill and Wang, 1982); Leon Fink, *Workingmen's Democracy: The Knights of Labor and American Politics* (Urbana: University of Illinois Press, 1983); William R. Brock, *Investigation and Responsibility: Public Responsibility in the United States,*

*1865–1900* (Cambridge: Cambridge University Press, 1984); Peri E. Arnold, *Making the Managerial Presidency: Comprehensive Reorganization Planning, 1905–1980* (Princeton, NJ: Princeton University Press, 1986); Don S. Kirschner, *The Paradox of Professionalism: Reform and Public Service in Urban America, 1900–1940* (Westport, CT: Greenwood Press, 1986); Michael E. McGerr, *The Decline of Popular Politics: The American North, 1865–1928* (New York: Oxford University Press, 1986); Nell I. Painter, *Standing at Armageddon: The United States, 1877–1919* (New York: W. W. Norton, 1987); Sean D. Cashman, *America in the Gilded Age: From the Death of Lincoln to the Rise of Theodore Roosevelt,* 2d ed., rev. (New York: New York University Press, 1988), and Cashman, *America in the Age of the Titans: The Progressive Era and World War I* (New York: New York University Press, 1988); Richard E. Welch, Jr., *The Presidencies of Grover Cleveland* (Lawrence: University Press of Kansas, 1988); Vincent P. DeSantis, *The Shaping of Modern America: 1877–1920,* 2d ed., rev. (Arlington Heights, IL: Forum Press, 1989); David Sarasohn, *The Party of Reform: Democrats in the Progressive Era* (Jackson: University Press of Mississippi, 1989); relevant essays in Mary O. Furner and Barry Supple, eds., *The State and Economic Knowledge: The American and British Experiences* (New York: Woodrow Wilson International Center for Scholars and Cambridge University Press, 1990); Richard L. McCormick, "Public Life in Industrial America, 1877–1917," in *The New American History,* ed. Eric Foner, pp. 93–117 (Philadelphia: Temple University Press, 1990); Joel L. Silbey, *The American Political Nation, 1838–1893* (Stanford, CA: Stanford University Press, 1991), pp. 141–251; Peter H. Argersinger, *Structure, Process, and Party: Essays in American Political History* (Armonk, NY: M. E. Sharpe, 1992); Mark W. Summers, *The Era of Good Stealings* (New York: Oxford University Press, 1993); Ballard C. Campbell, *The Growth of American Government: Governance from the Cleveland Era to the Present* (Bloomington: Indiana University Press, 1995), pp. 1–82; Charles W. Calhoun, ed., *The Gilded Age: Essays on the Origins of Modern America* (Wilmington, DE: Scholarly Resources, 1996); and Lewis L. Gould, *The Presidency of Theodore Roosevelt* (Lawrence: University Press of Kansas, 1991), and Gould, *Reform and Regulation: American Politics from Roosevelt to Wilson,* 3d ed., rev. (Prospect Heights, IL: Waveland Press, 1996).

2. Some of the volumes cited in note 1 are relevant to Progressivism. For additional sources, see chapter 6, note 1, and the analysis of Progressivism involving numerous citations in chapters 6 and 7.

3. I have treated with the nature of antebellum elites at length in volume 1, Paul A. C. Koistinen, *Beating Plowshares into Swords: The Political Economy of American Warfare, 1606–1865* (Lawrence: University Press of Kansas, 1996). Consult the index and see chapter 3, notes 6 and 7, and chapter 4, note 8. Moreover, in chapters 2, 5, and 8 elites are the focus, with multiple citations.

4. I have already written about and cited a number of sources on concentrated corporate power in previous studies, and with a few exceptions I will not repeat here volumes previously noted. See *The Military-Industrial Complex: A Historical Perspective* (New York: Praeger, 1980), pp. 14–16 and n. 12, and "Warfare and Power Relations in America: Mobilizing the World War II Economy," in *The Home Front and War in the Twentieth Century: The American Experience in Comparative Perspective,* ed. James Titus, pp. 98–103 and nn. 4 and 20 (Colorado Springs: U.S. Air Force Academy, 1984). A number of the studies cited in note 1 of this chapter are also relevant to economic development. Various statistics are taken from U.S. Department of Commerce,

Bureau of the Census, *Historical Statistics of the United States: Colonial Times to 1970,* 2 parts (Washington, DC: U.S. Government Printing Office, 1975).

In addition to these sources, the discussion-analysis of the maturation of the economy during the Gilded Age is based on Emory R. Johnson et al., *History of Domestic and Foreign Commerce of the United States,* 2 vols. (Washington, DC: Carnegie Institution of Washington, 1915), 1: 254–323; Victor S. Clark, *History of Manufactures in the United States,* vol. 2, *1860–1893,* vol. 3, *1893–1928* (Washington, DC: Carnegie Institution of Washington, 1929); Solomon Fabricant, *The Output of Manufacturing Industries, 1899–1937* (New York: National Bureau of Economic Research, 1940); Edward C. Kirkland, *Men, Cities, and Transportation: A Study in New England History, 1820–1900,* 2 vols. (Cambridge: Harvard University Press, 1948); Harold F. Williamson, ed., *The Growth of the American Economy,* 2d ed., rev. (Englewood Cliffs, NJ: Prentice-Hall, 1951); Paul Studenski and Herman E. Krooss, *Financial History of the United States: Fiscal, Monetary, Banking, and Tariff, Including Financial Administration and State and Local Finance* (New York: McGraw-Hill, 1952), pp. 161–279; Herman E. Krooss, *American Economic Development* (Englewood Cliffs, NJ: Prentice-Hall, 1955); Krooss and Martin R. Blyn, *A History of Financial Intermediaries* (New York: Random House, 1971), pp. 91–148; Krooss and Charles Gilbert, *American Business History* (Englewood Cliffs, NJ: Prentice-Hall, 1972), pp. 144–242; Thomas C. Cochran, *The American Business System: A Historical Perspective, 1900–1955* (Cambridge: Harvard University Press, 1957), pp. 1–100, Cochran, *Business in American Life: A History* (New York: McGraw-Hill, 1972), pp. 145–241, Cochran, *200 Years of American Business* (New York: Dell, 1977), pp. 51–170, and Cochran and William Miller, *The Age of Enterprise: A Social History of Industrial America,* 2d ed., rev. (New York: Harper and Row, 1961); Robert Fogel, *The Union Pacific Railroad: A Case in Premature Enterprise* (Baltimore: Johns Hopkins University Press, 1960), and Fogel, *Railroads and American Economic Growth: Essays in Econometric History* (Baltimore: Johns Hopkins University Press, 1964); Carter Goodrich, *Government Promotion of American Canals and Railroads, 1800–1890* (New York: Columbia University Press, 1960); Conference on Research in Income and Wealth, *Trends in the American Economy in the Nineteenth Century,* vol. 24, *Studies in Income and Wealth* (Princeton, NJ: Princeton University Press, 1960), and *Output, Employment, and Productivity in the United States After 1800,* vol. 30, *Studies in Income and Wealth* (New York: National Bureau of Economic Research, 1966); Walter Adams, ed., *The Structure of American Industry: Some Case Studies* (New York: Macmillan, 1961); William Appleman Williams, *The Contours of American History* (Cleveland, OH: World, 1961), pp. 320–450; Alfred D. Chandler, Jr., *Strategy and Structure: Chapters in the History of American Industrial Enterprise* (Cambridge: MIT Press, 1962), Chandler, ed., *The Railroads: The Nation's First Big Business* (New York: Harcourt, Brace and World, 1965), Chandler, *The Visible Hand: The Managerial Revolution in American Business* (Cambridge: Belknap Press, 1977), Chandler, *Scale and Scope: The Dynamics of Industrial Capitalism* (Cambridge: Belknap Press, 1990), Chandler, "The Beginning of 'Big Business' in American Industry," *Business History Review* 33 (Spring 1959): 1–31, Chandler, "The Emergence of Managerial Capitalism," *Business History Review* 58 (Winter 1984): 475–503, and Chandler and Louis Galambos, "The Development of Large-Scale Economic Organizations in Modern America," *Journal of Economic History* 30 (March 1970): 201–17; Milton Friedman and Anna Jacobson

Schwartz, *A Monetary History of the United States, 1867–1960* (Princeton, NJ: Princeton University Press, 1963), pp. 15–188; Peter Temin, *Iron and Steel in Nineteenth-Century America: An Economic Inquiry* (Cambridge: MIT Press, 1964); Albert Fishlow, *American Railroads and the Transformation of the Ante-bellum Economy* (Cambridge: Harvard University Press, 1965); Robert Averitt, *The Dual Economy: The Dynamics of American Industry Structure* (New York: W. W. Norton, 1968); Fritz Redlich, *The Molding of American Banking: Men and Ideas,* 2d ed., rev. (New York: Johnson Reprint Company, 1968), part 2, *1840–1910,* pp. 99–438; Jonathan Hughes, *Industrialization and Economic History: Theses and Conjectures* (New York: McGraw-Hill, 1970), and Hughes, *American Economic History* (Glenview, IL: Scott, Foresman, 1983), pp. 259–447; Vincent Carosso, *Investment Banking in America: A History* (Cambridge: Harvard University Press, 1970), and Carosso, *The Morgans: Private International Bankers, 1854–1913* (Cambridge: Harvard University Press, 1987); Robert Higgs, *The Transformation of the American Economy, 1865–1914: An Essay in Interpretation* (New York: John Wiley and Sons, 1971), and Higgs, *Crisis and Leviathan: Critical Episodes in the Growth of American Government* (New York: Oxford University Press, 1987); Glenn Porter and Harold C. Livesay, *Merchants and Manufacturers: Studies in the Changing Structure of Nineteenth-Century Marketing* (Baltimore: Johns Hopkins University Press, 1971), and Porter, *The Rise of Big Business, 1860–1910* (Arlington Heights, IL: AHM Publishing, 1973); Elisha P. Douglass, *The Coming of Age of American Business: Three Centuries of Enterprise, 1600–1900* (Chapel Hill: University of North Carolina Press, 1971), pp. 287–539; Lance E. Davis et al., *American Economic Growth: An Economist's History of the United States* (New York: Harper and Row, 1972); Nathan Rosenberg, *Technology and American Economic Growth* (New York: Harper and Row, 1972), and Rosenberg, "Technological Change in the Machine Tool Industry, 1840–1910," *Journal of Economic History* 23 (December 1963): 414–46; Louis P. Cain and Paul J. Uselding, eds., *Business Enterprise and Economic Change: Essays in Honor of Harold F. Williamson* (Kent, OH: Kent State University Press, 1973); David Bunting, *Statistical View of the Trusts: A Manual of Large American Industrial and Mining Corporations Active Around 1900* (Westport, CT: Greenwood Press, 1974), and Bunting, *The Rise of the Large Corporations, 1889–1919* (New York: Garland, 1986); Stuart Bruchey, *Growth of the Modern American Economy* (New York: Dodd, Mead, 1975), pp. 39–113, and Bruchey, *Enterprise: The Dynamic Economy of a Free People* (Cambridge: Harvard University Press, 1990), pp. 308–80; Louis Galambos, *The Public Image of Big Business in America, 1880–1940* (Baltimore: Johns Hopkins University Press, 1975), Galambos, "The Emerging Organizational Synthesis in Modern American History," *Business History Review* 44 (Autumn 1970): 279–90, Galambos, "Technology, Political Economy, and Professionalization: Central Themes of the Organizational Synthesis," *Business History Review* 57 (Winter 1983): 471–93, Galambos, "The Triumph of Oligopoly," in *American Economic Development in Historical Perspective,* ed. Thomas Weiss and Donald Schaefer, pp. 241–53, 307–13 (Stanford, CA: Stanford University Press, 1994), and Galambos and Joseph Pratt, *The Rise of the Corporate Commonwealth: U.S., Business and Public Policy in the Twentieth Century* (New York: Basic Books, 1988); David Klingaman and Richard Vedder, eds., *Essays in Nineteenth-Century Economic History: The Old Northwest* (Athens: Ohio University Press, 1975); Harold G. Vatter, *The Drive to Industrial Maturity: The U.S. Economy, 1860–1914* (Westport, CT: Greenwood Press,

1975); Gabriel Kolko, *Main Currents in Modern American History* (New York: Harper and Row, 1976), pp. 1–99; Harry N. Scheiber, Harold G. Vatter, and Harold Underwood Faulkner, *American Economic History* (New York: Harper and Row, 1976), pp. 193–316; Carol Campbell, *Economic Growth, Capital Gains and Income Distribution, 1897–1956* (New York: Arno Press, 1977); David F. Noble, *America by Design: Science, Technology, and the Rise of Corporate Capitalism* (New York: Oxford University Press, 1977); W. Elliot Brownlee, *Dynamics of Ascent: A History of the American Economy,* 2d ed., rev. (New York: Alfred A. Knopf, 1979), pp. 267–362; Susan P. Lee and Peter Passell, *A New Economic View of American History* (New York: W. W. Norton, 1979), pp. 266–361; Sidney Ratner, James H. Soltow, and Richard Sylla, *The Evolution of the American Economy* (New York: Basic Books, 1979), pp. 253–395; Joseph R. Frese and Jacob Judd, eds., *An Emerging Independent American Economy, 1815–1875* (Tarrytown, NY: Sleepy Hollow Press, 1980); Barry W. Poulson, *Economic History of the United States* (New York: Macmillan, 1981), pp. 141–657; William H. Becker, *The Dynamics of Business-Government Relations: Industry and Exports, 1893–1921* (Chicago: University of Chicago Press, 1982); R. Jeffrey Lustig, *Corporate Liberalism: The Origins of Modern American Political Theory, 1890–1920* (Berkeley: University of California Press, 1982); John A. James, "Structural Change in American Manufacturing, 1850–1890," *Journal of Economic History* 43 (June 1983): 433–59; David O. Whitten, *The Emergence of Giant Enterprise, 1860–1914* (Westport, CT: Greenwood Press, 1983); Douglass C. North, Terry L. Anderson, and Peter J. Hill, *Growth and Welfare in the American Past: A New Economic History,* 3d ed., rev. (Englewood Cliffs, NJ: Prentice-Hall, 1983), pp. 63–148; Larry G. Gerber, *The Limits of Liberalism: Josephus Daniels, Henry Stimson, Bernard Baruch, Donald Richberg, Felix Frankfurter, and the Development of the Modern American Political Economy* (New York: New York University Press, 1984); David A. Hounshell, *From the American System to Mass Production, 1800–1932* (Baltimore: Johns Hopkins University Press, 1984); Stanley Lebergott, *The Americans: An Economic Record* (New York: W. W. Norton, 1984), pp. 268–400; Thomas K. McCraw, *Prophets of Regulation: Charles Francis Adams, Louis D. Brandeis, and Alfred E. Kahn* (Cambridge: Belknap Press, 1984), pp. 1–79, and McCraw, ed., *Regulation in Perspective: Historical Essays* (Cambridge: Harvard University Press, 1981); C. Joseph Pusateri, *A History of American Business* (Arlington Heights, IL: Harlan Davidson, 1984), pp. 144–257; Peter George, *The Emergence of Industrial America: Strategic Factors in American Economic Growth Since 1870* (Albany: State University of New York Press, 1982); Harold Van B. Cleveland et al., *Citibank, 1812–1970* (Cambridge: Harvard University Press, 1985); Naomi Lamoreaux, *The Great Merger Movement in American Business, 1895–1904* (Cambridge: Cambridge University Press, 1985), and Lamoreaux, *Insider Trading: Banks, Personal Connections, and Economic Development in Industrial New England* (New York: Cambridge University Press in association with the National Bureau of Economic Research, 1994); James O. Robertson, *America's Business* (New York: Hill and Wang, 1985), pp. 121–87; James Livingston, *Origins of the Federal Reserve System: Money, Class, and Corporate Capitalism, 1890–1913* (Ithaca, NY: Cornell University Press, 1986), Livingston, "The Social Analysis of Economic History and Theory: Conjectures on Late Nineteenth-Century American Development," *American Historical Review* 92 (February 1987): 69–95, and Livingston, *Pragmatism and the Political*

*Economy of Cultural Revolution, 1850–1940* (Chapel Hill: University of North Carolina Press, 1994); Fred Block, *Revising State Theory: Essays in Politics and Postindustrialism* (Philadelphia: Temple University Press, 1987); Mansel G. Blackford, *The Rise of Modern Business in Great Britain, the United States, and Japan* (Chapel Hill: University of North Carolina Press, 1988), pp. 1–93; Blackford and K. Austin Kerr, *Business Enterprise in American History,* 2d ed., rev. (Boston: Houghton Mifflin, 1990); David A. Lake, *Power, Protection, and Free Trade: International Sources of U.S. Commercial Strategy, 1887–1939* (Ithaca, NY: Cornell University Press, 1988); David C. Mowery and Nathan Rosenberg, *Technology and the Pursuit of Economic Growth* (New York: Cambridge University Press, 1989); JoAnne Yates, *Control Through Communication: The Rise of System in American Management* (Baltimore: Johns Hopkins University Press, 1989); Martin J. Sklar, *The Corporate Reconstruction of American Capitalism, 1890–1916: The Market, the Law, and Politics* (New York: Cambridge University Press, 1988)—see also Sklar's related volume, *The United States as a Developing Country: Studies in U.S. History in the Progressive Era and the 1920s* (New York: Cambridge University Press, 1992); Richard B. Du Boff, *Accumulation and Power: An Economic History of the United States* (Armonk, NY: M. E. Sharpe, 1989); Alan I. Marcus and Howard P. Segal, *Technology in America: A Brief History* (San Diego, CA: Harcourt Brace Jovanovich, 1989), pp. 88–254; Mira Wilkins, *The History of Foreign Investments in the United States to 1914* (Cambridge: Harvard University Press, 1989); Neil Fligstein, *The Transformation of Corporate Control* (Cambridge: Harvard University Press, 1990), pp. 1–115; Oliver Zunc, *Making America Corporate, 1870–1920* (Chicago: University of Chicago Press, 1990); John L. Campbell, J. Roger Hollingsworth, and Leon N. Lindberg, eds., *Governance of the American Economy* (New York: Cambridge University Press, 1991); Larry Schweikart, "U.S. Commercial Banking: A Historiographical Survey," *Business History Review* 65 (Autumn 1991): 626–33; Albro Martin, *The Growth, Rejection, and Rebirth of a Vital American Force* (New York: Oxford University Press, 1992); Tony Freyer, *Regulating Big Business: Antitrust in Great Britain and America, 1880–1990* (Cambridge: Cambridge University Press, 1992); Maury Klein, *The Flowering of the Third America: The Making of an Organizational Society* (Chicago: Ivan R. Dee, 1993); Claudia Goldin and Gary D. Libecap, eds., *The Regulated Economy: A Historical Approach to Political Economy* (Chicago: University of Chicago Press, 1994); Gerald Berk, *Alternative Tracks: The Constitution of American Industrial Order, 1865–1917* (Baltimore: Johns Hopkins University Press, 1994), and Berk, "Corporate Liberalism Reconsidered: A Review Essay," *Journal of Policy History* 3 (Winter, 1991): 70–84, with reply of James Livingston, pp. 85–89; Robert F. Himmelberg, ed., *The Rise of Big Business and the Beginnings of Antitrust and Railroad Regulation, 1870–1900* (New York: Garland, 1994), Himmelberg, ed., *The Monopoly Issue and Antitrust, 1900–1917* (New York: Garland, 1994), and Himmelberg, ed., *Growth of the Regulatory State, 1900–1917: State and Federal Regulation of Railroads and Other Enterprises* (New York: Garland, 1994); Mark J. Roe, *Strong Managers, Weak Owners: The Political Roots of American Corporate Finance* (Princeton, NJ: Princeton University Press, 1994); and Walter Licht, *Industrializing America: The Nineteenth Century* (Baltimore: Johns Hopkins University Press, 1995).

5. Chandler, *Visible Hand.*

## CHAPTER THREE. MODERNIZING THE NAVY

1. The analysis of the navy from 1865 to 1917 is based on U.S. Congress, Senate, Committee on Naval Affairs, *Hearings, the Navy Department: Methods of Conducting Business and Departmental Changes,* S. Doc. 693, 60th Cong., 2d sess., 1909, pp. 1–31; U.S. Congress, House, *Report of the Committee to Investigate the Cost of an Armor Plant for the United States,* H. Doc. 1620, 63d Cong., 3d sess., 1915, pp. 1–139; U.S. Congress, House, Committee on Naval Affairs, *Report, Government Armor-Plate Factory,* H. Doc. 497, parts 1–2, 64th Cong. 1st sess., 1916; and U.S. Bureau of the Census, *Historical Statistics of the United States, Colonial Times to 1970* (Washington, DC: Government Printing Office, 1975), 2: 1114–15, 1141–43.

W. H. Jaques, "The Establishment of Steel Gun Factories in the United States," *Proceedings of the United States Naval Institute* 10, no. 4 (1884): 527–909; American Iron and Steel Association, *History of the Manufacture of Armor Plate for the United States Navy* (Philadelphia: American Iron and Steel Association, 1899); Robley D. Evans, *A Sailor's Log: Recollections of Forty Years of Naval Life* (New York: D. Appleton, 1901); John D. Long, *The New American Navy* (New York: Outlook, 1903); A. T. Mahan, *Naval Administration and Warfare: Some General Principles* (Boston: Little, Brown, and Company, 1908); French E. Chadwick, *The American Navy* (New York: Doubleday, Page, 1915), pp. 249–79; Bradley A. Fiske, *From Midshipman to Rear-Admiral* (New York: Century, 1919); Herman F. Krafft and Walter B. Norris, *Sea Power in American History: The Influence of the Navy and Merchant Marine upon American Development* (New York: Century, 1920), pp. 181–94, 297–343; Thomas Hunt, *The Life of William H. Hunt* (Brattleboro, VT: privately printed, 1922); Lawrence S. Mayo, ed., *America of Yesterday: As Reflected in the Journal of John Davis Long* (Boston: Atlantic Monthly Press, 1923); Albert Gleaves, *Life and Letters of Rear Admiral Stephen B. Luce, U.S. Navy: Founder of the Naval War College* (New York: G. P. Putnam's Sons, 1925); Fitzhugh Green, *Our Naval Heritage* (New York: Century, 1925), pp. 246–402; Victor S. Clark, *History of Manufactures in the United States* (Washington, DC: Carnegie Institution of Washington, 1929), vol. 2, *1860–1893,* pp. 73–99, 264–76, 312–66, vol. 3, *1893–1928,* pp. 15–156; Frederick Moore, *America's Naval Challenge* (New York: Macmillan, 1929); Edwin A. Falk, *Fighting Bob Evans* (New York: Jonathan Cape and Harrison Smith, 1931); Allan Nevins, *Grover Cleveland: A Study in Courage* (New York: Dodd, Mead, 1932), pp. 217–23, 514, 518–19, 673–74; George F. Howe, *Chester A. Arthur: A Quarter-Century of Machine Politics* (New York: Dodd, Mead, 1934), pp. 232–40; Dudley W. Knox, *A History of the United States Navy* (New York: G. P. Putnam's Sons, 1936), pp. 317–421; Fletcher Pratt, *The Navy, a History: The Story of a Service in Action* (New York: Doubleday, Doran, 1938), pp. 343–411, and Pratt and Hartley E. Howe, *The Compact History of the United States Navy,* rev. ed. (New York: Hawthorn Books, 1962), pp. 175–205; George R. Clark et al., *A Short History of the United States Navy,* rev. ed. (Philadelphia: J. B. Lippincott, 1939), pp. 406–82; George T. Davis, *A Navy Second to None: The Development of Modern Navy Policy* (New York: Harcourt, Brace, 1940), pp. 1–232; Holden A. Evans, *One Man's Fight for a Better Navy* (New York: Dodd, Mead, 1940); Bernard Brodie, *Sea Power in the Machine Age* (Princeton, NJ: Princeton University Press, 1941); Elting E. Morison, *Admiral Sims and the Modern American Navy* (Boston: Houghton-Mifflin, 1942), pp. 1–469, and various chapters in Morison, *Men,*

*Machines, and Modern Times* (Cambridge: MIT Press, 1966); Gordon C. O'Gara, *Theodore Roosevelt and the Rise of the Modern Navy* (Princeton, NJ: Princeton University Press, 1943); Josephus Daniels, *The Wilson Era: Years of Peace, 1910–1917* (Chapel Hill: University of North Carolina Press, 1944); Seward W. Livermore, "American Naval-Base Policy in the Far East, 1850–1914," *Pacific Historical Review* 13 (June 1944): 113–35, and Livermore, "The American Navy as a Factor in World Politics, 1903–1913," *American Historical Review* 63 (July 1958): 863–79; Donald W. Mitchell, *History of the Modern American Navy: 1883 Through Pearl Harbor* (New York: Alfred A. Knopf, 1946), pp. 1–210; Harold and Margaret Sprout, *The Rise of American Naval Power, 1776–1918,* rev. ed. (Princeton, NJ: Princeton University Press, 1946), pp. 1–346; Mark D. Hirsch, *William C. Whitney: Modern Warwick* (New York: Dodd, Mead, 1948); Archibald D. Turnbull and Clifford L. Lord, *History of United States Naval Aviation* (New Haven: Yale University Press, 1949), pp. 1–68; Allan Westcott, ed., *American Seapower Since 1775* (Philadelphia: J. B. Lippincott, 1947), pp. 206–334; Frank Freidel, *Franklin D. Roosevelt: The Apprenticeship* (Boston: Little, Brown), pp. 207–372; Harold G. Bowen, *Ships, Machinery, and Mossbacks: The Autobiography of a Naval Engineer* (Princeton, NJ: Princeton University Press, 1954), pp. 1–46; E. B. Potter, ed., *The United States and World Sea Power* (Englewood Cliffs, NJ: Prentice-Hall, 1955), pp. 383–470; Samuel P. Huntington, *The Soldier and the State: The Theory and Politics of Civil-Military Relations* (Cambridge: Harvard University Press, 1957), pp. 222–88; William R. Braisted, *The United States Navy in the Pacific, 1897–1909* (Austin: University of Texas Press, 1958), and Braisted, *The United States Navy in the Pacific, 1909–1922* (Austin: University of Texas Press, 1971); Dean C. Allard, "The Influence of the United States Navy upon the American Steel Industry, 1880–1900" (master's thesis, Georgetown University, 1959); Armin Rappaport, *The Navy League of the United States* (Detroit: Wayne State University Press, 1962); E. David Cronon, ed., *The Cabinet Diaries of Josephus Daniels* (Lincoln: University of Nebraska Press, 1963), pp. 1–126; Walter LaFeber, *The New Empire: An Interpretation of American Expansion, 1860–1898* (Ithaca, NY: Cornell University Press, 1963), pp. 58–60, 80–101, 121–49, 229–41; Peter Temin, *Iron and Steel in Nineteenth-Century America: An Economic Inquiry* (Cambridge: MIT Press, 1964); Daniel J. Carrison, *The Navy from Wood to Steel, 1860–1890* (New York: Franklin Watts, 1965), pp. 169–78; Brayton Harris, *The Age of the Battleship, 1890–1922* (New York: Franklin Watts, 1965); Edward W. Sloan III, *Benjamin Franklin Isherwood, Naval Engineer: The Years as Engineer in Chief, 1861–1869* (Annapolis, MD: U.S. Naval Institute, 1965); Leonard A. Swann, Jr., *John Roach, Maritime Entrepreneur: The Years as Naval Contractor, 1862–1886* (Annapolis, MD: U.S. Naval Institute, 1965); John A. S. Grenville and George B. Young, *Politics, Strategy, and American Diplomacy: Studies in Foreign Policy, 1873–1917* (New Haven: Yale University Press, 1966); Walter R. Herrick, Jr., *The American Naval Revolution* (Baton Rouge: Louisiana State University Press, 1966); Joseph L. Morrison, *Josephus Daniels: The Small-d Democrat* (Chapel Hill: University of North Carolina Press, 1966), pp. 3–79; George van Deurs, *Wings for the Fleet: A Narrative of Naval Aviation's Early Development, 1910-1916* (Annapolis, MD: U.S. Naval Institute, 1966); Daniel J. Costello, "Planning for War: A History of the General Board of the Navy, 1900–1914" (Ph.D. diss., Fletcher School of Law and Diplomacy, 1968); Louis M. Hacker, *The World of Andrew Carnegie: 1865–1901* (Philadelphia: J. B. Lippincott, 1968), pp. 31–32; Charles O. Paullin,

*Paullin's History of Naval Administration, 1775–1911* (Annapolis, MD: U.S. Naval Institute, 1968), pp. 309–485; Melvin I. Urofsky, *Big Steel and the Wilson Administration: A Study in Business-Government Relations* (Columbus: Ohio State University Press, 1969), pp. 117–51; John D. Alden, *The American Steel Navy* (Annapolis, MD: Naval Institute Press, 1972); Peter Karsten, *The Naval Aristocracy: The Golden Age of Annapolis and the Emergence of Modern American Navalism* (New York: Free Press, 1972); Benjamin F. Cooling, *Benjamin Franklin Tracy: Father of the Modern American Fighting Navy* (Hamden, CT: Archon Books, 1973), Cooling, "The Formative Years of the Naval-Industrial Complex: Their Meaning for Studies of Institutions Today," *Naval War College Review* 27 (March/April 1975): 53–62, and Cooling, *Gray Steel and Blue Water Navy: The Formative Years of America's Military-Industrial Complex, 1881–1917* (Hamden, CT: Archon Books, 1979); Kenneth J. Hagan, *American Gunboat Diplomacy and the Old Navy, 1877–1889* (Westport:, CT Greenwood Press, 1973), and Hagan, *This People's Navy: The Making of American Sea Power* (New York: Free Press, 1991), pp. 161–258; Lance C. Buhl, "Mariners and Machines: Resistance to Technological Change in the American Navy, 1865–1869," *Journal of American History* 61 (December 1974): 703–27, and Buhl, "Maintaining 'An American Navy,' 1865–1889," in *In Peace and War: Interpretations of American Naval History, 1775–1984*, ed. Kenneth J. Hagen, pp. 145–73, 2d ed. (Westport, CT: Greenwood Press, 1984); Ronald Spector, *Admiral of the New Empire: The Life and Career of George Dewey* (Baton Rouge: Louisiana State University Press, 1974), Spector, *Professors of War: The Naval War College and the Development of the Naval Profession* (Newport, RI: Naval War College Press, 1977), and Spector, "The Triumph of Professional Ideology: The U.S. Navy in the 1890s," in Hagen, ed., *In Peace and War*, pp. 174–204; Donal J. Sexton, "Forging the Sword: Congress and the American Naval Renaissance, 1880–1890" (Ph.D. diss., University of Tennessee, 1976); Johannes R. Lischka, "Armor Plate: Nickel and Steel, Monopoly and Profit," in *War, Business, and American Society: Historical Perspectives on the Military-Industrial Complex*, ed. Benjamin Franklin Cooling, pp. 43–58 (Port Washington, NY: Kennikat Press, 1977); Henry C. Ferrell, Jr., "Regional Rivalries, Congress, and MIC; The Norfolk and Charleston Navy Yards, 1913–1920," in Cooling, ed., *War, Business, and American Society*, pp. 59–72; Robert Seager II, *Alfred Thayer Mahan: The Man and His Letters* (Annapolis, MD: Naval Institute Press, 1977), and Seager, "Ten Years Before Mahan: The Unofficial Case for the New Navy, 1880–1890," *Mississippi Valley Historical Review* 60 (December 1953): 491–512; Lawrence C. Allin, *The United States Naval Institute, Intellectual Forum of the New Navy: 1873–1889* (Manhattan, KS: MA/AH Publishing, 1978); Paolo E. Coletta, *The American Naval Heritage in Brief* (Washington, DC: University Press of America, 1978), pp. 138–94, Coletta, ed., *American Secretaries of the Navy*, vol. 1, *1775–1913*, and vol. 2, *1913–1972* (Annapolis, MD: Naval Institute Press, 1980), Coletta, *A Survey of Naval Affairs, 1865–1917* (Lanham, MD: University Press of America, 1987), and Coletta, "The American Naval Leaders' Preparations for War," in *The Great War, 1914–18: Essays on the Military, Political and Social History of the First World War*, ed. R. J. Q. Adams, pp. 160–82 (College Station: Texas A&M University Press, 1990); Jeffrey M. Dorwart, *The Office of Naval Intelligence: The Birth of America's First Intelligence Agency, 1865–1918* (Annapolis, MD: Naval Institute Press, 1979), and Dorwart, "Naval Attaches, Intelligence Officers, and the Rise of the 'New American Navy,' 1882–1914," in *Changing Interpretations and New*

*Sources in Naval History: Papers from the Third United States Naval Academy History Symposium,* ed. Robert W. Love, Jr., pp. 260–69 (New York: Garland, 1980); Robert G. Albion, *Makers of Naval Policy, 1798–1947* (Annapolis, MD: Naval Institute Press, 1980), pp. 1–376; James L. Abrahamson, *America Arms for a New Century: The Making of a Great Military Power* (New York: Free Press, 1981); David F. Trask, *The War with Spain in 1898* (New York: Macmillan, 1981), and Trask, "William Shepherd Benson, 11 May 1915—25 September 1919," in *The Chiefs of Naval Operations,* ed. Robert W. Love, Jr., pp. 3–20 (Annapolis, MD: Naval Institute Press, 1980); Dennis A. Daellenbach, "Senators, the Navy, and the Politics of American Expansionism, 1881–1890" (Ph.D. diss., University of Kansas, 1982); Allan R. Millett and Peter Maslowski, *For the Common Defense: A Military History of the United States of America* (New York: Free Press, 1984), pp. 233–327; James C. Bradford, ed., *Captains of the Old Steam Navy: Makers of the American Naval Tradition, 1840–1880* (Annapolis, MD: Naval Institute Press, 1986), and Bradford, ed., *Admirals of the New Steel Navy: Makers of the American Naval Tradition, 1880–1930* (Annapolis, MD: Naval Institute Press, 1990); Mary Klachko, *Admiral William Shepherd Benson: First Chief of Naval Operations* (Annapolis, MD: Naval Institute Press, 1987); Richard W. Turk, *The Ambiguous Relationship: Theodore Roosevelt and Alfred Thayer Mahan* (Westport, CT: Greenwood Press, 1987); John Keegan, *The Price of Admiralty: The Evolution of Naval Warfare* (New York: Viking Penguin, 1988), pp. 97–155; William S. Petersen, "Congressional Politics: Building the New Navy, 1876–86," *Armed Services and Society* 14 (Summer 1988): 489–509; Mark R. Shulman, "The Emergence of American Sea Power: Politics and the Creation of a U.S. Naval Strategy, 1882–1893" (Ph.D. diss., University of California, Berkeley, 1990), and Shulman, *Navalism and the Emergence of American Sea Power, 1882–1893* (Annapolis, MD: Naval Institute Press, 1995); Robert L. O'Connell, *Sacred Vessels: The Cult of the Battleship and the Rise of the U.S. Navy* (New York: Oxford University Press, 1991); Gary E. Weir, *Building American Submarines, 1914–1940* (Washington, DC: Naval Historical Center, 1991), and Weir, "The Navy, Industry, and Conflicting Expectations: Fried. Krupp of Essen and the Electric Boat Company, 1890–1925," in *New Interpretations in Naval History,* ed. William R. Roberts and Jack Sweetman, pp. 350–68 (Annapolis, MD: Naval Institute Press, 1991); Donald A. Yerxa, *Admirals and Empire: The United States Navy and the Caribbean, 1898–1945* (Columbia: University of South Carolina Press, 1991), pp. 1–76; Colin S. Gray, *The Leverage of Sea Power: The Strategic Advantage of Navies in War* (New York: Free Press, 1992); and William J. Williams, "Josephus Daniels and the U.S. Navy's Shipbuilding Program during World War I," *Journal of Military History* 60 (January 1996): 7–38. A number of surveys of the navy have been published in the last decade and are cited in volume 1 of this series, Paul A. C. Koistinen, *Beating Plowshares into Swords: The Political Economy of Warfare, 1606–1865* (Lawrence: University Press of Kansas, 1996), chap. 4, n. 43. The most recent is George W. Baer, *One Hundred Years of Sea Power: The U.S. Navy, 1890–1990* (Stanford, CA: Stanford University Press, 1994).

2. Hagan, *Gunboat Diplomacy,* pp. 3–10, 188–91; Buhl, "Maintaining 'An American Navy,' 1865–1889," pp. 145–73 (quotation, p. 169). See also Buhl, "Mariners and Machines."

3. For example, see Hagan, *People's Navy,* pp. 233–34, 242–43.

4. Karsten, *Naval Aristocracy.*

5. The analysis of armor and heavy ordnance draws heavily, although not exclusively, on Allard's study, "The Influence of the U.S. Navy upon the American Steel Industry."

6. For some representative views of the Navy League, see Davis, *Navy Second to None,* pp. 147–49, 202, 210; Mitchell, *Modern American Navy,* pp. 136–38, 166–67, 192–97, 325–26, 332–34; and Karsten, *Naval Aristocracy,* pp. 174–78, 298–99, 362–79. The one monograph on the Navy League by Rappaport is useful but too biased and defensive to be reliable.

7. Cooling has done the most scholarship in this regard; see "The Formative Years of the Naval-Industrial Complex," and *Gray Steel and Blue Water Navy.* For a historiographical approach to the subject, see Kurt Hackemer, "The U.S. Navy and the Late Nineteenth-Century Steel Industry," *Historian* 57 (Spring 1995): 703–12.

## CHAPTER FOUR. MODERNIZING THE ARMY

1. The discussion and analysis of the army from 1865 to 1917 is based on Maj. Gen. William Harding Carter, *Creation of the American General Staff: Personal Narrative of the General Staff System of the American Army,* S. Doc. no. 119, 68th Cong., 1st sess., pp. 1–65; U.S. Bureau of the Census, *Historical Statistics of the United States, Colonial Times to 1970* (Washington, DC: U.S. Government Printing Office, 1975) 2: 1114–15, 1141–42; Ira L. Reeves, *Military Education in the United States* (Burlington, VT: Free Press Printing, 1914); William H. Carter, *The American Army* (Indianapolis, IN: Bobbs-Merrill, 1915); Arthur P. Van Gelder and Hugo Schlatter, *History of the Explosives Industry in America* (New York: Columbia University Press, 1927), pp. 121–73, 767–97; Oliver L. Spaulding, *The United States Army in War and Peace* (New York: G. P. Putnam's Sons, 1937), pp. 337–457; Philip C. Jessup, *Elihu Root,* 2 vols. (New York: Dodd, Mead, 1938), 1: 215–407; William A. Ganoe, *The History of the United States Army* (New York: D. Appleton-Century, 1942), pp. 298–476; Otto L. Nelson, Jr., *National Security and the General Staff* (Washington, DC: Infantry Journal Press, 1946), pp. 1–186; Henry L. Stimson and McGeorge Bundy, *On Active Service in Peace and War* (New York: Harper and Brothers, 1948), pp. 3–81; Mark S. Watson, *Chief of Staff: Prewar Plans and Preparations* (Washington, DC: Department of the Army, 1950), pp. 57–62; Richard W. Leopold, *Elihu Root and the Conservative Tradition* (Boston: Little, Brown, 1954), pp. 3–46, 191–98; Marvin A. Kreidberg and Merton G. Henry, *History of Military Mobilization in the United States Army, 1775–1945* (Washington, DC: Department of the Army, 1955), pp. 141–213; David A. Lockmiller, *Enoch H. Crowder: Soldier, Lawyer and Statesman* (Columbia: University of Missouri Studies, 1955), pp. 14–178; Arthur A. Ekirch, Jr., *The Civilian and the Military* (New York: Oxford University Press, 1956), pp. 107–75; Walter Millis, *Arms and Men: A Study in American Military History* (New York: Putnam, 1956), pp. 131–210; Samuel P. Huntington, *Soldier and the State: The Theory and Politics of Civil-Military Relations* (Cambridge: Harvard University Press, 1957), pp. 222–303; Juliette A. Hennessy, *The United States Army Air Arm, April 1861 to April 1917* (Colorado Springs: USAF Historical Division, 1958); Margaret Leech, *In the Days of McKinley* (New York: Harper and Brothers, 1959), pp. 151–431; Elting E. Morison, *Turmoil and Tradition: A Study of the Life and Times of Henry L. Stimson* (Boston: Houghton Mifflin, 1960), pp. 144–77;

C. Joseph Bernardo and Eugene H. Bacon, *American Military Policy: Its Development Since 1775*, 2d ed. (Harrisburg: Stackpole, 1961), pp. 234–352; Paul Y. Hammond, *Organizing for Defense: The American Military Establishment in the Twentieth Century* (Princeton, NJ: Princeton University Press, 1961), pp. 10–38; J. D. Hittle, *The Military Staff: Its History and Development* (Harrisburg: Stackpole, 1961); Mabel E. Deutrich, *Struggle for Supremacy: The Career of General Fred C. Ainsworth* (Washington, DC: Public Affairs Press, 1962); Virginia W. M. Johnson, *The Unregimented General: A Biography of Nelson A. Miles* (Boston: Houghton Mifflin, 1962); Erna Risch, *Quartermaster Support of the Army: A History of the Corps, 1775–1939* (Washington, DC: Office of the Quartermaster General, 1962), pp. 453–598; Russell F. Weigley, *Towards An American Army: Military Thought from Washington to Marshall* (New York: Columbia University Press, 1962), pp. 100–254, Weigley, *History of the United States Army* (New York: Macmillan, 1967), pp. 265–354, and Weigley, *The American Way of War: A History of United States Military Strategy and Policy* (New York: Macmillan, 1973), pp. 153–91; H. Wayne Morgan, *William McKinley and His America* (Syracuse, NY: Syracuse University Press, 1969), pp. 326–474, and Morgan, *America's Road to Empire: The War with Spain and Overseas Expansion* (New York: John Wiley and Sons, 1965); Don Rickey, Jr., *Forty Miles a Day on Beans and Hay: The Enlisted Soldier Fighting the Indian Wars* (Norman: University of Oklahoma Press, 1963); Philip L. Semsch, "Elihu Root and the General Staff," *Military Affairs* 27 (Spring 1963): 16–27; Stephen E. Ambrose, *Upton and the Army* (Baton Rouge: Louisiana State University Press, 1964), and Ambrose, *Duty, Honor, Country: A History of West Point* (Baltimore: Johns Hopkins University Press, 1966), pp. 191–260; Jim D. Hill, *The Minute Man in Peace and War: A History of the National Guard* (Harrisburg: Stackpole, 1964), pp. 99–223; Martha Derthick, *The National Guard in Politics* (Cambridge: Harvard University Press, 1965), pp. 1–44; James A. Huston, *The Sinews of War: Army Logistics, 1775–1953* (Washington, DC: Office of the Chief of Military History, 1966), pp. 253–307; George S. Pappas, *Prudens Futuri: The U.S. Army War College, 1901–1967* (Carlisle Barracks: Alumni Association of the U.S. Army War College, 1967), pp. 1–83; Edward Ranson, "The Endicott Board of 1885–1886, and the Coast Defense," *Military Affairs* 31 (Summer 1967): 74–84; Jack D. Foner, *The United States Soldier Between Two Wars: Army Life and Reforms, 1865–1898* (New York: Humanities Press, 1970); Samuel E. Morrison, Frederick Merk, and Frank Freidel, *Dissent in Three American Wars* (Cambridge: Harvard University Press, 1970), pp. 67–95; E. Berkeley Tomkins, *Anti-imperialism in the United States: The Great Debate, 1890–1920* (Philadelphia: University of Pennsylvania Press, 1970); Graham A. Cosmas, *An Army for Empire: The United States Army in the Spanish-American War* (Columbia: University of Missouri Press, 1971), Cosmas, "From Order to Chaos: The War Department, the National Guard, and Military Policy, 1898," *Military Affairs* 29 (Fall 1965): 105–21, and Cosmas, "Military Reform After the Spanish-American War: The Army Reorganization Fight of 1898–1899," *Military Affairs* 35 (February 1971): 12–18; John G. Clifford, *The Citizen Soldiers: The Plattsburg Training Camp Movement, 1913–1920* (Lexington: University Press of Kentucky, 1972), pp. 1–227; Peter Karsten, "Armed Progressives: The Military Reorganizes for the American Century," in *Building the Organization Society: Essays on Associational Activities in Modern America*, ed. Jerry Israel, pp. 197–232 (New York: Free Press, 1972); Richard D. Challener, *Admirals, Generals, and American Foreign Policy, 1898–1914* (Princeton, NJ: Princeton University Press, 1973); John M.

Gates, *Schoolbooks and Krags: The United States Army in the Philippines, 1898–1902* (Westport, CT: Greenwood Press, 1973), Gates, "The Alleged Isolation of U.S. Army Officers in the Late 19th Century," *Parameters* 10 (September 1980): 32–45, and Gates, "The 'New' Military Professionalism," *Armed Forces and Society* 2 (Spring 1985): 427–36; Robert M. Utley, *Frontier Regulars: The United States Army and the Indian, 1866–1891* (New York: Macmillan, 1973); Gerald F. Linderman, *The Mirror of War: American Society and the Spanish-American War* (Ann Arbor: University of Michigan Press, 1974); James E. Hewes, *From Root to McNamara: Army Organization and Administration, 1900–1963* (Washington, DC: Center of Military History, 1975), pp. 4–21; Allan R. Millett, *The General: Robert L. Bullard and Officership in the United States Army, 1881–1925* (Westport, CT: Greenwood Press, 1975), pp. 3–298; Marc B. Powe, *Emergence of the War Department Intelligence Agency: 1885–1918* (Manhattan, KS: Sunflower University Press, 1974); Robert F. Stohlman, Jr., *The Powerless Position: The Commanding General of the Army of the United States, 1864–1903* (Manhattan, KS: MA/AH Publishing, 1975); Elbridge Colby, *The National Guard of the United States: A Half Century of Progress* (Manhattan, KS: MA/AH Publishing, 1977), chaps. 1–6; Merritt R. Smith, "Military Arsenals and Industry Before World War I," and Daniel R. Beaver, "The Problem of American Military Supply, 1890–1920," in *War, Business, and American Society: Historical Perspectives on the Military-Industrial Complex,* ed. Benjamin Franklin Cooling, 24–42, 73–92 (Port Washington, NY: Kennikat Press, 1977); Thomas C. Leonard, *Above the Battle: War-Making in America from Appomattox to Versailles* (New York: Oxford University Press, 1978); Timothy K. Nenninger, *The Leavenworth Schools and the Old Army: Education, Professionalism, and the Officer Corps of the United States Army, 1881–1918* (Westport, CT: Greenwood Press, 1978); Jack C. Lane, *Armed Progressive: General Leonard Wood* (San Rafael, CA: Presidio Press, 1978); Walter Karp, *The Politics of War: The Story of Two Wars Which Altered Forever the Political Life of the American Republic (1890–1920)* (New York: Harper and Row, 1979); William R. Roberts, "Loyalty and Expertise: The Transformation of the Nineteenth-Century American General Staff and the Creation of the Modern Military Establishment" (Ph.D. diss., Johns Hopkins University, 1979); Richard E. Welch, Jr., *Response to Imperialism: The United States and the Philippine-American War, 1899–1902* (Chapel Hill: University of North Carolina Press, 1979); Jerry M. Cooper, *The Army and Civil Disorder: Federal Military Intervention in Labor Disputes, 1877–1900* (Westport, CT: Greenwood Press, 1980), and Cooper, "National Guard Reform, the Army, and the Spanish-American War: The View from Wisconsin," *Military Affairs* 42 (February 1978): 20–23; Rowena A. Reed, "The Endicott Board—Vision and Reality," *Council on Abandoned Military Posts* 21 (Summer 1979): 4–17; Lewis L. Gould, *The Presidency of William McKinley* (Lawrence: Regents Press of Kansas, 1980), and Gould, "William McKinley: 'The Man at the Helm,'" in *Commanders in Chief: Presidential Leadership in Modern Wars,* ed. Joseph G. Dawson III, pp. 49–64 (Lawrence: University Press of Kansas, 1993); Donna M. E. Thomas, "Army Reform in America: The Crucial Years, 1876–1881" (Ph.D. diss., University of Florida, 1980); James L. Abrahamson, *America Arms for a New Century: The Making of a Great Military Power* (New York: Free Press, 1981); David F. Trask, *The War with Spain in 1898* (New York: Macmillan, 1981); Barrie E. Zais, "The Struggle for a 20th Century Army: Investigation and Reform of the United States Army After the Spanish-American War, 1898–1903" (Ph.D. diss., Duke University, 1981); Patrick J. Garrity, "The Debate over American

National Security, 1890–1900: A Study in the Foundation of United States Foreign Policy" (Ph.D. diss., Claremont Graduate School, 1982); I. B. Holley, Jr., *General John M. Palmer, Citizen Soldiers, and the Army of a Democracy* (Westport, CT: Greenwood Press, 1982), pp. 3–259; Stuart C. Miller, *"Benevolent Assimilation:" The American Conquest of the Philippines, 1899–1903* (New Haven: Yale University Press, 1982); Stephen Skowronek, *Building a New American State: The Expansion of National Administrative Capacities, 1877–1920* (New York: Cambridge University Press, 1982), 85–120, 212–47; John K. Mahon, *History of the Militia and the National Guard* (New York: Macmillan, 1983), pp. 108–53; Allan R. Millett and Peter Maslowski, *For the Common Defense: A Military History of the United States of America* (New York: Free Press, 1984), pp. 233–327; Edward M. Coffman, *The Old Army: A Portrait of the American Army in Peacetime, 1784–1898* (New York: Oxford University Press, 1986), pp. 215–404, and Coffman, "The AEF Leaders' Education for War," in *The Great War, 1914–18: Essays on the Military, Political and Social History of the First World War,* ed. R. J. Q. Adams, pp. 138–59 (College Station: Texas A&M University Press, 1990); Kenneth J. Hagan and William R. Roberts, eds., *Against All Enemies: Interpretation of American Military History from Colonial Times to the Present* (Westport, CT: Greenwood Press, 1986), pp. 155–234; John W. Chambers II, *To Raise an Army: The Draft Comes to Modern America* (New York: Free Press, 1987), pp. 41–124; David A. Clary and Joseph W. A. Whitehorne, *The Inspectors General of the United States Army, 1777–1903* (Washington, DC: Office of the Inspector General and Center of Military History, 1987), pp. 242–409; Garry D. Ryan and Timothy K. Nenninger, eds., *Soldiers and Civilians: The U.S. Army and the American People* (Washington, DC: National Archives and Records Administration, 1987), pp. 27–44; Robert M. Fogelson, *America's Armories: Architecture, Society, and Public Order* (Cambridge: Harvard University Press, 1989); Center of Military History, *American Military History* (Washington, DC: Center of Military History, 1989), pp. 281–357; Darlis A. Miller, *Soldiers and Settlers: Military Supply in the Southwest, 1861–1885* (Albuquerque: University of New Mexico Press, 1989); C. Kenneth Allard, *Command, Control, and the Common Defense* (New Haven: Yale University Press, 1990), chap. 3; Joseph G. Dawson III, *The Late 19th Century U.S. Army, 1865–1898: A Research Guide* (Westport, CT: Greenwood Press, 1990); Carol Reardon, *Soldiers and Scholars: The U.S. Army and the Uses of Military History, 1865–1920* (Lawrence: University Press of Kansas, 1990); John L. Offner, *An Unwanted War: The Diplomacy of the United States and Spain over Cuba, 1895–1898* (Chapel Hill: University of North Carolina Press, 1992); Robert Wooster, *Nelson A. Miles and the Twilight of the Frontier Army* (Lincoln: University of Nebraska Press, 1993); and Ronald J. Barr, "Neo-Hamiltonian Republicans and Military Reform in the Progressive Era: 1898–1912" (Ph.D. diss., Louisiana State University, 1994).

2. As quoted in Risch, *Quartermaster,* p. 487.

3. Ibid., p. 481.

4. Weigley, *U.S. Army,* p. 289.

5. Huntington, *Soldier and State,* chap. 9, and Gates, "Alleged Isolation of U.S. Army Officers," pp. 32–45. See also Edward M. Coffman, "The Long Shadow of *The Soldier and the State,*" *Journal of Military History* 55 (January 1991): 69–82, and Terrence J. Gough, "Isolation and Professionalism of the Army Officer Corps: A Post-revisionist View of *The Soldier and the State,*" *Social Science Quarterly* 73 (March 1992): 420–36. William B. Skelton, "Samuel P. Huntington and the Roots of the

American Military Tradition," *Journal of Military History* 60 (April 1996): 325–38, and Coffman, "The Long Shadow," note or discuss most of the other relevant literature on the subject.

6. See Cosmas, *Army for Empire,* and Trask, *War With Spain*. See also Huston, *Sinews of War,* pp. 273–91.

7. Weigley, *U.S. Army,* p. 333.

8. For example, see Huston, *Sinews of War,* pp. 296–300.

9. Risch, *Quartermaster,* p. 598.

## CHAPTER FIVE. THE ROLE OF AMERICAN ELITES

1. I have already addressed the elitist nature of American society from the colonial period through the Civil War in *Beating Plowshares into Swords: The Political Economy of American Warfare, 1606–1865* (Lawrence: University Press of Kansas, 1996). I have also analyzed and cited sources on the modern American "power elite" in previous publications. See *The Military-Industrial Complex: A Historical Perspective* (New York: Praeger, 1980), pp. 14–17 and nn. 11–17, and "Warfare and Power Relations in America: Mobilizing the World War II Economy," in *The Home Front and War in the Twentieth Century: The American Experience in Comparative Perspective,* ed. James Titus, pp. 91–110, 231–43 (Colorado Springs: U.S. Air Force Academy, 1984); the entire article dissects the operations of power in mobilizing the World War II economy, with notes 4 and 21 particularly important in terms of content and citations. Numerous volumes cited in chapters 3 and 4 of this book deal directly or indirectly with the issue of the military and power in America. See also Richard C. Brown, *Social Attitudes of American Generals, 1898–1940* (New York: Arno Press, 1979), and Philip H. Burch, Jr., *Elites in American History,* vol. 2, *The Civil War to the New Deal,* and vol. 3, *The New Deal to the Carter Administration* (New York: Holmes and Meier Publishers, 1980–1981).

Excellent and often pioneering work has been done on business elites in the late nineteenth and early twentieth centuries. See William Miller, "The Business Elite in Business Bureaucracies: Careers of Top Executives in the Early Twentieth Century," and Frances W. Gregory and Irene D. Neu, "The American Industrial Elite in the 1870s: Their Social Origins," in *Men in Business: Essays of Entrepreneurship,* ed. William Miller, pp. 286–305, 346–50, and 193–211, 329–32 (Cambridge: Harvard University Press, 1952)—Miller cites on p. 286 his other pathbreaking essays on the subject; Gabriel Kolko, "Brahmins and Business, 1870–1914: A Hypothesis on the Social Basis of Success in American History," in *The Critical Spirit: Essays in Honor of Herbert Marcuse,* ed. Kurt H. Wolffe and Barrington Moore, Jr., pp. 343–63 (Boston: Beacon Press, 1967); Ralph Andreano, "A Note on the Horatio Alger Legend: Statistical Studies of the Nineteenth-Century American Business Elite," in *Business Enterprise and Economic Change: Essays in Honor of Harold F. Williamson,* ed. Louis P. Cain and Paul J. Uselding, pp. 227–46 (Kent, OH: Kent State University Press, 1973); and Christopher Jencks et al., *Who Gets Ahead: The Determinants of Economic Success in America* (New York: Basic Books, 1979). Much of this scholarship is summarized and placed in historical perspective, with additional citations, by Peter George, *The Emergence of Industrial America: Strategic Factors in Economic Growth Since 1870* (Albany: State University of New York Press, 1982), pp. 55–76, 213–17.

2. I have dealt with the professionalizing process and results for both services, including full citation of sources, in *Beating Plowshares into Swords,* chap. 4.

## CHAPTER SIX. PREPAREDNESS AND PARTICIPATION

1. The literature on Progressivism is exceptionally rich. One of the best introductions to it is Robert H. Wiebe, "The Progressive Years, 1900–1917," in *The Reinterpretation of American History and Culture,* ed. William H. Cartwright and Richard L. Watson, Jr., pp. 425–42 (Washington, DC: National Council for the Social Studies, 1973). More recent publications update Wiebe's essay and provide additional insight on the subject. See Richard M. Abrams, *The Burdens of Progress, 1900–1929* (Glenview, IL: Scott, Foresman, 1978)—short bibliographic essays conclude each chapter; John Whiteclay Chambers II, *The Tyranny of Change: America in the Progressive Era, 1900–1920,* rev. ed. (New York: St. Martin's Press, 1992), 301–15; and Richard L. McCormick, "Public Life in Industrial America, 1877–1917," in *The New American History,* ed. Eric Foner, pp. 93–117 (Philadelphia: Temple University Press, 1990).

2. The discussion of Progressive foreign policy and divisions over it, particularly the preparedness debate before American entry into World War I, is based on John Milton Cooper, Jr., "Progressivism and American Foreign Policy: A Reconsideration," *Mid-America* 51 (October 1969): 260–77, Cooper, *The Vanity of Power: American Isolationism and the First World War, 1914–1917* (Westport, CT: Greenwood, 1969), and Cooper, *The Warrior and the Priest: Woodrow Wilson and Theodore Roosevelt* (Cambridge: Belknap Press, 1983); John W. Chambers, "Conscripting for Colossus: The Adoption of the Draft in the United States in World War I" (Ph.D. diss., Columbia University, 1973), and Chambers, *To Raise an Army: The Draft Comes to Modern America* (New York: Free Press, 1987), pp. 73–237; Allen F. Davis, "Welfare, Reform, and World War I," *American Quarterly* 19 (Fall 1967): 516–33; Richard D. Challener, *Admirals, Generals, and American Foreign Policy, 1898–1914* (Princeton, NJ: Princeton University Press, 1973); John Carver Edwards, *Patriots in Pinstripe: Men of the National Security League* (Washington, DC: University Press of America, 1982); Arthur A. Ekirch, Jr., *Progressivism in America: A Study of the Era from Theodore Roosevelt to Woodrow Wilson* (New York: New Viewpoints, 1974); John Patrick Finnegan, *Against the Specter of a Dragon: The Campaign for American Military Preparedness, 1914–1917* (Westport, CT: Greenwood Press, 1974); Otis L. Graham, Jr., *An Encore for Reform: The Old Progressives and the New Deal* (New York: Oxford University Press, 1967), and Graham, *The Great Campaigns: Reform and War in America, 1900–1928* (Englewood Cliffs, NJ: Prentice-Hall, 1971), pp. 1–117; Carol S. Gruber, *Mars and Minerva: World War I and the Uses of Higher Learning in America* (Baton Rouge: Louisiana State University Press, 1975); Charles Hirschfeld, "Nationalist Progressivism and World War I," *Mid-America* 45 (July 1963): 139–56; Barry D. Karl, *The Uneasy State: The United States from 1915 to 1945* (Chicago: University of Chicago Press, 1983), pp. 16–49; Burton I. Kaufman, *Efficiency and Expansion: Foreign Trade Organization in the Wilson Administration, 1913–1921* (Westport, CT: Greenwood Press, 1974); William E. Leuchtenburg, "Progressivism and Imperialism: The Progressive Movement and American Foreign Policy, 1898–1916," *Mississippi Valley Historical Review* 39 (December 1952): 483–504; Arthur S. Link, *Woodrow Wilson and the Progressive Era, 1910–1917*

(New York: Harper and Row, 1954), and Link's multivolume study, *Wilson: The Struggle for Neutrality, 1914–1915* (Princeton, NJ: Princeton University Press, 1960), *Wilson: Confusion and Crises, 1915–1916* (Princeton, NJ: Princeton University Press, 1964), and *Wilson: Campaigns for Progressivism and Peace, 1916–1917* (Princeton, NJ: Princeton University Press, 1965); Herbert F. Margulies, "Recent Opinion on the Decline of the Progressive Movement," *Mid-America* 45 (October 1963): 250–68; James P. Martin, "The American Peace Movement and the Progressive Era, 1910–1917" (Ph.D. diss., Rice University, 1975); Michael Pearlman, *To Make Democracy Safe for America: Patricians and Preparedness in the Progressive Era* (Urbana: University of Illinois Press, 1984); Page Smith, *America Enters the World: A People's History of the Progressive Era and World War I,* 8 vols. (New York: McGraw-Hill, 1985), vol. 7; John A. Thompson, *Reformers and War: American Progressive Publicists and the First World War* (Cambridge: Cambridge University Press, 1987); Walter I. Trattner, "Progressivism and World War I: A Re-appraisal," *Mid-America* 44 (July 1962): 131–45; Richard L. Watson, Jr., *The Development of National Power: The United States, 1900–1919* (Boston: Houghton Mifflin, 1976); Nancy K. Bristow, "Creating Crusaders: The Commission on Training Camp Activities and the Pursuit of the Progressive Social Vision During World War One" (Ph.D. diss., University of California, Berkeley, 1989); Ernest A. McKay, *Against Wilson and War, 1914–1917* (Malabar, FL: Krieger, 1996). Ronald Schaffer, *America in the Great War: The Rise of the War Welfare State* (New York: Oxford University Press, 1991), presents the most systematic and insightful analysis of reform and war for this period; he also provides a thorough bibliography on World War I in *The United States in World War I: A Selected Bibliography* (Santa Barbara, CA: Clio Press, 1978). Kendrick A. Clements, *The Presidency of Woodrow Wilson* (Lawrence: University Press of Kansas, 1992), chap. 8, considers both reform and antireform impulses of World War I. John J. Broesamle, *Reform and Reaction in Twentieth Century American Politics* (New York: Greenwood Press, 1990), pp. 256–68, 289–96, perceptively examines war and reform from a broad base. In my analysis, only quotations, particularly important information, or other sources will be cited.

3. On Wilson and the Progressive synthesis, see chapter 2.

4. For background to the National Defense Act of 1916, see chapter 4; many of the sources cited relate to Progressive reform, foreign policy, and preparedness.

5. For the background to the Wilson administration and naval growth, see chapter 3.

6. Wood, Secretary of War Henry L. Stimson, and army reform are treated at length in chapter 4.

7. U.S. Congress, House, Committee on Military Affairs *Hearings, to Increase the Efficiency of the Military Establishment of the United States,* 64th Cong., 1st sess., 1916, pp. 115–24, 743–45; U.S. Congress, Senate, Committee on Military Affairs, *Hearings, Preparedness for National Defense,* 64th Cong., 1st sess., 1916, p. 993; "Statement of Martin Gillen," to Grosvenor B. Clarkson, 12/12/20, "Statements of Men in War Work," 1920–1922, Bernard M. Baruch Papers, Princeton University, Princeton, NJ; Hermann Hagedorn, *Leonard Wood: A Biography,* 2 vols. (New York: Harper, 1931); Ralph Barton Perry, *The Plattsburg Movement* (New York: E. P. Dutton, 1921); John Garry Clifford, *The Citizen Soldier: The Plattsburg Training Camp Movement, 1913–1920* (Lexington: University Press of Kentucky, 1972); and Frederick Palmer, *Newton D. Baker: America at War,* 2 vols. (New York: Dodd, Mead, 1931), 1: 46–47.

8. A bibliographic note and a selected list of the more significant works on the American peace movement, particularly in its modern phase, is included in volume 3 (forthcoming) of this series in an analysis of the Special Senate Committee Investigating the Munitions Industry, chaired by Sen. Gerald P. Nye.

9. Finnegan, *Specter of a Dragon,* p. 192. This is a major theme of the author's study.

10. Ibid., p. 191.

11. I have dealt at length with the subject of America's dual military heritage throughout volume 1 of this series, *Beating Plowshares into Swords: The Political Economy of American Warfare, 1606–1865* (Lawrence: University Press of Kansas, 1996); consult the index. The modernization of the army and navy in the late nineteenth and early twentieth centuries is analyzed in chapters 3 and 4 of this volume. The background to and the significance of the Selective Service Act of May 1917 is treated in depth by Chambers, *To Raise an Army*—a summary of his analysis is presented in "Conscripting for Colossus: The Progressive Era and the Origin of the Modern Draft in the United States in World War I," in *The Military in America: From the Colonial Era to the Present,* ed. Peter Karsten, pp. 297–311, rev. ed. (New York: Free Press, 1986)—and by Russell F. Weigley, *Towards An American Army: Military Thought from Washington to Marshall* (New York: Columbia University Press, 1962), pp. 177–241. Chambers covers thoroughly the numerous sources on the subject.

12. The rudimentary proposals for industrial mobilization and the response of the opponents of preparedness are covered to some degree in the preceding sources. In chapter 7, the subject will be treated in more detail.

13. These figures are from F. Carrington Weems, *America and Munitions: The Work of Messrs. J. P. Morgan & Co. in the World War,* 2 vols. (New York: privately printed, 1923), pp. 268–72, 345–46. Since the pagination for these volumes is continuous, future citations will be without reference to the volume. Weems was related by marriage to Edward R. Stettinius, head of the Morgan purchasing division for the Allies, and served as personal assistant to the latter throughout most of the war years. After hostilities, he cataloged the Export Department's documents and wrote what became the two-volume study for the benefit of J. P. Morgan & Co. Only six copies were printed. A copy is now available in the Pierpont Morgan Library in New York, which microfilmed it. These volumes are indispensable for studying the operations of J. P. Morgan & Co. from 1914 into 1917 and beyond in terms of purchasing, disbursing, and financing. The work must be treated with caution, however, because it draws a picture of a high-minded financial banking house working for years under killing pressure in a nearly flawless fashion and without concern for its own gain. Whole sections of relevant history are left out or written in such an opaque manner (rather typical of official administrative history) as to be nearly unintelligible. Nonetheless, if the volumes are approached with information, insight, and patience, they yield a great deal of crucial information unavailable elsewhere. The Senate Special Committee Investigating the Munitions Industry (chaired by Gerald P. Nye [R-ND], hereafter the Nye Committee) covered some of the same ground as Weems's volumes and provides one way of checking on the accuracy and coverage of Weems's work. J. P. Morgan & Co. did not make these volumes available to the Nye Committee. Had it done so, the committee would have had a much fuller and better picture of World War I economic developments, and so too would the public, because Nye and his colleagues undoubtedly would have published Weems's study. Some of the

figures on Morgan purchasing for the Allies between 1915 and 1917 and total U.S. trade with the Allies are verified in the Nye Committee work: U.S. Congress, Senate, Special Committee Investigating the Munitions Industry, *Munitions Industry,* Report no. 944, part 6, 74th Cong., 2d sess., 1936, p. 9, and *Hearings, Munitions Industry,* part 26, 74th Cong., 2d sess., 1936, pp. 7929–40 (hereafter Nye Committee, Report, and Nye Committee, *Hearings*). Accurate figures and information on such basic matters as trade, financing, and so forth are not easy to acquire and are often either contradictory within the same source, vary from source to source, or are exceptionally difficult to calculate in terms of the presentation. I have attempted to check at least two sources before reporting figures, but in some instances that has not been possible.

14. Weems, *America and Munitions,* p. 268.

15. Accounts of Allied buying in the United States in 1914 are limited and come mostly from Morgan sources. See ibid, pp. 7–26; "Memorandum, Regarding Activities of J. P. Morgan & Co., as purchasing agents for the British and French Governments," 4/17/22, "Allied Purchases," General File, 1921–37, Planning Branch (PB), Assistant Secretary of War (ASW), Office of the Secretary of War (OSW), RG 107, National Archives, Washington, DC—this memorandum came from Stettinius at the request of the assistant secretary of war and was probably written by Weems (see Wainwright to Stettinius, 12/10/21, and other correspondence, "Allied Purchases," General File 1921–37, PB, ASW, OSW); "Memorandum Regarding Commercial Agency Agreement Between British and French governments and J. P. Morgan & Co.," 7/26/35, Nye Committee, *Hearings,* part 26, pp. 8092–97—this memorandum was prepared for the Nye Committee by J. P. Morgan & Co., although the committee itself did very little with the period before the Morgan Commercial Agency Contract of 1915; and "Statement of Martin Gillen," to Clarkson, "Statements of Men in War Work," 1920–1922, Baruch Papers.

16. Weems, *America and Munitions,* pp. 27–39 and appendix 1; Nye Committee, *Hearings,* part 25, pp. 7482–86, 7675–77, and part 26, pp. 7796–7811, 8092–99; and Nye Committee, Report 944, part 6, pp. 66–70.

17. Weems, *America and Munitions,* pp. 39–46 and appendix 2; Nye Committee, *Hearings,* part 26, pp. 7805–10; and Nye Committee, Report 944, part 6, pp. 69–70.

18. Weems, *America and Munitions,* pp. 37, 40.

19. The thrust of the Weems volumes, *America and Munitions,* involves many of the points just discussed. The Nye Committee also constantly addresses the issue throughout its hearings and reports dealing with J. P. Morgan & Co. during the so-called neutrality years. John Douglas Forbes, *J. P. Morgan, Jr., 1867–1943* (Charlottesville: University Press of Virginia, 1981), casts some light on Morgan's personal relations with the British. Roberta A. Dayer, "Strange Bedfellows: J. P. Morgan & Co., Whitehall and the Wilson Administration During World War I," *Business History* 18 (July 1976): 128–30, focuses on why Britain selected Morgan.

20. Nye Committee, *Hearings,* part 25, pp. 7581–83, 7683–89, 7691–7714, and part 26, 7799–7804, 8092–98. The full Nye Committee *Hearings,* parts 25–35, and Report 944, parts 5 and 6, involving J. P. Morgan & Co., must be read in order to understand how much the committee was able to grasp of wartime economics, despite the extremely complex nature of the subject and the intense resistance, obstruction, and obfuscation of the Morgan partners. Dayer, "Strange Bedfellows," pp. 141–42, believes that the Nye Committee was thrown off on the issue of the U.S. government's

payment of the so-called Demand Loan after April 1917. As is indicated below (and also in n. 52), that is not exactly the case. Regrettably, Report 944, parts 5 and 6, which deal with American-British relations in the neutrality years, 1914–1917, were written under extreme pressure when Congress ended the committee's funding. Hence, these critically important reports are less complete, more inconsistent and contradictory, and less accomplished than the earlier ones. The same is true for Report 944, part 7. The Nye Committee is analyzed in depth, with these subjects treated in a larger context, in volume 3 (forthcoming) of this series.

For the official Morgan statement, and figures on profits from services performed for the Allies from 1915 to 1917 and beyond, see Weems, *America and Munitions,* pp. 361–82 and appendices 1, 2, 22, 24, 25, 26, 27, and 28. Weems, pp. 378–79, asserts that most Morgan profit from 1915 to 1917 came from the Export Department, and continues, "For the other activities which had to do with the flotation of loans, sales of securities, exchange operations, etc., it made only the ordinary banking charges and in very many instances, like that of the Anglo-French Loan, performed these duties without any charge whatsoever. No attempt, therefore, has been made to review these items of income in any detail." Dayer, "Strange Bedfellows," claims that Morgan "benefitted enormously in terms of pure financial profit from the war" (p. 143) yet offers no substantiation. The Nye Committee, Report 944, part 5, p. 75, says that J. P. Morgan's wartime "banking commissions were substantial" from services for the Allies but offers no further analysis or proof concerning the matter. The committee pursued profits only for the Export Department. However, some measure of the profit possibilities in World War I financing are indicated by the so-called de Rothchild Freres loan to France for a total of $44 million in June 1915. The loan was eventually liquidated by selling French-owned American railroad securities on this transaction. The Nye Committee calculated that J. P. Morgan & Co. and its branches realized almost $.5 million in profits on commission and underwriting fees. On a similar transaction, also involving railroad bonds with a "nominal value of $14,118,529 at par of exchange," Morgan made $273,192.74 (see Report 944, part 6, pp. 99–101).

J. P. Morgan & Co.'s operations, affiliates, alliances, and the like as the nation's dominant financial bank are explored in numerous works, including Vincent P. Carosso, *Investment Banking in America: A History* (Cambridge: Harvard University Press, 1970), Carosso, *More Than a Century of Investment Banking: The Kidder, Peabody & Co. Story* (New York: McGraw-Hill, 1979); Carosso, *The Morgans: Private International Bankers, 1854–1913* (Cambridge: Harvard University Press, 1987); Ron Charnow, *The House of Morgan: An American Banking Dynasty and the Rise of Modern Finance* (New York: Atlantic Monthly Press, 1990); Mark S. Mizruchi, *The American Corporate Network, 1904–1974* (Beverly Hills, CA: Sage Publications, 1982); Ferdinand Lundberg, *The Rich and the Super Rich: A Study in the Power of Money Today* (New York: Lyle Stuart, 1968); and Victor Perlo, *The Empire of High Finance* (New York: International Publishers, 1957). One of the very best sources on this subject is the multivolume series published under the aegis of the Temporary National Economic Committee.

21. This is the principal point of Dayer, "Strange Bedfellows," pp. 127–51.

22. For the larger thrust of twentieth-century American foreign policy, I am referring to the so-called Wisconsin school of diplomatic history. I have referred to and commented upon this interpretation in my earlier work: *The Military-Industrial Complex: A Historical Perspective* (New York: Praeger, 1980), pp. 15–16, and p. 21, n. 16.

An excellent analysis of American international ambitions, World War I, and the role of the House of Morgan is presented by John Milton Cooper, Jr., "The Command of Gold Reversed: American Loans to Britain, 1915–1917," *Pacific Historical Review* 45 (May 1976): 209–30. Another fine article that addresses the issue from an even broader base is Harry N. Scheiber, "World War I as Entrepreneurial Opportunity: Willard Straight and the American International Corporation," *Political Science Quarterly* 84 (September 1969): 486–511. David Kennedy, *Over Here: The First World War and American Society* (New York: Oxford University Press, 1980), chap. 6, maintains, in counterdistinction to the New Left historians, that although World War I had made the United States the world's dominant economic power, the nation was not ready and willing to take on the responsibilities of that position until World War II. Gerd Hardach, *The First World War, 1914–1918* (Berkeley: University of California Press, 1977), analyzes the operations of the international economy before, during, and after World War I, including the comparative position of the United States.

23. Progressive reforms as they relate to economic mobilization for war will be highlighted in the chapters that follow on the economics of World War I.

24. Nye Committee, *Hearings,* part 25, pp. 7482–85.

25. Nye Committee, *Hearings,* part 26, p. 8098. The figures are based on information provided by the Nye Committee. Most of the data, sometimes in different forms, is available in Weems, *America and Munitions.* I prefer the Nye Committee source because it reviewed the information provided by the Morgan partners and allowed them to go over and correct any errors. If a source other than the Nye Committee is used or if there is a significant difference between the committee and Weems, the difference will be noted.

26. Nye Committee, *Hearings,* part 25, exhibit 2080, pp. 7691–7714, is the most valuable source for analyzing Morgan contracting patterns. It summarizes total contracts with each firm, the value of the contracts when placed and when delivered, and Morgan interests and financing involving the contractors. Other exhibits have the same or very similar information but in a form much less refined and, hence, much more difficult to use. In this regard see pp. 7593–95, and part 26, pp. 7941–8090 and 7811–13, 7933–40, 8092–97, 8102–03.

27. Nye Committee, *Hearings,* part 26, pp. 7783–95, 7929–40. The figures for J. P. Morgan & Co. are based on existing contracts rather than actual shipment and, therefore, distort to some degree what occurred. The figures that the Nye Committee gathered with the assistance of the Bureau of Foreign and Domestic Commerce, Department of Commerce, on overall U.S. trade between 1913 and 1917 are somewhat lower than those in the U.S. Bureau of the Census, *Historical Statistics of the United States* (Washington, DC: U.S. Government Printing Office, 1975), 2: 864. Nonetheless, I have used the Nye Committee's figures in order to keep the analysis consistent.

28. John Douglas Forbes, *Stettinius, Sr.: Portrait of a Morgan Partner* (Charlottesville: University Press of Virginia, 1974), pp. 9–28, 36–37, 44–47, and Weems, *America and Munitions,* appendix 3.

29. There is very little information about the Export Department in general and little that has not come from within J. P. Morgan & Co. or those close to or uncritical of it. Nye and his colleagues did little with the day-to-day operations of the Export Department. The best and most extensive account is found in Weems, *America and*

*Munitions.* The appendixes of these volumes often contain especially valuable information. Forbes, *Stettinius,* chap. 6, provides additional information based on sources unavailable to others. (Weems wrote a thirty-six-page account of Stettinius's role in the Export Department that Forbes draws upon but that the Weems family would not make available to me.) The memorandums of Stettinius to the assistant secretary of war in 1922 and from J. P. Morgan & Co. to the Nye Committee in 1935, as cited in n. 15, are also helpful. B. C. Forbes, "The Biggest Buyer in the World," *American Magazine,* September 1917, pp. 15–17, 76–82, provides some additional insight as does Almon R. Wright, "Arsenal of Democracy, 1917–1918" (manuscript, [circa] 1945), pp. 1–15, copy in Baruch Papers.

A British scholar casts new light on the operations of the Export Department: Kathleen Burk, *Britain, America and the Sinews of War, 1914–1918* (Boston: George Allen and Unwin, 1985). Burk explains that the British government was displeased with the Export Department's handling of transportation, evaluating prospective contractors, and following up and expediting production. Britain took corrective action to deal with these deficiencies. The author has worked in American archives, but she draws principally on British sources. This approach gives a new perspective on the Export Department, but it is limited by the fact that Burk works mostly on a policy level rather than dealing at any length with the details of British purchasing and American production for Britain. Burk's articles on and related to this subject are included in her bibliography. See also her edited volume, *War and the State: The Transformation of British Government, 1914–1919* (London: George Allen and Unwin, 1982). See also W. G. Lyddon, *British War Missions to the United States, 1914–1918* (London: Oxford University Press, 1938), and E. Victor Morgan, *Studies in British Financial Policy, 1914–25* (London: Macmillan, 1952). The discussion and analysis of the Export Department is based on these sources. Any exceptions will be noted and preceding sources recited if emphasis is required.

30. For additional information on creating a munitions industry in the United States from 1914 to 1917, see Stettinius to Baker, 5/4/18, Correspondence File, Jan.–July, 1918–S, Newton D. Baker Papers, Library of Congress, Washington, DC; "Statement of H. P. Ingels," 12/30/20, Clarkson, "Statements of Men in War Work," 1920–1922; "Final Report upon Condition of the Forgings, Ordnance, Small Arms and Small Arms Ammunition Industries. . . . War Industries Board," World War I Records, part 2, vol. 7, all in Baruch Papers; *Final Report of the Chairman of the United States War Industries Board to the President of the United States, February, 1919* [author, Hugh S. Johnson], Nye Committee, Senate Committee Print no. 3, 74th Cong., 1st sess., 1935, pp. 531–42, 882–96 (hereafter, *Final Report, WIB–Johnson*); Bernard M. Baruch, *American Industry in the War: A Report of the War Industries Board* (Washington, DC: U.S. Government Printing Office, 1921), pp. 174–80, 262–64; and Grosvenor B. Clarkson, *Industrial America in the World War: The Strategy Behind the Line, 1917–1918* (Boston: Houghton Mifflin, 1923), pp. 397–411.

31. The information is based on a Nye Committee document that summarizes J. P. Morgan & Co. contracts by firm, product, and unadjusted and adjusted compensation (*Hearings,* part 25, pp. 7691–7714).

32. In Table 6.1 I have used David Bunting's *Statistical View of the Trusts* (Westport, CT: Greenwood Press, 1974) for identifying the 100 largest industrial and mining corporations for any year between 1896 and 1905. The top four that I list also appear

in the largest 100 category set forth by Alfred D. Chandler, Jr., *The Visible Hand: The Managerial Revolution in American Business* (Cambridge: Belknap Press, 1977), pp. 503–12. The seventh and tenth largest contractors for the Allies through the services of J. P. Morgan & Co. were Baldwin Locomotive Works and Midvale Steel & Ordnance Co. They did not appear under that name on Bunting's list but ranked seventy-fifth and sixth on Chandler's classifications for 1917. For Stettinius's procurement principles, see "Memorandum Regarding Activities of J. P. Morgan & Co. as purchasing agents for the British and French Governments," 4/17/22, "Allied Purchases," General File, 1921–1937, PB, ASW, OSW.

33. Weems, *America and Munitions,* p. 221. (The statistics in the above paragraph are from chapter 10 of this volume.)

34. The figures came from "Memorandum Regarding Activities of J. P. Morgan & Co. as purchasing agents for the British and French Governments," 4/17/22, "Allied Purchases," General File, 1921–1937, PB, ASW, OSW; Weems, *America and Munitions,* chap. 20; and Forbes, *Stettinius,* pp. 62–63.

35. The Morgan partners' stance is repeated throughout the hearings. For one of the best examples, see Nye Committee, *Hearings,* part 26, pp. 7795–7804. See also Nye Committee, *Hearings,* part 25, p. 7484, and Nye Committee, Report 944, part 6, pp. 66–69. Members of the Nye Committee and staff rather regularly tripped up the Morgan partners in their attempts to disassociate completely purchasing from financing. In this regard, see Nye Committee, *Hearings,* part 25, pp. 7627–34, and Nye Committee, Report 944, part 6, p. 42. Weems, *America and Munitions,* pp. 267–68, also denies once that J. P. Morgan & Co.'s buying and financing were tied one to another. Yet the entire thrust of his volumes contradicts this statement, and the author reverses himself on the same page to state that the two functions are inseparable. The Morgan partners were especially anxious to prove that winning the Commercial Agency Contract was not tied to financing in the belief that that fact would give greater legitimacy, even morality, to the buying for the Allies. In that light, the partners would be taking up a function they were not experts at and did not want but accepted for the sake of the nation and the Allies. Technically, of course, nothing in the contract or agreement with Britain or France for procuring goods included commitments for financing. But the understandings were there and even in print.

36. Nye Committee, Report 944, part 6, pp. 13–15. Nye Committee, part 5, pp. 59–77, also covers the financing of the Allies. These reports are based on Nye Committee, *Hearings,* parts 25–35. Whenever possible, I have taken direct quotations from the reports instead of the hearings or exhibits to the hearings since the former are more available and easier to use. Any document or part of it appearing in the reports is included in its entirety either in the text of the hearings or in the exhibits to them.

The Nye Committee hearings on the neutrality years, which involved principally the Morgan partners and their governmental, financial, and industrial relations and contacts at home and abroad, and particularly the exhibits to these hearings, are an especially rich document depository that has been largely untapped. The committee staff gathered the material, collated, and analyzed some of it but obviously never had an opportunity to put together a fully coherent and complete digest and summary of its work. Included in these parts of the hearings are a full breakdown of the Morgan partners and their economic affiliations; data and analysis of the various accounts J. P. Morgan & Co. maintained for the Allies; complete data on all or most contracting done for the Allies; a full accounting on most of the myriad forms of financing Morgan and its associated houses carried out for the Allies, including total lists of syndicate members and their subscribers, demand-loan participants, acceptances, and so forth; a copy of the questionnaire the Nye Committee sent to select contractors for the Allies and their responses and consolidated information based on them; extensive communications among members of the War Industries Board and related agencies concerning overseas operations; and thousands of cables, letters, documents, and other materials of J. P. Morgan & Co. involving the Export Department and Allied financing, which are available nowhere else since the company destroyed its files around 1959 when the merger with Guaranty Trust took place. In addition, of course, the Nye Committee hearings record the careful, informed, and often incisive examination of key witnesses about crucial events—an examination either never before undertaken or incompetently handled. (Another enormously helpful tool for the scholar is the Nye Committee's 1,000-page-plus full and competent index of the thirty-nine volumes of hearing and exhibits and the nine often lengthy reports. The index constitutes volume 40 of the committee's published work.) Much of this information is still in a very rough form, requiring years of work involving auditors, accountants, and experts in international finance in order fully to understand what occurred, if that is possible. In short, here is a researcher's gold mine that remains still today largely untouched or only selectively used. I have had neither the time nor the expertise to do the subject justice. Perhaps other scholars will someday thoroughly research and analyze this material.

37. Nye Committee, Report 944, part 6, pp. 9–29, 121 (quotation, p. 21), and Dayer, "Strange Bedfellows," p. 129, p. 144, n. 9. See also Weems, *America and Munitions,* pp. 267–94. The subject is briefly but authoritatively covered in Link, *Wilson, Struggle for Neutrality,* pp. 62–64, 131–36. It is difficult to get two sources to agree exactly and clearly on what would seem to be a straightforward matter of financing for the Allies. The Nye Committee presents figures in the most accessible way. For other sources, which involve much greater difficulty in usage, see Alexander D. Noyes, *The War Period of American Finance, 1908–1925* (New York: G. P. Putnam's Sons, 1926), pp. 92–161, and Cleona Lewis, *America's Stake in International Investments* (Washington, DC: Brookings Institution, 1938), pp. 114–30, 351–75. Burk, *Britain, America, and Sinews,* also deals extensively with financing throughout her volume and adds many fine insights and valuable information to the subject. Her contribution is less than it could have been because her monograph is a narrative more than an analysis of developments.

38. Weems, *America and Munitions,* pp. 267–75, 329–30, and Nye Committee, Report 944, part 6, p. 125. Who ultimately paid for the British Demand Loan after the United States entered the war is still a matter of controversy and uncertainty. Weems, *America and Munitions,* appendix 19, has graphed the course of the British Demand Loan from January 1915 to July 1919.

39. Nye Committee, Report 944, part 6, p. 44.

40. The analysis of Allied financing from late 1914 to October 1915 is based on Nye Committee, Report 944, part 5, p. 73, and part 6, pp. 31–64, 121; Nye Committee, *Hearings,* part 26, pp. 7792–93 (parts 25–35 cover financing for the Allies in its entirety); Link, *Wilson, Struggle for Neutrality,* pp. 616–25; and Weems, *America and Munitions,* pp. 279–308. For additional information on the publicly floated Allied loans and particularly their distribution patterns, see Richard W. Van Alstyne, "Private

Loans to the Allies, 1914–1916," *Pacific Historical Review* 2 (1933): 180–93. Van Alstyne says that inquiries he made to J. P. Morgan and other large banks revealed that no records had been kept on the details of publicly floated loans for the Allies, but this is actually not the case (see note 36).

41. The discussion and analysis of the 1916 rifle crisis is based on Nye Committee, *Hearings,* part 25, pp. 7557–7643, 7670–7779, and Nye Committee, Report 944, part 6, pp. 79–98. A somewhat different and truncated version of this situation is related in Weems, *America and Munitions,* pp. 194–202.

42. Nye Committee, *Hearings,* part 25, pp. 7643–54, 7770–81. After the United States entered the war, the Wilson administration bought the rifle companies from Britain to meet its own needs. See Burk, *Britain, America and Sinews,* p. 118.

43. Nye Committee, *Hearings,* part 27, pp. 8185–90, and part 36, p. 11907.

44. The analysis of J. P. Morgan & Co. and Allied financing between November 1916 and April 1917 is based on Nye Committee, Report 944, part 5, pp. 59–77, and part 6, pp. 31–64, 99–113, 121–59 (the two reports are based on Nye Committee, *Hearings,* parts 25–35); Link, *Wilson: Confusions and Crises,* p. 148, and *Wilson: Campaigns for Progressivism and Peace,* pp. 178–84, 200–206, 379–82; Cooper, "Command of Gold Reversed," pp. 209–30; Dayer, "Strange Bedfellows," pp. 127–51; Scheiber, "World War I as Entrepreneurial Opportunity," pp. 486–511; Kennedy, *Over Here,* chap. 6; and Burk, *Britain, America and Sinews.* Link, Cooper, Dayer, and Kennedy are especially valuable because they are based on British and American sources. Burk provides the most extensive account from the British side. Weems, *America and Munitions,* is typically weak in these areas. Only quotations, additional sources, and especially relevant material will be cited in the following notes.

45. Nye Committee, Report 944, part 6, pp. 129–30.

46. Harding to Strong, 11/16/16, as quoted in Nye Committee, Report 944, part 6, pp. 122–23.

47. Cooper, "Command of Gold Reversed," pp. 218–21, is indispensable on this topic. John Maynard Keynes was the principal analyst forcing Britain's resistive leaders to confront the nation's desperate plight; his volume, *The Economic Consequences of the Peace* (London: Macmillan, 1920), is generally enlightening in this regard (for the most direct statement on British dependence on the United States, see pp. 255–57). Recent biographies of Keynes cover the war years and the writing of *Economic Consequences* and cite other relevant studies. See Robert Skidelsky, *John Maynard Keynes,* vol. 1, *Hopes Betrayed, 1883–1920* (New York: Viking, 1986), pp. 333–53, 376–402, and D. E. Moggridge, *Maynard Keynes: An Economist's Biography* (London: Routledge, 1992), 264–87, 319–47. Britain's financial plight and humiliating dependence on the United States is the principal theme of Burk, *Britain, America and Sinews.*

48. Nye Committee, Report 944, part 5, p. 73, and part 6, pp. 155–56. Exhibit 3364, Nye Committee, *Hearings,* part 30, p. 9755, gives monthly figures on Allied private indebtedness from 12/1/14 to 11/1/20. For 4/1917, the figure is just short of $2.7 billion. Exhibit 2776, Nye Committee, *Hearings,* part 29, p. 9205, adds up the indebtedness of Great Britain (including the Demand Loan), France, Russia, and Italy, but not Canada, to almost $2.257 billion.

49. The Nye Committee summary is presented in Report 944, part 6, pp. 158–59. Its line of reasoning with documentation and edited testimony is set forth on pp. 121–58.

50. Copper, "Command of Gold Reversed," p. 229–30, argues that Great Britain's economic dependence on the United States, not vice versa, was key to America's entering the war. This seems to be much too compartmentalized a view of British-American relations and the international operations of power. America's tie to the Allies from the outset of hostilities involved circumstances and choice, including American ambitions for world dominance, as Cooper himself notes. If the United States generally viewed its world role, as I believe is the case, as one of first working with Britain as the overwhelmingly preeminent imperialist power and of later subordinating the British to American power, then America's need to ensure an Allied victory is not easily divisible into matters of strength and dependence when assessing motivation. Both Great Britain and the United States had strengths and characteristics that the other wanted and needed: Britain relied on America's sheer economic wealth; the latter wanted the former's global reach and all that it involved. For example, the Morgan partners argued that American investors did not want Britain's worldwide securities because, although they trusted the British to run an economic empire, they believed the United States lacked the necessary experience for doing so should that become necessary (Nye Committee, Report 944, part 6, pp. 152–53). The war, after all, had not made Britain helpless and hopeless overnight. These observations are in no way intended to distract from the overall quality of Cooper's first-rate article. Burk, *Britain, America and Sinews,* pp. 221–25, presents an approach similar to mine but from the British point of view.

51. The Nye Committee touched upon, but never explored in depth, the fact that the securities provided as collateral by Britain for some of the loans were of questionable value. Moreover, if even the sound American securities were suddenly dumped in large numbers on the market, and certainly if there had been an attempt to market them in tumultuous economic times—which a defeat of Britain would no doubt have created—their worth would have been greatly diminished, causing grave injury to the American economy. On these points, see Nye Committee, Report 944, part 6, pp. 142–57.

52. The analysis of the refinancing of the British Demand Loan is based on Dayer, "Strange Bedfellows," pp. 134–51. Dayer claims that the Nye Committee did not have the time, perhaps the expertise, to uncover the labyrinthine path that led to the United States paying off the British Demand Loan. Actually, this is not quite the case. Although the committee was studying the matter and writing its analysis of it, Congress was cutting off its funding; hence, the work was hurried and often inconsistent, piecemeal, and incomplete. In Report 944, part 5, pp. 69–70, the committee says that no public funds were used to pay off the Demand Loan, but on pp. 73–75, the committee claims that American financing after April 1917 paid for $775 million of the prewar debt. However, the references and details are quite vague so that it is difficult to determine exactly what Nye, his colleagues, and his staff had in mind. In Report 944, part 6, p. 6, the committee asserts that of the loans floated to the Allies after American entry into the war, $650 million was used to pay off private debt holders (without further details provided) and an additional sum for Russian debt held by Americans. On p. 73 of that same report, the figure was dropped to $600 million. On pp. 144 and 149–50, the committee again raises the issue of the Demand Loan and in an uncertain and unfocused discussion concludes that, despite Morgan's anticipation, the Demand Loan was not paid by publicly floated American governmental loans after 1917. The Nye Committee presents a rushed and confused rendition of American financing and the Demand Loan rather than a simple and clear account. Kennedy, *Over Here,* maintains that the

United States never paid off the Demand Loan and appears unaware of the work of Dayer and not fully conversant with the Nye Committee work. Dayer, on her part, begins by asserting that Washington paid off all private debt contracted before April 1917, later falls back to covering just the Demand Loan, and ends the analysis appearing to be lost in the maze of complexities and details the subject involves. Burk, *Britain, America, and Sinews,* provides information on the complex conditions imposed by the United States for using financial advances to make payments on the Demand Loan. The author's information is extremely valuable, but her narrative leaves many questions unanswered and critically important material undeveloped. The $650 million figure used in the text as the amount of Washington loans after April 1917 applied to debt is not meant to include the Demand Loan and comes from the Nye Committee, Report 944, part 6, pp. 6–7, 161, 167. A Morgan witness, in a confusing presentation, set the figure at around $300 million (*Hearings,* part 26, p. 7811). The fullest analysis of the general financing policy of the United States involving its Allies after April 1917 is presented in the Nye Committee, Report 944, part 6, pp. 161–84. My observations on the Allied use of loans for supporting currency and neutral buying and the responses of the Wilson administration to these realities are based on this source.

The assistant secretary of the treasury who became a Morgan partner is Russell Cornell Leffingwell. He was an attorney who was appointed to a partnership in June 1923. Leffingwell joined the Treasury Department in May 1917 without prior experience with or knowledge about international finance. Nonetheless, he was soon advising McAdoo to adopt flexible policies that would give the Allies maximum latitude in using the American loans. He resigned his post as assistant secretary of the treasury in June 1920. Leffingwell and his fellow former assistant secretary of the treasury, Albert Rathbone, sounded more like witnesses for J. P. Morgan & Co. before the Nye Committee than as witnesses for the American government. Both men were exceptionally vehement and vocal in defending wartime policies under the justification that anything and everything had to be subordinated to winning the war. On Leffingwell and Rathbone, see Nye Committee, Report 944, part 6, pp. 161–84, and Forbes, *Morgan,* p. 128.

The Nye Committee, Report 944, part 6, pp. 149, 153, places the British Demand Loan at $345 million but is vague or varying concerning the exact date. Both Dayer and Weems, *America and Munitions,* pp. 329–30, give the $400 million figure. I have used both in the text out of the realization that the apparent contradiction is resolvable in terms of exact dates. Within a matter of months, weeks, or even days, the Demand Loan could easily increase by $55 million. Weems relates that the British activity pushed the Demand Loan to its peak of $437 million on April 25, 1917. He says that it was thereafter reduced by U.S. Treasury advances, sale of securities, shipment of gold, and issuance of Treasury bills. He claims that the Demand Loan was down to $217 million on January 31, 1918, and then drops the subject, although in an appendix he has plotted the course of the Demand Loan to July 24, 1919 (appendix 19). Concerning proposals for Washington's paying off the entire loan, Weems goes no further than to state that a proposal for Washington to liquidate the debt "fell through for some reason." J. P. Morgan & Co. and Britain explain that the Demand Loan was about $345 million early in April 1917, rose to nearly $400 million in May 1917, and was fully paid off (exactly when is left unspecified), without U.S. government aid (see Nye Committee, *Hearings,* part 29, pp. 9234–64. Exactly how much of the outstanding Allied debt of $2.7 billion owed to American citizens in April 1917 (a sizable portion of which involved publicly floated securities) was covered by Washington financing after April 1917 is by no means certain and, to my knowledge, has never been authoritatively settled. Weems generally covers the matter in chapter 16, but his treatment of it is dense and opaque to the point of being impenetrable. The basic point is that much of the fundamental information on Allied financing in America from 1914 into 1917 and the liquidation of that debt is simply unavailable. This is a critically important subject that cries out for attention. Whether private and public records exist to research and analyze the topic with some authority I do not know. However, because such a study does not exist and those that are available, along with the primary documentation relating to the subject, are so incomplete, inconsistent, and contradictory, my own analysis by necessity also suffers.

53. Weems, *America and Munitions,* p. 242. Copies of the letters are available in appendix 10.

54. Ibid., chapter 11, is the only available account that has any details about the J. P. Morgan & Co. activities after the United States entered the war and about the way in which the Export Department was ultimately terminated.

55. A copy of the Stettinius letter, dated 5/19/17, is in the "Allied Purchases," General File, 1921–1937, PB, ASW, OSW. Weems also duplicates the letter in appendix 12, *America and Munitions* (see also pp. 246–47).

56. These matters will be treated in detail in the chapters that follow. For now it is enough to say that Summers was a key adviser to Baruch, and Catchings held an important post in the Council of National Defense–National Defense Advisory Commission structure and played a leading role in forcing the Wilson administration to reorganize the War Industries Board early in 1918. To reverse matters, see n. 52 on a Wilson administration official who appears to have used his wartime experience to gain a partnership in J. P. Morgan & Co.

57. Lamont's qualities became clear during the Nye Committee hearings. He was far and away the most aggressive, evasive, and contentious of the Morgan partners who testified. At one point, Stephen Rauschenbush, apparently aiming his remarks primarily at Lamont, stated: "You seem to think that in every question we ask that we are trying to hold somebody to blame, but we are trying to find out the mechanism or the function [of J. P. Morgan & Co.'s buying and financing activities for the Allies]" (Nye Committee, *Hearings,* part 27, p. 8190). J. P. Morgan, Jr., in contrast, was a much more forthright and straightforward witness. The Nye Committee staff often sought to draw him out, as others, especially Lamont, constantly jumped in either to answer questions, make statements, or interrupt Morgan's response, obviously intending to protect the firm from the candor of its namesake. Lamont's qualities are also revealed in his biography of Davison, *Henry P. Davison, the Record of a Useful Life* (New York: Harper and Brothers, 1933). See also a biography by Lamont's grandson, Edward M. Lamont, *The Ambassador from Wall Street: The Story of Thomas W. Lamont, J. P. Morgan's Chief Executive* (Lanham, MD: Madison Books, 1994).

58. Dayer, "Strange Bedfellows," pp. 127, 143, and n. 5. The author wants to include government appointments for Dwight D. Morrow and Stettinius as well as Lamont as an indication of the House of Morgan's influence. As was pointed out, at least for Stettinius, the position in the War Department was more ceremonial than substantial.

## CHAPTER SEVEN. ECONOMIC MOBILIZATION, 1914–1916

1. I am drawing on Robert H. Wiebe, *Businessmen and Reform: A Study of the Progressive Movement* (Cambridge: Harvard University Press, 1962), and Wiebe, *The Search for Order, 1877–1920* (New York: Hill and Wang, 1967); Gabriel Kolko, *The Triumph of Conservatism: A Reinterpretation of American History, 1900–1916* (New York: Free Press, 1963); James Weinstein, *The Corporate Ideal in the Liberal State, 1900–1918* (Boston: Beacon Press, 1968); and James Weinstein and David W. Eakins, eds., *For a New America: Essays in History and Politics from Studies on the Left, 1959–1967* (New York: Random House, 1970), especially Martin J. Sklar, "Woodrow Wilson and the Political Economy of Modern United States Liberalism," pp. 46–100; and Jerry Israel, ed., *Building the Organizational Society: Essays on Associational Activities in Modern America* (New York: Free Press, 1972), particularly David W. Eakins, "The Origins of Corporate Liberal Policy Research, 1916–1922: The Political-Economic Expert and the Decline of Public Debate," pp. 163–79. See also Guy Alchon, *The Invisible Hand of Planning: Capitalism, Social Science, and the State in the 1920s* (Princeton, NJ: Princeton University Press, 1985); Donald T. Critchlow, *The Brookings Institution, 1916–1952* (DeKalb: Northern Illinois University Press, 1985); and Ellen C. Lagemann, *The Politics of Knowledge: The Carnegie Corporation, Philanthropy, and Public Policy* (Middletown: Wesleyan University Press, 1989). Harold C. Syrett, "The Business Press and American Neutrality, 1914–1917," *Mississippi Valley Historical Review* 32 (September 1945): 215–29, is helpful in terms of more limited business views on the war.

2. Frank A. Vanderlip, "The Size of the Job," in *Readings in the Economics of War*, ed. J. Maurice Clark, Walton H. Hamilton, and Harold G. Moulton (Chicago: University of Chicago Press, 1918), p. 173.

3. The analysis of the Chamber of Commerce is based on Galen Reid Fisher, "The Chamber of Commerce of the United States and the Laissez-Faire Rationale, 1912–1919" (Ph.D. diss., University of California, Berkeley, 1960); Harwood Lawrence Childs, *Labor and Capital in National Politics* (Columbus: Ohio State University Press, 1930); Richard H. Werking, "Bureaucrats, Businessmen, and Foreign Trade: The Origins of the United States Chamber of Commerce," *Business History* Review 52 (Autumn 1978): 321–41; and Wiebe, *Businessmen and Reform*. (Several of Wiebe's articles preceding publication of the book are also helpful: "Business Disunity and the Progressive Movement, 1901–1914," *Mississippi Valley Historical Review* 44 (March 1958): 664–85, and "The House of Morgan and the Executive, 1905–1913," *American Historical Review* 65 (October 1959): 49–60.) Childs's work is valuable for providing details on the organization and function of the Chamber of Commerce and statistics concerning it. Fisher is virtually a primary source since he includes extensive and lengthy quotations from numerous documents throughout his study. Werking provides fresh insights on the chamber's founding. Wiebe's comments on the chamber are brief and scattered but nonetheless very useful. Overall, the secondary work on the chamber is surprisingly sparse. I have reached many of the generalizations and analytical points—such as the Chamber of Commerce leadership's acting to adapt small- to medium-sized businesses to elite modes of political economy—on my own through these and other sources. Work on the National Association of Manufacturers is also helpful for understanding the Chamber of Commerce. See Albert K. Steigerwalt, *The National Associa-*

*tion of Manufacturers, 1895–1914: A Study in Business Leadership* (Ann Arbor: Bureau of Business Research, University of Michigan, 1964); Alfred S. Cleveland, "Some Political Aspects of Organized Industry" (Ph.D. diss., Harvard University, 1946); and John Nellis Stalker, Jr., "The National Association of Manufacturers: A Study in Ideology" (Ph.D. diss., University of Wisconsin, 1950). See also H. M. Gitelman, "Management's Crisis of Confidence and the Origin of the National Industrial Conference Board, 1914–1916," *Business History Review* 58 (Summer 1984): 153–77, and Sarah L. Watts, *Order Against Chaos: Business Culture and Labor Ideology in America, 1800–1915* (Westport, CT: Greenwood, 1991), chap. 4. Only quotations, especially important information, and primary sources will be cited in the following notes.

4. The subject of combination and competition is stressed throughout Fisher, "Chamber of Commerce," but is treated specifically in chapters 3 and 4, pp. 26–110.

5. Childs, *Politics and People,* pp. 134–46, 157–73, 197–98, and elsewhere in his volume treats extensively with the chamber's referenda and substantiates these points.

6. The term is that of Wiebe, *Businessmen and Reform,* p. 81.

7. The chamber's methods of financing itself may have subtly reinforced the discrepancy between the leadership and the led. From the outset, chamber officials recognized that the low dues necessary to draw and hold enough organizational members essential for making the chamber authentically representative could never be relied upon to finance their effort. At first, the association depended on private contributions, later a capital fund, to assist its operations. For permanent financing, it solicited "individual" and "associate" membership fees primarily from firms that already belonged to the chamber through affiliated organizations (membership through affiliated organizations was the basic form of chamber membership). Such membership produced little income because the constituent bodies paid only modest sums based on a sliding scale. Naturally, the more financially sound, even prosperous, businesses would be more likely to be individual or associate members. Technically, this did not affect power relations within the chamber since additional forms of membership were strictly a matter of fund-raising, which did not alter voting procedures in any way. However, indirect influence, prestige, and power may well have been affected by the additional monetary contributions. In 1920, out of annual revenue totaling about $1.3 million, organizational dues accounted for only a little over 6 percent of chamber income, and individual and associational dues involved just under 60 percent; in 1927, with overall revenue at $2.04 million, the figures were around 4 and 40 percent. The entire subject of Chamber of Commerce financing, and especially how it affected policymaking, is a topic deserving further study and analysis. These figures and statistics are from or based on material presented in Childs, *Politics and People,* pp. 26–29, 31–36, and Fisher, "Chamber of Commerce," pp. 462–82.

8. *Minutes, Fourth Annual Meeting of the Chamber of Commerce of the United States,* February 8–10, 1916, pp. 296–303, and *Fifth Annual Meeting,* January 31–February 2, 1917, pp. 46–67, Archives of the Chamber of Commerce of the United States, Washington, DC (hereafter Chamber of Commerce Recds.); *Nation's Business* 4, 4 (April 1916): 15, 21; and Fisher, "Chamber of Commerce," chap. 10 (quotation, p. 288). See chapter 6 for an analysis of the movement for UMT.

9. See note 8. It is important to distinguish between what Germany did prior to World War I in terms of industrial preparedness and what American perceptions or fantasies about such activities were. Some information along this line is available in

Lloyd O. Scott, *Naval Consulting Board of the United States* (Washington, DC: U.S. Government Printing Office, 1920), pp. 28–29; see also n. 39. Some indication of Coffin's outlook is evident in a speech to the Chamber of Commerce, *Minutes, Fifth Annual Meeting,* pp. 46–51, Chamber of Commerce Recds.

10. *Nation's Business,* 4, 3 (March 1916): 2, and 4, 6 (June 1916): 4.

11. Reproduced in Nye Committee, *Hearings,* part 15, p. 3661.

12. *Nation's Business,* 5, 2 (February 1917): 70 (emphasis added).

13. This theme was stressed by Waddill Catchings, who played an important role in economic mobilization for World War I. See Chamber of Commerce, *Minutes, Sixth Annual Meeting,* and *Eighth Meeting, National Council,* April 1918, pp. 88–93, Chamber of Commerce Recds., and *Nation's Business,* 5, 11(November 1917): 36–37, and 6, 5 (May 1918): 43, 82.

14. This theme is addressed throughout Fisher, "Chamber of Commerce," especially, chap. 11. See also Price to Rutter, 1/22/17, and other correspondence, file 2–A–3, Raymond B. Price, Records of Council of National Defense, RG 62, National Archives, Washington, DC (hereafter CND Recds.).

15. Goodwin to Gifford, 3/1/17, w/enc., and other correspondence and documents, file 2–A–3, Chamber of Commerce, CND Recds.; U.S. Council of National Defense, *First Annual Report of the Council of National Defense* (Washington, DC: U.S. Government Printing Office, 1917), pp. 54–55; Nye Committee, *Minutes of the Council of National Defense,* 74th Cong., 2d sess., 1936, Senate Committee Print no. 7, pp. 29–30; Chamber of Commerce, *Minutes, War Convention of American Business, Seventh Meeting, National Council,* September 1917, p. 26, and *Annual Report of the Board of Directors,* U.S. Chamber of Commerce, April 1918, pp. 5–6, Chamber of Commerce Recds.; and Fisher, "Chamber of Commerce," pp. 331–34.

16. The fullest account of the Naval Consulting Board is still Scott, *Naval Consulting Board,* which contains, besides a narrative about the organization and its functions, numerous reproduced documents and collected data, making it as much a primary as a secondary source. See particularly pp. 3–63, 114–21, 160–61, 220–23, 232–59, and 286–88. Although much briefer, Robert D. Cuff, *The War Industries Board: Business-Government Relations During World War I* (Baltimore: Johns Hopkins University Press, 1973), pp. 15–25, presents a much more sophisticated account of the NCB that is also based on greater work in primary sources. See also U.S. Congress, House, Committee on Naval Affairs, *Hearings, Estimates Submitted by the Secretary of the Navy—1916,* 64th Cong., 1st sess., 1916, pp. 3343–55, 3573–77, 3660–63, testimony of Daniels and Edison (hereafter HNAC, *Hearings, 1916*), and William Franklin Willoughby, *Government Organization in War Time and After: A Survey of the Federal Civil Agencies Created for the Prosecution of the War* (New York: D. Appleton, 1919), pp. 30–32, 69–70. The Naval Consulting Board was actually unofficial until August 1916, when it was granted official status through an appropriations act, which led to the board members taking an oath of office in September 1916.

17. U.S. Congress, House, Select Committee on Expenditures in the War Department, *Hearings, War Expenditures,* serial 1, vol. 1, 66th Cong., 1921, pp. 336–37, Clarkson, and vol. 2, 1919, pp. 878–79, Gifford (hereafter Graham Committee, *Hearings*). The committee hearings are confusing in terms of citation, a fact, along with the importance of the committee, that is discussed in volume 3 (forthcoming) of this series. Carty to Gifford, 2/3/17, and other correspondence and documents, file 2–A–3,

American Telephone and Telegraph Co., CND Recds. Documents cited here and in note 16 constitute the best sources on the NCB.

18. Coffin's work with the SAE is related in George V. Thompson, "Intercompany Technical Standardization in the Early American Automobile Industry," *Journal of Economic History* 14 (Winter 1954): 1–2. The Taylorite Movement, its adherents, and its implications are analyzed in Samuel Haber, *Efficiency and Uplift: Scientific Management in the Progressive Era, 1890–1920* (Chicago: University of Chicago Press, 1964), quotation, p. 10. The linkage between the IPC and the Plattsburg Movement can be traced through Scott, *Naval Consulting Board,* and the sources on the Plattsburgites cited in chap. 6, n. 7.

19. Quoted in Franklin H. Martin, *Digest of the Proceedings of the Council of National Defense During the World War,* U.S. Congress, Senate, 73d Cong., 2d sess., doc. no. 193 (1934), p. 512.

20. U.S. Congress, Senate, Committee on Military Affairs, *Hearings, Investigation of the War Department,* 65th Cong., 2d sess., 1917–1918 (hereafter SMAC, *Hearings, 1917–1918*), p. 2281 (Coffin's entire testimony is on pp. 2253–89), and HNAC, *Hearings, 1916,* p. 3360 (Coffin's full testimony is on pp. 3356–73).

21. Educational orders were actually introduced as a well-defined practice with World War I. They resulted from the recognition that the requirements of technologically advanced, industrialized warfare created new imperatives. Educational orders were intended to help industry and the military either to prepare for or to institute large-scale munitions output. Without the restrictions of competitive bidding, the military could award contracts to select firms for the limited production of various munitions items. Thus industry accumulated the tools and worked out the techniques for quantity production, and the armed services tested munitions designs and procurement methods. For citations and bibliography on the origins of educational orders and information concerning them during World War I and in the interwar years, see Paul A. C. Koistinen, "The 'Industrial-Military Complex' in Historical Perspective: The InterWar Years," *Journal of American History* 56 (March 1970): 838, n. 58.

22. Grosvenor B. Clarkson was the brother of Coker Clarkson, who, along with Coffin, was instrumental in the standardization and efficiency work of the SAE. Grosvenor had done some publicity work for the society and was therefore known to Coffin. See Publicity Release on Coker F. Clarkson, file "Clarkson, G.B.," CND Recds. Clarkson exchanged some of his ideas with Coffin and Gifford about publicity and educational work involving preparedness in Clarkson to Coffin, 1/29/17, and in other correspondence, file "Council of National Defense (W.S.G./H.E.C.) Before Moving to Washington," CND Recds. See also Grosvenor B. Clarkson, *Industrial America in the World War: The Strategy Behind the Line, 1917–1918* (Boston: Houghton Mifflin, 1923), pp. 12–14.

23. The ideas of Coffin, Gifford, and the men around them would become clearer in the operations and controversies of the Council of National Defense–National Defense Advisory Commission. The quest for a broad base for industrial preparedness and economic mobilization is evident not only in the publicity work of the NCB but also in the close ties of Coffin and Gifford with the Chamber of Commerce and the cultivation of the organization by the two men. See Coffin's appearances and speeches before the Chamber of Commerce, *Fourth Annual Meeting,* February 1916, pp. 300–302, and *Fifth Annual Meeting,* January 1917, pp. 46–51, Chamber of Com-

merce Recds. See also Coffin to Gifford, 1/19/17, file 2–A–3 no. 257 Munitions and Manufacturing–Mr. Coffin, CND Recds.

24. Army War College, *Mobilization of Industries and Utilization of the Commercial and Industrial Resources of the Country for War Purposes in Emergency*, November 1915 (Washington, DC: U.S. Government Printing Office, 1916), copy in box no. 240, Records of the War Department General Staff, RG 165, National Archives, Washington, DC (quotations, p. 12). This document was a supplement to the larger "Statement of a Proper Military Policy for the United States"; Clarkson to Baker, 12/29/22, Selected Correspondence, Baruch Papers; SMAC, *Hearings, 1916*, pp. 83–85, 90, 126, 136–38, 165–67, 239–40, 519–30, 605, 677, 856–83, 1026–47; SMAC, *Hearings, 1917–1918*, pp. 2253–89; U.S. Congress, House, Committee on Military Affairs, *Hearings, to Increase the Efficiency of the Military Establishment of the United States*, 64th Cong., 1st sess., 1916, pp. 44, 52–76 (intermittent), 110–11, 115–24, 130–31, 201–13, 256–59, 281–315, 342–47, 475–572, 738–83, 852–70, 1147–56, 1194–1213, 1232–69, 1280–1317, 1365, 1451–57 (hereafter HMAC, *Hearings, 1916);* U.S. Congress, House, Committee on Military Affairs *Hearings, Making Appropriations for the Support of the Army for the Fiscal Year, 1917*, 64th Cong., 1st sess., 1916, pp. 791–93, 848–50; U.S. Congress, House, Committee of Military Affairs, *Increasing the Efficiency of the Military Establishment*, 64th Cong., 1st sess., 1916, House Report no. 297 to accompany H.R. 12766; U.S. Congress, Senate, *Preparedness for National Defense*, 64th Cong., 1st sess., 1916, Sen. Report no. 263, parts 1 and 2, to accompany S. 4840; U.S. *Statutes at Large*, vol. 39, part 1, pp. 213–15; U.S. Congress, *Congressional Record*, 64th Cong., 1st sess., vol. 53, part 5, pp. 4303, 4325–57, 4581–4583, 4725, 5061–66, 5083–91, part 8, 8027–47, part 9, 8375–8407, part 10, 9709–10 (hereafter *Cong. Rec.*); and War Department, *Report of the Secretary of War to the President, 1915* (Washington, 1915) (hereafter *ARSW*), *ARSW, 1916*, and *ARSW, 1917.*

25. Failure to use Sections 120 and 123 of the National Defense Act, 1916, is covered in the sources cited in note 24. See also Graham Committee, *Hearings*, serial 1, vol. 1, pp. 452–99; Frederick Palmer, *Newton D. Baker: America at War*, 2 vols. (New York: Dodd, Mead, 1931), 1: 58–61; and J. Franklin Crowell, *Government War Contracts* (New York: Oxford University Press, 1920), pp. 98–99.

26. U.S. Congress, Senate, *Government Manufacture of Arms, Munitions, and Equipment*, 64th Cong., 2d sess., 1917, Sen. Doc. 664, pp. 5–17; F. Carrington Weems, *America and Munitions: The World of Messrs. J. P. Morgan & Co. in the World War*, 2 vols. (New York: privately printed, 1923), 1: 429; and Marvin A. Kreidberg and Merton G. Henry, *History of Military Mobilization in the United States Army, 1775–1945* (Washington, DC: Department of the Army, 1955), pp. 336–37. The Kernan Board was virtually an extension of the Chamber of Commerce's Committee on National Defense. The criticism of the opponents of preparedness is contained in HMAC, *Hearings, 1916*, and SMAC, *Hearings, 1916*, cited in note 24. This topic is treated extensively in volume 3 (forthcoming) of this series, along with numerous publications and bibliographic essays on antiwar, peace, pacifist, and related topics.

27. The views of members of Congress, the armed services, and the advocates and opponents of war are made manifestly clear in the sources cited in note 24. Some of the keenest insights about the imperatives of modern warfare were entered into the public record but appeared to be ignored. See the testimony and/or documents of

Walter L. Fisher, HMAC, *Hearings, 1916,* pp. 1280–1317, and Walter R. Stiness (R-RI), *Cong. Rec.,* vol. 53, appendix, p. 2064.

28. Baruch to House, 10/26/15, House to Baruch, 10/28/15, Baruch to House, 4/24/16, Wilson to Baruch, 5/5/16, Baruch to Wilson, 8/17/16, Baruch to House, [circa] 12/1916, reproduced portions of House Diary, May–Dec. 1916, Selected Correspondence; "Statement of L. L. Summers," 4/17/20, Grosvenor B. Clarkson, "Statements of Men in War Work," 1920–1922, all in Baruch Papers; Graham Committee, *Hearings,* serial 1, vol. 1, pp. 1831–33; Bernard M. Baruch, *Baruch: My Own Story* (New York: Holt, Rinehart, and Winston, 1957), pp. 308–9, and Baruch, *Baruch: The Public Years* (New York: Holt, Rinehart, and Winston, 1960), pp. 20–25; Jordan A. Schwarz, *The Speculator: Bernard M. Baruch in Washington, 1917–1965* (Chapel Hill: University of North Carolina Press, 1981), pp. 43–49.

29. Martin, *Digest of the Proceedings of the Council of National Defense,* pp. 1–50.

30. Willoughby, *Government Organization in War Time and After,* pp. 22–32, and Cuff, *War Industries Board,* pp. 14–15.

31. Graham Committee, *Hearings,* serial 3, vol. 1, pp. 880–90, serial 1, vol. 1, pp. 1831–33; *Cong. Rec.,* 64th Cong., 1st sess., vol. 53, 1916, part 9, pp. 8620, 8920, part 10, pp. 10035–36, part 11, pp. 11501–504, part 12, pp. 11563–565, 11772–773, 11813, 12233–234, part 13, pp. 12844–845; excerpts from House Diary, January 1917, reproduced in Selected Correspondence, Baruch Papers; Palmer, *Baker,* 1: 48–51; Cuff, *War Industries Board,* pp. 27–30, 34–39. Haber, *Efficiency and Uplift,* is especially important for understanding the true-believer, quirky quality of Godfrey. Others had similar proposals for agencies such as the Council of National Defense but failed to achieve Godfrey's notoriety for their efforts. See George Frederick Kunz, "Preparedness, Scientific Efficiency, and Industrial Museums: Our Safeguards in Peace and War," 12/26/16, file 72–A–3, CND Recds.; Coffin to Gifford, 1/19/17, file 2–A–3 no. 257, Munitions and Manufacturing–Mr. Coffin, CND Recds.; and "Statement of Martin Gillen," 12/12/20, Clarkson, "Statements of Men in War Work," 1920–1922, Baruch Papers.

It is important to realize that the idea of a Council of National Defense to formulate, perhaps implement, a military policy consistent with the nation's foreign policy dated back to the late nineteenth century. Such a proposed council involved crucial matters of civil-military relations for the nation as a world power. There is substantial literature on this subject. For some of the better volumes, see Paul Y. Hammond, *Organizing for Defense: The American Military Establishment in the Twentieth Century* (Princeton, NJ: Princeton University Press, 1961), pp. 49–77; Samuel P. Huntington, *The Soldier and the State: The Theory and Politics of Civil-Military Relations* (Cambridge: Belknap Press, 1957), pp. 260–63; William James Breen, "The Council of National Defense: Industrial and Social Mobilization in the United States, 1916–1920" (Ph.D. diss., Duke University, 1968), pp. 18–23; John M. Peoples, "The Genesis of the War Industries Board" (Ph.D. diss., University of California, Berkeley, 1948), pp. 6–10; and Willoughby, *Government Organization in War Time and After,* pp. 9–11. See also the discussion in chapter 3 of this volume. Wood and the responses of Congress to legislation involving industrial mobilization have been discussed in terms of the National Defense Act, 1916. The same observations hold true for the enabling legislation for the Council of National Defense.

32. U.S. *Statutes at Large,* vol. 39, part 1, pp. 649–50. The section is conveniently reproduced in Clarkson, *Industrial America in the World War,* pp. 491–92.

33. Baker to Redfield, 7/5/16, w/enc. and other correspondence and documents, file 74405, General Correspondence, General Records, Office of the Secretary, Department of Commerce, RG 40, National Archives, College Park, MD (hereafter Dept. of Commerce Recds.); Martin, *Digest of Proceedings of Council of National Defense,* pp. 36–43; Baker to members of CND–NDAC, 11/13/16, file 2–A–3 no. 88, CND Recds.; Breen, "Council of National Defense," pp. 55–64; and Cuff, *War Industries Board,* pp. 38–40.

34. The elaborate ties among those participating in the economic mobilization movement before and during World War I is evident throughout the primary sources I have cited. For the secondary material, some idea of this small world is well illustrated by the same names and organizations repeatedly appearing, for example, in Scott, *Naval Consulting Board,* Fisher, "Chamber of Commerce," and Clarkson, *Industrial America in the World War.*

35. These points are covered, expanded upon, and documented in Koistinen, "The 'Industrial-Military Complex' in Historical Perspective," 380, 385–86. Coffin articulated these ideas best. See his testimony, SMAC, *Hearings, 1917–1918,* pp. 2253–89. Before, during, and after World War I, Baruch persistently hammered away at these points. For one example, see Baruch to Thompkins, 6/16/17, part I, vol. 55, World War I Recds., Baruch Papers.

36. U.S. *Statutes at Large,* vol. 34, part 1, p. 49; Scott, *Naval Consulting Board,* p. 43; Martin, *Digest of Proceedings of the Council of National Defense,* p. 121; Michael D. Reagan, "Serving Two Masters: Problems in the Employment of Dollar-a-Year and Without Compensation Personnel" (Ph.D. diss., Princeton University, 1959), pp. 2–19; and James A. McAleer, *Dollar-a-Year and Without Compensation Personnel Policies of the War Production Board and Predecessor Agencies, August 1939 to November 1945* (Washington, DC: War Production Board, 1947), pp. 1–6.

37. Peoples, "Genesis of the War Industries Board," pp. 43–47; and Wiebe, *Businessmen and Reform,* pp. 203–4.

38. Excerpts from the House Diary, May–Dec., 1916, Jan.–Sept., 1917. House was willing to use Baruch's money and his connections but recorded his contempt for the speculator and, in the process, revealed his anti-Semitism. On 9/23/17, House spoke of suffering Baruch's presence and then observed, "[Baruch] is a curious mixture of patriotism and egotism. He wishes to serve, and is willing to serve under any condition, but his admiration for Baruch and his methods are wonderful to contemplate." When the NDAC appointments were announced, House complained in his diary, 10/12/16, about Baruch's selection and added, "As it is, it places two Jews on the Council." On 5/27/17, House records his agreement with Vance McCormick, chairman of the Democratic National Committee, that Baruch should not be appointed as purchasing agent for the United States and the Allies. "He will have an expenditure of nearly a billion a week, and McCormick agrees with me that he is not the type of man the President should appoint. I believe Baruch is able and I believe he is honest, but I do not believe the country will take kindly to having a Hebrew Wall Street speculator given so much power. He is not the type that inspires confidence." See also Baruch to House [circa] 12/1916. The quotations are in Selected Correspondence, Baruch Papers. Charles Seymour, *The Intimate Papers of Colonel House,*

4 vols. (Boston: Houghton Mifflin Company, 1926–1928) contains virtually nothing on the prewar and wartime economic mobilization. See also "Statement of H. P. Ingels," 12/30/20, Clarkson, "Statements of Men in War Work," 1920–1922, Baruch Papers; Margaret L. Coit, *Mr. Baruch* (Boston: Houghton Mifflin, 1957), pp. 147–52; and other sources cited in Koistinen, "Industrial-Military Complex, World War I," 399, n. 47. The people investigating war mobilization in the interwar years frequently charged that Baruch and others were guilty of blatant conflicts of interest (see volume 3 [forthcoming] of this series).

39. There are numerous examples of this phenomenon. For some instances, see Nye Committee, *Minutes of the Advisory Commission of the Council of National Defense and Minutes of the Munitions Standards Board,* 74th Cong., 2d sess., 1936, Senate Committee Print no. 8, pp. 119–21 (hereafter NDAC or MSB *Minutes*); Nye Committee, *Final Report, WIB–Johnson,* Senate Committee Print no. 3, pp. 1–2, 39–40; HMAC, *Hearings, 1916,* pp. 1150–51, 1156; and U.S. Council of National Defense, *Third Annual Report of the United States Council of National Defense* (Washington, DC: U.S. Government Printing Office, 1919), pp. 16–17.

40. Scholars have come to appreciate that various groups and classes looked to the war as furthering their gains, goals, and interests. This theme is stated and developed by Allen F. Davis, "Welfare, Reform, and World War I," *American Quarterly* 19 (Fall 1967): 516–33. The best and most insightful book-length treatment of the subject is found in Ronald Schaffer, *America in the Great War: The Rise of the War Welfare State* (New York: Oxford University Press, 1991). See also Arthur A. Stein, *The Nation at War* (Baltimore: Johns Hopkins University Press, 1978), chap. 7; John F. McClymer, *War and Welfare: Social Engineering in America, 1890–1945* (Westport, CT: Greenwood Press, 1980); John M. Jordan, *Machine Age Ideology: Social Engineering and American Liberalism, 1911–1939* (Chapel Hill: University of North Carolina Press, 1994), chap. 4; and James L. Abrahamson, *The American Home Front: Revolutionary War, Civil War, World War I, and World War II* (Washington, DC: National Defense University Press, 1983), pp. 87–130.

41. This theme is discussed most authoritatively by Alfred D. Chandler, Jr., *The Visible Hand: The Managerial Revolution in American Business* (Cambridge: Belknap Press, 1977), pp. 345–48.

42. *New York Times,* Oct. 12, 1916, p. 10. This statement was written, and issued with only minor changes, by Clarkson. See Breen, "Council of National Defense," pp. 64–65.

43. Reproduced in Nye Committee, *Hearings,* part 16, pp. 4056–57.

44. For an excellent example of this type of thinking, see U.S. Congress, Subcommittee of the House Committee on Appropriations, *Hearings, Council of National Defense,* 65th Cong., 1st sess., 1917, pp. 37–38, 42–43.

## CHAPTER EIGHT. THE NATIONAL DEFENSE ADVISORY COMMISSION

1. Secretary of War to CND–NDAC, 11/13/16, and other documents, file 2–A3, no. 88, Godfrey to Coffin, 1/5/17, and other documents, file 2–A3, CND Recds.; Lane to Baker, 12/9/16, and numerous other correspondence and documents, file 74405, Dept. of Commerce Recds.; and "Statement of Daniel Willard," 3/11/21, Grosvenor

Clarkson, "Statements of Men in War Work," 1920–1922, Baruch Papers. The evolution of the CND–NDAC can be traced through the *Minutes* of those organizations. See Nye Committee, CND, NDAC, and MSB, *Minutes,* Committee Prints 7 and 8. Franklin H. Martin, *Digest of the Proceedings of the Council of National Defense During the World War,* 73d Cong., 2d sess., 1934, S. Doc. 193 is also helpful.

2. See chapter 7 on the Industrial Preparedness Committee. Secretary of Commerce William C. Redfield had some good insights into CND–NDAC operations (see Redfield to Baker, 12/28/16, and other correspondence and documents, file 74405, Dept. of Commerce Recds.).

3. The discussion of business representation in the NDAC is based on CND, *Minutes,* 2/12/17, 2/13/17, 2/16/17, 2/28/17; NDAC, *Minutes,* 12/6/16, 1/8/17, 3/3/17, Godfrey to Coffin, 1/5/17, and other correspondence, file 2–A3, Engineering and Education, and Verbatim Minutes of NDAC, 1/8/17, file 2–A3, CND Recds.; Pratt to Secretary of Commerce, 2/23/17, and other correspondence and documents, file 74405, Dept. of Commerce Recds.; Baruch to Gifford, 1/12/17, and other correspondence and documents, file part 1, vol. 4, "Excerpts from Wilson-Baruch Correspondence," part 2, sec. 2, "Diary of Bernard M. Baruch," 1/2/17, file part 2, Additional Materials, WWI; Baruch to Wilson, [circa] 1920, Selected Correspondence; Martin Gillen, L. L. Summers, and Willard statements, Clarkson, "Statements of Men in War Work," 1920–1922, all in Baruch Papers; *Minutes, War Conventions of American Business and Seventh Meeting, National Council, September, 1917,* pp. 186–89, *Annual Report of the Board of Directors, Fifth Annual Meeting,* Jan.–Feb., 1917, pp. 3–9, Archives, Chamber of Commerce Recds.; U.S. Congress, Senate, Committee on Military Affairs, *Hearings, Investigation of the War Department,* 65th Cong., 2d sess., 1917–1918, pp. 1850–84 (hereafter Chamberlain Committee, *Hearings*); Graham Committee, serial 1, *Hearings,* pp. 1793–1857. Some of the secondary sources cited treat with this subject. The most authoritative and extensive analysis is presented in Robert D. Cuff, *The War Industries Board: Business-Government Relations During World War I* (Baltimore: Johns Hopkins University Press, 1973), chap. 3.

4. For a complete list of NDAC committees, see U.S. Council of National Defense, *First Annual Report* (Washington, DC: U.S. Government Printing Office, 1917), pp. 97–127. Baruch's cooperative committees and their members are conveniently available in Grosvenor B. Clarkson, *Industrial America in the World War: The Strategy Behind the Line, 1917–1918* (Boston: Houghton Mifflin Company, 1923), pp. 495–500. The evolution of the cooperative committees can be traced through the CND's *Annual Reports,* the CND and the NDAC *Minutes,* Bernard M. Baruch, *American Industry in the War: A Report of the War Industries Board* (Washington, DC: U.S. Government Printing Office, 1921), Nye Committee, *Final Report, WIB–Johnson,* Senate Committee Print 3, and the sources in note 3. The business advisory bodies to the mobilization agencies gradually evolved from 1916 through 1918 and are not neatly divisible in terms of time, name, or the mobilization agency or agencies with which they were affiliated.

5. In the analysis of the NDAC commissioners, I have benefited greatly from the extensive research and keen analysis of Cuff, *War Industries Board,* which is also the best secondary source on economic mobilization for World War I. Two other secondary works are also important: Clarkson, *Industrial America in the World War,* and

John M. Peoples, "The Genesis of the War Industries Board" (Ph.D. diss., University of California, Berkeley, 1942).

6. For Gifford's congressional testimony, see Chamberlain Committee, *Hearings,* 1850–84, and Graham Committee, *Hearings,* serial 3, vol. 1, pp. 867–79; CND, *First and Second Annual Reports;* Gifford to Redfield, 4/5/17, w/enc. and other correspondence and documents, file 74405, Dept. of Commerce Recds.; Gifford to Baruch, 3/5/18, part 2, sec. 2, vol. 9, part 3, Washington Correspondence–Misc., WWI, House Diary, 3/21/18, Selected Correspondence, and Hugh Frayne statement, Clarkson, "Statements of Men in War Work," 1920–1922, Baruch Papers.

7. For Godfrey's congressional testimony, see Graham Committee, *Hearings,* serial 3, pp. 880–90; House Diary, Jan. 1917, Selected Correspondence, Baruch Papers; Martin, *Digest, Proceedings, CND,* pp. 65–67; and CND, *First Annual Report,* pp. 111–13.

8. For Coffin's congressional testimony, see Chamberlain Committee, *Hearings,* pp. 2253–89; MSB, *Minutes;* Nye Committee, *Minutes of the General Munitions Board from April 4 to August 9, 1917,* 74th Cong., 2d sess., 1936, Senate Committee Print 6 (hereafter GMB, *Minutes*); CND, *First Annual Report,* pp. 104–5; Coffin to Gifford, 1/19/17, file 2–A3, no. 257, Coffin to Rose, 2/17/17, w/enc. and other correspondence, file 2–A3, no. 262, Coffin to Pierce, 8/14/16, and other correspondence, file 2–A3, no. 382, CND Recds.; Frank A. Scott statement, Clarkson, "Statements of Men in War Work," 1920–1922, Baruch Papers. Aircraft production and the controversies it caused are discussed in volume 3 (forthcoming) of this series.

9. Martin provides the best running account of his activities and those of the CND–NDAC in his publication, *Digest, Proceedings, CND.* See also CND, *First Annual Report,* pp. 120–27.

10. For the cooperative committees organized under Gompers's direction, see CND, *First Annual Report,* pp. 113–20. Labor during World War I and Gompers's role in that regard are treated separately in chapter 11.

11. The operations of the Committee on Supplies were covered in great detail by congressional investigations, more than any other subdivision of the CND–NDAC. See Chamberlain Committee, *Hearings,* pp. 516–633, 869–921, and other relevant sections, and Graham Committee, *Hearings,* serial 1, pp. 341, 403–47, 517–518, and other relevant sections. (The Graham Committee's overall investigation is analyzed in depth in volume 3 [forthcoming] of this series.) See CND, *First Annual Report,* pp. 65–68, 105–7; CND, *Second Annual Report,* pp. 222–30; Crowder to Secretary of War, 8/18/17, w/enc., "Correspondence File 1917, C," Baker Papers; Verbatim Minutes of a Joint Meeting of the Council of National Defense and the Advisory Commission, 2/17/18, file part 2, sec. 2, Additional Material, Baruch's "Daily Record," WWI, and General Hugh S. Johnson and Herbert E. Peabody statements, Clarkson, "Statements of Men in War Work," 1920–1922, Baruch Papers.

12. Willard and Samuel M. Vauclain statements, Clarkson, "Statements of Men in War Work," 1920–1922, Baruch Papers; Willard testimony, Chamberlain Committee, *Hearings,* pp. 1799–1836; CND, *First Annual Report,* pp. 56–65, 102–4; "Memorandum to Mr. Clarkson," 2/26/17, file 2–A3, "Conference Committee on Nat'l Preparedness," Verbatim Minutes of NDAC, 1/8/17, file 2–A7, "CND & Adv. Com.," CND Recds.; Willard to Wilson, 1/11/18, and other correspondence, file 206 B, War Industries Board 1918 (Jan.–March), Memorandum for Clarkson, 5/17/19, and

Willard to Clarkson, 5/14/23, file "Grosvenor B. Clarkson Papers, 1917–1925," Series 4, Woodrow Wilson Papers, Library of Congress, Washington, DC; Willard to Baruch, 12/23/18, file part 2, sec. 2, vol. 9–part 8, Wash. Corr., Misc. T–Z, WWI, Baruch Papers; William J. Breen, "The Council of National Defense: Industrial and Social Mobilization in the United States, 1916–1920" (Ph.D. diss., Duke University, 1968), pp. 120–22. Breen has reworked his dissertation principally as a study of the CND at the state level, *Uncle Sam at Home: Civilian Mobilization, Wartime Federalism, and the Council of National Defense, 1917–1919* (Westport, CT: Greenwood Press, 1984).

13. Alfred D. Chandler, Jr., *The Visible Hand: The Managerial Revolution in American Business* (Cambridge: Belknap Press, 1977), quotation, p. 372. The analysis evolves throughout the volume, but for my purposes chapter 11 is the most relevant. The figures on Baruch's cooperative committees were calculated by using Chandler's appendix on leading industrial enterprises in 1917, pp. 503–12, and the list of Baruch's committees in CND, *First Annual Report,* pp. 107–11.

14. The discussion of Baruch draws on numerous primary sources. The World War I collection and the Clarkson, "Statements of Men in War Work," 1920–1922, Baruch Papers, are a rich source. The CND and NDAC *Minutes* and the CND *Annual Reports* are also helpful. For secondary sources, Cuff, *War Industries Board,* Clarkson, *Industrial America in the World War,* and Jordan A. Schwarz, *The Speculator: Bernard M. Baruch in Washington, 1917–1965* (Chapel Hill: University of North Carolina Press, 1981) are among the best available. Edward M. House often expressed a biting and derogatory view of Baruch in his unpublished diaries. Excerpts from the typescript are included in Selected Correspondence, 1916–1919, Baruch Papers.

15. John Kenneth Galbraith, *A Life in Our Times: Memoirs* (Boston: Houghton Mifflin, 1981), pp. 130–31, claims that many of the people involved in economic mobilization for World War I believed that Baruch was only a front person for Alexander Legge of International Harvester, who was the genuine brains and boss. My own research does not validate that conclusion. If anyone came close to playing such a role, it was Summers. However, the truth seems to be that Baruch tapped an enormous range and number of advisers to guide and inform his work. During World War I, Baruch managed to synthesize information and ideas from and to direct effectively the efforts of a wide and disparate group, a performance he doggedly and unsuccessfully attempted to match for the rest of a long public life. For insights about Summers, see his statement, Clarkson, "Statements of Men in War Work," 1920–1922, Baruch Papers. See also my discussion of Baruch and his coterie during the interwar years in volume 3 (forthcoming) of this series.

16. Martin provides a detailed account of his operations in *Digest, Proceedings, CND.*

17. Testimony before congressional committees and the postwar interviews conducted by Clarkson usually provide better and more coherent information about the cooperative committees than the spotty records found in the correspondence and related documents and *Minutes* of the CND and NDAC. The CND *Annual Reports* and the various *Reports* of the War Industries Board are helpful, however. In terms of congressional testimony and Clarkson's "Statements of Men in War Work," 1920–1922, the cooperative committees under Rosenwald are covered best. See Spencer Turner (one of the best statements for tracing the course of a cooperative committee to its reorganization as a war service committee), Peabody, and Lincoln Cromwell statements, Clark-

son, "Statements of Men in War Work," 1920–1922, Baruch Papers; Chamberlain Committee, *Hearings,* pp. 516–633, 869–921, and other relevant sections; Graham Committee, *Hearings,* serial 1, pp. 341, 403–77, 517–18, and other relevant portions; "Final Report . . . Cotton Goods Industry . . . and Cotton Goods Section," and Report on "Knit Goods," part 2, vol. 13, part 1, WWI, Baruch Papers.

18. For documentation on Willard's cooperative committees, see note 12.

19. "Report of the Activities of the Chemicals Division of the War Industries Board . . . with Chas. H. MacDowell as Director," [circa] 1918, file part 2, vol. 6, part 1, R. H. Downman memorandum, "Exhibit 'B,'" undated, file part 2, vol. 9, Memorandum on Nonferrous Metals, undated, part 2, vol. 11, Baruch to McAdoo, 5/2/17, and other documents, file part 2, sec. 2, vol. 9, part 7, Washington Corr., Misc.–S, Summers to Baruch, 10/23/17, and other correspondence, WIB–Copies of Important Letters, 1917–vol. 1, WWI; Baruch to Daniels, 3/21/17, Selected Correspondence; Charles Edgar, Charles H. MacDowell, and Summers statements, Clarkson, "Statements of Men in War Work," 1920–1922, all in Baruch Papers: and Graham Committee, *Hearings,* serial 1, pp. 1793–1857.

20. Some cooperative committees varied from the patterns sketched out. For example, what became the Electrical Wire and Cable Section of the WIB functioned, in effect, as a cooperative committee but without being formally under a commissioner or the CND–NDAC. For information on this curious situation, see LeRoy Clark to Baruch, 12/2/18, file part 2, vol. 7, WWI, and LeRoy Clark statement, Clarkson, "Statements of Men in War Work," 1920–1922, Baruch Papers. The board of directors of the U.S. Chamber of Commerce also assisted in selecting members for the cooperative committees whenever possible. See *Minutes, War Convention of American Business and Seventh Meeting, National Council, September, 1917, National Council Minutes,* p. 26, Chamber of Commerce Recds.

21. Willard statement, Clarkson, "Statements of Men in War Work," 1920–1922, Baruch Papers.

22. Graham Committee, *Hearings,* serial 1, pp. 559–61; U.S. *Cong. Rec.,* 65th Cong., 1st sess., vol. 55, part 4, pp. 3335–41, part 5, pp. 4590–4610, 4651–79, 4814–15, 5001–49 (intermittent), 5169–89 (intermittent), 5214–25; and Turner statement, Clarkson, "Statements of Men in War Work," 1920–1922, Baruch Papers.

23. See notes 16–20. The gradual evolution of various mobilization policies and procedures can be traced through the CND *Minutes,* NDAC and MSB *Minutes,* GMB *Minutes,* the CND *Annual Reports,* Baruch, *American Industry in the War, Final Report, WIB–Johnson,* and Clarkson, *Industrial America in the World War.*

24. See note 23.

25. William Denman statement, Clarkson, "Statements of Men in War Work," 1920–1922, Baruch Papers. The U.S. Shipping Board and the Emergency Fleet Corporation will be treated in greater length in chapter 11. Richard L. Watson, Jr., *The Development of National Power: The United States, 1900–1919* (Boston: Houghton Mifflin, 1976), provides a good overview of most World War I mobilization agencies. A much earlier survey is still useful: William Franklin Willoughby, *Government Organization in War Time and After* (New York: D. Appleton, 1919). A perceptive analysis of the Food Administration is presented by Robert D. Cuff, "Herbert Hoover, the Ideology of Voluntarism and War Organization During the Great War," *Journal of American History* 66 (September 1977): 358–72.

26. For additional general and specific information on the Navy Department during World War I, see John M. Hancock statement and George E. Merryweather statement, Clarkson, "Statements of Men in War Work," 1920–1922, Baruch Papers; Peoples, "Genesis of the War Industries Board," pp. 172–75; John K. Ohl, "The Navy, the War Industries Board, and the Industrial Mobilization for War, 1917–1918," *Military Affairs* 40 (February 1976): 17–22; William J. Williams, "Josephus Daniels and the U.S. Navy's Shipbuilding Program During World War I," *Journal of Military History* 60 (January 1996): 7–38; and J. Franklin Crowell, *Government War Contracts* (New York: Oxford University Press, 1920), pp. 135–136, 150–58. Many of the sources cited in chapter 3 on the navy to 1917 are also relevant for the war years. The annual reports of the Navy Department are useful for understanding the department's supply and procurement structure and its adaptation to war. See U.S. Navy Department, *Report of the Secretary of Navy to the President,* 1914 (Washington, DC, 1915) (hereafter *ARSN*). Especially important are the "Reports of Paymaster General of the Navy, Chief of Bureau of Supplies and Accounts" and particularly the report of 1918. The annual reports of the Navy Department tend to be general and even elliptical where critical matters are involved. Nonetheless, the reports contain an enormous amount of often very detailed and useful information. Moreover, unlike the War Department reports, those of the Navy Department conveniently include the reports of its subdivisions instead of publishing them separately.

27. The reorganization and operation of the War Department in the late nineteenth and early twentieth centuries has already been analyzed in chapter 4, with much of the documentation and sources relevant to the World War I situation. The discussion and analysis of the War Department during World War I is based on those and the following sources. The testimony of military and other witnesses before congressional committees is an exceptionally rich source for military supply operations both before and during World War I, which is simply unmatched in document collections and secondary sources. See the relevant portions of U.S. Congress, House, Committee on Military Affairs, *Hearings, to Increase the Efficiency of the Military Establishment of the United States,* 64th Cong., 1st sess., 1916; U.S. Congress, Senate, Committee on Military Affairs, *Hearings, Preparedness for National Defense,* 64th Cong., 1st sess., 1916; Chamberlain Committee, *Hearings;* Graham Committee, *Hearings,* serial 1 and 3; U.S. Congress, Senate Subcommittee of the Committee on Military Affairs, *Hearings, Reorganization of the Army,* 66th Cong., 2d sess., 1919; U.S. Congress, House, Committee on Military Affairs, *Hearings, Army Reorganization,* 66th Cong., 1st sess., 1919–1920.

The *Annual Reports* of the Secretary of War can also be insightful and provide some helpful detail. See *ARSW,* 1915, *ARSW,* 1916, *ARSW,* 1917, *ARSW,* 1918, and *ARSW,* 1919. The reports of the two principal supply bureaus, the Quartermaster Corps and the Ordnance Department, are even more useful for grasping the general and detailed prewar and wartime supply matters. See *Report of the Quartermaster General to the Secretary of War,* 1914, serial set 6798, H. Doc. 1409, pp. 277–331 (hereafter *QMGR*), and *QMGR,* 1915, serial set 6967, H. Doc. 92, pp. 261–375, *QMGR,* 1916, serial set 7140, H. Doc. 1378, pp. 329–462, *QMGR,* 1917, serial set 7341, H. Doc. 856, pp. 245–334, *QMGR,* 1918, serial set 7479, H. Doc. 1432, pp. 265–327, *QMGR,* 1919, serial set 7688, H. Doc. 433, pp. 2–173, and *QMGR,* 1920, serial set 7806, H. Doc. 863, pp. 379–441. See also *Report of the Chief of Ordnance to the Secretary of War,* 1914, serial set 6798, H. Doc. 1409, pp. 445–501 (hereafter *OR*), and *OR,* 1915, serial set 6967, H. Doc. 92, pp. 675–734, *OR,* 1916, serial set 7140, H. Doc. 1378, pp. 803–56, *OR,* 1917, serial set 7341, H. Doc. 856, pp. 791–833, *OR,* 1918, serial set 7479, H. Doc. 1432, pp. 1041–70, *OR,* 1919, serial set 7685, H. Doc. 426, pp. 3867–3955, and *OR,* 1920, serial set 7806, H. Doc. 863, pp. 1173–1236.

See also R. S. Lovett, Col. Charles A. McKenney, George N. Peek, Gen. Palmer E. Pierce, Scott, and Summers statements, Clarkson, "Statements of Men in War Work," 1920–1922, Baruch Papers; *Final Report, WIB–Johnson,* pp. 8–11; and Crowell, *Government War Contracts,* pp. 96–106. For more general secondary sources on the War Department and the army, see Paul Y. Hammond, *Organizing for Defense: The American Military Establishment in the Twentieth Century* (Princeton, NJ: Princeton University Press, 1961); Marvin A. Kreidberg and Merton G. Henry, *History of Military Mobilization in the United States Army, 1775–1945* (Washington, DC: Department of the Army, 1955); Otto L. Nelson, Jr., *National Security and the General Staff* (Washington, DC: Infantry Journal Press, 1946); Peoples, "Genesis of the War Industries Board"; and Russell F. Weigley, *History of the United States Army* (New York: Macmillan, 1967). Additional information on the supply bureaus is available in Erna Risch, *The Quartermaster Corps: Organization, Supply, and Services* (Washington, DC: Office of the Chief of Military History, 1953), and Risch, *Quartermaster Support of the Army: A History of the Corps, 1775–1939* (Washington, DC: Office of the Quartermaster General, 1962); Constance McLaughlin Green, Henry C. Thomson, and Peter C. Roots, *The Ordnance Department: Planning Munitions for War* (Washington, DC: Office of the Chief of Military History, 1955).

28. The Root reforms from 1899 to World War I are analyzed in chapter 4.

29. For the General Staff efforts involving economic mobilization prior to World War I, see chapter 7. For a discussion of the navy and the economy, see chapter 3.

30. John M. Clark, *The Cost of the World War to the American People* (New Haven: Yale University Press, 1931), p. 30. For comparative purposes, the War Department figures would be slightly lower if estimated normal expenses for the war years were subtracted.

31. Hancock statement, Clarkson, "Statements of Men in War Work," 1920–1922, Baruch Papers.

32. U.S. War Department, Purchase, Storage, and Traffic Division, General Staff, *Supply Bulletin no. 29,* Nov. 7, 1918—reproduced in Graham Committee, *Hearings,* serial 1, pp. 128–39. See also Hancock statement, Clarkson, "Statements of Men in War Work," 1920–1922, Baruch Papers.

33. See the conflicting views of Baker provided in the Scott statement and in the Hancock statement, Clarkson, "Statements of Men in War Work," 1920–1922, Baruch Papers. See also Frederick Palmer, *Newton D. Baker: America at War,* 2 vols. (New York: Dodd, Mead, 1931), 1: 372.

34. Gifford to Pratt, 2/21/17, file 2–A3, Gifford Correspondence 10–241, CND Recds.; Clarkson to "Secretary," 4/2/17, file 74405, Dept. of Commerce Recds.; Willard to Baker, [circa] March 1917, file part 2, sec. 2, vol. 9, part 1, Wash. Corr., Misc.–A–B, WWI, and Willard, Pierce, Scott, and Vauclain statements, Clarkson, "Statements of Men in War Work," 1920–1922, Baruch Papers; and CND, *Minutes,* 2/28/17, 3/24/17.

35. See Verbatim "Meeting of the Allied Industries of the Supply Committee," [circa] April 1917, file 21A–A7, Records of the War Industries Board, Record Group

61, National Archives, Washington, DC (hereafter WIB Recds.); Kirstein Committee to Secretary of War, 8/13/17, "Correspondence File, 1917–C," Baker Papers; Turner statement, Clarkson, "Statements of Men in War Work," 1920–1922, Baruch Papers; Graham Committee, *Hearings,* serial 1, pp. 333–447; Martin, *Digest, Proceedings, CND,* pp. 352–62; and Crowell, *Government War Contracts,* pp. 52–61, 99–100.

36. NDAC Resolution to CND, [circa] 1917, file 74405, Dept. of Commerce Recds.; Willard to Baker, 3/31/17, "Correspondence File, Misc., Jan.–June 1917," Baker Papers; Willard to Baker, [circa] March 1917, and other correspondence and documents, file part 2, sec. 2, vol. 9, part 1, Wash. Corr., Misc. A–B, WWI, and Willard statement, Clarkson, "Statements of Men in War Work," 1920–1922, all in Baruch Papers.

37. CND, *Minutes,* 2/16/17; NDAC and MSB, *Minutes,* 3/3/17; CND, *First Annual Report,* pp. 20–23, 30–32, 100–101; Verbatim Minutes, NDAC, 1/8/17, 2/16/17, and [circa] March 1917, file 2–A7, CND and Advisory Commission, CND Recds.; statements of Scott, Vauclain, and Willard, Clarkson, "Statements of Men in War Work," 1920–1922, Baruch Papers; and U.S. Congress, House, Subcommittee of Committee on Appropriations, *Hearings, Council of National Defense,* 65th Cong., 1st sess., 1917, pp. 36–43 (hereafter Appropriations Subcommittee, *Hearings*).

38. Scott statement, Clarkson, "Statements of Men in War Work," 1920–1922, Baruch Papers; Scott testimony, Graham Committee, *Hearings,* serial 3, pp. 987–1019. Scott's papers are disappointing for the World War I period, but some material of interest and relevance is included in the files "Council of National Defense," "'War Industries Board,' GMB, MSB," "History of the War Industries Board," and "'WIB,' Resignation-Ltrs re: health," Box 1, Frank A. Scott Papers, Princeton University. In contrast, Scott's papers for the interwar years are very rich. Scott lectured on economic mobilization at the Army War College and the Army Industrial Colleges during the 1920s and into the 1930s. In these presentations, he provided a great deal of information about mobilizing the World War I economy and his role in the endeavor. In volume 3 (forthcoming) of this series, I discuss at length and document fully Scott's interwar role in the economic preparedness movement and his reflections on the World War I experience.

39. MSB, *Minutes,* 3/21/17; CND, *First Annual Report,* pp. 20–23, 30–32, 100–101; and Vauclain and Scott statements, Clarkson, "Statements of Men in War Work," 1920–1922, Baruch Papers.

40. CND, *Minutes,* 3/31/17, 4/28/17, and 5/5/17; NDAC and MSB, *Minutes,* 3/23/17 and 3/30/17; GMB, *Minutes,* 4/4/17; CND, *First Annual Report,* pp. 20–23, 99–100; Graham Committee, *Hearings,* serial 3, pp. 867–79, 987–1019; and Pierce, Scott, and Vauclain statements, Clarkson, "Statements of Men in War Work," 1920–1922, Baruch Papers.

41. See note 40. See also memorandum to Baker, [circa] July 1917, file "Report, Unfinished, Report to Baker," CND Recds.; "Excerpts from Reports for the Week Ending June 2d, 1917," to Gifford, 6/16/17, and other documents, file 74405, Dept. of Commerce Recds.; and Hancock, H. P. Ingels, McKenney, and Summers statements, Clarkson, "Statements of Men in War Work," 1920–1922, Baruch Papers.

42. J. C. Musser, "Clearance Office," [circa] December 1918, file I–D–I, Chairman's Office, Final Reports, WIB Recds.; J. C. Musser, Report on Clearance Committee, [circa] December 1918, file part 2, vol. 1, part 1, WWI, Baruch Papers; GMB,

*Minutes,* 4/4/17, 4/7/17, 4/9/17, 4/17/17, 4/18/17, 4/24/17, 4/25/17, 4/26/17, 4/30/17, 7/13/17, 7/18/17; CND, *Minutes,* 4/28/17; NDAC, *Minutes,* 5/1/17; CND, *First Annual Report,* p. 23; Baruch, *American Industry in the War,* pp. 32–35, 316–20; and *Final Report, WIB–Johnson,* pp. 11–17, 67–70.

43. Gifford to Priority Committee, GMB, 5/11/18, w/encs. and "Report of the Priorities Committee of War Industries Board to . . . Baruch," [circa] December 1918, file I–D–I, "Chairman's Office, Final Reports," WIB Recds.; CND, *Minutes,* 4/28/17 and 5/5/17; NDAC, *Minutes,* 5/1/17, 7/8/17, and 7/9/17; GMB, *Minutes,* 4/25/17, 4/26/17, 5/3/17, 5/7/17, 5/12/17, 5/21/17, and 5/29/17; CND, *First Annual Report,* pp. 23, 100; Hancock statement, Clarkson, "Statements of Men in War Work," 1920–1922, Baruch Papers; Baruch, *American Industry in the War,* pp. 47–60; and *Final Report, WIB–Johnson,* pp. 12–37, 52–62.

44. The analysis of price control policy and activity is based on Colver to Brookings, 9/30/18, w/encs. and memorandum, "Price Fixing," [circa] December 1918, file "Price Fixing Committee," Misc. Correspondence and Papers, no. 2 and no. 4, WIB Recds.; Fahey to Wilson, 7/16/17 and other correspondence, file 206, series 4, Wilson Papers; Baruch to Wilson, 5/15/17, and other correspondence and documents, file part 1, vol. 4, and Baruch to Daniels, 4/13/17, file part 2, sec. 2, vol. 9, part 2, Wash. Corr., Misc. C–D, WWI; Baruch to Daniels, 4/14/17, and numerous other correspondence, Selected Correspondence, 1917; Denman, Hancock, J. Leonard Replogle, Scott, Summers, and Pope Yeatman statements, Clarkson, "Statements of Men in War Work," 1920–1922, all in Baruch Papers; Graham Committee, *Hearings,* serial 1, pp. 333–447; NDAC, *Minutes,* 5/1/17, 7/8/17, 7/9/17, 7/12/17; CND, *Minutes,* 4/28/17 and 5/5/17; GMB, *Minutes,* 4/14/17, 4/16/17, 4/17/17, 4/18/17, 4/24/17, 4/25/17, 4/26/17, 4/30/17 and 5/21/17; CND, *First Annual Report,* pp. 56–72; and Baruch, *American Industry in the War,* pp. 70–81.

45. Most of the preceding primary and secondary sources in one way or another deal with the requirements issue. Good discussions of the subject are provided in *Final Report, WIB–Johnson,* pp. 8–17, and Baruch, *American Industry in the War,* pp. 30–37. The statements of World War I mobilization participants involved in Clarkson, "Statements of Men in War Work," 1920–1922, Baruch Papers, provide a rather consistent lament about the requirements problem throughout the war years and the drastic complications that it caused. For some specific examples of the civilian mobilization agencies' attempts to deal with the critical issue of requirements, see CND, *Minutes,* 2/28/17, 3/24/17, 4/28/17, 7/10/17, and GMB, *Minutes,* 4/4/17, 4/9/17, 4/24/17, 4/26/17, 7/18/17.

46. As with requirements, most of the preceding primary and secondary sources treat with the civilian mobilizers' quest for adequate mobilization authority. For some examples, see Fahey to Wilson, 7/16/17, and other correspondence, file 206, and Rhett to Wilson, 7/18/17, and other correspondence, file 1019; Willard to Clarkson, 5/14/23, file "Grosvenor B. Clarkson Papers, 1917–1925," all in series 4, Wilson Papers; Baruch to Daniels, 6/14/17, and Baruch to Wilson, 5/20/17, 6/4/17, and 6/19/17, Selected Correspondence; Meyer to Baruch, 5/30/17, and other correspondence, file part 2, section 2–Additional Material–BMB Personal–Price Policy, Baruch to Wilson, 6/4/17, part 2, sec. 2–Additional Material–Wilson Correspondence Excerpts, and Baruch to Scott, 5/4/17, and numerous other correspondence and documents, file part 1, vol. 4, WWI: Spencer statement, Clarkson, "Statements of

Men in War Work," 1920–1922, all in Baruch Papers; Scott to Baker, 8/30/17, file 21, Box 1, Scott Papers; and Bernard M. Baruch, *Baruch, the Public Years* (New York: Holt, Rinehart and Winston, 1960), pp. 43–44.

## CHAPTER NINE. THE WAR INDUSTRIES BOARD, AUGUST 1917–MARCH 1918

1. CND, *Minutes,* Senate Committee Print 7, May 31 and June 8, 1917; *Minutes,* NDAC and MSB, Senate Committee Print 8, June 1, 1917. See also GMB, *Minutes,* Senate Committee Print 6. In the *Minutes* of the CND, NDAC, and GMB during June and July 1917 can be traced the stalemate and tension that gripped the economic mobilization structure.

2. Chadbourne to McAdoo, 5/12/17, w/enc., part 2, sec. 2, vol. 9, part 2, Wash. Corr. Misc. C–D, WWI, and Frank A. Scott statement, Grosvenor Clarkson "Statements of Men in War Work," 1920–1922, Baruch Papers; E. David Cronon, ed., *The Cabinet Diaries of Josephus Daniels, 1913–1921* (Lincoln: University of Nebraska Press, 1963), p. 148. Lane's response, attitudes, and activity about economic mobilization are recorded in Anne W. Lane and Louise H. Wall, eds., *The Letters of Franklin K. Lane, Personal and Political* (Boston: Houghton Mifflin, 1922). Baruch and McAdoo had been political allies, if not friends, prior to World War I. See Melvin I. Urofsky, *Big Steel and the Wilson Administration: A Study in Business-Government Relations* (Columbus: Ohio State University Press, 1969), p. 158; Bernard M. Baruch, *Baruch: My Own Story,* pp. 308–9, and *Baruch: The Public Years,* pp. 22–23 (New York: Holt, Rinehart and Winston, 1957, 1960). See also Wilson to Baker, 5/5/16, and other correspondence, Letterbook 29, series 3, Wilson Papers.

3. Baker to president, 5/28/17, and numerous other correspondence, file "Correspondence, W. Wilson, May, 1917," Baker Papers; Baruch to Wilson, 6/19/17, and numerous other correspondence and documents, file part 1, vol. 4 and Baruch to Scott, 5/4/17, and other correspondence, file part 2, sec. 2, vol. 9, part 7–Wash. Corr., Misc. S, WWI; and Edward M. House Diary, May 27, 28, 31, 1917—excerpts in Selected Correspondence, all in Baruch Papers; Cronon, ed., *Daniels Diaries,* p. 158.

4. For congressional criticism, see Appropriations Subcommittee, *Hearings;* Chamberlain Committee, *Hearings;* and Graham Committee, *Hearings,* serials 1 and 3; U.S. Congress, *Cong. Rec.,* 65th Cong., 1st sess., 1917, vol. 55, part 3, pp. 3183–87, part 4, 3335–41, part 5, pp. 4590–4610, 4651–79, 4814–15, 5001–4, 5021, 5030–49, 5169–89, 5214–25.

For other primary sources, see Newlands to Secretary of Commerce, 6/13/17, w/enc. and numerous other correspondence and documents, file 74405, Dept. of Commerce Recds.; Clarkson to Ellsworth, 8/14/17, and other correspondence, file "ATT," Clarkson to Gifford, 1/22/17, file "Council of N.D. (W.S.G. & /H.E.C.)—Before Moving to Wash.," Clarkson to Penrose, 7/19/17, file "Penrose, Hon. Boise," Meyer to Baruch, 8/8/17, and numerous other correspondence and documents, file, "Prices, Publication of," Clarkson to Young, 4/26/17, file, "Young, Lafayette," CND Recds.; Scott, L. L. Summers, and Spencer Turner statements, Clarkson, "Statements of Men in War Work," 1920–1922, Baruch Papers; U.S. Council of National Defense, *First Annual Report* (Washington, DC: U.S. Government Printing Office, 1917), and *Second Annual Report* (Washington, DC: U.S. Government Printing Office, 1918); NDAC, *Minutes,* 7/18/17; and Franklin H. Martin, *Digest of the Proceedings of the Council of National Defense During the World War,* U.S. Congress, Senate, 73d Cong., 2d sess., Doc. 193, 1934, pp. 224–26.

5. Besides the documentation in note 4, these secondary sources cover the passage of the Lever Food and Fuel Control Act: Seward W. Livermore, *Politics Is Adjourned: Woodrow Wilson and the War Congress, 1916–1918* (Middletown: Wesleyan University Press, 1966), pp. 15–16, 48–57; Frederick Palmer, *Newton D. Baker: America at War,* 2 vols. (New York: Dodd, Mead, 1931), 2: 37; Frederick L. Paxson, *American Democracy and the World War,* 3 vols. (Boston and Berkeley: Houghton Mifflin and the University of California Press, 1936–1948), 2: 77–87; and Daniel R. Beaver, *Newton D. Baker and the American War Effort, 1917–1919* (Lincoln: University of Nebraska Press, 1966), pp. 87–89.

6. Rosenwald to Wilson, 7/2/17, and Wilson to Rosenwald, 7/3/17, file 4010, series 4, Wilson Papers, and *Cong. Rec.,* 65th Cong., 1st sess., 1917, vol. 55, part 5, pp. 4655–57.

7. Wilson to McKellar, 7/9/17, file 4010, series 4, Wilson Papers.

8. See the documentation in note 4; see also Wilson to McKellar, 7/6/17, and numerous other correspondence, file 4010, series 4, and Wilson to McKellar, 7/9/17, and other correspondence, Letterbook 42, series 3, Wilson Papers; Baker to Gifford, 10/23/17, w/ encs., file 2–A7, CND and Advisory Commission, CND Recds.; Thomas to Baruch, 6/12/17, and numerous other correspondence and documents, file part 2, sec. 2, Wash. Corr. 3 (Contracts), WWI, Baruch Papers. The Pomerene amendment is conveniently reproduced in its entirety in William Franklin Willoughby, *Government Organization in Wartime and After: A Survey of the Federal Civil Agencies Created for the Prosecution of the War* (New York: D. Appleton, 1919), pp. 84–85. For the origins of the Pomerene amendment, see Robert Dennis George Cuff, "Business, Government and the War Industries Board" (Ph.D. diss., Princeton University, 1966), pp. 102–3 and n. 72.

9. Most relevant primary and secondary sources on the process that produced the WIB have already been cited in this chapter; only new or additional sources of importance will be listed.

10. For conflicting views on Wilson's understanding of and leadership involving economic mobilization, see House Diary, 1/17/18, excerpted in Selected Correspondence, and R. S. Lovett statement, Clarkson, "Statements of Men in War Work," 1920–1922, both in Baruch Papers.

11. Fahey to Wilson, 7/16/17, and other correspondence, file 206, series 4, Wilson Papers; Wilson to Baker, 7/17/17, and other correspondence, file "Correspondence, W. Wilson, July, 1917," and Baker to Wilson, 8/1/17, file "Correspondence, W. Wilson, Aug. 1917," Baker Papers; House Diary, May 27, May 29, May 31, July 5, July 11, July 2, 1917, excerpts in Selected Correspondence; "Diary of Bernard M. Baruch," 7/13/17, file part 2–Additional Material, WWI, and Daniel Willard statement, Clarkson, "Statements of Men in War Work," 1920–1922, all in Baruch Papers; GMB, *Minutes,* 6/19/17; NDAC, *Minutes,* July 8, 9, 12, 18, 1917; CND, *Minutes,* July 9, 10, 1917; Martin, *Digest, Proceedings, CND,* pp. 218–26; and CND, *Second Annual Report.*

12. Memorandum, "Appointment of War Industries Board," undated, and other documents, file 2–A5, Gen'l Category, Gifford's Correspondence, Apr. 1917–May 1921, CND Recds.

13. Ibid.; Baker to Wilson, 6/27/17, and other correspondence, file, "Correspondence, W. Wilson, May, 1917," and Wilson to Baker, 7/17/17, and other correspondence, file, "Correspondence, W. Wilson, July, 1917," Baker Papers; Baruch to Crosby, 7/13/17, file, "Copies of Important Letters, 1917–vol. 1," WWI, and Robert S. Brookings, Charles K. Foster, Hugh Frayne, Lovett, and Summers statements, Clarkson, "Statements of Men in War Work," 1920–1922, Baruch Papers.

14. Memorandum, "Appointment of War Industries Board," undated, file 2–A5, Gen'l Category, Gifford's Correspondence, Apr. 1917–May 21, CND Recds. (emphasis added).

15. Gregory to Scott, 8/29/17, file "Attorney General, Office of," CND Recds.; Palmer to president, 9/20/17, and other correspondence and documents, file 206, series 4, Wilson Papers; Graham Committee, *Hearings,* serial 1, pp. 333–402; CND, *Minutes,* 9/5/17; and Martin, *Digest, Proceedings, CND,* pp. 325–28.

16. CND, *First Annual Report,* pp. 54–55; Chamber of Commerce of the United States, *War Convention of American Business,* September 18–21, 1917, pp. 23–42, and Board of Directors, *Annual Report,* Sixth Annual Meeting, April 10–12, 1918, pp. 3–17, *Minutes* of the Executive Committee of the Chamber of Commerce of the United States, May–August 1917 and Thirty-fourth Meeting, Board of Directors, 6/28/17, Chamber of Commerce Recds.; George N. Peek statement, Clarkson, "Statements of Men in War Work," 1920–1922, Baruch Papers; F. Carrington Weems, *America and Munitions: The Work of Messrs. J. P. Morgan & Co. in the World War,* 2 vols. (New York: privately printed, 1923), 2: appendix 3, p. 4.

17. The Chamber of Commerce's attitudes, policies, and actions on behalf of economic mobilization in general and business representation in particular can be traced through the *Minutes of the Annual Meetings and National Councils, Minutes of the War Convention,* Board of Directors, *Minutes* of Meetings and *Annual Reports, Minutes* of the Executive Committee, 1915–1918, Chamber of Commerce Recds.; Clarkson to Catchings, 8/17/17, and other correspondence and documents, file "Chamber of Commerce, U.S.," CND Recds.; Henry to Brookings, 10/4/18, file, "Price Fixing Committee, Misc. Correspondence and Papers, no. 2," WIB Recds.; Chamber of Commerce of the United States, *War Service Executive Committee of American Industries, Members of the Advisory Council,* February 1919, in file part 2, vol. 15 (Special Papers), WWI, Baruch Papers; CND, *Second Annual Report,* pp. 9–11, 79–81; Bernard M. Baruch, *American Industry in the War: A Report of the War Industries Board* (Washington, DC: U.S. Government Printing Office, 1921), pp. 23–24.

18. *Nation's Business,* August 1918, pp. 9–10. There is no one outstanding and comprehensive work on trade associations. Several of the better volumes include Joseph H. Foth, *Trade Associations: Their Service to Industry* (New York: Ronald Press, 1930); Simon N. Whitney, *Trade Associations and Industrial Control: A Critique of the N.R.A.* (New York: Central Book, 1934); Charles A. Pearce, *Trade Association Survey* (Washington, DC: U.S. Government Printing Office, 1941); National Industrial Conference Board, *Trade Associations: Their Economic Significance and Legal Status* (New York: National Industrial Conference Board, 1925); and U.S. Department of Commerce, *Trade Association Activities* (Washington, DC: U.S. Government Printing Office, 1927). Most of the studies on trade associations view the World War I years as critically important for shaping the growth and development of these institutions. These same sources also recognize that the difficulty in defining and identifying trade associations and the

paucity of information about them create extraordinary problems for presenting reliable statistics on the prevalence of trade associations at any particular time.

19. On this development see chapter 7.

20. Lovett to Gifford, 10/31/17, reproduced in Nye Committee, *Minutes of the War Industries Board from August 1, 1917 to December 19, 1918,* 74th Cong., 1st sess., 1935, Senate Committee Print 4, 11/l/17 and 2/11/18 (hereafter WIB, *Minutes*), and Lovett statement, Clarkson, "Statements of Men in War Work," 1920–1922, Baruch Papers. Even if Baruch had desired to work with the Chamber of Commerce, it would have been difficult since the chamber included numerous manufacturers but few firms dealing in raw materials, Baruch's specialty. Through George N. Peek and others, however, Baruch typically kept the door open and maintained communication with the chamber and its leaders. Wilson's attitude toward the chamber was curious and shifting. Chamber leaders worked with his administration on key bills involving political economy during 1913 and 1914, and the White House remained solicitous of and interested in the chamber's views and activities throughout 1917 and 1918. However, the president, Baker, and others were seriously at odds with the Chamber of Commerce during the economic mobilization crisis in winter 1917–1918. Thereafter, Wilson rather typically refused to have much to do with the business association, going so far as to decline an invitation to attend an important association conference late in 1918 and even refusing to send a message to the gathering. Wilson seemed to have a particular animus toward Wheeler, which he made little effort to hide. See Wilson to Tumulty, 8/22/18, and numerous other correspondence and documents, file 1019, series 4, Wilson Papers.

21. WIB, *Minutes,* August 17, 29, 1917, September 7, 21, 27, 28, 1917, October 5, 19, 25, 1917, November 1, 1917; CND, *Minutes,* 9/5/17, 11/19/17; Bradley to Baruch, 9/13/17, part 1, vol. 4, Baruch to Scott, 10/24/17, w/enc., file, "Copies of Important Letters, 1917, vol. 1," and Alexander C. Brown, George E. Merryweather, E. E. Parsonage, Turner, and Pope Yeatman statements, Clarkson, "Statements of Men in War Work," 1920–1922, all in Baruch Papers. Actually, many other statements in the Clarkson work provide good insights into the formation, evolution, and operation of the commodity sections–war service committees, but that of Spencer is outstanding in that regard. "Final Report of Alkali and Chlorine Section," 12/28/18, "Brief History and Record of the Activities of the Advisory Committee on Plants and Munitions," 11/22/18, "Acids and Heavy Chemicals Section and Sulphur and Pyrites Section," [circa] 12/1918, and "Tentative Draft of Report—The Cotton Committee," 11/7/18, file IDI, Chairman's Office, Final reports, WIB Recds.; and Graham Committee, *Hearings,* serial 1, pp. 403–47, 1793–1857. The war service committees and their members are included in Baruch, *American Industry in the War,* appendix 44, pp. 395–409. That publication and *Final Report, WIB–Johnson,* give a full narrative and analysis of the war service committees and their antecedents, prepared largely by the war mobilizers themselves.

22. These developments are covered in full in Baruch, *American Industry in the War,* and *Final Report, WIB–Johnson.* See also Charles H. MacDowell, Peek, J. Leonard Replogle, Scott, and Summers statements, Clarkson, "Statements of Men in War Work," 1920–1922, Baruch Papers.

23. Grosvenor B. Clarkson, *Industrial America in the World War: The Strategy Behind the Line, 1917–1918* (New York: Houghton Mifflin, 1923), pp. 98 (quotation), pp. 303–11.

24. The analysis of the operation of the WIB draws on the wide base of sources already cited for this chapter. For published work, especially important are *Final Report, WIB–Johnson,* Baruch, *American Industry in the War,* and Clarkson, *Industrial America in the World War.* Clarkson's interviews, "Statements of Men in War Work," 1920–1922, Baruch Papers, are also useful and especially so in this regard for Edwin P. Gay, Herbert E. Peabody, Replogle, and Yeatman. Robert D. Cuff, *The War Industries Board: Business-Government Relations During World War I* (Baltimore: Johns Hopkins University Press, 1973), as the most recent and best secondary source is indispensable for analyzing the WIB. Board personnel, including war service committee membership, is conveniently available in Baruch, *American Industry in the War,* and Clarkson, *Industrial America in the World War.* Chamber of Commerce of the United States, *War Service Executive Committee of American Industries,* 2/1919, copy in part 2, vol. 15 (Special Papers), WWI, Baruch Papers, also provides good information in a convenient form. The Nye Committee, *Hearings, Munitions Industry,* 73d Cong., 1934, part 16, pp. 4121–45, provides a list of top WIB personnel, their business affiliations and, when available, their wartime sources of income. Also included in this source is the same information on the chief army procurement officers, who were often civilians on temporary duty, along with brief summaries of their entire careers. I have analyzed the corporations that served as contractors for the Export Department of J. P. Morgan & Co. (Nye Committee, *Munitions Industry,* part 25, 74th Cong., 2d sess., 1936, pp. 7691–7714), which provided personnel for the CND–NDAC, MSB, GMB, and WIB structures (CND, *First and Second Annual Reports,* pp. 97–127 and pp. 256–66), and the war service committees as represented in the Chamber of Commerce publication on those committees. Although this approach is rather crude, it establishes a significant level of continuity of personnel and firms in economic mobilization from the operations of J. P. Morgan & Co. through the WIB.

25. Michael D. Reagan, "Serving Two Masters: Problems in the Employment of Dollar-a-Year and Without Compensation Personnel" (Ph.D. diss., Princeton University, 1959), pp. 2–19, examines this matter for World War I as an introduction to World War II and after. See also "Daily Record of Mr. Baruch's Activities at Office from Jan. 16th to Feb. 12th Inclusive," 2/8/18, file part 2, sec. 2–Additional Material, and McAdoo to Baruch 10/10/18, file part 2, Section 2, vol. 9, part 3, Wash. Corr., Misc. E–G, WWI; Baruch to Wilson, 9/18/19, Selected Correspondence, all in Baruch Papers; and WIB, *Minutes,* 6/18/18, 10/22/18. For differing views about abuse and potential abuse in the WIB, see William Denman, John M. Hancock, and Merryweather in Clarkson, "Statements of Men in War Work," 1920–1922, Baruch Papers.

26. The ideology of the business mobilizers and the business community will be analyzed further in volume 3 (forthcoming) of this series. Clarkson best articulated many of these ideas and attitudes. See his testimony, Graham Committee, *Hearings,* serial 1, pp. 333–402. More important, his influential volume, secretly financed by Baruch, *Industrial America in the World War,* although containing invaluable information and insights, is nonetheless a propaganda piece on behalf of Baruch and the business ideology of World War I (see volume three).

27. This critical point is further substantiated in Beaver, *Baker,* which is basically sympathetic to Baker but is meticulously researched and balanced in interpretation (see pp. 71–75).

28. The general state and condition of the WIB from August 1917 to March 1918 can be traced in WIB, *Minutes,* Baruch, *American Industry in the War,* and *Final Report, WIB–Johnson.*

29. Baruch to Members of Allied Purchasing Commission, 9/28/17, file "Copies of Important Letters, 1917–vol. 1," WWI; "Diary of Bernard M. Baruch," 9/9/17 and other entries, file part 2–Additional Material, WWI; House Diary, 9/23/17 and 9/24/17, excerpted in Selected Correspondence, all in Baruch Papers; and WIB, *Minutes,* 8/1/17, 8/2/17, 8/3/17.

30. See note 28. See also Baruch to McGowan, 9/14/17, and other correspondence, file, part 1, vol. 4, Baruch to Crowell, 2/16/18, and other correspondence, file "Copies of Important Letters, 1918–vol. II," Baruch to Scott, 8/30/17, and other correspondence, file "Copies of Important Letters, 1917–vol. I," WWI, Baruch Papers; and WIB, *Minutes,* 8/1/17.

31. J. C. Musser, "Clearance Office," [circa] December 1918, file IDI, Chairman's Office, Final Reports, WIB Recds.; J. C. Musser, Report on Clearance Committee, [circa] December 1918, file part 2, vol. 1, part 1, WWI, Baruch Papers; Scott to Musser, 1/13/19, w/enc. correspondence and report on "Clearance Office" [this is the most complete version of the report available], file 21, "History of War Industries Board," Box 1, Scott Papers; Director of Purchases to Acting Quartermaster General, 2/12/18, file "Copies of Important Letters, 1918–vol. II," WWI, Baruch Papers; Baruch, *American Industry in the War,* pp. 32–35, 316–20; *Final Report, WIB–Johnson,* pp. 11–17, 67–70; and WIB, *Minutes,* 8/8/17, 9/26/17.

32. Gifford to Priority Committee of GMB, 5/11/18, w/encs. and "History of the Establishment, Organization, Functions, Procedure, and Operation of the Priorities Board of the War Industries Board," [circa] December 1918, file IDI, Chairman's Office, Final Report, WIB Recds.; Baruch to Baker, 7/13/17, file, "Copies of Important Letters, 1917–vol. I," WWI, Baruch Papers; WIB, *Minutes,* 8/8/17, 9/26/17; Foster and Lovett statements, Clarkson, "Statements of Men in War Work," 1920–1922, Baruch Papers; Baruch, *American Industry in the War,* pp. 47–60; *Final Report, WIB–Johnson,* pp. 12–37, 52–62; and Cuff, *War Industries Board,* pp. 119–22.

33. The analysis of price policy is based on Wilson to Baker, 6/29/17, and other correspondence, file "Correspondence, W. Wilson, May, 1917," Wilson to Baker, 8/9/17, w/enc. and other correspondence, file "Correspondence, W. Wilson, August, 1917," Baker Papers; Baruch "Diary," 11/5/17, file part 2, sec. 2–Additional material–Diary, from 11/5/17 to 10/30/18, Baruch to Singer, 7/13/17, file part 1, vol. 4, Baruch to Scott, 8/8/17, file "Copies of Important Letters, 1917–vol. I," and Baruch to Crowell, 2/16/18, file, "Copies of Important Letters, 1918–vol. II," WWI; Hancock, Lovett, Summers, and Daniel Willard statements, Clarkson, "Statements of Men in War Work," 1920–1922, all in Baruch Papers; Baruch, *American Industry in the War,* pp. 70–81; Livermore, *Politics Is Adjourned,* pp. 48–52; Robert D. Cuff and Melvin I. Urofsky, "The Steel Industry and Price-Fixing During World War I," *Business History Review* 44 (August 1970): 291–306. See also the discussion, analysis, and documentation of pricing in chapter 8.

34. For some examples of WIB executives' efforts for change, see Brookings to Willard, 1/16/18, w/enc., "Memorandum Concerning Functions of the War Industries Board," and correspondence concerning it and other correspondence and documents, file 4–AI, WIB Recds.

35. Morgan to Scott, 10/25/17, file "WIB Resignation–Ltrs re: Health," and Drain to Scott, 11/17/28, w/enc., file "Aftermath, 1930 thru 1940," Scott Papers.

36. Baker to Wilson, 11/17/17, and other correspondence, file 206, Council of National Defense–1917 (Sept.), Willard to Wilson, 1/11/18, file 206B, War Industries Board, 1918 (Jan.–March), and Willard to Clarkson, 5/14/23, file Grosvenor B. Clarkson Papers, 1917–1925, series 4, Wilson Papers; Wilson to Baker, 9/18/17, and other correspondence, file "Correspondence–W. Wilson–September 1917," and Willard to CND, 11/28/17, and other correspondence and documents, file "Correspondence, 1917–A," Baker Papers; Clarkson to Lovett, 2/27/18, file, "Lovett, Judge R. S.," CND Recds.; Willard to Chamberlain, 1/14/18, reproduced by CND, 1/15/18, file 74405, Dept. of Commerce Recds.; "Diary of Bernard M. Baruch," 11/19/17, and numerous other entries for months of November, December 1917 and January, February 1918, file part 2–Additional Material, WWI; "Daily Record of Mr. Baruch's Activities at Office from Jan. 16th to Feb. 12th Inclusive," various entries for January, February, and March 1918, file part 2, sec. 2–Additional Material"; Baruch to Assistant Secretary of War, 1/30/18, and other correspondence, file "Copies of Important Letters, 1918–vol. II"; Lovett, Peek, Palmer E. Pierce, and Willard statements, Clarkson, "Statements of Men in War Work," 1920–1922, all in Baruch Papers; CND, *Minutes,* 11/27/17; WIB, *Minutes,* 12/10/17; and Palmer, *Baker,* 1: 378–79.

37. The winter crisis of 1917–1918 is covered fully in Baker to Wilson, 11/3/17, and other correspondence, file "Correspondence, W. Wilson–Nov., 1917," Baker Papers; Gifford to Redfield, 12/1/17, w/enc. memorandums, file 74405, Dept. of Commerce Recds.; "Some Railroad Difficulties–A Memoranda," 12/10/17, and "Memoranda by R. S. Lovett," undated, file part 1, vol. 4, WWI; "Daily Record of Mr. Baruch's Activities at Office from Jan. 16th to Feb. 12th Inclusive," 1/31/18, part 2, sec. 2, Additional Material; Baruch, "Diary," various entries October, 1917–March 1918, part 2, sec. 2–Additional Material–Diary from 11/5/17 to 10/30/18; Peek and Willard statements, Clarkson, "Statements of Men in War Work," 1920–1922, all in Baruch Papers.

See these secondary sources for the winter crisis and its resolution: Beaver, *Baker,* pp. 79–109; Alexander D. Noyes, *The War Period of American Finance, 1908–1925* (New York: G. P. Putnam's Sons, 1926), pp. 244–78; L. C. Marshall, "A Nation of Economic Amateurs," in *Readings in the Economics of War,* ed. J. Maurice Clark, Walter H. Hamilton, and Harold G. Moulton, pp. 221–24 (Chicago: University of Chicago Press, 1918); Benedict Crowell and Robert F. Wilson, *How America Went to War,* 6 vols. (New Haven: Yale University Press, 1921), vol. 4, *The Armies of Industry,* pp. 1–19; Livermore, *Politics Is Adjourned,* pp. 62–104; Palmer, *Baker,* 2: 66–84; Paxson, *American Democracy and the World War,* 2: 210–28, 250–53; Clarkson, *Industrial America in the World War,* pp. 42–45, 51–59, 138–39, 199–200, 234–35, 453; and Cuff, *War Industries Board,* pp. 131–47.

38. Chamberlain Committee, *Hearings,* pp. 1885–1924; Chamber of Commerce of the United States, *Minutes, War Convention of American Business,* and *Seventh Meeting, National Council,* September 1917, *Minutes, Sixth Annual Meeting,* and *Eighth Meeting, National Council,* April 1918, Board of Directors, *Annual Report,* Fifth Annual Meeting, January–February 1917, Board of Directors, *Annual Report,* Sixth Annual Report, April 1918, and *Minutes,* Meetings, Board of Directors and Meetings, Executive Committee, 1917–1918, Chamber of Commerce Recds.; Galen Reid Fisher,

"The Chamber of Commerce of the United States and the Laissez Faire-Rationale, 1912–1919" (Ph.D. diss., University of California, Berkeley, 1960), chaps. 12–14; Tumulty to Wilson, 11/14/17, and other correspondence, file 1019, series 4, Wilson Papers; Baker to president, 12/10/17, and other correspondence, file "Correspondence, W. Wilson, Dec., 1917," Baker Papers; Clarkson to Catchings, 8/7/17, and other correspondence and documents, file "Chamber of Commerce of the U.S.," CND Recds.; Chamber of Commerce, *War Bulletin no. 12,* 8/10/17, and other documents, file part 2, vol. 15 (Special Papers), Brand to Baruch, 11/26/17, file part 1, vol. 3, and Allen to Baruch [circa] June 1917, file part 2, sec. 2–Additional Material–BMB Personal–Price Policy, WWI, Baruch Papers; CND, *Minutes,* 11/19/17, 1/7/18, 2/4/18, 2/7/18, 2/21/18, 2/25/18, 3/4/18, 5/27/18; and Martin, *Digest, Proceedings, CND,* pp. 348–65, 370–72.

After Catchings resigned from the CND, the chamber committee he headed, the Committee on Cooperation with the Council of National Defense, was renamed the War Committee of the Chamber and even later the War Committee and the Executive Committee on Industrial War Service Committees. For a time, the Chamber of Commerce's Executive Committee was also called the War Committee of the Chamber, which creates some confusion in trying to follow Catchings's path in the Chamber of Commerce hierarchy. In May 1918 Catchings was rather abruptly dropped from the Chamber of Commerce leadership involving economic mobilization, which he had held at least since mid-1917. Why this occurred is not clear. It probably resulted from the chamber's strained relations with the sensitive Wilson administration during the winter crisis of 1917–1918, when the chamber assumed the preeminent role in forcing the administration fundamentally to change its mobilization structure and policies. As the principal spokesperson and leader of the Chamber of Commerce in this regard, Catchings was probably sacrificed for the cause of reconciliation with the Wilson administration after the reorganization of the WIB between March and May 1918, in which Catchings and the chamber had achieved much of what they wanted.

39. U.S. Congress, Senate, Committee on Military Affairs, *Director of Munitions,* 65th Cong., 2d sess., 1918, Senate Report no. 200 to accompany S. 3311, pp. 1–2; *Cong. Rec.,* 65th Cong., 2d sess., vol. 56, part 1, 1918, pp. 557–58, 977–79, 980–83, 1004, part 2, pp. 1194–1211, 1242–44, 1607–21, 1686–95, 1747, 1819–32, 1842–52, 2095–2105, part 3, pp. 2136–49, part 4, p. 3815, part 5, pp. 4504–26, 4572–83, 4945–4973, 5013–23, part 6, pp. 5551–71, 5739–66, part 9, p. 8616; Baker to Wilson, 1/25/18, w/enc., file, "Correspondence, W. Wilson, Jan., 1918," Baker Papers; House Diary, 1/17/18, excerpts in Selected Correspondence, and Peek statement, Clarkson, "Statements of Men in War Work," 1920–1922, both in Baruch Papers; and Palmer, *Baker,* 2: 82.

40. Wilson to Baker, 3/4/18, w/enc., "Correspondence, W. Wilson, March–April 1918–W," Baker Papers; Wilson to Baruch, 3/4/18, Selected Correspondence; Baruch to Wilson, 5/24/18, and other correspondence and documents, file "Copies of Important Letters, 1918–vol. IV," WWI; Peek and Willard statements, Clarkson, "Statements of Men in War Work," 1920–1922, Baruch Papers; Baruch, *American Industry in the War,* pp. 22–29; and Wilson to Clarkson, 3/26/18, file 206, series 4, Wilson Papers.

41. E. M. H. Lloyd, *Experiments in State Control at the War Office and the Ministry of Food* (Oxford: Clarendon Press, 1924); John A. Fairle, *British War Administration* (New York: Oxford University Press, 1919); Pierre Renouvin, *The Forms of*

*War Government in France* (New Haven: Yale University Press, 1927); S. O. Zagorsky, *State Control of Industry in Russia During the War* (New Haven: Yale University Press, 1928); and Robert B. Armeson, *Total Warfare and Compulsory Labor: A Study of the Military-Industrial Complex in Germany During World War I* (The Hague: M. Nijhoff, 1964). See also the relevant portions of Gabriel Kolko, *Century of War: Politics, Conflict, and Society Since 1914* (New York: New Press, 1994). Not only is this a rich and provocative study, but the author also cites most of the relevant bibliography on economic mobilization for war in Europe, including among others the work of Gerald D. Feldman and Arthur Marwick.

42. Beaver, *Baker,* pp. 52, 96, n. 64, 105–6. Revering yet suspecting the business community has been a long-run trend in American life. See Thomas C. Cochran, *The American Business System: A Historical Perspective, 1900–1955* (Cambridge: Harvard University Press, 1957), pp. 2–10, 194–205.

43. *Cong. Rec.,* 65th Cong., 2d sess., vol. 56, part 1, p. 558; *New York Times,* January 5, 1918, p. 3. See also the citations for the *Cong. Rec.,* nn. 4 and 39.

44. See testimony of Willard, Baruch, Gifford, and Coffin in Chamberlain Committee, *Hearings,* pp. 1799–1847, 1850–84, 2253–89. See also Brookings to Wilson, 2/16/18, w/enc., file 206B, series 4, Wilson Papers.

45. Willard to Baker, 12/7/17, and numerous other correspondence and documents, file 1019, U.S. Chamber of Commerce, series 4, Wilson Papers, and *Nation's Business,* February 1918, pp. 7–9.

46. Clarkson, *Industrial America in the World War,* pp. 5–9, 20, 215–16, and *Final Report, WIB–Johnson,* pp. 3–4. Most businessmen serving in the mobilization structure agreed that an evolutionary process was essential for the economic mobilization machinery, with maximum latitude left to the business mobilizers to work out the proper techniques. See Hugh S. Johnson, Lovett, Charles A. Otis, Parsonage, Peek, Pierce, Replogle, A. W. Shaw, Turner, Samuel M. Vauclain, and Willard statements, Clarkson, "Statements of Men in War Work," 1920–1922, Baruch Papers, and Appropriations Subcommittee, *Hearings,* pp. 36–43. In order to protect military prerogatives, the War Department was generally opposed to legislative solutions to the mobilization crisis. See Beaver, *Baker,* pp. 93–97.

47. *New York Times,* February 27, 1918, p. 4, and Fisher, "Chamber of Commerce," pp. 378–80. See also the citations in notes 38 and 45.

48. The winter crisis and its effects and consequences are covered in the secondary and some of the primary sources cited in note 37. See also Lovett and Otis statements, Clarkson, "Statements of Men in War Work," 1920–1922, Baruch Papers.

49. The discussion and analysis of Baruch's selection as chairman of the WIB is based on McAdoo to Wilson, 1/17/18, and numerous other correspondence and documents, file 206B, and Baker to Clarkson, 10/22/25, file "Grosvenor B. Clarkson Papers, 1917–1925," series 4, Wilson Papers; Frankfurter to Baker, 1/4/18, w/enc., file, "Correspondence, 1918–F," Baker to Wilson, 1/24/18 w/enc., and other correspondence, file, "Correspondence, W. Wilson–Jan., 1918," Baker to Wilson, 2/1/18, and other correspondence, file "Correspondence, W. Wilson, Feb., 1918," and Wilson to Baker, 3/4/18, w/enc., file "Correspondence, W. Wilson, March–April, 1918–W," Baker Papers; Baruch to Wilson, 2/5/18, and other correspondence, file part 1, vol. 4, Baker to Baruch, 2/2/18, file part 2, sec. 2, vol. 9, part 1, Washington Correspondence, Misc. A–G, Baruch to Wilson, 2/8/18, and other correspondence,

file "Copies of Important Letters, 1918–vol. II," "Daily Record of Mr. Baruch's Activities at Office from Jan. 16th to Feb. 12th Inclusive," entries Jan.–March 1918, part 2, sec. 2, Additional Materials, F. W. Allen, Memo. to Baruch, "Centralized Purchasing," undated and other correspondence and documents, file, part 2, sec. 2–Additional Material–BMB Personal–Price Policy, WWI; Pierce and Willard statements, Clarkson, "Statements of Men in War Work," 1920–1922; Baruch to Baker, 2/4/18, and numerous other correspondence and documents, including excerpts from the House Diary, Selected Correspondence, all in Baruch Papers; J. P. Miller, Jr., "Memorandum of Confidential Conference with Bernard M. Baruch," 4/2/18, file "Assistant Secretary," Box 155, CND Recds.; Brookings to Willard, 1/16/18, w/enc. and other correspondence and documents, file 4–AI–Price Fixing Committee, Misc. Correspondence and Papers, WIB Recds.; Chamberlain Committee, *Hearings,* pp. 1605–1797, 1925–86, 2069–2103; CND, *Minutes,* 2/21/18; Cronon, ed., *Daniels Cabinet Diaries,* December 1917–March 1918, numerous entries, pp. 244–94; Palmer, *Baker,* 2: 82–84, 201–2; Beaver, *Baker,* pp. 79–109; and Baruch, *Baruch: The Public Years,* pp. 44–52.

## CHAPTER TEN. THE WAR INDUSTRIES BOARD, MARCH–NOVEMBER 1918

1. The final structure and membership of the WIB is set forth in Bernard M. Baruch, *American Industry in the War: A Report of the War Industries Board* (Washington, DC: Government Printing Office, 1921); *Final Report, WIB–Johnson;* and Grosvenor B. Clarkson, *Industrial America in the World War: The Strategy Behind the Line, 1917–1918* (New York: Houghton Mifflin, 1923). The structure and membership as of May 1918 is included in U.S. Council of National Defense, *Second Annual Report* (Washington, DC: U.S. Government Printing Office, 1918), pp. 256–61.

2. Baruch's style and mode of operation are best examined through the views of WIB executives. The most valuable in this regard is the L. L. Summers statement in Grosvenor Clarkson, "Statements of Men in War Work," 1920–1922, Baruch Papers. But also worthwhile are the statements of Charles K. Foster, H. P. Ingels, Spencer Turner, Samuel M. Vauclain, and Pope Yeatman, ibid. The Frank A. Scott interview establishes that the frequently made charge of Baruch's not tapping the nation's "strongest" talent was a code word for those in the J. P. Morgan & Co. circles. See also Clarkson, *Industrial America in the World War,* chap. 4.

3. The rise of the commodity section–war service committee system to the point of dominance is a major theme of *Final Report, WIB–Johnson.* This approach is also evident in Baruch, *American Industry in the War,* and is highlighted in Clarkson, *Industrial America in the World War.* For Baruch's views on the strengthened WIB shortly after his appointment to the chair, see J. P. Miller, Jr., "Memorandum of Confidential Conference with Bernard M. Baruch," 4/2/18, file "Assistant Secretary," Box 155, CND Recds. File 2–A5, "General Category, Gifford's Correspondence, April 1917–May 1921," Box 83, CND Recds., has several lengthy and informative memorandums on the evolution of the WIB. See also Council of National Defense, "Commodity Organization," March 1918, and Parker, "War Industries Board: Its Functions, Organization, and Personnel," 6/1/18, and other correspondence and documents,

file 21A–Al, WIB Recds. Many of the key commodity sections–war service committees will be analyzed in greater depth in volume 3 (forthcoming) of this series.

4. See chap. 9, n. 31. See also WIB, *Minutes,* Senate Committee Print 4, 7/9/18; CND, *Second Annual Report,* pp. 121–22; Baruch to Hurley, 4/3/18, and numerous other correspondence and documents, file "Copies of Important Letters, 1918–vol. III," and Baruch to Johnson, 8/2/18, file "Copies of Important Letters, 1918–vol. IV," WWI; Baruch to Baker, 7/24/18, Selected Correspondence, all in Baruch Papers; and Baruch, *American Industry in the War,* pp. 106–9.

5. Baruch to Wilson, [circa] January 1920, Selected Correspondence, and Baruch to WIB, 11/14/17, part 1, vol. 4, WWI, Baruch Papers; Frost to Gay, 9/27/18, and other correspondence, file 21A–A7, WIB Recds.; Baruch, *American Industry in the War,* pp. 30–37, 106–9, 320–23; WIB, *Minutes,* 7/9/18; *Final Report, WIB–Johnson,* pp. 8–23; CND, *Second Annual Report,* pp. 119–21; and Clarkson, *American Industry in the World War,* pp. 121–37. Clarkson, "Statements of Men in War Work," 1920–1922, Baruch Papers, gives both rich detail and varying assessments of the functioning and value of the Requirements Division. See the statements of Samuel P. Bush, Lincoln Cromwell, Foster, John M. Hancock, Charles A. Otis, Herbert E. Peabody, George N. Peek, J. Leonard Replogle, Turner, Vauclain, and Yeatman.

6. The discussion and analysis of the priority system under the strengthened WIB is based on "History of the Establishment, Organization, Functions, Procedure, and Operation of the Priorities Board of the War Industries Board," [circa] Dec. 1918, and "Report of the Priorities Committee of War Industries Board to Mr. Baruch, Chairman, War Industries Board," [circa] Dec. 1918, file IDI, Chairman's Office, Final Reports; "Minutes, WIB with . . . the Wire-Bound Box Industry," 9/5/18, file "Priority," 18G–Al, Papers Assembled by AIC, all in WIB Recds.; Baruch to Baker, 4/24/18, file "Copies of Important Letters, 1918–vol. IV," WWI; Baruch to Wilson, 8/30/18, and other correspondence, Selected Correspondence; Foster, Hancock, R. S. Lovett, Chas. A. McKenney, Peek, Replogle, Summers, Turner, and Vauclain statements, Clarkson, "Statements of Men in War Work," 1920–1922, all in Baruch Papers; Graham Committee, *Hearings,* serial 1, pp. 1793–1857; *Final Report, WIB–Johnson,* pp. 24–37, 52–67; Baruch, *American Industry in the War,* pp. 47–60, 325–54; CND, *Second Annual Report,* pp. 124–28; and WIB, *Minutes,* 5/16/18 and 5/17/18.

7. Actually, the old Priorities Committee was continued, a new Priorities Board created, and both were within the new Priorities Division. To simplify matters, this new structure will be referred to as the Priorities Division, without in any way sacrificing a reasonable level of accuracy.

8. The discussion and analysis of price control is based on Brookings to Wilson, 2/22/19, and report, "Price Fixing," [circa] Dec. 1918, file IDI, Chairman's Office, Final Reports; Montgomery to Price Fixing Committee, 7/1/18, and numerous other correspondence and documents, file 4–AI–Price Fixing Committee, Misc. Corr. and Papers–1, Brookings to Wilson, 10/4/18, and numerous other correspondence and documents, file "Price Fixing Committee, Misc. Corr. and Papers–2," Brookings to Colver, 8/2/18, and other correspondence, file "Price Fixing Committee, Misc. Corr. and Papers–3," all in WIB Recds.; Edgar to Baruch, 7/22/18, w/enc., file part 2, sec. 2, vol. 9, part 3, Wash. Corr.–Misc. E–G, Wilson to Baruch, 3/12/18, file "Copies of Important Letters, 1918–vol. III," Daniels to Baruch, 3/4/18, w/enc., file "Copies of Important Letters, 1918–vol. IV," "Daily Record of Mr. Baruch's Activities at Office

from Jan. 16th to Feb. 12th Inclusive," various entries from March–June 1918, part 2, sec. 2—Additional Material, Memorandum on Price Fixing, undated, unsigned and numerous other correspondence and documents, file part 2, sec. 2–Additional Material, BMB Personal–Price Policy, WWI; Daniels to Baruch, 3/4/18, and other correspondence; Robert S. Brookings, William Denman, Edwin P. Gay, Hancock, Charles H. MacDowell, Peabody, Peek, Replogle, A. W. Shaw, Summers, Turner, and Yeatman statements, Clarkson, "Statements of Men in War Work," 1920–1922, all in Baruch Papers; Willard to Wilson, 12/7/17, and other correspondence, file 206, and Daniels to Wilson, 3/11/18, and other correspondence, file 206B, series 4, Wilson Papers; Graham Committee, *Hearings,* serial 1, pp. 1793–1857; CND, *Second Annual Report,* pp. 122–24; WIB, *Minutes,* 3/14/18; Baruch, *American Industry in the War,* pp. 70–81, and various portions on commodity section analysis, pp. 103–284; *Final Report, WIB–Johnson,* pp. 37–39, and various portions on commodity section analysis, pp. 111–1110; and Benedict Crowell and Robert F. Wilson, *How America Went to War,* 6 vols. (New Haven: Yale University Press, 1921), vol. 1, *The Giant Hand,* p. 77.

The most basic and important documents of the wartime price-fixing procedures are the verbatim minutes of the Price Fixing Committee, which are readily accessible because they were published in three volumes by the Nye Committee. See *Minutes of the Price Fixing Committee of the War Industries Board,* parts l–4, March 14–December 30, 1918, 74th Cong., 2d sess., 1936, Senate Committee Print no. 5 (hereafter Price Fixing Committee, *Minutes*). Various secondary works that deal exclusively or primarily with the price-fixing process are also valuable. For some of the better ones, see Frank W. Taussig, "Price-Fixing as Seen by a Price-Fixer," *Quarterly Journal of Economics* 33 (February 1919): 205–41; Lewis H. Haney, "Price Fixing in the United States During the War, I, II, and III," *Political Science Quarterly* 34 (March, June, and September 1919): 104–26, 262–89, and 434–53; Simon Litman, *Prices and Price Control in Great Britain and the United States During the World War* (New York: Oxford University Press, 1920); Herbert Stein, *Government Price Policy in the United States During the World War* (Williamstown: Williams College, 1939); Charles O. Hardy, *Wartime Control of Prices* (Washington, DC: Brookings Institution, 1940); George P. Adams, Jr., *Wartime Price Control* (Washington, DC: American Council on Public Affairs 1942); and Hugh Rockoff, *Drastic Measures: A History of Wage and Price Controls in the United States* (New York: Cambridge University Press, 1984), pp. 43–84.

9. Shaw statement and statements of Gay, Peabody, and Peek, Clarkson, "Statements of Men in War Work," 1920–1922, and Baruch to Shaw, 3/14/18, file "Copies of Important Letters, 1918–vol. III," WWI, Baruch Papers; Wilson to Baker, 7/24/18, file 206B, series 4, Wilson Papers; Shaw to Baruch, 12/15/1–Report on Conservation Division and its antecedents–file IDI, Chairman's Office, Final Reports, WIB Recds.; Baruch, *American Industry in the War,* pp. 61–69; *Final Report, WIB–Johnson,* pp. 33–37, 70–86; CND, *Second Annual Report,* pp. 131, 193–200; and Clarkson, *Industrial America in the War,* pp. 181–82, 209–31.

10. Bush to Peek, "Outline of Activities and Problems of the Facilities Division," 12/14/18, "History of the Division of Planning and Statistics, War Industries Board," [circa] December 1918, and Paul W. Garrett, "Report of the Work of the Price Section of the Division of Planning and Statistics," 12/31/18, file IDI, Chairman's Office, Final Reports, WIB Recds.; "Diary of Bernard M. Baruch," various entries for late 1917 and early 1918, file part 2–Additional Materials, WWI, Baruch to Baker,

5/4/18, and other correspondence, file "Copies of Important Letters, 1918–vol. IV," and "*Minutes,* Meeting [of WIB] with representatives of the National Federation of Building Industries," 8/22/18, and other documents, file part 2, sec. 2–Additional Material, WWI; Bush and Gay statements, Clarkson, "Statements of Men in War Work," 1920–1922, all in Baruch Papers; Baruch, *American Industry in the War,* pp. 38–40, 43–46, 61–69; *Final Report, WIB–Johnson,* pp. 33–37, 70–86, 105–10; Clarkson, *Industrial America in the World War,* pp. 200–206, 209–31; Robert D. Cuff, "Creating Control Systems: Edwin F. Gay and the Central Bureau of Planning and Statistics, 1917–1919," *Business History Review* 63 (Autumn 1989): 588–613; William J. Breen, "Foundations, Statistics, and State-Building: Leonard P. Ayers, the Russell Sage Foundation, and U.S. Government Statistics in the First World War," *Business History Review* 68 (Winter 1994): 451–82; and James R. Beniger, *The Control Revolution: Technological and Economic Origins of the Informational Society* (Cambridge: Harvard University Press, 1986), chap. 9.

11. The discussion of the Resources and Conservation Section is based on Otis, "Resources and Conservation Section," Final Report, 12/5/18, file IDI, Chairman's Office, Final Reports, WIB Recds.; Perry to Clarkson, 5/7/18, file "B–Misc.," Box 156, CND Recds.; Otis to Baruch, 12/5/18 w/enc., "Partial Minutes of the . . . Resources and Conservation Section," WIB, July 18, 19, 1918, and other correspondence and documents, file part 2, vol. 3, Peek to Baruch, 2/15/18, file "Copies of Important Letters, 1918–vol. II," Baruch to Willard, 4/15/18, file "Copies of Important Letters, 1918–vol. III," WWI; Daniels to Baruch, 4/27/18, and other correspondence, Selected Correspondence; Otis statement and also those of Bush, Martin Gillen, Hugh S. Johnson, and McKenney, Clarkson, "Statements of Men in War Work," 1920–1922, all in Baruch Papers; CND, *Second Annual Report,* pp. 201–2; Baruch, *American Industry in the War,* pp. 40–42; *Final Report, WIB–Johnson,* pp. 86–91; and Robert D. Cuff, *War Industries Board: Business-Government Relations During World War I* (Baltimore: Johns Hopkins University Press, 1973), pp. 182–90. See also chap. 9, nn. 17–20 and 38 for sources on the Chamber of Commerce.

12. "Baruch Diary," 1/10/18, file part 2, sec. 2–Additional Material–Diary from 11/5/17 to 10/30/18, and Baruch to WIB, 8/31/17, file part 1, vol. 4, WWI; Replogle statement, Clarkson, "Statements of Men in War Work," 1920–1922, all in Baruch Papers; Baruch, *American Industry in the War,* pp. 57–60; *Final Report, WIB–Johnson,* pp. 25–37; and Clarkson, *Industrial America in the World War,* pp. 181–86.

13. Replogle to Baruch, 5/2/18, and other correspondence, file "Conservation and Substitution," file group 18–E–A1 Papers, WIB Recds.; Replogle to Baruch, 12/6/17, file part 1, vol. 4, Minutes, "Meeting of the War Industries Board with Representatives of the Automobile Industry," May 7, 1918, and other documents, file part 2, vol. 4, WIB Minutes, Baruch to Pierce, 2/18/18, and other correspondence, file "Copies of Important Letters, 1918–vol. II," and Baruch to Lodge, 3/28/18, and other correspondence, file "Copies of Important Letters, 1918–vol. III," WWI; Replogle and Summers statements, Clarkson, "Statements of Men in War Work," 1920–1922, all in Baruch Papers; WIB, *Minutes,* 7/16/18, 8/6/18, 8/13/18, and other entries; Baruch, *American Industry in the World War,* pp. 271–73; *Final Report, WIB–Johnson,* pp. 764–80; Clarkson, *Industrial America in the World War,* pp. 331–43; and Cuff, *War Industries Board,* pp. 204–19.

14. The discussion and analysis of attempts at price controls for the civilian population are based on Brookings to Wilson, 5/2/18, and other correspondence, file 206B, series 4, Wilson Papers; Scott to Ely, 9/9/18, and numerous other correspondence and documents, file "Price Fixing Committee, Misc. Corr. and Papers no. 2," WIB Recds.; "Daily Records of Mr. Baruch's Activities at Office from Jan. 16th to Feb. 12th Inclusive," 6/15/18, and other entries, file sec. 2, Additional Material, WWI, and Brookings, Cromwell, and Shaw statements, Clarkson, "Statements of Men in War Work," 1920–1922, Baruch Papers; WIB, *Minutes,* August 1, 6, 13, 1918; Baruch, *American Industry in the War,* pp. 252–54; *Final Report, WIB–Johnson,* pp. 923–27; Clarkson, *Industrial America in the World War,* pp. 432–36; and Cuff, *War Industries Board,* pp. 232–40.

15. Parker to Baruch, 4/5/18, and other correspondence, file 4–AI Price Fixing Committee, Misc. Correspondence and Papers, WIB Recds.; Miller, "Memorandum of Confidential Conference with Bernard Baruch," 4/2/18, file "Ass't sec.," and Clarkson to Catchings, 8/7/17, file, "Chamber of Commerce of the U.S.," CND Recds.; "Daily Record of Mr. Baruch's Activities at Office from Jan. 16th to Feb. 12th Inclusive," 2/14/18, and other entries, file part 2, sec. 2, Additional Material, WWI, and Lovett, Peek, and Daniel Willard statements, Clarkson, "Statements of Men in War Work," 1920–1922, Baruch Papers; WIB, *Minutes,* 5/16/18; Baruch, *American Industry in the War,* pp. 27–29; and Cuff, *War Industries Board,* pp. 223–24. See also chap. 9, nn. 45 and 46 and the relevant text.

16. The description and analysis of War Department–army supply reforms in 1917–1918 draws on Daniel R. Beaver, *Newton D. Baker and the American War Effort, 1917–1919* (Lincoln: University of Nebraska Press, 1966), pp. 79–109, 161–71 (and some references before and after this analysis), Beaver, "Newton D. Baker and the Genesis of the War Industries Board, 1917–1918," *Journal of American History* 52 (June 1965): 43–58, and Beaver, "George W. Goethals and the Problem of Military Supply," in *Some Pathways in Twentieth-Century History: Essays in Honor of Charles McGrane,* ed. Beaver, pp. 95–109 (Detroit: Wayne State University Press, 1969); John Dickinson, *The Building of An Army: A Detailed Account of Legislation, Administration and Opinion in the United States, 1915–1920* (New York: Century, 1922), pp. 247–322; Edward M. Coffman, *The Hilt of the Sword: The Career of Peyton C. March* (Madison: University of Wisconsin Press, 1966), pp. 67–68, 76–77, 149, 151, 247–48, and Coffman, *The War to End All Wars: The American Military Experience in World War I* (New York: Oxford University Press, 1968), pp. 10–211; Frederick Palmer, *Newton D. Baker: America at War,* 2 vols. (New York: Dodd, Mead, 1931), 2: 2–3, 22–88, 330–40; Crowell and Wilson, *How America Went to War,* vol. 1, *The Giant Hand,* pp. 99–103, vol. 2, *The Road to France,* pp. 227–28, vol. 4, *The Armies of Industry,* pp. 1–19; J. Franklin Crowell, *Government War Contracts* (New York: Oxford University Press, 1920), pp. 22–30, 64–73, 104–6; James E. Hewes, Jr., *From Root to McNamara: Army Organization and Administration, 1900–1963* (Washington, DC: Center of Military History, 1975), pp. 21–50; James A. Huston, *The Sinews of War: Army Logistics, 1775–1953* (Washington, DC: Office of the Chief of Military History, 1966), pp. 308–28; Erna Risch, *Quartermaster Support of the Army: A History of the Corps, 1775–1939* (Washington, DC: Office of the Quartermaster General, 1962), pp. 599–644; Hugh S. Johnson, *The Blue Eagle from Egg to Earth* (New York: Doubleday, Doran, 1935), pp. 86–101, 115; Otto L. Nelson, Jr., *National Security and*

*the General Staff* (Washington, DC: Infantry Journal Press, 1946), pp. 217–71; Peyton C. March, *The Nation at War* (New York: Doubleday, Doran, 1932), pp. 38–56, 74–75, 165, 187–88; Harvey A. DeWeerd, *President Wilson Fights His War: World War I and the American Intervention* (New York: Macmillan, 1968), pp. 206–10, 220–29, 394–99; Jordan A. Schwarz, *The Speculator: Bernard M. Baruch in Washington, 1917–1965* (Chapel Hill: University of North Carolina Press, 1981), chap. 2; Joseph B. Bishop and Farnham Bishop, *Goethals: Genius of the Panama Canal—A Biography* (New York: Harper and Brothers, 1930), pp. 374–98; John Kennedy Ohl, "'Old Iron Pants': The Wartime Career of General Hugh S. Johnson" (Ph.D. diss., University of Cincinnati, 1971), Ohl, "General Hugh S. Johnson and the War Industries Board," *Military Review* 55 (May 1975): 35–48, and Ohl, *Hugh S. Johnson and the New Deal* (DeKalb: Northern Illinois University Press, 1985), pp. 36–53; Phyllis A. Zimmerman, "George W. Goethals and the Reorganization of the United States Army Supply System, 1917–1918" (Ph.D. diss., Indiana University, 1987), and Zimmerman, *The Neck of the Bottle: George W. Goethals and the Reorganization of the U.S. Army Supply System, 1917–1918* (College Station: Texas A&M University Press, 1992). See also David F. Trask, *The AEF and Coalition Warmaking, 1917–1918* (Lawrence: University Press of Kansas, 1993), and Timothy K. Nenninger, "American Military Effectiveness in the First World War," in *Military Effectiveness,* vol. 1, *The First World War,* ed. Allan R. Millett and Williamson Murray, pp. 116–56 (Boston: Allen and Unwin, 1988).

17. Baker to Reed, 5/11/18, file, "Correspondence File, Jan.–Aug., 1918–R," and Baker to Wilson, 1/15/18, file, "Correspondence–W. Wilson–January 1918," Baker Papers; "Diary of Bernard M. Baruch," January 24, 25, 1918, file part 2–Additional Materials, WWI, and Palmer E. Pierce and Willard statements, Clarkson, "Statements of Men in War Work," 1920–1922, both in Baruch Papers; Brewster to Baker, 1/25/18, file "Unanswerable Matters," Box 162, CND Recds.; U.S. Congress, Senate, Committee on Military Affairs, *Hearings, Investigation of the War Department,* 65th Cong., 2d Sess, 1917–1918, pp. 1605–1798; SMAC, *Hearings, 1920,* pp. 78–83; and HMAC, *Hearings, 1920,* pp. 65–75, 142–49.

18. The creation of the Purchase, Storage, and Traffic Division between January and November 1919 is an extremely complex and detailed matter that is treated with varying degrees of quality and insight in some of the secondary sources cited in note 16. Primary sources, however, are indispensable for grasping the intricacy and significance of what occurred. A personal, running account of developments is recorded in Goethals's letters to his son Dody, December 1917–December 1918, file "Family Correspondence, 1916–1927," file 1918, and see also Johnson to Goethals, 7/5/18, and other correspondence, file, "General Correspondence, 1917–1929," file Jan.–Nov.–1918, George W. Goethals Papers, Library of Congress, Washington, DC.

The records of the Purchase, Storage, and Traffic Division are rather disappointing in terms of general policy formulation and implementation, as opposed to day-to-day administrative details. Nonetheless, valuable information and data about the division and its staffing and functioning are found there. See "Information Requested in Senate Resolution of February 28, 1919" (a breakdown of wartime purchases, including name, rank, location, and business connections of procuring officers), file 032.2, and Ross to Fair, 1/10/19, w/ enc., consolidated figure on "Personnel as of January 1, 1919" by the Office of the Director of Purchase, Storage and Traffic, file 200 and other documents, and correspondence in these two files and files 230.38, 330.3, and

022; stenographic Report of "Conference on a War Program," 3/30/18, and other documents and correspondence, Box 509, and Crowell to Williams, 8/26/18, w/encs. and other correspondence and documents, Box 508, file "Papers from Mr. Swope's File"; Thorne to Goethals, 1/28/19, and other correspondence and documents, file "Organizational Papers from Col. Fair's File," and Stettinius to Pierce, 4/4/18, and other correspondence and documents, Box 3, file "Hugh S. Johnson Papers," all in Records of the War Department General and Special Staffs, General Staff—Purchase, Storage, and Traffic Division, 1918–1920, Series 441, Record Group 165, National Archives, Washington, DC.

The yearly reports of the secretary of war also provide both general and specific information about the operations, modifications, and reforms of the army's supply system. See *ARSW*, 1914–1919. The reports of the two principal army supply bureaus, the Quartermaster Corps and the Ordnance Department *(QMGR* and *OR)* are even more useful for grasping the general and detailed prewar and wartime supply matters (see chap. 8, n. 27). The *QMGR*s from 1914 through 1917 reflect well the ossified state of the bureau. Despite impending hostilities and the burdens of war, the Quartermaster General continued to focus on day-to-day operations and minutiae much more than on the crisis at hand. However, the 1918 and 1919 reports, once army supply reforms were under way and a new quartermaster general was in place, are of a totally different quality. In fact, the two reports together constitute among the best sources for describing and analyzing the emergence and operation of the Purchase, Storage, and Traffic Division. The 1919 report indicates the increased tension between the General Staff and the supply bureaus that the wartime reforms generated. Because the Ordnance Department experienced less stress and trauma than the Quartermaster Corps before and during America's entry into the war, its reports are both less revealing and less informative. From 1915, the Ordnance Department was more aware than the Quartermaster Corps of how the war would influence its operations, and it began to prepare itself accordingly. Hence, when war came, the department was able to meet its vast new burdens better than the corps and, therefore, was in a more favorable position for protecting its interests and keeping its organization intact despite increased power for the civilian mobilization agencies and the General Staff. Some of the best information on the evolution and operations of the Purchase, Storage, and Traffic Division, with both supporting and detracting points of view, are presented in congressional hearings. See SMAC, *Hearings, 1920,* particularly the testimony of Goethals, pp. 1025–41. However, almost all principal bureau chiefs and many of the key army supply personnel also testified, which makes this a valuable source that requires reading from the beginning to the end. The same is true for *HMAC, Hearings, 1920.* Moreover, in the Graham Committee, *Hearings,* Serial 1, vol. 1, pp. 128–54, are reproduced many of the important documents that set forth and explain the evolution and functioning of the Purchase, Storage, and Traffic Division. These *Hearings* also contain invaluable testimony on the army's supply situation. Most significant, again, is the testimony of Goethals, pp. 517–57. However, numerous other military and civilian war mobilizers provide excellent material and insight throughout this extended and comprehensive congressional investigation; see both Serials 1 and 3 in this regard. See also Crowder to Baker, 12/8/17, w/enc., Correspondence File 1917–C, and Stettinius to Baker, 5/4/18, Correspondence File, Jan.–July, 1918–S, Baker Papers; Summers to Baruch, 9/1/18, and numerous other correspondence, file part 2, sec. 2, vol. 9, part 7, Wash. Corr.–Misc. S, and "Diary of Mr. Bernard M. Baruch," 12/6/17, 4/18/18, and numerous other entries, file part 2–Additional Material, WWI; and Johnson and McKenney statements, Clarkson, "Statements of Men in War Work," 1920–1922, all in Baruch Papers.

19. The staffing of the Purchase, Storage, and Traffic Division can be traced through HMAC, *Hearings, 1920,* p. 447; Graham Committee, *Hearings,* Serial 1, pp. 147–52, 293; Dickinson, *Building of an Army,* pp. 305–6; Risch, *Quartermaster Support of the Army,* pp. 630; David Loth, *Swope of G.E.: The Story of Gerard Swope and General Electric in American Business* (New York: Simon and Schuster, 1958), pp. 80–92; and CND, *Second Annual Report,* pp. 200–201. See also the Purchase, Storage, and Traffic Division Records pertinent to staffing and personnel, note 18, and Goethals to Dody, 7/14/18, and other letters, Goethals Papers; Hatfield, "History of the Division of Planning and Statistics, War Industries Board," [circa] December 1918, file IDI, Chairman's Office, Final Reports, WIB Recds.; Baruch to Crowell, 5/8/18, file "Copies of Important Letters, 1918–vol. IV," and "Daily Record of Mr. Baruch's Activities at Office from Jan. 16th to Feb. 12th Inclusive," 2/14/18, and other entries, file part 2, section 2–Additional Material; and Gay, Peabody, Pierce, and Willard statements, Clarkson, "Statements of Men in War Work," 1920–1922, all in Baruch Papers. See also Cuff, "Creating Control Systems," *Business History Review,* and Breen, "Foundations, Statistics, and State-Building," *Business History Review.*

20. Stettinius to Baruch, 3/18/18, w/enc., file part 2, sec. 2, vol. 9–part 7, Wash. Corr.–Misc. S, Stettinius to Baruch, 4/2/18, file "Copies of Important Letters, 1918"–vol. III," Baruch to Baker, 5/8/18, file "Copies of Important Letters, 1918–vol. IV," and "Daily Record of Mr. Baruch's Activities at Office from Jan. 16th to Feb. 12th Inclusive," 2/1/18, 3/5/18, 3/6/18, 3/11/18, and 3/25/18, file part 2, sec. 2–Additional Material; Hancock statement, Clarkson, "Statements of Men in War Work," 1920–1922, all in Baruch Papers; Graham Committee, *Hearings,* serial 1, pp. 528–29; and Cuff, *War Industries Board,* pp. 162–69.

21. The account of integrating the procurement agencies, and particularly the army, into the restructured WIB after March 1918 is based on Goethals to Dody, 7/14/18, and other letters, Goethals Papers; Fletcher to Baruch, "Activities of the [Navy with] the Different Divisions and Sections of the War Industries Board," 11/22/18, file IDI, Chairman's Office, Final Reports, WIB Recds.; Pierce to Baruch, 3/20/18, and other documents and correspondence, file "Copies of Important Letters, 1918–vol. III," "Daily Record of Mr. Baruch's Activities at Office from Jan. 16th to Feb. 12th Inclusive," 7/9/18, and other entries, file part 2, sec. 2–Additional Material, WWI; Bush, Foster, Gay, Hancock, Johnson, McDowell, McKenney, Peek, and Summers statements, Clarkson, "Statements of Men in War Work," 1920–1922, all in Baruch Papers; WIB, *Minutes,* 8/16/18; *Final Report, WIB–Johnson,* pp. 14–15, 40–52; and Baruch, *American Industry in the War,* pp. 105–6. For additional sources on the navy, see chap. 8, n. 26.

22. King to Baker, 11/8/18, file, "Correspondence–Nov.–Dec. 1918–K," Baker Papers; Baruch to Baker, 11/2/18, and other correspondence, file part 2, sec. 2, vol. 9, part 1, Wash. Corr., Misc. A–B, Baruch to Wilson, 5/28/18, and other correspondence, "Copies of Important Letters, 1918–vol. IV," "Daily Record of Mr. Baruch's Activities at Office from Jan. 16th to Feb. 12th Inclusive," 6/13/18, and other entries, file part 2, section 2–Additional Material, Wilson to Baruch, 5/24/18, "Excerpts from Wilson-Baruch Correspondence, an Unknown Date," file part 2, sec.

2–Additional Material, WWI; Wilson to Baker, 7/24/18, Selected Correspondence; Denman, Foster, Gay, McKenney, George E. Merryweather, and Peek statements, Clarkson, "Statements of Men in War Work," 1920–1922, all in Baruch Papers; CND, *Second Annual Report,* p. 7; *Final Report, WIB–Johnson,* pp. 46–48; David Novick, Melvin Anshen, and W. C. Truppner, *Wartime Production Controls* (New York: Columbia University Press, 1949), pp. 28–30; and Beaver, *Baker,* pp. 172–73.

23. Goethals to Dody, 6/23/18, and numerous other letters, Goethals Papers; Frost to Gay, 9/27/18, file 21A–A7, and Parker to Baruch, 5/27/18, w/enc., file 21A–Al, WIB Recds.; Baker to Wilson, l/5/18, file "Correspondence, W. Wilson–Jan. 1918," Baker Papers; O'Laughlin to Baruch, 8/14/18, file part 2, sec. 2, vol. 9–part 6, Wash. Corr.–Misc.–N–R, and "Diary of Mr. Bernard M. Baruch," 10/29/18 and 10/30/18, file part 2–Additional Material, WWI; Gay, Johnson, McKenney, Otis, Pierce, Vauclain, and Yeatman statements, Clarkson, "Statements of Men in War Work," 1920-1922, all in Baruch Papers; SMAC, *Hearings, 1920,* p. 81; *Final Report, WIB–Johnson,* pp. 10–11; Beaver, *Baker,* pp. 156–61, 165–69, 171–78, 186–88; Coffman, *Hilt of Sword,* pp. 73–74, 76, 84–89, 104–10, 136–41; Bernard M. Baruch, *Baruch: The Public Years* (New York: Holt, Rinehart and Winston, 1957), pp. 56–58; and Clarkson, *Industrial America in the World War,* pp. 100–103, 125, 128, 132–35.

## CHAPTER ELEVEN. OTHER AGENCIES

1. Several authors either survey all or most mobilization agencies for World War I or treat with the congressional response to wartime imperatives. These books are helpful in dealing with the agencies other than the WIB and its predecessor bodies, which I briefly discuss. See William Franklin Willoughby, *Government Organization in War Time and After: A Survey of the Federal Civil Agencies Created for the Prosecution of the War* (New York: D. Appleton, 1919); Seward W. Livermore, *Politics Is Adjourned: Woodrow Wilson and the War Congress, 1916–1918* (Middletown: Wesleyan University Press, 1966); Richard L. Watson, Jr., *The Development of National Power: The United States 1900–1919* (Boston: Houghton Mifflin, 1976); Robert H. Ferrell, *Woodrow Wilson and World War I, 1917–1921* (New York: Harper and Row, 1985); and Peter Fearon, *War, Prosperity and Depression: The U.S. Economy 1917–45* (Lawrence: University Press of Kansas, 1987), pp. 3–27. Almost all the agencies mentioned are the subject of discussion in the numerous document collections cited in the previous five chapters. Since I have already made clear to the reader the range of sources I have drawn upon, I will cite primary documents only infrequently.

2. There is a substantial literature on agriculture and food during World War I. For some of the better publications, see Frank M. Surface and R. L. Bland, *American Food in the World War and Reconstruction Period* (Stanford, CA: Stanford University Press, 1931); William C. Mullendore, *History of the United States Food Administration, 1917–1919* (Stanford, CA: Stanford University Press, 1941); Maxcy R. Dickson, *The Food Front in World War I* (Washington, DC: American Council on Public Affairs 1944); Robert D. Cuff, "Herbert Hoover, the Ideology of Voluntarism and War Organization During the Great War," *Journal of American History* 64 (September 1977): 358–72; and James L. Guth, "Herbert Hoover, the U.S. Food Administration, and the Dairy Industry, 1917–1918," *Business History Review* 55 (Summer 1981): 170–87.

Hoover, his ideology, and public leadership are basic to any understanding of the nature and operations of the Food Administration. For an extensive list of the recent literature on Hoover and American life, see volume 3 (forthcoming) of this series.

3. Not much secondary work has been done on the Fuel Administration; see the sources in note 1. See also U.S. Fuel Administration, *Final Report of the United States Fuel Administrator, 1917–1919,* by H. A. Garfield (Washington, DC: U.S. Government Printing Office, 1921). See also U.S. Council of Defense, *First Annual Report* (Washington, DC: U.S. Government Printing Office, 1917), pp. 32–37. Robert D. Cuff, "Harry Garfield, the Fuel Administration, and the Search for a Cooperative Order During World War I," *American Quarterly* 30 (Spring 1978): 39–53, is helpful in terms of Garfield's goals and approaches.

4. This theme is examined in depth in William J. Breen, *Uncle Sam at Home: Civilian Mobilization, Wartime Federalism, and the Council of National Defense, 1917–1919* (Westport, CT: Greenwood Press, 1984).

5. Unlike the Fuel Administration, there are numerous sources on the Railroad Administration. For some of the better and standard works, see Frank H. Dixon, *Railroads and Government: Their Relations in the United States, 1910–1921* (New York: Scribner's Sons, 1922); Walker D. Hines, *War History of American Railroads* (New Haven: Yale University Press, 1928); K. Austin Kerr, *American Railroad Politics, 1914–1920: Rates, Wages and Efficiency* (Pittsburgh: University of Pittsburgh Press, 1968); Aaron Austin Godfrey, *Government Operation of the Railroads: Its Necessity, Success, and Consequences, 1918–1920* (Austin, TX: San Felipe Press, 1974); and Robert D. Cuff, "United States Mobilization and Railroad Transportation: Lessons in Coordination and Control, 1917–1945," *Journal of Military History* 53 (January 1989): 33–50. See also Maury Klein, "Competition and Regulation: The Railroad Model," *Business History Review* 64 (Summer 1990): 311–25.

6. William S. Culbertson, *Commercial Policy in War Time and After: A Study of the Application of Democratic Ideas to International Commercial Relations* (New York: D. Appleton, 1919), and James A. Salter, *Allied Shipping Control* (Oxford: Clarendon Press, 1921). For a broader interpretative scheme for America's wartime trade policies, see Carl P. Parrini, *Heir to Empire: United States Economic Diplomacy, 1916–1923* (Pittsburgh: University of Pittsburgh Press, 1969), and Burton I. Kaufman, *Efficiency and Expansion: Foreign Trade Organization in the Wilson Administration, 1913–1921* (Westport, CT: Greenwood Press, 1974). See also C. M. Wooley statement, in Grosvenor B. Clarkson, "Statements of Men in War Work," 1920–1922, Baruch Papers.

7. W. C. Mattox, *Building the Emergency Fleet: A Historical Narrative of the Problems and Achievements of the United States Shipping Board Emergency Fleet Corporation* (Cleveland, OH: Penton Publishing, 1920); Edward N. Hurley, *The Bridge to France* (Philadelphia: J. B. Lippincott, 1927); Joseph B. and Farnham Bishop, *Goethals, Genius of the Panama Canal: A Biography* (New York: Harper and Brothers, 1930), pp. 271–370; Darrell H. Smith and P. V. Betters, *The United States Shipping Board* (Washington, DC: Brookings Institution, 1931); John J. Broesamle, *William Gibbs McAdoo: A Passion for Change, 1863–1917* (Port Washington, NY: Kennikat Press, 1973), pp. 212–36; Robert Hessen, *Steel Titan: The Life of Charles M. Schwab* (New York: Oxford University Press, 1975), pp. 211–46; Barnard Mergen, "The Government as Manager: Emergency Fleet Shipbuilding, 1917–1919," in *Business and Its Environment: Essays for Thomas C. Cochran,* ed. Harold I. Sharlin, pp. 49–80 (West-

port, CT: Greenwood Press, 1983); and William J. Williams, *The Wilson Administration and the Shipbuilding Crisis of 1917: Steel Ships and Wooden Steamers* (Lampeter, UK: Edwin Mellen Press, 1992). See also William Denman statement, Clarkson, "Statements of Men in War Work," 1920–1922, Baruch Papers.

8. Ernest L. Bogart, *War Costs and Their Financing: A Study of the Financing of the War and After-war Problems of Debt and Taxation* (New York: D. Appleton, 1921); Alexander D. Noyes, *The War Period of American Finance, 1908–1925* (New York: G. P. Putnam's Sons, 1926); Woodbury Willoughby, *The Capital Issues Committee and War Finance Corporation* (Baltimore: Johns Hopkins University Press, 1934); and Charles Gilbert, *American Financing of World War I* (Westport, CT: Greenwood Publishing, 1970).

9. The discussion and analysis of labor during World War I is based on a range of sources. CND, *Minutes,* NDAC, *Minutes,* MSB, *Minutes,* WIB, *Minutes,* and Price Fixing Committee, *Minutes,* Senate Committee Prints 7, 8, 4, and 5, are helpful in tracing labor's role in mobilization. The same is true of U.S. Council of Defense, *First and Second Annual Reports* (Washington, DC: U.S. Government Printing Office, 1917–1918). Also useful are the Annual Reports of the Secretary of War, the Secretary of the Navy, and the Ordnance Department and Quartermaster Corps cited in chapter 8, nn. 26 and 27, and chapter 10, n. 18. See also Bernard M. Baruch, *American Industry in the War: A Report of the War Industries Board* (Washington, DC: U.S. Government Printing Office, 1921), pp. 82–91.

No definitive secondary work on labor during the World War I years has yet been written; existing works are of mixed quality. See Gordon S. Watkins, *Labor Problems and Labor Administration in the United States During the World War* (Urbana: University of Illinois, 1919); Robert D. Cuff, "The Politics of Labor Administration During World War I," *Labor History* 21 (Fall 1980): 546–69; Valerie Jean Conner, *The National War Labor Board: Stability, Social Justice, and the Voluntary State in World War I* (Chapel Hill: University of North Carolina Press, 1983); Joseph Anthony McCartin, "Labor's 'Great War': American Workers, Unions, and the State, 1916–1920" (Ph.D. diss., State University of New York at Binghamton, 1990); Ronald Schaffer, *America in the Great War: The Rise of the War Welfare State* (New York: Oxford University Press, 1991), pp. 64–74; Melvyn Dubofsky, *The State and Labor in Modern America* (Chapel Hill: University of North Carolina Press, 1994), pp. 37–81; and Eric J. Karolak, "'Work or Fight': Federal Labor Policy and the First World War, 1913–1920" (Ph.D. diss., Ohio State University, 1994), the latest and broadest study of wartime labor policy and includes the most up-to-date bibliography. Some more general works are also helpful. See George Soule, *Prosperity Decade: From War to Depression, 1917–1929* (New York: Holt, Rinehart and Winston, 1947), pp. 64–76; James Weinstein, *The Corporate Ideal in the Liberal State, 1900–1918* (Boston: Beacon Press, 1968), particularly chap. 8; Daniel R. Beaver, *Newton D. Baker and the American War Effort, 1917–1919* (Lincoln: University of Nebraska Press, 1966), intermittent; Melvin I. Urofsky, *Big Steel and the Wilson Administration: A Study in Business-Government Relations* (Columbus: Ohio State University Press, 1969), chap. 7; Daniel Nelson, *Managers and Workers: Origins of the New Factory System in the United States, 1880–1920* (Madison: University of Wisconsin Press, 1975), chap. 8; David M. Gordon, Richard Edwards, and Michael Reich, *Segmented Work, Divided Workers: The Historical Transformation of Labor in the United States* (New York: Cambridge University Press, 1982), pp. 1–164; various essays in James E. Cronin and Carmen Sirianni, eds., *Work, Community, and Power: The Experience of Labor in Europe and America, 1900–1925* (Philadelphia: Temple University Press, 1983); Frederick W. Smith, *The Amazing Storm: Business Answers to the Labor Question, 1900–1920* (New York: Garland, 1986); Neil A. Wynn, *From Progressivism to Prosperity: World War I and American Society* (New York: Holmes and Meier, 1986), pp. 86–132; and Larry G. Gerber, "Corporatism in Comparative Perspective: The Impact of the First World War on American and British Labor Relations," *Business History Review* 62 (Spring 1988): 93–127.

Since Gompers played such a dominant role as labor's representative and spokesperson during World War I, any assessment of labor during hostilities must deal with the president of the AFL. Here the literature is rich and varied in interpretation. Any sampling of it must include Gompers, *Seventy Years of Life and Labour,* 2 vols. (New York: E. P. Dutton, 1925). For other works, see Bernard Mandel, *Samuel Gompers: A Biography* (Yellow Springs, OH: Antioch Press, 1963); Frank L. Grubbs, Jr., *The Struggle for Labor Loyalty: Gompers, the A.F. of L., and the Pacifists, 1917–1920* (Durham, NC: Duke University Press, 1968); Ronald Radosh, *American Labor and United States Foreign Policy* (New York: Random House, 1969); Will Chasan, *Samuel Gompers: Leader of American Labor* (New York: Praeger Publishers, 1971); William M. Dick, *Labor and Socialism in America: The Gompers Era* (Port Washington, NY: Kennikat Press, 1972); Stuart Bruce Kaufman, *Samuel Gompers and the Origins of the American Federation of Labor, 1848–1896* (Westport, CT: Greenwood Press, 1973); Simon Larson, *Labor and Foreign Policy: Gompers, the AFL, and World War, 1914–1918* (Rutherford, NJ: Fairleigh Dickinson University Press, 1975); Harold C. Livesay, *Samuel Gompers and Organized Labor in America* (Boston: Little, Brown, 1978); and Philip S. Foner, *The Labor Movement in the United States,* vol. 5, *The AFL in the Progressive Era, 1910–1915* (New York: International Publishers, 1980). See also Mary O. Furner, "Knowing Capitalism: Public Investigation and the Labor Question in the Long Progressive Era," in *The State and Economic Knowledge: The American and British Experiences,* eds. Furner and Barry Supple, pp. 241–86 (New York: Woodrow Wilson International Center for Scholars and Cambridge University Press, 1990); Sarah L. Watts, *Order Against Chaos: Business Culture and Labor Ideology in America, 1800–1915* (Westport, CT: Greenwood Press, 1991); and Clarence E. Wunderlin, Jr., *Visions of a New Industrial Order: Social Science and Labor Theory in America's Progressive Era* (New York: Columbia University Press, 1992). Some basic information on the U.S. Employment Service (USES) is provided in I. W. Litchfield, "The United States Employment Service and Demobilization," *Annals of the American Academy of Political and Social Science* 81 (January 1919): 19–27; William J. Breen, "Administrative Politics and Labor Policy in World War: The U.S. Employment Service and the Seattle Labor Market Experiment," *Business History Review* 61 (Winter 1987): 582–605; and Karolak, "'Work or Fight,'" pp. 116–31.

10. The neo-Hamiltonians as reformers, expansionists, and preparedness advocates are analyzed in chapter 6, along with the Progressive reformers in general and their suspicious attitudes about the state. The positions of Howard E. Coffin, the Chamber of Commerce, and others on a type of national service proposal are included in the sources cited in chapters 7–10 involving those individuals and institutions. Volume 3 (forthcoming) of this series treats at length with the national service, or universal conscription, movement.

11. Wilford I. King, Oswald W. Knauth, and Frederick R. Macaulay, *Income in the United States: Its Amount and Distribution, 1909–1919,* 2 vols. (New York: National Bureau of Economic Research, 1922) 2: 298–313, and Soule, *Prosperity Decade,* pp. 77–78.

12. *Report of Federal Trade Commission Regarding Profiteering,* June 29, 1918, 65th Cong., 2d sess., S. Doc. 248, quotation, p. 5. See also U.S. Federal Trade Commission, *Report on War-Time Costs and Profits of Southern Pine Lumber Companies* (Washington, DC: U.S. Government Printing Office, 1922); U.S. Federal Trade Commission, *Report on War-Time Profits and Costs of the Steel Industry* (Washington, DC: U.S. Government Printing Office, 1925); and King, Knauth, and Macaulay, *Income in the United States,* pp. 298–329. U.S. Congress, House, Committee on Military Affairs, *Hearings, Universal Mobilization for War Purposes,* 68th Cong., 1st sess., March 1924, pp. 590–638, includes a copy of the FTC 1918 report on profiteering, an extensive bibliography on profiteering, and other relevant sources and documents. General and scattered figures on wartime corporate profits cannot accurately measure what took place during hostilities. This point was a major matter of concern and study during interwar congressional investigations of economic mobilization for World War I. The work of the Nye Committee is particularly important.

13. The analysis is based on extensive data and its analysis in Simon Kuznets, *National Product in Wartime* (New York: National Bureau of Economic Research, 1945); John Maurice Clark, *The Costs of the World War to the American People* (New Haven: Yale University Press, 1931); Arthur F. Burns, *Production Trends in the United States Since 1870* (New York: National Bureau of Economic Research, 1934); and Frederick C. Mills, *Economic Tendencies in the United States: Aspects of the Pre-War and Post-War Changes* (New York: National Bureau of Economic Research, 1932). A convenient summary of some of this data is found in Soule, *Prosperity Decade,* pp. 46–80.

14. Statistics on World War I vary considerably from source to source. The most thorough study of World War I financing and spending is Gilbert, *American Financing of World War I.* I have filled out somewhat Gilbert's figures and cited other relevant sources in *The Military-Industrial Complex: A Historical Perspective* (New York: Praeger Publishers, 1980), pp. 107–8. On inflationary forces during the war, see Mills, *Economic Tendencies,* p. 584.

15. Ralph L. Nelson, *Merger Movements in American Industry, 1895–1956* (Princeton, NJ: Princeton University Press, 1959). Nelson's data and analysis is further developed for the 1920s by his student Carl Eis, *The 1919–1930 Merger Movement in American Industry* (New York: Arno Press, 1978). See also Samuel Richardson Reid, *Mergers, Managers, and the Economy* (New York: McGraw-Hill, 1968), pp. 1–72, and Naomi R. Lamoreaux, *The Great Merger Movement in American Business, 1895–1904* (New York: Cambridge University Press, 1985).

16. Definitions and quotations are from Nelson, *Merger Movements,* pp. 58–59.

17. The expansion and growth of the munitions trade for the Allies in the United States from 1914 to 1917 and after is discussed and documented in chapter 6 and will be further analyzed in volume 3 (forthcoming) of this series.

18. The figures on war spending as a composition of the GNP are from Kuznets, *National Product in Wartime,* pp. 96, 102, 132–34. Clark, *Costs of the World War,* is also helpful in this regard. The estimate of specialized munitions for World War I comes

from Murray L. Weidenbaum, *The Economics of Peacetime Defense* (New York: Praeger Publishers, 1974), p. 134.

19. These developments are traced and discussed in numerous sources. For an introduction to the subject, including the citation and discussion of varying or differing interpretations, see Vincent P. Carosso, *Investment Banking in America: A History* (Cambridge: Harvard University Press, 1970), pp. 1–299; Carosso, *The Morgans: Private Bankers, 1854–1913* (Cambridge: Harvard University Press, 1987); David M. Kotz, *Bank Control of Larger Corporations in the United States* (Berkeley: University of California Press, 1978), pp. 1–71; Mark S. Mizruchi, *The American Corporate Network, 1904–1974* (Beverly Hills, CA: Sage, 1982); and Ron Chernow, *The House of Morgan: An American Banking Dynasty and the Rise of Modern Finance* (New York: Atlantic Monthly Press, 1990).

20. Alfred D. Chandler, Jr., *The Visible Hand: The Managerial Revolution in American Business* (Cambridge: Belknap Press, 1977). Chandler's entire volume is necessary to appreciate his full analysis; most of what I have discussed is found on pp. 411–97. On the theme of business and planning, see also Michael D. Reagan, *The Managed Economy* (New York: Oxford University Press, 1963); David Ira Cleland, *The Origins and Development of a Philosophy of Long-Range Planning in American Business* (New York: Arno Press, 1976); Otis L. Graham, Jr., *Toward a Planned Society: From Roosevelt to Nixon* (New York: Oxford University Press, 1976); Robert F. Himmelberg, *The Origins of the National Recovery Administration: Business, Government, and the Trade Association Issue, 1921–1933* (New York: Fordham University Press, 1976); Philip W. Warken, *A History of the National Resources Planning Board, 1933–1943* (New York: Garland, 1979); and Anthony S. Campagna, *U.S. National Economic Policy, 1917–1985* (New York: Praeger Publishers, 1987).

## CHAPTER TWELVE. RECONVERSION

1. Gompers to Gifford, 11/27/18, w/enc., file 2–A7, Clarkson to Ely, 7/12/18, file "Ely, Richard T.," Clarkson to House, 9/10/18, file "House, Col. E.M.," Clarkson to Wilson, 5/29/18, and other correspondence and documents, file "President," CND Recds.; Clarkson to Redfield, 4/27/18, w/encs. and numerous other correspondence and documents, file 74405, General Correspondence, General Records, Dept. of Commerce Recds.; Wilson to Clarkson, 3/26/18, and other correspondence and documents, file 206, Baker to Clarkson, 10/2/25, file "Grosvenor B. Clarkson Papers, 1917–1925," series 4, Wilson Papers; Baker to Wilson, 6/ll/18, and other correspondence, file "Correspondence–W. Wilson, 1918–W," Baker to Wilson, 11/9/18, and other correspondence, file "Correspondence–W. Wilson, Nov.–Dec., 1918–W," Baker Papers: Gifford to Baruch, 5/28/18, w/enc. and numerous other correspondence and documents, part 1, vol. 3, WWI, and House Diary, 8/13/18 (excerpted), Selected Correspondence, Baruch Papers; NDAC, *Minutes,* and MSB, *Minutes,* Senate Committee Print 8, 5/2/18, 5/6/18, 6/3/18, 7/l/18, 8/5/18; CND, *Minutes,* Senate Committee Print 7, 4/15/18, 5/6/18, 6/3/18, 6/10/18, 6/24/18, 7/l/18, 11/29/18, and 12/2/18–2/21/21 (all quotations can be located in this source); U.S. Council of National Defense, *Third and Fourth Annual Report* (Washington, DC: U.S. Government Printing Office, 1919 and 1920); Franklin H. Martin, *Digest of the Pro-*

*ceedings of the Council of National Defense During the World War,* U.S. Congress, Senate, 73d Cong., 2d sess., S. Doc. 193, pp. 446–47; and Graham Committee, *Hearings,* Serial 1, p. 355. Reconversion planning in the later months of World War I tended to blend in with proposals for postwar industrial mobilization planning. The latter topic will be treated extensively in volume 3 (forthcoming) of this series.

2. Until the 1960s the most important and informed scholarship on reconversion or readjustment was presented by E. Jay Howenstein, Jr., in a series of articles and a book: "The Industrial Board, Precursor of the N.R.A.: The Price-Reduction Movement After World War I," *Journal of Political Economy* 51 (June 1943): 235–50; "Demobilization After World War," *Quarterly Journal of Economics* 58 (November 1943): 91–105; "Public Works Program After World War I," *Journal of Political Economy* 51 (December 1943): 523–37; "Federal Planning for Demobilization During World War I," *American Journal of Economics and Sociology* 3 (July 1944): 631–46; "Lessons of World War I," *Annals of the American Academy of Political and Social Sciences* 238 (March 1945): 180–87; and *The Economics of Demobilization* (Washington, DC: American Council on Public Affairs 1944). Another competent and quite comprehensive survey of demobilization efforts is provided in James R. Mock and Evangeline Thurber, *Report on Demobilization* (Norman: University of Oklahoma Press, 1944). William J. Breen, *Uncle Sam at Home: Civilian Mobilization, Wartime Federalism, and the Council of National Defense, 1917-1919* (Westport, CT: Greenwood Press, 1984), provides insight and information about reconversion efforts and attitudes at the local, state, and regional levels, especially as they involved the State Councils of National Defense. *The Annals of the American Academy of Political and Social Science* 82 (March 1919) is devoted to reconstruction and contains numerous articles of value.

3. Wilson's attitudes and responses concerning reconversion are set forth or examined in many of the citations in notes 1 and 2. More particularly, see Wilson to Gompers, 11/27/18, and related correspondence, file 744405, Wilson to Redfield, 11/8/18, and 11/16/18, Wilson to Wheeler, 10/5/18, and related correspondence, file 77270, Dept. of Commerce Recds.; Wilson to Baker, 12/2/18, and related correspondence, file "Correspondence–W. Wilson, Nov.–Dec., 1918–W," Baker Papers; and *New York Times,* December 3, 1918, pp. 1–2. The most complete and sophisticated scholarship on the reconversion-reconstruction issue and its consequences has been presented in the last thirty years or so. See Robert F. Himmelberg, "Relaxation of the Federal Anti-trust Policy as a Goal of the Business Community During the Period 1918–1933" (Ph. D. diss., Pennsylvania State University, 1963), Himmelberg, "The War Industries Board and the Antitrust Question in November 1918," *Journal of American History* 52 (June 1965): 59–74, Himmelberg, "Business, Antitrust Policy, and the Industrial Board of the Department of Commerce, 1919," *Business History Review* 62 (Spring 1968): 1–23, Himmelberg, *The Origins of the National Recovery Administration: Business, Government, and the Trade Association Issue, 1921–1933* (New York: Fordham University Press, 1976); and Robert D. Cuff, *The War Industries Board: Business-Government Relations During World War I* (Baltimore: Johns Hopkins University Press, 1973), chap. 9. Wilson is covered in detail in these sources. I draw heavily on this scholarship and develop the analysis in depth because it is essential for enlightening not only the transition of the economy to peace but also the war mobilization process and the nation's political economy in the interwar years.

4. The analysis of Baruch, the WIB, and the business community involving reconversion is based on a number of primary sources. Grosvenor Clarkson, "Statements of

Men in War Work," 1920–1922, Baruch Papers, is a rich source about what wartime mobilization executives thought about reconversion and the legacy of the mobilization experience for the future; of particular interest are the interviews involving Edwin F. Gay, John M. Hancock, Charles H. MacDowell, Charles A. Otis, E. E. Parsonage, George N. Peek, J. Leonard Replogle, A. W. Shaw, and L. L. Summers. For other primary sources, see Hecker to Baruch, 10/8/18, and other correspondence, file "Price Fixing Committee, Misc. Correspondence and Papers no. 2," Purnell to Replogle, 11/20/18, file "Allocations," file Group 18–E–Al, Peek to Baruch, 11/18/18, and "Memorandum Concerning Post War Program–War Industries Board," undated, unsigned, file 21A–A7, Correspondence and Papers, WIB Recds. The numerous final reports of the WIB divisions, sections, and other subdivisions are found in the WIB Records, file IDI–Chairman's Office–Final Reports, and are a rich source on industry and WIB attitudes, proposals, action, and attempted action concerning reconversion. See also Peek to Baruch, "Report of the Finished Products Division," 12/17/18, file part 2, vol. 1, D. R. McLennan, "Report of Non War Construction Section," [circa] December 1918, file part 2, vol. 2, part 1, "Meeting of the War Industries Board, November 19, 1918," file part 2, vol. 4, WIB Minutes, M. L. Requa, "Peace—Not the End But the Beginning," an address, 12/5/18, and Verbatim Report of the War Industries Board "With Committee Representing the American Iron and Steel Institute, for the Purpose of Discussing Means for Stabilizing the Industry During the Transition Period Following the Signing of the Armistice," 11/13/18, H. P. Engels, Secretary, file part 2, vol. 14, Howard to Brookings, 12/11/18, file part 2, sec. 2, vol. 14, part 1, Wash. Corr., Misc. A–B, WWI; Baruch to Wilson, 11/11/18, and other related correspondence, Selected Correspondence, all in Baruch Papers; Redfield to Wilson, 11/25/18, and related correspondence, file 206B, series 4, Wilson Papers; and Chamber of Commerce of the United States, George N. Peek address, "Government Organization in Relation to War," *Minutes, Sixth Annual Meeting,* April 1918; *Minutes, War Emergency and Reconstruction Congress under Auspices of the Chamber of Commerce of the United States of America,* December 1918, Chamber of Commerce Recds. See also the extended analysis and documentation concerning the Chamber of Commerce in chapter 7, and WIB, *Minutes,* Senate Committee Print 4, 10/31/18, 12/19/18, and appendixes. In terms of secondary sources, Cuff, *War Industries Board,* chapter 9, and Himmelberg, "War Industries Board and the Antitrust Question," are invaluable.

5. Himmelberg, "War Industries Board and the Antitrust Question," pp. 64–66, proposes that Baruch and his lieutenants may have attempted to persuade Wilson to accept an active role for the WIB in reconstruction, but his line of analysis and the evidence is weak and unconvincing.

6. Baruch to Wilson, 11/21/18, Selected Correspondence, Baruch Papers. In March 1919, through the efforts of Ritchie and Peek, legislation was passed by Congress that validated informal contracts. The subject of seeking legislation for the WIB as a reconstruction agency and passage of the informal contracts bill is discussed and documented in Cuff, *War Industries Board,* pp. 248–49, 261–62.

7. Himmelberg, "War Industries Board and the Antitrust Question," pp. 64–65.

8. Baruch to Wilson, 11/27/18, with enclosed letter to president of the same date, file 206B, series 4, Wilson Papers. The letter and Wilson's response are published in WIB, *Minutes,* 12/10/18, but with Baruch's letter dated November 29 and Wil-

son's response, November 30. An earlier version of Baruch's letter with a November 19 date is available in Selected Correspondence, Baruch Papers.

9. Baker to Wilson, 11/30/18, Baruch to Baker, 11/30/18, and Wilson to Baker, 12/2/18, file "Correspondence–W. Wilson–Nov.–Dec., 1918–W" Baker Papers, and CND, *Minutes,* 11/29/18.

10. WIB, *Minutes,* 12/12/18, 12/2/19, and appendixes. These developments are addressed in the surveys of war mobilization and demobilization: William Franklin Willoughby, *Government Organization in Wartime and After: A Survey of the Federal Civil Agencies Created for the Prosecution of the War* (New York: D. Appleton, 1919), and Mock and Thurber, *Report on Demobilization.*

11. Chamber of Commerce, *Minutes, War Emergency and Reconstruction Congress,* Chamber of Commerce Recds., and Himmelberg, "War Industries Board and the Antitrust Question," pp. 60–64.

12. Himmelberg, "War Industries Board and the Antitrust Question," pp. 70–74.

13. Himmelberg, "Business, Antitrust Policy, and the Industrial Board," pp. 4–5, quotations, p. 5. Himmelberg's work is the best and most recent on the Industrial Board. However, Willoughby, *Government Organization in War Time and After,* pp. 116–20, briefly discusses the board's origins and operations, and Howenstein, "The Industrial Board," has set forth the first, extended, and scholarly treatment of this organization.

14. Himmelberg, "Business, Antitrust Policy, and the Industrial Board," pp. 5–9; unless otherwise indicated or supplemented, the description/analysis of the Industrial Board is based on this article.

15. Peek to Baruch, 11/18/18, file 21A–A7, WIB Recds. For a fuller background to the Peek-favored discharge/furlough program, see Howenstein, "Demobilization After World War," and Mock and Thurber, *Report on Demobilization,* pp. 126–44.

16. Redfield to Wilson, 11/25/18, and Wilson to Redfield, 11/26/18, file 206B, series 4, Wilson Papers. Baruch's letter to Wilson of November 27 (published in WIB, *Minutes,* 12/10/18, as dated November 29) in which the chairman recommended disestablishing the WIB by January 1, 1919, is ambiguous and subject to endless interpretations. Moreover, the version of the letter in the Wilson Papers, file 206B, dated November 27, is missing the following key paragraph, which appears in the WIB, *Minutes,* version and in an earlier version of the letter, dated November 19, contained in Selected Correspondence, Baruch Papers: "I feel sure that the businessmen who have been acting as commodity heads will, if requested, be willing to remain here or be subject to call if they can be of service to the departments or other Governmental agencies as points of contact between them and industry."

17. Howenstein, "The Industrial Board," has the best and most extended discussion of the Industrial Board's approach and action on pricing and the controversies that they generated.

## CHAPTER THIRTEEN. THE CHALLENGE AND EFFECT OF MOBILIZING FOR MODERN WAR

1. "Industrial self-government" is used by many scholars and is discussed and analyzed in a most intelligent and insightful way by Ellis W. Hawley, *The New Deal*

*and the Problem of Monopoly: A Study in Economic Ambivalence* (Princeton, NJ: Princeton University Press, 1966), pp. 3–16. I adopted the term myself in "The 'Industrial-Military Complex' in Historical Perspective: World War I," *Business History Review* 61 (Winter 1967): 379–80, but I have since somewhat modified my position.

2. Grosvenor B. Clarkson, *Industrial America in the World War: The Strategy Behind the Line, 1917–1918* (Boston: Houghton Mifflin, 1923), and Bernard M. Baruch, *American Industry in the War: A Report of the War Industries Board* (Washington, DC: Government Printing Office, 1921). This theme, including related publications on economic mobilization for World War I, will be treated in length in volume 3 (forthcoming).

3. Robert D. Cuff, *The War Industries Board: Business-Government Relations During World War I* (Baltimore: Johns Hopkins University Press, 1973), uses terms similar to these throughout his work (for examples, see pp. 3–6, 30–31, and 113).

4. The neo-Jeffersonians' critique of the political economy of World War I and their solutions to avoid perceived dangers in the future are examined fully in volume 3 (forthcoming).

5. For a contrary interpretation on the radical potential in America during the Progressive Era and after, see James Weinstein, *The Decline of Socialism in America, 1912–1925* (New York: Monthly Review Press, 1967).

6. This subject will be examined fully and in depth in volume 3 (forthcoming) on the interwar years and in volume 4 on World War II.

7. On this critically important point, see the keen insights offered by Otis L. Graham, Jr., *An Encore for Reform: The Old Progressives and the New Deal* (New York: Oxford University Press, 1967), particularly pp. 3–23.

8. Civil-military relations during World War II and after will be addressed in volumes 4 and 5 (forthcoming) of this series. The one best source for examining control over the military during World War I is Edward M. Coffman, *The War to End All Wars: The American Military Experience in World War I* (New York: Oxford University Press, 1968).

9. Such an interpretation is rather widespread throughout the literature. For one example, see Daniel R. Beaver, *Newton D. Baker and the American War Effort, 1917–1919* (Lincoln: University of Nebraska Press, 1966), p. 76.

10. Cuff, *War Industries Board,* pp. 6–7. Richard Polenberg, *War and Society: The United States, 1941–1945* (Philadelphia: J. B. Lippincott, 1972), similarly argues that World War I mobilization and the New Deal had little or no relevance for mobilizing the economic structure for World War II. See in particular pp. 2–3. Cuff appears to have modified his views on the singularity of the World War I economic mobilization in "War Mobilization, Institutional Learning, and State Building in the United States, 1917–1941," in *The State and Social Investigation in Britain and the United States,* ed. Michael J. Lacey and Mary O. Furner, pp. 388–425 (New York: Woodrow Wilson Center Press and Cambridge University Press, 1993). Other articles in Lacey and Furner's work are relevant to this volume, as is Fred Block, *Revising State Theory: Essays in Politics and Postindustrialism* (Philadelphia: Temple University Press, 1987), and numerous other sources cited in volume 3 (forthcoming).

11. Developments during the interwar years and economic mobilization for World War II will be analyzed in depth in volumes 3 and 4 (forthcoming) in this series. I have already published on the interwar years and on World War II. See "Mobilizing the

World War II Economy: Labor and the Industrial-Military Alliance," *Pacific Historical Review* 62 (November 1973): 443–78, *The Hammer and the Sword* (New York: Arno Press, 1979), *The Military-Industrial Complex: A Historical Perspective* (New York: Praeger, 1980), "Warfare and Power Relations in America: Mobilizing the World War II Economy," in *The Home Front and War in the Twentieth Century: The American Experience in Comparative Perspective,* ed. James Titus, pp. 91–110, 231–43 (Colorado Springs: U.S. Air Force Academy, 1984), and "Toward a Warfare State: Militarization in America During the Period of the World Wars," in *Militarization of the Western World,* ed. John R. Gillis, pp. 47–64, 175–79 (New Brunswick, NJ: Rutgers University Press, 1989). My reference to Chandler is from *The Visible Hand: The Managerial Revolution in American Business* (Cambridge: Belknap Press, 1977), p. 455.

12. Here I am agreeing with the numerous scholars who see war as the handmaiden of reform during World War I. In the long run, for the twentieth century as a whole, however, I see war as a deadly enemy, not a close friend, of movements to create a more equitable, responsible society. I have made this point earlier. See "Mobilizing the World War II Economy," and "Warfare and Power Relations in America." In a larger sense, my entire analysis of war mobilization, along with many of the cited primary and secondary sources, directly or indirectly involves the critical interaction of war and reform.

# BIBLIOGRAPHICAL ESSAY

## PART ONE—GILDED AGE TO WORLD WAR I

The secondary literature relevant to the political economy of warfare for this period is enormous. I have already cited a great deal of it in the notes, including numerous Ph.D. dissertations. An introduction to the political developments of the era is provided by Richard L. McCormick, "Public Life in Industrial America, 1877–1917," in *The New American History,* ed. Eric Foner, pp. 93–117 (Philadelphia: Temple University Press, 1990. Also helpful is Charles W. Calhoun, ed., *The Gilded Age: Essays on the Origins of Modern America* (Wilmington, DE: Scholarly Resources, 1996). One of the best sources on the bibliography of the Progressive Era is Robert E. Wiebe, "The Progressive Years, 1900–1917," in *The Reinterpretation of American History and Culture,* ed. William H. Cartwright and Richard L. Watson, Jr., pp. 425–42 (Washington, DC: National Council for the Social Studies, 1973). More recent publications revise Wiebe's essay and provide additional insights into the subject. See Richard M. Abrams, *The Burdens of Progress, 1900–1929* (Glenview, IL: Scott, Foresman, 1978); John Whiteclay Chambers II, *The Tyranny of Change: America in the Progressive Era, 1900–1920,* rev. ed. (New York: St Martin's, 1992); and Lewis L. Gould, *Reform and Regulation: American Politics from Roosevelt to Wilson,* 3d ed., rev. (Prospect Heights, IL: Waveland, 1996).

Some of the preceding sources cover economics as well as politics for the years from the Civil War to World War I. In chapter 2, note 4, I cite my own work related to the economy and most other major publications dealing with subject matter, interpretive trends, and bibliography. A fine and thorough work on industry is available in David O. Whitten, ed., *Manufacturing: A Historiographical and Bibliographical Guide* (Westport, CT: Greenwood Press, 1990). I include references to publications on America's major industries and bibliographic aids involving them in volume 3 (forthcoming) of this series.

Essays by Lance C. Buhl, Ronald Spector, and Richard W. Turk, in *In Peace and War: Interpretations of American Naval History, 1775–1984,* ed. Kenneth J. Hagan, 2d ed., rev. (Westport, CT: Greenwood Press, 1984), pp. 145–204, are a way to commence study of the navy from 1865 to 1914. The subject matter and bibliography are further enhanced by a number of useful surveys published in the last decade: Edward L. Beach, *The United States Navy: 200 Years* (New York: Henry Holt, 1986); Kenneth J. Hagan, *This People's Navy: The Making of American Sea Power* (New York: Free Press,

1991); Stephen Howarth, *To Shining Sea: A History of the United States Navy, 1775–1991* (New York: Random House, 1991); Robert W. Love, Jr., *History of the U.S. Navy, 1775–1941* (Harrisburg, PA: Stackpole Books, 1992); George W. Baer, *One Hundred Years of Sea Power: The U.S. Navy, 1890–1990* (Stanford, CA: Stanford University Press, 1994); and Frank Uhlig, Jr., *How Navies Fight: The U.S. Navy and Its Allies* (Annapolis, MD: Naval Institute Press, 1994).

There are two bibliographies on the army during the Gilded Age and Progressive Era: Joseph G. Dawson III, *The Late 19th Century U.S. Army, 1865–1898: A Research Guide* (Westport, CT: Greenwood Press, 1990), and Marvin Fletcher, *The Peacetime Army, 1900–1941: A Research Guide* (Westport, CT: Greenwood Press, 1988). Relevant essays in Kenneth J. Hagan and William R. Roberts, eds., *Against All Enemies: Interpretations of American Military History from Colonial Times to the Present* (Westport, CT: Greenwood Press, 1986), pp. 173–234, are also helpful.

In notes for chapters 3 and 4 I cite the extensive literature on the Spanish-American War.

## PART TWO—WORLD WAR I

Primary documents are essential for analyzing the political economy of World War I. The Woodrow Wilson, Newton D. Baker, and George W. Goethals Papers in the Library of Congress, Washington, DC, and the Bernard M. Baruch and Frank A. Scott Papers at Princeton University, Princeton, NJ, are of great importance. The same is true for the following document collections at the National Archives in Washington, DC, and in College Park, MD: Records of the Council of National Defense (Record Group 62), Records of the War Industries Board (Record Group 61), Records of the Department of Commerce (Record Group 40), Records of the Office of the Secretary of War (Record Group 107), and Records of the War Department General and Special Staffs (Record Group 165). The U.S. Chamber of Commerce Archives in Washington, DC, also houses crucial documents on mobilizing the World War I economy.

The federal government has facilitated research on the World War I economy by publishing a host of significant documents. The Nye Committee, named after its chair, Sen. Gerald P. Nye (R-ND), stands out in that regard. See U.S. Congress, Senate, Special Committee Investigating the Munitions Industry, 74th Cong., 1st and 2d sess., 1935–1936, *Final Report of the Chairman of the United States War Industries Board to the President of the United States, February, 1919* [author, Hugh S. Johnson], Committee Print no. 3; *Minutes of the War Industries Board from August 1, 1917 to December 19, 1918,* Committee Print no. 4; *Minutes of the Price Fixing Committee of the War Industries Board,* parts 1–4, March 14–December 30, 1918, Committee Print no. 5; *Minutes of the General Munitions Board from April 4 to August 9, 1917,* Committee Print no. 6; *Minutes of the Council of National Defense,* Committee Print no. 7; and *Minutes of the Advisory Commission of the Council of National Defense and Minutes of the Munitions Standards Board,* Committee Print no. 8. See also U.S. Council of National Defense, *First, Second, Third, and Fourth Annual Report of the United States Council of National Defense* (Washington, DC: U.S. Government Printing Office, 1917–1920); U.S. War Department, *Report of the Secretary of War to the President,* 1914–1920; *Report of the Quartermaster General to the Secretary of War,* 1914–1920;

*Report of the Chief of Ordnance to the Secretary of War,* 1914–1920; and U.S. Navy Department, *Report of the Secretary of Navy to the President,* 1914–1920; Bernard M. Baruch, *American Industry in the War: A Report of the War Industries Board* (Washington, DC: U.S. Government Printing Office, 1921); Lloyd N. Scott, *Naval Consulting Board* (Washington, DC: U.S. Government Printing Office, 1920); Franklin H. Martin, *Digest of the Proceedings of the Council of National Defense During the World War,* 73d Cong., 2d sess., 1934, S. Doc. 193; U.S. Fuel Administration, *Final Report of the United States Fuel Administration, 1917–1919,* by H. A. Garfield (Washington, DC: U.S. Government Printing Office, 1921); U.S. Congress, Senate, *Government Manufacture of Arms, Munitions, and Equipment,* 64th Cong., 2d sess., 1917, S. Doc. 664; U.S. Federal Trade Commission, *Report on War-Time Costs and Profits of Southern Pine Lumber Companies* (Washington, DC: U.S. Government Printing Office, 1922), *Report on War-Time Profits and Costs of the Steel Industry* (Washington, DC: U.S. Government Printing Office, 1925), and *Report of the Federal Trade Commission Regarding Profiteering,* June 29, 1918, 65th Cong., 2d sess., S. Doc. 248.

Congressional hearings and reports, 1916–1920, are an exceptionally rewarding source for grasping the dynamics of mobilizing the World War I economy. See the House and Senate Military Affairs Committees and various subcommittees; the House and Senate Naval Affairs Committees and various subcommittees, 1916–1920; and the House Appropriations Committees and various subcommittees. Additionally, the House Select Committee on Expenditures in the War Department, 1919–1921, and the Senate Special Committee Investigating the Munitions Industry, 1934–1936, are indispensable for understanding the economics of World War I at home. (I analyze the two committees at length in volume 3 [forthcoming] of this series.) See also the relevant issues of the U.S. *Statutes at Large,* and U.S. Congress, *Congressional Record* (full citations for these sources are provided in the notes, chapters 6–10).

The secondary literature that directly or indirectly deals with mobilizing the World War I economy is extensive. Most of it is covered in two bibliographies: Ronald Schaffer, *The United States in World War I: A Selected Bibliography* (Santa Barbara, CA: Clio Press, 1978), and David R. Woodward and Robert Franklin Maddox, *America and World War I: A Selected Annotated Bibliography of English-Language Sources* (New York: Garland, 1985). Most of the books, articles, and dissertations involving the subject are cited in the notes, chapters 5–13.

# INDEX

ABCDs (naval vessels), 29, 30, 48, 49
Adams, Harry M., 248
Addams, Jane, 153
Advisory Council (navy), 42, 46
AEF. *See* American Expeditionary Forces
Aero Club, 110
Aero Squadron (Signal Corps), 96
Aetna Explosives Company, 125 (table)
AFL. *See* American Federation of Labor
Agrarian protest movements, 13. *See also* Populist Era
Agrarian society, 12, 15, 111
Agriculture
  gross farm output increase (1860–1910), 15, 16
  income, 262–63
  mechanization, 15
  regional specialization, 15
Agriculture Department, 158, 194, 201, 206
Ainsworth, Fred C., 91, 92
Aircraft Production Board, 218
Airplanes, 95–96, 249
Aldrich, Nelson W., 25
Aleshire, James B., 153, 192
Alger, Russell A., 66, 75, 76, 81, 84, 86–87
Allied Purchasing Commission, 136, 217
Aluminum Company of America, 175
Ambulances, 78
American Alliance for Labor and Democracy, 260
American Bankers' Association, 140
American Brass Company, 175
American Expeditionary Forces (AEF), 71, 183, 252–53
American Federation of Labor (AFL), 158, 258, 259, 260, 269
American Indians, 59. *See also under* Army
American Iron and Steel Institute, 178, 180
American Railway Association, 98, 173, 190
American Smelting and Refining Company, 124, 125 (table)
American Society of Electrical Engineers, 147
American Society of Mechanical Engineers, 189
American Telephone and Telegraph Company (ATT), 128, 147
Amphibious warfare, 37
Anaconda Copper Company, 175, 249
Anglophilia, 111
Annapolis Proving Ground, 53
Antielite attitudes, 6
Antiexpansionists, 32, 34, 48, 107, 111
Antitrust strategies, 279–81, 283
Antiwar attitudes, 6, 107, 153–54. *See also* Pacifists
Appointed officials, 15, 100
Arizona, 61
*Armies of Asia and Europe, The* (Upton), 69
Armor, 19, 20, 28, 33, 50, 52–55. *See also under* Navy; Steel
Armor-piercing shells, 30
Army
  adjutant general, 91
  airplanes, 95–96, 249
  and American Indians, 59, 62
  appropriations for, 59, 63, 68, 73, 95, 97, 184–85
  cars and trucks, 95
  colonial duties, 94, 97
  commanding general, 62, 63, 65–67, 87
  command system, 64, 65, 69, 75, 88, 91, 102, 105
  Commissary Department, 79
  and Congress, 41, 58, 63, 65, 67, 68–69, 103, 184–85
  Corps of Engineers, 63, 71, 73, 79, 93
  desertion, 62
  Eighth Corps, 85
  Endicott Board, 51, 73–74
  and executive branch, 58, 69, 76, 103
  Fifth Corps, 86
  food, 59–60, 79

Army *(continued)*
- frontier duty, 19, 58, 59, 61, 62, 91
- General Staff/Chief of Staff, 72, 88, 89, 90, 91–92, 95, 97, 109, 151–54, 183, 184, 245–48, 249, 296
- Hospital Corps, 63
- and industrial conflicts, 58–59
- in industrial stage, 4, 9
- Inspector General, 86
- intelligence (*see* Army War College; Military Information Division)
- manpower, 59, 62, 76, 94, 95, 108, 113, 182, 184
- medical care, 60, 63
- Medical Corps, 155
- Medical Department, 79, 86
- militia, 69 (*see also subentry* reserves; National Guard)
- mobilization, 94, 98–99
- modern, 4, 65, 71, 102–3
- and navy, coordination with, 37–38, 72, 76
- officers, 72, 74, 92–93, 184
- Ordnance Department, 60, 63, 77, 78–79, 153, 245, 248
- post–Civil War, 19, 58
- posts, 62, 72, 104
- professionalism, 2–3, 5, 9, 64, 69, 72, 74–75, 88, 92
- Quartermaster Department/Corps, 60–61, 63, 77–78, 80, 82, 84, 95, 96–98, 146, 153, 173, 183, 184, 246, 248
- reforms, 62, 64–75, 88–99, 247
- reorganization of, 64, 245
- reserves, 74 (*see also subentry* militia; National Guard)
- retirement, 72
- schools, 70–71, 80, 88, 92–93
- Signal Corps, 63, 79, 93, 95–96
- Subsistence Department, 82, 96
- supply depots and arsenals, 60, 73, 77, 78, 79, 80, 95
- supply restructuring, 246–49, 358 (n18)
- technology, 64, 72–73, 95–96, 102 (*see also subentry* weapons)
- tradition, 70
- training, 70, 93, 109, 113
- training for students, 109 (*see also* Reserve Officers' Training Corps)
- in transitional stage, 2–3
- transportation, 60–62, 80–85, 87, 97, 248–49
- volunteers, 76
- weapons, 72–73, 78, 95, 96, 223 (*see also subentry* technology)
- Western barracks and posts, 59, 62
- and WIB, 206, 218, 233, 249–51
- *See also* War Department; *under* Civil-military relations; Congress; Democratic party; Executive branch; Railroads; Spanish-American War; Wilson, Woodrow; World War I; World War II

Army and Navy Coast Defense Board, 76. *See also* Coastal defense
Army Appropriations Act (1916, 1918), 256
Army Gun Factory (Watervliet, N.Y.), 73
Army League, 109, 110
*Army-Navy Journal,* 25, 32
Army School of the Line, 70, 71
Army Staff College, 70, 71
Army War College, 72, 90, 92, 151, 184
Arthur, Chester A., 28
Articles of Confederation, 2, 6
Artillery, 73, 78, 93, 95, 123, 126
Asia, 97
Asquith, Herbert, 116
Association for National Service, 110
ATT. *See* American Telephone and Telegraph Company
Augur, Christopher C., 67
Automobile, 95, 241, 265
Ayers, Leonard P., 249

Bacon, Robert, 109–10
Baker, Newton D., 92, 108, 114, 146, 151, 157, 158, 160, 198, 199, 203, 204–5, 219, 228, 244, 245, 246, 269, 291, 292, 295, 296
- and NDAC, 166, 167, 170, 183, 187, 190
- *See also* Council of National Defense; General Munitions Board; Munitions Standards Board; War Industries Board

Balance of power, 26, 27
Baldwin Locomotive Works, 119, 125 (table), 130, 188
Baltimore and Ohio Railroad, 158
Banking, 2, 5, 11, 17, 114, 115–16, 117, 130, 142, 266
Bank of England, 116, 132
Banning, Henry, 68
Barber, F. M., 52
Baruch, Bernard M., 140, 154–55, 157, 269, 286, 289, 291, 294
- big business outlook, 290
- and chamber of commerce, 210, 347 (n20)
- and CND, 158, 160, 162, 166–67, 168–69, 170, 171, 174, 175–77, 178, 190, 193, 196, 199, 200, 205, 334 (n38), 338 (n15)
- and WIB, 198, 206, 207, 211, 215, 216, 222–23, 227–28, 230–31, 239–40, 252, 273–78, 280, 281, 289

Bates, John C., 90

Battle cruisers, 40
Battleships, 19, 31, 34, 37, 38, 39, 40
  first-class, 35
  sea-going, coast-line, 32
  second-class, 29, 35
Bedford, Alfred C., 175
Belknap, William W., 62, 65, 68
Bell, J. Franklin, 71, 90
Benson, William Shepherd, 42
Berle, Adolf A., Jr., 100
Bethlehem Iron Company, 30, 33, 34, 51, 52, 53, 54
Bethlehem Steel Company, 124, 125 (table), 131
Bigelow, John, Jr., 71
Billings, John S., 59
Bird, Charles, 84
Blacks, 12
Bliss, Tasker H., 183, 245
Board on Fortifications and Other Defenses. *See* Army, Endicott Board
Bolton, Chester C., 218
Borie, Adolph E., 20
Boston (Mass.) navy yard, 29, 45
Boutelle, Charles A., 31, 32
Boxer Rebellion (1900), 94
Brazil, 34
Breckinridge, Henry, 153
Breech-loaders, 72
Brooker, Charles S., 175
Brookings, Robert S., 206, 207, 217, 230, 242, 244
Brown-water war, 37
Bryan, William Jennings, 107, 127
Buhl, Lance C., 21
Bunting List of 100 Corporations, 125 (table)
Bureau of Steam Engineering, 20
Burnside, Ambrose E., 68
Burnside Committee hearings (1878), 70
Bush, Samuel P., 281
Business associations, 139, 140, 154
Business sector. *See* Civil-military relations; Corporations; Federal government, and business; Mergers
Butler, Nicholas Murray, 157
Butterworth Judson Company, 125 (table)

Calhoun, John C., 70
Cambria Iron Company, 53
Cameron, James D., 68
*Campaign of Chancellorsville, The: A Strategic and Tactical Study* (Bigelow), 71
Canada, 54, 121
Cannon, 28, 73, 78
Cantonment Adjustment Commission (1917), 260
Capital-intensive industries, 16–17
Capitalism, 3
Carbines, 72–73
Caribbean, 21, 37, 38, 41
Carnegie, Phipps and Company, 33, 34, 53, 54
Carnegie Endowment for International Peace, 112
Carter, William H., 89, 93
Carty, John J., 147
Catchings, Waddill, 137, 208, 222, 225, 226, 350 (n38)
Cattell, Alexander G., 20
Cavalry, 72
Cavalry Association, 71
*Cavalry Journal*, 71
Central Trust Company of Chicago, 249
Chaffee, Adna R., 90
Chamberlain, George E., 110, 151, 153, 157, 221–22, 292
Chamberlain Committee, 221, 224, 226
Chamber of Commerce, U.S., 109, 110, 140–46, 160, 163, 168, 208–9, 210, 225, 259, 279, 329 (n7), 347 (n20)
  Committee on National Defense, 144, 145
  Reconstruction Congress of American Industries (1918), 272, 280
Chandler, Alfred D., Jr., 16, 174, 267, 297
Chandler, William E., 25, 28, 29, 32
*Charleston* (U.S. cruiser), 29
Chase Manhattan Bank, 130
Chemicals, 17
Chester (Pa.) shipyard, 29
Chile, 32
China, 34, 38, 94
Citizen soldiers. *See* Army, reserves; Militia; National Guard
Civil-military relations, 1, 295, 297, 298
  and army, 10, 65, 69, 74–75, 102–3, 109
  in industrial stage, 3, 4, 5, 104
  and navy, 10, 21, 22, 23, 26, 28, 29, 33, 41, 42, 48–55, 56, 57, 102–3
  power, 101, 104, 114, 191
  in preindustrial stage, 2, 4, 5
  in transitional stage, 3, 5
Civil War (1861–1865), 3, 6–7, 9, 64, 80
Cleveland, Grover, 29, 33–34, 47
Cleveland Rolling Mills, 53
Clothing industry, 17
CND. *See* Council of National Defense
Coal, 256
Coaling stations, 32
Coastal defense, 48, 51, 73–74, 76, 112
Coffin, Howard E., 148–50, 151, 157, 188, 189–90, 206, 226, 238, 259, 262
  and NDAC, 158, 159, 160, 162, 163, 164, 167, 171–72, 177, 190, 196

Cold War (1945–1991), 5, 6, 57, 297
Collective bargaining, 261
Command of the Army Act repeal, 68
Commerce Department, 168, 194, 269, 276, 278
  secretary, 158, 210
Commercial Agency Agreement, 116, 117, 118, 119, 120, 138
Commercialism, 21
Committee of American Physicians for Medical Preparedness, 155
Committee on Public Information, 260
Confederacy, 3, 7
Congress, 12, 66
  and army, 41, 58, 63, 67, 68, 103, 184–85
  and navy, 21–22, 25, 26, 29, 31, 34, 37, 39, 40, 41, 42, 43, 47–48, 103, 185
  and World War I, mobilization agencies, 111, 140, 153, 200, 201–3, 293, 294
Constitution, 6
Continental Army Plan, 94
Continentalism, 21, 27
Conversion. *See* Production, conversion for military
Cooke, Jay, and Company, 20
Corbin, Henry C., 76, 81
Corporate capitalism, 14, 17, 100, 163
Corporations, 3, 5, 9, 11, 13, 102, 123–24, 125 (table), 288
  Bunting List, 125 (table)
  competition, 16, 17, 174, 279 (*see also* Antitrust strategies)
  elite, 100
  management, 16, 17, 100, 101, 174
  ownership, 100–101
  profit, 263
  size, 17
  structure, 16, 101, 267
  and wartime mobilization, 139, 174, 196–97, 198, 263, 289–90
  *See also* Economic maturity; Economic regulation; Elites; Federal government, and business; Holding companies; Mergers; Military-industrial complex; Oligopolies; World War I, and government-business regulatory alliance; *under* War Department
Council of National Defense (CND) (1916), 105, 154, 156–58, 167, 187
  business participation, 168–70, 200
  committees and operation, 167–82, 193, 200–205, 211, 249
  National Defense Advisory Commission (NDAC), 158–65, 166–67, 187–88, 191, 196, 200–205, 290, 293 (*see also under* War Department)
  price controls, 193–95
  proposal (1912), 41
  and reconversion, 268–71, 278
  and states, 256, 269
  *See also* Baker, Newton D.; General Munitions Board; Munitions Standards Board; War Industries Board
Cramp and Sons (shipbuilder), 49
Crampton, Henry E., 156, 157
Croly, Herbert, 111
Crowder, Enoch H., 157, 222
Crowell, Benedict, 152, 244–45, 247
Crozier, William, 153, 245
Cruisers, 28, 31, 32, 35, 40
  armored, 39
  gunned, 29, 31
  protected, 39
  scout, 39
  torpedo-, 31, 32
Cuba, 23, 34, 76, 83–84, 85
Cuff, Robert D., 289, 297
Cummings, Albert B., 111
Cunliffe, Lord, 116

Dana, Charles A., 31
Daniels, Josephus, 39, 42–43, 45, 46, 49, 147, 151, 170, 191, 203, 240, 295
Davis, Arthur V., 175
Davison, Henry P., 116, 129, 132
Dawes, Charles G., 249
Day, Charles R., 250
Dayton Engineering Laboratories Company (Delco), 189
Deeds, Edward A., 189
Defense Department, 201
Delaware River shipyards, 48
Delco. *See* Dayton Engineering Laboratories Company
Democratic ideology, 5–6, 12, 15, 108, 111
Democratic party
  and army, 58, 68
  and military, 29, 67, 112–13
  and navy, 47, 48
Depression (1917–1921), 278
Destroyers, torpedo boat, 37, 39
Dewey, George, 36, 37, 39, 40–41, 77
Dewey, John, 111
Dick, Charles W., 93
Dickinson, Jacob M., 90
Dispatch boat, 28
Dodge, Grenville M., 87
Dodge Commission, 87, 96, 97
Dollar-a-year-man system, 143, 151, 161, 201, 215. *See also* Council of National Defense; War Industries Board
Dollar Decade (1920s), 294
Downman, Robert H., 175, 180
Dreadnoughts, 38–39

Drum, R. C., 62
Dunn, Harry T., 212
Du Pont de Nemours, E. I., Powder Company, 121, 124, 125 (table)
Dysentery, 85, 86

Eagan, Charles P., 77, 79
Economic maturity, 1
  and ethnocultural issues, 14
  and industrial economy, 15, 17, 102, 229, 262–64, 298
  in industrial stage, 2, 102
  in transitional stage, 2, 3
  *See also* Corporations; Federal government, and business
Economic mobilization for war. *See* Political economy of warfare; *under* World War I; World War II
Economic regulation
  in industrial stage, 3, 4, 11, 13, 102, 105
  in transitional stage, 3
  twentieth century, 14, 108
Eddystone Ammunition Corporation, 130–31
Edison, Thomas A., 147
EFC. *See* Emergency Fleet Corporation
Eight-hour-day law (1912), 260
Eisenman, Charles, 173, 177
Election
  1876, 58, 68
  1918, 271
Electric Boat Company, 49
Elites, 5–6, 114, 143, 229
  and democratic ideology, 12, 15
  modern, 12, 148
  political, 11–12, 15, 100
  power, 100, 101, 253
  states, 7
  *See also* Civil-military relations; Federal government, and business; Middle class; Progressive era, and elitism; Upper class; Wealth distribution; *under* Corporations; Foreign policy; Military
Emergency Fleet Corporation (EFC), 182, 190, 233, 252, 257
Employment Service, U.S. (USES), 261, 262, 278
Endicott, William C., 51, 73
Endicott Board. *See under* Army
Engineer Corps (1842), 43. *See also* Army, Corps of Engineers
Engineering, 148
Evans, Holden A., 46
Executive branch, 12–13, 14, 27, 41, 48, 57
  and army, 58, 69, 103
  growth, 15
  and navy, 76, 103
  *See also* Overman Act
Explosives, 123

Fahey, John H., 140, 141
Federal government
  and business, 3, 4, 5, 11, 14, 30, 34, 49, 50, 54–55, 61, 77, 80, 101, 114–15, 146, 160–61, 165, 200, 201–2, 267, 288, 289, 298 (*see also* Economic regulation; Military-industrial complex)
  changes, 12–13
  domestic reform, 107
  and economic mobilization, 1, 3, 5 (*see also* Council of National Defense; General Munitions Board; Munitions Standards Board; War Industries Board)
  foreign policy (1890s–1920), 26–27, 38, 107
  growth, 12, 14, 18, 102, 298
  in industrial stage, 3, 4, 102
  in preindustrial stage, 2, 3
  *See also* Congress; Executive branch; *under specific departments*
Federalists, 2
Federal Reserve Bank of New York, 132
Federal Reserve Banks, 142
Federal Reserve Board (FRB), 15, 132, 133, 134, 142, 143, 145, 257
Federal Trade Commission (FTC), 15, 142, 143, 145, 194, 256, 280
  Act (1914), 142, 279
  and wartime profiteering, 263
Filene, Edward A., 140
Finance. *See* Banking
Finnegan, John Patrick, 113
First National Bank of New York, 118, 130, 249
Fiske, Bradley A., 42, 44
Fisk Rubber Company, 212
Flagler, Daniel W., 77
Fletcher, Frank F., 206
Food Administration (U.S.), 173, 182, 254, 255–56, 257
Ford Motor Company, 241
Foreign policy, 26–27, 38, 104, 157, 333 (n31)
  and domestic policy, 107, 108
  and elites, 12, 101
  and navy, 56
Fort Leavenworth (Kans.) military prison, 60
Fortress Monroe Artillery School, 70
Fourth party system (1896–1932), 14
France
  steel, 52
  and World War I, 114, 117, 120, 121, 124, 223

Franco-Prussian War (1870–1871), 65
Frankfurter, Felix, 260, 261
Frayne, Hugh A., 206, 207, 230, 258, 259, 270
FRB. *See* Federal Reserve Board
Freight companies, 61
FTC. *See* Federal Trade Commission
Fuel Administration (U.S.), 182, 254, 255, 256, 257

Gardner, Augustus P., 42, 109
Garfield, Harry A., 226, 255, 256, 285
Garfield, James A., 26, 66, 67, 68
Garrison, Lindley M., 92, 94, 108, 153, 156
Gary, Elbert H., 175, 179–80, 236, 273, 284
Gates, John M., 74, 75
General Board (navy), 30, 40, 42, 44, 46
  phased out (1951), 47
General Electric Company, 119, 188
General Motors Corporation, 241
General Munitions Board (GMB), 190–96, 205. *See also* Council of National Defense; Munitions Standards Board; War Industries Board; *under* Navy Department; War Department
General Rubber Company, 175
General Trade-Union Conference (1917), 258
Germany, 26, 38, 41, 223
  as military model, 69, 70, 144, 145
  navy, 39, 110, 130
Gifford, Walter S., 147, 148, 149, 159, 168–70, 171, 208, 210, 269, 290, 291
Gilded Age (1865–1899), 11, 12, 15, 19
  and military, 21, 23, 32, 55, 59, 62, 74, 75, 103
Glass, Carter, 281, 283, 285
Glass-Owen Act (1913), 142
Glenn, Thomas, 282
GMB. *See* General Munitions Board
GNP. *See* Gross National Product
Godfrey, Hollis, 156–57, 158, 160, 162, 171, 177, 205, 269
Goethals, George W., 246–48, 250, 253
Gold notes, 118
Gompers, Samuel, 111, 158, 162, 168, 172–73, 177, 206, 258–59, 269
Gorgas, William C., 155
Grant, Ulysses S., 13, 20, 64, 65, 67, 80
Great Britain, 20, 34, 38, 111, 120
  defense, 73
  steel, 52
  Treasury Bills, 132, 133
  and World War I, 114, 115–18, 120, 121, 122, 124, 126, 127–32, 156, 223, 242, 325 (nn50,52)
Great Depression (1930s), 101
Great Lakes shipyards, 49
Great Plains, 15
Greene, Frank L., 156
Gregory, Thomas W., 208
Gross National Product (GNP)
  1870 and 1910, 15
  1918, 263–64, 265
Guam, 38
Guaranty Trust Company, 130
Gunboats, 31, 37
Gun Foundry Board (1883), 50, 51, 52, 73

Hagan, Kenneth J., 21
Haiti, 32
Hale, Eugene, 31
Hale, George Ellery, 155
Halleck, Henry W., 64
Hanch, Charles C., 212
Hancock, John M., 182
Hancock, Winfield Scott, 71
Hanna, Marcus A., 14
Harding, W. P. G., 133
Harrison, Benjamin, 30
Harvard Club, Committee of One Hundred, 109
Harvard University, 109
Harvey, Augustus, 54
Haupt, Herman, 80
Hawaii, 32, 38
Hay, John, 91, 157
Hayes, R. H., 249
Hayes, Rutherford B., 12, 66, 68
Hecker, Frank J., 84
Herbert, Hilary A., 31, 33–35, 45
Hercules Powder Company, 125 (table)
Hillquit, Morris, 111
Himmelberg, Robert F., 277
Hines, Walker D., 281, 283, 285
Hobson, Richmond P., 41, 42, 48
Holding companies, 16
Hoover, Herbert, 173, 255
Horses, 78
Hotchkiss, H. Stuart, 176
House, Edward M., 39, 129, 138, 154, 157, 205, 334 (n38)
House Banking and Currency Committee, 119
House Commission on Ordnance and Gunnery, 51
House Committee on Military Affairs, 67, 68, 91, 111
House Naval Affairs Committee, 25, 31, 33, 111
Houston, David F., 206, 269
Huidekoper, Frederick L., 109
Hull, John A. T., 76
Humphrey, Charles F., 83

Hunt, William H., 26, 27, 28
Huntington, Samuel P., 74, 75
Hurley, Edward N., 257
Hydraulic press, 54

Immigrants, 13, 14, 62
Imperialism, 26–27, 32, 38, 57, 107
Industrial Board (1919), 268, 281–87, 290. *See also* Reconstruction; Reconversion; *under* Wilson, Woodrow
Industrial Cooperation Service, 281
Industrialization, 2, 3, 7, 9, 11
  political adjustment to, 12–15, 104
Industrial mobilization. *See* Congress, and World War I, mobilization agencies; Corporations, and wartime mobilization; Munitions Standards Board; Naval Consulting Board; Production; War Industries Board; Wilson, Woodrow, and World War I mobilization; World War I, and industrial preparedness
Industrial Preparedness Committee (IPC) (NCB), 147, 148–50, 151, 152, 159–61, 189. *See also under* World War I
Industrial production (1910), 15
Industrial self-regulation, 180, 288
Industrial stage, 1, 3–5, 6, 7. *See also* Political economy of warfare; *under* Economic maturity; Economic regulation; Federal government; Military; Military technology
Industrial Workers of the World (IWW), 258, 259, 262
Infantry, 72
Infantry Association, 71
*Infantry Journal,* 71
Inflation, 193, 278, 281
*Influence of Sea Power upon History, A, 1660–1783* (Mahan), 25, 33
Ingraham, William M., 245
Inland water vessels, 48
Innovation, 15
Insurance companies, 17
Interest groups, 6, 262, 294
Interior Department, 194
  secretary, 158, 199, 281
International Harvester Company, 119, 128
Internationalists, 112
International Nickel Company, 175
Interstate Commerce Act (1887), 13
Interstate Commerce Commission (ICC), 15, 142
Interwar years (1919–1939), 4, 6, 154, 297
IPC. *See* Industrial Preparedness Committee
Iron, 19, 48
Isolationists, 32, 111
Isthmian Canal, 25
Italy, 26, 115, 121
IWW. *See* Industrial Workers of the World

James, George R., 281
Japan, 26, 38, 41
  navy, 34
Jaques, William H., 52
Jeffersonians, 107
Jeffersonville (Ind.) depot, 77
Jingoist, 34
John Deere Wagon Company, 212
Johnson, Andrew, 13, 58, 66
Johnson, Hugh S., 225, 244, 250, 251
Joint Army-Navy Board (1903), 41
*Journal of the United States Military Service Institution,* 71

Kahn, Julius, 153
Kahn, Otto, 249
Karsten, Peter, 42
Kernan, Francis J., 152
Kernan Board, 152, 153, 163
Key, Albert L., 44
Key West (Fla.) naval base, 37
Kidder, Peabody and Company, 130
King, Stanley, 260
Kitchen, Claude, 111
Krag-Jorgensen rifle and carbine, 73, 78
Kuhn, Loeb, and Company, 249

Labor Department, 261
  secretary, 158, 261, 281
Labor-intensive industries, 17
Labor strife (1919–1921), 278
Labor unions, 14, 111, 158, 258–63
LaFollette, Robert M., 107–8, 111
Lake Torpedo Boat Company, 49
Lamont, Thomas H., 138
Landis, J. F. Reynolds, 187
Lane, Franklin K., 199, 204, 281
Lansing, Robert, 39, 127, 129
Latin America, and U.S., 26, 32, 34, 38, 97
League to Enforce the Peace, 112
Leavenworth (Kans.)
  School of Application for Cavalry and Infantry, 70, 71
  School of the Line, 93
  Staff College, 93
Lee, Higginson and Company, 130
Le Ferro Nickel (company), 53–54
Legge, Alexander, 176, 230, 252
Lehman, Herbert H., 249
Lehman Brothers, 249
Lesseps, Ferdinand de, 21
Lever Food and Fuel Control Act (1917), 173, 200–201, 207–8, 255

Liberty loans, 135
Liberty products, 242–43
Lincoln, Abraham, 64
Lincoln, Robert Todd, 66
Lippmann, Walter, 111, 260
Little, Bascom, 144, 152–53
Lloyd George, David, 116
Lodge, Henry Cabot, 25, 29, 31, 48, 107
Logan, John A., 67–68
Long, John D., 23, 35, 36, 37, 38, 40, 76
Lovett, Robert S., 206, 207, 217, 218, 226, 230, 244
Luce, Stephen B., 23–24, 25, 31, 41, 44, 70
Ludington, Marshall I., 77, 82, 84
Lumber, 17
*Lusitania* crisis (1915), 112

McAdoo, William, 31, 34
McAdoo, William G., 129, 135, 138, 174, 199, 205, 256–57
McCallum, Daniel C., 80
McCann, William P., 31
*McClure's Magazine,* 44
McCormick, Vance C., 257
Machine guns, 95, 126
McKellar, Kenneth D., 202, 292
McKinley, William, 9, 13, 35, 36, 54, 88
  and labor, 14
  and Spanish-American War, 76, 82, 87
Mahan, Alfred Thayer, 21, 24, 25, 26, 31, 33, 36
Mahan, Dennis Hart, 64
Malaria, 85
Manchu Law, 92
Manila Bay (Philippines), 36
Manufacturing, 2, 5, 15, 17
March, Peyton C., 246, 247, 296
Marine Corps, 37, 42
Marine steam engines, 29
Market forces, 3, 4, 6, 7, 267
Marketing, 2, 16
Martin, Franklin H., 155, 158, 162, 168, 172, 177, 190, 196, 205, 269
Massachusetts Institute of Technology School of Naval Architecture, 44
Mass distribution, 17
Mass production, 17
Means, Gardiner C., 100
Medical associations, 155, 159
Meigs, J. F., 54
Meigs, Montgomery C., 60, 63, 68
Menken, S. Stanwood, 109
Merchant Marine, 25, 48
Mergers, 17, 264–65
Merritt, Wesley, 77, 85, 88
Mexican War (1846–1848), 3, 9
Mexico, 92, 93, 110
Meyer, Eugene, Jr., 176
Meyer, George von Lengerke, 39, 41–42, 46
MIC. *See* Military-industrial complex
MID. *See* Military Information Division
Middle class, 13, 15. *See also* Elites
Middleman, 17
Midvale Iron and Steel Company, 53, 55
Midvale Steel and Ordnance Company, 119, 125 (table), 129, 131
Midwestern businessmen, 231
Miles, Nelson A., 66, 75–76, 77, 81, 85, 87, 88, 89
Military, 1
  conscription (*see* Selective Service Act)
  and democratic ideology, 6
  elites, 12, 101, 102
  in industrial stage, 6, 19
  officer corps, 101
  peacetime (Cold War), 5
  peacetime (post-1865), 19, 21
  in preindustrial stage, 2
  preparedness and civilian support, 109–11, 288, 295–96
  reserves, 44
  in transitional stage, 2–3
  *See also* Army; Civil-military relations; Marine Corps; Military technology; Navy; Navy Department; War Department; World War I; World War II; *under* Democratic party
Military Academy, U.S. (West Point, N.Y.), 71, 101. *See also* Naval Academy, U.S.
Military-industrial complex (MIC), 55–57, 103–4, 296, 297
Military Information Division (MID) (1885), 72
*Military Policy of the United States, The* (Upton), 69
Military prison. *See* Fort Leavenworth
Military Service Institution (army) (1878), 71
Military technology, 1, 102
  and Cold War, 5
  1888–1898, 10, 50, 96
  in industrial stage, 4, 6, 9, 103
  in preindustrial stage, 2
  in transitional stage, 3
  World War I, 64, 96, 147, 148–49, 265–66, 298
  *See also* Army, technology; National Guard, weapons; Navy, and technological change; World War I, and weapons technology
Military Training Camps Association (MTCA), 109
Militia, 37, 69. *See also* Army, reserves; National Guard

Militia Act (Dick Act) (1903), 89, 93
Minell, Ambrose, 175
Mississippi River shipyards, 49
Missouri Pacific Railroad, 248–49
Montagu, Edwin S., 116
Montauk, Long Island, 86
Montgomery Ward and Company, 248
Moody, William H., 41
Morgan, Grenfell and Company, 116, 122
Morgan, J. P., Jr., 110, 136
Morgan, J. P., and Company, 17, 199, 266
  Export Department, 121–22, 123, 124, 126, 127, 320 (n29)
  as financier and purchasing agent for Allies, 114–18, 120–21, 122, 124, 125 (table), 126–38, 178, 189
  and Nye Committee, 120, 127, 322 (n36)
  wartime profits, 118–19, 120
Morrison, John F., 71
Moseley, George Van Horn, 110
MSB. *See* Munitions Standards Board
MTCA. *See* Military Training Camps Association
Mugwumps, 13
Mules, 61, 78, 84
Munitions industry, 123, 126, 130–31, 149–50, 151
  and educational orders, 149, 331 (n21)
Munitions Standards Board (MSB), 188–90. *See also* Council of National Defense; General Munitions Board; War Industries Board
Muskets, 72

Nagel, Charles, 140
NAM. *See* National Association of Manufacturers
National Academy of Sciences, 155
  National Research Council, 159
National Association of Manufacturers (NAM), 140, 143, 279, 280
National Board of Trade, 140
National City Bank, 117, 127
National Civic Federation (NCF), 109, 143, 259, 260
National Defense Act (1916), 92, 108, 112, 151, 152, 155, 184
National Defense Advisory Commission. *See under* Council of National Defense
National Guard, 74, 75, 76, 87, 88, 89, 93, 94, 97, 108
  and Mexico, 110
  weapons, 95
  *See also* Militia
National Guard Association (1877), 74
National Implement and Vehicle Association, 212
National Industrial Conference Board, 172
National Lumber Manufacturers' Association, 175
National Recovery Administration, 101, 287
National Research Council, 155, 190
National Security League (NSL), 109, 110
National security state, 298. *See also* Military-industrial complex
National Tariff Commission League, 141
National War Labor Board (NWLB), 260–61
*Nation's Business* (Chamber of Commerce), 145, 209
Naval Academy, U.S. (Annapolis, Md.), 24, 35, 43, 101
  Postgraduate Department, 44
  *See also* Military Academy, U.S.
Naval Advisory Board, 28
Naval Appropriations Act (1916), 152
Naval Consulting Board (NCB) (1915), 105, 147–51, 154, 155, 160
Naval Institute (1873), 22, 23, 24, 71
  *Proceedings*, 23
Naval War Board, 23, 36, 40
Naval War College (NWC) (1884), 22, 24–25, 29, 30, 31, 32, 35, 40, 44
Navy
  administration, 43–47
  appropriations for, 22, 29, 38, 39, 40, 53
  armored ships, 28, 29, 34, 50
  and army, coordination, 37–38
  Asiatic squadron, 36, 37
  Atlantic squadron, 36
  bases, 25, 32, 38, 45, 104
  and change, 103
  chief of naval operations (1915), 23, 42, 46, 47
  command system, 37, 40, 41–43, 46
  for commerce raiding, 21
  doctrines, 30, 31, 39
  enlisted men, 24, 35–36, 37, 39, 40, 43
  expansion (Civil War), 19
  expansion (1890s), 27, 32, 37, 38
  expansion (1900s), 38–39, 40, 108, 182
  gunnery hit record, 37
  gun placement, 30
  guns, 30
  for harbor defense, 21
  in industrial stage, 4, 6, 9
  iron ships, 27, 48 (*see also* Steel)
  militia, 37 (*see subentry* reserves)
  modern, 4, 6, 9, 10, 23, 25, 26, 102–3
  new, 55–57
  offensive role, 27, 30, 31, 32, 38, 56–57
  officers, 19, 20, 22, 24, 28, 29, 32, 35, 37, 39, 40, 43
  ordnance, 28, 29–30, 50, 52, 53, 189
  peacetime duties, 19

Navy *(continued)*
permanent fleet, 31
personnel reform, 43
professionalism, 2–3, 5, 19, 22, 26
promotion, 43
rankings, 19, 28, 38, 39, 46, 48
repair limit, 28
reserves, 43–44
ship construction and design, 20–21, 22, 26, 28, 30, 32–33, 34, 35, 38–39, 43, 44, 47, 48–50, 106
ship purchase, 37
ship types, 19, 27, 28, 29, 31, 32, 35, 37, 38–39
supply system, 182, 195, 223
and technological change, 19–20, 26, 28, 102, 103, 147, 266
in transitional stage, 2–3
war plans, 41
and WIB, 206, 217–18, 219, 233, 249–50
*See also under* Congress; Democratic party; Executive branch; Republican party; Spanish-American War; Wilson, Woodrow; World War I
Navy Department, 9, 295–96
aide system, 41–42
Board of Construction/Board on the Design of Ships, 32–33, 37, 44
bureaus, 32, 33, 35, 40, 42, 43, 45, 46, 182, 185, 252
and corporations, 101
corruption, 20–21, 54–55
and GMB, 192, 195
secretaries, 20, 21, 22, 23, 25, 26, 29, 30, 39, 41, 45, 57, 158 *(see also individual names)*
*See also* Advisory Council; General Board; Joint Army-Navy Board
Navy League, 55, 110
Navy yards, 20, 28, 29, 30, 33, 43, 44–46
and large ships, 36
specialization, 45
NCB. *See* Naval Consulting Board
NCF. *See* National Civic Federation
NDAC. *See* Council of National Defense, National Defense Advisory Commission
Nelson, Ralph L., 265
Neo-Hamiltonians, 107, 143, 145, 162, 262, 294
Neo-Jeffersonians, 107, 143, 202, 203, 293–94
Newberry, Truman H., 45–46
New Competition, 279
New Deal, 295
New England Westinghouse Company, 125 (table)
New Freedom, 14, 108
New Jersey Zinc Company, 175
New London (Conn.) navy yard, 29
New Mexico, 61
New Nationalism, 14, 107, 108, 162
New Orleans (La.), 60
Newport (R.I.), 44
Newport News (Va.) Shipbuilding and Dry Dock Company, 49
*New Republic group,* 111
New York City, 60
New York Dry Dock no. 2, 36
New York Port Authority, 246
New York State, 110
Nicaragua, 34
Nonessential industries, 226, 240, 241
Norton, Christopher C., 249
NSL. *See* National Security League
Nurses' Corps, 60
NWC. *See* Naval War College
NWLB. *See* National War Labor Board
Nye, Gerald P., 317 (n13)
Nye Committee, 119, 120, 127, 134, 317 (n13), 318 (n20), 322 (n36), 325 (n51)

Office of Naval Intelligence (ONI) (1882), 22, 23, 24, 28, 30, 40
and MID, 72
and Spanish-American War, 37, 72
Ohio River shipyard, 49
Oil, 16
Oil tankers, 49
Oligopolies, 16, 174, 179–80, 267, 279
ONI. *See* Office of Naval Intelligence
Ore ships, 49
*Organization and Tactics* (Wagner), 71
Otis, Charles A., 238–40
Otis, Elwell S., 85
Otterson, John E., 188
Overman, Lee S., 222, 270
Overman Act (1918), 222, 223–24, 296
Overseas naval bases, 25, 32, 38, 45

Pacific area, 21, 26–27, 34, 38, 96
Pacifists, 32, 111–12. *See also* Antiwar attitudes
Packet ships, 48
Pago Pago (Samoa), 32
Palmer, Edgar, 175
Palmer, John McAuley, 94, 113
Panama Coal Company, 21
Parker, Edwin B., 218, 230, 233, 244, 249, 280
Parker, Foxhall A., 24
Parsonage, Edward E., 212
Parsons, Lewis B., 80
Passenger ships, 48

Peace societies, 111–12
Peek, George N., 176, 230, 231, 238–39, 240, 242, 251, 273, 278, 280, 281, 282, 284–85, 286, 291, 347 (n20)
Penquet, Ramsey, 212–13
Pensacola (Fla.) navy yard, 29
Perkins, George H., 110
Perkins, Thomas N., 250
Pershing, John J., 96
Philadelphia (Pa.), 60
  depot, 77
  Frankfurt Arsenal, 78
Philippines, 26, 36, 37, 38, 77, 85, 94
Picatinny (N.J.) Arsenal, 95
Pierce, Palmer E., 206
Platt, Thomas C., 30–33
Plattsburg Movement, 94, 109, 113, 148, 160
Political economy of warfare
  defined, 1
  and democratic ideology, 5–6
  factors, 1 (*see also* Federal government; Military; Military technology)
  institutions, 1, 4, 106, 159, 229, 295
  stages, 2–5 *(see also individual stages)*
  *See also* Spanish-American War; World War I
Political machines, 12, 13, 29, 30
Political parties, 12
  elections versus issues, 12, 13, 14
  and government contracts, 20–21
  realignment (1894–1896), 13
Political reform, 12–13, 14, 102
Pomerene, Atlee, 202
Pomerene Amendment, 203, 207
Population (1865, 1914), 15
Populist Era (1870–1890s), 55, 107. *See also* Agrarian protest movements
Porter, David Dixon, 20, 28, 43
Portsmouth (N.H.) naval shipyard, 29, 49
Post, Louis F., 261
Powder
  brown, 30
  nitrocellulose, 124
  smokeless, 78, 95
Powell, Thomas C., 282
Pratt, Francis C., 188
Pratt, John T., 110
Preindustrial stage (colonial period–1815), 1, 2, 7
  and elites, 6
Price controls, 193–94, 219–20, 234–37, 241–43, 244
Price fixing, 283, 284
Princeton University, 109
*Principles of Strategy, The* (Bigelow), 71
Proctor, Redfield, 62
Production
  civilian diversion for military, 2, 3, 151, 266
  conversion for military, 4, 151, 240, 241
Professional groups, 139, 148, 150
Progressive era (1900–1920), 3, 11, 12, 14–15, 19, 55, 102, 103, 141, 164, 266, 293, 295, 298
  and elitism, 148
  policies, 38, 39, 107, 108, 111, 139, 140
Propaganda, 260
Propeller, 19
Prussia, 65
Puerto Rico, 65
Pujo, Arsene, 119
Pujo Committee, 119

Railroad Administration, U.S., 174, 254, 255, 256–57, 284–85
Railroads, 3, 5, 11, 174
  and army, 61, 81–82, 84, 97–98
  federal control, 256
  and national markets, 16
  strike (1877), 58–59
Rainey Act (1916), 141
Rams, 28, 30
Rawlings, John A., 65
Reconstruction, 58, 66, 67
Reconversion, 268–78. *See also under* Wilson, Woodrow
Redfield, William C., 156, 210, 280, 281, 282, 285, 286, 292
Reed, Thomas R., 29, 31
Refrigeration, 79, 84
Regionalism. *See* Sectional ideology
Remington Arms Company, 123, 129
Remington Arms–Union Metallic Cartridge Company, 118
Replogle, J. Leonard, 211, 217, 230
Republican party, 21, 28, 58
  as majority party (1894–1896), 13
  and navy, 47, 48
  and World War I, 112
Republicans, 2, 6, 110, 112
  progressive, 107–8
Requa, Mark L., 280
Reserve Officers' Training Corps (ROTC), 109
Revolutionary War (1775–1783), 2, 5, 6
Rhett, R. Goodwyn, 153
Rifles, 72–73, 78, 95, 126, 129, 130
Ritchie, Albert C., 244, 275, 278, 280, 281, 291
Ritchie, S. J., 54
Ritter, William M., 281, 282
Roach, John, 21, 28, 29
Robeson, George M., 20, 21

Rock Island (Ill.) Arsenal, 78
Rocky Mountains, 61
Roosevelt, Franklin D., 291
Roosevelt, Theodore, 14, 25, 31, 90, 114
  as assistant secretary of the navy, 34, 35, 36
  and foreign policy, 107, 112
  and navy, 38–39, 44, 48, 103
Roosevelt, Theodore, Jr., 109
Root, Elihu, 9–10, 62, 64, 66, 70, 88–89, 91, 92, 94–96, 103, 157
Root, Elihu, Jr., 109
Root and Van Dervoort Engineering Company, 188
Rosenwald, Julius, 158, 162, 163, 168, 173, 177–78, 190, 196, 201–2, 206
ROTC. *See* Reserve Officers' Training Corps
Rough Riders regiment, 78
Russia (tsarist), 115, 121, 130, 223
Ryan, John D., 175, 249

SAE. *See* Society of Automobile Engineers
Sail power, 20, 27
Saint Louis (Mo.), 60
Samoa, 32, 38
Sanford, Rollin B., 157
San Francisco (Calif.), 49, 60, 85
  depot, 77
Santo Domingo, 32
Sargent, Murray, 212
Saunders, William L., 160
Schneider, Henri, 52, 53, 54
Schofield, John M., 62, 66, 88
Schwab, Charles M., 257
Scientific management, 140, 156
Scientists, 155, 159
Scott, Frank A., 189, 193, 195–96, 206, 220–21
Scott, Hugh L., 92, 183, 245
Scott, Winfield, 65, 94, 113
*Seamanship* (Luce), 24
Sears, Roebuck, and Company, 158
Sectional ideology, 12, 107, 108
Seger, C. B., 249
Selective Service Act (1917), 113, 261
Selective Service System, 250
Self-propelled "automobile torpedo," 29–30
Senate Military Affairs Committee, 221
Senate Naval Affairs Committee, 25, 31
Senate Select Committee on Ordnance and War Ships, 51
Senate Special Committee Investigating the Munitions Industry. *See* Nye Committee
*Service of Security and Information, The* (Wagner), 71
Service vessels, 29, 82–85
Shafter, William R., 76, 77, 82
Sharpe, Henry G., 98, 246
Shaw, Arch W., 231, 237, 275
Sheridan, Philip H., 62, 66, 67
Sherman, William T., 24, 62, 64, 65, 66, 67, 68, 69, 70, 71
Sherman Antitrust Act (1890), 13, 142, 280
Shipbuilders, 21, 49
Shipping Act (1916), 141
Shipping Board, U.S. (USSB), 182, 218, 254, 257
Shipyards (private), 20–21, 28, 48–51. *See also* Armor; Navy yards; Steel
Shoulder arms, 73
Silk Association of America, 213
Simpson, Franklin F., 155
Sims, William S., 42, 44
Sino-Japanese War (1894–1895), 34
Social control, 111
Social Darwinism, 24
Socialists, 111, 259, 260, 293
Social reform, 13, 14–15, 298, 371 (n12)
Society of Automobile Engineers (SAE), 148
Society of the National Reserve Corps, 109
Soley, James R., 31
South, 3, 7, 263
  railroads, 81
  and reconstruction, 58
Spain, 23, 34, 37, 77
Spanish-American War (1898), 4, 9, 23, 26, 107
  and army, 36, 37–38, 64, 65, 72, 75–88, 102
  casualties, 85
  cost, 88
  disease, 85–86
  and MID, 72
  and navy, 35–38, 40, 43–44, 49, 57, 102
  nurses' corps, 60
  ships, 82–83
  strategy, 76–77
  uniforms, 77, 78
Spencer and Sharps (gun manufacturer), 73
Spoils system, 33, 45
Springfield (Mass.) arsenal, 60, 78
Springfield rifles and carbines, 72, 73, 95
"Squadron of evolution." *See* Navy, permanent fleet
Standard Oil Company of New Jersey, 175
Stanton, Edwin M., 62, 64
State capitalism, 293
State Department, 41, 101
Steam, 10, 19, 20, 28, 29
  hammer, 54
Steam engineers, 43
Steel, 10, 16, 28, 29, 32, 34, 36, 48, 49–50, 51, 241, 273, 284
  armor and ordnance plants, 50–53, 56

Corey process, 54
forging plants, 30, 53
Harveyized, 33, 54
nickel-, 33, 53–54
prices, 34, 36, 273
rolled, open-hearth, 49
technology, 50, 56
*See also* Armor
Sternberg, George M., 86
Stettinius, Edward R., 121, 122, 123, 124, 131, 137–38, 189, 245, 247, 317 (n13)
Stimson, Henry L., 90–91, 92, 94, 103, 114
Stone, C. A., 54
Stone, Webster, and Company, 249
Stout, Charles F. C., 275
Street, Oliver D., 248
Strong, Benjamin, 129, 132–33, 135, 157
Studebaker Corporation, 212
Submarines, 39, 49, 110, 112, 130
Suffrage, 12
Summers, Leland L., 137, 175–76, 211, 230
Supply and demand, 15
Supply transportation, 37, 60–62, 95–96, 124
Surgeon general, 86
*Sussex* crisis (1916), 130
Swift, Eben, 70
Swope, Gerard, 248, 250

Taft, Alphonso, 65–66
Taft, William Howard, 14, 39, 90, 91, 103, 260
Tampa (Fla.), 76–77, 80, 81–82, 83–84
Tariff (1890, 1913), 54, 141
Taylor, Frederick W., 156, 163
Taylor, Henry C., 24, 25, 41
Taylorite Movement, 148, 156
Technology, 15, 50. *See also* Military technology; Navy, and technological change; *under* Army
Telegraph, 3, 63
Telephone lines, 63
Textile industry, 17
Third party system, 13
Thompson, Richard W., 21
Thorne, Robert J., 248
Tilden, Samuel J., 29
Tilson, John P., 153
Torpedo boats, 28, 31, 32, 37
submarine, 39
Torpedoes, self-propelled, 29–30, 31
Torpedo School (Newport, R.I.), 44
Tracy, Benjamin F., 30–33, 44, 45, 46, 47, 53, 54
Trade associations, 140, 168–69, 175, 209, 210, 279, 346 (n18)
Transitional stage (1816–1865), 1, 2–3, 6–7
Treasury Department, 257
secretaries, 199, 281
Tripp, Guy E., 239
Troop transportation, 37, 83–84, 85, 95–96
Tumulty, Joseph P., 228, 283
Tweed ring, 29
Typhoid, 85, 86

UMT. *See* Universal military training
Underwood Tariff (1913), 141
Union, 3, 6–7, 9
Union Iron Works (company), 49
Union Pacific Railroad, 61, 249
*United Service* (army journal), 71
United States, as creditor nation, 119. *See also* Latin America, and U.S.
United States Steel Corporation, 119, 124, 125 (table), 175, 263
Universal military training (UMT), 110, 113, 144
Universal Military Training League, 110
Upper class, 13, 15, 148. *See also* Elites
Upton, Emory, 24, 69–70, 74, 89, 94
Urban sector, 13, 14
USES. *See* Employment Service
USSB. *See* Shipping Board

Vanderlip, Frank A., 139
Van Dervoort, W. H., 188
Vardaman, James K., 111
Vauclain, Samuel L., 188
Veblen, Thorstein, 163
Venezuela, 34
Voluntary service, 150

Wagner, Arthur L., 70, 71
Wagons, 61, 78
Wake Island, 38
Wald, Lillian, 153
Walsh, Frank P., 260
War
inevitability of, 24
and reform, 298, 371 (n12)
War College Board, 89–90
War Council, 255
War Department, 62
bureaus, 63–64, 92, 183, 184, 185, 188
centralization, 106
and Chamber of Commerce, 146
and corporations, 101
and corruption, 62
and GMB, 195
investigation of, 87
and NDAC, 166, 183, 186–87
secretaries, 9, 41, 51, 62–63, 90, 92, 158 *(see also individual names)*

War Department *(continued)*
and transportation, distribution, and camps, 9, 80, 86–87, 95
and weapons and supplies, 9, 80, 106, 183–87, 189, 195, 197, 224, 253
and World War I, 108, 197, 198, 251, 295, 296
*See also* Army; Joint Army-Navy Board; Spanish-American War, and army; World War I, army
War Finance Corporation (1918), 254, 257
Capital Issues Committee, 257
War Industries Board (WIB) (1917), 4, 14, 105, 106, 136, 171, 174, 254–55, 269, 287
authority, 216–29
commodity sections, 211, 212–13, 214, 219, 220, 249, 250–51, 253, 273, 277, 289
compared to GMB, MSB, and NDAC, 209
members, 206, 234
operations, 205–10, 213–16, 231–34, 288–89, 290, 291, 292, 296, 297
policy, 230, 235–44
and reconversion, 270, 272, 273–79 (*see also* Reconstruction; Reconversion)
war service committees, 208–11, 212, 214, 218, 231–34, 253, 289
*See also under* Army; Navy; Wilson, Woodrow
War Labor Policies Board (WLPB), 261, 269
Warner and Swasey Company, 189
War of 1812, 2, 6
War Trade Board (1917), 252, 257
Washington (D.C.) Navy Yard, 30
Naval Gun Factory, 45, 53
Watervliet (N.Y.) Arsenal, 73
Wealth distribution, 11–12. *See also* Elites
Weather Bureau, 63
Weeks, John W., 157, 201, 270, 293
Weems, F. Carrington, 249
Weigley, Russell F., 66, 92
Welfare state, 14, 15
Welles, Gideon, 20, 22
Wells Fargo (stagecoach line), 61
West Point. *See* Military Academy, U.S.
Wheeler, Harry A., 140–41, 142, 209, 272
White, Weld, and Company, 249
Whitney, William C., 29, 30, 51–53
Whitworth, Joseph, 52, 54
WIB. *See* War Industries Board
Willard, Daniel, 158, 162, 163, 167, 173–74, 178, 179, 221, 225, 256
Williams, William Appleman, 27
Wilson, William B., 261, 281
Wilson, Woodrow, 14, 177
and army, 48, 106, 108
and Industrial Board, 283, 285, 292
and interventionism, 108
and navy, 39–40, 48, 103, 108, 147
and reconversion, 269, 270–72, 286
and WIB, 207, 208–9, 220–23, 292
and World War I mobilization, 110, 112–13, 114, 129, 133, 147, 155, 158, 161, 165, 166, 191, 194, 198, 199, 204, 252, 291–92, 297–98
Winchester Repeating Arms Company, 123, 129, 188–89
Winter crisis (1917–1918), 256, 293
Women, 12
Wood, Leonard, 90–91, 92, 94, 108–9, 110, 113, 153, 156, 160
"Work-or-fight" (Selective Service Act), 261, 262
World War I (1914–1918)
and airplanes, 96 (*see also* Airplanes)
antipreparedness sentiment, 111–12
army, 71, 72, 92, 94, 106, 108
economic mobilization, 139–40, 148, 158–65 (*see also* Council of National Defense; General Munitions Board; Munitions Standards Board; Naval Consulting Board; War Industries Board; Wilson, Woodrow, and World War I mobilization)
financing, 264
and government-business regulatory alliance, 14, 105, 108, 142–44, 145, 160–61, 198, 266, 267, 288, 295–96, 298
income, 262–63
and industrial preparedness, 114, 115, 148, 150, 234, 253, 293
and military preparedness, 108, 110, 113, 114, 253
mobilization agencies, 254–58 (*see also* Labor unions)
navy, 40, 106
and neutrality, 127, 131, 133
political economy, 4, 6, 101
post- (*see* Reconversion)
and prices, 193
and professionalized military, 19, 113, 114
and ships, 98
and weapons technology, 64, 96, 149–50
*See also under* Military technology; War Department
World War II (1939–1945), 4
army, 94
economic mobilization, 4–5, 6, 101, 297
post- (*see* Cold War)

Wotherspoon, William W., 92
Wright, Luke E., 90

Yachts, 37
Yale University, 109
Yeatman, Pope, 217
Yellow fever, 85, 86
Young, Samuel B. M., 90

Wotherspoon, William W., 92
Wright, Luke E., 90

Yachts, 37
Yale University, 109
Yeatman, Pope, 217
Yellow fever, 85, 86
Young, Samuel B. M., 90